T-SQL Querying

Itzik Ben-Gan
Dejan Sarka
Adam Machanic
Kevin Farlee

PUBLISHED BY
Microsoft Press
A Division of Microsoft Corporation
One Microsoft Way
Redmond, Washington 98052-6399

Library of Congress Control Number: 2014951866
ISBN: 978-0-7356-8504-8

Printed and bound in the United States of America.

3 17

Microsoft Press books are available through booksellers and distributors worldwide. If you need support related to this book, email Microsoft Press Support at mspinput@microsoft.com. Please tell us what you think of this book at http://aka.ms/tellpress.

Acquisitions Editor: Devon Musgrave
Developmental Editor: Devon Musgrave
Project Editor: Carol Dillingham
Editorial Production: Curtis Philips, Publishing.com
Technical Reviewer: Alejandro Mesa; Technical Review services provided by
                    Content Master, a member of CM Group, Ltd.
Copyeditor: Roger LeBlanc
Proofreader: Andrea Fox
Indexer: William P. Meyers
Cover: Twist Creative • Seattle and Joel Panchot

To Lilach, for giving meaning to everything that I do.

—Itzik

Contents at a glance

Contents

What do you think of this book? We want to hear from you!

Microsoft is interested in hearing your feedback so we can continually improve our books and learning resources for you. To participate in a brief online survey, please visit:

microsoft.com/learning/booksurvey

Chapter 3 Multi-table queries 187

Chapter 6 Data modification   373

Chapter 10 In-Memory OLTP   671

Chapter 11   Graphs and recursive queries   707

What do you think of this book? We want to hear from you!

Microsoft is interested in hearing your feedback so we can continually improve our books and learning resources for you. To participate in a brief online survey, please visit:

microsoft.com/learning/booksurvey

Foreword

I have been with Microsoft and working with the Microsoft SQL Server team since 1993. It has been one heck of a ride to watch this product mature into what it is today. It has been exciting to watch how the Microsoft SQL Server customer base uses SQL Server to run their mission-critical businesses. Most of all, it has been an honor to support the most vibrant, passionate technology community I have ever seen.

The Microsoft SQL Server community is filled with truly amazing, smart people. They take pride in sharing their great knowledge with others, all for making the community stronger. Anyone in the world can jump on Twitter and ask any question to #sqlhelp, and within seconds one of the smartest experts in the world will be responding. If you are looking for expertise in performance, storage, query optimization, large-scale design, modeling, or any data-related topic, these experts are in the community today sharing their expertise. You will get to know them not only by their expertise but by their unique, friendly personalities as well. We in the SQL Server community world refer to this as our SQL family.

Everyone in the community knows the major contributors by their expertise in particular areas. If you ask who the best database performance expert is, people in the community will give you the same four or five names. If you ask for the best storage expert, again people will give you the same four or five storage expert names. You'll always find a few experts in the community who are the very best for a specific area of database domain expertise. There is only one exception to this that I am aware of, and that is the T-SQL language. There are a lot of talented T-SQL experts, but if you ask for the best everyone will give you one name: Itzik Ben-Gan.

Itzik asked me to write this foreword for his new book, and I am honored to do so. His previous books—*Inside Microsoft SQL Server: T-SQL Querying* (Microsoft Press, 2009), *Inside Microsoft SQL Server: T-SQL Programming* (Microsoft Press, 2009), and *Microsoft SQL Server High-Performance T-SQL Using Window Functions* (Microsoft Press, 2012)—are sitting on the shelves of every DBA I know. These books add up to over 2,000 pages of top-notch technical knowledge about Microsoft SQL Server T-SQL, and they set the standard for high-quality database content.

I am excited about this new book, *T-SQL Querying*. Not only does it combine material from his three previous books, but it also adds material from SQL Server 2012 and 2014, including window functions, the new cardinality estimator, sequences, column-store, In-Memory OLTP, and much more. Itzik has a few exciting co-authors as well: Kevin Farlee, Adam Machanic, and Dejan Sarka. Kevin is part of the Microsoft SQL

Server engineering team and someone I have been working with for many years. Adam is one of those few names that I refer to above as one of the best database performance experts in the world, and Dejan is well known for his BI and data-modeling expertise.

I fully expect this book to be the standard T-SQL guide for the Microsoft SQL Server community.

Mark Souza
General Manager, Cloud and Enterprise Engineering
Microsoft

Introduction

Updating both *Inside Microsoft SQL Server 2008: T-SQL Querying* (Microsoft Press, 2009) and parts of *Inside Microsoft SQL Server 2008: T-SQL Programming* (Microsoft Press, 2009), this book gives database developers and administrators a detailed look at the internal architecture of T-SQL and a comprehensive programming reference. It includes coverage of SQL Server 2012 and 2014, but in many cases deals with areas that are not version-specific and will likely be relevant in future versions of SQL Server. Tackle the toughest set-based querying and query-tuning problems—guided by an author team with in-depth, inside knowledge of T-SQL. Deepen your understanding of architecture and internals—and learn practical approaches and advanced techniques to optimize your code's performance. This book covers many unique techniques that were developed, improved, and polished by the authors over their many years of experience, providing highly efficient solutions for common challenges. There's a deep focus on the performance and efficiency of the techniques and solutions covered. The book also emphasizes the need to have a correct understanding of the language and its underlying mathematical foundations.

Who should read this book

This book is designed to help experienced T-SQL practitioners become more knowledgeable and efficient in this field. The book's target audience is T-SQL developers, DBAs, BI pros, data scientists, and anyone who is serious about T-SQL. Its main purpose is to prepare you for real-life needs, as far as T-SQL is concerned. Its main focus is not to help you pass certification exams. That said, it just so happens that the book covers many of the topics that exams 70-461 and 70-464 test you on. So, even though you shouldn't consider this book as the only learning tool to prepare for these exams, it is certainly a tool that will help you in this process.

Assumptions

This book assumes that you have at least a year of solid experience working with SQL Server, writing and tuning T-SQL code. It assumes that you have a good grasp of T-SQL coding and tuning fundamentals, and that you are ready to tackle more advanced challenges. This book could still be relevant to you if you have similar experience with a different database platform and its dialect of SQL, but actual knowledge and experience with SQL Server and T-SQL is preferred.

This book might not be for you if...

This book might not be for you if you are fairly new to databases and SQL.

Organization of this book

The book starts with two chapters that lay the foundation of logical and physical query processing required to gain the most from the rest of the chapters.

The first chapter covers logical query processing. It describes in detail the logical phases involved in processing queries, the unique aspects of SQL querying, and the special mindset you need to adopt to program in a relational, set-oriented environment.

The second chapter covers query tuning and the physical layer. It describes internal data structures, tools to measure query performance, access methods, cardinality estimates, indexing features, prioritizing queries with extended events, columnstore technology, use of temporary tables and table variables, sets versus cursors, query tuning with query revisions, and parallel query execution. (The part about parallel query execution was written by Adam Machanic.)

The next five chapters deal with various data manipulation–related topics. The coverage of these topics is extensive; beyond explaining the features, they focus a lot on the performance of the code and the use of the features to solve common tasks. Chapter 3 covers multi-table queries using subqueries, the APPLY operator, joins, and the UNION, INTERSECT, and EXCEPT relational operators. Chapter 4 covers data analysis using grouping, pivoting, and window functions. Chapter 5 covers the TOP and OFFSET-FETCH filters, and solving *top N per group* tasks. Chapter 6 covers data-modification topics like minimally logged operations, using the sequence object efficiently, merging data, and the OUTPUT clause. Chapter 7 covers date and time treatment, including the handling of date and time intervals.

Chapter 8 covers T-SQL for BI practitioners and was written by Dejan Sarka. It describes how to prepare data for analysis and how to use T-SQL to handle statistical data analysis tasks. Those include frequencies, descriptive statistics for continuous variables, linear dependencies, and moving averages and entropy.

Chapter 9 covers the programmability constructs that T-SQL supports. Those are dynamic SQL, user-defined functions, stored procedures, triggers, SQLCLR programming (written by Adam Machanic), transactions and concurrency, and error handling.

Previously, these topics were covered in the book *Inside Microsoft SQL Server: T-SQL Programming*.

Chapter 10 covers one of the major improvements in SQL Server 2014—the In-Memory OLTP engine. This chapter was written by Microsoft's Kevin Farlee, who was involved in the actual development of this feature.

Chapter 11 covers graphs and recursive queries. It shows how to handle graph structures such as employee hierarchies, bill of materials, and maps in SQL Server using T-SQL. It shows how to implement models such as the enumerated path model (using your own custom solution and using the HIERARCHYID data type) and the nested sets model. It also shows how to use recursive queries to manipulate data in graphs.

System requirements

You will need the following software to run the code samples in this book:

- Microsoft SQL Server 2014:

  - Edition: 64-bit Enterprise, Developer, or Evaluation; other editions do not support the In-Memory OLTP and columnstore technologies that are covered in the book. You can download a trial version here: *http://www.microsoft.com/sql*.

  - For hardware and software requirements see *http://msdn.microsoft.com/en-us/library/ms143506(v=sql.120).aspx*.

  - In the Feature Selection dialog of the SQL Server 2014 setup program, choose the following components: Database Engine Services, Client Tools Connectivity, Documentation Components, Management Tools – Basic, Management Tools – Complete.

- Microsoft Visual Studio 2013 with Microsoft SQL Server Data Tools (SSDT):

  - You can find the system requirements and platform compatibility for Visual Studio 2013 here: *http://www.visualstudio.com/products/visual-studio-2013-compatibility-vs*.

  - For information about installing SSDT, see *http://msdn.microsoft.com/en-us/data/tools.aspx*.

Depending on your Windows configuration, you might require Local Administrator rights to install or configure SQL Server 2014 and Visual Studio 2013.

Downloads: Code samples

This book contains many code samples. You can download the source code for this book from the authors' site: *http://tsql.solidq.com/books/tq3*.

The source code is organized in a compressed file named *T-SQL Querying - YYYYMMDD.zip*, where *YYYYMMDD* stands for the last update date of the content. Follow the instructions in the Readme.txt file that is included in the compressed file to install the code samples.

Acknowledgments

A number of people contributed to making this book a reality, whether directly or indirectly, and deserve thanks and recognition. It's certainly possible that I omitted some names unintentionally and I apologize for this ahead of time.

To Lilach: you're the one who makes me want to be good at what I do. Besides being my inspiration in life, you had an active unofficial role in this book. You were the book's first reader! So many hours we spent reading the text together looking for errors before I sent it to the editors. I have a feeling that you know some things about T-SQL better than people who are professionals in the field.

To my parents, Mila and Gabi, and to my siblings, Mickey and Ina, for the constant support and for accepting the fact that I'm away. You experienced so much turbulence in the last few years, and I'm hoping that the coming years will be healthy and happy.

To the coauthors of the book, Dejan Sarka, Adam Machanic, and Kevin Farlee. It's a true privilege to be part of such a knowledgeable and experienced group of people. Each of you are such experts in your areas that I felt that your topics would be best served if covered by you: Dejan with the chapter on T-SQL for BI practitioners, Adam with the sections on parallel query execution and SQL CLR programming, and Kevin with the chapter on In-Memory OLTP. Thanks for taking part in this book.

To the technical reviewer of the book, Alejandro Mesa: you read and unofficially reviewed my previous books. You're so passionate about the topic that I'm glad with this book you took a more official reviewer role. I also want to thank the reviewer of the former edition of the book, Steve Kass: you did such thorough and brilliant work that a lot of it echoes in this one.

To Mark Souza: you were there pretty much since the inception of the product, being involved in technical, management, and community-related roles. If anyone feels the heartbeat of the SQL Server community, it is you. We're all grateful for what you do, and it is a great honor to have you write the foreword.

Many thanks to the editors at Microsoft Press. To Devon Musgrave, who played both the acquisitions editor and developmental editor roles: you are the one who made this book a reality and handled all the initial stages. I realize that this book is very likely one of many you were responsible for, and I'd like to thank you for dedicating the time and effort that you did. To Carol Dillingham, the book's project editor: you spent so many hours on this project, and you coordinated it delightfully. It was a pleasure working with you. Also, thanks to Curtis Philips, the project manager from Publishing.com. It was a complex project, and I'm sure it wasn't a picnic for you. Also, many thanks to the copyeditor, Roger LeBlanc, who worked on my previous books, and to the proofreader, Andrea Fox. It was a pleasure to work with you guys.

To SolidQ, my company for over a decade: it's gratifying to be part of such a great company that evolved into what it is today. The members of this company are much more than colleagues to me; they are partners, friends, and family. Thanks to Fernando G. Guerrero, Douglas McDowell, Herbert Albert, Dejan Sarka, Gianluca Hotz, Antonio Soto, Jeanne Reeves, Glenn McCoin, Fritz Lechnitz, Eric Van Soldt, Berry Walker, Marilyn Templeton, Joelle Budd, Gwen White, Jan Taylor, Judy Dyess, Alberto Martin, Lorena Jimenez, Ron Talmage, Andy Kelly, Rushabh Mehta, Joe Chang, Mark Tabladillo, Eladio Rincón, Miguel Egea, Alejandro J. Rocchi, Daniel A. Seara, Javier Loria, Paco González, Enrique Catalá, Esther Nolasco Andreu, Rocío Guerrero, Javier Torrenteras, Rubén Garrigós, Victor Vale Diaz, Davide Mauri, Danilo Dominici, Erik Veerman, Jay Hackney, Grega Jerkič, Matija Lah, Richard Waymire, Carl Rabeler, Chris Randall, Tony Rogerson, Christian Rise, Raoul Illyés, Johan Åhlén, Peter Larsson, Paul Turley, Bill Haenlin, Blythe Gietz, Nigel Semmi, Paras Doshi, and so many others.

To members of the Microsoft SQL Server development team, past and present: Tobias Ternstrom, Lubor Kollar, Umachandar Jayachandran (UC), Boris Baryshnikov, Conor Cunningham, Kevin Farlee, Marc Friedman, Milan Stojic, Craig Freedman, Campbell Fraser, Mark Souza, T. K. Rengarajan, Dave Campbell, César Galindo-Legaria, and I'm sure many others. I know it wasn't a trivial effort to add support for window functions in SQL Server. Thanks for the great effort, and thanks for all the time you spent meeting with me and responding to my emails, addressing my questions, and answering my requests for clarification.

To members of the *SQL Server Pro* editorial team, past and present: Megan Keller, Lavon Peters, Michele Crockett, Mike Otey, Jayleen Heft, and I'm sure many others. I've been writing for the magazine for over a decade and a half, and I am grateful for the opportunity to share my knowledge with the magazine's readers.

To SQL Server MVPs, past and present: Paul White, Alejandro Mesa, Erland Sommarskog, Aaron Bertrand, Tibor Karaszi, Benjamin Nevarez, Simon Sabin, Darren Green, Allan Mitchell, Tony Rogerson, and many others—and to the MVP lead, Simon Tien. This is a great program that I'm grateful and proud to be part of. The level of expertise of this group is amazing, and I'm always excited when we all get to meet, both to share ideas and just to catch up at a personal level over beer. I have to extend special thanks to Paul White. I've learned so much from you, and I thoroughly enjoy reading your work. I think it's safe to say that you're my favorite author. Who knows, maybe one day we'll get to work on something together.

Finally, to my students: teaching about T-SQL is what drives me. It's my passion. Thanks for allowing me to fulfill my calling and for all the great questions that make me seek more knowledge.

—Cheers, *Itzik*

Errata, updates, & book support

We've made every effort to ensure the accuracy of this book. If you discover an error, please submit it to us via *mspinput@microsoft.com*. You can also reach the Microsoft Press Book Support team for other assistance via the same email address. Please note that product support for Microsoft software and hardware is not offered through the previous addresses. For help with Microsoft software or hardware, go to *http://support.microsoft.com*.

Free ebooks from Microsoft Press

From technical overviews to in-depth information on special topics, the free ebooks from Microsoft Press cover a wide range of topics. These ebooks are available in PDF, EPUB, and Mobi for Kindle formats, ready for you to download at:

http://aka.ms/mspressfree

Check back often to see what is new!

We want to hear from you

At Microsoft Press, your satisfaction is our top priority, and your feedback our most valuable asset. Please tell us what you think of this book at:

http://aka.ms/tellpress

We know you're busy, so we've kept it short with just a few questions. Your answers go directly to the editors at Microsoft Press. (No personal information will be requested.) Thanks in advance for your input!

Stay in touch

Let's keep the conversation going! We're on Twitter: *http://twitter.com/MicrosoftPress*.

CHAPTER 1

Logical query processing

Observing true experts in different fields, you find a common practice that they all share—mastering the basics. One way or another, all professions deal with problem solving. All solutions to problems, complex as they may be, involve applying a mix of fundamental techniques. If you want to master a profession, you need to build your knowledge upon strong foundations. Put a lot of effort into perfecting your techniques, master the basics, and you'll be able to solve any problem.

This book is about Transact-SQL (T-SQL) querying—learning key techniques and applying them to solve problems. I can't think of a better way to start the book than with a chapter on the fundamentals of logical query processing. I find this chapter the most important in the book—not just because it covers the essentials of query processing but also because SQL programming is conceptually very different than any other sort of programming.

> **Note** This book is in its third edition. The previous edition was in two volumes that are now merged into one. For details about the changes, plus information about getting the source code and sample data, make sure you visit the book's introduction.

T-SQL is the Microsoft SQL Server dialect of, or extension to, the ANSI and ISO SQL standards. Throughout the book, I'll use the terms *SQL* and *T-SQL* interchangeably. When discussing aspects of the language that originated from ANSI/ISO SQL and are relevant to most dialects, I'll typically use the term *SQL* or *standard SQL*. When discussing aspects of the language with the implementation of SQL Server in mind, I'll typically use the term *T-SQL*. Note that the formal language name is *Transact-SQL*, although it's commonly called *T-SQL*. Most programmers, including myself, feel more comfortable calling it T-SQL, so I and the other authors made a conscious choice to use the term *T-SQL* throughout the book.

Origin of SQL pronunciation

Many English-speaking database professionals pronounce *SQL* as *sequel,* although the correct pronunciation of the language is *S-Q-L* ("ess kyoo ell"). One can make educated guesses about the reasoning behind the incorrect pronunciation. My guess is that there are both historical and linguistic reasons.

As for historical reasons, in the 1970s, IBM developed a language named SEQUEL, which was an acronym for Structured English QUEry Language. The language was designed to manipulate data stored in a database system named System R, which was based on Dr. Edgar F. Codd's model for relational database management systems (RDBMS). The acronym SEQUEL was later shortened to SQL because of a trademark dispute. ANSI adopted SQL as a standard in 1986, and ISO did so in 1987. ANSI declared that the official pronunciation of the language is "ess kyoo ell," but it seems that this fact is not common knowledge.

As for linguistic reasons, the *sequel* pronunciation is simply more fluent, mainly for English speakers. I often use it myself for this reason.

More Info The coverage of SQL history in this chapter is based on an article from Wikipedia, the free encyclopedia, and can be found at *http://en.wikipedia.org/wiki/SQL*.

SQL programming has many unique aspects, such as thinking in sets, the logical processing order of query elements, and three-valued logic. Trying to program in SQL without this knowledge is a straight path to lengthy, poor-performing code that is difficult to maintain. This chapter's purpose is to help you understand SQL the way its designers envisioned it. You need to create strong roots upon which all the rest will be built. Where relevant, I'll explicitly indicate elements that are specific to T-SQL.

Throughout the book, I'll cover complex problems and advanced techniques. But in this chapter, as mentioned, I'll deal only with the fundamentals of querying. Throughout the book, I'll also focus on performance. But in this chapter, I'll deal only with the logical aspects of query processing. I ask you to make an effort while reading this chapter not to think about performance at all. You'll find plenty of performance coverage later in the book. Some of the logical query-processing phases that I'll describe in this chapter might seem very inefficient. But keep in mind that in practice, the physical processing of a query in the database platform where it executes might be very different than the logical one.

The component in SQL Server in charge of generating the physical-query execution plan for a query is the *query optimizer*. In the plan, the optimizer determines in which order to access the tables, which access methods and indexes to use, which join algorithms to apply, and so on. The optimizer generates multiple valid execution plans and chooses the one with the lowest cost. The phases in the logical processing of a query have a specific order. In contrast, the optimizer can often make shortcuts in the physical execution plan that it generates. Of course, it will make shortcuts only if the result set is guaranteed to be the correct one—in other words, the same result set you would get by following the logical processing phases. For example, to use an index, the optimizer can decide to apply a filter much sooner than dictated by logical processing. I'll refer to the processing order of the elements in the physical-query execution plan as *physical processing order*.

For the aforementioned reasons, you need to make a clear distinction between logical and physical processing of a query.

Without further ado, let's delve into logical query-processing phases.

Logical query-processing phases

This section introduces the phases involved in the logical processing of a query. I'll first briefly describe each step. Then, in the following sections, I'll describe the steps in much more detail and apply them to a sample query. You can use this section as a quick reference whenever you need to recall the order and general meaning of the different phases.

Listing 1-1 contains a general form of a query, along with step numbers assigned according to the order in which the different clauses are logically processed.

LISTING 1-1 Logical query-processing step numbers

```
(5) SELECT (5-2) DISTINCT (7) TOP(<top_specification>) (5-1) <select_list>
(1) FROM (1-J) <left_table> <join_type> JOIN <right_table> ON <on_predicate>
    | (1-A) <left_table> <apply_type> APPLY <right_input_table> AS <alias>
    | (1-P) <left_table> PIVOT(<pivot_specification>) AS <alias>
    | (1-U) <left_table> UNPIVOT(<unpivot_specification>) AS <alias>
(2) WHERE <where_predicate>
(3) GROUP BY <group_by_specification>
(4) HAVING <having_predicate>
(6) ORDER BY <order_by_list>
(7) OFFSET <offset_specification> ROWS FETCH NEXT <fetch_specification> ROWS ONLY;
```

The first noticeable aspect of SQL that is different from other programming languages is the logical order in which the code is processed. In most programming languages, the code is processed in the order in which it is written (call its *typed order*). In SQL, the first clause that is processed is the FROM clause, whereas the SELECT clause, which is typed first, is processed almost last. I refer to this order as *logical processing order* to distinguish it from both typed order and physical processing order.

There's a reason for the difference between logical processing order and typed order. Remember that prior to SQL the language was named SEQUEL, and in the original name the first *E* stood for *English*. The designers of the language had in mind a declarative language where you declare your instructions in a language similar to English. Consider the manner in which you provide an instruction in English: "Bring me the T-SQL Querying book from the office." You indicate the object (the book) before indicating the location of the object (the office). But clearly, the person carrying out the instruction would have to first go to the office, and then from there obtain the book. In a similar manner, in SQL the typed order indicates the SELECT clause with the desired columns before the FROM clause with the source tables. But logical query processing starts with the FROM clause. This realization tends to generate many *a-ha* moments for people, explaining so many things about SQL that might otherwise seem obscure.

Each step in logical query processing generates a virtual table that is used as the input to the following step. These virtual tables are not available to the caller (client application or outer query). Only the table generated by the final step is returned to the caller. If a certain clause is not specified in a query, the corresponding step is simply skipped. The following section briefly describes the different logical steps.

Logical query-processing phases in brief

Don't worry too much if the description of the steps doesn't seem to make much sense for now. These descriptions are provided as a reference. Sections that come after the scenario example will cover the steps in much more detail. Also, here I describe only the join table operator because it's the most commonly used one and therefore easy to relate to. The other table operators (APPLY, PIVOT, and UNPIVOT) are covered later in the chapter in the section "Further aspects of logical query processing."

Figure 1-1 contains a flow diagram representing logical query-processing phases in detail. Throughout the chapter, I'll refer to the step numbers that appear in the diagram.

- **(1) FROM**   This phase identifies the query's source tables and processes table operators. Each table operator applies a series of subphases. For example, the phases involved in a join are (1-J1) Cartesian Product, (1-J2) ON Predicate, (1-J3) Add Outer Rows. This phase generates virtual table VT1.

- **(1-J1) Cartesian Product**   This phase performs a Cartesian product (cross join) between the two tables involved in the table operator, generating VT1-J1.

- **(1-J2) ON Predicate**   This phase filters the rows from VT1-J1 based on the predicate that appears in the ON clause (<*on_predicate*>). Only rows for which the predicate evaluates to TRUE are inserted into VT1-J2.

- **(1-J3) Add Outer Rows**   If OUTER JOIN is specified (as opposed to CROSS JOIN or INNER JOIN), rows from the preserved table or tables for which a match was not found are added to the rows from VT1-J2 as outer rows, generating VT1-J3.

- **(2) WHERE**   This phase filters the rows from VT1 based on the predicate that appears in the WHERE clause (<*where_predicate*>). Only rows for which the predicate evaluates to TRUE are inserted into VT2.

- **(3) GROUP BY**   This phase arranges the rows from VT2 in groups based on the set of expressions (aka, *grouping set*) specified in the GROUP BY clause, generating VT3. Ultimately, there will be one result row per qualifying group.

- **(4) HAVING**   This phase filters the groups from VT3 based on the predicate that appears in the HAVING clause (<*having_predicate*>). Only groups for which the predicate evaluates to TRUE are inserted into VT4.

- **(5) SELECT**   This phase processes the elements in the SELECT clause, generating VT5.

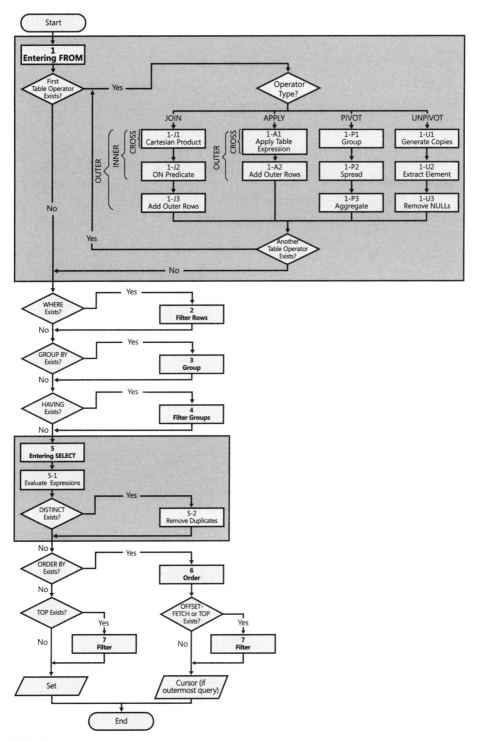

FIGURE 1-1 Logical query-processing flow diagram.

- **(5-1) Evaluate Expressions** This phase evaluates the expressions in the SELECT list, generating VT5-1.

- **(5-2) DISTINCT** This phase removes duplicate rows from VT5-1, generating VT5-2.

- **(6) ORDER BY** This phase orders the rows from VT5-2 according to the list specified in the ORDER BY clause, generating the cursor VC6. Absent an ORDER BY clause, VT5-2 becomes VT6.

- **(7) TOP | OFFSET-FETCH** This phase filters rows from VC6 or VT6 based on the top or offset-fetch specification, generating VC7 or VT7, respectively. With TOP, this phase filters the specified number of rows based on the ordering in the ORDER BY clause, or based on arbitrary order if an ORDER BY clause is absent. With OFFSET-FETCH, this phase skips the specified number of rows, and then filters the next specified number of rows, based on the ordering in the ORDER BY clause. The OFFSET-FETCH filter was introduced in SQL Server 2012.

Sample query based on customers/orders scenario

To describe the logical processing phases in detail, I'll walk you through a sample query. First run the following code to create the dbo.Customers and dbo.Orders tables, populate them with sample data, and query them to show their contents:

```
SET NOCOUNT ON;
USE tempdb;

IF OBJECT_ID(N'dbo.Orders', N'U') IS NOT NULL DROP TABLE dbo.Orders;

IF OBJECT_ID(N'dbo.Customers', N'U') IS NOT NULL DROP TABLE dbo.Customers;

CREATE TABLE dbo.Customers
(
  custid  CHAR(5)     NOT NULL,
  city    VARCHAR(10) NOT NULL,
  CONSTRAINT PK_Customers PRIMARY KEY(custid)
);

CREATE TABLE dbo.Orders
(
  orderid INT     NOT NULL,
  custid  CHAR(5)     NULL,
  CONSTRAINT PK_Orders PRIMARY KEY(orderid),
  CONSTRAINT FK_Orders_Customers FOREIGN KEY(custid)
    REFERENCES dbo.Customers(custid)
);
GO

INSERT INTO dbo.Customers(custid, city) VALUES
  ('FISSA', 'Madrid'),
  ('FRNDO', 'Madrid'),
  ('KRLOS', 'Madrid'),
  ('MRPHS', 'Zion' );
```

```
INSERT INTO dbo.Orders(orderid, custid) VALUES
  (1, 'FRNDO'),
  (2, 'FRNDO'),
  (3, 'KRLOS'),
  (4, 'KRLOS'),
  (5, 'KRLOS'),
  (6, 'MRPHS'),
  (7, NULL   );

SELECT * FROM dbo.Customers;
SELECT * FROM dbo.Orders;
```

This code generates the following output:

```
custid city
------ ----------
FISSA  Madrid
FRNDO  Madrid
KRLOS  Madrid
MRPHS  Zion


orderid     custid
----------- ------
1           FRNDO
2           FRNDO
3           KRLOS
4           KRLOS
5           KRLOS
6           MRPHS
7           NULL
```

I'll use the query shown in Listing 1-2 as my example. The query returns customers from Madrid who placed fewer than three orders (including zero orders), along with their order counts. The result is sorted by order count, from smallest to largest.

LISTING 1-2 Query: Madrid customers with fewer than three orders

```
SELECT C.custid, COUNT(O.orderid) AS numorders
FROM dbo.Customers AS C
  LEFT OUTER JOIN dbo.Orders AS O
    ON C.custid = O.custid
WHERE C.city = 'Madrid'
GROUP BY C.custid
HAVING COUNT(O.orderid) < 3
ORDER BY numorders;
```

This query returns the following output:

```
custid numorders
------ -----------
FISSA  0
FRNDO  2
```

Both FISSA and FRNDO are customers from Madrid who placed fewer than three orders. Examine the query and try to read it while following the steps and phases described in Listing 1-1, Figure 1-1, and the section "Logical query-processing phases in brief." If this is your first time thinking of a query in such terms, you might be confused. The following section should help you understand the nitty-gritty details.

Logical query-processing phase details

This section describes the logical query-processing phases in detail by applying them to the given sample query.

Step 1: The FROM phase

The FROM phase identifies the table or tables that need to be queried, and if table operators are specified, this phase processes those operators from left to right. Each table operator operates on one or two input tables and returns an output table. The result of a table operator is used as the left input to the next table operator—if one exists—and as the input to the next logical query-processing phase otherwise. Each table operator has its own set of processing subphases. For example, the sub-phases involved in a join are (1-J1) Cartesian Product, (1-J2) ON Predicate, (1-J3) Add Outer Rows. As mentioned, other table operators will be described separately later in this chapter. The FROM phase generates virtual table VT1.

Step 1-J1: Perform Cartesian product (cross join)

This is the first of three subphases that are applicable to a join table operator. This subphase per-forms a Cartesian product (a cross join, or an unrestricted join) between the two tables involved in the join and, as a result, generates virtual table VT1-J1. This table contains one row for every possible choice of a row from the left table and a row from the right table. If the left table contains n rows and the right table contains m rows, VT1-J1 will contain $n \times m$ rows. The columns in VT1-J1 are qualified (prefixed) with their source table names (or table aliases, if you specified them in the query). In the subsequent steps (step 1-J2 and on), a reference to a column name that is ambiguous (appears in more than one input table) must be table-qualified (for example, *C.custid*). Specifying the table quali-fier for column names that appear in only one of the inputs is optional (for example, *O.orderid* or just *orderid*).

Apply step 1-J1 to the sample query (shown in Listing 1-2):

```
FROM dbo.Customers AS C ... JOIN dbo.Orders AS O
```

As a result, you get the virtual table VT1-J1 (shown in Table 1-1) with 28 rows (4×7).

TABLE 1-1 Virtual table VT1-J1 returned from step 1-J1

C.custid	C.city	O.orderid	O.custid
FISSA	Madrid	1	FRNDO
FISSA	Madrid	2	FRNDO
FISSA	Madrid	3	KRLOS
FISSA	Madrid	4	KRLOS
FISSA	Madrid	5	KRLOS
FISSA	Madrid	6	MRPHS
FISSA	Madrid	7	NULL
FRNDO	Madrid	1	FRNDO
FRNDO	Madrid	2	FRNDO
FRNDO	Madrid	3	KRLOS
FRNDO	Madrid	4	KRLOS
FRNDO	Madrid	5	KRLOS
FRNDO	Madrid	6	MRPHS
FRNDO	Madrid	7	NULL
KRLOS	Madrid	1	FRNDO
KRLOS	Madrid	2	FRNDO
KRLOS	Madrid	3	KRLOS
KRLOS	Madrid	4	KRLOS
KRLOS	Madrid	5	KRLOS
KRLOS	Madrid	6	MRPHS
KRLOS	Madrid	7	NULL
MRPHS	Zion	1	FRNDO
MRPHS	Zion	2	FRNDO
MRPHS	Zion	3	KRLOS
MRPHS	Zion	4	KRLOS
MRPHS	Zion	5	KRLOS
MRPHS	Zion	6	MRPHS
MRPHS	Zion	7	NULL

Step 1-J2: Apply ON predicate (join condition)

The ON clause is the first of three query clauses (ON, WHERE, and HAVING) that filter rows based on a predicate. The predicate in the ON clause is applied to all rows in the virtual table returned by the previous step (VT1-J1). Only rows for which the *<on_predicate>* is TRUE become part of the virtual table returned by this step (VT1-J2).

NULLs and the three-valued logic

Allow me to digress a bit to cover some important aspects of SQL related to this step. The relational model defines two marks representing missing values: an A-Mark (missing and applicable) and an I-Mark (missing and inapplicable). The former represents a case where a value is generally applicable, but for some reason is missing. For example, consider the attribute *birth-date* of the People relation. For most people this information is known, but in some rare cases it isn't, as my wife's grandpa will attest. Obviously, he was born on some date, but no one knows which date it was. The latter represents a case where a value is irrelevant. For example, consider the attribute *custid* of the Orders relation. Suppose that when you perform inventory in your company, if you find inconsistency between the expected and actual stock levels of an item, you add a dummy order to the database to compensate for it. In such a transaction, the customer ID is irrelevant.

Unlike the relational model, the SQL standard doesn't make a distinction between different kinds of missing values, rather it uses only one general-purpose mark—the NULL mark. NULLs are a source for quite a lot of confusion and trouble in SQL and should be understood well to avoid errors. For starters, a common mistake that people make is to use the term "NULL value," but a NULL is not a value; rather, it's a mark for a missing value. So the correct terminology is either "NULL mark" or just "NULL." Also, because SQL uses only one mark for missing values, when you use a NULL, there's no way for SQL to know whether it is supposed to represent a missing and applicable case or a missing and inapplicable case. For example, in our sample data one of the orders has a NULL mark in the *custid* column. Suppose that this is a dummy order that is not related to any customer like the scenario I described earlier. So your use of a NULL here records the fact that the value is missing, but not the fact that it's missing and inapplicable.

A big part of the confusion in working with NULLs in SQL is related to predicates you use in query filters, CHECK constraints, and elsewhere. The possible values of a predicate in SQL are TRUE, FALSE, and UNKNOWN. This is referred to as *three-valued logic* and is unique to SQL. Logical expressions in most programming languages can be only TRUE or FALSE. The UNKNOWN logical value in SQL typically occurs in a logical expression that involves a *NULL*. (For example, the logical value of each of these three expressions is UNKNOWN: *NULL* > 1759; *NULL = NULL; X + NULL > Y*.) Remember that the NULL mark represents a missing value. According to SQL, when comparing a missing value to another value (even another NULL), the logical result is always UNKNOWN.

Dealing with UNKNOWN logical results and NULLs can be very confusing. While *NOT* TRUE is FALSE, and NOT FALSE is TRUE, the opposite of UNKNOWN (NOT UNKNOWN) is still UNKNOWN.

UNKNOWN logical results and NULLs are treated inconsistently in different elements of the language. For example, all query filters (ON, WHERE, and HAVING) treat UNKNOWN like FALSE. A row for which a filter is UNKNOWN is eliminated from the result set. In other words, query filters return TRUE cases. On the other hand, an UNKNOWN value in a CHECK constraint is actually treated like TRUE. Suppose you have a CHECK constraint in a table to require that the salary column be greater than zero. A row entered into the table with a NULL salary is accepted because (*NULL > 0*) is UNKNOWN and treated like TRUE in the CHECK constraint. In other words, CHECK constraints reject FALSE cases.

A comparison between two NULLs in a filter yields UNKNOWN, which, as I mentioned earlier, is treated like FALSE—as if one NULL is different than another.

On the other hand, for UNIQUE constraints, some relational operators, and sorting or grouping operations, NULLs are treated as equal:

- You cannot insert into a table two rows with a NULL in a column that has a UNIQUE constraint defined on it. T-SQL violates the standard on this point.

- A GROUP BY clause groups all NULLs into one group.

- An ORDER BY clause sorts all NULLs together.

- The UNION, EXCEPT, and INTERSECT operators treat NULLs as equal when comparing rows from the two sets.

Interestingly, the SQL standard doesn't use the terms *equal to* and *not equal to* when describing the way the UNION, EXCEPT, and INTERSECT relational operators compare rows; rather, it uses *is not distinct from* and *is distinct from*, respectively. In fact, the standard defines an explicit *distinct predicate* using the form: IS [NOT] DISTINCT FROM. These relational operators use the distinct predicate implicitly. It differs from predicates using = and <> operators in that it uses two-valued logic. The following expressions are true: *NULL IS NOT DISTINCT FROM NULL, NULL IS DISTINCT FROM 1759.* As of SQL Server 2014, T-SQL doesn't support the explicit distinct predicate, but I hope very much that such support will be added in the future. (See the feature request: *http://connect.microsoft.com/SQLServer/feedback/details/286422/*.)

In short, to spare yourself some grief you should be aware of the way UNKNOWN logical results and NULLs are treated in the different elements of the language.

Apply step 1-J2 to the sample query:

```
ON C.custid = O.custid
```

The first column of Table 1-2 shows the value of the logical expression in the ON clause for the rows from VT1-J1.

TABLE 1-2 Logical value of ON predicate for rows from VT1-J1

Logical value	C.custid	C.city	O.orderid	O.custid
FALSE	FISSA	Madrid	1	FRNDO
FALSE	FISSA	Madrid	2	FRNDO
FALSE	FISSA	Madrid	3	KRLOS
FALSE	FISSA	Madrid	4	KRLOS
FALSE	FISSA	Madrid	5	KRLOS
FALSE	FISSA	Madrid	6	MRPHS
UNKNOWN	FISSA	Madrid	7	NULL
TRUE	FRNDO	Madrid	1	FRNDO
TRUE	FRNDO	Madrid	2	FRNDO
FALSE	FRNDO	Madrid	3	KRLOS
FALSE	FRNDO	Madrid	4	KRLOS
FALSE	FRNDO	Madrid	5	KRLOS
FALSE	FRNDO	Madrid	6	MRPHS
UNKNOWN	FRNDO	Madrid	7	NULL
FALSE	KRLOS	Madrid	1	FRNDO
FALSE	KRLOS	Madrid	2	FRNDO
TRUE	KRLOS	Madrid	3	KRLOS
TRUE	KRLOS	Madrid	4	KRLOS
TRUE	KRLOS	Madrid	5	KRLOS
FALSE	KRLOS	Madrid	6	MRPHS
UNKNOWN	KRLOS	Madrid	7	NULL
FALSE	MRPHS	Zion	1	FRNDO
FALSE	MRPHS	Zion	2	FRNDO
FALSE	MRPHS	Zion	3	KRLOS
FALSE	MRPHS	Zion	4	KRLOS
FALSE	MRPHS	Zion	5	KRLOS
TRUE	MRPHS	Zion	6	MRPHS
UNKNOWN	MRPHS	Zion	7	NULL

Only rows for which the *<on_predicate>* is TRUE are inserted into VT1-J2, as shown in Table 1-3.

TABLE 1-3 Virtual table VT1-J2 returned from step 1-J2

Logical value	C.custid	C.city	O.orderid	O.custid
TRUE	FRNDO	Madrid	1	FRNDO
TRUE	FRNDO	Madrid	2	FRNDO
TRUE	KRLOS	Madrid	3	KRLOS
TRUE	KRLOS	Madrid	4	KRLOS
TRUE	KRLOS	Madrid	5	KRLOS
TRUE	MRPHS	Zion	6	MRPHS

Step 1-J3: Add outer rows

This step occurs only for an outer join. For an outer join, you mark one or both input tables as *preserved* by specifying the type of outer join (LEFT, RIGHT, or FULL). Marking a table as preserved means you want all its rows returned, even when filtered out by the *<on_predicate>*. A left outer join marks the left table as preserved, a right outer join marks the right one, and a full outer join marks both. Step 1-J3 returns the rows from VT1-J2, plus rows from the preserved table or tables for which a match was not found in step 1-J2. These added rows are referred to as *outer rows*. NULLs are assigned to the attributes of the nonpreserved table in the outer rows. As a result, virtual table VT1-J3 is generated.

In our example, the preserved table is Customers:

```
Customers AS C LEFT OUTER JOIN Orders AS O
```

Only customer FISSA did not yield any matching orders (and thus wasn't part of VT1-J2). Therefore, a row for FISSA is added to VT1-J2, with NULLs for the Orders attributes. The result is virtual table VT1-J3 (shown in Table 1-4). Because the FROM clause of the sample query has no more table operators, the virtual table VT1-J3 is also the virtual table VT1 returned from the FROM phase.

TABLE 1-4 Virtual table VT1-J3 (also VT1) returned from step 1-J3

C.custid	C.city	O.orderid	O.custid
FRNDO	Madrid	1	FRNDO
FRNDO	Madrid	2	FRNDO
KRLOS	Madrid	3	KRLOS
KRLOS	Madrid	4	KRLOS
KRLOS	Madrid	5	KRLOS
MRPHS	Zion	6	MRPHS
FISSA	Madrid	NULL	NULL

Note If multiple table operators appear in the FROM clause, they are processed from left to right—that's at least the case in terms of the logical query-processing order. The result of each table operator is provided as the left input to the next table operator. The final virtual table will be used as the input for the next step.

Step 2: The WHERE phase

The WHERE filter is applied to all rows in the virtual table returned by the previous step. Those rows for which *<where_predicate>* is TRUE make up the virtual table returned by this step (VT2).

Caution You cannot refer to column aliases created by the SELECT list because the SELECT list was not processed yet—for example, you cannot write *SELECT YEAR(orderdate) AS orderyear ... WHERE orderyear > 2014*. Ironically, some people think that this behavior is a bug in SQL Server, but it can be easily explained when you understand logical query processing. Also, because the data is not yet grouped, you cannot use grouped aggregates here—for example, you cannot write *WHERE orderdate = MAX(orderdate)*.

Apply the filter in the sample query:

```
WHERE C.city = 'Madrid'
```

The row for customer MRPHS from VT1 is removed because the city is not Madrid, and virtual table VT2, which is shown in Table 1-5, is generated.

TABLE 1-5 Virtual table VT2 returned from step 2

C.custid	C.city	O.orderid	O.custid
FRNDO	Madrid	1	FRNDO
FRNDO	Madrid	2	FRNDO
KRLOS	Madrid	3	KRLOS
KRLOS	Madrid	4	KRLOS
KRLOS	Madrid	5	KRLOS
FISSA	Madrid	NULL	NULL

A confusing aspect of queries containing outer joins is whether to specify a predicate in the ON clause or in the WHERE clause. The main difference between the two is that ON is applied before adding outer rows (step 1-J3), whereas WHERE is applied afterward. An elimination of a row from the preserved table by the ON clause is not final because step 1-J3 will add it back; an elimination of a row by the WHERE clause, by contrast, is final. Another way to look at it is to think of the ON predicate as serving a matching purpose, and of the WHERE predicate as serving a more basic filtering purpose. Regarding the rows from the preserved side of the join, the ON clause cannot discard those; it can only determine which rows from the nonpreserved side to match them with. However, the WHERE clause can certainly discard rows from the preserved side. Bearing this in mind should help you make the right choice.

For example, suppose you want to return certain customers and their orders from the Customers and Orders tables. The customers you want to return are only Madrid customers—both those who placed orders and those who did not. An outer join is designed exactly for such a request. You perform a left outer join between Customers and Orders, marking the Customers table as the preserved table. To be able to return customers who placed no orders, you must specify the correlation between Customers and Orders in the ON clause (*ON C.custid = O.custid*). Customers with no orders are eliminated in step 1-J2 but added back in step 1-J3 as outer rows. However, because you want to return only Madrid customers, you must specify the city predicate in the WHERE clause (*WHERE C.city = 'Madrid'*). Specifying the city predicate in the ON clause would cause non-Madrid customers to be added back to the result set by step 1-J3.

> **Tip** This logical difference between the ON and WHERE clauses exists only when using an outer join. When you use an inner join, it doesn't matter where you specify your predicate because step 1-J3 is skipped. The predicates are applied one after the other with no intermediate step between them, both serving a basic filtering purpose.

Step 3: The GROUP BY phase

The GROUP BY phase associates rows from the table returned by the previous step to groups according to the grouping set, or sets, defined in the GROUP BY clause. For simplicity, assume that you have a single set of expressions to group by. This set is called the *grouping set*.

In this phase, the rows from the table returned by the previous step are arranged in groups. Each unique combination of values of the expressions that belong to the grouping set identifies a group. Each row from the previous step is associated with one and only one group. Virtual table VT3 consists of the rows of VT2 arranged in groups (the *raw* information) along with the group identifiers (the *groups* information).

Apply step 3 to the following sample query:

```
GROUP BY C.custid
```

You get the virtual table VT3 shown in Table 1-6.

TABLE 1-6 Virtual table VT3 returned from step 3

Groups	Raw			
C.custid	C.custid	C.city	O.orderid	O.custid
FRNDO	FRNDO FRNDO	Madrid Madrid	1 2	FRNDO FRNDO
KRLOS	KRLOS KRLOS KRLOS	Madrid Madrid Madrid	3 4 5	KRLOS KRLOS KRLOS
FISSA	FISSA	Madrid	NULL	NULL

Eventually, a grouped query will generate one row per group (unless that group is filtered out). Consequently, when GROUP BY is specified in a query, all subsequent steps (HAVING, SELECT, and so on) can specify only expressions that result in a scalar (singular) value per group. These expressions can include columns or expressions from the GROUP BY list—such as *C.custid* in the sample query here—or aggregate functions, such as COUNT(O.orderid).

Examine VT3 in Table 1-6 and think what the query should return for customer FRNDO's group if the SELECT list you specify is *SELECT C.custid, O.orderid*. There are two different *orderid* values in the group; therefore, the answer is not a scalar. SQL doesn't allow such a request. On the other hand, if you specify *SELECT C.custid, COUNT(O.orderid) AS numorders*, the answer for FRNDO is a scalar: it's 2.

This phase considers NULLs as equal. That is, all NULLs are grouped into one group, just like a known value.

Step 4: The HAVING phase

The HAVING filter is applied to the groups in the table returned by the previous step. Only groups for which the *<having_predicate>* is TRUE become part of the virtual table returned by this step (VT4). The HAVING filter is the only filter that applies to the grouped data.

Apply this step to the sample query:

```
HAVING COUNT(O.orderid) < 3
```

The group for KRLOS is removed because it contains three orders. Virtual table VT4, which is shown in Table 1-7, is generated.

TABLE 1-7 Virtual table VT4 returned from step 4

C.custid	C.custid	C.city	O.orderid	O.custid
FRNDO	FRNDO FRNDO	Madrid Madrid	1 2	FRNDO FRNDO
FISSA	FISSA	Madrid	NULL	NULL

Note You must specify *COUNT(O.orderid)* here and not *COUNT(*)*. Because the join is an outer one, outer rows were added for customers with no orders. *COUNT(*)* would have added outer rows to the count, undesirably producing a count of one order for FISSA. *COUNT(O.orderid)* correctly counts the number of orders for each customer, producing the desired value 0 for FISSA. Remember that *COUNT(<expression>)* ignores NULLs just like any other aggregate function.

Note An aggregate function does not accept a subquery as an input—for example, *HAVING SUM((SELECT . . .)) > 10*.

Step 5: The SELECT phase

Though specified first in the query, the SELECT clause is processed only at the fifth step. The SELECT phase constructs the table that will eventually be returned to the caller. This phase involves two sub-phases: (5-1) Evaluate Expressions and (5-2) Apply DISTINCT Clause.

Step 5-1: Evaluate expressions

The expressions in the SELECT list can return columns and manipulations of columns from the virtual table returned by the previous step. Remember that if the query is an aggregate query, after step 3 you can refer to columns from the previous step only if they are part of the groups section (GROUP BY list). If you refer to columns from the raw section, they must be aggregated. Nonmanipulated columns selected from the previous step maintain their original names unless you alias them (for example, *col1 AS c1*). Expressions involving manipulations of columns should be aliased to have a column name in the result table—for example, *YEAR(orderdate) AS orderyear*.

Important As mentioned earlier, aliases created by the SELECT list cannot be used by earlier steps—for example, in the WHERE phase. When you understand the logical processing order of the query clauses, this makes perfect sense. In addition, expression aliases cannot even be used by other expressions within the same SELECT list. The reasoning behind this limitation is another unique aspect of SQL; many operations are all-at-once operations. For example, in the following SELECT list, the logical order in which the expressions are evaluated should not matter and is not guaranteed: *SELECT c1 + 1 AS e1, c2 + 1 AS e2*. Therefore, the following SELECT list is not supported: *SELECT c1 + 1 AS e1, e1 + 1 AS e2*. You're allowed to use column aliases only in steps following the step that defined them. If you define a column alias in the SELECT phase, you can refer to that alias in the ORDER BY phase—for example, *SELECT YEAR(orderdate) AS orderyear . . . ORDER BY orderyear*.

The concept of an all-at-once operation can be hard to grasp. For example, in most pro-gramming environments, to swap values between variables you use a temporary variable. However, to swap table column values in SQL, you can use the following:

```
UPDATE dbo.T1 SET c1 = c2, c2 = c1;
```

Logically, you should assume that the whole operation takes place at once. It is as if the source table is not modified until the whole operation finishes and then the result replaces the source. For similar reasons, the following UPDATE would update all of T1's rows, adding to c1 the same maximum c1 value from T1 when the update started:

```
UPDATE dbo.T1 SET c1 = c1 + (SELECT MAX(c1) FROM dbo.T1);
```

Don't be concerned that the maximum c1 value might keep changing as the operation proceeds; it does not because the operation occurs all at once.

Apply this step to the sample query:

```
SELECT C.custid, COUNT(O.orderid) AS numorders
```

You get the virtual table VT5-1, which is shown in Table 1-8. Because the other possible subphase (DISTINCT) of the SELECT phase isn't applied in the sample query, the virtual table VT5-1 returned by this subphase is also the virtual table VT5 returned by the SELECT phase.

TABLE 1-8 Virtual table VT5-1 (also VT5) returned from step 5

C.custid	numorders
FRNDO	2
FISSA	0

Step 5-2: Apply the DISTINCT clause

If a DISTINCT clause is specified in the query, duplicate rows are removed from the virtual table returned by the previous step, and virtual table VT5-2 is generated.

Note SQL deviates from the relational model by allowing a table to have duplicate rows (when a primary key or unique constraint is not enforced) and a query to return duplicate rows in the result. According to the relational model, the body of a relation is a set of *tuples* (what SQL calls *rows*), and according to mathematical set theory, a *set* (as opposed to a *multiset*) has no duplicates. Using the DISTINCT clause, you can ensure that a query returns unique rows and, in this sense, conform to the relational model.

You should realize that the SELECT phase first evaluates expressions (subphase 5-1) and only after-ward removes duplicate rows (subphase 5-2). If you don't realize this, you might be surprised by the

results of some queries. As an example, the following query returns distinct customer IDs of customers who placed orders:

```
SELECT DISTINCT custid
FROM dbo.Orders
WHERE custid IS NOT NULL;
```

As you probably expected, this query returns three rows in the result set:

```
custid
------
FRNDO
KRLOS
MRPHS
```

Suppose you wanted to add row numbers to the result rows based on *custid* ordering. Not realizing the problem, you add to the query an expression based on the ROW_NUMBER function, like so
(don't run the query yet):

```
SELECT DISTINCT custid, ROW_NUMBER() OVER(ORDER BY custid) AS rownum
FROM dbo.Orders
WHERE custid IS NOT NULL;
```

Before you run the query, how many rows do you expect to get in the result? If your answer is
3, you're wrong. That's because phase 5-1 evaluates all expressions, including the one based on the
ROW_NUMBER function, before duplicates are removed. In this example, the SELECT phase operates
on table VT4, which has five rows (after the WHERE filter was applied). Therefore, phase 5-1 generates
a table VT5-1 with five rows with row numbers 1 through 5. Including the row numbers, those rows
are already unique. So when phase 5-2 is applied, it finds no duplicates to remove. Here's the result of
this query:

```
custid rownum
------ --------------------
FRNDO  1
FRNDO  2
KRLOS  3
KRLOS  4
KRLOS  5
MRPHS  6
```

If you want to assign row numbers to distinct customer IDs, you have to get rid of duplicate customer IDs before you assign the row numbers. This can be achieved by using a table expression such
as a common table expression (CTE), like so:

```
WITH C AS
(
  SELECT DISTINCT custid
  FROM dbo.Orders
  WHERE custid IS NOT NULL
)
SELECT custid, ROW_NUMBER() OVER(ORDER BY custid) AS rownum
FROM C;
```

This time you do get the desired output:

```
custid rownum
------ --------------------
FRNDO  1
KRLOS  2
MRPHS  3
```

Back to our original sample query from Listing 1-2, step 5-2 is skipped because DISTINCT is not specified. In this query, it would remove no rows anyway.

Step 6: The ORDER BY phase

The rows from the previous step are sorted according to the column list specified in the ORDER BY clause, returning the cursor VC6. The ORDER BY clause is the only step where column aliases created in the SELECT phase can be reused.

If DISTINCT is specified, the expressions in the ORDER BY clause have access only to the virtual table returned by the SELECT phase (VT5). If DISTINCT is not specified, expressions in the ORDER BY clause can access both the input and the output virtual tables of the SELECT phase (VT4 and VT5). Moreover, if DISTINCT isn't present, you can specify in the ORDER BY clause any expression that would have been allowed in the SELECT clause. Namely, you can sort by expressions that you don't end up returning in the final result set.

There is a reason for not allowing access to expressions you're not returning if DISTINCT is specified. When adding expressions to the SELECT list, DISTINCT can potentially change the number of rows returned. Without DISTINCT, of course, changes in the SELECT list don't affect the number of rows returned.

In our example, because DISTINCT is not specified, the ORDER BY clause has access to both VT4, shown in Table 1-7, and VT5, shown in Table 1-8.

In the ORDER BY clause, you can also specify ordinal positions of result columns from the SELECT list. For example, the following query sorts the orders first by *custid* and then by *orderid*:

```
SELECT orderid, custid FROM dbo.Orders ORDER BY 2, 1;
```

However, this practice is not recommended because you might make changes to the SELECT list and forget to revise the ORDER BY list accordingly. Also, when the query strings are long, it's hard to figure out which item in the ORDER BY list corresponds to which item in the SELECT list.

When describing the contents of a table, most people (including me) routinely depict the rows in a certain order. But because a table is a set of rows with no particular order, such depiction can cause some confusion by implying otherwise. Figure 1-2 shows an example for depicting the content of tables in a more correct way that doesn't imply order.

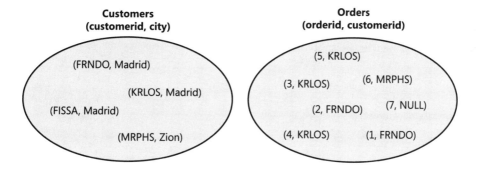

FIGURE 1-2 Customers and Orders sets.

Because this step doesn't return a table (it returns a cursor), a query with an ORDER BY clause that serves only a presentation ordering purpose cannot be used to define a table expression—that is, a view, an inline table-valued function, a derived table, or a CTE. Rather, the result must be consumed by a target that can handle the records one at a time, in order. Such a target can be a client application, or T-SQL code using a CURSOR object. An attempt to consume a cursor result by a target that expects a relational input will fail. For example, the following attempt to define a derived table is invalid and produces an error:

```
SELECT orderid, custid
FROM ( SELECT orderid, custid
       FROM dbo.Orders
       ORDER BY orderid DESC  ) AS D;
```

Similarly, the following attempt to define a view is invalid:

```
CREATE VIEW dbo.MyOrders
AS

SELECT orderid, custid
FROM dbo.Orders
ORDER BY orderid DESC;
GO
```

There is an exceptional case in which T-SQL allows defining a table expression based on a query with an ORDER BY clause—when the query also specifies the TOP or OFFSET-FETCH filter. I'll explain this exceptional case shortly after describing these filters.

The ORDER BY clause considers NULLs as equal. That is, NULLs are sorted together. Standard SQL leaves the question of whether NULLs are sorted lower or higher than known values up to implementations, which must be consistent. T-SQL sorts NULLs as lower than known values (first).

Apply this step to the sample query from Listing 1-2:

```
ORDER BY numorders
```

You get the cursor VC6 shown in Table 1-9.

TABLE 1-9 Cursor VC6 returned from step 6

C.custid	numorders
FISSA	0
FRNDO	2

Step 7: Apply the TOP or OFFSET-FETCH filter

TOP and OFFSET-FETCH are query filters that are based on a count of rows and order. This is in contrast to the more classic query filters (ON, WHERE, and HAVING), which are based on a predicate. TOP is a T-SQL specific filter, whereas OFFSET-FETCH is standard. As mentioned, OFFSET-FETCH was introduced in SQL Server 2012. This section describes these filters in the context of logical query processing.

The TOP filter involves two elements in its specification. One (required) is the number or percentage of rows (rounded up) to be filtered. The other (optional) is the order defining which rows to filter. Unfortunately, the ordering specification for TOP (and the same goes for OFFSET-FETCH) is defined by the classic presentation ORDER BY clause in the query, as opposed to being disconnected from it and independent of it. I'll explain in a moment why this design choice is problematic and leads to confusion. If order is not specified, you should assume it to be arbitrary, yielding a nondeterministic result. This means that if you run the query multiple times, you're not guaranteed to get repeatable results even if the underlying data remains unchanged. Virtual table VT7 is generated. If the order is specified, cursor VC7 is generated. As an example, the following query returns the three orders with the highest *orderid* values:

```
SELECT TOP (3) orderid, custid
FROM dbo.Orders
ORDER BY orderid DESC;
```

This query generates the following output:

```
orderid     custid
----------- ------
7           NULL
6           MRPHS
5           KRLOS
```

Even when order is specified, this fact alone doesn't guarantee determinism. If the ordering isn't unique (for example, if you change *orderid* in the preceding query to *custid*), the order between rows with the same sort values should be considered arbitrary. There are two ways to make a TOP filter deterministic. One is to specify a unique ORDER BY list (for example, *custid, orderid*). Another is to use a non-unique ORDER BY list and add the WITH TIES option. This option causes the filter to include also all other rows from the underlying query result that have the same sort values as the last row returned. With this option, the choice of which rows to return becomes deterministic, but the presentation ordering still isn't in terms of rows with the same sort values.

The OFFSET-FETCH filter is similar to TOP, but it adds the option to indicate how many rows to skip (OFFSET clause) before indicating how many rows to filter (FETCH clause). Both the OFFSET and FETCH clauses are specified after the mandatory ORDER BY clause. As an example, the following query specifies the order based on *orderid*, descending, and it skips four rows and filters the next two rows:

```
SELECT orderid, custid
FROM dbo.Orders
ORDER BY orderid DESC
OFFSET 4 ROWS FETCH NEXT 2 ROWS ONLY;
```

This query returns the following output:

```
orderid     custid
----------- ------
3           KRLOS
2           FRNDO
```

As of SQL Server 2014, the implementation of OFFSET-FETCH in T-SQL doesn't yet support the PERCENT and WITH TIES options even though standard SQL does. This step generates cursor VC7.

Step 7 is skipped in our example because TOP and OFFSET-FETCH are not specified.

I mentioned earlier that the ordering for TOP and OFFSET-FETCH is defined by the same ORDER BY clause that traditionally defines presentation ordering, and that this causes confusion. Consider the following query as an example:

```
SELECT TOP (3) orderid, custid
FROM dbo.Orders
ORDER BY orderid DESC;
```

Here the ORDER BY clause serves two different purposes. One is the traditional presentation ordering (present the returned rows based on *orderid*, descending ordering). The other is to define for the TOP filter which three rows to pick (the three rows with the highest *orderid* values). But things get confusing if you want to define a table expression based on such a query. Recall from the section "Step 6: The ORDER BY phase," that normally you are not allowed to define a table expression based on a query with an ORDER BY clause because such a query generates a cursor. I demonstrated attempts to define a derived table and a view that failed because the inner query had an ORDER BY clause.

There is an exception to this restriction, but it needs to be well understood to avoid incorrect expectations. The exception says that the inner query is allowed to have an ORDER BY clause to support a TOP or OFFSET-FETCH filter. But what's important to remember in such a case is that if the outer query doesn't have a presentation ORDER BY clause, the presentation ordering of the result is not guaranteed. The ordering is relevant only for the immediate query that contains the ORDER BY clause. If you want to guarantee presentation ordering of the result, the outermost query must include an ORDER BY clause. Here's the exact language in the standard that indicates this fact, from ISO/IEC 9075-2:2011(E), section 4.15.3 Derived Tables:

A <query expression> can contain an optional <order by clause>. The ordering of the rows of the table specified by the <query expression> is guaranteed only for the <query expression> that immediately contains the <order by clause>.

Despite what you observe in practice, in the following example presentation ordering of the result is not guaranteed because the outermost query doesn't have an ORDER BY clause:

```
SELECT orderid, custid
FROM ( SELECT TOP (3) orderid, custid
       FROM dbo.Orders
       ORDER BY orderid DESC          ) AS D;
```

Suppose you run the preceding query and get a result that seems to be sorted in accordance with the inner query's ordering specification. It doesn't mean that the behavior is guaranteed to be repeatable. It could be a result of optimization aspects, and those are not guaranteed to be repeatable. This is one of the most common traps that SQL practitioners fall into—drawing a conclusion and basing expectations on observed behavior as opposed to correctly understanding the theory.

Along similar lines, a common mistake that people make is to attempt to create a "sorted view." Remember that if you specify the TOP or OFFSET-FETCH options, you are allowed to include an ORDER BY clause in the inner query. So one way some try to achieve this without actually filtering rows is to specify the TOP (100) PERCENT option, like so:

```
-- Attempt to create a sorted view
IF OBJECT_ID(N'dbo.MyOrders', N'V') IS NOT NULL DROP VIEW dbo.MyOrders;
GO
```

```
-- Note: This does not create a "sorted view"!
CREATE VIEW dbo.MyOrders
AS

SELECT TOP (100) PERCENT orderid, custid
FROM dbo.Orders
ORDER BY orderid DESC;
GO
```

Consider the following query against the view:

```
SELECT orderid, custid FROM dbo.MyOrders;
```

According to what I just explained, if you query such a view and do not specify an ORDER BY clause in the outer query, you don't get any presentation ordering assurances. When I ran this query on my system, I got the result in the following order:

```
orderid     custid
----------- ------
1           FRNDO
2           FRNDO
3           KRLOS
4           KRLOS
5           KRLOS
6           MRPHS
7           NULL
```

As you can see, the result wasn't returned based on *orderid*, descending ordering. Here the SQL Server query optimizer was smart enough to realize that because the outer query doesn't have an ORDER BY clause, and *TOP (100) PERCENT* doesn't really filter any rows, it can ignore both the filter and its ordering specification.

Another attempt to create a sorted view is to specify an OFFSET clause with 0 rows and omit the FETCH clause, like so:

```
-- Attempt to create a sorted view
IF OBJECT_ID(N'dbo.MyOrders', N'V') IS NOT NULL DROP VIEW dbo.MyOrders;
GO

-- Note: This does not create a "sorted view"!
CREATE VIEW dbo.MyOrders
AS

SELECT orderid, custid
FROM dbo.Orders
ORDER BY orderid DESC
OFFSET 0 ROWS;
GO

-- Query view
SELECT orderid, custid FROM dbo.MyOrders;
```

When I ran this query on my system, I got the result in the following order:

```
orderid      custid
-----------  ------
7            NULL
6            MRPHS
5            KRLOS
4            KRLOS
3            KRLOS
2            FRNDO
1            FRNDO
```

The result seems to be sorted by *orderid*, descending, but you still need to remember that this is not guaranteed behavior. It's just that with this case the optimizer doesn't have logic embedded in it yet to ignore the filter with its ordering specification like in the previous case.

All this confusion can be avoided if the filters are designed with their own ordering specification, independent of, and disconnected from, the presentation ORDER BY clause. An example for a good design that makes this separation is that of window functions like ROW_NUMBER. You specify the order for the ranking calculation, independent of any ordering that you may or may not want to define in the query for presentation purposes. But alas, for TOP and OFFSET-FETCH, that ship has sailed already. So the responsibility is now on us, the users, to understand the existing design well, and to know what to expect from it, and more importantly, what not to expect from it.

When you're done, run the following code for cleanup:

```
IF OBJECT_ID(N'dbo.MyOrders', N'V') IS NOT NULL DROP VIEW dbo.MyOrders;
```

Further aspects of logical query processing

This section covers further aspects of logical query processing, including table operators (JOIN, APPLY, PIVOT, and UNPIVOT), window functions, and additional relational operators (UNION, EXCEPT, and INTERSECT). Note that I could say much more about these language elements besides their logical query-processing aspects, but that's the focus of this chapter. Also, if a language element described in this section is completely new to you (for example, PIVOT, UNPIVOT, or APPLY), it might be a bit hard to fully comprehend its meaning at this point. Later in the book, I'll conduct more detailed discussions, including uses, performance aspects, and so on. You can then return to this chapter and read about the logical query-processing aspects of that language element again to better comprehend its meaning.

Table operators

T-SQL supports four table operators in the FROM clause of a query: JOIN, APPLY, PIVOT, and UNPIVOT.

Note APPLY, PIVOT, and UNPIVOT are not standard operators; rather, they are extensions specific to T-SQL. APPLY has a similar parallel in the standard called LATERAL, but PIVOT and UNPIVOT don't.

I covered the logical processing phases involved with joins earlier. Here I'll briefly describe the other three operators and the way they fit in the logical query-processing model.

Table operators get one or two tables as inputs. Call them *left input* and *right input* based on their position with respect to the table operator keyword (*JOIN, APPLY, PIVOT, UNPIVOT*). An input table could be, without being restricted, one of many options: a regular table, a temporary table, table variable, derived table, CTE, view, or table-valued function. In logical query-processing terms, table operators are evaluated from left to right, with the virtual table returned by one table operator becoming the left input table of the next table operator.

Each table operator involves a different set of steps. For convenience and clarity, I'll prefix the step numbers with the initial of the table operator (J for JOIN, A for APPLY, P for PIVOT, and U for UNPIVOT).

Following are the four table operators along with their elements:

```
(J) <left_input_table>
      {CROSS | INNER | OUTER} JOIN <right_input_table>
        ON <on_predicate>

(A) <left_input_table>
      {CROSS | OUTER} APPLY <right_input_table>

(P) <left_input_table>
      PIVOT (<aggregate_func(<aggregation_element>)> FOR
        <spreading_element> IN(<target_col_list>))
          AS <result_table_alias>

(U) <left_input_table>
      UNPIVOT (<target_values_col> FOR
        <target_names_col> IN(<source_col_list>))
          AS <result_table_alias>
```

As a reminder, a *join* involves a subset (depending on the join type) of the following steps:

- J1: Apply Cartesian Product

- J2: Apply ON Predicate

- J3: Add Outer Rows

APPLY

The APPLY operator (depending on the apply type) involves one or both of the following two steps:

1. **A1:** Apply Right Table Expression to Left Table Rows

2. **A2:** Add Outer Rows

The APPLY operator applies the right table expression to every row from the left input. The right table expression can refer to the left input's columns. The right input is evaluated once for each row from the left. This step unifies the sets produced by matching each left row with the corresponding rows from the right table expression, and this step returns the combined result.

Step A1 is applied in both CROSS APPLY and OUTER APPLY. Step A2 is applied only for OUTER APPLY. CROSS APPLY doesn't return an outer (left) row if the inner (right) table expression returns an empty set for it. OUTER APPLY will return such a row, with NULLs as placeholders for the inner table expression's attributes.

For example, the following query returns the two orders with the highest order IDs for each customer:

```
SELECT C.custid, C.city, A.orderid
FROM dbo.Customers AS C
  CROSS APPLY
    ( SELECT TOP (2) O.orderid, O.custid
      FROM dbo.Orders AS O
      WHERE O.custid = C.custid
      ORDER BY orderid DESC              ) AS A;
```

This query generates the following output:

```
custid     city       orderid
---------- ---------- -----------
FRNDO      Madrid     2
FRNDO      Madrid     1
KRLOS      Madrid     5
KRLOS      Madrid     4
MRPHS      Zion       6
```

Notice that FISSA is missing from the output because the table expression A returned an empty set for it. If you also want to return customers who placed no orders, use OUTER APPLY as follows:

```
SELECT C.custid, C.city, A.orderid
FROM dbo.Customers AS C
  OUTER APPLY
    ( SELECT TOP (2) O.orderid, O.custid
      FROM dbo.Orders AS O
      WHERE O.custid = C.custid
      ORDER BY orderid DESC              ) AS A;
```

This query generates the following output:

```
custid       city        orderid
----------   ----------  -----------
FISSA        Madrid      NULL
FRNDO        Madrid      2
FRNDO        Madrid      1
KRLOS        Madrid      5
KRLOS        Madrid      4
MRPHS        Zion        6
```

PIVOT

You use the PIVOT operator to rotate, or pivot, data from rows to columns, performing aggregations along the way.

Suppose you want to query the Sales.OrderValues view in the TSQLV3 sample database (see the book's introduction for details on the sample database) and return the total value of orders handled by each employee for each order year. You want the output to have a row for each employee, a column for each order year, and the total value in the intersection of each employee and year. The following PIVOT query allows you to achieve this:

```
USE TSQLV3;

SELECT empid, [2013], [2014], [2015]
FROM ( SELECT empid, YEAR(orderdate) AS orderyear, val
       FROM Sales.OrderValues                          ) AS D
  PIVOT( SUM(val) FOR orderyear IN([2013],[2014],[2015]) ) AS P;
```

This query generates the following output:

```
empid  2013      2014       2015
------ --------- ---------- ---------
9      9894.52   26310.39   41103.17
3      18223.96  108026.17  76562.75
6      16642.61  43126.38   14144.16
7      15232.16  60471.19   48864.89
1      35764.52  93148.11   63195.02
4      49945.12  128809.81  54135.94
5      18383.92  30716.48   19691.90
2      21757.06  70444.14   74336.56
8      22240.12  56032.63   48589.54
```

Don't get distracted by the subquery that generates the derived table D. As far as you're concerned, the PIVOT operator gets a table expression called D as its left input, with a row for each order, with the employee ID (*empid*), order year (*orderyear*), and order value (*val*). The PIVOT operator involves the following three logical phases:

1. P1: Grouping

2. P2: Spreading

3. P3: Aggregating

The first phase (P1) is tricky. You can see in the query that the PIVOT operator refers to two of the columns from D as input arguments (*val* and *orderyear*). The first phase implicitly groups the rows from D based on all columns that weren't mentioned in PIVOT's inputs, as though a hidden GROUP BY were there. In our case, only the *empid* column wasn't mentioned anywhere in PIVOT's input arguments. So you get a group for each employee.

> **Note** PIVOT's implicit grouping phase doesn't affect any explicit GROUP BY clause in a query. The PIVOT operation will yield a virtual result table as input to the next logical phase, be it another table operator or the WHERE phase. And as I described earlier in the chapter, a GROUP BY phase might follow the WHERE phase. So when both PIVOT and GROUP BY appear in a query, you get two separate grouping phases—one as the first phase of PIVOT (P1) and a later one as the query's GROUP BY phase.

PIVOT's second phase (P2) spreads values of *<spreading_col>* to their corresponding target columns. Logically, it uses the following CASE expression for each target column specified in the IN clause:

```
CASE WHEN <spreading_col> = <target_col_element> THEN <expression> END
```

In this situation, the following three expressions are logically applied:

```
CASE WHEN orderyear = 2013 THEN val END,
CASE WHEN orderyear = 2014 THEN val END,
CASE WHEN orderyear = 2015 THEN val END
```

> **Note** A CASE expression with no ELSE clause has an implicit ELSE NULL.

For each target column, the CASE expression will return the value (*val* column) only if the source row had the corresponding order year; otherwise, the CASE expression will return NULL.

PIVOT's third phase (P3) applies the specified aggregate function on top of each CASE expression, generating the result columns. In our case, the expressions logically become the following:

```
SUM(CASE WHEN orderyear = 2013 THEN val END) AS [2013],
SUM(CASE WHEN orderyear = 2014 THEN val END) AS [2014],
SUM(CASE WHEN orderyear = 2015 THEN val END) AS [2015]
```

In summary, the previous PIVOT query is logically equivalent to the following query:

```
SELECT empid,
  SUM(CASE WHEN orderyear = 2013 THEN val END) AS [2013],
  SUM(CASE WHEN orderyear = 2014 THEN val END) AS [2014],
  SUM(CASE WHEN orderyear = 2015 THEN val END) AS [2015]
FROM ( SELECT empid, YEAR(orderdate) AS orderyear, val
       FROM Sales.OrderValues                          ) AS D
GROUP BY empid;
```

UNPIVOT

Recall that the PIVOT operator rotates data from rows to columns. Inversely, the UNPIVOT operator rotates data from columns to rows.

Before I demonstrate UNPIVOT's logical phases, first run the following code, which creates and populates the dbo.EmpYearValues table and queries it to present its content:

```
SELECT empid, [2013], [2014], [2015]
INTO dbo.EmpYearValues
FROM ( SELECT empid, YEAR(orderdate) AS orderyear, val
       FROM Sales.OrderValues                          ) AS D
  PIVOT( SUM(val) FOR orderyear IN([2013],[2014],[2015]) ) AS P;

UPDATE dbo.EmpYearValues
  SET [2013] = NULL
WHERE empid IN(1, 2);

SELECT empid, [2013], [2014], [2015] FROM dbo.EmpYearValues;
```

This code returns the following output:

```
empid       2013        2014        2015
----------- ----------- ----------- -----------
3           18223.96    108026.17   76562.75
6           16642.61    43126.38    14144.16
9           9894.52     26310.39    41103.17
7           15232.16    60471.19    48864.89
1           NULL        93148.11    63195.02
4           49945.12    128809.81   54135.94
2           NULL        70444.14    74336.56
5           18383.92    30716.48    19691.90
8           22240.12    56032.63    48589.54
```

I'll use the following query as an example to describe the logical processing phases involved with the UNPIVOT operator:

```
SELECT empid, orderyear, val
FROM dbo.EmpYearValues
  UNPIVOT( val FOR orderyear IN([2013],[2014],[2015]) ) AS U;
```

This query unpivots (or splits) the employee yearly values from each source row to a separate row per order year, generating the following output:

```
empid       orderyear   val
----------- ----------  -----------
3           2013        18223.96
3           2014        108026.17
3           2015        76562.75
6           2013        16642.61
6           2014        43126.38
6           2015        14144.16
9           2013        9894.52
9           2014        26310.39
9           2015        41103.17
7           2013        15232.16
7           2014        60471.19
7           2015        48864.89
1           2014        93148.11
1           2015        63195.02
4           2013        49945.12
4           2014        128809.81
4           2015        54135.94
2           2014        70444.14
2           2015        74336.56
5           2013        18383.92
5           2014        30716.48
5           2015        19691.90
8           2013        22240.12
8           2014        56032.63
8           2015        48589.54
```

The following three logical processing phases are involved in an UNPIVOT operation:

1. U1: Generating Copies

2. U2: Extracting Element

3. U3: Removing Rows with NULLs

The first step (U1) generates copies of the rows from the left table expression provided to UNPIVOT as an input (EmpYearValues, in our case). This step generates a copy for each column that is unpivoted (appears in the IN clause of the UNPIVOT operator). Because there are three column names in the IN clause, three copies are produced from each source row. The resulting virtual table will contain a new column holding the source column names as character strings. The name of this column will be the one specified right before the IN clause (*orderyear*, in our case). The virtual table returned from the first step in our example is shown in Table 1-10.

TABLE 1-10 Virtual table returned from UNPIVOT's first step

empid	2013	2014	2015	orderyear
3	18223.96	108026.17	76562.75	2013
3	18223.96	108026.17	76562.75	2014
3	18223.96	108026.17	76562. 75	2015
6	16642.61	43126.38	14144.16	2013
6	16642.61	43126.38	14144.16	2014
6	16642.61	43126.38	14144.16	2015
9	9894.52	26310.39	41103.17	2013
9	9894.52	26310.39	41103.17	2014
9	9894.52	26310.39	41103.17	2015
7	15232.16	60471.19	48864.89	2013
7	15232.16	60471.19	48864.89	2014
7	15232.16	60471.19	48864.89	2015
1	NULL	93148.11	63195.02	2013
1	NULL	93148.11	63195.02	2014
1	NULL	93148.11	63195.02	2015
4	49945.12	128809.81	54135.94	2013
4	49945.12	128809.81	54135.94	2014
4	49945.12	128809.81	54135.94	2015
2	NULL	70444.14	74336.56	2013
2	NULL	70444.14	74336.56	2014
2	NULL	70444.14	74336.56	2015
5	18383.92	30716.48	19691.90	2013
5	18383.92	30716.48	19691.90	2014
5	18383.92	30716.48	19691.90	2015
8	22240.12	56032.63	48589.54	2013
8	22240.12	56032.63	48589.54	2014
8	22240.12	56032.63	48589.54	2015

The second step (U2) extracts the value from the source column corresponding to the unpivoted element that the current copy of the row represents. The name of the target column that will hold the values is specified right before the FOR clause (*val* in our case). The target column will contain the value from the source column corresponding to the current row's order year from the virtual table. The virtual table returned from this step in our example is shown in Table 1-11.

TABLE 1-11 Virtual table returned from UNPIVOT's second step

empid	val	orderyear
3	18223.96	2013
3	108026.17	2014
3	76562.75	2015
6	16642.61	2013
6	43126.38	2014
6	14144.16	2015
9	9894.52	2013
9	26310.39	2014
9	41103.17	2015
7	15232.16	2013
7	60471.19	2014
7	48864.89	2015
1	NULL	2013
1	93148.11	2014
1	63195.02	2015
4	49945.12	2013
4	128809.81	2014
4	54135.94	2015
2	NULL	2013
2	70444.14	2014
2	74336.56	2015
5	18383.92	2013
5	30716.48	2014
5	19691.90	2015
8	22240.12	2013
8	56032.63	2014
8	48589.54	2015

UNPIVOT's third and final step (U3) is to remove rows with NULLs in the result value column (*val,* in our case). The virtual table returned from this step in our example is shown in Table 1-12.

TABLE 1-12 Virtual table returned from UNPIVOT's third step

empid	val	orderyear
3	18223.96	2013
3	108026.17	2014
3	76562.75	2015
6	16642.61	2013
6	43126.38	2014
6	14144.16	2015
9	9894.52	2013
9	26310.39	2014
9	41103.17	2015
7	15232.16	2013
7	60471.19	2014
7	48864.89	2015
1	93148.11	2014
1	63195.02	2015
4	49945.12	2013
4	128809.81	2014
4	54135.94	2015
2	70444.14	2014
2	74336.56	2015
5	18383.92	2013
5	30716.48	2014
5	19691.90	2015
8	22240.12	2013
8	56032.63	2014
8	48589.54	2015

When you're done, run the following code for cleanup:

```
IF OBJECT_ID(N'dbo.EmpYearValues', N'U') IS NOT NULL DROP TABLE dbo.EmpYearValues;
```

Window functions

You use window functions to apply a data-analysis calculation against a set (a *window*) derived from the underlying query result set, per underlying row. You use a clause called OVER to define the window specification. T-SQL supports a number of types of window functions: aggregate, ranking, offset, and statistical. As is the practice with other features described in this chapter, the focus here will be just on the logical query-processing context.

As mentioned, the set that the window function applies to is derived from the underlying query result set. If you think about it in terms of logical query processing, the underlying query result set is achieved only when you get to the SELECT phase (5). Before this phase, the result is still shaping. For this reason, window functions are restricted only to the SELECT (5) and ORDER BY (6) phases, as Listing 1-3 highlights.

LISTING 1-3 Window functions in logical query processing

```
(5) SELECT (5-2) DISTINCT (7) TOP(<top_specification>) (5-1) <select_list>
(1) FROM (1-J) <left_table> <join_type> JOIN <right_table> ON <on_predicate>
      | (1-A) <left_table> <apply_type> APPLY <right_input_table> AS <alias>
      | (1-P) <left_table> PIVOT(<pivot_specification>) AS <alias>
      | (1-U) <left_table> UNPIVOT(<unpivot_specification>) AS <alias>
(2) WHERE <where_predicate>
(3) GROUP BY <group_by_specification>
(4) HAVING <having_predicate>
(6) ORDER BY <order_by_list>
(7) OFFSET <offset_specification> ROWS FETCH NEXT <fetch_specification> ROWS ONLY;
```

Even though I didn't really explain in detail yet how window functions work, I'd like to demonstrate their use in both phases where they are allowed. The following example includes the *COUNT* window aggregate function in the SELECT list:

```
USE TSQLV3;

SELECT orderid, custid,
  COUNT(*) OVER(PARTITION BY custid) AS numordersforcust
FROM Sales.Orders
WHERE shipcountry = N'Spain';
```

This query produces the following output:

```
orderid     custid      numordersforcust
----------- ----------- ----------------
10326       8           3
10801       8           3
10970       8           3
10928       29          5
10568       29          5
10887       29          5
10366       29          5
10426       29          5
10550       30          10
10303       30          10
10888       30          10
10911       30          10
10629       30          10
10872       30          10
10874       30          10
```

10948	30	10
11009	30	10
11037	30	10
11013	69	5
10917	69	5
10306	69	5
10281	69	5
10282	69	5

Before any restrictions are applied, the starting set that the window function operates on is the virtual table provided to the SELECT phase as input—namely, VT4. The window partition clause restricts the rows from the starting set to only those that have the same *custid* value as in the current row. The *COUNT(*)* function counts the number of rows in that set. Remember that the virtual table that the SELECT phase operates on has already undergone WHERE filtering—that is, only orders shipped to Spain have been filtered.

You can also specify window functions in the ORDER BY list. For example, the following query sorts the rows according to the total number of output rows for the customer (in descending order):

```
SELECT orderid, custid,
   COUNT(*) OVER(PARTITION BY custid) AS numordersforcust
FROM Sales.Orders
WHERE shipcountry = N'Spain'
ORDER BY COUNT(*) OVER(PARTITION BY custid) DESC;
```

This query generates the following output:

orderid	custid	numordersforcust
10550	30	10
10303	30	10
10888	30	10
10911	30	10
10629	30	10
10872	30	10
10874	30	10
10948	30	10
11009	30	10
11037	30	10
11013	69	5
10917	69	5
10306	69	5
10281	69	5
10282	69	5
10928	29	5
10568	29	5
10887	29	5
10366	29	5
10426	29	5
10326	8	3
10801	8	3
10970	8	3

The UNION, EXCEPT, and INTERSECT operators

This section focuses on the logical query-processing aspects of the operators UNION (both ALL and implied distinct versions), EXCEPT, and INTERSECT. These operators correspond to similar operators in mathematical set theory, but in SQL's case are applied to relations, which are a special kind of a set. Listing 1-4 contains a general form of a query applying one of these operators, along with numbers assigned according to the order in which the different elements of the code are logically processed.

LISTING 1-4 General form of a query applying a UNION, EXCEPT, or INTERSECT operator

```
(1) query1
(2) <operator>
(1) query2
(3) [ORDER BY <order_by_list>]
```

The UNION, EXCEPT, and INTERSECT operators compare complete rows between the two inputs. There are two kinds of UNION operators supported in T-SQL. The UNION ALL operator returns one result set with all rows from both inputs combined. The UNION operator returns one result set with the distinct rows from both inputs combined (no duplicates). The EXCEPT operator returns distinct rows that appear in the first input but not in the second. The INTERSECT operator returns the distinct rows that appear in both inputs.

An ORDER BY clause is not allowed in the individual queries because the queries are supposed to return sets (unordered). You are allowed to specify an ORDER BY clause at the end of the query, and it will apply to the result of the operator.

In terms of logical processing, each input query is first processed separately with all its relevant phases (minus a presentation ORDER BY, which is not allowed). The operator is then applied, and if an ORDER BY clause is specified, it is applied to the result set.

Take the following query as an example:

```
USE TSQLV3;

SELECT region, city
FROM Sales.Customers
WHERE country = N'USA'

INTERSECT

SELECT region, city
FROM HR.Employees
WHERE country = N'USA'

ORDER BY region, city;
```

This query generates the following output:

```
region          city
--------------- ---------------
WA              Kirkland
WA              Seattle
```

First, each input query is processed separately following all the relevant logical processing phases. The first query returns locations (*region*, *city*) of customers from the United States. The second query returns locations of employees from the United States. The INTERSECT operator returns distinct rows that appear in both inputs—in our case, locations that are both customer locations and employee locations. Finally, the ORDER BY clause sorts the rows by *region* and *city*.

As another example for logical processing phases, the following query uses the EXCEPT operator to return customers that have made no orders:

```
SELECT custid FROM Sales.Customers
EXCEPT
SELECT custid FROM Sales.Orders;
```

The first query returns the set of customer IDs from Customers, and the second query returns the set of customer IDs from Orders. The EXCEPT operator returns the set of rows from the first set that do not appear in the second set. Remember that a set has no duplicates; the EXCEPT operator returns distinct occurrences of rows from the first set that do not appear in the second set.

The result set's column names are determined by the operator's first input. Columns in corresponding positions must have compatible data types. Finally, when comparing rows, the UNION, EXCEPT, and INTERSECT operators implicitly use the distinct predicate. (One NULL is not distinct from another NULL; a NULL is distinct from a non-NULL value.)

Conclusion

Understanding logical query processing and the unique aspects of SQL is essential to SQL practitioners. By being familiar with those aspects of the language, you can produce correct solutions and explain your choices. Remember, the idea is to master the basics.

CHAPTER 2

Query tuning

Chapter 1, "Logical query processing," focused on the logical design of SQL. This chapter focuses on the physical implementation in the Microsoft SQL Server platform. Because SQL is based on a standard, you will find that the core language elements look the same in the different database platforms. However, because the physical layer is not based on a standard, there you will see bigger differences between the different platforms. Therefore, to be good at query tuning you need to get intimately familiar with the physical layer in the particular platform you are working with. This chapter covers various aspects of the physical layer in SQL Server to give you a foundation for query tuning.

To tune queries, you need to analyze query execution plans and look at performance measures that different performance tools give you. A critical step in this process is to try and identify which activities in the plan represent more work, and somehow connect the relevant parts of the performance measures to those activities. Once you have this part figured out, you need to try and eliminate or reduce the activities that represent the majority of the work.

To understand what you see in the query execution plans, you need to be very familiar with access methods. To understand access methods, well, you need to be very familiar with the internal data structures that SQL Server uses.

This chapter starts by covering internal data structures. It then describes tools you will use to measure query performance. Those topics are followed by a detailed discussion of access methods and an examination of query-execution plans involving those. This chapter also covers cardinality estimates, indexing features, prioritizing queries for tuning, index and query information and statistics, temporary tables, set-based versus iterative solutions, query tuning with query revisions, and parallel query execution.

This chapter focuses on the traditional disk-based tables. Memory-optimized tables are covered separately in Chapter 10, "In-Memory OLTP."

Internals

This section focuses on internal data structures in SQL Server. It starts with a description of pages and extents. It then goes into a discussion about organizing tables as a heap versus as a B-tree and nonclustered indexes.

Pages and extents

A *page* is an 8-KB unit where SQL Server stores data. With disk-based tables, the page is the smallest I/O unit that SQL Server can read or write. Things change in this respect with memory-optimized tables, but as mentioned, those issues are discussed separately in Chapter 10. Figure 2-1 shows an illustration of the page structure.

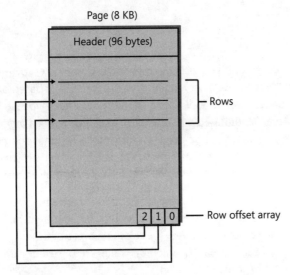

FIGURE 2-1 A diagram of a page.

The 96-byte header of the page holds information such as which allocation unit the page belongs to, pointers to the previous and next pages in the linked list in case the page is part of an index, the amount of free space in the page, and more. Based on the allocation unit, you can eventually figure out which object the page belongs to through the views sys.allocation_units and sys.partitions. For data and index pages, the body of the page contains the data or index records. At the end of the page, there's the row-offset array, which is an array of two-byte pointers that point to the individual records in the page. The combination of the previous and next pointers in the page header and the row-offset array enforce index key order.

To work with a page for read or write purposes, SQL Server needs the page in the buffer pool (the data cache in memory). SQL Server cannot interact with a page directly in the data file on disk. If SQL Server needs to read a page and the page in question is already in the data cache as the result of some previous activity, it will perform only a logical read (read from memory). If the page is not already in memory, SQL Server will first perform a physical read, which pulls the page from the data file to memory, and then it will perform the logical read. Similarly, if SQL Server needs to write a page and the page is already in memory, it will perform a logical write. It will also set the dirty flag in the header of the page in memory to indicate that the state in memory is more recent than the state in the data file.

SQL Server periodically runs processes called *lazywriter* and *checkpoint* to write dirty pages from cache to disk, and it will sometimes use other threads to aid in this task. SQL Server uses an algorithm called *LRU-K2* to prioritize which pages to free from the data cache based on the last two visits (recorded in the page header in memory). SQL Server uses mainly the lazywriter process to mark pages as free based on this algorithm.

An *extent* is a unit that contains eight contiguous pages, as shown in Figure 2-2.

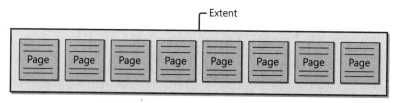

FIGURE 2-2 A diagram of an extent.

SQL Server supports two types of extents, called *mixed* and *uniform*. For new objects (tables or indexes), SQL Server allocates one page at a time from mixed extents until they reach a size of eight pages. So different pages of the same mixed extent can belong to different objects. SQL Server uses bitmap pages called *shared global allocation maps* (SGAMs) to keep track of which extents are mixed and have a page available for allocation. Once an object reaches a size of eight pages, SQL Server applies all future allocations of pages for it from uniform extents. A uniform extent is entirely owned by the same object. SQL Server uses bitmap pages called *global allocation maps* (GAMs) to keep track of which extents are free for allocation.

Table organization

A table can be organized in one of two ways—either as a heap or as a B-tree. Technically, the table is organized as a B-tree when it has a clustered index defined on it and as a heap when it doesn't. You can create a clustered index directly using the CREATE CLUSTERED INDEX command or, starting with SQL Server 2014, using an inline clustered index definition *INDEX <index_name> CLUSTERED*. You can also create a clustered index indirectly through a primary key or unique constraint definition. When you add a primary-key constraint to a table, SQL Server will enforce it using a clustered index unless either you specify the NONCLUSTERED keyword explicitly or a clustered index already exists on the table. When you add a unique constraint to a table, SQL Server will enforce it using a nonclustered index unless you specify the CLUSTERED keyword. Either way, as mentioned, with a clustered index the table is organized as a B-tree and without one it is organized as a heap. Because a table must be organized in one of these two ways—heap or B-tree—the table organization is known as HOBT.

It's far more common to see tables organized as B-trees in SQL Server. The main reason is probably that when you define a primary-key constraint, SQL Server enforces it with a clustered index by default. So, in cases where people create tables without thinking of the physical organization and define primary keys with their defaults, they end up with B-trees. As a result, there's much more experience in SQL Server with B-trees than with heaps. Also, a clustered index gives a lot of control both on insertion patterns and on read patterns. For these reasons, with all other things being equal, I will generally prefer the B-tree organization by default.

There are cases where a heap can give you benefits. For example, in Chapter 6, "Data modification," I describe bulk-import tools and the conditions you need to meet for the import to be processed with minimal logging. If the target table is a B-tree, it must be empty when you start the import if you want to get minimal logging. If it's a heap, you can get minimal logging even if it already contains data. So, when the target table already contains some data and you're adding a lot more, you can get better import performance if you first drop the indexes, do the import into a heap, and then re-create the indexes. In this example, you use a heap as a temporary state.

Regardless of how the table is organized, it can have zero or more nonclustered indexes defined on it. Nonclustered indexes are always organized as B-trees. The HOBT, as well as the nonclustered indexes, can be made of one or more units called *partitions*. Technically, the HOBT and each of the nonclustered indexes can be partitioned differently. Each partition of each HOBT and nonclustered index stores data in collections of pages known as *allocation units*. The three types of allocation units are known as IN_ROW_DATA, ROW_OVERFLOW_DATA, and LOB_DATA.

IN_ROW_DATA holds all fixed-length columns; it also holds variable-length columns as long as the row size does not exceed the 8,060-byte limit. ROW_OVERFLOW_DATA holds VARCHAR, NVARCHAR, VARBINARY, SQL_VARIANT, or CLR user-defined typed data that does not exceed 8,000 bytes but was moved from the original row because it exceeded the 8,060-row size limit. LOB_DATA holds large object values—VARCHAR(MAX), NVARCHAR(MAX), VARBINARY(MAX) that exceed 8,000 bytes, XML, or CLR UDTs. The system view sys.system_internals_allocation_units holds the anchors pointing to the page collections stored in the allocation units.

In the following sections, I describe the heap, clustered index, and nonclustered index structures. For simplicity's sake, I'll assume that the data is nonpartitioned; but if it is partitioned, the description is still applicable to a single partition.

Heap

A *heap* is a table that has no clustered index. The structure is called a *heap* because the data is not organized in any order; rather, it is laid out as a bunch of pages and extents. The Orders table in the sample database PerformanceV3 (see this book's intro for details on how to install the sample database) is actually organized as a B-tree, but Figure 2-3 illustrates what it might look like when organized as a heap.

SQL Server maps the data that belongs to a heap using one or more bitmap pages called *index allocation maps* (IAMs). The header of the IAM page has pointers to the first eight pages that SQL Server allocated for the heap from mixed extents. The header also has a pointer to a starting location of a range of 4 GB that the IAM page maps in the data file. The body of the IAM page has a representative bit for each extent in that range. The bit is 0 if the extent it represents does not belong to the object owning the IAM page and 1 if it does. If one IAM is not enough to cover all the object's data, SQL Server will maintain a chain of IAM pages. When SQL Server needs to scan a heap, it relies on the information in the IAM pages to figure out which pages and extents it needs to read. I will refer to this type of scan as an *allocation order scan*. This scan is done in file order and, therefore, when the data is not cached it usually applies sequential reads.

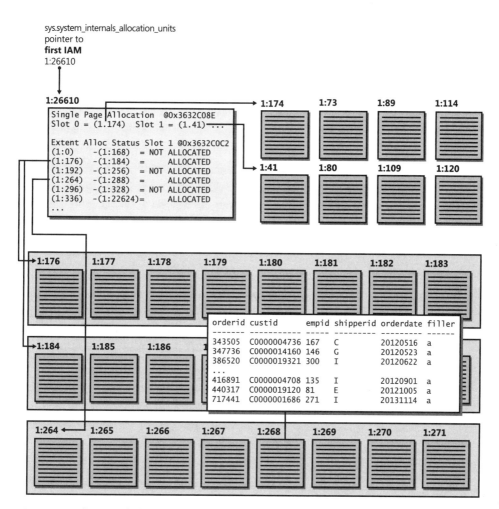

FIGURE 2-3 A diagram of a heap.

As you can see in Figure 2-3, SQL Server maintains internal pointers to the first IAM page and the first data page of a heap. Those pointers can be found in the system view sys.system_internals_allocation_units.

Because a heap doesn't maintain the data in any particular order, new rows that are added to the table can go anywhere. SQL Server uses bitmap pages called *page free space* (PFS) to keep track of free space in pages so that it can quickly find a page with enough free space to accommodate a new row or allocate a new one if no such page exists.

When a row expands as a result of an update to a variable-length column and the page has no room for the row to expand, SQL Server moves the expanded row to a page with enough space to accommodate it and leaves behind what's known as a *forwarding pointer* that points to the new location of the row. The purpose of forwarding pointers is to avoid the need to modify pointers to the row from nonclustered indexes when data rows move.

I didn't yet explain a concept called a *page split* (because page splits can happen only in B-trees), but it suffices to say for now that heaps do not incur page splits.

B-tree (clustered index)

All indexes in SQL Server on disk-based tables are structured as *B-trees*, which are a special case of *balanced trees*. A balanced tree is a tree where no leaf is much farther away from the root than any other leaf.

A *clustered index* is structured as a B-tree, and it maintains the entire table's data in its leaf level. The clustered index is not a copy of the data; rather, it *is* the data. Figure 2-4 illustrates how the Orders table might look when organized as a B-tree with the *orderdate* column defined as the key.

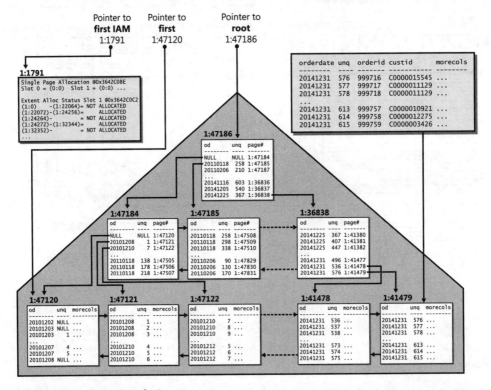

FIGURE 2-4 An illustration of a B-tree.

As you can see in the figure, the full data rows of the Orders table are stored in the index *leaf level*. The data rows are organized in the leaf in key order (*orderdate* in our case). A doubly linked list maintains the key order between the pages, and the row-offset array at the end of the page maintains this order within the page. When SQL Server needs to perform an ordered scan (or a range scan) operation in the leaf level of the index, it does so by following the linked list. I'll refer to this type of scan as an *index order scan*.

Notice in Figure 2-4 that with each leaf row, the index maintains a column called *uniquifier* (abbreviated to *unq* in the illustration). The value in this column enumerates rows that have the same key value, and it is used together with the key value to uniquely identify rows when the index's key columns are not unique. I'll elaborate on the purpose of the uniquifier later when discussing nonclustered indexes.

When the optimizer optimizes a query, it needs to choose algorithms to handle operations such as joins, grouping and aggregating, distinct, window functions, and presentation order. Some operations can be processed only by using an order-based algorithm, like presentation order (ORDER BY clause in query). Some operations can be processed using more than one algorithm, including an order-based one. For example, grouping/aggregating and distinct can be processed either with an order-based algorithm or a hash-based one. Joins can be processed with an order-based algorithm, a hash-based algorithm, or a loop-based one. To use an order-based algorithm, the data needs to be arranged as ordered. One way for the optimizer to get the data ordered is to add an explicit sort operation to the plan. However, an explicit sort operation requires a memory grant and doesn't scale well (N log N scaling).

Another way to get the data ordered is to perform an index order scan, assuming the right index exists. This option tends to be more efficient than the alternatives. Also, it doesn't require a memory grant like explicit sort and hash operators do. When an index doesn't exist, the optimizer is then left with just the remaining options. For operations that can be processed only with an order-based algorithm, like presentation order, the optimizer will have to add an explicit sort operation. For operations that can be processed with more than one algorithm, like grouping and aggregating, the optimizer will make a choice based on cost estimates. Because sorting doesn't scale well, the optimizer tends to choose a strategy based on sorting with a small number of rows. Hash algorithms tend to scale better than sorting, so the optimizer tends to prefer hashing with a large number of rows.

Regarding the data in the leaf level of the index, the order of the pages in the file might not match the index key order. If page *x* points to next page *y*, and page *y* appears before page *x* in the file, page *y* is considered an *out-of-order page*. Logical scan fragmentation (also known as *average fragmentation in percent*) is measured as the percentage of out-of-order pages. So if there are 25,000 pages in the leaf level of the index and 5,000 of them are out of order, you have 20 percent of logical scan fragmentation. The main cause of logical scan fragmentation is page splits, which I'll describe shortly. The higher the logical scan fragmentation of an index is, the slower an index order scan operation is when the data isn't cached. This fragmentation tends to have little if any impact on index order scans when the data is cached.

Interestingly, in addition to the linked list, SQL Server also maintains IAM pages to map the data stored in the index in file order like it does in the heap organization. Recall that I referred to a scan of the data that is based on IAM pages as an *allocation order scan*. SQL Server might use this type of scan when it needs to perform unordered scans of the index's leaf level. Because an allocation order scan reads the data in file order, its performance is unaffected by logical scan fragmentation, unlike with index order scans. Therefore, allocation order scans tend to be more efficient than index order scans, especially when the data isn't cached and there's a high level of logical scan fragmentation.

As mentioned, the main cause of logical scan fragmentation is page splits. A split of a leaf page occurs when a row needs to be inserted into the page and the target page does not have room to accommodate the row. Remember that an index maintains the data in key order. A row must enter a certain page based on its key value. If the target page is full, SQL Server will split the page. SQL Server supports two kinds of splits: one for an ascending key pattern and another for a nonascending key pattern.

If the new key is greater than or equal to the maximum key, SQL Server assumes that the insert pattern is an ascending key pattern. It allocates a new page and inserts the new row into that page. An ascending key pattern tends to be efficient when a single session adds new rows and the disk subsystem has a small number of drives. The new page is allocated in cache and filled with new rows. However, the ascending key pattern is not efficient when multiple sessions add new rows and your disk subsystem has many drives. With this pattern, there's constant page-latch contention on the rightmost index page and insert performance tends to be suboptimal. An insert pattern with a random distribution of new keys tends to be much more efficient in such a scenario.

If the new key is less than the maximum key, SQL Server assumes that the insert pattern is a nonascending key pattern. It allocates a new page, moves half the rows from the original page to the new one, and adjusts the linked list to reflect the right logical order of the pages. It inserts the new row either to the original page or to the new one based on its key value. The new page is not guaranteed to come right after the one that split—it could be somewhere later in the file, and it could also be somewhere earlier in the file.

Page splits are expensive, and they tend to result in logical scan fragmentation. You can measure the level of fragmentation in your index by querying the *avg_fragmentation_in_percent* attribute of the function sys.dm_db_index_physical_stats. To remove fragmentation, you rebuild the index using an ALTER INDEX REBUILD command. You can specify an option called FILLFACTOR with the percent that you want to fill leaf-level pages at the end of the rebuild. For example, using *FILLFACTOR = 70* you request to fill leaf pages to 70 percent. With indexes that have a nonascending key insert pattern, it could be a good idea to leave some free space in the leaf pages to reduce occurrences of splits and to not let logical scan fragmentation evolve to high levels. You decide which fill factor value to use based on the rate of additions and frequency of rebuilds. With indexes that have an ascending key insert pattern, it's pointless to leave empty space in the leaf pages because all new rows go to the right edge of the index anyway.

On top of the leaf level of the index, the index maintains additional levels, each summarizing the level below it. Each row in a nonleaf index page points to a whole page in the level below it, and together with the next row has information about the range of keys that the target page is responsible for. The row contains two elements: the minimum key column value in the index page being pointed to (assuming an ascending order) and a 6-byte pointer to that page. This way, you know that the target page is responsible for the range of keys that are greater than or equal to the key in the current row and less than the key in the next row. Note that in the row that points to the first page in the level below, the first element is NULL to indicate that there's no minimum. As for the page pointer, it consists of the file number in the database and the page number in the file. When SQL Server builds an index, it starts from the leaf level and adds levels on top. It stops as soon as a level contains a single page, also known as the *root* page.

When SQL Server needs to find a certain key or range of keys at the leaf level of the index, it performs an access method called *index seek*. The access method starts by reading the root page and identifies the row that represents the range that contains the key being sought. It then navigates down the levels, reading one page in each level, until it reaches the page in the leaf level that contains the first matching key. The access method then performs a range scan in the leaf level to find all matching keys. Remember that all leaf pages are the same distance from the root. This means that the access method will read as many pages as the number of levels in the index to reach the first matching key. The I/O pattern of these reads is *random I/O*, as opposed to *sequential I/O*, because naturally the pages read by a seek operation until it reaches the leaf level will seldom reside next to each other.

In terms of our performance estimations, it is important to know the number of levels in an index because that number will be the cost of a seek operation in terms of page reads, and some execution plans invoke multiple seek operations repeatedly (for example, a Nested Loops join operator). For an existing index, you can get this number by invoking the INDEXPROPERTY function with the IndexDepth property. But for an index that you haven't created yet, you need to be familiar with the calculations you can use to estimate the number of levels the index will contain.

The operands and steps required for calculating the number of levels in an index (call it *L*) are as follows (remember that these calculations apply to clustered and nonclustered indexes unless explicitly stated otherwise):

- **The number of rows in the table (call it *num_rows*)** This is 1,000,000 in our case.

- **The average gross leaf row size (call it *leaf_row_size*)** In a clustered index, this is actually the data row size. By "gross," I mean that you need to take into consideration the internal overhead of the row and the 2-byte pointer in the row-offset array. The row overhead typically involves a few bytes. In our Orders table, the gross average data row size is roughly 200 bytes.

- **The average leaf page density (call it *page_density*)** This value is the average percentage of population of leaf pages. Page density is affected by things like data deletion, page splits, and rebuilding the index with a *fillfactor* value that is lower than 100. The clustered index in our table is based on an ascending key pattern; therefore, *page_density* in our case is likely going to be close to 100 percent.

- **The number of rows that fit in a leaf page (call it *rows_per_leaf_page*)** The formula to calculate this value is *FLOOR((page_size – header_size) * page_density / leaf_row_size)*. In our case, *rows_per_leaf_page* amount to *FLOOR((8192 – 96) * 1 / 200) = 40*.

- **The number of leaf pages (call it *num_leaf_pages*)** This is a simple formula: *num_rows / rows_per_leaf_page*. In our case, it amounts to *1,000,000 / 40 = 25,000*.

- **The average gross nonleaf row size (call it *non_leaf_row_size*)** A nonleaf row contains the key columns of the index (in our case, only *orderdate*, which is 3 bytes); the 4-byte *uniquifier* (which exists only in a clustered index that is not unique); the page pointer, which is 6 bytes; a few additional bytes of internal overhead, which total 5 bytes in our case; and the row offset pointer at the end of the page, which is 2 bytes. In our case, the gross nonleaf row size is 20 bytes.

- **The number of rows that fit in a nonleaf page (call it *rows_per_non_leaf_page*)** The formula to calculate this value is similar to calculating *rows_per_leaf_page*. It's *FLOOR((page_size – header_size) / non_leaf_row_size)*, which in our case amounts to *FLOOR((8192 – 96) / 20) = 404*.

- **The number of levels above the leaf (call it *L–1*)** This value is calculated with the following formula: *CEILING(LOG(num_leaf_pages, rows_per_non_leaf_page))*. In our case, *L–1* amounts to *CEILING(LOG(25000, 404)) = 2*.

- **The index depth (call it *L*)** To get *L* you simply add 1 to *L–1*, which you computed in the previous step. The complete formula to compute *L* is *CEILING(LOG(num_leaf_pages, rows_per_non_leaf_page)) + 1*. In our case *L* amounts to 3.

- **The number of rows that can be represented by an index with *L* levels (call it *N*)** Suppose you are after the inverse computation of *L*. Namely, how many rows can be represented by an index with *L* levels. You compute *rows_per_non_leaf_page* and *rows_per_leaf_page* just like before. Then to compute *N*, use the formula: *POWER(rows_per_non_leaf_page, L–1) * rows_per_leaf_page*. For *L = 3*, *rows_per_non_leaf_page = 404*, and *rows_per_leaf_page = 40*, you get 6,528,540 rows.

You can play with the preceding formulas for *L* and *N* and see that with up to about 16,000 rows, our index will have two levels. Three levels would support up to about 6,500,000 rows, and four levels would support up to about 2,600,000,000 rows. With nonclustered indexes, the formulas are the same—it's just that you can fit more rows in each leaf page, as I will describe later. So with nonclustered indexes, the upper bound for each number of levels covers even more rows in the table. Our table has 1,000,000 rows, and all current indexes on our table have three levels. Therefore, the cost of a seek operation in any of the indexes on our table is three reads. Remember this number for later performance-related discussions in the chapter. As you can understand from this discussion, the number of levels in the index depends on the row size and the key size. But unless we're talking about extreme sizes, as ballpark numbers you will probably get two levels with small tables (up to a few dozens of thousands of rows), three levels with medium tables (up to a few million rows), and four levels with large ones (up to a few billion rows).

Nonclustered index on a heap

A nonclustered index is also structured as a B-tree and in many respects is similar to a clustered index. The main difference is that a leaf row in a nonclustered index contains only the index key columns and a *row locator* value representing a particular data row. The content of the row locator depends on whether the underlying table is organized as a heap or as a B-tree. This section describes nonclustered indexes on a heap, and the following section will describe nonclustered indexes on a B-tree (clustered table).

Figure 2-5 illustrates the nonclustered index that SQL Server created to enforce our primary-key constraint (*PK_Orders*) with the *orderid* column as the key column. SQL Server assigned the index with the same name as the constraint, *PK_Orders*.

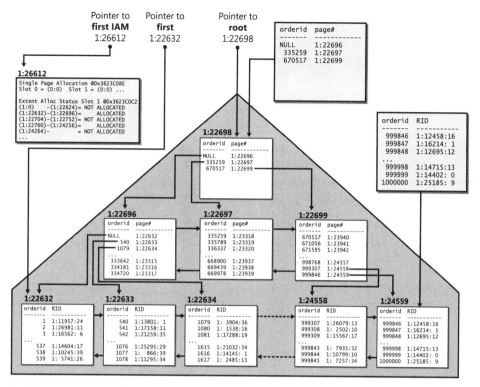

FIGURE 2-5 Nonclustered index on a heap.

The row locator used by a nonclustered index leaf row to point to a data row is an 8-byte physi-cal pointer called a *row identifier*, or *RID* for short. It consists of the file number in the database, the target page number in the file, and the zero-based entry number in the row-offset array in the target page. When looking for a data row based on a given nonclustered index key, SQL Server first per-forms a seek operation in the index to find the leaf row with the key being sought. SQL Server then performs a *RID lookup* operation, which translates to reading the page that contains the data row, and then it pulls the row of interest from that page. Therefore, the cost of a RID lookup is one page read.

If you're looking for a range of keys, SQL Server will perform a range scan in the index leaf and then a RID lookup per matching key. For a single lookup or a small number of lookups, the cost is not high, but for a large number of lookups, the cost can be very high because SQL Server ends up read-ing one whole page for each row being sought. For range queries that use a nonclustered index and a series of lookups—one per qualifying key—the cumulative cost of the lookup operations typically makes up the bulk of the cost of the query. I'll demonstrate this point in the "Access methods" sec-tion. As for the cost of a seek operation, remember that the formulas I provided earlier for clustered indexes are just as relevant to nonclustered indexes. It's just that the *leaf_row_size* is smaller, and therefore the *rows_per_leaf_page* will be higher. But the formulas are the same.

Nonclustered index on a B-tree

Nonclustered indexes created on a B-tree (clustered table) are architected differently than on a heap. The difference is that the row locator in a nonclustered index created on a B-tree is a value called a *clustering key*, as opposed to being a RID. The clustering key consists of the values of the clustered index keys from the row being pointed to and the *uniquifier* (if present). The idea is to point to a row *logically* as opposed to *physically*. This architecture was designed mainly for OLTP systems, where clustered indexes tend to incur frequent page splits upon data insertions and updates. If nonclustered indexes used RIDs as row locators, all pointers to the data rows that moved would have to be changed to reflect their new RIDs. Imagine the performance impact this would have with multiple nonclustered indexes defined on the table. Instead, SQL Server maintains logical pointers that don't change when data rows move between leaf pages in the clustered index.

Figure 2-6 illustrates what the *PK_Orders* nonclustered index might look like; the index is defined with *orderid* as the key column, and the Orders table has a clustered index defined with *orderdate* as the key column.

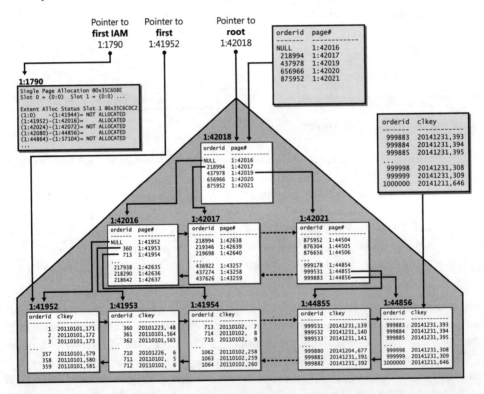

FIGURE 2-6 Nonclustered index on a B-tree.

A seek operation looking for a particular key in the nonclustered index (some *orderid* value) will end up reaching the relevant leaf row and have access to the row locator. The row locator in this case is the clustering key of the row being pointed to. To actually get to the row being pointed to, the lookup operation will need to perform a seek in the clustered index based on the acquired clustering key. This type of lookup is known as a *key lookup*, as opposed to a RID lookup. I will demonstrate this access method later in the chapter. The cost of each lookup operation (in terms of the number of page reads) is as high as the number of levels in the clustered index (3 in our case). That's compared to a single page read for a RID lookup when the table is a heap. Of course, with range queries that use a nonclustered index and a series of lookups, the ratio between the number of logical reads in a heap case and a clustered table case will be close to *1:L*, where *L* is the number of levels in the clustered index.

Tools to measure query performance

SQL Server gives you a number of tools to measure query performance, but one thing to keep in mind is that ultimately what matters is the user experience. The user mainly cares about two things: response time (the time it takes the first row to return) and throughput (the time it takes the query to complete). Naturally, as technical people we want to identify different performance measures that we believe are the major contributors to the eventual user experience. So we tend to look at things like number of reads (mainly interesting in I/O intensive activities), as well as CPU time and elapsed time.

The examples I will use in this chapter will be against a sample database called PerformanceV3. (See the book's intro for details on how to install it.) Run the following code to connect to the sample database:

```
SET NOCOUNT ON;
USE PerformanceV3;
```

I will use the following query to demonstrate tools to measure query performance:

```
SELECT orderid, custid, empid, shipperid, orderdate, filler
FROM dbo.Orders
WHERE orderid <= 10000;
```

When you want to measure query performance in a test environment, you need to think about whether you expect the production environment to have hot or cold cache for the query. If the former, you want to execute the query twice and measure the performance of the second execution. The first execution will cause all pages to be brought into the data cache, and therefore the second execution will run against hot cache. If the latter, before you run your query, you want to run a manual checkpoint to write dirty buffers to disk and then drop all clean buffers from cache, like so:

```
CHECKPOINT;
DBCC DROPCLEANBUFFERS;
```

Note, though, that you should manually clear the data cache only in isolated test environments, because obviously this action will have a negative impact on the performance of queries. Both commands require elevated permissions.

I use three main, built-in tools to analyze and measure query performance: a graphical execution plan, the STATISTICS IO and STATISTICS TIME session options, and an Extended Events session with *statement completed* events. I use the graphical execution plan to analyze the plan that the optimizer created for the query. I use the session options when I need to measure the performance of a single query or a small number of queries. I use an Extended Events session when I need to measure the performance of a large number of queries.

Regarding the execution plan, you request to see the estimated plan in SQL Server Management Studio (SSMS) by highlighting your query and clicking the Display Estimated Execution Plan (Ctrl+L) button on the SQL Editor toolbar. You request to see the actual plan by enabling the Include Actual Execution Plan (Ctrl+M) button and executing the query. I generally prefer to analyze the actual plan because it includes run-time information like the actual number of rows returned by, and the actual number of executions of, each operator. Suboptimal choices made by the optimizer are often a result of inaccurate cardinality estimates, and those can be detected by comparing estimated and actual numbers in an actual execution plan.

Use the following code to enable measuring query performance with the session options STATISTICS IO (for I/O information) and STATISTICS TIME (for time information):

```
SET STATISTICS IO, TIME ON;
```

When you run a query, SSMS will report performance information in the Messages pane.

To measure the performance of ad hoc queries that you submit from SSMS using an Extended Events session, capture the event *sql_statement_completed* and filter the session ID of the SSMS session that you're submitting the queries from. Use the following code to create and start such an Extended Events session after replacing the session ID with that of your SSMS session:

```
CREATE EVENT SESSION query_performance ON SERVER
ADD EVENT sqlserver.sql_statement_completed(
    WHERE (sqlserver.session_id=(53))); -- replace with your session ID;

ALTER EVENT SESSION query_performance ON SERVER STATE = START;
```

To watch the event information, go to Object Explorer in SSMS. Navigate through the folder hierarchy Management\Extended Events\Sessions. Expand the Sessions folder, right-click the session *query_performance*, and choose Watch Live Data.

To show the output of the different performance-measuring tools, run the sample query after clearing the data cache. I got the actual query plan shown in Figure 2-7.

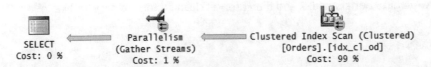

FIGURE 2-7 Execution plan for the sample query.

The plan is parallel. You can tell that an operator uses parallelism if it has a yellow circle with two arrows. The plan performs a parallel clustered index scan, which also applies a filter, and then it gathers the streams of rows returned by the different threads. An interesting point to note here is that the data flows in the plan from right to left as depicted by the direction of the arrows; however, the internal execution of the plan starts with the leftmost node, which is known as the *root node*. This node executes the node to its right requesting rows, and in turn that node executes the node to its right, requesting rows.

Following is the output generated by the STATISTICS IO option for this query:

```
Table 'Orders'. Scan count 9, logical reads 25339, physical reads 1, read-ahead reads 25138, lob
logical reads 0, lob physical reads 0, lob read-ahead reads 0.
```

The measure *Scan count* indicates how many times the object was accessed during the processing of the query. I think that the name of this measure is a bit misleading because any kind of access to the object adds to the count, not necessarily a scan. A name like *Access count* probably would have been more appropriate. In our case, the scan count is 9 because there were 8 threads that accessed the object in the parallel scan, plus a separate thread accessed the object for the serial parts of the plan.

The *logical reads* measure (25,339 in our case) indicates how many pages were read from the data cache. Note that if a page is read twice from cache, it is counted twice. Unfortunately, the STATISTICS IO tool does not indicate how many distinct pages were read. The measures *physical reads* (1 in our case) and *read-ahead reads* (25,138 in our case) indicate how many pages were read physically from disk into the data cache. As you can imagine, a physical read is much more expensive than a logical read. The *physical reads* measure represents a regular read mechanism. This mechanism uses synchronous reads of single-page units. By *synchronous*, I mean that the query processing cannot continue until the read is completed. The *read-ahead reads* measure represents a specialized read mechanism that anticipates the data that is needed for the query. This mechanism is referred to as *read-ahead* or *prefetch*. SQL Server usually uses this mechanism when a large-enough scan is involved. This mechanism applies asynchronous reads and might read chunks greater than a single page, all the way up to 512 KB per read. To help with troubleshooting, you can disable read-ahead by using trace flag 652. (Turn it on with DBCC TRACEON, and turn it off with DBCC TRACEOFF.) To find out the total number of physical reads that were involved in the processing of the query, sum the measures *physical reads* and *read-ahead reads*. In our case, the total is 25,139.

The STATISTICS IO output also shows logical reads, physical reads, and read-ahead reads for large object types separately. In our case, there are no large object types involved; therefore, all three measures are zeros.

The STATISTICS TIME option reports the following time statistics for our query:

```
SQL Server Execution Times:
   CPU time = 170 ms,  elapsed time = 765 ms.
```

Note that you will get multiple outputs from this option. In addition to getting the output for the execution of the query, you will also get output for the parsing and compilation of the query. You also will get outputs for every element you enable in SSMS that involves work that is submitted behind the scenes to SQL Server, like when you enable the graphical execution plan. The STATISTICS TIME output row that appears right after the STATISTICS IO output row is the one representing the query execution. To process our query against cold cache, SQL Server used 170 ms of CPU time and it took the query 765 ms of wall-clock time to complete.

Figure 2-8 shows the Watch Live Data window for the Extended Events session *query_performance*, with the execution of the sample query against cold cache highlighted.

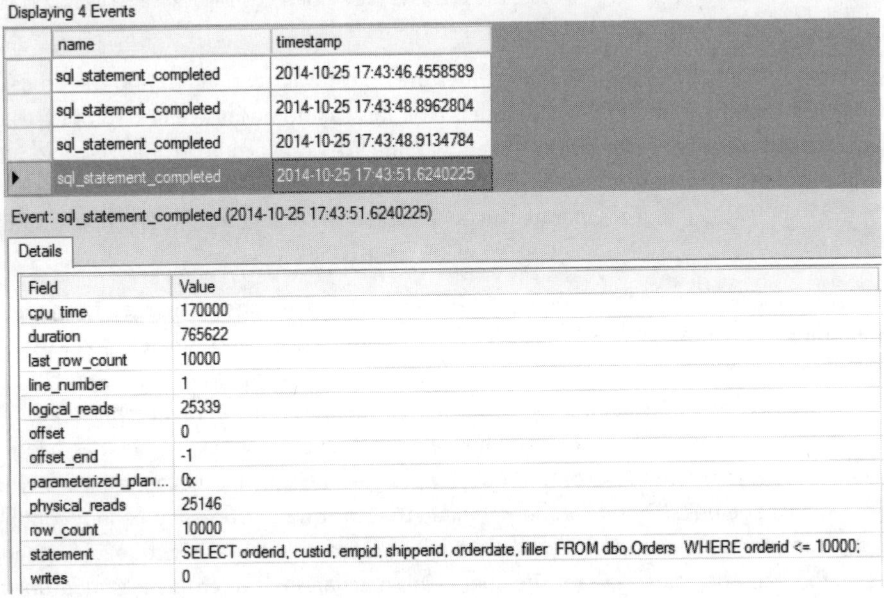

FIGURE 2-8 Information from the Extended Events session.

Now that the cache is hot, run the query a second time. I got the following output from STATISTICS IO:

```
Table 'Orders'. Scan count 9, logical reads 25339, physical reads 0, read-ahead reads 0, lob
logical reads 0, lob physical reads 0, lob read-ahead reads 0.
```

Notice that the measures representing physical reads are zeros. I got the following output from STATISTICS TIME:

```
CPU time = 265 ms,  elapsed time = 299 ms.
```

Naturally, with hot cache the query finishes more quickly.

Access methods

This section provides a description of the various methods SQL Server uses to access data; it is designed to be used as a reference for discussions throughout this book involving the analysis of execution plans.

The examples in this section will use queries against the Orders table in the PerfromanceV3 database. This table is organized as a B-tree with the clustered index defined based on *orderdate* as the key. Use the following code to create a copy of the Orders table called *Orders2*, organized as a heap:

```
IF OBJECT_ID(N'dbo.Orders2', N'U') IS NOT NULL DROP TABLE dbo.Orders2;
SELECT * INTO dbo.Orders2 FROM dbo.Orders;
ALTER TABLE dbo.Orders2 ADD CONSTRAINT PK_Orders2 PRIMARY KEY NONCLUSTERED (orderid);
```

When I want to show access methods against a B-tree–organized table, I'll query Orders. When I want to show access methods against a heap-organized table, I'll query Orders2.

 Important I used randomization to generate the sample data in the PerformanceV3 database. This means that when you query objects in this database, your results probably will be slightly different than mine.

Most of the cost associated with access methods is related to I/O activity. Therefore, I'll provide the number of logical reads as the main measure of the access methods' performance.

Table scan/unordered clustered index scan

The first access method I'll describe is a full scan of the table when there's no requirement to return the data in any particular order. You get such a full scan in two main cases. One is when you really need all rows from the table. Another is when you need only a subset of the rows but don't have a good index to support your filter. The tricky thing is that the query plan for such a full scan looks different depending on the underlying table's organization (heap or B-tree). When the underlying table is a heap, the plan will show an operator called Table Scan. When the underlying table is a B-tree, the plan will show an operator called Clustered Index Scan with an Ordered: False property. I'll refer to the former as a *table scan* and to the latter as an *unordered clustered index scan*.

A *table scan* or an *unordered clustered index scan* involves a scan of all data pages that belong to the table. The following query against the Orders2 table, which is structured as a heap, would require a table scan:

```
SELECT orderid, custid, empid, shipperid, orderdate, filler
FROM dbo.Orders2;
```

Figure 2-9 shows the graphical execution plan produced by the relational engine's optimizer for this query, and Figure 2-10 shows an illustration of the way this access method is processed by the storage engine.

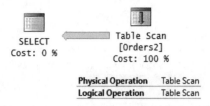

FIGURE 2-9 Heap scan (execution plan).

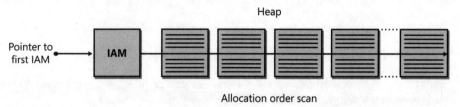

FIGURE 2-10 Heap scan (storage engine).

SQL Server reported 24,396 logical reads for this query on my system.

If you find it a bit confusing that both the Physical Operation and Logical Operation properties show Table Scan, you're not alone. To me, the logical operation is a table scan and the physical operation is a heap scan.

The only option that the storage engine has to process a Table Scan operator is to use an allocation order scan. Recall from the section "Table organization" that an allocation order scan is performed based on IAM pages in file order.

The following query against the Orders table, which is structured as a B-tree, would require an unordered clustered index scan:

```
SELECT orderid, custid, empid, shipperid, orderdate, filler
FROM dbo.Orders;
```

Figure 2-11 shows the execution plan that the optimizer will produce for this query. Notice that the Ordered property of the Clustered Index Scan operator indicates False. Figure 2-12 shows an illustration of the two ways that the storage engine can carry out this access method.

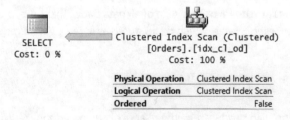

FIGURE 2-11 B-tree scan (execution plan).

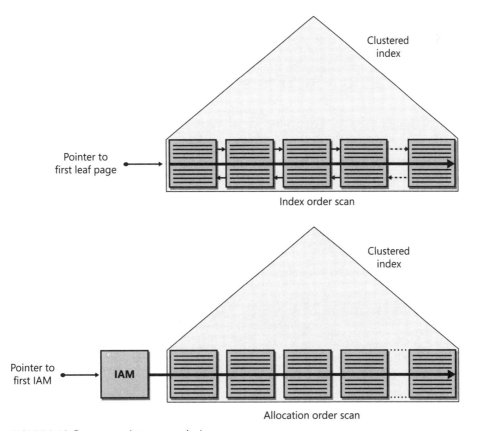

FIGURE 2-12 B-tree scan (storage engine).

SQL Server reported 25,073 logical reads for this query on my system.

Also, here I find it a bit confusing that the plan shows the same value in the Physical Operation and Logical Operation properties. This time, both properties show Clustered Index Scan. To me, the logical operation is still a table scan and the physical operation is a clustered index scan.

The fact that the Ordered property of the Clustered Index Scan operator indicates False means that as far as the relational engine is concerned, the data does not need to be returned from the operator in key order. This doesn't mean that it is a problem if it is returned ordered; instead, it means that any order would be fine. This leaves the storage engine with some maneuvering space in the sense that it is free to choose between two types of scans: an index order scan (a scan of the leaf of the index following the linked list) and an allocation order scan (a scan based on IAM pages). The factors that the storage engine takes into consideration when choosing which type of scan to employ include performance and data consistency. I'll provide more details about the storage engine's decision-making process after I describe ordered index scans (Clustered Index Scan and Index Scan operators with the property Ordered: True).

Unordered covering nonclustered index scan

An *unordered covering nonclustered index scan* is similar to an unordered clustered index scan. The concept of a *covering index* means that a nonclustered index contains all columns specified in a query. In other words, a covering index is not an index with special properties; rather, it becomes a covering index with respect to a particular query. SQL Server can find all the data it needs to satisfy the query by accessing solely the index data, without needing to access the full data rows. Other than that, the access method is the same as an unordered clustered index scan, only, obviously, the leaf level of the covering nonclustered index contains fewer pages than the leaf of the clustered index because the row size is smaller and more rows fit in each page. I explained earlier how to calculate the number of pages in the leaf level of an index (clustered or nonclustered).

As an example of this access method, the following query requests all *orderid* values from the Orders table:

```
SELECT orderid
FROM dbo.Orders;
```

Our Orders table has a nonclustered index on the *orderid* column (*PK_Orders*), meaning that all the table's order IDs reside in the index's leaf level. The index covers our query. Figure 2-13 shows the graphical execution plan you would get for this query, and Figure 2-14 illustrates the two ways in which the storage engine can process it.

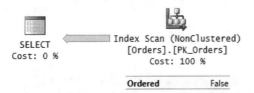

```
                                    Index Scan (NonClustered)
    SELECT                              [Orders].[PK_Orders]
    Cost: 0 %                               Cost: 100 %

                                    ─────────────────────────────
                                    Ordered              False
```

FIGURE 2-13 Unordered covering nonclustered index scan (execution plan).

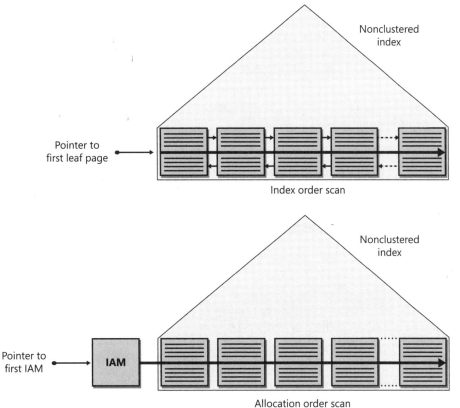

FIGURE 2-14 Unordered covering nonclustered index scan (storage engine).

SQL Server reported 2,611 logical reads for this query on my system. This is the number of pages making the leaf level of the *PK_Orders* index.

As a small puzzle for you, add the *orderdate* column to the query, like so:

```
SELECT orderid, orderdate
FROM dbo.Orders;
```

Examine the execution plan for this query as shown in Figure 2-15.

Output List
[PerformanceV3].[dbo].[Orders].orderid,
[PerformanceV3].[dbo].[Orders].orderdate

FIGURE 2-15 Index that includes a clustering key.

Observe that the *PK_Orders* index is still considered a covering one with respect to this query. The question is, how can this be the case when the index was defined explicitly only on the *orderid* column as the key? The answer is the table has a clustered index defined with the *orderdate* column as the key. As you might recall, SQL Server uses the clustered index key as the row locator in nonclustered indexes. So, even though you defined the *PK_Orders* index explicitly only with the *orderid* column, SQL Server internally defined it with the columns *orderid* and *orderdate.* Never mind that SQL Server added the *orderdate* column to be used as the row locator—once it's there, SQL Server can use it for other query-processing purposes.

Ordered clustered index scan

An *ordered clustered index scan* is a full scan of the leaf level of the clustered index that guarantees that the data will be returned to the next operator in index order. For example, the following query, which requests all orders sorted by *orderdate*, will get such an access method in its plan:

```
SELECT orderid, custid, empid, shipperid, orderdate, filler
FROM dbo.Orders
ORDER BY orderdate;
```

You can find the execution plan for this query in Figure 2-16 and an illustration of how the storage engine carries out this access method in Figure 2-17.

FIGURE 2-16 Ordered clustered index scan (execution plan).

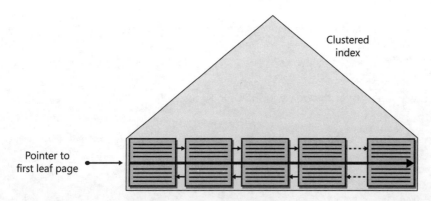

FIGURE 2-17 Ordered clustered index scan (storage engine).

SQL Server reported 25,073 logical reads for this query on my system.

Notice in the plan that the Ordered property is True. This indicates that the data needs to be returned from the operator ordered. When the operator has the property Ordered: True, the scan can be carried out by the storage engine only in one way—by using an index order scan (a scan based on the index linked list), as shown in Figure 2-17. Unlike an allocation order scan, the performance of an index order scan depends on the fragmentation level of the index. With no fragmentation at all, the performance of an index order scan should be very close to the performance of an allocation order scan because both will end up reading the data in file order sequentially. However, with cold cache, as the fragmentation level grows, the performance difference will be more substantial—in favor of the allocation order scan, of course. The natural deductions are that you shouldn't request the data sorted if you don't need it sorted, to allow the potential for using an allocation order scan, and that you should resolve fragmentation issues in indexes that incur large index order scans against cold cache. I'll elaborate on fragmentation and its treatment later.

Note that the optimizer is not limited to ordered-forward scans. Remember that the linked list is a doubly linked list, where each page contains both a *next* pointer and a *previous* pointer. Had you requested a descending sort order, you would have still gotten an ordered index scan, only ordered backward (from tail to head) instead of ordered forward (from head to tail). Interestingly, though, as of SQL Server 2014, the storage engine will consider using parallelism only with an ordered-forward scan. It always processes an ordered-backward scan serially.

SQL Server also supports descending indexes. One reason to use those is to enable parallel scans when parallelism is an important factor in the performance of the query. Another reason to use those is to support multiple key columns that have opposite directions in their sort requirements—for example, sorting by *col1, col2 DESC*. I'll demonstrate using descending indexes later in the chapter in the section "Indexing features."

Ordered covering nonclustered index scan

An *ordered covering nonclustered index scan* is similar to an ordered clustered index scan, with the former performing the access method in a nonclustered index—typically, when covering a query. The cost is, of course, lower than a clustered index scan because fewer pages are involved. For example, the *PK_Orders* index on our clustered Orders table covers the following query, and it has the data in the desired order:

```
SELECT orderid, orderdate
FROM dbo.Orders
ORDER BY orderid;
```

Figure 2-18 shows the query's execution plan, and Figure 2-19 illustrates the way the storage engine processes the access method.

FIGURE 2-18 Ordered covering nonclustered index scan (execution plan).

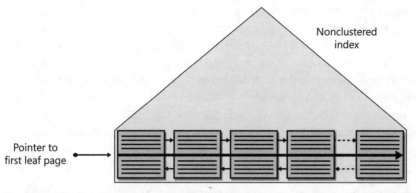

FIGURE 2-19 Ordered covering nonclustered index scan (storage engine).

Notice in the plan that the Ordered property of the Index Scan operator shows True.

An ordered index scan is used not only when you explicitly request the data sorted, but also when the plan uses an operator that can benefit from sorted input data. This can be the case when processing GROUP BY, DISTINCT, joins, and other requests. This can also happen in less obvious cases. For example, check out the execution plan shown in Figure 2-20 for the following query:

```
SELECT orderid, custid, empid, orderdate
FROM dbo.Orders AS O1
WHERE orderid =
  (SELECT MAX(orderid)
   FROM dbo.Orders AS O2
   WHERE O2.orderdate = O1.orderdate);
```

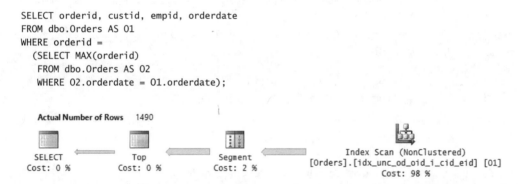

FIGURE 2-20 Ordered covering nonclustered index scan with segmentation.

The Segment operator arranges the data in groups and emits a group at a time to the next operator (Top in our case). Our query requests the orders with the maximum *orderid* per *orderdate*. Fortunately, we have a covering index for the task (*idx_unc_od_oid_i_cid_eid*), with the key columns being (*orderdate, orderid*) and included nonkey columns being (*custid, empid*). I'll elaborate on included nonkey columns later in the chapter. The important point for our discussion is that the Segment operator organizes the data by groups of *orderdate* values and emits the data, a group at a time, where the last row in each group is the maximum *orderid* in the group; because *orderid* is the second key column right after *orderdate*. Therefore, the plan doesn't need to sort the data; rather, the plan just collects it with an ordered scan from the covering index, which is already sorted by *orderdate* and *orderid*. The Top operator has a simple task of just collecting the last row (TOP 1 descending), which is the row of interest for the group. The number of rows reported by the Top operator is 1490, which is the number of unique groups (*orderdate* values), each of which got a single row from the operator.

Because our nonclustered index covers the query by including in its leaf level all other columns that are mentioned in the query (*custid, empid*), there's no need to look up the data rows; the query is satisfied by the index data alone.

The storage engine's treatment of scans

Before I continue the coverage of additional access methods, I'm going to explain the way the storage engine treats the relational engine's instructions to perform scans. The *relational engine* is like the brains of SQL Server; it includes the optimizer, which is in charge of producing execution plans for queries. The *storage engine* is like the muscles of SQL Server; it needs to carry out the instructions provided to it by the relational engine in the execution plan and perform the actual row operations. Sometimes the optimizer's instructions leave the storage engine with some room for maneuvering, and then the storage engine determines the best of several possible options based on factors such as performance and consistency.

Allocation order scans vs. index order scans

When the plan shows a Table Scan operator, the storage engine has only one option: to use an allocation order scan. When the plan shows an Index Scan operator (clustered or nonclustered) with the property Ordered: True, the storage engine can use only an index order scan.

When the plan shows an Index Scan operator with Ordered: False, the relational engine doesn't care in what order the rows are returned. In this case, there are two options to scan the data: allocation order scan and index order scan. It is up to the storage engine to determine which to employ. Unfortunately, the storage engine's actual choice is not indicated in the execution plan, or anywhere else. I will explain the storage engine's decision-making process, but it's important to understand that what the plan shows is the relational engine's instructions and not what the storage engine did.

The performance of an allocation order scan is not affected by logical fragmentation in the index because it's done in file order, anyway. However, the performance of an index order scan that involves physical reads is affected by fragmentation—the higher the fragmentation, the slower the scan. Therefore, as far as performance is concerned, the storage engine considers the allocation order scan the preferable option. The exception is when the index is very small (up to 64 pages). In that case, the cost of interpreting IAM pages becomes significant with respect to the rest of the work, and the storage engine considers the index order scan to be preferable. Small tables aside, in terms of performance the allocation order scan is considered preferable.

However, performance is not the only aspect that the storage engine needs to take into consideration; it also needs to account for data-consistency expectations based on the effective isolation level. When there's more than one option to carry out a request, the storage engine opts for the fastest option that meets the consistency requirements.

In certain circumstances, scans can end up returning multiple occurrences of rows or even skipping rows. Allocation order scans are more prone to such behavior than index order scans. I'll first describe how such a phenomenon can happen with allocation order scans and in which circumstances. Then I'll explain how it can happen with index order scans.

Allocation order scans

Figure 2-21 demonstrate in three steps how an allocation order scan can return multiple occurrences of rows.

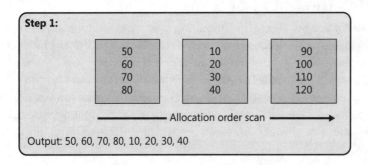

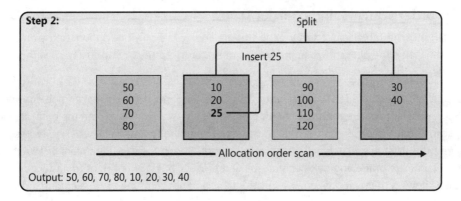

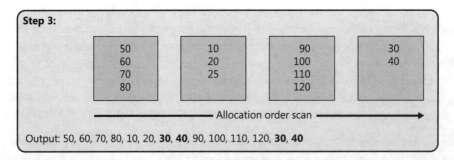

FIGURE 2-21 Allocation order scan: getting multiple occurrences of rows.

Step 1 shows an allocation order scan in progress, reading the leaf pages of some index in file order (not index order). Two pages were already read (keys 50, 60, 70, 80, 10, 20, 30, 40). At this point, before the third page of the index is read, someone inserts a row into the table with key 25.

Step 2 shows a split that took place in the page that was the target for the insert because it was full. As a result of the split, a new page was allocated—in our case, later in the file at a point that the scan did not yet reach. Half the rows from the original page move to the new page (keys 30, 40), and the new row with key 25 was added to the original page because of its key value.

Step 3 shows the continuation of the scan: reading the remaining two pages (keys 90, 100, 110, 120, 30, 40), including the one that was added because of the split. Notice that the rows with keys 30 and 40 were read a second time.

Of course, in a similar fashion, depending on how far the scan reaches by the time this split happens and where the new page is allocated, the scan might end up skipping rows. Figure 2-22 demonstrates how this can happen in three steps.

Allocation order scan: skipping rows

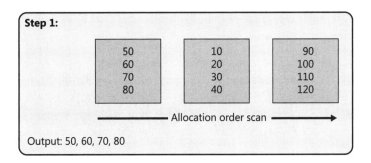

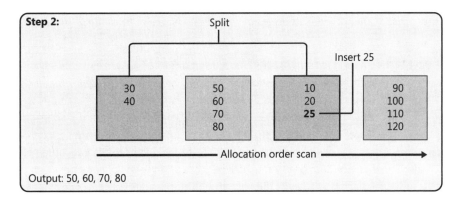

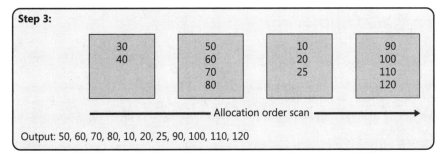

FIGURE 2-22 Allocation order scan: skipping rows.

Step 1 shows an allocation order scan in progress that manages to read one page (keys 50, 60, 70, 80) before the insert takes place.

Step 2 shows the split of the target page, only this time the new page is allocated earlier in the file at a point that the scan already passed. Like in the previous split example, the rows with keys 30 and 40 move to the new page, and the new row with key 25 is added to the original page.

Step 3 shows the continuation of the scan: reading the remaining two pages (keys 10, 20, 25, 90, 100, 110, 120). As you can see, the rows with keys 30 and 40 were completely skipped.

In short, an allocation order scan can return multiple occurrences of rows and skip rows resulting from splits that take place during the scan. A split can take place because of an insert of a new row, an update of an index key causing the row to move, or an update of a variable-length column causing the row to expand. Remember that splits take place only in indexes; heaps do not incur splits. Therefore, such phenomena cannot happen in heaps.

An index order scan is safer in the sense that it won't read multiple occurrences of the same row or skip rows because of splits. Remember that an index order scan follows the index linked list in order. If a page that the scan hasn't yet reached splits, the scan ends up reading both pages; therefore, it won't skip rows. If a page that the scan already passed splits, the scan doesn't read the new one; therefore, it won't return multiple occurrences of rows.

The storage engine is well aware that allocation order scans are prone to such inconsistent reads because of splits, while index order scans aren't. It will carry out an Index Scan *Ordered: False* with an allocation order scan in one of two categories of cases that I will refer to as the *unsafe* and *safe* categories.

The unsafe category is when the scan actually can return multiple occurrences of rows or skip rows because of splits. The storage engine opts for this option when the index size is greater than 64 pages and the request is running under the Read Uncommitted isolation level (for example, when you specify NOLOCK in the query). Most people's perception of Read Uncommitted is simply that the query does not request a shared lock and therefore it can read uncommitted changes (dirty reads). This perception is true, but unfortunately most people don't realize that to the storage engine, Read Uncommitted is also an indication that pretty much all bets are off in terms of consistency. In other words, it will opt for the faster option even at the cost of returning multiple occurrences of rows or skipping rows. When the query is running under the default Read Committed isolation level or higher, the storage engine will opt for an index order scan to prevent such phenomena from happening because of splits. To recap, the storage engine employs allocation order scans of the unsafe category when all the following conditions are true:

- The index size is greater than 64 pages.

- The plan shows Index Scan, Ordered: False.

- The query is running under the Read Uncommitted isolation level.

- Changes are allowed to the data.

In terms of the safe category, the storage engine also opts for allocation order scans with higher isolation levels than Read Uncommitted when it knows that it is safe to do so without sacrificing the consistency of the read (at least as far as splits are concerned). For example, when you run the query using the TABLOCK hint, the storage engine knows that no one can change the data while the read is in progress. Therefore, it is safe to use an allocation order scan. Of course, this means that attempts by other sessions to modify the table will be blocked during the read. Another example where the storage engine knows that it is safe to employ an allocation order scan is when the index resides in a read-only filegroup or database. To summarize, the storage engine will use an allocation order scan of the safe category when the index size is greater than 64 pages and the data is read-only (because of the TABLOCK hint, read-only filegroup, or database).

Keep in mind that logical fragmentation has an impact on the performance of index order scans but not on that of allocation order scans. And based on the preceding information, you should realize that the storage engine will sometimes use index order scans to process an Index Scan operator with the Ordered: False property.

The next section will demonstrate both unsafe and safe allocation order scans.

Run the following code to create a table called T1:

```
SET NOCOUNT ON;
USE tempdb;
GO

-- Create table T1
IF OBJECT_ID(N'dbo.T1', N'U') IS NOT NULL DROP TABLE dbo.T1;

CREATE TABLE dbo.T1
(
  clcol UNIQUEIDENTIFIER NOT NULL DEFAULT(NEWID()),
  filler CHAR(2000) NOT NULL DEFAULT('a')
);
GO
CREATE UNIQUE CLUSTERED INDEX idx_clcol ON dbo.T1(clcol);
```

A unique clustered index is created on *clcol*, which will be populated with random GUIDs by the default expression *NEWID()*. Populating the clustered index key with random GUIDs should cause a large number of splits, which in turn should cause a high level of logical fragmentation in the index.

Run the following code to insert rows into the table using an infinite loop, and stop it after a few seconds (say 5, to allow more than 64 pages in the table):

```
SET NOCOUNT ON;
USE tempdb;

TRUNCATE TABLE dbo.T1;

WHILE 1 = 1
  INSERT INTO dbo.T1 DEFAULT VALUES;
```

Run the following code to check the fragmentation level of the index:

```
SELECT avg_fragmentation_in_percent FROM sys.dm_db_index_physical_stats
(
  DB_ID(N'tempdb'),
  OBJECT_ID(N'dbo.T1'),
  1,
  NULL,
  NULL
);
```

When I ran this code on my system, I got more than 99 percent fragmentation, which of course is very high. If you need more evidence to support the fact that the order of the pages in the linked list is different from their order in the file, you can use the undocumented DBCC IND command, which gives you the B-tree layout of the index:

```
DBCC IND(N'tempdb', N'dbo.T1', 0);
```

I prepared the following piece of code to spare you from having to browse through the output of DBCC IND in an attempt to figure out the index leaf layout:

```
CREATE TABLE #DBCCIND
(
  PageFID INT,
  PagePID INT,
  IAMFID INT,
  IAMPID INT,
  ObjectID INT,
  IndexID INT,
  PartitionNumber INT,
  PartitionID BIGINT,
  iam_chain_type VARCHAR(100),
  PageType INT,
  IndexLevel INT,
  NextPageFID INT,
  NextPagePID INT,
  PrevPageFID INT,
  PrevPagePID INT
);

INSERT INTO #DBCCIND
  EXEC (N'DBCC IND(N''tempdb'', N''dbo.T1'', 0)');

CREATE CLUSTERED INDEX idx_cl_prevpage ON #DBCCIND(PrevPageFID, PrevPagePID);

WITH LinkedList
AS
(
  SELECT 1 AS RowNum, PageFID, PagePID
  FROM #DBCCIND
  WHERE IndexID = 1
    AND IndexLevel = 0
    AND PrevPageFID = 0
    AND PrevPagePID = 0
```

```
    UNION ALL

    SELECT PrevLevel.RowNum + 1,
      CurLevel.PageFID, CurLevel.PagePID
    FROM LinkedList AS PrevLevel
      JOIN #DBCCIND AS CurLevel
        ON CurLevel.PrevPageFID = PrevLevel.PageFID
        AND CurLevel.PrevPagePID = PrevLevel.PagePID
)
SELECT
  CAST(PageFID AS VARCHAR(MAX)) + ':'
  + CAST(PagePID AS VARCHAR(MAX)) + ' ' AS [text()]
FROM LinkedList
ORDER BY RowNum
FOR XML PATH('')
OPTION (MAXRECURSION 0);

DROP TABLE #DBCCIND;
```

The code stores the output of DBCC IND in a temp table, then it uses a recursive query to follow the linked list from head to tail, and then it uses a technique based on the *FOR XML PATH* option to concatenate the addresses of the leaf pages into a single string in linked list order. I got the following output on my system:

```
1:132098 1:111372 1:133098 1:125591 1:137567 1:118198 1:128938 1:117929 1:136036 1:128595...
```

It's easy to observe logical fragmentation here. For example, page 1:132098 points to the page 1:111372, which is earlier in the file.

Next, run the following code to query T1:

```
SELECT SUBSTRING(CAST(clcol AS BINARY(16)), 11, 6) AS segment1, *
FROM dbo.T1;
```

The last 6 bytes of a *UNIQUEIDENTIFIER* value represent the first segment that determines ordering; therefore, I extracted that segment with the *SUBSTRING* function so that it would be easy to see whether the rows are returned in index order. The execution plan of this query indicates a Clustered Index Scan, Ordered: False. However, because the environment is not read-only and the isolation level is the default Read Committed, the storage engine uses an index order scan. This query returns the rows in the output in index order. For example, here's the output that I got on my system:

```
segment1        clcol                                 filler
-------------   ------------------------------------  -------
0x0000ED83A06E  F5F5CA72-48F6-4716-BBDC-0000ED83A06E  a
0x0002672771DF  7B3D64FE-9197-487E-A354-0002672771DF  a
0x0002EE4AF130  7D4A671D-5FBD-4B37-831C-0002EE4AF130  a
0x000395E30408  2A670CC5-5459-4506-9DCE-000395E30408  a
0x0004BD69D4ED  40CB1A42-48C7-4D9C-A5F4-0004BD69D4ED  a
0x0005E14203C0  DCFFE73A-2125-490F-913B-0005E14203C0  a
0x00067DD63977  B49C5103-01E7-4745-B1C3-00067DD63977  a
0x0007B82DD187  1157F2E9-AD7E-4795-850F-0007B82DD187  a
0x0007BC012CC0  93ED4A5C-3AAD-4686-8CA1-0007BC012CC0  a
0x0007E73BEFB8  732072E7-A767-48A3-B2CF-0007E73BEFB8  a
...
```

Query the table again, this time with the NOLOCK hint:

```
SELECT SUBSTRING(CAST(clcol AS BINARY(16)), 11, 6) AS segment1, *
FROM dbo.T1 WITH (NOLOCK);
```

This time, the storage engine employs an allocation order scan of the unsafe category. Here's the output I got from this code on my system:

```
segment1        clcol                                 filler
--------------  ------------------------------------  -------
0x03D5CA43F8AE  7E1A28DE-B712-4F71-A553-03D5CA43F8AE  a
0x426CDFD8DDB3  003EFE48-180E-4A8D-B6E1-426CDFD8DDB3  a
0x426D6A3FFC2C  9239BF31-1AA2-47F0-8B50-426D6A3FFC2C  a
0x426E5C9673AD  2F0A49B8-2A7E-4C20-A22E-426E5C9673AD  a
0x5EEBC295A84A  3743277C-0C72-48CF-A6B5-5EEBC295A84A  a
0x97A52864E1D8  131BDF97-E015-42E2-B884-97A52864E1D8  a
0x78D967590D8C  7AA0F5BF-0BF1-4689-B851-78D967590D8C  a
0x78DA17132327  F40CC88B-FC08-4534-842C-78DA17132327  a
0x78DACE8A159E  90BE7781-301F-48AB-A398-78DACE8A159E  a
0x20C225A8A10D  547BD309-7804-4969-8A7F-20C225A8A10D  a
...
```

Notice that this time the rows are not returned in index order. If splits occur while such a read is in progress, the read might end up returning multiple occurrences of rows and skipping rows.

As an example of an allocation order scan of the safe category, run the query with the TABLOCK hint:

```
SELECT SUBSTRING(CAST(clcol AS BINARY(16)), 11, 6) AS segment1, *
FROM dbo.T1 WITH (TABLOCK);
```

Here, even though the code is running under the Read Committed isolation level, the storage engine knows that it is safe to use an allocation order scan because no one can change the data during the read. I got the following output back from this query:

```
segment1        clcol                                 filler
--------------  ------------------------------------  -------
0x03D5CA43F8AE  7E1A28DE-B712-4F71-A553-03D5CA43F8AE  a
0x426CDFD8DDB3  003EFE48-180E-4A8D-B6E1-426CDFD8DDB3  a
0x426D6A3FFC2C  9239BF31-1AA2-47F0-8B50-426D6A3FFC2C  a
0x426E5C9673AD  2F0A49B8-2A7E-4C20-A22E-426E5C9673AD  a
0x5EEBC295A84A  3743277C-0C72-48CF-A6B5-5EEBC295A84A  a
0x97A52864E1D8  131BDF97-E015-42E2-B884-97A52864E1D8  a
0x78D967590D8C  7AA0F5BF-0BF1-4689-B851-78D967590D8C  a
0x78DA17132327  F40CC88B-FC08-4534-842C-78DA17132327  a
0x78DACE8A159E  90BE7781-301F-48AB-A398-78DACE8A159E  a
0x20C225A8A10D  547BD309-7804-4969-8A7F-20C225A8A10D  a
...
```

Next I'll demonstrate how an unsafe allocation order scan can return multiple occurrences of rows. Open two connections (call them *connection 1* and *connection 2*). Run the following code in connection 1 to insert rows into T1 in an infinite loop, causing frequent splits:

```
SET NOCOUNT ON;
USE tempdb;

TRUNCATE TABLE dbo.T1;

WHILE 1 = 1
  INSERT INTO dbo.T1 DEFAULT VALUES;
```

Run the following code in connection 2 to read the data in a loop while connection 1 is inserting data:

```
SET NOCOUNT ON;
USE tempdb;

WHILE 1 = 1
BEGIN
  SELECT * INTO #T1 FROM dbo.T1 WITH(NOLOCK);

  IF EXISTS(
    SELECT clcol
    FROM #T1
    GROUP BY clcol
    HAVING COUNT(*) > 1) BREAK;

  DROP TABLE #T1;
END

SELECT clcol, COUNT(*) AS cnt
FROM #T1
GROUP BY clcol
HAVING COUNT(*) > 1;

DROP TABLE #T1;
```

The SELECT statement uses the NOLOCK hint, and the plan shows Clustered Index Scan, Ordered: False, meaning that the storage engine will likely use an allocation order scan of the unsafe category. The SELECT INTO statement stores the output in a temporary table so that it will be easy to prove that rows were read multiple times. In each iteration of the loop, after reading the data into the temp table, the code checks for multiple occurrences of the same GUID in the temp table. This can happen only if the same row was read more than once. If duplicates are found, the code breaks from the loop and returns the GUIDs that appear more than once in the temp table. When I ran this code, after a few seconds I got the following output in connection 2 showing all the GUIDs that were read more than once:

```
clcol                                 cnt
------------------------------------  -----------
F144911F-44B8-4AC7-9396-D2C26DBB9E2E  2
990B829E-739D-4AA1-BD59-F55DFF8E9530  2
9A02C46B-389E-45A1-AC07-90DB4115D43B  2
B5BAF81C-B2B5-492A-9E9A-DB566E4A5A98  2
132255C8-63F5-4DB7-9126-D37C1F321868  2
69A77E96-B748-48A8-94A2-85B6A270F5D1  2
7F3C7E7A-8181-44BB-8D0F-0F39AA001DC2  2
B5C5C70D-B721-4225-8455-F56910DA2CD1  2
9E2588DA-CB57-4CA0-A10D-F08B0306B6A6  2
F50AA680-E754-4B61-8335-F08A3C965924  2
...
```

At this point, you can stop the code in connection 1.

If you want, you can rerun the test without the NOLOCK hint and see that the code in connection 2 doesn't stop, because duplicate GUIDs are not found.

Next I'll demonstrate an unsafe allocation order scan that skips rows. Run the following code to create the tables T1 and MySequence:

```
-- Create table T1
SET NOCOUNT ON;
USE tempdb;

IF OBJECT_ID(N'dbo.T1', N'U') IS NOT NULL DROP TABLE dbo.T1;

CREATE TABLE dbo.T1
(
  clcol UNIQUEIDENTIFIER NOT NULL DEFAULT(NEWID()),
  seqval INT NOT NULL,
  filler CHAR(2000) NOT NULL DEFAULT('a')
);
CREATE UNIQUE CLUSTERED INDEX idx_clcol ON dbo.T1(clcol);

-- Create table MySequence
IF OBJECT_ID(N'dbo.MySequence', N'U') IS NOT NULL DROP TABLE dbo.MySequence;

CREATE TABLE dbo.MySequence(val INT NOT NULL);
INSERT INTO dbo.MySequence(val) VALUES(0);
```

The table T1 is similar to the one used in the previous demonstration, but this one has an additional column called *seqval* that will be populated with sequential integers. The table MySequence holds the last-used sequence value (populated initially with 0), which will be incremented by 1 before each insert to T1. To prove that a scan skipped rows, you simply need to show that the output of the scan has gaps between contiguous values in the *seqval* column. I'm not using the built-in sequence object in my test because SQL Server doesn't guarantee that you won't have gaps between sequence values, regardless of the cache setting you use. To demonstrate this behavior, open two connections (again, call them *connection 1* and *connection 2*). Run the following code from connection 1 to insert rows into T1 in an infinite loop, and increment the sequence value by 1 in each iteration:

```
SET NOCOUNT ON;
USE tempdb;

UPDATE dbo.MySequence SET val = 0;
TRUNCATE TABLE dbo.T1;

DECLARE @nextval AS INT;

WHILE 1 = 1
BEGIN
  UPDATE dbo.MySequence SET @nextval = val += 1;
  INSERT INTO dbo.T1(seqval) VALUES(@nextval);
END
```

Run the following code in connection 2 while the inserts are running in connection 1:

```
SET NOCOUNT ON;
USE tempdb;

DECLARE @max AS INT;
WHILE 1 = 1
BEGIN
  SET @max = (SELECT MAX(seqval) FROM dbo.T1);
  SELECT * INTO #T1 FROM dbo.T1 WITH(NOLOCK);
  CREATE NONCLUSTERED INDEX idx_seqval ON #T1(seqval);

  IF EXISTS(
    SELECT *
    FROM (SELECT seqval AS cur,
             (SELECT MIN(seqval)
              FROM #T1 AS N
              WHERE N.seqval > C.seqval) AS nxt
          FROM #T1 AS C
          WHERE seqval <= @max) AS D
    WHERE nxt - cur > 1) BREAK;

  DROP TABLE #T1;
END

SELECT *
FROM (SELECT seqval AS cur,
         (SELECT MIN(seqval)
          FROM #T1 AS N
          WHERE N.seqval > C.seqval) AS nxt
      FROM #T1 AS C
      WHERE seqval <= @max) AS D
WHERE nxt - cur > 1;

DROP TABLE #T1;
```

This code runs an infinite loop that in each iteration reads the data using NOLOCK into a temp table and breaks from the loop as soon as contiguous values with a gap between them are found in the *seqval* column. The code then presents the pairs of contiguous values that have a gap between them. After a few seconds, I got the following output in connection 2, shown here in abbreviated form:

```
cur          nxt
-----------  -----------
8128         8130
12378        12380
13502        13504
17901        17903
25257        25259
27515        27517
29782        29784
32764        32766
32945        32947
...
```

You can stop the code in connection 1.

You can run the test again without the NOLOCK hint, in which case the storage engine will use an index order scan. The code in connection 2 should not break from the loop, because gaps won't be found.

Index order scans

If you think that index order scans are safe from phenomena such as returning multiple occurrences of rows or skipping rows, think again. It is true that index order scans are safe from such phenomena because of page splits, but page splits are not the only reason for data to move around in the index leaf.

Another cause of movement in the leaf is update of an index key. If an index key is modified after the row was read by an index order scan and the row is moved to a point in the leaf that the scan hasn't reached yet, the scan will read the row a second time. Similarly, if an index key is modified before the row is read by an index order scan and the row is moved to a point in the leaf that the scan has already passed, the scan will never reach that row.

For example, suppose you have an Employees table that currently has four employee rows (employee A with a salary of 2000, employee B with a salary of 4000, employee C with a salary of 3000, and employee D with a salary of 1000). A clustered index is defined on the *salary* column as the key. Figure 2-23 shows in three steps how an index order scan can return multiple occurrences of the same row because of an update that takes place during the read.

Index order scan: getting multiple occurrences of rows

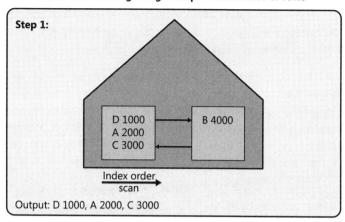

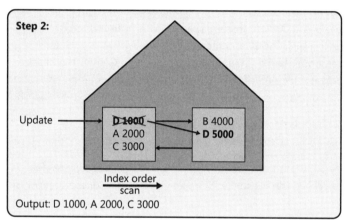

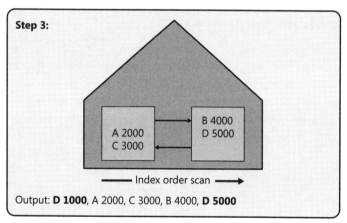

FIGURE 2-23 Index order scan: getting multiple occurrences of rows.

You issue a query against the table, and the storage engine uses an index order scan. Remember that an index order scan is always used when the plan shows Index Scan: Ordered: True (for example, when the query has an ORDER BY clause), but it also does so when the Ordered property is False, the environment is read/write, and the isolation level is not Read Uncommitted.

Step 1 shows that the scan already read the first page in the leaf level and returned the rows for employees D, A, and C. If the query is running under Read Uncommitted, no shared locks are acquired on the rows. If the query is running under Read Committed, shared locks are acquired, but they are released as soon as the query is done with the resource (for example, a row or page), even though the query hasn't finished yet. This means that at the point in time that the scan is done with the page, under both isolation levels no locks are held on the rows that were read.

Step 2 shows an update of the row for employee D, increasing the salary from 1000 to 5000. The row moves to the second page in the leaf level because of the index key change.

Step 3 shows the continuation of the scan, reading the second page in the leaf of the index, and returning the rows for employees B and D. Note that employee D was returned a second time. The first time, the row was returned with salary 1000 and the second time with salary 5000. Note that this phenomenon cannot happen under higher isolation levels than Read Committed because those isolation levels keep shared locks until the end of the transaction. This phenomenon also cannot happen under the two isolation levels that are based on row versioning: Read Committed Snapshot and Snapshot.

Similarly, an index order scan can skip rows. Figure 2-24 shows how this can happen in three steps.

Employee D starts with salary 5000 this time, and its row resides in the second index leaf page. Step 1 shows that the scan already read the first page in the leaf level and returned the rows for employees A and C.

Step 2 shows an update of the row for employee D, decreasing the salary from 5000 to 1000. The row moves to the first page in the leaf level because of the index key change.

Step 3 shows the continuation of the scan, reading the second page in the leaf of the index, returning the rows for employee B. Note that the row for employee D was not returned at all—neither with the salary 5000 nor with 1000. Note that this phenomenon can happen in Read Uncommitted, Read Committed, and even Repeatable Read because the update was done to a row that was not yet read. This phenomenon cannot happen under the isolation levels Serializable, Read Committed Snapshot, and Snapshot.

Index order scan: skipping rows

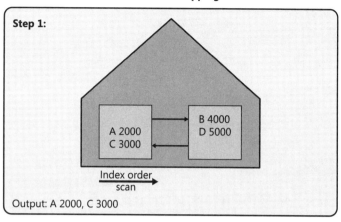

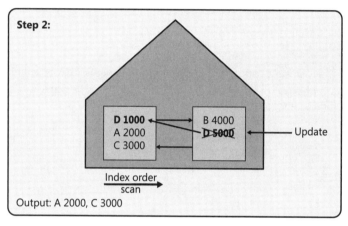

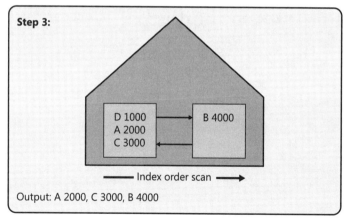

FIGURE 2-24 Index order scan: skipping rows.

To see both phenomena for yourself, you can run a simple test. First, execute the following code to create and populate the Employees table:

```
SET NOCOUNT ON;
USE tempdb;

IF OBJECT_ID(N'dbo.Employees', N'U') IS NOT NULL DROP TABLE dbo.Employees;

CREATE TABLE dbo.Employees
(
  empid VARCHAR(10) NOT NULL,
  salary MONEY NOT NULL,
  filler CHAR(2500) NOT NULL DEFAULT('a')
);

CREATE CLUSTERED INDEX idx_cl_salary ON dbo.Employees(salary);
ALTER TABLE dbo.Employees
  ADD CONSTRAINT PK_Employees PRIMARY KEY NONCLUSTERED(empid);

INSERT INTO dbo.Employees(empid, salary) VALUES
  ('D', 1000.00),('A', 2000.00),('C', 3000.00),('B', 4000.00);
```

Open two connections. Run the following code in connection 1 to run an infinite loop that in each iteration updates the salary of employee D from its current value to 6000 minus its current value (switching between the values 1000 and 5000):

```
SET NOCOUNT ON;
USE tempdb;

WHILE 1=1
  UPDATE dbo.Employees
    SET salary = 6000.00 - salary
  WHERE empid = 'D';
```

This code causes the row for employee D to keep moving between the two index leaf pages. Run the following code in connection 2:

```
SET NOCOUNT ON;
USE tempdb;

WHILE 1 = 1
BEGIN
  SELECT * INTO #Employees FROM dbo.Employees;

  IF @@rowcount <> 4 BREAK; -- use < 4 for skipping, > 4 for multi occur

  DROP TABLE #Employees;
END

SELECT * FROM #Employees;

DROP TABLE #Employees;
```

The code runs an infinite loop that reads the contents of the Employees table into a temp table. Because the code doesn't specify the NOLOCK hint and the environment is read/write, the storage engine uses an index order scan. The code breaks from the loop when the number of rows read is different than the expected number (four). In cases where the scan reads the same row twice, this code returns five rows in the output:

```
empid       salary               filler
----------  -------------------- ------
D           1000.00              a
A           2000.00              a
C           3000.00              a
B           4000.00              a
D           5000.00              a
```

In cases where the scan skips a row, this code returns three rows in the output:

```
empid       salary               filler
----------  -------------------- ------
A           2000.00              a
C           3000.00              a
B           4000.00              a
```

You can change the filter to < *4* to wait for a case where the row is skipped, and you can change it to > *4* to wait for a case where the row is read twice.

I hope this section gave you a better understanding of how the storage engine handles scans and, most importantly, the implications of running your code under the Read Uncommitted isolation level. The next sections continue the coverage of access methods.

Nonclustered index seek + range scan + lookups

The access method *nonclustered index seek + range scan + lookups* is typically used for small-range queries (including a point query) using a nonclustered index that doesn't cover the query. For example, suppose you want to query orders with an order ID that falls within a small range of order IDs, like *orderid <= 25*. For qualifying orders, you want to return the columns *orderid, custid, empid, shipperid, orderdate,* and *filler*. We do have a nonclustered noncovering index called *PK_Orders*, which is defined with the *orderid* column as the key. The index can support the filter; however, because the index doesn't cover the query, lookups will be required to obtain the remaining columns from the respective data rows. If the target table is a heap, the lookups will be RID lookups, each costing one page read. If the underlying table is a B-tree, the lookups will be key lookups, each costing as many reads as the number of levels in the clustered index.

To demonstrate this access method against a heap, I will use the following query:

```
USE PerformanceV3;
```

```
SELECT orderid, custid, empid, shipperid, orderdate, filler
FROM dbo.Orders2
WHERE orderid <= 25;
```

Figure 2-25 shows the query's execution plan, and Figure 2-26 illustrates the way the storage engine processes the access method.

At the top right of the plan, the Index Seek operator against the *PK_Orders2* index performs a seek in the index to the first matching row, and then it performs a range scan to identify all qualifying rows (25 in our case). The purpose of this activity is to collect the row locators (RIDs in the heap case) of the target data rows. The seek costs three reads. As for the cost of the range scan, it depends on how many qualifying rows there are and how many fit in a leaf page. This index can fit close to 400 rows per leaf page. So, in our case, the 25 qualifying rows probably reside in the first page in the leaf that the seek operation reached. So it's very likely no additional page reads will be required for the range scan. The third part of the access method is to apply lookups based on the returned row locators to collect the remaining columns from the respective data rows. The lookups are activated by the Nested Loops operator per row that is returned from the Index Seek operator. Because this example involves a heap, the lookups are RID lookups, each costing one page read. With 25 qualifying rows, the lookups cost 25 reads in total. All in all, the total number of reads our query performs is 3 + 0 + 25 = 28. That's exactly the number of reads that SQL Server reported for this query on my system.

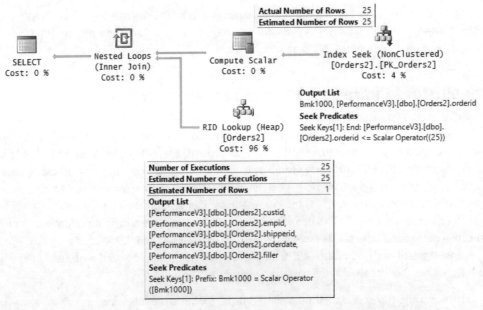

FIGURE 2-25 Nonclustered index seek + range scan + lookups against a heap (execution plan).

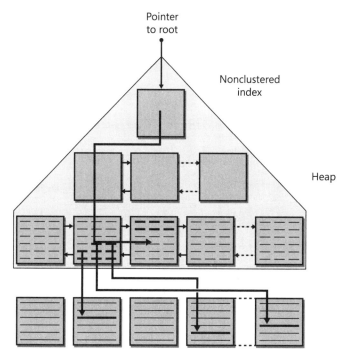

Pointer
to root

Nonclustered
index

Heap

FIGURE 2-26 Nonclustered index seek + range scan + lookups against a heap (storage engine).

To demonstrate this access method against a B-tree, I will use the following query:

```
SELECT orderid, custid, empid, shipperid, orderdate, filler
FROM dbo.Orders
WHERE orderid <= 25;
```

Figure 2-27 shows the query's execution plan, and Figure 2-28 illustrates the way the storage engine processes the access method.

The key difference in this access method compared to the previous one is that instead of applying RID lookups, it applies key lookups. Remember that a key lookup translates to a seek in the clustered index and costs as many reads as the number of levels in the clustered index (3 in our case). So the total number of reads that our query performs is 3 + 0 + 25 * 3 = 78. That's exactly the number of reads that SQL Server reported for this query on my system.

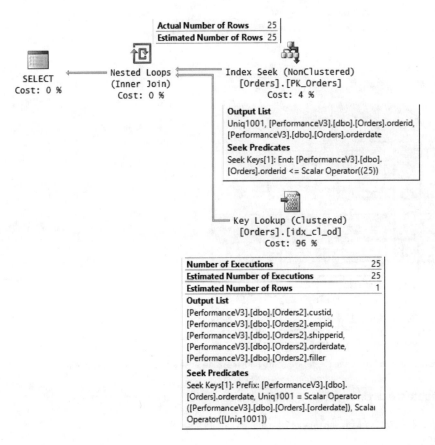

| Actual Number of Rows | 25 |
| Estimated Number of Rows | 25 |

SELECT
Cost: 0 %

Nested Loops
(Inner Join)
Cost: 0 %

Index Seek (NonClustered)
[Orders].[PK_Orders]
Cost: 4 %

Output List
Uniq1001, [PerformanceV3].[dbo].[Orders].orderid,
[PerformanceV3].[dbo].[Orders].orderdate
Seek Predicates
Seek Keys[1]: End: [PerformanceV3].[dbo].
[Orders].orderid <= Scalar Operator((25))

Key Lookup (Clustered)
[Orders].[idx_cl_od]
Cost: 96 %

Number of Executions	25
Estimated Number of Executions	25
Estimated Number of Rows	1

Output List
[PerformanceV3].[dbo].[Orders2].custid,
[PerformanceV3].[dbo].[Orders2].empid,
[PerformanceV3].[dbo].[Orders2].shipperid,
[PerformanceV3].[dbo].[Orders2].orderdate,
[PerformanceV3].[dbo].[Orders2].filler
Seek Predicates
Seek Keys[1]: Prefix: [PerformanceV3].[dbo].
[Orders].orderdate, Uniq1001 = Scalar Operator
([PerformanceV3].[dbo].[Orders].[orderdate]), Scalar
Operator([Uniq1001])

FIGURE 2-27 Nonclustered index seek + range scan + lookups against a B-tree (execution plan).

Now that the fundamental aspects of this access method have been covered, we can move on to some more interesting aspects, like cardinality estimates, prefetch, and tipping points.

When optimizing a query like the one in our example, the optimizer needs to make a number of choices that depend on the estimated cardinality of the filter (the estimated number of rows returned). Before I describe the specific choices the optimizer needs to make here, I'll first describe the cardinality estimation method that it uses for this query. Generally, making cardinality estimates is quite a tricky business, as I will elaborate on later in this chapter in the section "Cardinality estimates." Our particular case is pretty straightforward, though.

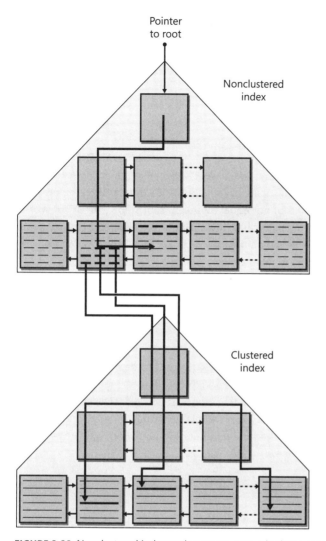

FIGURE 2-28 Nonclustered index seek + range scan + lookups against a B-tree (storage engine).

When you create an index, SQL Server also creates statistics about the data in the index. The statistics include a header with general information, density information about vectors of leading key columns in the index, and a histogram on the leading key column in the index. The histogram represents the distribution of key values within the column. Run the following code to show the histogram that SQL Server created based on the *orderid* column as part of the statistics for the *PK_Orders* index on the Orders table:

```
DBCC SHOW_STATISTICS (N'dbo.Orders', N'PK_Orders') WITH HISTOGRAM;
```

This code generated the following output on my system:

RANGE_HI_KEY	RANGE_ROWS	EQ_ROWS	DISTINCT_RANGE_ROWS	AVG_RANGE_ROWS
1	0	1	0	1
1000000	999998	1	999998	1

SQL Server supports histograms with up to 200 steps. But in our case, because the table has a consecutive range of order IDs between 1 and 1,000,000, SQL Server figured that it can adequately represent such data distribution with only two steps. Each step represents the keys greater than the previous step's *RANGE_HI_KEY* value and less than or equal to the current step's *RANGE_HI_KEY* value. The *EQ_ROWS* value represents how many rows have a key value equal to the *RANGE_HI_KEY* value. The *RANGE_ROWS* value indicates how many rows have a value greater than the previous step's *RANGE_HI_KEY* value and less than (but not equal to) the current step's *RANGE_HI_KEY* value. Similarly, the *DISTINCT_RANGE_ROWS* value indicates how many distinct values are greater than the previous step's *RANGE_HI_KEY* value and less than the current step's *RANGE_HI_KEY* value. The *AVG_RANGE_ROWS* value indicates the average number of rows per distinct value in the step.

You can see in Figure 2-27 (and the same in Figure 2-25) that the optimizer made an accurate cardinality estimate for our query filter based on this histogram. The estimated number of rows is 25 just like the actual number.

As for the choices the optimizer needs to make based on the cardinality estimate, there are a number of those. Assuming the optimizer chose to use the index, it needs to decide whether to employ a prefetch (read-ahead) in the range scan to speed up the lookups. If it does, the Nested Loops operator will have a property indicating that it uses a prefetch; otherwise, it won't. The condition to employ a prefetch is to have more than 25 qualifying rows. Our sample query has 25 qualifying rows, so the plan does not involve a prefetch. Remember, the total number of reads for our query was 3 + 0 + 25 * 3 = 78. Change the filter in our query to *orderid <= 26*, like so:

```
SELECT orderid, custid, empid, shipperid, orderdate, filler
FROM dbo.Orders
WHERE orderid <= 26;
```

Now the condition to employ a prefetch is met. If you examine the properties of the Nested Loops operator in the execution plan for this query, you will find a new property called *WithUnordered-Prefetch* with the value True. The *unordered* part of this property indicates that the rows do not need to be returned in key order. When I ran this query on my system, SQL Server reported 90 reads. Three reads can be attributed to the seek, 78 reads can be attributed to the lookups, and the remaining nine reads can be attributed to the prefetch. Recall that the read-ahead operation can read data in bigger chunks than a page, so the operation might end up reading some pages that don't contain qualifying rows, as is the case in this example.

To see an example of an ordered prefetch, which requires the rows to be returned in key order, add *ORDER BY orderid* to the query, like so:

```
SELECT orderid, custid, empid, shipperid, orderdate, filler
FROM dbo.Orders
WHERE orderid <= 26
ORDER BY orderid;
```

The properties of the Nested Loops operator now include a property called *WithOrderedPrefetch* with the value True.

If you want to troubleshoot the effect of the prefetch, you can disable it by using query trace flag 8744, like so:

```
SELECT orderid, custid, empid, shipperid, orderdate, filler
FROM dbo.Orders
WHERE orderid <= 26
OPTION(QUERYTRACEON 8744);
```

Now the Nested Loops operator has no property indicating a prefetch. SQL Server reported 81 logical reads for this query on my system.

Another choice the optimizer needs to make based on the cardinality estimate is whether to use this access method (*nonclustered index seek + range scan + lookups*) at all or rather opt for the alternative, which is a full scan of the table (heap or B-tree). Remember that this access method tends to be efficient compared to the alternative for a small percent of matches. That's mainly because the cost of each lookup is quite high. Think about it; per qualifying row, a key lookup involves three random page reads. When I experimented with different range sizes, the tipping point for me was 6,505 matches. Namely, for up to 6,505 matches the optimizer chose a plan that performed a seek and a range scan in the *PK_Orders* index and applied key lookups, and beyond that point it used a clustered index scan. For example, when I used a filter that has 10,000 matching rows (1 percent), I got a plan with a full clustered index scan. The tipping point is less than one percent of matching rows, which some might find as surprisingly low. But ultimately, the optimizer chooses the plan with the lowest estimated query cost between the ones that it explores. Naturally, things like row size and key size can affect where the tipping point is, so when you do similar experiments with your data, the percentage you will get could be lower or higher.

The important conclusion from this exercise is that a nonclustered index that doesn't cover a query is efficient only for highly selective filters. If your users tend to filter such percentages of rows that are beyond the tipping point, the optimizer won't bother using the index. So you need to think carefully whether it makes sense to create such an index after considering the extra costs that modifications will incur.

Note The next part requires familiarity with how SQL Server handles parallelism, a topic that is covered later in the chapter in the section "Parallel query execution." In fact, the next part repeats some of the concepts from the parallelism section. The discussion here is connected directly to the topic of access methods and explains when SQL Server chooses a serial scan rather than a parallel scan. It is provided here so that you can use it in the future as a reference. If you start reading this section and feel a bit overwhelmed, feel free to skip it for now. After reading the section on parallelism later in the chapter, you might feel more comfortable reading the next part.

As mentioned, if the percentage of matches is beyond the aforementioned tipping point, the optimizer will choose a full scan of the clustered index (or heap). But then another choice that the optimizer needs to make is whether to go with a parallel plan or a serial plan. Contrary to the intuitive assumption that parallelism should always improve the performance of a scan, a serial scan can sometimes be more efficient than a parallel one. The scan itself can be handled quite efficiently by the read-ahead mechanism. What can benefit from parallelism is processing the filter, which is an operation that requires CPU cycles. The more threads there are, the faster the scan with the filter is. The thing is, after the parallel scan supplier assigns the packets of rows to the different threads, and each thread applies the filter, a Parallelism (Gather Streams) operator needs to gather the streams of qualifying rows that are returned by the different threads. There's a constant cost for each row that needs to be gathered. So the more rows that remain after the filter, the more expensive the Gather Streams operation is. If the sum of the costs of the parallel scan with the filter and the Gather Streams operation is lower than the cost of the serial scan, the optimizer will choose the former; otherwise, it will choose the latter.

Let me be more specific. To reflect the fact that more threads will allow the scan with the filter to finish more quickly, the optimizer computes the CPU cost of the parallel scan (call it *CPUParallel*) as the CPU cost of the serial scan (call it *CPUSerial*) divided by the *degree of parallelism for costing* (call it *DOPForCosting*). You can find the CPU cost of the serial scan by issuing a query against Orders without a filter and looking at the properties of the serial scan in the query plan. I get a *CPUSerial* cost of 1.1 optimizer units. The *DOPForCosting* measure is computed as the *degree of parallelism for execution* (call it *DOPForExecution*) divided by 2 using integer division. The *DOPForExecution* measure is a property of the execution plan; it represents the maximum number of threads that SQL Server can use to process a parallel zone in the plan, and it is mainly based on the number of logical CPUs that are available to SQL Server. The *DOPForExecution* measure can be seen as the *Degree of Parallelism* property of the root node in an actual query plan. For example, in my system I have 8 logical CPUs, and I usually get *Degree of Parallelism* 8 in parallel plans. So, in my case, *DOPForCosting* is 8 / 2 = 4. Therefore, *CPUParallel* is 1.1 / 4 = 0.275.

The Gather Streams operation involves some constant startup cost (call it *CPUGatherStreamsStartup*) and an additional constant cost per row (call it *CPUGatherStreamsRow*).

The CPU part of the cost of a plan with a serial scan is *CPUSerial*. The cost of this plan is not affected by the number of rows you filter. The CPU part of the cost of a plan with a parallel scan is

*CPUSerial / (DOPForExecution / 2) + CPUGatherStreamsStartup + CPUGatherStreamsRow * FilteredRows*

The greater *DOPForExecution* is, the more rows you can filter before the cost of the parallel plan becomes higher than the cost of the serial plan. On my system with *DOPForExecution* 8, the tipping point between a parallel plan and a serial plan is somewhere between 272,000 rows and 273,000 rows.

For example, the following query got a parallel plan on my system:

```
SELECT orderid, custid, empid, shipperid, orderdate, filler
FROM dbo.Orders
WHERE orderid <= 10000;
```

The execution plan I got for this query is shown in Figure 2-29.

FIGURE 2-29 Parallel query plan with a scan.

With 272,000 rows, I still get a parallel plan. With 273,000 rows and beyond, I get a serial plan. For example, the following query got a serial plan on my system:

```
SELECT orderid, custid, empid, shipperid, orderdate, filler
FROM dbo.Orders
WHERE orderid <= 300000;
```

The execution plan I got for this query is shown in Figure 2-30.

FIGURE 2-30 Serial query plan with a scan.

Because the costing formulas for parallel plans depend on the number of logical CPUs you have in the system, it can be tricky to troubleshoot a query on a test system that has a different number of CPUs than in the production system. There are a couple of tools you can use to make the optimizer assume a different number of CPUs than there really are, but unfortunately those tools are undocumented and unsupported, and their behavior should be considered unpredictable. So I use them strictly for experimentation and research purposes. I feel that experimenting with those tools helps me better understand how the SQL Server engine works, and I recommend that you refrain from using them in any capacity in production systems.

One tool is a DBCC command called OPTIMIZER_WHATIF. This tool makes the optimizer assume for the current session that the system has certain available resources just for costing purposes. To assume a certain number of CPUs, specify *CPUs* as the first parameter and the number as the second parameter. For example, to assume 16 CPUs, run the following code:

```
DBCC OPTIMIZER_WHATIF(CPUs, 16);
```

Examine the plan for the following query, which filters 300,000 rows:

```
SELECT orderid, custid, empid, shipperid, orderdate, filler
FROM dbo.Orders
WHERE orderid <= 300000
OPTION(RECOMPILE);
```

This time, I got a parallel plan. That's because now *CPUParallel* is lower than before, allowing more rows to be filtered before reaching the tipping point between a parallel plan and a serial plan.

Note that this tool affects only the number of CPUs that will be considered for costing purposes; so the *DOPForCosting* measure will be computed as this number divided by 2, with integer division. The actual degree of parallelism for execution will still be based on the number of logical CPUs in the system. More precisely, it will be based on the number of schedulers that SQL Server creates; but normally, SQL Server creates one scheduler per logical CPU.

To revert back to the default number of CPUs in the system, specify 0 as the second parameter, like so:

```
DBCC OPTIMIZER_WHATIF(CPUs, 0);
```

The DBCC OPTIMIZER_WHATIF command has a local effect on the session. There's a tool that has a more global impact on the entire system, but again, it's undocumented and unsupported. As mentioned, normally SQL Server creates a scheduler for each logical CPU in the system, and the number of schedulers determines *DOPForExecution*. You can start the SQL Server service with startup parameter −*Pn*, where *P* has to be uppercase and *n* represents the number of schedulers you want SQL Server to use. You can query the sys.dm_os_schedulers view and filter only the rows with *scheduler_id < 255* to see how many user schedulers SQL Server uses. Both the *DOPForExecution* measure and, consequently, the *DOPForCosting* measure will be determined by the number of schedulers, as if you have that many logical CPUs in the system. However, from a physical execution perspective, remember that you still have only as many CPUs as the number you actually have in the system.

Finally, a third undocumented and unsupported tool that affects parallelism treatment is query trace flag 8649. This trace flag causes SQL Server to use a parallel plan even if it has a higher cost than the alternative serial plan. Again, this is a tool I use for experimentation and research to see what the implications of using a parallel plan would be when SQL Server doesn't choose one by itself. Here's an example of using this trace flag in our query:

```
SELECT orderid, custid, empid, shipperid, orderdate, filler
FROM dbo.Orders
WHERE orderid <= 300000
OPTION(QUERYTRACEON 8649);
```

Remember that with 8 logical CPUs and the number of rows that this query filters, the optimizer would normally choose a serial plan. But with this trace flag, the optimizer chooses a parallel plan.

Unordered nonclustered index scan + lookups

The optimizer typically uses the *unordered nonclustered index scan + lookups* access method when the following conditions are in place:

- The query has a selective filter.

- There's a nonclustered index that contains the filtered column (or columns), but the index isn't a covering one.

- The filtered columns are not leading columns in the index key list.

For example, the plan for the following query uses such an access method against the index *idx_nc_sid_od_cid*, created on the key columns (*shipperid, orderdate, custid*):

```
SELECT orderid, custid, empid, shipperid, orderdate, filler
FROM dbo.Orders
WHERE custid = 'C0000000001';
```

What's important about this index is that the *custid* column appears in the index leaf rows but not as the first key column.

Figure 2-31 shows the query's execution plan, and Figure 2-32 illustrates the way the storage engine processes the access method.

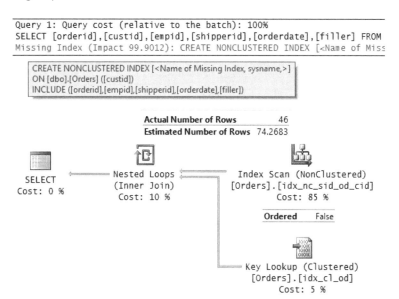

FIGURE 2-31 Unordered nonclustered index scan + lookups (execution plan).

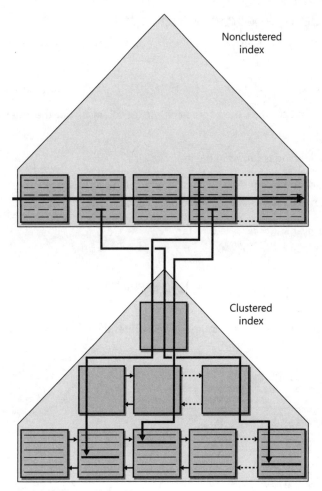

FIGURE 2-32 Unordered nonclustered index scan + lookups (storage engine).

SQL Server reported 4,006 logical reads for this query on my system.

Of course, you can get a much more efficient plan by creating a covering index with *custid* as the leading key column. Sure enough, the optimizer realizes this and reports such a missing index, as you can see in Figure 2-31. With such an index, you can get the desired result with probably three or four reads total. However, perhaps the query is so infrequent that you'd rather pay more when you do run it, but not incur the increase in the write costs resulting from the creation of another index. Also, perhaps you're not allowed to create new indexes in the target system.

The *unordered nonclustered index scan + lookups* access method performs a full unordered scan of the leaf level of the index, followed by lookups for qualifying keys. As I mentioned, the query must be selective enough to justify this access method; otherwise, with too many lookups it will be more expensive than simply scanning the whole table. To figure out the cardinality of the filter, SQL Server needs a histogram on the filtered column. Normally, when you create an index, SQL Server creates statistics that include a histogram on the leading key column. But in our example, the optimizer needs a histogram on *custid*, which is not a leading key column in an index. If such statistics do not exist, SQL Server creates them, provided that the database property *AUTO_CREATE_STATISTICS* is turned on, which it is by default.

So when you ran this query for the first time, SQL Server looked for distribution statistics on the *custid* column and realized that none existed. SQL Server then checked the state of the *AUTO_CREATE_STATISTICS* database option and found that it was turned on. SQL Server then triggered an automatic creation of statistics based on the *custid* column after sampling a percentage of the values in the column. The optimizer then made a cardinality estimate for the filter based on the histogram, which as you can see in the query plan was 74.2683. That's not very far from the actual number of matches, which is 46. Because of the selectivity of the filter, the optimizer estimated that using this access method is more efficient than using a full scan of the table. The scanning of the leaf level of the index cost 3,868 reads. The 46 key lookups cost 138 reads. That's why in total the query performed 4,006 reads. Later in the chapter, I'll elaborate on the cardinality estimation methods that the optimizer uses in the section "Cardinality estimates."

Clustered index seek + range scan

As I explained when I described the access method *nonclustered index seek + range scan + lookups*, lookups are quite expensive. Therefore, when you have a nonclustered noncovering index, the optimizer typically uses it along with lookups only for a very small percentage of qualifying rows. I explained that there's a tipping point beyond which the optimizer prefers a full scan of the table. If you have a query with a filter that tends to have a large number of matches and it's important for you to get good performance, your focus should be on eliminating the need for the expensive lookups. This can be achieved by arranging a covering index—namely, an index that includes in the leaf row all columns that the query refers to. There are two main ways to get a covering index: one is with a clustered index, and another is with a nonclustered index with included columns. This section focuses on the former, and the next section focuses on the latter.

A clustered index is obviously a covering index because the leaf row is the complete data row. The optimizer typically uses the access method *clustered index seek + range scan* for range queries where you filter based on the first key column (or columns) of the clustered index. This access method performs a seek operation to the first qualifying row in the leaf level, and then it applies a range scan until the last qualifying row. Without the expensive lookups, this access method is always more efficient than an alternative full scan of the table. This makes a plan based on this method a *trivial plan*, meaning that there's only one optimal plan for the query regardless of the number of matching rows.

The following query, which looks for all orders placed on a given *orderdate* (the clustered index key column), uses the access method, which is the focus of this discussion:

```
SELECT orderid, custid, empid, shipperid, orderdate
FROM dbo.Orders
WHERE orderdate = '20140212';
```

Figure 2-33 shows the query's execution plan, and Figure 2-34 illustrates the way the storage engine processes the access method.

FIGURE 2-33 Clustered index seek + range scan (execution plan).

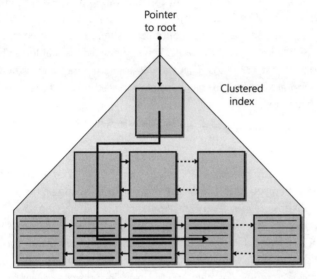

FIGURE 2-34 Clustered index seek + range scan (storage engine).

The filter uses an equality operator, but because the *orderdate* column isn't unique, the filter might have multiple matching rows. In my case, I got 703 matching rows. SQL Server reported 22 logical reads for this query on my system. Naturally, you will get a similar access method if you use the operators >, >=, <, <=, and BETWEEN.

Covering nonclustered index seek + range scan

The access method *covering nonclustered index seek + range scan* is similar to the access method *clustered index seek + range scan*, only it uses a nonclustered covering index. The access method with the nonclustered index is more efficient because with fewer columns in the leaf row, you can fit more rows per leaf page. Take the query in the previous section as an example. The clustered index can fit about 40 rows per leaf page. This means that if the query has 10,000 matching rows, it needs to scan about 250 pages in the index leaf. To get an optimal covering nonclustered index, you create the index with *orderdate* as the key column, and specify all remaining columns from the query (*orderid*, *custid*, *empid*, and *shipperid*) in the index INCLUDE clause. The leaf row size in such an index is about 40 bytes, meaning that you can fit about 200 rows per leaf page; that's compared to a leaf row size of about 200 bytes in the clustered index, with only 40 rows that fit in a leaf page. The row size ratio between the nonclustered index and the clustered index is one to five. This means that with the nonclustered index, the query can get the rows that it needs by scanning one-fifth of the pages compared to the clustered index. So, in the example with the 10,000 matching rows, the query would need to scan only about 50 pages in the nonclustered index leaf.

Besides coverage, there's another critical thing you need to consider when optimizing queries with supporting indexes. When the query filter involves multiple predicates, you need to consider carefully the order of the key columns in the index key list. Take the following query as an example:

```
SELECT orderid, shipperid, orderdate, custid
FROM dbo.Orders
WHERE shipperid = 'C'
  AND orderdate >= '20140101'
  AND orderdate < '20150101';
```

The guidelines for the order of the key columns in the index key list depend on the operators you use in the predicates (equality or range) and, in some cases, the selectivity of the filter.

If you have multiple equality predicates, you have the most flexibility in creating an efficient index. You can define the key list in any order you like. That's because with all key orders, the qualifying rows will appear in a consecutive range in the index leaf. For example, if the query filter was *shipperid = <some_shipper_ID> AND orderdate = <some_date>*, you can create the index with the key list *(shipperid, orderdate)* or *(orderdate, shipperid)*.

You will hear some recommendations that claim you will get better cardinality estimates if you place the column from the more selective predicate first in the key list because the optimizer creates a histogram on the first key column. This is not really true, because as I explained earlier, if SQL Server needs a histogram on a column that is not a leading key in the index, it creates one on the fly. What could be a factor in determining key order when you use only equality predicates is if one column is always specified in the query filter and another only sometimes. You want to make sure that the column that is always specified appears first in the index key list because to get an index seek, the query filter has to refer to leading key columns.

If you have at most one range predicate and all remaining predicates are equality ones, you have less flexibility compared to having only equality predicates. However, you can still create an optimal index. The guideline in this case is to place the columns that appear in the equality predicates first in the key list (in any order that you like among them), and to place the column that appears in the range predicate last in the key list. Only this way will you get the qualifying rows in a consecutive range in the index leaf. Our sample query falls into this category because it has one equality predicate and one range predicate. As usual, if you want the index to be a covering one to avoid the need for lookups, place the remaining columns that appear in the query in the INCLUDE clause of the index. Following the indexing guidelines for this category, use the following code to create the optimal index:

```
CREATE INDEX idx_nc_sid_od_i_cid_orderid
  ON dbo.Orders(shipperid, orderdate) INCLUDE(custid, orderid);
```

Figure 2-35 shows the execution plan for our sample query after creating this index, and Figure 2-36 illustrates the way the storage engine processes the access method.

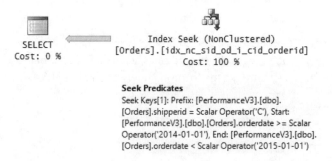

Seek Predicates
Seek Keys[1]: Prefix: [PerformanceV3].[dbo].
[Orders].shipperid = Scalar Operator('C'), Start:
[PerformanceV3].[dbo].[Orders].orderdate >= Scalar
Operator('2014-01-01'), End: [PerformanceV3].[dbo].
[Orders].orderdate < Scalar Operator('2015-01-01')

FIGURE 2-35 Covering nonclustered index seek + range scan (execution plan).

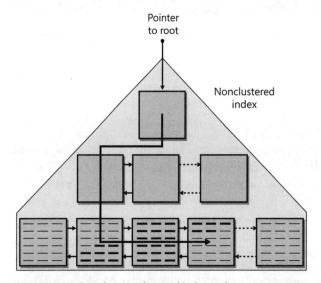

FIGURE 2-36 Covering nonclustered index seek + range scan (storage engine).

Observe the Seek Predicates property of the Index Seek operator in the plan: *Prefix: shipperid =* *'C', Start: orderdate >= '2014-01-01', End: orderdate < '2015-01-01'*. The seek operation finds the first row in the index leaf that satisfies the Prefix and Start predicates. The range scan continues until the last row that satisfies the Prefix and End predicates. When I ran this query on my system, I got 49,782 matching rows. SQL Server reported only 222 logical reads for the query. The range scan read only pages with qualifying rows. Had the index been created with the range column first in the key list and the equality column second, the situation would have been very different. SQL Server would have had to scan all rows that satisfy the range predicate (*orderdate >= '20140101' AND orderdate < '20150101'*) as a seek predicate, and evaluate the equality predicate (*shipperid = 'C'*) as a residual predicate.

If you have multiple range predicates, you're not in luck. In such a case, it's not possible to create an index that will arrange the qualifying rows in a consecutive range in the index leaf. Among the range predicates, only the one involving the leading key column among the ones that appear in the range predicates can be used as a seek predicate; all remaining range predicates will be used as residual predicates and will be applied to the scanned rows to determine whether to return them or not. For this reason, you want to make sure you place the column that is associated with the most selective range predicate right after the columns that are associated with equality predicates. Place all remaining columns from the range predicates last in the index key list.

For example, suppose that your filter has the predicates *col1 > 5 AND col2 > 10*. Suppose that the first predicate has 50 percent of matching rows and the second predicate has 2 percent. You want to make sure you define the index with the key list *(col2, col1)* and not the other way around. This way, SQL Server will need to scan only 2 percent of the pages in the index leaf instead of 50 percent. You will see a few examples in the book for performance problems that are associated with multiple range predicates and recommended ways to mitigate those problems. You will find such examples in Chapter 7, "Working with date and time," in the discussion about intervals, and in Chapter 11, "Graphs and recursive queries," in the discussion about the nested sets model.

To recap, when you have multiple equality predicates, place the columns from the predicates in any order that you like in the index key list. When you have at most one range predicate, place the columns from the equality predicates first in the key list and the column from the range predicate last. When you have multiple range predicates, place the column from the most selective range predicate before the columns from the remaining range predicates.

For more information about optimizing multiple predicates, see the series of articles "Optimization Tips for Multiple Range Predicates." Part 1 can be found here: *http://sqlmag.com/ database-development/optimization-tips-multiple-range-predicates-part-1*. Part 2 appears here: *http://sqlmag.com/t-sql/optimization-tips-multiple-range-predicates-part-2*. And Part 3 is here: *http://sqlmag.com/t-sql/optimization-tips-multiple-range-predicates-part-3*.

When you're done, run the following code for cleanup:

```
DROP INDEX idx_nc_sid_od_i_cid_orderid ON dbo.Orders;
```

Cardinality estimates

The main component within the SQL Server relational engine (also known as the *query processor*) is the query optimizer. This component is responsible for generating physical execution plans for the queries you submit to SQL Server. During the optimization of a query, the optimizer explores alternative plans and chooses one that it considers to be the most efficient out of the ones that it explored. The optimizer needs to make decisions about which access methods to use to access objects, which join algorithms to use, which aggregate and distinct algorithms to use, how much memory to allocate for sort and hash activities, and so on. In many cases, the choices that the optimizer needs to make at different points in the plan depend on cardinality estimates—namely, on how many rows are returned from the previous operator. To make cardinality estimates, the optimizer employs a component called the *cardinality estimator*.

When you analyze a graphical query execution plan, you can see the cardinality estimates by placing your mouse pointer on the arrows coming out of the operators. If you examine an estimated query plan, you will see only estimates. If you examine an actual plan, you will see both the estimated numbers of rows and the actual numbers side by side. Often suboptimal choices that the optimizer makes are connected to inaccurate cardinality estimates, and the main way to detect those is by comparing the estimated and actual numbers. Note that the cost percentages associated with the different operators reflect the estimated costs that are connected to the estimated numbers of rows. Therefore, when the optimizer makes inaccurate estimates, those percentages can be misleading. Conversely, the thickness of the arrows in an actual plan reflects the actual number of rows flowing, so thicker arrows mean more rows flowing. Moreover, when you have a Nested Loops operator involved, be aware that the estimated number of rows reported for the inner part of the loop is for one execution, whereas the actual number of rows reported is the sum of all executions. So if you have a case where the estimated number of rows is 10, the estimated number of executions is 100, and the actual number of rows is 1,000, it's actually an accurate estimate.

In the following sections, I go into the details of cardinality estimates. I cover major milestones in SQL Server regarding changes in the cardinality estimator, the implications of inaccurate estimates, statistics, multiple predicates, the ascending key problem, and the treatment of unknowns.

 Note As a reminder, I used randomization to create the sample data. Moreover, SQL Server samples only a percentage of the data using randomization when creating statistics for a column that is not a leading key in an index. So when you run the queries in my examples, you will most likely get slightly different results than mine.

Legacy estimator vs. 2014 cardinality estimator

The two major milestones for significant changes in the cardinality estimator were SQL Server 7.0 and SQL Server 2014. There's a 16-year difference between the release dates of these versions. The new cardinality estimator is the result of lots of learning, taking into consideration the changes that took place over the years in database workloads. These days, the volume of data and the types of queries are different than they were two decades ago.

There are many changes in the new cardinality estimator compared to the legacy one. Microsoft's goal was to improve the average case, with the understanding that there could be some cases with regression. SQL Server will use the new cardinality estimator by default when the database compatibility level is that of 2014 (120) or higher, and it will use the legacy estimator with lower compatibility levels. To make sure SQL Server uses the new cardinality estimator in our PerformanceV3 database, set the database compatibility level to 120 by running the following code:

```
USE PerformanceV3;
ALTER DATABASE PerformanceV3 SET COMPATIBILITY_LEVEL = 120;
```

If you identify certain queries that will benefit from the nondefault cardinality estimator, you can use a query trace flag to force a specific one. Use trace flag 9481 for the legacy cardinality estimator and trace flag 2312 for the new one. Because our database compatibility will cause SQL Server to use the new one by default, in my examples I will use query trace flag 9481 when I want to demonstrate using the old one. If you need your databases to use compatibility level 120 and up to enable new functionality but still use the old cardinality estimator by default, you can enable the trace flag at the server level with the startup parameter *–T9481* or the command *DBCC TRACEON(9481, –1)*.

I'm going to discuss a number of critical changes in cardinality estimation methods between the legacy estimator and the new cardinality estimator, but my coverage is not meant to be exhaustive. You can find more details in the following white paper: *http://msdn.microsoft.com/en-us/library/dn673537.aspx.*

Implications of underestimations and overestimations

Making accurate cardinality estimations is not a simple task you can do well without actually running the query and without a time machine. If you ever tried getting into the business of fortune telling, you know this. Even with the new cardinality estimator, you will still encounter cases where the estimations will be inaccurate. The implications of inaccurate estimations are generally that they might lead the optimizer to make suboptimal choices.

Underestimations and overestimations tend to have different implications. Underestimations will tend to result in the following (not an exhaustive list):

- For filters, preferring an index seek and lookups to a scan.

- For aggregates, joins, and distinct, preferring order-based algorithms to hash-based ones.

- For sort and hash operations, there might be spills to tempdb as a result of an insufficient memory grant.

- Preferring a serial plan over a parallel one.

To demonstrate an underestimation, I'll use a variable in the query and tell the optimizer to optimize the query for a specified value, like so:

```
DECLARE @i AS INT = 500000;

SELECT empid, COUNT(*) AS numorders
FROM dbo.Orders
WHERE orderid > @i
GROUP BY empid
OPTION(OPTIMIZE FOR (@i = 999900));
```

The execution plan for this query is shown in Figure 2-37.

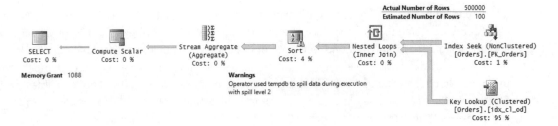

FIGURE 2-37 Plan with underestimated cardinality.

As instructed, the optimizer optimized the query for the variable value 999900, regardless of the run-time value. The optimizer used the histogram on the *orderid* column to estimate the cardinality of the filter for this input, and it came up with an estimation of 100 rows. In practice, the filter has 500,000 matches. Consequently, you see all four aforementioned implications of an underestimation on the optimizer's choices. It chose to use a seek in the index *PK_Orders* and lookups, even though a scan of the table would have been more efficient. It chose to sort the rows and use an order-based aggregate algorithm (Stream Aggregate) even though a hash aggregate would have been more efficient here. The memory grant for the sort operation was insufficient because it was based on the estimate of 100 rows, so the Sort operator ended up spilling to tempdb twice (spill level 2). It chose a serial plan even though a parallel plan would have been more efficient here.

Overestimations will tend to result in pretty much the inverse of underestimations (again, not an exhaustive list):

- For filters, preferring a scan to an index seek and lookups.

- For aggregates, joins, and distinct, preferring hash-based algorithms to order-based ones.

- For sort and hash operations, there won't be spills, but very likely there will be a larger memory grant than needed, resulting in wasting memory.

- Preferring a parallel plan over a serial one.

To demonstrate an overestimation, I'll simply use a variable in the query and assign it a value that results in a selective filter, like so:

```
DECLARE @i AS INT = 999900;

SELECT empid, COUNT(*) AS numorders
FROM dbo.Orders
WHERE orderid > @i
GROUP BY empid;
```

Unlike parameter values, variable values normally cannot be sniffed. That's because the initial optimization unit that the optimizer gets to work on is the entire batch. The optimizer is not supposed to execute the code preceding the query before optimizing it. In other words, it doesn't perform the variable assignment before it optimizes the query. So it has to make a cardinality estimate for the predicate *orderid* > *@i* based on an unknown variable value. Later, in the section "Unknowns," I provide a magic table of estimates for unknown inputs in Table 2-1. You will find that for the greater than (>) operator with an unknown input, the optimizer uses a hard-coded estimate of 30 percent matches. Apply 30 percent to the table's cardinality of 1,000,000 rows, and you get 300,000 rows. That's compared to an actual number of matches of 100. You can see these estimated and actual numbers in the execution plan for this query, which is shown in Figure 2-38.

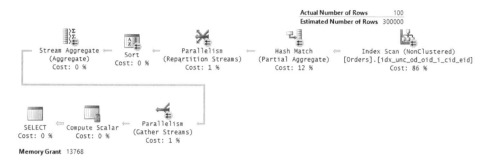

FIGURE 2-38 Plan with overestimated cardinality.

You can see the aforementioned implications of an overestimation of cardinality on the optimizer's choices. It chose to use a scan of some covering index instead of a seek in the index *PK_Orders* and lookups. It chose a local/global aggregate with a hash-based algorithm for the local aggregate instead of using an order-based aggregate. The memory grant for the hash and sort operations is exaggerated. It chose a parallel plan instead of a serial one.

Of course, it is best if the cardinality estimate is accurate, but between an underestimation and an overestimation, I generally prefer the latter. That's because I find that the impact of an overestimation on the performance of the query tends to be less severe.

Statistics

SQL Server relies on statistics about the data in its cardinality estimates. Whenever you create an index, SQL Server creates statistics using a full scan of the data. When additional statistics are needed, SQL Server might create them automatically using a sampled percentage of the data. SQL Server creates three main types of statistics: header, density vectors, and a histogram. To demonstrate those, run the following code, which creates an index with the key columns *(custid, empid)*:

```
CREATE INDEX idx_nc_cid_eid ON dbo.Orders(custid, empid);
```

SQL Server created the three aforementioned types of statistics to support the index. You can see those by running the DBCC SHOW_STATISTICS command, like so:

```
DBCC SHOW_STATISTICS(N'dbo.Orders', N'idx_nc_cid_eid');
```

I got the following output from this command (with the text for the header wrapped to fit in print):

```
Name            Updated               Rows      Rows Sampled  Steps  Density     Average key length
--------------  --------------------  --------  ------------  ------  ----------  ------------------
idx_nc_cid_eid  Oct 21 2014  7:17PM   1000000   1000000       187    0.02002646  18


String Index  Filter Expression  Unfiltered Rows
------------  -----------------  ---------------
YES           NULL               1000000


All density   Average Length  Columns
------------   --------------  -------------------------
5E-05         11              custid
1.050216E-06  15              custid, empid
1.000042E-06  18              custid, empid, orderdate


RANGE_HI_KEY  RANGE_ROWS  EQ_ROWS  DISTINCT_RANGE_ROWS  AVG_RANGE_ROWS
------------  ----------  -------  -------------------  --------------
C0000000001   0           46       0                    1
C0000000130   6437        37       128                  50.28906
C0000000252   6089        37       121                  50.32232
C0000000310   2918        67       57                   51.19298
C0000000539   11538       62       228                  50.60526
...
C0000019486   6307        66       126                  50.05556
C0000019704   10934       30       217                  50.3871
C0000019783   4045        66       78                   51.85897
C0000019904   5906        68       120                  49.21667
C0000020000   4733        46       95                   49.82105
```

The first part in the statistics is the header. It contains general information about the data, such as the cardinality of the table (1,000,000 rows in our example).

The second part in the statistics is the density vectors. This part records density information for all leading vectors of key columns. You created the index on *custid* and *empid*, but internally SQL Server added *orderdate* as the last key column; that's because the *orderdate* column is the clustered index key column and therefore nonclustered indexes use it as the row locator. So, with three key columns, you have three vectors of leading columns. The density of the column represents the average percentage of occurrences per distinct combination of values. For example, there are 20,000 distinct customer IDs in the table, so the average percentage per distinct value is 1 / 20,000 = 0.00005, or 5E-05 as it appears in the statistics. As you add more columns, the density reduces until you get uniqueness. So, for the vector (*custid, empid*), the density is 0.000001050216, or 1.050216E-06. SQL Server uses the density information when it needs to make cardinality estimates for unknown inputs, or when it considers that the average case is likely to be more accurate.

The third part of the statistics is the histogram. When you create an index, SQL Server creates a histogram on the leading key based on a full scan of the data. In addition, when SQL Server optimizes a query and needs a histogram on a column that is not a leading index key, it can create one on the fly as long as the database option *AUTO_CREATE_STATISTICS* is enabled. It samples a percentage of the rows for this purpose.

SQL Server supports only single-column histograms with up to 200 steps. Each step represents the range of keys that are greater than the previous step's *RANGE_HI_KEY* value and less than or equal to the current *RANGE_HI_KEY* value. For example, the second step in our histogram represents the range of customer IDs that are greater than C0000000001 and less than or equal to C0000000130. The *RANGE_ROWS* value indicates the number of rows represented by the step, excluding the ones with the *RANGE_HI_KEY* value. The *EQ_ROWS* value represents the number of rows with the *RANGE_HI_KEY* value. The sum of *RANGE_ROWS* and *EQ_ROWS* is the total number of rows that the step represents. The *DISTINCT_RANGE_ROWS* value represents the distinct count of the key values in the step, excluding the upper bound. The *AVG_RANGE_ROWS* value represents the average number of rows in the step per distinct key value, again, excluding the upper bound.

SQL Server uses the histogram to make cardinality estimates for known inputs. As an example, consider the following query:

```
SELECT orderid, custid, empid, shipperid, orderdate, filler
FROM dbo.Orders
WHERE custid = 'C0000000001';
```

The execution plan for this query is shown in Figure 2-39.

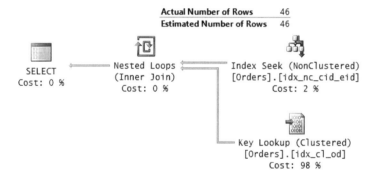

FIGURE 2-39 Plan that shows the use of a histogram on a single column based on *RANGE_HI_KEY*.

SQL Server looked for the step responsible for the input value C0000000001 and found that it belongs to step 1. It so happens that this input value is equal to the *RANGE_HI_KEY* value in the step, so the cardinality estimate for it is simply the *EQ_ROWS* value, which is 46. You can see in the query plan that 46 is the estimated number of rows after filtering.

As another example, consider the following query:

```
SELECT orderid, custid, empid, shipperid, orderdate, filler
FROM dbo.Orders
WHERE custid = 'C0000000002';
```

Observe the first two steps in the histogram:

RANGE_HI_KEY	RANGE_ROWS	EQ_ROWS	DISTINCT_RANGE_ROWS	AVG_RANGE_ROWS
C0000000001	0	46	0	1
C0000000130	6437	37	128	50.28906

The input value belongs to step 2. However, it is less than the *RANGE_HI_KEY* value of the step, so SQL Server uses the *AVG_RANGE_ROWS* value of 50.2891 as the cardinality estimate. The query plan I got for this query on my system showed an estimated number of rows of 50.2891 and an actual number of 57.

As you can see, with an equality predicate for a known input the cardinality estimate is pretty straightforward. If you have a range predicate, the estimate will be interpolated from the information in the histogram steps. If only one step is involved, the estimate will be interpolated from only that step's information. If multiple steps are involved, SQL Server will split the filter's range into the subintervals that intersect with the different steps, interpolate the estimate for each subinterval, and aggregate the estimates.

The next example demonstrates a case where the optimizer uses density vectors. Remember that unlike parameter values, variable values aren't sniffable. That's because the initial optimization unit is the batch and the optimizer isn't supposed to execute the assignments before it optimizes the query. Consider the following code:

```
DECLARE @cid AS VARCHAR(11) = 'C0000000001';

SELECT orderid, custid, empid, shipperid, orderdate, filler
FROM dbo.Orders
WHERE custid = @cid;
```

The optimizer cannot sniff the variable value here. Because density information is available for the *custid* column, the optimizer uses it. Remember that the density for this column is 0.00005. Multiply this value by the table's cardinality of 1,000,000 rows, and you get 50. The execution plan I got for this query showed an estimated number of rows of 50 and an actual number of 46.

Estimates for multiple predicates

As mentioned, SQL Server supports only single-column histograms. When the query filter involves more than one predicate, SQL Server can make an estimate for each of the predicates based on the respective histogram, but it will need to somehow combine the estimates into a single one. The legacy estimator and new cardinality estimator handle this differently.

I'll explain the estimation methods with both a conjunction of predicates (predicates separated by AND operators) and a disjunction of predicates (predicates separated by OR operators).

Before I describe estimation methods for multiple predicates, I'll make a note of the selectivity (percentage of matches) of two specific predicates so that I can use those in my examples. The following query has a filter with a predicate based on the *custid* column:

```
SELECT orderid, custid, empid, shipperid, orderdate, filler
FROM dbo.Orders
WHERE custid <= 'C0000001000';
```

On my system, the query plan shows an estimated number of rows of 52,800. This number translates to a selectivity of 5.28%.

The following query has a filter with a predicate based on the *empid* column:

```
SELECT orderid, custid, empid, shipperid, orderdate, filler
FROM dbo.Orders
WHERE empid <= 100;
```

If there are no statistics on the *empid* column before you run this query, the execution of this query triggers the creation of such statistics. On my system, the query plan showed an estimated number of rows of 19,800, translating to a selectivity of 19.8%.

The legacy cardinality estimator assumes that when your query has multiple predicates, they are independent of each other. Based on this assumption, for a conjunction of predicates it computes the result selectivity as the product of the individual ones. Consider the following query as an example (notice the trace flag forces the use of the legacy cardinality estimator):

```
SELECT orderid, custid, empid, shipperid, orderdate, filler
FROM dbo.Orders
WHERE custid <= 'C0000001000'
  AND empid <= 100
OPTION(QUERYTRACEON 9481);
```

On my system, I got the query plan shown in Figure 2-40.

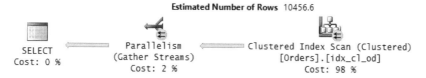

Estimated Number of Rows 10456.6

FIGURE 2-40 Estimate for the conjunction with the legacy cardinality estimator.

Remember that the individual estimates on my system were 5.28% and 19.8%, so the product is 5.28% * 19.8% = 10.4%. Indeed, the cardinality estimate in the plan reflects this.

After many years of experience with SQL Server, Microsoft learned that, in reality, there's usually some level of dependency between predicates. In the average case, predicates are neither completely independent nor completely dependent—rather, they are somewhere in between. Even though my sample data doesn't reflect this because I used simple randomization to create it, if you think about it, there will typically be some dependency between the customer who places an order and the employee who handles it. With complete independence, statistically a product of the individual estimates should be used. Under complete dependence, the most selective estimate should be used. But because the average case in reality is somewhere in between, Microsoft chose a method called *exponential backoff*, which is suitable in such a case. This method takes into consideration the most selective estimate as is, and then gradually reduces the effect of the less selective estimates by raising each to the power of a smaller fraction. Assuming S1 is the most selective estimate (expressed as a percentage), S2 is the next most selective, and so on, the exponential backoff formula is the following:

$$S1 * S2^{1/2} * S3^{1/4} * S4^{1/8} * \ldots$$

Of course, the cardinality estimator will multiply the final percentage by the input's cardinality (1,000,000 in our case) to produce an estimate in terms of a number of rows. In our example, when you apply this method to our two predicates, you get 5.28% * SQRT(19.8%) = 23.5%, which translates to 23,500 rows.

Here's our query without the trace flag, meaning that the new cardinality estimator will be used:

```
SELECT orderid, custid, empid, shipperid, orderdate, filler
FROM dbo.Orders
WHERE custid <= 'C0000001000'
  AND empid <= 100;
```

I got the plan shown in Figure 2-41.

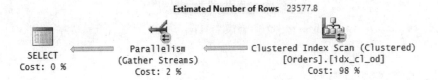

Estimated Number of Rows 23577.8

FIGURE 2-41 Estimate for the conjunction with the new cardinality estimator.

As you can see, the cardinality estimate here was based on the exponential backoff method, and as a result, you get a higher estimate compared to the legacy method, which is based on a simple product. If you have cases where predicates are truly independent of each other, you can always add trace flag 9481 to the query to force the legacy cardinality estimation method.

For a disjunction of predicates, the legacy cardinality estimator computes the sum of the individual estimates minus their product. Consider the following query as an example:

```
SELECT orderid, custid, empid, shipperid, orderdate, filler
FROM dbo.Orders
WHERE custid <= 'C0000001000'
  OR empid <= 100
OPTION(QUERYTRACEON 9481);
```

The estimate in this example is computed as 5.28% + 19.8% – (5.28% * 19.8%) = 24%.

The new cardinality estimator uses a method that is more aligned with the method for a conjunction of predicates. It negates (100% minus) the result of an exponential backoff formula that is based on the negation of the individual estimates. In our example, this translates to 100% − (100% − 19.8%) * SQRT(100% − 5.28%) = 21.9%. That's the estimate I got on my system for our sample query (about 21,900 rows):

```
SELECT orderid, custid, empid, shipperid, orderdate, filler
FROM dbo.Orders
WHERE custid <= 'C0000001000'
  OR empid <= 100;
```

If you have multiple predicates and you often get inaccurate estimates there are a couple of ways to get better estimates. That's assuming that all predicates are equality ones or that you have at most one range predicate but all the rest are equality ones. For example, suppose that users often filter the data by customer ID and employee ID, both with equality predicates. So the query filter might look like this: *WHERE custid = 'C0000000003' AND empid = 5*. You create a computed column (call it *custid_empid*) that concatenates the customer ID and employee ID values. Just the fact that a computed column exists allows SQL Server to create statistics on the column, regardless of whether you index it or not. Your query will need to filter the concatenated value to benefit from such statistics. You can filter by the computed column name or directly by the concatenated expression. In both cases, SQL Server can rely on the histogram on the computed column and on an index if you created one. So the query filter might look like this: *WHERE custid_empid = 'C0000000003_5'*.

Another method to use to get better estimates is working with filtered indexes. As long as you have a small number of distinct values in one of the columns, a solution that creates a filtered index per distinct value is maintainable. For example, suppose that in your organization only 10 distinct employees handle orders; in such a case, it's reasonable to create 10 filtered indexes, one per distinct employee ID. For example, the index for employee ID 5 will have the filter *WHERE empid = 5*. The index key will be based on the *custid* column. SQL Server will create a histogram based on the *custid* column for each filtered index. When the optimizer will need to make a cardinality estimate for a filter such as *WHERE custid = 'C0000000003' AND empid = 5*, it will use the histogram on the *custid* column in the filtered index for that employee ID (in this example, 5). Effectively, the quality of the estimates will be the same as if you had a multicolumn histogram. You can find more information on filtered indexes later in the chapter, in the section "Indexing features."

When you're done, run the following code for cleanup:

```
DROP INDEX idx_nc_cid_eid ON dbo.Orders;
```

Ascending key problem

SQL Server normally refreshes statistics once every 500 plus 20 percent of changes in the column in question. Any data added after the statistics were last refreshed is not modeled by the statistics. As an example, the following code creates a table called Orders2 with 900,000 rows and a nonclustered index through a primary key constraint called PK_Orders2:

```
IF OBJECT_ID(N'dbo.Orders2', N'U') IS NOT NULL DROP TABLE dbo.Orders2;
SELECT * INTO dbo.Orders2 FROM dbo.Orders WHERE orderid <= 900000;
ALTER TABLE dbo.Orders2 ADD CONSTRAINT PK_Orders2 PRIMARY KEY NONCLUSTERED(orderid);
```

SQL Server creates statistics for the index as part of the index creation; therefore, the histogram on the *orderid* column models all 900,000 rows from the table. Run the following code to show the statistics for the index:

```
DBCC SHOW_STATISTICS('dbo.Orders2', 'PK_Orders2');
```

I got the following output on my system:

Name	Updated	Rows	Rows Sampled	Steps	Density	Average key length
PK_Orders2	Oct 21 2014 9:29PM	900000	900000	2	1	4

String Index	Filter Expression	Unfiltered Rows
NO	NULL	900000

All density	Average Length	Columns
1.111111E-06	4	orderid

RANGE_HI_KEY	RANGE_ROWS	EQ_ROWS	DISTINCT_RANGE_ROWS	AVG_RANGE_ROWS
1	0	1	0	1
900000	899998	1	899998	1

The last part of the output is the histogram on the *orderid* column. Observe that the maximum order ID value recorded is 900,000, which is indeed currently the maximum value in the table. Next, run the following code to add 100,000 rows:

```
INSERT INTO dbo.Orders2
  SELECT *
  FROM dbo.Orders
  WHERE orderid > 900000 AND orderid <= 1000000;
```

Now query the table and filter the rows with an order ID that is greater than 900,000, like so (the trace flag ensures the legacy cardinality estimator is used):

```
SELECT orderid, custid, empid, shipperid, orderdate, filler
FROM dbo.Orders2
WHERE orderid > 900000
ORDER BY orderdate
OPTION(QUERYTRACEON 9481);
```

Because the extra 100,000 rows are less than the threshold for refreshing the statistics, the new rows are not modeled by the histogram. You can see this by running DBCC SHOW_STATISTICS again. You will see that the maximum value is still 900,000. The legacy cardinality estimator examines the histogram and sees that the filter's range is after the maximum value in the histogram. Based on just this information, the estimate should be zero matching rows, but the minimum allowed estimation is 1. Examine the execution plan for the query in Figure 2-42.

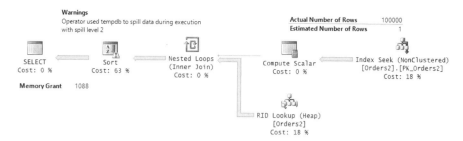

FIGURE 2-42 Plan showing the ascending key problem with the legacy cardinality estimator.

Observe that the estimated cardinality of the filter is 1 row, whereas the actual is 100,000. You can see a number of suboptimal choices that the optimizer made based on the inaccurate estimate. This problem typically happens when the column is an ascending key column and you filter recent data. Often the recent data isn't modeled by the histogram.

The new cardinality estimator handles the estimate differently. If it identifies that the filter's interval exceeds the recorded maximum, it interpolates the estimate by taking into consideration the count of modifications since the last statistics refresh. Run the sample query again, but this time allow SQL Server to use the new cardinality estimator:

```
SELECT orderid, custid, empid, shipperid, orderdate, filler
FROM dbo.Orders2
WHERE orderid > 900000
ORDER BY orderdate;
```

I got the execution plan shown in Figure 2-43.

FIGURE 2-43 Plan showing the ascending key problem solved with the new cardinality estimator.

This time, as you can see, the estimate is accurate. As a result, the choices that the optimizer made are much more optimal.

Another tool you can use to deal with the ascending key problem is trace flag 2389. Unlike the new cardinality estimator, this trace flag is available prior to SQL Server 2014. If you enable this trace flag, when SQL Server refreshes statistics it checks if the values in the source column keep increasing. If they keep increasing in three consecutive refreshes, SQL Server brands the source column as *ascending*. Then, at query compile time, SQL Server adds a ministep to the histogram to model the data that was added since the last refresh. You can find information about this trace flag here: *http://blogs. msdn.com/b/ianjo/archive/2006/04/24/582227.aspx*.

With very large tables, the default threshold for an automatic statistics update of every 500 plus 20 percent of changes could be insufficient. Think about it: for a table with 100,000,000 rows, the threshold is 20,000,500 changes. If you enable trace flag 2371, SQL Server will gradually reduce the percentage as the table grows. You can find details about this trace flag, including a graph showing the gradual change, here: *http://blogs.msdn.com/b/saponsqlserver/archive/2011/09/07/changes-to-automatic-update-statistics-in-sql-server-traceflag-2371.aspx*.

Unknowns

I described some cardinality estimation methods SQL Server uses when statistics are available and the input values are known (for example, when you use constants or parameters). In some cases, SQL Server uses cardinality estimation methods based on unknown inputs. Following are those cases:

- No statistics are available.

- You use variables (as opposed to parameters). As mentioned earlier, variable values aren't sniffable because the initial optimization unit is the entire batch.

- You use parameters with sniffing disabled (for example, when you specify the OPTIMIZE FOR UNKNOWN hint).

Table 2-1 shows the rules that SQL Server uses to make a cardinality estimate for unknown inputs based on the operator you use.

TABLE 2-1 Magic table of estimates for unknown inputs

Operator	Estimate
>, >=, <, <=	30%
BETWEEN/LIKE	9% Exception: in 2014 BETWEEN with variables/parameters with sniffing disabled the estimate is 16.4317%
= with a unique column	1 row
= with a nonunique column prior to SQL Server 2014	$C^{3/4}$ (C = table cardinality)
= with a nonunique column in SQL Server 2014	$C^{1/2}$

I should mention that there are a couple of exceptional cases in which SQL Server won't use this table. One exception is with variables. I mentioned that normally variable values aren't sniffable. However, if you force a statement-level recompile with a RECOMPILE query option or an automatic statement-level recompile happens, the query gets optimized after the variable values are assigned. Therefore, the variable values become sniffable to the optimizer, and then SQL Server can use its normal cardinality estimation methods based on statistics.

The other exception is when using variables or parameters with sniffing disabled, and the operator is an equality operator, and a density vector is available for the filtered columns. In such a case, the estimate will be based on the density vector.

Next, I'll demonstrate examples for estimates that are based on the rules in Table 2-1. Run the following code to check which indexes you currently have on the Orders table:

```
EXEC sp_helpindex N'dbo.Orders';
```

The output should show only the following indexes:

```
idx_cl_od
idx_nc_sid_od_cid
idx_unc_od_oid_i_cid_eid
PK_Orders
```

If you get any other indexes, drop them.

Run the following code to turn off the auto collection of statistics in the database:

```
ALTER DATABASE PerformanceV3 SET AUTO_CREATE_STATISTICS OFF;
```

Run the following query to identify statistics that were created automatically on the Orders table:

```
SELECT S.name AS stats_name,
    QUOTENAME(OBJECT_SCHEMA_NAME(S.object_id)) + N'.' + QUOTENAME(OBJECT_NAME(S.object_id)) AS
object,
    C.name AS column_name
FROM sys.stats AS S
  INNER JOIN sys.stats_columns AS SC
    ON S.object_id = SC.object_id
    AND S.stats_id = SC.stats_id
  INNER JOIN sys.columns AS C
    ON SC.object_id = C.object_id
    AND SC.column_id = C.column_id
WHERE S.object_id = OBJECT_ID(N'dbo.Orders')
  AND auto_created = 1;
```

Drop all statistics that this query reports. In my case, I used the following code based on the output of the query; of course, you should drop the statistics that the query reports for you:

```
DROP STATISTICS dbo.Orders._WA_Sys_00000002_38EE7070;
DROP STATISTICS dbo.Orders._WA_Sys_00000003_38EE7070;
```

Observe in Table 2-1 that the estimate for unknown with any of the operators >, >=, <, <= is 30%. The following queries demonstrate this estimation method:

```
-- Query 1
DECLARE @i AS INT = 999900;

SELECT orderid, custid, empid, shipperid, orderdate, filler
FROM dbo.Orders
WHERE orderid > @i;

-- Query 2
SELECT orderid, custid, empid, shipperid, orderdate, filler
FROM dbo.Orders
WHERE custid <= 'C0000000010';
```

Figure 2-44 shows the plans for these queries.

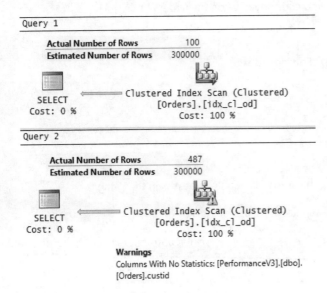

FIGURE 2-44 Plans showing an estimate of 30 percent.

The first query uses a variable whose value cannot be sniffed. The second uses a constant, but statistics are not available, and you disabled the option to create new ones.

For the BETWEEN and LIKE predicates, Table 2-1 shows an estimate of 9%. An exception to this rule is that in SQL Server 2014 when you use BETWEEN with variables, or parameters with sniffing disabled, the estimate is 16.4317%. The following queries demonstrate these rules:

```
-- Query 1
DECLARE @i AS INT = 999901, @j AS INT = 1000000;

SELECT orderid, custid, empid, shipperid, orderdate, filler
FROM dbo.Orders
WHERE orderid BETWEEN @i AND @j;

-- Query 2
SELECT orderid, custid, empid, shipperid, orderdate, filler
FROM dbo.Orders
WHERE orderid BETWEEN @i AND @j
OPTION(QUERYTRACEON 9481);

-- Query 3
SELECT orderid, custid, empid, shipperid, orderdate, filler
FROM dbo.Orders
WHERE custid BETWEEN 'C0000000001' AND 'C0000000010';

-- Query 4
SELECT orderid, custid, empid, shipperid, orderdate, filler
FROM dbo.Orders
WHERE custid LIKE '%9999';
```

The execution plans for these queries are shown in Figure 2-45.

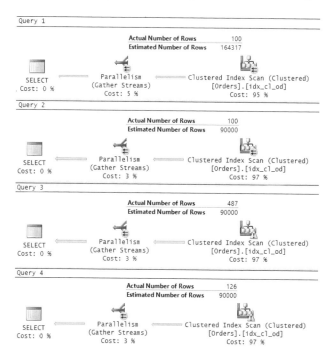

FIGURE 2-45 Plans showing estimates for BETWEEN and LIKE.

The first query falls into the exception that I just described, so it gets an estimate of 16.4317%. The second query is the same as the first, but because you force using the legacy cardinality estimator, you get an estimate of 9%. The third and fourth queries use constants, but there are no statistics available. As an aside, query 4 normally causes string statistics, which contain information about occurrences of substrings, to be created. However, because you disabled automatic creation of statistics in the database, SQL Server did not create those statistics, and it used the estimation method based on unknown inputs instead.

With the equality operator, the estimation method for an unknown input depends on the uniqueness of the column and the version of SQL Server. When the column is unique, the estimate is 1 row. When it's not unique, in SQL Server 2014 the estimate is $C^{1/2}$, where C is the input's cardinality, and prior to SQL Server 2014 it's $C^{3/4}$.

The following queries demonstrate all three methods:

```
-- Query 1
DECLARE @i AS INT = 1000000;

SELECT orderid, custid, empid, shipperid, orderdate, filler
FROM dbo.Orders
WHERE orderid = @i;
```

```
-- Query 2
SELECT orderid, custid, empid, shipperid, orderdate, filler
FROM dbo.Orders
WHERE custid = 'C0000000001';

-- Query 3
SELECT orderid, custid, empid, shipperid, orderdate, filler
FROM dbo.Orders
WHERE custid = 'C0000000001'
OPTION(QUERYTRACEON 9481);
```

The execution plans with the estimates for these queries are shown in Figure 2-46.

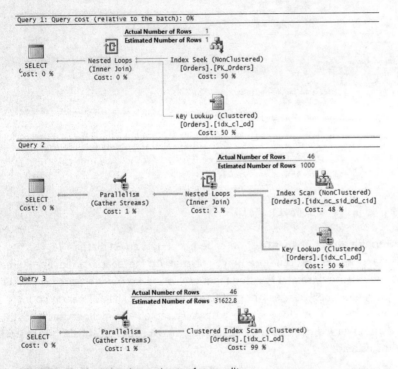

FIGURE 2-46 Plans showing estimates for equality.

When you're done experimenting, run the following code to turn the automatic creation of statistics back on:

```
ALTER DATABASE PerformanceV3 SET AUTO_CREATE_STATISTICS ON;
```

Feel free to rerun the queries to see how the estimations change when SQL Server automatically creates statistics when it needs those. For example, rerun the query with the LIKE predicate:

```
SELECT orderid, custid, empid, shipperid, orderdate, filler
FROM dbo.Orders
WHERE custid LIKE '%9999';
```

I got the query plan shown in Figure 2-47.

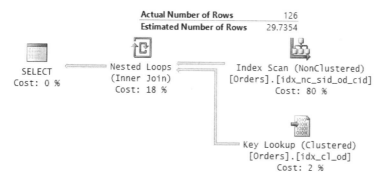

FIGURE 2-47 Plan for a query using LIKE with string statistics available.

SQL Server first created string statistics on the *custid* column and then performed the estimate based on those statistics. Compared to the previous estimate you got for this query in Figure 2-45 (it was Query 4 in that figure), this time the estimate is much more accurate.

Another curious difference between the legacy and new cardinality estimators is in how they handle a filter with an expression that manipulates a column. Take the expression *orderid % 2 = 0* as an example. The legacy cardinality estimator simply treats the case as an unknown input. As such, the estimate for an equality operator is $C^{3/4}$. With our Orders table, this translates to $1,000,000^{3/4} = 31,622$. That's likely to be a significant underestimation. The new cardinality estimator is more sophisticated. Here, it actually realizes that the expression uses the modulo (%) operator. Statistically, with % 2 = 0, you're going to get 50% matches. Accordingly, the estimation for this case is 500,000 rows. This will likely be much closer to the actual number than the estimation made by the legacy cardinality estimator.

Indexing features

This section covers various indexing features. It includes information about descending indexes, included non-key columns, filtered indexes and statistics, columnstore indexes, and inline index definition. The features are covered in the order in which they were added to SQL Server.

Descending indexes

With SQL Server, you can indicate the direction of key columns in an index definition. By default, the direction is ascending, but using the DESC keyword you can request descending order, as in *(col1, col2 DESC)*.

Indexes on disk-based tables have a doubly linked list in their leaf level. So SQL Server can scan the rows in the leaf in forward and backward order. As an aside, as you will learn in Chapter 10, BW-Tree indexes on memory-optimized tables are unidirectional. But back to B-tree-based indexes on disk-based tables, at the beginning it might seem like there's no need for descending indexes, but there are a few use cases.

As it turns out, the storage engine is currently able to process only forward scans with parallelism. Whenever you have a backward scan, it is processed serially. Take the following queries as an example:

```
-- Query 1, parallel
SELECT orderid, custid, empid, shipperid, orderdate, filler
FROM dbo.Orders
WHERE orderid <= 100000
ORDER BY orderdate;

-- Query 2, serial
SELECT orderid, custid, empid, shipperid, orderdate, filler
FROM dbo.Orders
WHERE orderid <= 100000
ORDER BY orderdate DESC;
```

Figure 2-48 shows the execution plans for these queries.

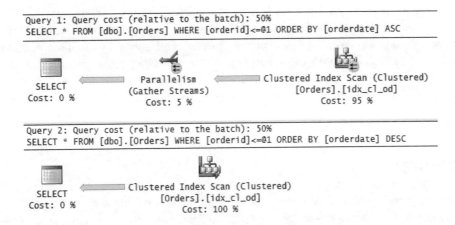

FIGURE 2-48 Plans showing that there's no parallel backward scan.

I have 8 logical CPUs on my machine. According to SQL Server's costing formulas, with that many CPUs, a query against a table with 1,000,000 rows that filters 100,000 rows should get a parallel plan. That's why the plan for the first query uses a parallel scan. However, because a backward scan cannot be processed with parallelism, the plan for the second query uses a serial one.

It's interesting to see what the optimizer does when you try to force parallelism with the second query using query trace flag 8649, like so:

```
SELECT orderid, custid, empid, shipperid, orderdate, filler
FROM dbo.Orders
WHERE orderid <= 100000
ORDER BY orderdate DESC
OPTION(QUERYTRACEON 8649);
```

The plan for this query is shown in Figure 2-49.

FIGURE 2-49 Plan with forced parallelism.

Not being able to use a parallel backward-order scan, the optimizer chose a plan that uses a parallel unordered scan, and then an explicit sort operation. Clearly, it's a very inefficient plan. If you find that parallelism is a critical factor in the performance of the query, you can arrange a descending index. Of course, if at some point Microsoft introduces support for parallel backward scans, you won't need descending indexes for this purpose anymore.

Another curious case where descending indexes are useful is with window functions that have both a window partition clause and a window order clause. Consider the following queries:

```
-- Query 1
SELECT shipperid, orderdate, custid,
  ROW_NUMBER() OVER(PARTITION BY shipperid ORDER BY orderdate) AS rownum
FROM dbo.Orders;

-- Query 2
SELECT shipperid, orderdate, custid,
  ROW_NUMBER() OVER(PARTITION BY shipperid ORDER BY orderdate DESC) AS rownum
FROM dbo.Orders;

-- Query 3
SELECT shipperid, orderdate, custid,
  ROW_NUMBER() OVER(PARTITION BY shipperid ORDER BY orderdate DESC) AS rownum
FROM dbo.Orders
ORDER BY shipperid DESC;
```

Currently, there is a covering index called idx_nc_sid_od_cid on the table, defined with the key list *(shipperid, orderdate, custid)*. Examine the execution plans for these queries as shown in Figure 2-50.

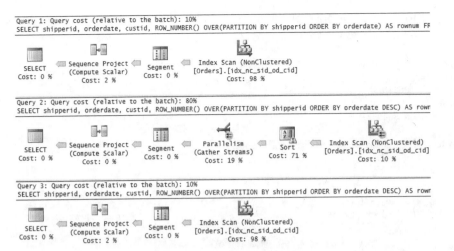

Query 1: Query cost (relative to the batch): 10%
SELECT shipperid, orderdate, custid, ROW_NUMBER() OVER(PARTITION BY shipperid ORDER BY orderdate) AS rownum FF

SELECT   Sequence Project   Segment   Index Scan (NonClustered)
Cost: 0 %   (Compute Scalar)   Cost: 0 % [Orders].[idx_nc_sid_od_cid]
                Cost: 2 %   Cost: 98 %

Query 2: Query cost (relative to the batch): 80%
SELECT shipperid, orderdate, custid, ROW_NUMBER() OVER(PARTITION BY shipperid ORDER BY orderdate DESC) AS rownm

SELECT   Sequence Project   Segment   Parallelism   Sort   Index Scan (NonClustered)
Cost: 0 %   (Compute Scalar)   Cost: 0 % (Gather Streams) Cost: 71 % [Orders].[idx_nc_sid_od_cid]
              Cost: 0 %   Cost: 19 %   Cost: 10 %

Query 3: Query cost (relative to the batch): 10%
SELECT shipperid, orderdate, custid, ROW_NUMBER() OVER(PARTITION BY shipperid ORDER BY orderdate DESC) AS rownm

SELECT   Sequence Project   Segment   Index Scan (NonClustered)
Cost: 0 %   (Compute Scalar)   Cost: 0 % [Orders].[idx_nc_sid_od_cid]
                Cost: 2 %   Cost: 98 %

FIGURE 2-50 Plans for queries with a window function.

The plan for query 1 shows that as long as there's a covering index with a key list that starts with the partition columns in ascending order, and continues with the order columns in the order specified in the window function, the optimizer chooses an ordered scan of the index and avoids an explicit sort operation.

In query 2, the window function's specification is similar to the one in query 1, but with descending order for the window order column *orderdate*. Theoretically, the optimizer could have chosen a plan that scans our covering index in descending order. After all, absent a presentation ORDER BY clause, SQL Server might return the rows in any order in the output. But it seems like SQL Server somehow wants to process the rows in ascending order of the window partition elements, so it adds an explicit sort operation.

Oddly, as you can see in the plan for query 3, if you do add a presentation ORDER BY clause with the *shipperid* column in descending order, suddenly the optimizer figures that it can use a backward scan both to compute the window function and to support the desired presentation order. I learned this last bit from Brad Shultz, mind you, while presenting a session in front of hundreds of people.

Another use case for descending indexes is when SQL Server needs to process rows based on multiple columns with opposite directions. For example, if your query has an ORDER BY clause with *col1, col2 DESC*, it can benefit from an index with the key list *col1, col2 DESC* or *col1 DESC, col2*. An index with both columns in ascending order isn't optimal; SQL Server would still need to explicitly sort the rows.

As an anecdote, almost two decades ago, shortly after SQL Server 2000 was released, my friend Wayne Snyder discovered one of the most amazing bugs I've seen in SQL Server. If you created a clustered index with *col1 DESC* as the key, and issued a DELETE statement with the filter *col1 > @n*, SQL Server deleted all rows where *col1 < @n*. This bug existed in SQL Server 2000 RTM and, of course, was fixed in Service Pack 1.

Included non-key columns

When you define a nonclustered index, you specify a vector of columns as the key list to determine the order of the rows in the index. SQL Server can perform ordered scans and range scans based on this key list to support operations such as ordering, filtering, grouping, joining, and others. However, if you need to add columns to the index for coverage purposes (to avoid lookups) and those columns don't serve any ordering-related purpose, you add those columns in a designated INCLUDE clause.

Unlike key columns, included columns appear only in the index leaf rows. Also, SQL Server imposes fewer restrictions on those. For example, the key list cannot have more than 16 columns, whereas included columns can. The key list cannot have more than 900 bytes, whereas included columns can. The key list cannot have special types like XML and other large object types, whereas the include list can. Moreover, when you update a row in the table, naturally SQL Server needs to update all respective index rows that contain the updated columns. If an index key column value changes, the sort position of the row might change, in which case SQL Server will need to relocate the row. If an included column value changes, the sort position remains the same, and the update can happen in place (assuming the row doesn't expand).

As an example for a use case for the INCLUDE clause, consider the following query:

```
SELECT orderid, custid, empid, shipperid, orderdate, filler
FROM dbo.Orders
WHERE custid = 'C0000000001';
```

I showed this query earlier as part of the discussion about the access method *unordered nonclustered index scan + lookups*, and I provided the query execution plan in Figure 2-31. At the moment, there is no optimal index for this query. The plan scans the entire leaf level of some noncovering nonclustered index that contains the *custid* column as a nonleading key, and then it applies lookups for the matching cases. The execution of this plan performed 4,006 logical reads on my system.

A far more optimal index is one defined with *custid* as the key column to support the filter, and all remaining columns defined as included columns to avoid lookups, like so:

```
CREATE INDEX idx_nc_cid_i_oid_eid_sid_od_flr ON dbo.Orders(custid)
  INCLUDE(orderid, empid, shipperid, orderdate, filler);
```

Run the query again:

```
SELECT orderid, custid, empid, orderdate, filler
FROM dbo.Orders
WHERE custid = 'C0000000001';
```

The plan for this query is shown in Figure 2-51.

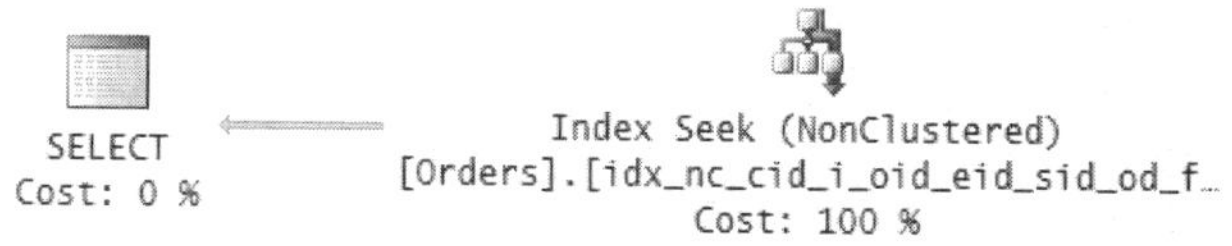

FIGURE 2-51 Plan that uses an index with included columns.

I got only 5 logical reads reported for this query.

When you're done, run the following code for cleanup:

```
DROP INDEX dbo.Orders.idx_nc_cid_i_oid_eid_sid_od_flr;
```

Filtered indexes and statistics

A filtered index is an index on a subset of rows from the underlying table defined based on a predicate. You specify the predicate in a WHERE clause as part of the index definition. Filtered indexes are cheaper to create and maintain than nonfiltered ones because only modifications to the relevant subset of rows need to be reflected in the index. Also, filtered distribution statistics (histograms) are more accurate than nonfiltered statistics. That's because the maximum number of steps in a histogram is 200, and with filtered statistics that number is used to represent a smaller set of rows. Furthermore, because the histogram is created on the leading key of the index only for the subset of rows that satisfy the index filter, effectively you get a quality of estimates as if you had a multicolumn histogram.

In cases where the index itself is not really important but statistics are, you can also create filtered statistics. You do so using the CREATE STATISTICS command, and specify the filter predicate in a WHERE clause.

As an example of a filtered index, suppose that you often query orders for the ship country USA and a certain order date period (since the beginning of the week, month, year). Perhaps you don't issue similar queries for other ship countries as frequently. You need to speed up the queries specifically for the USA. You create an index with a filter based on the predicate *shipcountry = N'USA'* and specify the *orderdate* column as the key. If it's important for you to avoid lookups, you will want to specify all remaining columns from the query as included columns. Run the following code to create such a filtered index:

```
USE TSQLV3;

CREATE NONCLUSTERED INDEX idx_USA_orderdate
  ON Sales.Orders(orderdate)
  INCLUDE(orderid, custid, requireddate)
  WHERE shipcountry = N'USA';
```

Queries such as the following will then greatly benefit from the new index:

```
SELECT orderid, custid, orderdate, requireddate
FROM Sales.Orders
WHERE shipcountry = N'USA'
  AND orderdate >= '20140101';
```

The execution plan for this query is shown in Figure 2-52.

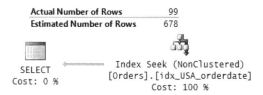

FIGURE 2-52 Plan with a filtered index and an inaccurate cardinality estimate.

Because the index filter matches the query filter, the optimizer considered the index as potentially useful. By the way, if the query filter is a subinterval of the index filter, the index can still be used. For example, if the index filter is *col1 > 10* and the query filter is *col1 > 20*, the index can be used. Back to our example, because the index key column matches the column in the query's range predicate, the optimizer could use a seek and a range scan to get the qualifying rows. Because the index covers the query, there was no need for lookups. The index is optimal for this query.

Curiously, despite what I said about the improved quality of cardinality estimates with filtered indexes, if you look at the query plan in Figure 2-52, the estimate doesn't seem to be very accurate. In fact, it reflects the estimate for the filter based on the *orderdate* column alone. The thing is that here you're not doing anything with the filtered rows, so the optimizer doesn't really need a more accurate estimate. For example, if you add *ORDER BY orderid* to the query, you will see that the estimated number of rows coming out of the sort will be accurate.

An interesting tip I learned from Paul White is that if you add the filtered column (*shipcountry* in our case) to the index—for example, as an included column—the estimate will be based on the filtered statistics to begin with. With this in mind, re-create the index with *shipcountry* as an included column, like so:

```
CREATE NONCLUSTERED INDEX idx_USA_orderdate
  ON Sales.Orders(orderdate)
  INCLUDE(orderid, custid, requireddate, shipcountry)
  WHERE shipcountry = N'USA'
WITH ( DROP_EXISTING = ON );
```

Rerun the query:

```
SELECT orderid, custid, orderdate, requireddate
FROM Sales.Orders
WHERE shipcountry = N'USA'
  AND orderdate >= '20140101';
```

The execution plan for this query is shown in Figure 2-53.

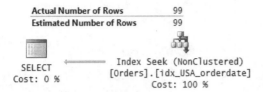

FIGURE 2-53 Plan with a filtered index and an accurate cardinality estimate.

Observe that this time the estimate is accurate.

You can also use filtered indexes to solve a common request related to enforcing data integrity. The *UNIQUE* constraint supported by SQL Server treats two NULLs as equal for the purposes of enforcing uniqueness. This means that if you define a *UNIQUE* constraint on a NULLable column, you are allowed only one row with a NULL in that column. In some cases, though, you might need to enforce the uniqueness only of non-NULL values but allow multiple NULLs. Standard SQL does support such a kind of *UNIQUE* constraint, but SQL Server never implemented it. With filtered indexes, it's quite easy to handle this need. Simply create a unique filtered index based on a predicate in the form *WHERE <column> IS NOT NULL*. As an example, run the following code to create a table called T1 with such a filtered index on the column *col1*:

```
IF OBJECT_ID(N'dbo.T1', N'U') IS NOT NULL DROP TABLE dbo.T1;
CREATE TABLE dbo.T1(col1 INT NULL, col2 VARCHAR(10) NOT NULL);
GO
CREATE UNIQUE NONCLUSTERED INDEX idx_col1_notnull ON dbo.T1(col1) WHERE col1 IS NOT NULL;
```

Run the following code in an attempt to insert two rows with the same non-NULL *col1* value:

```
INSERT INTO dbo.T1(col1, col2) VALUES(1, 'a'), (1, 'b');
```

The attempt fails with the following error:

```
Msg 2601, Level 14, State 1, Line 1023
Cannot insert duplicate key row in object 'dbo.T1' with unique index 'idx_col1_notnull'. The
duplicate key value is (1).
The statement has been terminated.
```

Try to insert two rows with a NULL in *col1*:

```
INSERT INTO dbo.T1(col1, col2) VALUES(NULL, 'c'), (NULL, 'd');
```

This time the code succeeds.

When you're done, run the following code for cleanup:

```
USE TSQLV3;
DROP INDEX idx_USA_orderdate ON Sales.Orders;
DROP TABLE dbo.T1;
```

Columnstore indexes

Columnstore technology is a game changer in the database world. It was introduced initially in SQL Server 2012 and significantly improved in SQL Server 2014. This technology targets mainly data-warehousing workloads. Consider the classic star schema model for data warehouses as shown in Figure 2-54.

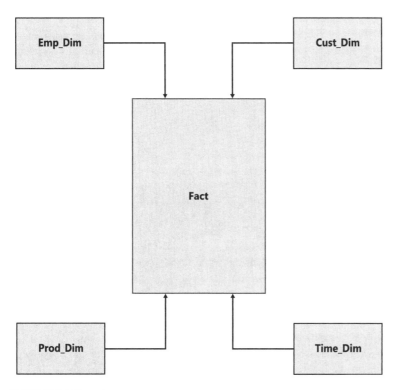

FIGURE 2-54 Star schema.

You have the dimension tables that keep track of the subjects you analyze the data by, like customers, employees, products, and time. Each dimension table has a surrogate key. The bulk of the data resides in the Fact table. This table has a column for the surrogate key of each of the dimension tables, plus columns representing measures like quantities and amounts. The traditional internal representation of the data in SQL Server before the introduction of columnstore technology has always been based on rowstore technology. This means that the data is stored and processed in a row-oriented mode. With the growing volume of data in data warehouses in recent years, rowstore technology tends to be inefficient on a number of levels, and columnstore technology addresses those inefficiencies.

To understand why rowstore is inefficient for large data warehouse environments, consider the typical data warehouse queries (also known as *star join queries*). They usually join the Fact table with some of the dimension tables, filter, group, and aggregate. Here's an example of a typical data warehouse query in our PerformanceV3 database:

```
USE PerformanceV3;
SET STATISTICS IO, TIME ON; -- turn on performance statistics

SELECT D1.attr1 AS x, D2.attr1 AS y, D3.attr1 AS z,
  COUNT(*) AS cnt, SUM(F.measure1) AS total
FROM dbo.Fact AS F
  INNER JOIN dbo.Dim1 AS D1
    ON F.key1 = D1.key1
  INNER JOIN dbo.Dim2 AS D2
    ON F.key2 = D2.key2
  INNER JOIN dbo.Dim3 AS D3
    ON F.key3 = D3.key3
WHERE D1.attr1 <= 10
  AND D2.attr1 <= 15
  AND D3.attr1 <= 10
GROUP BY D1.attr1, D2.attr1, D3.attr1;
```

The execution plan for this query is shown in Figure 2-55.

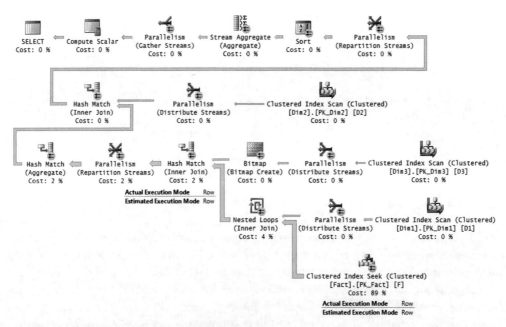

FIGURE 2-55 Plan for a star join query against a rowstore.

I got the following performance statistics for this query on my system:

```
Table 'Fact'. Scan count 122, logical reads 29300
CPU time = 890 ms,  elapsed time = 490 ms.
```

The Fact table in the sample database has only 2,500,000 rows. Usually, data warehouses have much bigger tables. Our table is big enough, though, to justify a parallel plan and to allow me to illustrate the differences between rowstore and columnstore technologies. The bigger the tables are, the more advantageous it is to use columnstore technology, so keep in mind that in reality you will see much bigger differences than what you will see in my examples.

As mentioned, the rowstore technology has a number of drawbacks. There are so many possibilities in terms of indexing, causing you to spend a lot of time and energy on index tuning. If you have lots of query patterns in the system, it's not going to be very practical for you to create the perfect covering index on the Fact table per query. You'll end up with too many indexes. In an attempt to limit the number of indexes you create, you prioritize queries for tuning and also try to consolidate multiple queries with roughly similar indexing requirements. For example, if you have a number of queries that can benefit from indexes with the same key list but different include lists, you will probably prefer to create one index with a superset of the included columns. The result is that many queries won't have truly optimal indexes to support them, and each query will likely end up using indexes that contain more than just the columns that are relevant to it. As you can realize, this means that queries will tend to perform more reads than the optimal number.

With rowstore, data is not compressed by default; rather, you need to explicitly request to compress it with row or page compression. Even if you do, because the data is stored a row at a time, the compression levels SQL Server can achieve are nowhere near what it can achieve with columnstore.

Another drawback of the rowstore technology is that currently the execution model for it is a row-execution model. This means that the different operators in the query plan are all limited to processing one row at a time. You can see this in the execution plan for our sample query in Figure 2-55. All operators in the plan will show the execution mode Row. (I highlighted this property for the clustered index seek against the Fact table and one of the hash joins.) A lot of CPU cycles are wasted because the operators process one row at a time. Any metadata information the operator needs to evaluate is evaluated per row. Any internal functions the operator needs to invoke are invoked per row.

Columnstore technology changes things quite dramatically. Note though that SQL Server 2012 is limited only to nonclustered, nonupdateable, columnstore indexes. SQL Server 2014 adds support for clustered, updateable indexes, making the technology much more accessible.

Use the following code to create a nonclustered columnstore index on our Fact table:

```
CREATE NONCLUSTERED COLUMNSTORE INDEX idx_nc_cs
  ON dbo.Fact(key1, key2, key3, measure1, measure2, measure3, measure4);
```

You want to list all columns from the Fact table in the index. The order in which you list them isn't significant. Unlike the key list in a rowstore index, which defines order, there is no similar concept of ordering in a columnstore index. Figure 2-56 illustrates how the data is organized in the columnstore index.

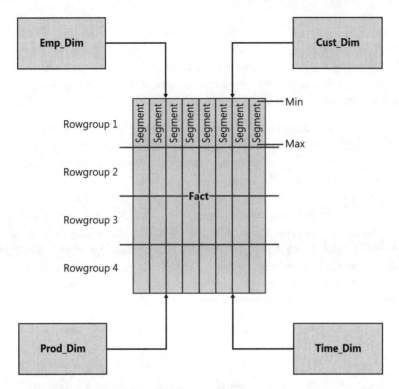

FIGURE 2-56 Columnstore applied to the Fact table.

SQL Server arranges the data in units called *rowgroups*. Each rowgroup has up to about 1,000,000 rows (more precisely, up to 2^{20}). You can find information about the rowgroups by querying the view sys.column_store_row_groups. Each rowgroup is split into the individual *column segments*, and each column segment is stored in a highly compressed form on a separate set of pages. You can find information about the column segments in the view sys.column_store_segments, including the minimum and maximum values in the column segment. SQL Server reduces storage requirements by using *dictionaries* that map entry numbers to the actual larger values. SQL Server always uses dictionaries for strings, and sometimes also for other types when there are few enough distinct values. You can find information about the dictionaries in the view sys.column_store_dictionaries.

Run our sample query again after creating the columnstore index:

```
SELECT D1.attr1 AS x, D2.attr1 AS y, D3.attr1 AS z,
  COUNT(*) AS cnt, SUM(F.measure1) AS total
FROM dbo.Fact AS F
  INNER JOIN dbo.Dim1 AS D1
    ON F.key1 = D1.key1
  INNER JOIN dbo.Dim2 AS D2
    ON F.key2 = D2.key2
  INNER JOIN dbo.Dim3 AS D3
    ON F.key3 = D3.key3
WHERE D1.attr1 <= 10
  AND D2.attr1 <= 15
  AND D3.attr1 <= 10
GROUP BY D1.attr1, D2.attr1, D3.attr1;
```

The execution plan for this query is shown in Figure 2-57.

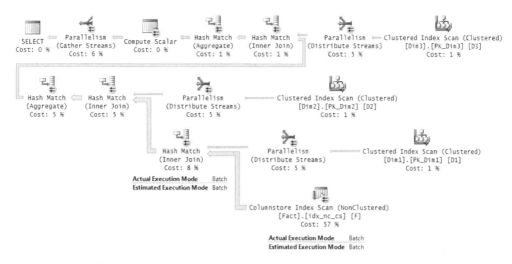

FIGURE 2-57 Plan for a star join query against a columnstore.

I got the following performance statistics for this query on my system:

```
Table 'Fact'. Scan count 8, logical reads 13235
CPU time = 172 ms,  elapsed time = 185 ms.
```

As mentioned, our Fact table is pretty small in data warehousing terms. In practice, you will tend to work with much bigger tables and you will get much bigger performance differences between rowstore and columnstore.

One of the greatest things about the columnstore technology is that it pretty much eliminates the need to do index tuning on the Fact table. You just create one index. To fulfill a query, SQL Server constructs the result set only from the relevant columns. This is quite profound if you think about it; it's as if you have all possible covering indexes without really needing to create a separate index for each case. Also, the fact that SQL Server constructs the result set only from the relevant columns tends to result in a significant reduction of I/O costs compared to rowstore.

Two other aspects of the columnstore technology tend to further reduce I/O costs. As mentioned, the level of compression that Microsoft managed to achieve with columnstore is much higher than with rowstore. Furthermore, remember that SQL Server records internally the minimum and maximum values of each column segment. If your query filters by a certain column, and the filtered values fall outside of the range covered by a column segment, the entire respective rowgroup is excluded. This capability is known as *segment elimination*.

An interesting aspect of the way the columnstore technology was implemented in SQL Server is that it is memory optimized, but it doesn't require the entire data set to fit in memory. The columnstore technology also greatly benefits from parallel processing.

I described some aspects of the technology that tend to reduce I/O costs. There's an aspect of the technology that tends to reduce CPU costs. Along with the columnstore technology, Microsoft introduced *batch execution* in SQL Server. A batch consists of a vectorized form of the relevant columns for a subset of the rows. Usually, the batch size is close to a thousand rows. Operators that were enhanced to support batch mode process a batch at a time instead of a row at a time. Internal functions that the operator executes use a batch as their input instead of a row. In the plan for our sample query, the operators that use batch mode are Columnstore Index Scan, all Hash operators, and the Compute Scalar operator. Figure 2-57 highlights two of the operators that use batch mode in this plan. Such operators will apply fewer iterations. Also, they evaluate the metadata information per batch instead of per row. All this translates to fewer CPU cycles. Currently, batch mode is used only when the data is organized as columnstore, but there's nothing inherent in the technology that prevents it from being used also with rowstore. So perhaps we will see such support in the future.

As mentioned, support for columnstore in SQL Server 2012 was limited in a number of ways. You could create only a nonclustered columnstore index, which meant you had to create it in addition to the main rowstore-based representation of the data. With very large data warehouses, you have to consider the extra space requirements and the maintenance of two different representations of your data. The biggest limitation, though, is that once you create a nonclustered columnstore index, the table becomes nonupdateable. One way around this limitation is to maintain two tables with the same structure. One is a static partitioned table with a nonclustered columnstore index. Another is a trickle table without a columnstore index that absorbs the real-time changes. As soon as you are ready to make the trickle table part of the partitioned table, you create the nonclustered columnstore index on it, switch it into the partitioned table, and create a new trickle table to absorb the real-time changes. This solution also requires you to query both tables and unify the results.

The SQL Server 2012 implementation also has a number of limitations with the batch-execution feature. There's a limited set of operators that support batch execution, and those that do, in some cases, will have to revert to row mode. For example, take the classic hash join algorithm, which is typically used in star join queries. The hash join operator can use batch execution only if the logical join type is an inner join; it always uses row mode with outer joins. Similarly, scalar aggregates are limited to row mode. In addition, if an operator doesn't have enough memory and has to spill to tempdb, it switches to row mode. The process of switching from one mode to another is very static and can be done only at very specific points in the plan.

The SQL Server 2012 implementation is also more limited in its data type support with columnstore indexes. For example, it doesn't support NUMERIC with a precision beyond 18, DATETIMEOFFSET with a precision beyond 2, BINARY, VARBINARY, UNIQUEIDENTIFIER, and others.

SQL Server 2014 has a number of significant improvements to the columnstore technology. The biggest one is support for clustered, updateable, columnstore indexes. Note, though, that if you create one, it cannot be unique, and you cannot create any other indexes on the table. As an example, the following code creates a table called FactCS with a clustered columnstore index and populates it with the rows from the table Fact:

```
CREATE TABLE dbo.FactCS
(
  key1     INT NOT NULL,
  key2     INT NOT NULL,
  key3     INT NOT NULL,
  measure1 INT NOT NULL,
  measure2 INT NOT NULL,
  measure3 INT NOT NULL,
  measure4 NVARCHAR(50) NULL,
  filler   BINARY(100) NOT NULL DEFAULT (0x)
);

CREATE CLUSTERED COLUMNSTORE INDEX idx_cl_cs ON dbo.FactCS;

INSERT INTO dbo.FactCS WITH (TABLOCK) SELECT * FROM dbo.Fact;
```

When you use large-enough bulk inserts (102,400 rows or more) to add data to the table, SQL Server converts batches of up to 1,048,576 rows to columnstore format. When you perform nonbulk trickle inserts, SQL Server stores those in a rowgroup that uses a normal B-tree rowstore representation. Such a rowgroup is also known as a *deltastore*. As long as the deltastore keeps accepting new data, it will appear in the sys.column_store_row_groups view with the state description OPEN. Once the deltastore reaches the maximum size allowed for a rowgroup (1,048,576), it will stop accepting new data and SQL Server will mark it as CLOSED. A background process called *tuple mover* will then convert the data from the deltastore to the compressed columnstore format. When the process is done, the state of the rowgroup will appear as COMPRESSED.

SQL Server also supports deletes and updates. A delete of a row that resides in a deltastore is processed as a regular delete from a B-tree. A delete of a row from a compressed rowgroup causes the row ID of the deleted row to be written to a *delete bitmap* (an actual bitmap in memory and a B-tree on disk). When you query the data, SQL Server consults the delete bitmap to know which rows to consider as deleted. An update is handled as a delete followed by an insert.

The best thing about all this is that the query-processing layer is oblivious to this split between compressed rowgroups and deltastores; the storage-engine layer takes care of the details. This means that from the user's perspective, it's business as usual. The user submits reads and writes against the table, and behind the scenes the storage engine handles the writing to and reading from the deltastores and compressed rowgroups. One thing you do need to be aware of is that a large delete bitmap will slow down your queries. So, after a large number of deletes and updates, it would be a good idea to rebuild the table, like so:

```
ALTER TABLE dbo.FactCS REBUILD;
```

If the table is partitioned, you can rebuild the relevant partition by adding to the code *PARTITION = <partition_number>*.

SQL Server 2014 makes a number of improvements in batch-mode processing. For example, it can use batch mode in hash join operators that handle outer joins, in scalar aggregates, and in operators that spill to tempdb. It also handles cases where it needs to switch from one mode to another more dynamically. SQL Server 2014 also relaxes some of the restrictions related to data types. For example, it supports NUMERIC beyond precision 18, DATETIMEOFFSET beyond precision 2, BINARY and VARBINARY (although not with the MAX specifier), and UNIQUEIDENTIFIER.

Run the following star join query with the FactCS table this time:

```
SELECT D1.attr1 AS x, D2.attr1 AS y, D3.attr1 AS z,
  COUNT(*) AS cnt, SUM(F.measure1) AS total
FROM dbo.FactCS AS F
  INNER JOIN dbo.Dim1 AS D1
    ON F.key1 = D1.key1
  INNER JOIN dbo.Dim2 AS D2
    ON F.key2 = D2.key2
  INNER JOIN dbo.Dim3 AS D3
    ON F.key3 = D3.key3
WHERE D1.attr1 <= 10
  AND D2.attr1 <= 15
  AND D3.attr1 <= 10
GROUP BY D1.attr1, D2.attr1, D3.attr1;
```

Note that the first time you run the query SQL Server will likely need to refresh existing statistics and create new ones, so the parse and compile time might take a bit longer. Run the query a second time to get a sense of the more typical run time. SQL Server reported the following performance statistics for this query on my system:

```
Table 'FactCS'. Scan count 8, logical reads 13556
CPU time = 139 ms,  elapsed time = 219 ms.
```

For more information about the columnstore technology and the improvements in SQL Server 2014, see the following white paper: *http://research.microsoft.com/apps/pubs/default.aspx?id=193599*.

When you're done, run the following code for cleanup:

```
SET STATISTICS IO OFF;
SET STATISTICS TIME OFF;
DROP INDEX idx_nc_cs ON dbo.Fact;
DROP TABLE dbo.FactCS;
```

Inline index definition

As you will learn in Chapter 10, SQL Server 2014 introduces support for memory-optimized tables as part of the In-Memory OLTP feature. In this first implementation, DDL changes are not allowed after the table creation. To allow you to define indexes on such tables as part of the table creation, Microsoft introduced syntax for inline index definition. Because Microsoft already made the effort mainly in the parser component, it extended the support for such a syntax also for disk-based tables, including table variables.

Remember that you cannot alter the definition of table variables once you declare them, so you cannot define indexes on existing table variables. Previously, you could define indexes only on table variables through PRIMARY KEY and UNIQUE constraints as part of the table definition, and therefore the indexes had to be unique. Now with the new inline index syntax, you can define nonunique indexes as part of the table variable definition, like so:

```
DECLARE @T1 AS TABLE
(
  col1 INT NOT NULL
    INDEX idx_cl_col1 CLUSTERED, -- column index
  col2 INT NOT NULL,
  col3 INT NOT NULL,
  INDEX idx_nc_col2_col3 NONCLUSTERED (col2, col3) -- table index
);
```

Just like with constraints, you can define column-level indexes as part of a column definition and table-level indexes based on a composite key list as a separate item. Note that in the SQL Server 2014 implementation, inline indexes do not support the options UNIQUE, INCLUDE, and WHERE. For uniqueness, define the indexes like you used to indirectly through PRIMARY KEY or UNIQUE constraints.

Prioritizing queries for tuning with extended events

If you experience general performance problems in your system, besides trying to find and fix the bottlenecks, a common thing to do is to tune queries to be more efficient. The tricky part is that if you have lots of query patterns in the system, it's not realistic to try and tune them all. You want to prioritize the queries for tuning so that you can spend more time on cases that, when tuned, will have a bigger impact on the system as a whole.

You need to decide which performance measure to use to prioritize the queries. It could be duration because that's the user's perception of performance. But it could also be that you identified a specific bottleneck in the system and need to rely on related measures. For example, if you identify a bottleneck in the I/O subsystem, you naturally will want to focus on I/O-related measures like writes and reads.

To measure query performance, you can capture a typical workload in your system using an Extended Events session with *statement completed* events. Remember that statement completed events carry performance information. For demonstration purposes, I'll submit the sample workload with ad hoc queries from a specific SSMS session, so I'll capture the *sql_statement_completed* event and filter by the session ID of the session in question. If the queries are submitted in your environment from stored procedures, you will need to capture the *sp_statement_completed* event and apply any filters that are relevant to you.

A critical element that can help you prioritize which queries to tune is the *query_hash* action. It's available to statement completed events starting with SQL Server 2012. This is a hash value that represents the template, or parameterized, form of the query string. Query strings that have the same template will get the same query hash value even if their input values are different. After you capture the workload, you group the events by the query hash value and order the groups (query templates) by the total relevant performance measure (say, duration in our example), descending. Then you spend more time and energy on the top templates.

Use the following code to create an Extended Events session that will capture the performance workload from the specified session into the specified target file (make sure to replace the session ID and file path with the ones relevant to you):

```
CREATE EVENT SESSION query_perf ON SERVER
ADD EVENT sqlserver.sp_statement_completed(
    ACTION(sqlserver.query_hash)
    WHERE (sqlserver.session_id=(54))),
ADD EVENT sqlserver.sql_statement_completed(
    ACTION(sqlserver.query_hash)
    WHERE (sqlserver.session_id=(54)))
ADD TARGET package0.event_file(SET filename=N'C:\Temp\query_perf.xel');
```

Use the following code to start the session:

```
ALTER EVENT SESSION query_perf ON SERVER STATE = START;
```

Assuming that the following set of queries represents your typical workload, run it a few times from the source SSMS session (54 in my case):

```
SELECT orderid, custid, empid, shipperid, orderdate
FROM dbo.Orders
WHERE orderid >= 1000000;

SELECT orderid, custid, empid, shipperid, orderdate
FROM dbo.Orders
WHERE custid = 'C0000000001';

SELECT orderid, custid, empid, shipperid, orderdate
FROM dbo.Orders
WHERE orderdate = '20140101';

SELECT orderid, custid, empid, shipperid, orderdate
FROM dbo.Orders
WHERE orderid >= 1000001;

SELECT orderid, custid, empid, shipperid, orderdate
FROM dbo.Orders
WHERE custid = 'C0000001000';

SELECT orderid, custid, empid, shipperid, orderdate
FROM dbo.Orders
WHERE orderdate = '20140201';
```

When you're done running the workload, run the following code to stop the session:

```
ALTER EVENT SESSION query_perf ON SERVER STATE = STOP;
```

The event data was captured in the target file in XML format. Use the following code to copy the data from the file through the table function *sys.fn_xe_file_target_read_file* into a temporary table called #Events:

```
SELECT CAST(event_data AS XML) AS event_data_XML
INTO #Events
FROM sys.fn_xe_file_target_read_file('C:\Temp\query_perf*.xel', null, null, null) AS F;
```

Query the #Events table, and then extract the event columns from the XML using the *value()* method, placing them into a temporary table called #Queries, like so:

```
SELECT
  event_data_XML.value ('(/event/action[@name=''query_hash''    ]/value)[1]', 'NUMERIC(38, 0)')
    AS query_hash,
  event_data_XML.value ('(/event/data  [@name=''duration''      ]/value)[1]', 'BIGINT'        )
    AS duration,
  event_data_XML.value ('(/event/data  [@name=''cpu_time''       ]/value)[1]', 'BIGINT'        )
    AS cpu_time,
  event_data_XML.value ('(/event/data  [@name=''physical_reads'']/value)[1]', 'BIGINT'        )
    AS physical_reads,
  event_data_XML.value ('(/event/data  [@name=''logical_reads'' ]/value)[1]', 'BIGINT'        )
    AS logical_reads,
  event_data_XML.value ('(/event/data  [@name=''writes''        ]/value)[1]', 'BIGINT'        )
    AS writes,
  event_data_XML.value ('(/event/data  [@name=''row_count''     ]/value)[1]', 'BIGINT'        )
    AS row_count,
  event_data_XML.value ('(/event/data  [@name=''statement''      ]/value)[1]', 'NVARCHAR(4000)')
    AS statement
INTO #Queries
FROM #Events;
```

```
CREATE CLUSTERED INDEX idx_cl_query_hash ON #Queries(query_hash);
```

You can now examine the query performance information conveniently by querying the #Queries table, like so:

```
SELECT query_hash, duration, cpu_time, physical_reads AS physreads,
  logical_reads AS logreads, writes, row_count AS rowcnt, statement
FROM #Queries;
```

I got the following output on my system (the *statement* column is displayed on two lines to fit the printed page):

Query_hash	duration	cpu_time	physreads	logreads	writes	rowcnt	statement
3195161633580410947	234514	0	0	22	0	692	... orderdate = '20140101'
3195161633580410947	189375	0	0	21	0	671	... orderdate = '20140201'
...							
14791727431994962596	272909	281000	0	4028	0	46	... custid = 'C0000000001'
14791727431994962596	270893	281000	0	4016	0	42	... custid = 'C0000001000'
...							
15020196184001629514	405	0	0	6	0	1	... orderid >= 1000000
15020196184001629514	354	0	0	3	0	0	... orderid >= 1000001
...							

Observe that queries that are based on the same template got the same query hash value even though their input values were different.

The final step is to issue a query against the table #Queries that groups the events by the query hash value and orders the groups by the sum of the desired performance measure (in this example, based on duration), descending, like so:

```
SELECT
  query_hash, SUM(duration) AS sumduration,
  CAST(100. * SUM(duration) / SUM(SUM(duration)) OVER() AS NUMERIC(5, 2)) AS pct,
  (SELECT TOP (1) statement
   FROM #Queries AS Q2
   WHERE Q2.query_hash = Q1.query_hash) AS queryexample
FROM #Queries AS Q1
GROUP BY query_hash
ORDER BY SUM(duration) DESC;
```

I got the following output on my system:

```
query_hash             sumduration  pct     queryexample
---------------------  -----------  ------  ------------------------------------------------
14791727431994962596   3159476      58.13   SELECT orderid, custid, empid, shipperid, orderdate
                                            FROM dbo.Orders
                                            WHERE custid = 'C0000000001'

31951616335804110947   2267599      41.72   SELECT orderid, custid, empid, shipperid, orderdate
                                            FROM dbo.Orders
                                            WHERE orderdate = '20140101'

15020196184001629514   7963         0.15    SELECT orderid, custid, empid, shipperid, orderdate
                                            FROM dbo.Orders
                                            WHERE orderid >= 1000001
```

I had only three query templates in my sample workload. Naturally, in an active system you will have many more. At this point, you know which queries are more important to tune in terms of the potential effect on the system as a whole.

When you're done, drop the temporary tables and the Extended Events session by running the following code:

```
DROP TABLE #Events, #Queries;
DROP EVENT SESSION query_perf ON SERVER;
```

Index and query information and statistics

SQL Server provides you with a wealth of performance-related information about your indexes and queries through dynamic management views (DMVs) and dynamic management functions (DMFs). This section describes some objects I find particularly useful.

Earlier in the chapter, I discussed index fragmentation. You can query the *sys.dm_db_index_physical_stats* function to get physical statistics about your indexes, including fragmentation levels. For example, the following code returns information about all indexes in the PerformanceV3 database (the NULLs stand for all tables, all indexes, and all partitions):

```
SELECT database_id, object_id, index_id, partition_number,
  avg_fragmentation_in_percent, avg_page_space_used_in_percent
FROM sys.dm_db_index_physical_stats( DB_ID('PerformanceV3'), NULL, NULL, NULL, 'SAMPLED' );
```

To evaluate fragmentation, I examine two measures: *avg_fragmentation_in_percent* is the percentage of out-of-order pages (also known as *logical scan fragmentation*), and *avg_page_space_used_in_percent* is the average page population expressed as a percentage.

You want to be careful when you run such code in a production environment because the information is actually gathered when you query this object. The DETAILED mode is the most expensive one because it involves full scans of the data. The LIMITED mode is the cheapest because it examines only parent index pages (nonleaf), but for this reason it cannot report the average page population. The SAMPLED mode scans one percent of the data, and therefore is a good compromise between the two.

When you have a high level of logical scan fragmentation and you find that it negatively affects your query performance, the remedy is to rebuild or reorganize the index. Similarly, if you have too much free space, or too little (which results in splits), you rebuild the index and, if relevant, specify the desired fill factor.

Use ALTER INDEX REBUILD to rebuild the index, like so:

```
ALTER INDEX <index_name> ON <table_name> REBUILD WITH (FILLFACTOR = 70 /*, ONLINE = ON */);
```

Use ALTER INDEX REORGANIZE to reorganize the index, like so:

```
ALTER INDEX <index_name> ON <table_name> REORGANIZE;
```

The REBUILD option allows specifying a fill factor, and its result tends to be more effective than the REORGANIZE option; however, the former is an offline operation, whereas the latter is an online one. You can rebuild an index as a mostly online operation if you're using the Enterprise edition of SQL Server by adding the ONLINE = ON option; however, an online rebuild is a longer and more expensive operation, so you better do it as an offline one if you can allow some downtime.

You need to be able to identify which indexes are used more often and which are rarely or never used. You don't want to keep indexes that are rarely used, because they do have a negative performance effect on modifications. SQL Server collects index-usage information in the background and enables you to query it through dynamic management objects called *dm_db_index_operational_stats* and *dm_db_index_usage_stats*. The *dm_db_index_operational_stats* function gives you low-level I/O, locking, latching, and access-method activity information. For example, to get information about all objects, indexes, and partitions in the PerformanceV3 database, you query the function like so:

```
SELECT * FROM sys.dm_db_index_operational_stats( DB_ID('PerformanceV3'), null, null, null );
```

The *dm_db_index_usage_stats* view gives you usage counts of the different access methods (scan, seek, lookup):

```
SELECT * FROM sys.dm_db_index_usage_stats;
```

Recall from earlier examples, such as in Figure 2-31, that in some plans SQL Server identifies missing indexes. SQL Server also records such missing index information internally and exposes it through the dynamic management objects *sys.dm_db_missing_index_details*, *sys.dm_db_missing_index_group_stats*, *sys.dm_db_missing_index_groups*, and *sys.dm_db_missing_index_columns*. Query those objects to get missing index information that was collected since SQL Server was last restarted.

The *sys.dm_db_missing_index_details* view contains most of the interesting information. Run the following code to query the view in your system:

```
SELECT * FROM sys.dm_db_missing_index_details;
```

This view has a row for each missing index. The attributes *equality_columns* and *inequality_columns* report the columns that are candidates as key columns in the index. The *included_columns* attribute reports the columns that are candidates as included columns in the index if it's important for you to avoid lookups.

Make sure, though, that you apply your knowledge, your experience, and some common sense in choosing which recommendations to follow. You might find redundant recommendations. For example, if two queries look the same but only slightly differ in the returned set of columns (for example, one returns *col1* and *col2* and the other returns *col1* and *col3*), you will get different missing index recommendations. You can easily consolidate such recommendations and create one index with the superset of included columns (*col1*, *col2*, and *col3*).

The view *sys.dm_db_missing_index_group_stats* gives you summary statistics about groups of missing indexes, like the average user impact. At the moment, an index group contains only one index. Perhaps the thinking was to allow the future arrangement of multiple indexes in groups. Run the following code to query the view in your system:

```
SELECT * FROM sys.dm_db_missing_index_group_stats;
```

The view *sys.dm_db_missing_index_groups* gives you a group-to-index connection (again, at the moment, it is a one-to-one relationship). Use the following code to query the view in your system:

```
SELECT * FROM sys.dm_db_missing_index_groups;
```

Query the *sys.dm_db_missing_index_columns* function with a specific index handle you obtain from the *sys.dm_db_missing_index_details* view to get information about the columns of the missing index individually. The result will tell you if the column role is equality or inequality. Such information can help you determine which columns to specify in the index key list and which to specify in the include list. Query the function like so:

```
SELECT * FROM sys.dm_db_missing_index_columns(<handle>);
```

SQL Server supports a handy view called *sys.dm_exec_query_stats* that aggregates query performance information for queries whose plans are in cache. Querying such a view is so much easier than working with an Extended Events session to get query performance information, but keep in mind that this view won't report information for queries whose plans are not in cache. The information that this view provides for each cached query plan includes, among other things, the following:

- A SQL handle that you can provide as input to the function *sys.dm_exec_sql_text* to get the text of the parent query or batch of the current query. You also get the start and end offsets of the query that the current row represents so that you can extract it from the full parent query or batch text. Note that the offsets are zero based and are specified in bytes, although the text is Unicode (meaning two bytes of storage per character).

- A plan handle that you can provide as input to the function *sys.dm_exec_query_plan* to get the XML form of the plan.

- The creation time and last execution time.

- The execution count.

- Performance information, including worker (CPU) time, physical reads, logical reads, CLR time, and elapsed time. For each performance counter, you get the total for all invocations of the plan: last, minimum, and maximum.

- Query hash and plan hash values. You use the former to identify queries with the same query template (similar to the *query_hash* action in Extended Events). With the latter, you can identify similar query execution plans.

- Row counts.

Run the following code to query the view in your system:

```
SELECT * FROM sys.dm_exec_query_stats;
```

If you want to isolate top query templates that represent more work, you can group the data in the view by the *query_hash* attribute, and order the groups by the sum of the performance measure of interest, descending, like so (using duration in this example):

```
SELECT TOP (5)
  MAX(query) AS sample_query,
  SUM(execution_count) AS cnt,
  SUM(total_worker_time) AS cpu,
  SUM(total_physical_reads) AS reads,
  SUM(total_logical_reads) AS logical_reads,
  SUM(total_elapsed_time) AS duration
```

```
FROM (SELECT
        QS.*,
        SUBSTRING(ST.text, (QS.statement_start_offset/2) + 1,
          ((CASE statement_end_offset
              WHEN -1 THEN DATALENGTH(ST.text)
              ELSE QS.statement_end_offset END
                - QS.statement_start_offset)/2) + 1
        ) AS query
      FROM sys.dm_exec_query_stats AS QS
        CROSS APPLY sys.dm_exec_sql_text(QS.sql_handle) AS ST
        CROSS APPLY sys.dm_exec_plan_attributes(QS.plan_handle) AS PA
        WHERE PA.attribute = 'dbid'
          AND PA.value = DB_ID('PerformanceV3')) AS D
GROUP BY query_hash
ORDER BY duration DESC;
```

This query generated the following output on my system:

sample_query	cnt	cpu	reads	logical_reads	duration
SELECT ... WHERE custid = 'C0000001000'	10	3155513	92	40305	3158897
SELECT ... FROM dbo.FactCS AS F	8	2021766	1	110332	2929692
SELECT ... WHERE orderid <= 100000	1	463615	0	25339	2805217
SELECT ... WHERE orderdate = '20140201'	10	15054	0	215	2266620
SELECT ... WHERE custid LIKE '%9999'	1	1828461	0	4283	1887095

SQL Server provides you with similar views called *sys.dm_exec_procedure_stats* and *sys.dm_exec_trigger_stats* to query procedure and trigger performance statistics. Run the following code to query these views in your system:

```
SELECT * FROM sys.dm_exec_procedure_stats;
SELECT * FROM sys.dm_exec_trigger_stats;
```

SQL Server 2014 introduces a curious new DMV called *sys.dm_exec_query_profiles*. This view provides real-time query plan progress. It returns a row for every operator in an active actual query plan or, more precisely, for every operator and thread in the plan, with progress information. It shows the estimated row count as well as the actual row count produced so far, I/O, CPU and elapsed time information, open and close times, first and last times the operator was active, first and last times it produced a row, and more. It's a supercool feature. Note, though, that you need to have some form of an actual query plan enabled for the view to report information about the plan. To achieve this, you can enable the Include Actual Execution Plan option in SSMS, turn on the STATISTICS PROFILE or STATISTICS XML session options, run an Extended Events session with the event *query_post_execution_showplan*, or a trace with the events *Showplan Statistics Profile* or *Showplan XML Statistics Profile*.

As an example, enable the Include Actual Execution Plan option in SSMS and run the following expensive query:

```
SELECT O1.orderid, O1.orderdate, MAX(O2.orderdate) AS mxdate
FROM dbo.Orders AS O1
  INNER JOIN dbo.Orders AS O2
    ON O2.orderid <= O1.orderid
GROUP BY O1.orderid, O1.orderdate;
```

To see the live query progress, query the view in a different query pane, like so:

```
SELECT * FROM sys.dm_exec_query_profiles;
```

I'm just waiting for some company like SQL Sentry, which developed the popular Plan Explorer tool, to come forward and, based on the information in the view, provide a graphical animated view of the real-time progress of a query plan. Who knows, perhaps by the time you read these words some company will have already done this.

Temporary objects

This section covers the use of temporary tables and table variables as tools to aid in query tuning. These objects are often misunderstood, and this misunderstanding tends to lead to suboptimal solutions. Hopefully, with the information in this section you will be equipped with correct understanding of these objects, and will use them efficiently. I'll refer to temporary tables and table variables collectively as temporary objects.

Temporary objects are used for various purposes, not just performance related. For example, you need such objects when you have a process that requires you to set aside intermediate result sets for further processing. Because the focus of this chapter is query tuning, I'll discuss the use of such objects mainly for query tuning purposes.

In a number of cases, you'll find it beneficial to use temporary objects from a query-tuning perspective. One case is when you have an expensive query that generates a small result set and you need to refer to this result set multiple times. Naturally, you want to avoid repeating the work. Another case is to help improve cardinality estimates. SQL Server uses statistics to make cardinality estimates mainly in the leaf nodes of the plan, but the farther the data flows in the plan, the more likely it is that the quality of cardinality estimates will degrade. If you have a query that involves a lot of tables and a lot of manipulation, and you observe suboptimal choices in the plan that you connect to inaccurate cardinality estimates, one way to deal with those is to split the original solution into steps. Extract the part of the work, like a subset of the joins, up to the point where you see the problem in the plan, and write the result to a temporary object. Then apply the next step between the temporary object and the rest of the tables. This will give the optimizer a fresh start and, I hope, lead to a more efficient solution overall.

In the upcoming sections, I compare and contrast the different types of temporary objects that SQL Server supports. I compare local temporary tables (named with a number sign as prefix, as in #MyTable), table variables (named with the at sign as prefix, as in @MyTable), and table expressions such as derived tables and CTEs. For reference purposes, Table 2-2 has a summary of the comparison.

TABLE 2-2 Temporary objects

Functionality/Object type	Local temp table	Table variable	Table expression (derived table/CTE)
Physical representation in tempdb	Yes	Yes	No
Typically suitable when you need to query once or multiple times	Multi	Multi	Once
Distribution statistics (histograms, density vectors)/Plan optimality recompiles	Yes	No	#NA
Typically suitable for table size	Big	Small	Any
Scope/visibility	Current and inner levels	Batch	Statement
Part of outer transaction/Affected by outer transaction rollback	Yes	No	#NA
Logging	To support transaction rollback	To support statement rollback	#NA

There are a number of common misconceptions concerning the use of temporary objects. Probably the oldest one is that some people incorrectly believe that table variables reside only in memory and have no disk-based representation. The source for this misconception is probably that people intuitively think that a variable is always a memory-only resident object. The reality is that temporary tables and table variables are represented the same way as a set of pages in tempdb and can incur disk activity.

Interestingly, the technology seems to be catching up with the misconception. Certain improvements in recent versions of SQL Server could result in reduced activity or no disk activity. For example, starting with SQL Server 2014 you can define a table type as a memory-optimized one (using the MEMORY_OPTIMIZED = ON option). Then, when you declare a table variable of this type, it is represented as a memory-optimized table. This feature is part of the In-Memory OLTP engine and is described in Chapter 10.

Another improvement in SQL Server 2014 (also backported to SQL Server 2012) is related to how SQL Server handles what's called *eager writes* for bulk operations like SELECT INTO in tempdb. Normally, eager writes eagerly flush dirty pages associated with bulk operations to disk to prevent such operations from flooding the memory with new pages. With the new feature, when you perform bulk operations in tempdb, the eager-writing behavior is relaxed, not forcing the flushing of dirty pages as quickly as before. This improvement can be beneficial when you create and populate a temporary object with a bulk operation, query it, and drop it quickly. Now such work can be done with reduced activity or no disk activity.

Another common misconception concerns table expressions like derived tables and CTEs. Some intuitively think that when you use a table expression, SQL Server persists the inner query's result in a work table if it is beneficial to do so from a performance perspective. Theoretically, such potential exists, but the reality is that, so far, Microsoft has not introduced such a capability to the engine. Any reference to a table expression gets unnested (inlined), and the query plan interacts with the underlying objects directly. This fact is especially important to remember when you have an expensive query and you need to interact with its result set multiple times—perhaps even with the same query. All references to the table expression will be inlined, and the expensive work will be repeated. It's easy to demonstrate this behavior. Start by running the following code to enable reporting performance statistics:

```
SET STATISTICS IO, TIME ON;
```

Consider the following query, which computes yearly order counts:

```
SELECT YEAR(orderdate) AS orderyear, COUNT(*) AS numorders
FROM dbo.Orders
GROUP BY YEAR(orderdate);
```

I got the following performance statistics for this query on my system: logical reads = 2,641, CPU time = 861 ms, elapsed time = 289 ms.

You need to come up with a solution that, for each current year, returns the year with the closest count of orders and the difference between the order counts between the two years. To achieve this, you use the following query (if you're not familiar with the CROSS APPLY operator, you can find details in Chapter 3):

```
WITH C AS
(
  SELECT YEAR(orderdate) AS orderyear, COUNT(*) AS numorders
  FROM dbo.Orders
  GROUP BY YEAR(orderdate)
)
SELECT C1.orderyear, C1.numorders,
  A.orderyear AS otheryear, C1.numorders - A.numorders AS diff
FROM C AS C1 CROSS APPLY
  (SELECT TOP (1) C2.orderyear, C2.numorders
   FROM C AS C2
   WHERE C2.orderyear <> C1.orderyear
   ORDER BY ABS(C1.numorders - C2.numorders)) AS A
ORDER BY C1.orderyear;
```

Examine the query plan for this query as shown in Figure 2-58.

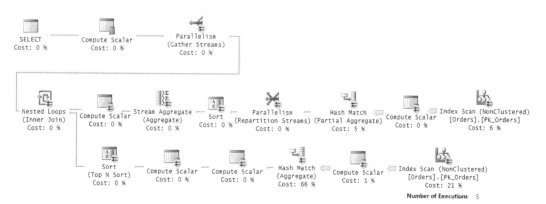

FIGURE 2-58 Query plan with a CTE shows the expensive work is repeated.

The middle branch in the plan (outer input of the Nested Loops operator) represents the instance of the CTE called C1, which is referenced in the FROM clause of the outer query. It involves scanning, grouping, and aggregating the data from the Orders table once. The bottom branch in the plan (the inner input of the Nested Loops operator) represents the instance of the CTE called C2, which is referenced by the TOP (1) subquery. This branch also involves scanning, grouping, and aggregating the data from the Orders table. Because there are five years currently in the outer table C1, this branch is activated five times. In total, the expensive work was repeated six times. I got the following performance statistics from this query: logical reads = 15,696 (6 scans), CPU time = 4763 ms, elapsed time = 1938 ms.

To avoid repeating the expensive work, you should persist the result of the grouped query in a temporary table or a table variable. Here's an example of how you can achieve this using a table variable:

```
DECLARE @T AS TABLE
(
  orderyear INT,
  numorders INT
);

INSERT INTO @T(orderyear, numorders)
  SELECT YEAR(orderdate) AS orderyear, COUNT(*) AS numorders
  FROM dbo.Orders
  GROUP BY YEAR(orderdate)

SELECT T1.orderyear, T1.numorders,
  A.orderyear AS otheryear, T1.numorders - A.numorders AS diff
FROM @T AS T1 CROSS APPLY
  (SELECT TOP (1) T2.orderyear, T2.numorders
   FROM @T AS T2
   WHERE T2.orderyear <> T1.orderyear
   ORDER BY ABS(T1.numorders - T2.numorders)) AS A
ORDER BY T1.orderyear;
```

The execution plans for these statements are shown in Figure 2-59.

The first execution plan is for the code that computes the yearly aggregates and writes those to the table variable. Observe that 100 percent of the cost of the batch (in reality it's almost 100 percent) is associated with this activity. The second execution plan is for the query against the table variable. The important thing here is that this solution executes the bulk of the work only once. The table variable is accessed six times by the second query, but it's so tiny that this part of the work is negligible. Here are the performance statistics I got for this solution: logical reads = 2,622, CPU time = 468 ms, elapsed time = 572 ms. That's one-sixth of the reads and less than one-third of the run time of the solution with the CTE. In short, remember that table expressions don't have a physical side to them; they don't get persisted anywhere. When you query them, SQL Server translates the work directly to the underlying objects. If you need to persist the result somewhere, you should be using temporary tables or table variables.

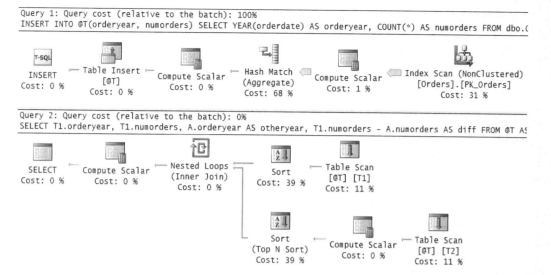

Query 1: Query cost (relative to the batch): 100%
INSERT INTO @T(orderyear, numorders) SELECT YEAR(orderdate) AS orderyear, COUNT(*) AS numorders FROM dbo.(

INSERT
Cost: 0 %

Table Insert
[@T]
Cost: 0 %

Compute Scalar
Cost: 0 %

Hash Match
(Aggregate)
Cost: 68 %

Compute Scalar
Cost: 1 %

Index Scan (NonClustered)
[Orders].[PK_Orders]
Cost: 31 %

Query 2: Query cost (relative to the batch): 0%
SELECT T1.orderyear, T1.numorders, A.orderyear AS otheryear, T1.numorders - A.numorders AS diff FROM @T AS

SELECT
Cost: 0 %

Compute Scalar
Cost: 0 %

Nested Loops
(Inner Join)
Cost: 0 %

Sort
Cost: 39 %

Table Scan
[@T] [T1]
Cost: 11 %

Sort
(Top N Sort)
Cost: 39 %

Compute Scalar
Cost: 0 %

Table Scan
[@T] [T2]
Cost: 11 %

FIGURE 2-59 Query plan with a table variable shows the expensive work is not repeated.

The key difference between temporary tables and table variables from a performance perspective is in the kinds of statistics that SQL Server maintains for each. SQL Server maintains the same types of statistics for temporary tables that it does for permanent ones. This includes the statistics header, density vectors, and histogram. For table variables, SQL Server maintains only the table's cardinality, and even this limited information is typically not visible to the optimizer, as I will demonstrate shortly. Theoretically, because temporary tables have more statistics, queries involving them should get more accurate cardinality estimates, and therefore more optimal plans than table variables. In some cases, that's what you will experience. But you know what Einstein said about theory and practice: "In theory, theory and practice are the same. In practice, they are not." You should be aware that especially when using temporary tables in stored procedures, certain complications can lead to inaccurate estimates. I'll elaborate on this point later. Pro tem, for simplicity's sake, assume that with temporary tables, because of the existence of more statistics, you will tend to get better plans than with table variables.

If you tend to get better plans with temporary tables, why even bother with table variables? There are both performance reasons and logical ones. From a performance standpoint, because table variables don't have statistics, you don't pay the costs related to creating and maintaining those. Furthermore, you will tend to get fewer recompilations. If you think about it, when the volume of data you need to store in the temporary object is very small (just a few pages), you don't really care much about the accuracy of the estimates. Then you might as well use table variables and benefit from the fewer recompiles. Such is the case with our last solution. When working with data beyond just a few pages, you will typically care about the quality of the estimates, and the cost of maintaining statistics and the related recompilations associated with temporary tables will typically be worth it.

I mentioned that the table cardinality is recorded for table variables but that often it's not visible to the optimizer. This has much to do with the earlier discussion about cardinality estimates when variables are involved. I explained that because the initial optimization unit is the batch and not the statement, normally the optimizer cannot sniff variable values. The same applies to table variables. If the same batch declares, populates, and queries the table variable, the optimizer gets to optimize the query before the table variable is populated. So it cannot know what the cardinality of the table is. Like with regular variables, if you add the RECOMPILE query option, the query will get optimized after the table variable is populated; therefore, its cardinality will be visible to the optimizer. But this will cost you a recompile every time you execute the code. Another option to make the table cardinality visible is to pass the table variable as a table-valued parameter to a stored procedure, and this way get parameter sniffing.

I'll use the following code and the related query plans to demonstrate cardinality estimates with table variables:

```
DECLARE @T AS TABLE
(
  col1 INT NOT NULL PRIMARY KEY NONCLUSTERED,
  col2 INT NOT NULL,
  filler CHAR(200) NOT NULL
);

INSERT INTO @T(col1, col2, filler)
  SELECT n AS col1, n AS col2, 'a' AS filler
  FROM TSQLV3.dbo.GetNums(1, 100000) AS Nums;

-- Query 1
SELECT col1, col2, filler
FROM @T
WHERE col1 <= 100
ORDER BY col2;

-- Query 2
SELECT col1, col2, filler
FROM @T
WHERE col1 <= 100
ORDER BY col2
OPTION(RECOMPILE);

-- Query 3
SELECT col1, col2, filler
FROM @T
WHERE col1 >= 100
ORDER BY col2
OPTION(RECOMPILE);
```

The execution plans for these three queries are shown in Figure 2-60.

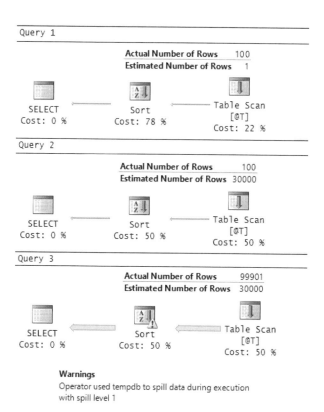

Query 1

Actual Number of Rows   100
Estimated Number of Rows   1

SELECT   Sort   Table Scan
Cost: 0 %   Cost: 78 %   [@T]
                                  Cost: 22 %

Query 2

Actual Number of Rows   100
Estimated Number of Rows   30000

SELECT   Sort   Table Scan
Cost: 0 %   Cost: 50 %   [@T]
                                  Cost: 50 %

Query 3

Actual Number of Rows   99901
Estimated Number of Rows   30000

SELECT   Sort   Table Scan
Cost: 0 %   Cost: 50 %   [@T]
                                  Cost: 50 %

Warnings
Operator used tempdb to spill data during execution
with spill level 1

FIGURE 2-60 Query plans with a table variable.

The code declares a table variable called *@T* with three columns called *col1*, *col2*, and *filler*, with a nonclustered index called *PK_T1* defined on *col1*. The code populates the table variable with 100,000 rows. The code then issues three queries. Query 1 filters the rows where *col1 <= 100*. Query 2 filters the rows where *col1 <= 100* and has the RECOMPILE option. Query 3 filters the rows where *col1 >= 100* and has the RECOMPILE option. All queries order the result rows by *col2*. The index *PK_T1* can support the query filters, but because it's not a covering index, if the optimizer decides to use it, lookups will be involved. Because the first two queries are very selective, they would benefit from a plan that uses the index and applies a few lookups. The last query is nonselective and would benefit from a scan.

Looking at the plans in Figure 2-60, you see inefficient choices in all three plans. In the first plan, the optimizer doesn't have the table cardinality available, so it assumes that it's very small. As a result, it uses a scan. In the second plan, thanks to the RECOMPILE query option, the optimizer does have the table cardinality available; however, because there's no histogram available and you used the <= operator, it estimates 30% matches. (Remember the magic table of estimates in Table 2-1?) In the third plan—again, thanks to the RECOMPILE query option—the optimizer does have the table cardinality available, and also here the estimate is 30% because you used the operator >=. However, in this case, 30% is an underestimate, which results in a spill of the sort operation to tempdb.

Another option to make the cardinality of a table variable visible is to use trace flag 2453, which is available in SQL Server 2014 RTM CU3 and later and in SQL Server 2012 SP2 and later. This trace flag causes SQL Server to trigger recompiles based on the same thresholds that it uses for normal tables. This means that instead of forcing a recompile explicitly in every execution of the query, you will get fewer automated recompiles. When an automated recompile does happen, the table cardinality becomes available. You can find details about this trace flag here: *http://support.microsoft.com/ kb/2952444/en-us*.

With temporary tables, you will tend to get better cardinality estimates and, consequently, better plans, as the following code demonstrates:

```
CREATE TABLE #T
(
  col1 INT NOT NULL PRIMARY KEY NONCLUSTERED,
  col2 INT NOT NULL,
  filler CHAR(200) NOT NULL
);

INSERT INTO #T(col1, col2, filler)
  SELECT n AS col1, n AS col2, 'a' AS filler
  FROM TSQLV3.dbo.GetNums(1, 100000) AS Nums
OPTION(MAXDOP 1);
GO

-- Query 1
SELECT col1, col2, filler
FROM #T
WHERE col1 <= 100
ORDER BY col2;

-- Query 2
SELECT col1, col2, filler
FROM #T
WHERE col1 >= 100
ORDER BY col2;
GO

-- Cleanup
DROP TABLE #T;
```

The execution plans for the two queries are shown in Figure 2-61.

You can see in the plans that the cardinality estimates are accurate. As expected, the plan for the first query performs a seek and lookups. The plan for the second query is a parallel plan that performs a scan, and the sort doesn't spill to tempdb.

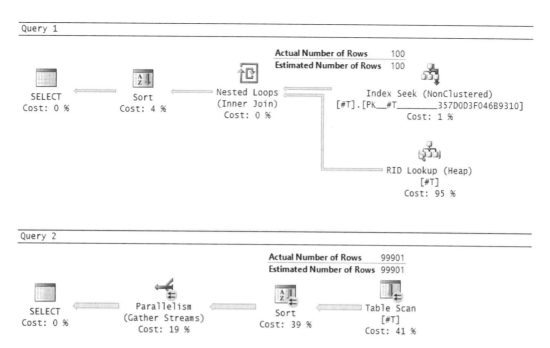

FIGURE 2-61 Query plans with a temporary table.

I mentioned that in theory queries involving temporary tables should get better cardinality estimates, but that in practice things are not always that simple. The complications have to do with a certain caching mechanism SQL Server uses for temporary tables, table variables, and worktables SQL Server creates as part of the query plan. Recall from the discussions about the internal data structures earlier in the book that, by default, the first eight page allocations for a new table are done from mixed extents. Also remember that SQL Server uses SGAM pages to map the extents in the file that are mixed and have a page available for allocation. Temporary objects start empty, and the first few allocations for those will tend to be single-page allocations from mixed extents. Every time your modification allocates a page from a mixed extent, it needs to obtain an update latch on the respective SGAM page. As you can realize, with many temporary objects created at the same time, the situation can potentially lead to a bottleneck as a result of page-latch contention against the SGAM pages.

SQL Server has an internal caching mechanism designed to reduce such contention. Say that you execute a stored procedure where you use a temporary table or a table variable. When the procedure finishes, the temporary object is normally supposed to be destroyed. With this caching mechanism, SQL Server keeps some resources of the temporary object in cache. Those include the metadata entries, one IAM page, and one data page. The next time you (or someone else) execute the stored procedure, if such resources are available in cache, SQL Server can connect your new logical temporary object to those cached physical resources. By doing so, some page allocations are avoided and, thus, contention is reduced.

All this sounds nice in theory. In practice, there's a small problem; apparently, SQL Server also caches and reuses the statistics for those temporary objects. The odd thing is that the internal modification counter of changes in the temporary objects, which SQL Server uses to know whether to trigger a refresh of the statistics, accumulates *across* procedure calls. Consequently, if SQL Server optimizes a query against a temporary object in a stored procedure and the recompilation threshold wasn't reached yet, it might end up using distribution information that was created earlier for a different execution of the procedure. You must be thinking, "No way!" Well, I'm afraid it's "Yes way!" Enough said by me. I cannot do this topic as good a service as Paul White did with the following two brilliant articles:

- *http://sqlblog.com/blogs/paul_white/archive/2012/08/15/temporary-tables-in-stored-procedures.aspx*

- *http://sqlblog.com/blogs/paul_white/archive/2012/08/17/temporary-object-caching-explained.aspx*

Not only is the information in these articles gold, the articles are also a sheer pleasure to read.

Paul's recommendation is that in those targeted cases where you find the problem, you can explicitly update statistics in the temporary table right before the query and add the RECOMPILE option to the query. This will trigger a refresh of the statistics and a recompile.

Back to the discussion about the differences between temporary tables and table variables: another difference is in scope and visibility. Like regular variables, a table variable is visible only to the batch that declared it. A local temporary table is visible only to the session that created it, including the entire level in which it was created as well as all inner levels in the call stack. It gets automatically destroyed (logically, at least) as soon as the level that created it goes out of scope. With ad hoc code, this means that the temporary table will even be able to cross batch boundaries. With stored procedures and triggers, as soon as the module that created the temporary table terminates, the temporary table is destroyed. This means that if you create a temporary table in one level, you will be able to interact with it in inner levels like an inner procedure, trigger, or dynamic batch. If your scope requirements dictate that the temporary object should be visible in an inner level in the call stack, you will have to use a temporary table. If you create a global temporary table (with two number signs as a prefix, as in ##MyTable), it's visible globally (not just to the session that created it) and destroyed as soon as the session that created it terminates and there are no active references.

Another curious difference between temporary tables and table variables is what happens when you modify them in a transaction that eventually rolls back. In such a case, changes against a temporary table are undone just like changes against a permanent table. But with table variables, only a single-statement change that doesn't complete is undone. As soon as a single-statement change completes, the changes survive a rollback. This capability of table variables makes them extremely useful in transactions and triggers that fail (or when you fail them) and where you need to keep information created by the transaction. For example, suppose that you make changes in a transaction within a TRY block. If the transaction fails, it enters a doomed state and control is passed to the CATCH block. You have to roll back the doomed transaction. But what if there's critical information that the transaction generated and you need to save. The trick is to copy the data you need to save into table variables in the CATCH block and then roll back the transaction. The data in the table variables survives the rollback, and you can then save it wherever you need in a new transaction.

In a similar manner, suppose that you have a trigger and, in certain conditions, you need to issue a rollback from the trigger. But you need to save the information from the inserted and deleted tables. If you issue a rollback, all data in inserted and deleted disappears. If you first copy the data from inserted and deleted to the target tables and then do the rollback, the copying to the target tables will be undone too. The solution is that before you issue the rollback, you copy the data from inserted and deleted into table variables. You then issue a rollback, and after the rollback you copy the data from the table variables to the target tables.

Set-based vs. iterative solutions

One of the common dilemmas people have when they need to solve a querying task is whether to use a set-based approach or an iterative one in their solution. The relational model is based, in part, on mathematical set theory. You solve a task using a set-based approach by applying principles that are based on set theory. Here's the definition of a set as formulated by Georg Cantor—the creator of set theory:

> By a "set" we mean any collection M *into a whole of definite, distinct objects* m *(which are called the "elements" of* M) *of our perception or of our thought.*

> —Joseph W. Dauben, Georg Cantor (Princeton University Press, 1990)

To me, a set-based solution interacts with an input table as a whole, and it doesn't make any assumptions about the physical order of the data in terms of the correctness of the solution. You can implement such solutions with T-SQL queries without iterations. Conversely, an iterative solution manipulates one row at a time and can rely on the order of the data. You can manipulate one row at a time using a cursor mechanism or a loop with TOP (1) queries.

There are two main reasons why I generally prefer to use the set-based approach as my default and consider the iterative approach only in exceptional cases. One reason is philosophical, and the other is pragmatic. The philosophical dimension is that I feel that an approach based on strong mathematical foundations is likely going to result in more stable and robust solutions. The relational model survived so many years probably because it is based on strong mathematical foundations, unlike so many other aspects of computing that are based more on intuition and tend to be shorter lasting.

The pragmatic dimension is that iterative constructs in T-SQL are very inefficient compared to iterative constructs in many other programming languages. For example, the T-SQL *WHILE* loop is much slower than a *while* loop in C#. Similarly, working with a T-SQL cursor is much slower than working with the *SQLDataReader* object in .NET. So T-SQL set-based solutions tend to perform better than T-SQL iterative ones.

Interestingly, the execution model SQL Server uses when it executes a query plan for a T-SQL set-based solution is, after all, iterative. When SQL Server executes a query plan, the various operators perform iterations (hence, they are also known as iterators) to process one row at a time. But the language that SQL Server uses to perform those iterations isn't T-SQL; rather, it is some low-level language that is highly efficient in applying them.

I consider iterative solutions in exceptional cases where the optimizer doesn't do a good job at optimizing my set-based solution and I feel that I exhausted my tuning options. But then, I can get much better performance by implementing a CLR-based iterative solution rather than a T-SQL-based one.

To demonstrate how expensive a T-SQL iterative solution can be compared to a set-based one, I'll use a task such as grouping and aggregating as my example. To make the problem a bit more interesting than just a basic grouping problem, I'll add a filtering dimension as well. The task involves the Shippers and Orders tables in the PerformanceV3 database. Use the following code to add a few more shippers and orders to the sample data:

```
SET NOCOUNT ON;
USE PerformanceV3;

INSERT INTO dbo.Shippers(shipperid, shippername)
  VALUES ('B', 'Shipper_B'),
         ('D', 'Shipper_D'),
         ('F', 'Shipper_F'),
         ('H', 'Shipper_H'),
         ('X', 'Shipper_X'),
         ('Y', 'Shipper_Y'),
         ('Z', 'Shipper_Z');

INSERT INTO dbo.Orders(orderid, custid, empid, shipperid, orderdate)
  VALUES (1000001, 'C0000000001', 1, 'B', '20090101'),
         (1000002, 'C0000000001', 1, 'D', '20090101'),
         (1000003, 'C0000000001', 1, 'F', '20090101'),
         (1000004, 'C0000000001', 1, 'H', '20090101');
```

The task is to identify shippers who handled orders placed prior to 2010 but haven't handled any orders placed since then. The bulk of the work in this task is to compute the maximum order date per shipper. The qualifying shippers are the ones with a maximum order date before January 1, 2010. The optimal index for this task is a nonclustered index on the Orders table with the key list *(shipperid, orderdate)*. Run the following code to create such an index:

```
CREATE NONCLUSTERED INDEX idx_nc_sid_od ON dbo.Orders(shipperid, orderdate);
```

The gross leaf row size in this index is about 20 bytes. So you can fit about 400 rows per leaf page. With 1,000,004 rows in the table, the index leaf level contains about 2,500 pages. There are 12 shippers in the Shippers table, out of which three are entirely new—namely, those three that have not shipped any orders yet. Nine of the shippers have shipped orders, but four of them have not shipped orders that were placed in 2010 or later. Those are the four shippers your solution should return.

One of the critical things you need to think about when tuning queries is the data characteristics. In our case, the grouping, or partitioning, column *shipperid* is very dense. There are only nine distinct shipper IDs in the index, each appears on average in over 100,000 rows. Your solution needs to somehow obtain the order date from the last row in each shipper section (that's the maximum order date for the shipper), and if that date is before 2010, return the shipper.

Remember that before you test your solutions, you need to determine whether to do a cold cache test or a hot cache one, depending on the cache state you expect to have in production. I'll assume a cold cache state for our example, so make sure to use the following code to clear the data cache before you run each solution:

```
CHECKPOINT;
DBCC DROPCLEANBUFFERS;
```

I'll first present a cursor-based solution and then a set-based one.

> **Note** Before you execute the cursor-based solution, make sure that you don't have the actual execution plan enabled in SSMS and that you don't have any session options reporting performance information enabled. That's because if these options are enabled, the information will be generated per fetch of a row from the cursor.

Here's the cursor-based solution:

```
DECLARE
  @sid     AS VARCHAR(5),
  @od      AS DATETIME,
  @prevsid AS VARCHAR(5),
  @prevod  AS DATETIME;

DECLARE ShipOrdersCursor CURSOR FAST_FORWARD FOR
  SELECT shipperid, orderdate
  FROM dbo.Orders
  ORDER BY shipperid, orderdate;

OPEN ShipOrdersCursor;

FETCH NEXT FROM ShipOrdersCursor INTO @sid, @od;

SELECT @prevsid = @sid, @prevod = @od;

WHILE @@fetch_status = 0
BEGIN
  IF @prevsid <> @sid AND @prevod < '20100101' PRINT @prevsid;
  SELECT @prevsid = @sid, @prevod = @od;
  FETCH NEXT FROM ShipOrdersCursor INTO @sid, @od;
END

IF @prevod < '20100101' PRINT @prevsid;

CLOSE ShipOrdersCursor;

DEALLOCATE ShipOrdersCursor;
```

This solution implements an order-based aggregate algorithm similar to the one that the optimizer calls Stream Aggregate. Observe that the query that feeds the data to the cursor arranges the data ordered by *shipperid* and *orderdate*. This means that the last row in each shipper group will be the one with the maximum order date. Naturally, the execution plan that the optimizer uses for this query is an ordered scan of the nonclustered index, as shown in Figure 2-62.

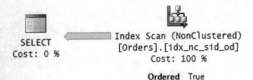

FIGURE 2-62 Execution plan for the query that the cursor is based on.

The important thing to observe in this plan is that the index scan is ordered; therefore, there's no need for explicit sorting to arrange the data in the order that the query specifies.

The code starts by declaring and opening the cursor. The code declares the cursor as a FAST_ FORWARD one, meaning that it's read-only and forward-only. The code then fetches the first row's values and puts them into the current row's variables, and it initially assigns the current row's variables to the previous row's variables. Then the code iterates while the last fetch hasn't reached the end of the cursor (@@*fetch_status* = 0). In each iteration, the code applies the following:

- It checks if the previous shipper ID is different than the current shipper ID. If so, the previous row has the maximum order date for the previous shipper. In such a case, the code checks if that date is before 2010, and if it is, the code returns that shipper ID as a qualifying one.

- It assigns the current row's variables to the previous row's variables.

- It fetches the next row's values and puts them into the current row's variables.

After the loop, the code needs to handle the last row separately to check if the last shipper is a qualifying shipper. Finally, the code closes and deallocates the cursor.

Normally, scanning about 2,500 pages on my system with cold cache takes about half a second. However, because of the high overhead of the iterations and the cursor fetches in T-SQL, it took this solution 17 seconds to complete on my system.

Before you test the set-based solution, run the following code to turn on reporting I/O and time statistics in the session:

```
SET STATISTICS IO, TIME ON;
```

You can also enable the Include Actual Execution Plan option in SSMS. It's OK to do so now because you're about to run a single statement.

Following is a simple set-based solution for our task (call it *set-based solution 1*):

```
SELECT shipperid
FROM dbo.Orders
GROUP BY shipperid
HAVING MAX(orderdate) < '20100101';
```

The solution uses a basic grouped query against the Orders table. The query groups the rows by shipper ID, and it filters only shipper groups having a maximum order date before 2010. The execution plan for this query is shown in Figure 2-63.

FIGURE 2-63 Query plan for set-based solution 1.

The optimizer created a plan that scans the nonclustered index in order. The plan then applies a stream aggregate based on this order without the need to explicitly sort the rows. Finally, the plan filters the rows that satisfy the HAVING predicate. I got the following performance statistics for this query on my system: logical reads = 2,487, CPU time = 375 ms, elapsed time = 602 ms.

Notice that the run time of this solution is only about half a second. That's compared with 17 seconds that it took the previous solution to complete. You realize that the plan for this solution uses the same order-based algorithm as in the cursor-based solution. Both solutions scan the same number of pages. The reason that the cursor solution is so much slower is mainly because of the expensive iterations and cursor fetching in T-SQL.

Query tuning with query revisions

Set-based solution 1 is much more efficient than the cursor-based solution. However, what if it's not efficient enough? Perhaps this is just small-scale test environment with 1,000,000 rows in the Orders table, but suppose the production environment has 100,000,000 rows.

The two operators in the plan in Figure 2-63 that do most of the work are the Index Scan and the Stream Aggregate operators. Both have linear scaling because their cost is proportional to the number of rows involved. Therefore, the whole plan has linear scaling. Simplifying things a bit for the purposes of our discussion, if it takes the query half a second to complete with 1,000,000 rows, it should take it about 50 seconds to complete with 100,000,000 rows. Suppose that you need the query to be much faster than that; say you need it to complete in under three seconds. You did the best you could with rowstore indexes. Now suppose that using columnstore indexing here is not really an option for you. At this point, you should evaluate query revisions that perhaps will result in a more optimal plan.

The idea behind query revisions is that the query optimizer isn't perfect. Don't get me wrong; I'm not trying to underestimate its capabilities. But the reality is that, in many cases, different queries that perform the same logical task get different execution plans. This has to do with a number of reasons. The optimizer limits the optimization process so that it won't become counterproductive. It computes both cost-based and time-based thresholds based on the sizes of the tables involved. If either of the thresholds is reached, the optimization process stops and the optimizer picks the best plan it generated up to that point. With different queries, the starting point for the optimization process is different, so the point where it stops in each case could be after exploring different sets of plans. Also, the use of certain query constructs might impose certain restrictions in terms of the optimizer's options.

In short, as mentioned, different queries that perform the same logical task can get different plans. Therefore, you have to think of query revisions as a query tuning tool. And if you'd like to improve your query-tuning skills, you should invest time in this area. You should learn how the optimizer tends to handle different query constructs and what changing conditions make the optimizer change its choices. Then, when you tune a query and want to achieve a certain effect on the plan, you will know what to try as opposed to shooting in the dark. I'll demonstrate this technique on our sample task, and I will show more examples throughout the book.

The first step is to identify the most expensive part in the existing plan. Clearly, that part is the full scan of the leaf level of the nonclustered index.

The second step is to try and identify a more efficient strategy, theoretically, even if you don't know yet how to achieve it. With a very dense partitioning column (remember, we have a small number of shipper IDs, each with many occurrences in average), the scan strategy isn't optimal. A far more optimal strategy is to scan the small Shippers table and, per shipper, apply a seek in the nonclustered index on Orders. The seek would reach the right edge of the current shipper's section in the index leaf and then scan backward one row. That row has the maximum order date for the current shipper. What's nice about this strategy is that its scaling depends on the number of shippers and not on the number of orders. So, as long as you have a very small number of shippers, that number dictates how many seek operations you will get. Remember that the cost of a seek in an index is as many reads as the number of levels in the index. The number of levels in an index doesn't change significantly when the number of rows increases. For example, with 1,000,000 rows the index will have three levels, and with 100,000,000 rows it will have four.

The third step is to come up with a query that will get a plan with the desired strategy. You could first try the following query, which returns the maximum order date for a single shipper, just to see if the optimizer will handle it with a seek:

```
SELECT MAX(orderdate) FROM dbo.Orders WHERE shipperid = 'A';
```

The plan for this query is shown in Figure 2-64.

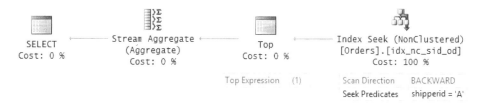

FIGURE 2-64 Query plan for a single shipper.

Sure enough, the plan performs a seek in the nonclustered index to the right edge of shipper A's section in the index leaf and then starts a backward range scan. The Top operator is the one request-ing the rows from the Index Seek operator and, as you can see in the plan, it requests only one row. Therefore, the range scan has no reason to proceed beyond that row. The order date from the filtered row is served to the Stream Aggregate operator, and this operator returns that date as the maximum order date. The execution of this query plan involved three logical reads on my system.

Now that you know that the optimizer applies the desired strategy for a single shipper, the next move is to get the same per shipper from the Shippers table. One way to achieve this is to query the Shippers table and, in the filter, invoke a correlated scalar aggregate subquery that returns the maxi-mum order date for the current shipper. Filter the shipper only if the returned date is before 2010. Here's the complete solution that implements this approach (call it *set-based solution 2*):

```
SELECT shipperid
FROM dbo.Shippers AS S
WHERE (SELECT MAX(orderdate)
       FROM dbo.Orders AS O
       WHERE O.shipperid = S.shipperid) < '20100101';
```

One would hope that the plan for this query will start by scanning some index from the Shippers table to get the shipper IDs, and then in a loop perform the activity you saw in Figure 2-64 per ship-per. But alas, it is not so, as you can see in the execution plan in Figure 2-65.

FIGURE 2-65 Query plan for set-based solution 2.

As you can see, the optimizer chose a plan that performs a full scan of the nonclustered index, which is what you were looking to avoid with this query revision. SQL Server reported the follow-ing performance statistics for this query on my system: logical reads = 8 + 2487, CPU time = 438 ms, elapsed time = 524 ms.

As it turns out, when the optimizer sees a scalar aggregate subquery like in our example, it first unnests it internally, turning it into a join form. This way, the optimizer can evaluate different plans that access the tables in a different order. The problem is that the optimizer needs to make a number of other decisions here, like which access methods to use to access the tables, which join algorithm to use, which aggregate algorithm to use, and so on. The search space becomes so large that if the optimizer tried to explore all possible plans, the optimization process would become so long that it would be counterproductive. It looks like the optimizer didn't explore the truly optimal plan here.

Normally, the unnesting of the subqueries that the optimizer performs leads to more efficient plans, but in our case it resulted in an inefficient one. So what you need in this case is to somehow prevent the optimizer from unnesting the subquery, causing it to go to Shippers first and then to Orders per shipper. It would have been handy if SQL Server supported a hint that instructs the optimizer not to unnest the inner query, but unfortunately there's no such hint. Curiously, there is an indirect way to achieve the same effect. When the subquery uses a TOP filter, SQL Server doesn't unnest it because, in some cases, such unnesting could change the meaning of the query. The one exception is when the inner query uses TOP (100) PERCENT; in such a case, SQL Server simply ignores the TOP option, knowing that it's meaningless. So in our query, if you change the subquery to use TOP (1) instead of MAX, it will prevent the undesired unnesting. Here's the revised solution (call it *set-based solution 3*):

```
SELECT shipperid
FROM dbo.Shippers AS S
WHERE (SELECT TOP (1) orderdate
       FROM dbo.Orders AS O
       WHERE O.shipperid = S.shipperid
       ORDER BY orderdate DESC) < '20100101';
```

The plan for this query is shown in Figure 2-66.

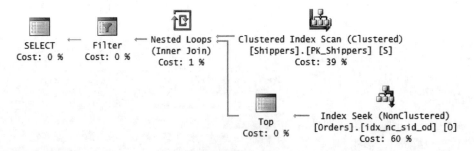

FIGURE 2-66 Query plan for set-based solution 3.

This time, the plan is precisely the desired one. It starts with a scan of the Shippers table, which costs just a couple of reads. This scan returns 12 shipper IDs. Then, per shipper, the loop performs a seek in the nonclustered index on Orders to retrieve the maximum order date for the current shipper. Then the filter keeps the shipper ID if the respective date is before 2010; otherwise, it discards it. Here are the performance statistics I got for this solution: logical reads against Shippers = 2, access count against Orders = 12, logical reads against Orders = 36, CPU time = 0 ms, elapsed time = 12 ms.

Following is another solution that gets an efficient plan (call it *set-based solution 4*):

```
SELECT shipperid
FROM dbo.Shippers AS S
WHERE NOT EXISTS
  (SELECT * FROM dbo.Orders AS O
   WHERE O.shipperid = S.shipperid
     AND O.orderdate >= '20100101')
  AND EXISTS
  (SELECT * FROM dbo.Orders AS O
   WHERE O.shipperid = S.shipperid);
```

You issue the query against the Shippers table. The filter uses a NOT EXISTS predicate with a correlated subquery that ensures that the outer shipper didn't handle orders placed in 2010 or later. The filter also uses an EXISTS predicate with a correlated subquery that ensures the outer shipper handled at least one order. The plan for this query is shown in Figure 2-67.

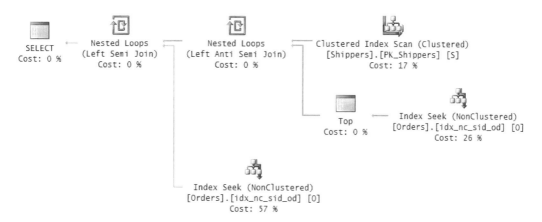

FIGURE 2-67 Query plan for set-based solution 4.

Like the plan for set-based solution 3, this plan also starts with a scan of the Shippers table, which returns 12 shipper IDs. For each of the 12 shippers, the first loop applies a seek in the nonclustered index to check the NOT EXISTS predicate in the query. For each of the remaining shipper IDs (which could be 0 to 12 in our case), the second loop applies a seek in the nonclustered index to check the EXISTS predicate in the query. This plan is a bit more expensive than the one for set-based solution 3, but it's still highly efficient, and its scaling is also tied to the number of shippers. The performance statistics I got for this query are as follows: logical reads against Shippers = 2, access count against Orders = 19, logical reads against Orders = 72, CPU time = 0 ms, elapsed time = 9 ms.

I covered four different solutions to the task, and each one got a different execution plan. The first was the simplest and most intuitive solution but not the most efficient one. You saw that the remaining attempts to tune the query were not just a matter of trying a bunch of other solutions until you get an efficient one. They were about understanding the inefficiencies in the plan for the first solution and, after thinking about what an efficient plan should look like, applying revisions in an attempt to get certain effects on the plan. The point of this exercise is to emphasize the importance of developing the skill to tune queries based on query revisions.

When you're done, run the following code to turn off reporting I/O and time statistics in the session:

```
SET STATISTICS IO, TIME OFF;
```

At this point, it's recommended that you rerun the script file PerformanceV3.sql from the book's source code to re-create the sample database as a clean one.

Parallel query execution

The changes to computer hardware over the past several years have been characterized by huge growth along virtually every possible metric: more and much faster storage, more and faster main memory, and most importantly, more and much more powerful CPUs. A similar set of changes have occurred in databases, with data volumes rapidly growing. Meanwhile, users are ever more demanding of data analytics, but they still expect split-second query times and reports that render at the click of a button.

Processing large volumes of data is naturally easier with a large amount of computing power, but the biggest performance improvements are made by using special algorithms that specifically take advantage of the increased power of newer servers. The key to these algorithms lies in splitting data into smaller chunks that can be distributed across many processor cores at once. Such techniques are referred to as *parallel query execution*, *intraquery parallelism*, or simply *parallelism*, and SQL Server has a mature and nuanced system for handling this kind of work.

This section delves into SQL Server's parallel query capabilities, focusing on key aspects of query optimization, query execution, and scheduling internals. Understanding these areas will allow you not only to analyze query plans and performance characteristics, but also to control parallelism when necessary, applying it or limiting it as is appropriate for your queries or workload.

 Note The examples in this section use the AdventureWorks2014 sample database. This database is available from CodePlex at *https://msftdbprodsamples.codeplex.com/releases/view/125550*.

How intraquery parallelism works

Parallel processing—the act of splitting work across multiple processor cores—can be done in several different ways. The most common models are the following:

- A factory line model, in which each core takes responsibility for a single action and data is passed from core to core. (Think of an automobile factory, where one person installs door handles, another installs windows, and so on.)

- A stream-based model, in which each core is responsible for a set of data and performs all the required operations. (This model is similar to a factory in which each car is built completely by a single person.)

Although the factory-line model seems intuitively better, especially when applied to cars and human workers, SQL Server and many other database products are based instead on streaming models. Computer processors, unlike humans, are able to quickly and efficiently switch between tasks, as long as the data is already in the processor's local cache. Acquiring data from main memory—or, worse, main storage—can be orders of magnitude more expensive than switching to a new task. This means that it is almost always advantageous to do as much work as possible on a given piece of data before moving it along to some other processor or memory location.

Stream-based models also often can scale much better than factory-line models, especially as data sizes grow. SQL Server's streaming model involves distributing rows across cores as evenly as possible using various algorithms (chosen depending on the scenario). Consider a situation in which a query plan has only three operations but tens of billions of rows on which to apply those operations. In a simple factory-line model, the query plan might be able to use only three processors, but in a streaming model the plan could, in theory, scale to millions or even billions of processor cores. Naturally, there are real-world limits on the number of processor cores that servers ship with, and there is also a point of diminishing returns when massively scaling a data set. But this type of flexibility helps even in smaller cases and is one of the key reasons that a stream-based model is commonly used in database systems.

Basics of parallelism in query plans

The idea of a *parallel query plan* is a bit of a misnomer. A query plan will be either entirely serial—processed using a single worker thread—or it will include one or more parallel branches, which are areas of the plan that are processed using multiple threads. This is an important distinction, because the query processor has the ability to either merge multiple parallel streams into a single stream or create parallel streams out of a single stream. These operations can be done an arbitrary number of times in a given query plan, meaning that a plan can have numerous parallel zones intermingled with numerous serial zones.

Every parallel zone in a given plan will use the same number of threads as every other parallel zone in the plan. The number of threads per zone is referred to as the *degree of parallelism* (DOP) for the plan and is determined based on a combination of server settings, plan hints, and run-time server conditions. A given set of threads might be reused by multiple zones over the course of the plan. For example, if your plan has a DOP of 4 and 4 parallel zones, it might use between 4 and 16 actual worker threads to do its work, depending on how the various parallel zones interrelate.

Determining whether or not a given operator is inside of a parallel zone can be done by looking at the icons in the graphical execution plan viewer. Operators that are in parallel zones will be adorned with a circle with two arrows, as shown in Figure 2-68; the Parallelism and Sort operators are in a parallel zone, whereas the Top operator is not.

FIGURE 2-68 Operators in parallel zones are decorated with a circle icon with two arrows.

Within a given parallel zone, each worker thread will process a single, unique stream of rows for the entire zone, after which those rows will be moved to another thread in the plan's next zone (whether that zone is serial or parallel). Therefore, each parallel zone is always bounded on one side by an operator that feeds multiple parallel streams and on the other side by an operator that either redistributes or serializes multiple parallel streams.

Exchange operators

The key feature of parallel query plans is the various parallel zones, and the key to parallel zones is an operator internally referred to as *Exchange* but exposed in graphical query plans as *Parallelism*. This operator controls both worker threads and streams of data in parallel plans and, therefore, is the core component that makes parallel plans work.

As a reminder, query plans can be read in two different ways: right to left or left to right. Reading the query plan starting from the right side follows data as it flows through the plan. On the other hand, reading the plan starting from the left side follows the operator logic, which is what actually pulls the data through. Each operator in a plan asks the next downstream operator for one row at a time, and so data streams through the plan.

Most query plan operators are concerned with asking only the next upstream operator for a row and then doing whatever operation or transformation is required before passing the row down the stream. (In the case of blocking operators, like Sort, that might mean acquiring many rows prior to passing one or more back.) Exchange operators deal with multiple streams of rows. However, virtually all other operators on the streams remain blissfully unaware that parallelism is involved.

The Exchange operator has three variants. Each of the three operators has two tasks, which are seemingly in opposition depending on whether you're reading the plan from a data-flow or operator-logic point of view.

- **Gather Streams** This operator bounds the end of a parallel zone (and the start of a serial zone) when looking at a plan from a data-flow point of view. It takes multiple parallel streams of data and merges them into a single serial stream. When reading a plan from an operator-logic perspective, the Gather Streams operator is actually the start of a parallel zone. Its job from this perspective is to invoke parallel worker threads and ask the operators on each thread for rows.

- **Distribute Streams** Reading from a data-flow perspective, this operator bounds the start of a parallel zone (likewise, the end of a serial zone). It takes a serial stream of rows and splits it into multiple parallel streams. Reading from an operator-logic perspective, this operator marks the end of a parallel zone; the next upstream operator will be part of a serial zone.

- **Repartition Streams** The role of this operator is to ingest multiple parallel streams and redistribute the rows onto different threads, based on a different scheme than was used to distribute them in the upstream parallel zone. As such, this operator bounds both the beginning and end of a parallel zone whether the plan is read from a data or logic perspective. Another way to think of this operator is that it joins together two adjacent parallel zones.

Figure 2-69 shows a query plan that includes all three types of Exchange operators.

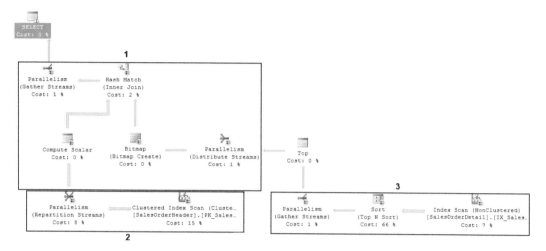

FIGURE 2-69 A query plan that uses all three types of Exchange operators.

The plan shown in Figure 2-69 has been edited and annotated to highlight the three parallel zones (and two serial zones) that are bounded by the various Exchange operators. Parallel zone 1 starts—from a logical perspective—with the Gather Streams operator. The Bitmap operator is fed from a Distribute Streams operator that bounds the zone with a serial zone containing a Top operator. Parallel zone 3 feeds this serial zone and is bounded by a Gather Streams operator. The final parallel zone in the plan—zone 2—is bounded by a Repartition Streams operator and is directly adjacent to zone 1, without an intermediate serial zone.

From a threading point of view, this plan will use a total of DOP * 2 worker threads for its parallel zones, plus a parent thread in the serial zones. The reason that it can use only twice as many worker threads as the DOP, rather than one set of threads per zone, is that the threads allocated for zone 3 will be able to be reused by zone 2.

Again, following the plan's logical sequence, if DOP is 4, zone 1 will begin and four worker threads will be allocated. The Hash Match operator blocks on its build side—the side that includes parallel zone 3. So this operator will start and will not return until all the work done by the four threads allocated for zone 3 is complete. At this point, the same four threads will be used to process zone 2.

It can be difficult to imagine exactly what is going on when looking at a parallel query plan, but it is somewhat simpler when put into a slightly different graphical form. Consider the plan fragment shown in Figure 2-70.

FIGURE 2-70 A parallel zone containing only a Sort operator.

The plan fragment shown in this figure is a complete parallel zone, containing only a Sort operator. If the graphical plan view were rendered in terms of what is really happening, and if the DOP for the plan was 4, the image might instead look similar to what is shown in Figure 2-71.

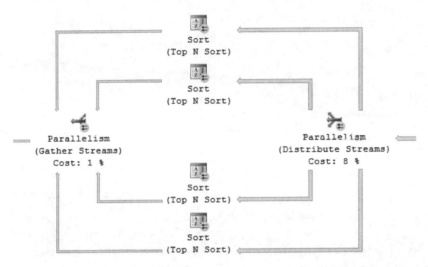

FIGURE 2-71 How parallelism really works.

Given a DOP 4 plan, the Gather Streams operator will allocate four worker threads. Each of these worker threads, in turn, will spawn a Sort operator, and each of these Sort operators will ask the Distribute Streams operator for rows. The important thing to realize is that each of the Sort operators operates entirely independently and completely unaware of what the other Sort operators are doing. Given this design, the DOP can be arbitrarily scaled up or down and the plan can still function the same way, albeit faster or slower.

Inside the Exchange operator

The prior section focused on Exchange operators from a worker-thread and row-stream perspective, but it left a core question unanswered: Why is an Exchange called an *Exchange*?

Each SQL Server query plan operator has, internally, two logical interfaces: a consumer interface, which takes rows from upstream, and a producer interface, which passes rows downstream. In most operators, these interfaces are handled on the same thread, but in the case of an Exchange, multiple threads will be involved. It is the job of the Exchange operator to take rows from threads on the consumer side and exchange those threads for different threads on the producer side. This is the basis of the name.

The actual exchange process takes place inside of a data structure called *CXPacket*, where *C* represents a C++ class (that implements the structure) and *XPacket* stands for *exchange packet*, which is the structure's actual name. As rows are consumed in the operator, they are stored in exchange packets. As the packets fill up with rows, they are passed across the exchange to the thread or threads waiting on the producer side. The number of threads on each side of the exchange depends on the type of exchange: Gather Streams operators will have DOP threads on the consumer side and one thread on the producer side; Distribute Streams operators will have one thread on the consumer side and DOP threads on the producer side; and Repartition Streams operators will have DOP threads on each side of the exchange.

If you have spent some time monitoring SQL Server wait statistics, you no doubt have encountered the CXPACKET wait type. This packet is so named because it involves threads in parallel plans waiting on the CXPacket data structure. Threads with this wait type set are usually waiting for rows on the producer side of the exchange. However, threads on the consumer side can also set the wait type if, for example, some synchronization is necessary prior to the threads beginning to produce rows.

Row-distribution strategies

Parallel query plans must cover a broad set of use cases. To increase the flexibility available to the query optimizer, there are a five options for distributing rows across the threads on the producer side of a Distribute or Repartition exchange:

- **Hash** This is the most common distribution scheme, and it involves each row getting assigned a consumer thread based on the result of a hash function. This scheme is generally used to align rows in logical groups on worker threads. For example, if the hash function is applied to the *ProductID* column, all rows with the same product ID will be assigned to the same worker thread. If the query includes an aggregation grouped by product ID, each thread will be able to independently handle aggregations of several products.

- **Round Robin** In this scheme, the first row consumed by the exchange will be distributed to the first thread waiting on the producer side, the second row will be distributed to the second waiting thread, and so on until all threads have received a row. Then the distribution will start again from the first thread. One example of when this scheme is commonly used is on the outside of a Nested Loops operator, where each row represents independent work to be done on the inner side of the loop.

- **Broadcast** This scheme sends all rows from the consumer side to all threads on the producer side. It is used only when there is a relatively small number of estimated rows and it is desirable for the entire set of rows to be present on each thread—for example, to build a hash table.

- **Demand** This scheme is unique in that it involves threads on the producer side receiving rows on request. Currently, this is used only in query plans involving aligned partitioned tables.

- **Range** In this scheme, each thread is given a unique and nonoverlapping range of keys to work with. This scheme is used only when building indexes.

To see the row distribution scheme and related information used by an Exchange operator, either hover the mouse pointer over the operator until the tooltip appears or, better, click F4 to get a properties window, as shown in Figure 2-72.

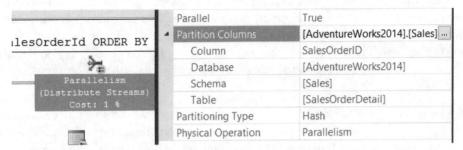

	Parallel	True
◢	Partition Columns	[AdventureWorks2014].[Sales] ...
	Column	SalesOrderID
	Database	[AdventureWorks2014]
	Schema	[Sales]
	Table	[SalesOrderDetail]
	Partitioning Type	Hash
	Physical Operation	Parallelism

FIGURE 2-72 Getting information about the Exchange operator's row-distribution scheme.

This figure shows that the selected Distribute Streams operator uses Hash partitioning, and the hash function will be applied to the *SalesOrderID* column from the AdventureWorks2014 Sales.SalesOrderDetail table.

The properties window has another useful feature for reading parallel query plans: when viewing an *actual* (as opposed to *estimated*) query plan, it shows for each operator in the plan—Exchange as well as others—the number of rows that were processed by each worker thread. This information is shown in Figure 2-73.

	Actual Execution Mode	Row
▷	Actual Number of Batches	0
◢	Actual Number of Rows	1000
	Thread 0	0
	Thread 1	201
	Thread 2	103
	Thread 3	149
	Thread 4	134
	Thread 5	179
	Thread 6	234

FIGURE 2-73 Viewing the number of rows processed per thread, in an *actual* query plan.

The number of rows per thread is available by expanding the dialog under the Actual Number Of Rows item. The plan shown here has a DOP of 6, meaning that in each parallel zone there are 6 worker threads. Here each thread processed over 100 rows, but some threads processed more than others; this is probably not a major issue for a plan that deals with only 1,000 rows, but potentially it can cause performance problems for a bigger plan.

Thread 0 here represents the parent thread (also known as the *distributor* or *coordinator* thread). This is the thread that is active in serial zones and that spawns the parallel worker threads. Its role here is not to process rows, but rather to control the life cycle of the worker threads; therefore, it does not show as having done any work on this particular operator.

Parallel sort and merging exchange

The main goal of parallelism, of course, is to break expensive units of work into smaller pieces that can run concurrently on more than one CPU. It might be reasonable to expect that if a given operation takes 1,000 ms running on a single processor, it might take only 250 ms running on four processors. This is somewhat naïve logic, but it might be correct—it depends on how expensive it is to split up the work to begin with, and how expensive it is to merge the results back into a single stream so that they can be consumed by the caller.

Surprisingly, there are also cases where splitting up units of work into smaller pieces can actually result in an even greater performance boost than would be expected based on the number of concurrent workers. In other words, for these types of operations, the 1,000-ms example, when run on four processors might take only 200 ms rather than 250 ms. The types of operations for which this works are those that mathematically scale extralinearly; given a working set of size N, these types of operations will perform over 10 times worse for a working set of size N * 10.

One such operation, and by far the most common in database scenarios, is sorting data. The best sort algorithms all scale at the rate of N * LOG(N). This is not a very steep curve: a set of 100,000,000 items will take just over 11 times longer to sort than a set of 10,000,000 items, a difference of only 10 percent compared to a linear scale. However, in the world of database performance, every bit counts. So it makes a lot of sense to take advantage of these kinds of mathematical gains in the query processor.

If a large set of rows needs to be sorted by a given key, the query plan will often put the sort into a parallel zone. If the sort is being done on more than one column, the data will often be distributed using the hash scheme, in order to keep like values together.

Once the data has been sorted, the order often needs to be preserved in a subsequent serial zone; there is little benefit to sorting the data in parallel if it can't be used. In these cases, the query plan will use a special variant of a Gather Streams operator, known as a *merging exchange*. A merging exchange consumes multiple streams of data ordered the same way, and it outputs a single stream of data that maintains the same order. This is done using a simple merge algorithm: if the data is sorted by *ProductID* ascending, rows are read off of each input stream and the minimum *ProductID* is recorded. Now rows are read off of each stream until there are no more rows for that minimum ID, at which point the next smallest ID is recorded. Rows are now read for that ID, and so on, thereby maintaining the input order.

Figure 2-74 displays a plan fragment for the following query:

```
SELECT TOP(1000)
    UnitPrice
FROM Sales.SalesOrderDetail
ORDER BY
    UnitPrice DESC;
```

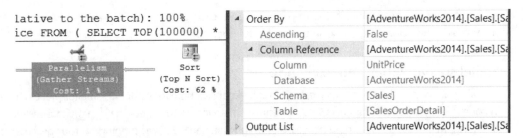

⊿ Order By	[AdventureWorks2014].[Sales].[Sa
Ascending	False
⊿ Column Reference	[AdventureWorks2014].[Sales].[Sa
Column	UnitPrice
Database	[AdventureWorks2014]
Schema	[Sales]
Table	[SalesOrderDetail]
▷ Output List	[AdventureWorks2014].[Sales].[Sa

FIGURE 2-74 Parallel sort with merging exchange.

The Gather Streams operator shown here includes an Order By property, indicating that it is a merging exchange. The data will be output ordered by the *UnitPrice* column from the Adventure-Works2014 Sales.SalesOrderDetail table, which is, in this plan, the same column that the upstream Sort operator uses.

Partial aggregation

When thinking about query plan performance, the most important consideration is generally not how many operators exist in the plan. Most operators process only a single row at a time, and do so very quickly. This is, in fact, the whole point of SQL Server's streaming query processor model.

The important thing, rather than the number of operators, is how many rows are passing through each operator. Performance problems occur in areas of plans where there are a lot of rows, meaning that the operators are doing a lot of work. It makes sense, therefore, that the earlier in a plan (from a data-flow perspective) that rows can be either filtered or aggregated, the faster that plan will be.

The benefit of early row reduction is more apparent with more expensive operations, and moving data across threads—as is done in Exchange operators—is a very expensive operation. This is because it requires putting the data into exchange packets and then copying those packets to new memory locations, rather than keeping everything in the same place.

To eliminate as much exchange cost as possible, many parallel plans that involve aggregates will use a strategy called *partial aggregation*. This strategy involves aggregating groups of rows on whatever thread they happen to be on at an earlier point in the plan, and then completing the full aggregation later, after the data has been properly repartitioned.

For example, consider a case where a query is using the MAX aggregate to find the highest price every product in the system has ever sold for. There are 1,000,000 rows for ProductID 123, and these rows are spread across 10 threads. The query processor could repartition all 1,000,000 rows—copying them to new memory locations—and then calculate the aggregate. Or, alternatively, the query processor could calculate one aggregate per thread—the maximum value of all the rows that happen to be on each thread—and then repartition only 10 threads prior to calculating the final aggregate. The answer in either case would be the same, but the cost of repartitioning would be greatly reduced in the latter.

Figure 2-75 shows partial aggregation as the result of the following query:

```
SELECT
    th.ProductID,
    th.TransactionDate,
    MAX(th.ActualCost) AS MaxCost
FROM
(
    SELECT
        tha.ProductID,
        tha.TransactionDate,
        tha.ActualCost
    FROM Production.TransactionHistoryArchive AS tha
    CROSS JOIN Production.TransactionHistory AS th
) AS th
GROUP BY
    th.ProductID,
    th.TransactionDate;
```

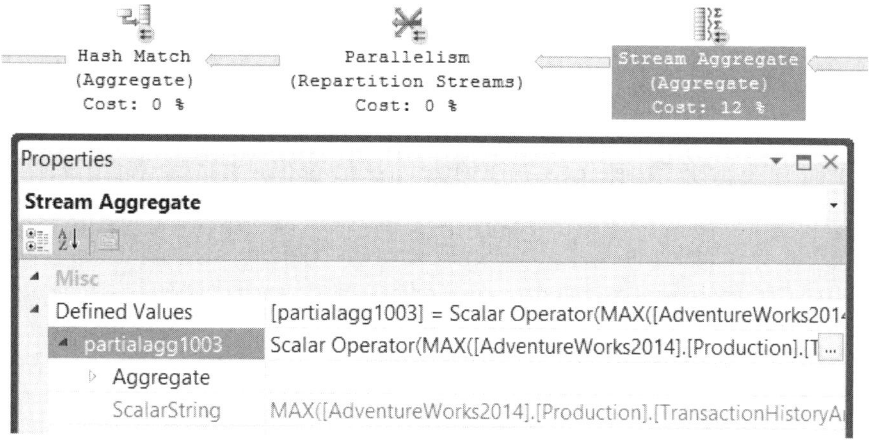

FIGURE 2-75 Partial aggregation.

Here the Stream Aggregate operator calculates a partial aggregate—named within the plan as *partialagg1003*—which greatly reduces the row count prior to the rows being consumed by the Repartition Streams operator. This plan is chosen because the row estimate is exceptionally large due to the two tables used in the plan being cross joined: An estimated 10,125,100,000 rows will be created by the cross join, but after the initial aggregation only an estimated 319,983 will remain. These rows will be repartitioned, using the Hash scheme, on the combination of the *ProductID* and *TransactionDate* columns. Then the Hash Match operator will finish the aggregation by taking the maximum value of *partialagg1003* for each group.

Note that here both Stream Aggregate and Hash Match operators are involved in this partial aggregation, but that is not always the case. Any combination of two aggregate operators can be used to perform partial aggregation.

Parallel scan

Prior to operating on a set of rows, those rows must be read from the heap or index in which they are contained. While this could be accomplished by having a single thread read the data, it is often faster, especially for large tables, to involve several threads in the process. This is done by using a parallel scan.

Figure 2-76 shows a parallel scan as the result of this query:

```
SELECT
    ActualCost
FROM Production.TransactionHistory AS th
ORDER BY
    ActualCost DESC;
```

FIGURE 2-76 Parallel scan.

A parallel scan can be a table scan, an index scan, or a range scan—the latter of which will use an operator called Index Seek. There is no special labeling, but a parallel scan is effectively any scan operation done in a parallel zone, except under a nested loop. (That is a special case covered later in this chapter.)

In this plan, the Gather Streams operator spawns worker threads, each of which instantiate a Sort operator. The Sort operators, in turn, ask the Index Scan operator for rows. Because this Index Scan is in a parallel zone, it is parallel aware, and it will not feed the same set of rows to each of the worker threads. Instead, it gives each worker thread a data page or a range of data pages to read, depending on how large the table is. The worker threads read the rows off of the data page or pages, after which they are consumed by the Sort operator. Once all the rows have been read, the worker thread will request more rows from the Scan operator. Scan will once again provide one or more data pages, and it will keep doing so until the entire table or range has been scanned.

The component inside of the Scan operator that takes care of providing the data pages is responsible for figuring out which pages each thread should read next, and also for ensuring that the pages read by each thread are unique so that no two threads will process duplicate rows. The decisions made by this component are largely based upon statistics, so it is even more important than usual to keep statistics up to date when working with large parallel plans.

Few outer rows

One of the key attributes of a high-performance parallel system is that every worker will be equally as busy, and for as long, as every other worker. This means that work has been properly distributed and the work being done in parallel will finish on every worker at about the same time, thereby reducing overall run duration.

Parallel scan works in terms of data pages rather than in terms of rows, and especially with smaller lookup tables there can be cases in which there are fewer data pages than there are worker threads. In such a case, some worker threads would be allocated but would have no work to do, which would mean not only that allocating those threads was a waste of time, but also that the remaining threads would each have to do more work than was expected.

To eliminate this situation, SQL Server implements a special optimization called *few outer rows*. This optimization occurs when a parallel scan is being used to feed the outer side of a Nested Loops operator. In this case, each row on each thread represents work to be done on the inner side of the loop, and ideally that work should be as evenly distributed among the threads as possible. To accomplish that in a case where the optimizer detects that there will be too few rows, a Repartition Streams operator is injected into the plan immediately following the parallel scan.

Figure 2-77 shows the result of this optimization on behalf of the following query:

```
SELECT
    p.ProductId,
    th0.TransactionID
FROM Production.Product AS p
CROSS APPLY
(
    SELECT TOP(1000)
        th.TransactionId
    FROM Production.TransactionHistory AS th
    WHERE
        th.ProductID = p.ProductID
    ORDER BY
        th.TransactionID
) AS th0
ORDER BY
    th0.TransactionId;
```

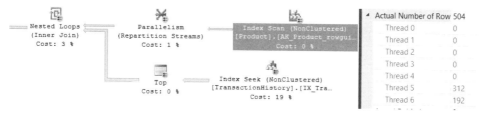

FIGURE 2-77 Without the few outer rows optimization, only two of six threads would have work to do.

In this plan, the index scan of the Product table results in only two of the six worker threads receiving rows. This is because there are only two data pages in the index; the table has only 504 rows. The query optimizer has foreseen this issue and included a Repartition Streams operator directly after the scan. This operator will repartition the rows using the Round Robin scheme, thereby producing perfect balance across the workers, as shown in Figure 2-78.

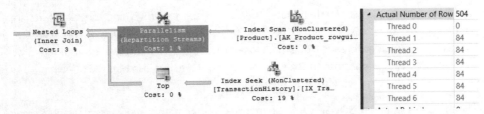

Actual Number of Row	504
Thread 0	0
Thread 1	84
Thread 2	84
Thread 3	84
Thread 4	84
Thread 5	84
Thread 6	84

FIGURE 2-78 The Round Robin scheme equally distributes rows among the worker threads.

Parallel hash join and bitmap

It is extremely common—given that parallel query plans tend to work with large sets of rows and that hash match is designed to join large sets of rows—to see Hash Join operators in parallel query plans. Therefore, it makes sense that these joins should be as optimized as possible.

The usual hash join algorithm involves hashing the outer (build-side) keys, hashing each inner (probe-side) key, finding the matching bucket in the hash table, and finally walking the bucket's linked list to find the matching row.

In parallel plans, an optimization can occur whereby each thread will build a bitmap with the same number of bits as the number of buckets in the hash table. A bit in the bitmask will be 0 if there are no rows in the corresponding hash bucket and 1 if there are rows in the hash bucket. At probe time, rather than going straight into the hash bucket, the query processor can instead first discover, by means of the bitmap, whether or not there might be a potential row in the hash table. This can greatly reduce the cost and overhead of hash join queries, especially in cases where a large proportion of probe-side rows do not match a build-side row.

The following query is optimized with a bitmap in the plan, as shown in Figure 2-79:

```
SELECT
    *
FROM
(
    SELECT
        sh.*,
        sd.ProductId
    FROM
    (
        SELECT TOP(1000)
            *
        FROM Sales.SalesOrderDetail
        ORDER BY
            SalesOrderDetailId
    ) AS sd
    INNER JOIN Sales.SalesOrderHeader AS sh ON
        sh.SalesOrderId = sd.SalesOrderId
) AS s;
```

FIGURE 2-79 A hash bitmap in a parallel plan.

The bitmap in these kinds of plans, as shown here, is based on the same hash keys as the subsequent Hash Match operator.

A further enhancement of the bitmap optimization can occur in data-warehouse queries that the query optimizer has determined to be part of a star join (one or more dimensions joining to a fact table). If the star join optimization occurs, each of the dimensions will be scanned and internally merged into a single bitmap (and hash table) that can be used on the probe side as a single filter. This approach can be significantly faster than separately probing a hash table for each dimension.

Parallelism and partitioned tables

In parallel plans involving tables with a large number of partitions, the query optimizer might choose to distribute threads and individually process each partition, rather than sequentially scanning the entire set of partitions using the typical parallel scan mechanism. This special case involves the Demand distribution scheme; each thread can work on a single partition at a time and request another partition to work on once the first one is done. In this way, the work is well balanced across worker threads, even when some partitions have fewer rows than others.

Seeing this in action requires a partitioned table, so some setup is needed. The following code creates a partition function, a partition scheme, and a table in tempdb:

```
USE tempdb;
GO

CREATE PARTITION FUNCTION pf_1 (INT)
AS RANGE LEFT FOR VALUES
(
    25000, 50000, 75000, 100000,
    125000, 150000, 175000, 200000,
    225000, 250000, 275000, 300000,
    325000, 350000, 375000, 400000,
    425000, 450000, 475000, 500000,
    525000, 550000, 575000, 600000,
    625000, 650000, 675000, 700000,
    725000, 750000, 775000, 800000,
    825000, 850000, 875000, 900000,
    925000, 950000, 975000, 1000000
);
GO
```

```
CREATE PARTITION SCHEME ps_1
AS PARTITION pf_1 ALL TO ([PRIMARY]);
GO

CREATE TABLE dbo.partitioned_table
(
  col1 INT NOT NULL,
  col2 INT NOT NULL,
  some_stuff CHAR(200) NOT NULL DEFAULT('')
) ON ps_1(col1);
GO

CREATE UNIQUE CLUSTERED INDEX ix_col1
ON dbo.partitioned_table
(
    col1
) ON ps_1(col1);
GO
```

The partition function specifies 41 partitions (including the implicit partition for values greater than 1,000,000), and the table is clustered based on *col1* used in conjunction with the partition scheme. The table includes two integer columns and a *CHAR(200)* column that is used to increase the query cost in order to influence the optimization process. (See the discussion later in this chapter for more detail.)

Once the table has been created, some data can be inserted:

```
WITH
n1 AS (SELECT 1 a UNION ALL SELECT 1),
n2 AS (SELECT 1 a FROM n1 b, n1 c),
n3 AS (SELECT 1 a FROM n2 b, n2 c),
n4 AS (SELECT 1 a FROM n3 b, n3 c),
n5 AS (SELECT 1 a FROM n4 b, n4 c),
n6 AS (SELECT 1 a FROM n5 b, n5 c)
INSERT INTO dbo.partitioned_table WITH (TABLOCK)
(
    col1,
    col2
)
SELECT TOP(1000000)
    ROW_NUMBER() OVER
    (
        ORDER BY
            (SELECT NULL)
    ) AS col1,
    CHECKSUM(NEWID()) AS col2
FROM n6;
GO
```

This query generates and inserts 1,000,000 rows into the table. The *col1* column will contain sequential values between 1 and 1,000,000, whereas the values in *col2* will be pseudorandom, based on a checksum of a unique identifier.

Once the table has been populated with data, the following query can be used, which produces the plan fragment shown in Figure 2-80:

```
SELECT
    COUNT(*)
FROM partitioned_table AS pt1
INNER JOIN partitioned_table AS pt2 ON
    pt1.col1 = pt2.col1
WHERE
    pt1.col1 BETWEEN 25000 AND 500000;
GO
```

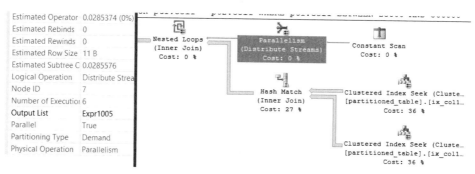

FIGURE 2-80 Demand-based row distribution in a plan involving partitioned tables.

The Constant Scan used in this plan returns one row per partition that will need to be accessed, as determined by the query optimizer based on the predicate in the WHERE clause of the query. The Distribute Streams operator consumes these rows and then distributes them based on the Demand scheme, as shown on the Properties tab to the left of the plan fragment.

Parallel SELECT INTO

For several years, it has been possible to do parallel bulk loads of data into tables by using the Bulk Copy API. A parallel bulk load does not involve query-processor parallelism, but rather enables client applications to spawn multiple concurrent bulk loads that can run together. This works because a minimally logged bulk copy deals only with page allocations; several streams allocating pages simultaneously has no risk of conflict nor requirement for concurrency except in the page allocation structures, so this is a low overhead and simple way to improve throughput.

Within the query engine itself, T-SQL developers have long been able to do minimally logged inserts by using the SELECT INTO syntax (as long as the target database uses either the Simple or Bulk Logged recovery model). However, these operations have always written data using a single stream even though the relational engine is capable of handling multiple concurrent streams.

Consider the following SELECT INTO query:

```
WITH
n1 AS (SELECT 1 a UNION ALL SELECT 1),
n2 AS (SELECT 1 a FROM n1 b, n1 c),
n3 AS (SELECT 1 a FROM n2 b, n2 c),
n4 AS (SELECT 1 a FROM n3 b, n3 c),
n5 AS (SELECT 1 a FROM n4 b, n4 c),
n6 AS (SELECT 1 a FROM n5 b, n5 c)
SELECT TOP(10000000)
    ROW_NUMBER() OVER
    (
        ORDER BY
            (SELECT NULL)
    ) AS col1,
    CHECKSUM(NEWID()) AS col2
INTO #test_table
FROM n6;
```

This query inserts 10,000,000 rows into a temporary table called #test_table. Figure 2-81 shows a fragment of the query plan when this query is run against a SQL Server 2012 instance.

FIGURE 2-81 In SQL Server 2012, SELECT INTO writes on a single thread.

Even though this query uses parallelism, prior to calculating the row number, the parallel streams are gathered. After the row number is calculated, the data is written to the temp table on a single serial stream.

The same query, run against a SQL Server 2014 instance, generates the plan fragment shown in Figure 2-82.

FIGURE 2-82 In SQL Server 2014, SELECT INTO can do multithreaded writes.

In SQL Server 2014, the row number is still generated in a serial zone. However, once it has been calculated, the rows are distributed to multiple threads (in this case, using the Round Robin scheme) and are then written to the destination temporary table from multiple simultaneous streams.

The performance benefit of this enhancement can be surprisingly large: on one test server that has both SQL Server 2012 and SQL Server 2014 installed, with identical disk systems and memory allocations, the query runs for 10 seconds in SQL Server 2012 and only for 4 seconds in SQL Server 2014.

Parallelism and query optimization

Prior to the query processor being able to exercise a parallel query plan, the query optimizer must generate one. The process that is used is somewhat more complex and nuanced than that used for serial query plans, and as a developer working with parallel queries you need to understand what is going on in order to effectively deal with problems as they occur.

The decision to use or not use parallelism in a query plan is mostly made prior to the query processor's role in plan execution. This decision is based on a combination of instance-level (or Resource Governor workload group-level) settings and the query in question. The execution engine that actually runs the plan has very little say in whether or not parallelism is used, and it will veto its use only when the SQL Server instance is under extreme resource pressure.

Parallelism settings

A discussion of the parallel query optimization process is impossible without an understanding of the instance-level and Resource Governor settings that influence the process.

There are four instance-level settings that can influence parallelism. These settings can be viewed in the sys.configurations catalog view and can be configured using the *sp_configure* system stored procedure. The settings are as follows:

- **Affinity Mask**   This setting controls which of the server's logical processors will be mapped to a SQLOS scheduler. A parallel query plan requires more than one SQLOS scheduler, so if the affinity mask is set such that there is only a single mapped processor, the query optimizer will not attempt to produce parallel query plans. That said, it is quite rare to see a single-scheduler SQL Server instance given the commonality of multicore processors in today's servers. The default value for this setting is 0, which indicates that all logical processors should be mapped to SQLOS schedulers.

- **Max Degree of Parallelism**   The maximum degree of parallelism is a default value that is used by parallel queries to determine how many worker threads to allocate per parallel zone (the DOP previously discussed). This setting can be overridden—either increased or decreased—using the query-level MAXDOP hint. The *maximum* in this setting's name and the query hint are both a bit misleading; if a query uses parallelism, it will use whatever DOP is specified at the query level, by this setting, or by the Resource Governor setting described later in this section. There is neither a query optimizer decision nor a run-time query processor decision made about what the "correct" DOP might be for a given query. The default for this setting is 0, which means that each zone of a parallel plan can use as many threads as there are online SQLOS schedulers, up to 64.

- **Cost Threshold for Parallelism**   When optimizing query plans, the query optimizer goes through multiple stages, each of which adds time and expense to the process. One of the central goals of the optimizer is to produce a good enough plan in a short amount of time, and this setting helps it achieve that goal by allowing it to exit the query-optimization process if a serial version of a query's plan does not have a high enough cost to warrant further optimization. The default for this setting is 5, which means that only serial plans with a cost higher than 5 will be put through the parallel-optimization phases.

- **Max Worker Threads**   SQLOS maintains an internal pool of operating system threads that are used (and reused) by queries as needed. Threads are finite resources and must be carefully controlled to avoid process starvation issues, so a given SQL Server instance is limited in how many threads it can create at any given time. This setting controls that limit, and this is the only setting that can have a run-time impact, rather than an optimization-time impact. If the query processor determines that the server is close to running out of worker threads, it will downgrade a parallel query plan to a serial query plan (by using a DOP of 1) in an attempt to keep the server from hitting the wall. The default for this setting is 0, which means that the instance controls the number of threads based on the number of logical processors. This system is fully documented at the following URL: *http://msdn.microsoft.com/en-us/library/ms190219.aspx*.

In addition to these instance-level settings, a given Resource Governor workload group can override the Max Degree Of Parallelism setting by using the Resource Governor *max_dop* setting. This setting has the same implications as the instance-level setting, except that it interacts differently with the query-level MAXDOP hint: the Resource Governor setting can be overridden by the query level hint, but it can be only lessened, and not increased. In other words, if *max_dop* is set to 10 by Resource Governor, a T-SQL developer can override it in a given query to 8, but not to 12. This is a useful way to control complex ad hoc workloads and ensure that a single query does not consume too many resources.

The optimization process

In the first phase of query optimization, the optimizer produces a serial version of a query plan for the query. The query plan has a total cost, which is the sum of the cost determined for each operator in the plan. These costs are further broken down, on each operator, into CPU and I/O costs, as shown in Figure 2-83.

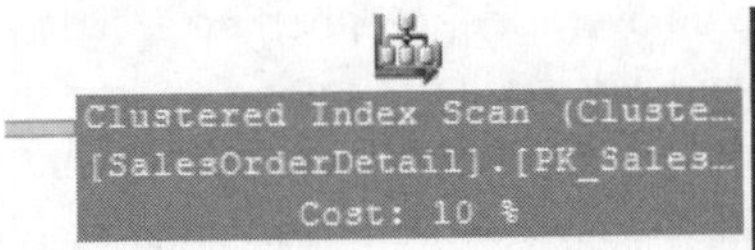

Estimated CPU Cost	0.133606
Estimated Execution Mode	Row
Estimated I/O Cost	0.918681
Estimated Number of Executions	1
Estimated Number of Rows	121317
Estimated Operator Cost	1.05229 (10%)

Clustered Index Scan (Cluste…
[SalesOrderDetail].[PK_Sales…
Cost: 10 %

FIGURE 2-83 The operator costs for an index scan in a serial plan.

In the plan fragment shown, this serial scan has an estimated CPU cost of 0.133606, an estimated I/O cost of 0.918681, and a total operator cost of 1.05229—the sum of the CPU and I/O costs.

Once the serial plan has been generated, the costs for each of the operators in the plan are added together. If the total is less than the value of the Cost Threshold For Parallelism setting, no further optimization is attempted and the plan is used as-is. If, however, the total exceeds the Cost Threshold For Parallelism, the query is subjected to further optimization phases, and parallel query plans are considered.

Once a parallel query plan has been generated for a query, additional math takes place. Each operator's CPU cost—but not its I/O cost—is divided by the number referred to as the *DOP for costing*. This number is the lesser of half of the number of SQLOS schedulers, or the MAXDOP that will be used by the plan as a result of settings or the MAXDOP query hint. For example, on an instance with 24 schedulers, the DOP for costing will be 12 if the Max Degree Of Parallelism setting is left untouched and the query is left unhinted. If the query-level MAXDOP hint is set to 8, that number will be used instead. However, on an instance with 12 schedulers, the DOP for costing will be 6 even if the MAXDOP hint is set to 8, because the lesser of the two values is used.

Figure 2-84 shows the same index scan as the prior figure, this time in a parallel plan.

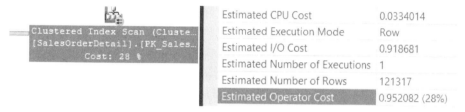

Clustered Index Scan (Cluste... [SalesOrderDetail].[PK_Sales... Cost: 28 %	Estimated CPU Cost	0.0334014
	Estimated Execution Mode	Row
	Estimated I/O Cost	0.918681
	Estimated Number of Executions	1
	Estimated Number of Rows	121317
	Estimated Operator Cost	0.952082 (28%)

FIGURE 2-84 The CPU cost has been divided by the DOP for costing.

In this case, the query was optimized on an instance with 8 SQLOS schedulers, but with the instance-level Max Degree Of Parallelism set to 6. The serial CPU cost of 0.133606 has been divided by 4—half of the number of schedulers—to yield an estimated parallel CPU cost of 0.0334014. The I/O cost remains untouched, because SQL Server takes a conservative approach in assuming that the I/O channel will be fully saturated. The result, even without touching the I/O cost, is a lower overall operator cost.

The new operator costs are all added together, in addition to the operator costs for any Exchange operators that were added to the plan to facilitate parallel processing. If the total operator cost of the parallel version of the plan is less than the total operator cost of the serial version of the plan, the query optimizer chooses the parallel version. Otherwise, the serial version is used.

Configuring an instance for parallelism

No discussion of settings would be complete without some advice for configuration. Unfortunately, there are no simple answers, but some general guidelines can be helpful.

The Affinity Mask and Max Worker Threads settings, in the vast majority of cases, should be left untouched.

Affinity Mask was primarily intended to control licensing agreements, but recent versions of SQL Server must be licensed for all the processors available on a given server. This leaves edge cases where, for example, SQL Server shares a server with an IIS instance and the administrator wants to give each process its own reserved CPUs. This use case does make some sense, but in today's world, server virtualization technologies are usually a better way to handle that situation.

The Max Worker Threads setting is designed to be automatically maintained and should generally need adjustment only in extreme cases with especially heavy parallel workloads and specific symptoms indicative of thread-pool exhaustion. These cases will generally necessitate a call to product support, and it is probably wise to allow the support person to decide how best to fix the situation.

Query cost is a metric that was first introduced in SQL Server 7.0, back in 1998. Now, 16 years later, as of the time of this writing, the computer industry has changed dramatically, but query costs still use the same basic structure. A query with a cost of 5, the default for Cost Threshold Of Parallelism, was quite large in 1998, but in today's massive databases it is relatively small. It is therefore recommended that this number be changed for most SQL Server instances. A value between 30 and 50 makes sense given today's typical hardware and data sizes. You might consider setting things even higher if you are seeing small queries (for your environment) using parallel plans.

Like Cost Threshold For Parallelism, the Max Degree Of Parallelism setting has an unfortunate default. This setting should be tuned for a given instance in an effort to balance the goals of fast query response time and allowing many queries to run concurrently. If Max Degree Of Parallelism is set too low, large queries will slow down; if it is set too high, concurrent queries will be forced to compete for processor time and therefore will interact negatively.

General guidelines for Max Degree Of Parallelism depend on the workload. For OLTP systems, which tend to have a much higher percentage of small serial query plans in addition to much lighter-weight larger queries, a smaller Max Degree Of Parallelism—as low as 2—might be advised.

For OLAP workloads, on the other hand, a smaller number of much larger queries is typical and a higher Max Degree Of Parallelism is usually a good idea. It is wise to start, on a four-socket server, with the number of processors per NUMA node (usually the same as the number of processors per socket), or half that number on a two-socket server. This gives each query a significant portion of the available CPU power, while allowing several concurrent queries to run without interacting.

If Hyper-Threading is enabled, it is recommended that you set Max Degree Of Parallelism to no more than 50 percent higher than the number of physical processors per node. In other words, if there are 6 physical processors per node and 12 logical processors (due to Hyper-Threading), it is generally advisable to set Max Degree Of Parallelism no higher than 9. This helps to keep query execution from overwhelming the additional boost provided by Hyper-Threading.

Parallelism inhibitors

In addition to the core query optimization and processing decisions, several query features can inhibit parallelism in one of two ways: either forcing a serial zone in an otherwise parallel query plan, or disabling parallelism entirely for a given query.

Following is a list of the common things that will cause a serial region to appear in a parallel query plan:

■ **Multistatement T-SQL UDF** A multistatement UDF returns a tabular value via a table variable. The logic in the user-defined function (UDF) will be processed in a serial zone, although the rest of the plan might use parallelism.

■ **Recursive CTEs** Recursive common table expressions are processed in serial zones, although downstream operators might still use parallelism.

■ **Backward scans** Indexes in SQL Server use doubly linked lists that can be scanned in either a forward or backward direction. Only forward scans are eligible for the parallel scan already described. Backward scans will be done in serial.

■ **Nonpartitioned TOP, aggregates, and windowing functions** Use of the TOP operator, aggregations, and windowing functions all involve creating groups of rows. If the group must be determined by analyzing the entire set of input rows at a given stage of the plan, the query optimizer has no choice but to use a serial zone. Examples include TOP outside of a correlated table expression, an ungrouped aggregate (also known as a *scalar aggregate*), and a windowing function that doesn't use partitioning.

The following list includes common features that will completely disable parallelism for a given plan:

■ **Scalar T-SQL UDF** Use of any scalar T-SQL UDF in a query will make that query unable to use parallelism. This should be a major red flag for any developer thinking of using T-SQL UDFs. Inline expressions or CLR scalar UDFs are often better options.

■ **Modification of table variables** In most cases, when inserting, updating, or deleting rows in a table using a query, the parts of the query prior to the actual data modification can be processed in a parallel zone. (The data modification will always be processed in a serial zone, with the exception of parallel SELECT INTO.) Table variables break this precedent; if rows in a table variable are being modified, the entire plan will run serially. Note that this is not the case if the table variable is merely used in some part of the plan not involving row modification.

■ **CLR UDFs with** *DataAccessKind.Read* CLR UDFs will not disable parallelism unless the UDF is marked with *DataAccessKind.Read*, which means that it has access to run a query in the hosting database.

■ **Memory-optimized tables** Memory-optimized tables cannot participate in parallel query plans.

To see the impact of one of these features, first consider the following query, the plan for which is shown in Figure 2-85:

```
SELECT TOP(1000)
    OrderQty
FROM Sales.SalesOrderDetail
ORDER BY
    OrderQty DESC;
GO
```

FIGURE 2-85 A parallel query plan.

This query generates a typical parallel plan; but what if a small modification is made? First create the following scalar UDF:

```
CREATE FUNCTION dbo.ReturnInput(@input INT)
RETURNS INT
AS
BEGIN
    RETURN(@input)
END
GO
```

Once the UDF is created, it can be used in the query:

```
SELECT TOP(1000)
    dbo.ReturnInput(OrderQty)
FROM Sales.SalesOrderDetail
ORDER BY
    OrderQty DESC;
GO
```

Despite the fact that it is probably the simplest UDF that can possibly be written, its impact on the query plan is extreme, as shown in Figure 2-86.

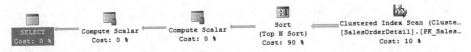

FIGURE 2-86 No longer a parallel query plan.

If you are trying to figure out whether your plan is not parallel as a result of the presence of an inhibitor, check the properties of the SELECT operator. Figure 2-87 highlights the *NonParallelPlan-Reason* property, which can help you understand what might be keeping parallelism at bay.

FIGURE 2-87 The *NonParallelPlanReason* node shows that an inhibitor is present.

In this case, the *NonParallelPlanReason* node shows that it is impossible to generate a valid parallel plan—in other words, the inhibitor is invalidating things. Looking at this property for a plan that you expect to be parallel tells you to look for and remove inhibitors.

The parallel APPLY query pattern

Given the extra-linear properties of scale described earlier in the chapter, in addition to the overhead associated with migrating rows between threads, large parallel query plans often don't scale as well as might be ideal.

Although the query optimizer is capable of performing a number of optimizations and transformations on any given query, its scope is somewhat limited based on its model. By using more extensive manual rewrites, you often can create plans that perform up to an order of magnitude faster, without hoping that the query optimizer will arrive at the right solution.

An example query

The AdventureWorks2014 sample database, although handy for example queries, is not quite big enough to illustrate the benefits or drawbacks of various performance techniques. To write a sample query, a few larger tables are required.

First, let's look at a table with five times more products than the standard version:

```
SELECT
    p.Name,
    p.ProductID + x.v AS ProductID
INTO #bigger_products
FROM Production.Product AS p
CROSS JOIN
(
    VALUES
        (0),(1000),(2000),(3000),(4000)
) AS x(v);

CREATE CLUSTERED INDEX i_ProductID
ON #bigger_products (ProductID);
GO
```

The #bigger_products table is created by cross-joining the 504 rows from Production.Product with five new rows, and then adding a number to each row to create a total of 2,520 rows. This table is clustered on *ProductID*.

Next, here's a table with 504 times more transactions than the standard version:

```
SELECT
    th.ProductID + x.v AS ProductID,
    th.ActualCost,
    th.TransactionDate
INTO #bigger_transactions
FROM Production.TransactionHistory AS th
CROSS JOIN
(
    SELECT
        (NTILE(5) OVER (ORDER BY p.ProductId) - 1) * 1000
    FROM Production.Product AS p
) AS x(v);

CREATE CLUSTERED INDEX i_ProductID
ON #bigger_transactions (ProductID);
GO
```

This table is created by cross-joining the 113,443 transactions in Production.TransactionHistory with 504 rows derived from Production.Product. The NTILE function is used to create five groups of rows that correspond to the five rows used to create the #bigger_products table. The resultant set has 57,175,272 rows and is also clustered on the *ProductID* column. This was chosen because the example query will use this column to join the two tables.

The scenario is as follows: a user would like to know, for each product, the top 10 highest prices (including ties) for which that product was sold, as well as the dates of the transactions. The following query answers the question:

```
SELECT
    p.Name,
    x.TransactionDate,
    x.ActualCost
FROM
(
    SELECT
        th.ProductID,
        th.TransactionDate,
        th.ActualCost,
        ROW_NUMBER() OVER
        (
            PARTITION BY
                th.ProductId
            ORDER BY
                th.ActualCost DESC
        ) AS rn
    FROM #bigger_transactions AS th
) AS x
INNER JOIN #bigger_products AS p ON
    p.ProductID = x.ProductID
WHERE
    x.rn <= 10;
```

This query works by calculating a row number in derived table *x*, partitioned by *ProductID* and ordered by ActualCost descending. On the outer side of the query, the rows are filtered to return only the top 10 per product, and a join is made to #bigger_products to obtain each product's name. Figure 2-88 shows a version of the plan that has been edited to fit in this book.

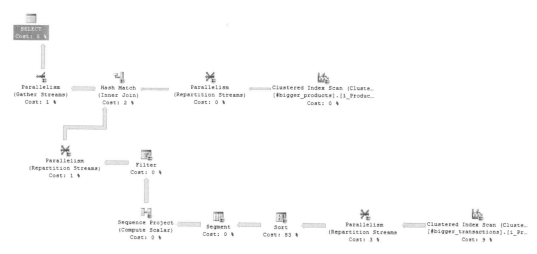

FIGURE 2-88 The query plan for finding the top 10 most expensive transactions.

This query plan uses parallelism, but it has a couple of potential bottlenecks that can be solved without modifying either indexes or table structure.

The first bottleneck is the sort on the probe side of the Hash Join operator. As already mentioned, Sort does not scale linearly, and in this case the number of input rows is quite large. The set will be split up because this is a parallel plan, but the reduction in size will be limited by the DOP of the plan. Splitting the set into even smaller working subsets could potentially yield a larger benefit. Furthermore, smaller subsets require less memory and have less of a chance of running out of memory and spilling to tempdb.

The second bottleneck is the Repartition Streams used just downstream from the parallel scan on the probe side of the Hash Join operator. This operator uses the Hash distribution methodology to distribute rows among the threads based on *ProductID*. This is done so that the rows for each product will be properly sorted together. Unfortunately, because this repartition is necessary so early in the plan, it must move every row produced by the scan—all 57,175,272 of them. That is a lot of data movement.

Parallel nested loops

The solution to both of these bottlenecks is to rethink the way data flows through a big plan like this one and work out a way to eliminate monolithic operations and instead do many more, but much smaller, operations. The query plan tool that can make this happen is the Nested Loops operator.

In any query plan, whether it is serial or parallel, a Nested Loops operator invokes its inner-side operators once per outer row. Nested Loops is often used with correlated subqueries or table expressions as a way to evaluate the correlated expression for every necessary row.

From the perspective of join performance, Nested Loops is generally not the best choice for large sets of data, because each inner-side evaluation requires another seek or scan of the data and the cost of these operations can add up. For this reason, Hash or Merge joins are usually used as data volumes increase.

That said, in many queries join performance is not the main thing that determines overall performance. Because of the scalability curve of both the Sort and Repartition Streams operator, the join performance in the plan shown in Figure 2-88 is greatly overshadowed by other elements. In this and similar examples, you are better off ignoring join performance and focusing on the bigger picture. Leveraging Nested Loops will allow you to properly handle this situation.

Reducing parallel plan overhead

The key to leveraging Nested Loops is a special query technique known as the *Parallel APPLY Pattern*. This pattern is shown in Listing 2-1.

LISTING 2-1 The Parallel APPLY Pattern

```
SELECT
    p.[columns]
FROM [driver_table] AS x
[CROSS | OUTER] APPLY
(
    SELECT
        [columns]
    FROM [correlated_table] AS c
    WHERE
        c.[key] = x.[key]
) AS p
```

The pattern has two primary elements:

- **Driver table**   This is a table (or set of rows) where each row represents a unique piece of work to be done in the inner table expression. For example, this table might be a set of products, customers, dates, or some similar element type over which you would like to do an analysis on a per-item basis.

- **Correlated table (or tables)**   The rows in the driver table should be able to correlate to rows in the table expression via a key. Ideally, correlation should be nonoverlapping, such that each row in the outer driver table represents a specific and unique set in the inner expression. Ideally, the inner table or tables should use covering indexes so that key lookups will be unnecessary.

Applying this pattern to the example query is simply a matter of rewriting the inner join using a CROSS APPLY, as follows:

```
SELECT
    p.Name,
    x.TransactionDate,
    x.ActualCost
FROM #bigger_products AS p
CROSS APPLY
(
    SELECT
        th.TransactionDate,
        th.ActualCost,
        ROW_NUMBER() OVER
        (
            ORDER BY
                th.ActualCost DESC
        ) AS rn
    FROM #bigger_transactions AS th
    WHERE
        th.ProductID = p.ProductID
) AS x
WHERE
    x.rn <= 10;
```

This version of the query starts with the #bigger_products table; because the join is done on *ProductID* and the row number is calculated by partitioning on *ProductID*, each product represents a unique piece of work in the query plan. By driving a loop off of rows from #bigger_products, the query will exercise the inner table expression once per product. The inner table expression is correlated on *ProductID*, so the explicit PARTITION BY clause is removed from the ROW_NUMBER function.

The resultant query has exactly the same logic as the prior version, but the query plan changes significantly, as shown in Figure 2-89.

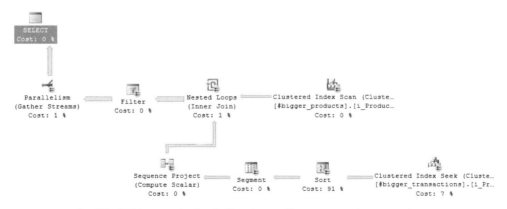

FIGURE 2-89 Parallel APPLY query plan for finding the top 10 most expensive transactions.

This query plan now includes one inner-side index operation per product. That is undoubtedly more expensive than the single parallel scan used in the previous version of the query. But that increased cost is much more than made up for by much smaller sorts and the lack of needing an inner-side repartition.

Running these queries side by side on a test server with Max Degree Of Parallelism set to 6 gives conclusive results: the initial version of the query runs for 31 seconds, and the rewritten version completes in 15. Bigger or more complex queries will see even greater performance improvements when this pattern is properly leveraged.

Conclusion

This chapter covered various query and index tuning topics. It introduced you to internal data structures, fundamental index access methods, tools to measure query performance, and other tuning aspects. So much is involved in tuning, and knowledge of the product's architecture and internals plays a big role in doing it well. But knowledge is not enough. I hope this chapter gave you the tools and guidance for putting your knowledge into action as you progress in this book—and, of course, in your production environments.

Multi-table queries

This chapter's focus is multi-table queries. It covers subqueries, table expressions, the APPLY operator, joins, and the relational operators UNION, EXCEPT, and INTERSECT.

Chapters 1 and 2 provided the foundation for the rest of the book. Chapter 1, "Logical query processing," described the logical layer of T-SQL, and Chapter 2, "Query tuning," described the physical layer. Each layer was described separately to emphasize its unique role—the logical layer's role is to define meaning, and the physical layer's role is to implement, or carry out, what the logical layer defines. The physical layer is not supposed to define meaning. Starting with this chapter, the coverage relies on the foundation provided in the previous chapters, with discussions revolving around both the logical and the physical aspects of the code.

Subqueries

Subqueries are a classic feature in SQL that you use to nest queries. Using subqueries is a convenient capability in the language when you want one query to operate on the result of another, and if you prefer not to use intermediate objects like variables for this purpose.

This section covers different aspects of subqueries. It covers self-contained versus correlated subqueries, the EXISTS predicate, and misbehaving subqueries. Subqueries can return three shapes of results: single-valued (scalar), multi-valued, and table-valued. This section covers the first two. The last type is covered later in the chapter in the "Table expressions" section.

Self-contained subqueries

A *self-contained subquery* is, as it sounds, independent of the outer query. In contrast, a *correlated subquery* has references (correlations) to columns of tables from the outer query. One of the advantages of self-contained subqueries compared to correlated ones is the ease of troubleshooting. You can always copy the inner query to a separate window and troubleshoot it independently. When you're done troubleshooting and fixing what you need, you paste the subquery back in the host query. I'll start by providing examples for scalar and multi-valued self-contained subqueries, and then transition to correlated ones.

The first example I'll discuss is of a self-contained, scalar subquery. A scalar subquery returns a single value and is allowed where a single-valued expression is expected—for example, as an operand in a comparison in the WHERE clause. As an example, the following query returns customers for whom all employees in the organization handled orders:

```
SET NOCOUNT ON;
USE TSQLV3;

SELECT custid
FROM Sales.Orders
GROUP BY custid
HAVING COUNT(DISTINCT empid) = (SELECT COUNT(*) FROM HR.Employees);
```

As an aside, this query handles a simple case of what relational algebra refers to as *relational division*. You are dividing the set of orders in the Orders table (which connects customers and employees) by the set of employees in the Employees table, and you get back qualifying customers.

The subquery returns the count of employees in the Employees table. The outer query groups the orders from the Orders table by customer ID, and it filters only customer groups having a distinct count of employee IDs that is equal to the count of employees returned by the subquery. Obviously, this query assumes that proper referential integrity is enforced in the database, preventing an order from having an employee ID that doesn't appear in the Employees table. The subquery returns 9 as the count of employees in the Employees table. The outer query returns customer ID 71 because that's the only customer with orders handled by 9 distinct employees.

Note that if a scalar subquery returns an empty set, it's converted to a NULL. If it returns more than one value, it fails at run time. Neither option is a possibility in our case, because the scalar aggregate subquery is guaranteed to return exactly one value, even if the source table is empty.

The next example is of a self-contained, multi-valued subquery. A multi-valued subquery returns multiple values in one column. It can be used where a multi-valued result is expected—for example, with the IN predicate.

The task in our example is to return orders that were placed on the last date of activity of the month. The last date of activity is not necessarily the last possible date of the month—for example, if the company doesn't handle orders on weekends and holidays. The first step in the solution is to write a grouped query that returns the last date of activity for each year and month group, like so:

```
SELECT MAX(orderdate) AS lastdate
FROM Sales.Orders
GROUP BY YEAR(orderdate), MONTH(orderdate);
```

This query returns the following output:

```
lastdate
----------
2014-01-31
2014-07-31
2015-05-06
2014-04-30
2014-10-31
2015-02-27
2013-12-31
```

```
2014-05-30
2015-03-31
2013-09-30
...
```

This query is a bit unusual for a grouped query. Usually, you group by certain elements and return the grouped elements and aggregates. Here you group by the order year and month, and you return only the aggregate without the group elements. But if you think about it, the maximum date for a year and month group preserves within it the year and month information, so the group information isn't really lost here.

The second and final step is to query the Orders table and filter only orders with order dates that appear in the set of dates returned by the query from the previous step. Here's the complete solution query:

```
SELECT orderid, orderdate, custid, empid
FROM Sales.Orders
WHERE orderdate IN
  (SELECT MAX(orderdate)
   FROM Sales.Orders
   GROUP BY YEAR(orderdate), MONTH(orderdate));
```

This query generates the following output:

```
orderid     orderdate   custid      empid
----------- ----------- ----------- -----------
10269       2013-07-31  89          5
10294       2013-08-30  65          4
10317       2013-09-30  48          6
10343       2013-10-31  44          4
10368       2013-11-29  20          2
...
```

Correlated subqueries

Correlated subqueries have references known as *correlations* to columns from tables in the outer query. They tend to be trickier to troubleshoot when problems occur because you cannot run them independently. If you copy the inner query and paste it in a new window (to make it runnable), you have to substitute the correlations with constants representing sample values from your data. But then when you're done troubleshooting and fixing what you need, you have to replace the constants back with the correlations. This makes troubleshooting correlated subqueries more complex and more prone to errors.

As the first example for a correlated subquery, consider a task similar to the last one in the previous section. The task was to return the orders that were placed on the last date of activity of the month. Our new task is to return the orders that were placed on the last date of activity of the *customer*. Seemingly, the only difference is that instead of the group being the year and month, it's now the customer. So if you take the last query and replace the grouping set from *YEAR(orderdate)*, *MONTH(orderdate)* with *custid*, you get the following subquery.

```
SELECT orderid, orderdate, custid, empid
FROM Sales.Orders
WHERE orderdate IN
  (SELECT MAX(orderdate)
   FROM Sales.Orders
   GROUP BY custid);
```

However, now there is a bug in the solution. The values returned by the subquery this time don't preserve the group (customer) information. Suppose that for customer 1 the maximum date is some *d1* date, and for customer 2, the maximum date is some later *d2* date; if customer 2 happens to place orders on d1, you will get those too, even though you're not supposed to. To fix the bug, you need the inner query to operate only on the orders that were placed by the customer from the outer row. For this, you need a correlation, like so:

```
SELECT orderid, orderdate, custid, empid
FROM Sales.Orders AS O1
WHERE orderdate IN
  (SELECT MAX(O2.orderdate)
   FROM Sales.Orders AS O2
   WHERE O2.custid = O1.custid
   GROUP BY custid);
```

Now the solution is correct, but there are a couple of awkward things about it. For one, you're filtering only one customer and also grouping by the customer, so you will get only one group. In such a case, it's more natural to express the aggregate as a scalar aggregate without the explicit GROUP BY clause. For another, the subquery will return only one value. So, even though the IN predicate is going to work correctly, it's more natural to use an equality operator in such a case. After applying these two changes, you get the following solution:

```
SELECT orderid, orderdate, custid, empid
FROM Sales.Orders AS O1
WHERE orderdate =
  (SELECT MAX(O2.orderdate)
   FROM Sales.Orders AS O2
   WHERE O2.custid = O1.custid);
```

This code generates the following output:

orderid	orderdate	custid	empid
11044	2015-04-23	91	4
11005	2015-04-07	90	2
11066	2015-05-01	89	7
10935	2015-03-09	88	4
11025	2015-04-15	87	6
...			
10972	2015-03-24	40	4
10973	2015-03-24	40	6
11028	2015-04-16	39	2
10933	2015-03-06	38	6
11063	2015-04-30	37	3
...			

Currently, if a customer placed multiple orders on its last date of activity, the query returns all those orders. As an example, observe that the query output contains multiple orders for customer 40. Suppose you are required to return only one order per customer. In such a case, you need to define a rule for breaking the ties in the order date. For example, the rule could be to break the ties based on the maximum primary key value (order ID, in our case). In the case of the two orders that were placed by customer 40 on March 24, 2015, the maximum primary key value is 10973. Note that that's the maximum primary key value from the customer's orders with the maximum order date—not from all the customer's orders.

You can use a number of methods to apply the tiebreaking logic. One method is to use a separate scalar aggregate subquery for each ordering and tiebreaking element. Here's a query demonstrating this technique:

```
SELECT orderid, orderdate, custid, empid
FROM Sales.Orders AS O1
WHERE orderdate =
  (SELECT MAX(orderdate)
   FROM Sales.Orders AS O2
   WHERE O2.custid = O1.custid)
  AND orderid =
  (SELECT MAX(orderid)
   FROM Sales.Orders AS O2
   WHERE O2.custid = O1.custid
     AND O2.orderdate = O1.orderdate);
```

The first subquery is the same as in the solution without the tiebreaker. It's responsible for returning the maximum order date for the outer customer. The second subquery returns the maximum order ID for the outer customer and order date. The problem with this approach is that you need as many subqueries as the number of ordering and tiebreaking elements. Each subquery needs to be correlated by all elements you correlated in the previous subqueries plus a new one. So, especially when multiple tiebreakers are involved, this solution becomes long and cumbersome.

To simplify the solution, you can collapse all subqueries into one by using TOP instead of scalar aggregates. The TOP filter has two interesting advantages in its design compared to aggregates. One advantage is that TOP can return one element while ordering by another, whereas aggregates consider the same element as both the ordering and returned element. Another advantage is that TOP can have a vector of elements defining order, whereas aggregates are limited to a single input element. These two advantages allow you to handle all ordering and tiebreaking elements in the same subquery, like so:

```
SELECT orderid, orderdate, custid, empid
FROM Sales.Orders AS O1
WHERE orderid =
  (SELECT TOP (1) orderid
   FROM Sales.Orders AS O2
   WHERE O2.custid = O1.custid
   ORDER BY orderdate DESC, orderid DESC);
```

The outer query filters only the orders where the key is equal to the key obtained by the TOP subquery representing the customer's most recent order, with the maximum key used as a tiebreaker.

To obtain the qualifying key, the subquery filters the orders for the outer customer, orders them by *orderdate DESC, orderid DESC*, and returns the key of the very top row.

This type of task is generally known as the *top N per group* task and is quite common in practice in different variations. It is discussed in a number of places in the book, with the most complete coverage conducted in Chapter 5, "TOP and OFFSET-FETCH." Here it is discussed mainly to demonstrate subqueries.

At this point, you have a simple and intuitive solution using the TOP filter. The question is, how well does it perform? In terms of indexing guidelines, solutions for *top N per group* tasks usually benefit from a specific indexing pattern that I like to think of as the *POC* pattern. That's an acronym for the elements involved in the task. *P* stands for the partitioning (the group) element, which in our case is *custid*. *O* stands for the ordering element, which in our case is *orderdate DESC, orderid DESC*. The *PO* elements make the index key list. *C* stands for the *covered* elements—namely, all remaining elements in the query that you want to include in the index to get query coverage. In our case, the C element is *empid*. If the index is nonclustered, you specify the C element in the index INCLUDE clause. If the index is clustered, the C element is implied. Run the following code to create a POC index to support your solution:

```
CREATE UNIQUE INDEX idx_poc
  ON Sales.Orders(custid, orderdate DESC, orderid DESC) INCLUDE(empid);
```

With the index created, you get the plan shown in Figure 3-1 for the solution with the TOP subquery.

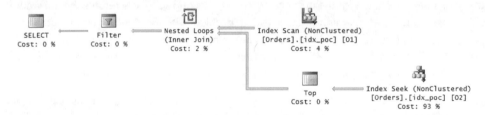

FIGURE 3-1 Plan with a seek per order.

The plan does a full scan of the POC index representing the instance O1 of the Orders table (the outer instance in the query). Then for each row from O1, the plan performs a seek in the POC index representing the instance O2 of the Orders table (the inner instance in the query). The seek reaches the beginning of the section in the leaf of the index for the current customer and scans one row to collect the key. The plan then filters only the rows from O1 where the O1 key is equal to the O2 key.

There is a certain inefficiency in this plan that can be optimized. Think about how many times the Index Seek operator is executed. Currently, you get a seek per order, but you are after only one row per customer. So a more efficient strategy is to apply a seek per customer. The denser the *custid* column, the fewer seeks such a strategy would require. To make the performance discussion more concrete, suppose the data has 10,000 customers with an average of 1,000 orders each, giving you 10,000,000 orders in total. The existing plan performs 10,000,000 seeks. With three levels in the index B-tree, this translates to 30,000,000 random reads. That's extremely inefficient. If you figure out a way to get a plan that performs a seek per customer, you would get only 10,000 seeks. Such a plan can be achieved using the CROSS APPLY operator, as I will demonstrate later in this chapter. For now, I'll limit the solution to using only plain subqueries because that's the focus of this section.

To get a more efficient plan using subqueries, you implement the solution in two steps. In one step, you query the Customers table, and with a TOP subquery similar to the previous one you return the qualifying order ID for each customer, like so:

```
SELECT
  (SELECT TOP (1) orderid
   FROM Sales.Orders AS O
   WHERE O.custid = C.custid
   ORDER BY orderdate DESC, orderid DESC) AS orderid
FROM Sales.Customers AS C;
```

This query generates the following output showing just the qualifying order IDs:

```
orderid
-----------
11011
10926
10856
11016
10924
11058
10826
10970
11076
11023
...
```

The plan for this query is shown in Figure 3-2.

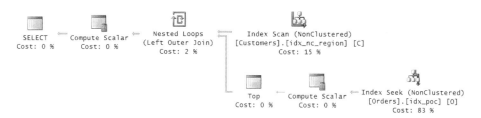

FIGURE 3-2 Plan with a seek per customer.

The critical difference between this plan and the one in Figure 3-1 is that this one applies a seek per customer, not per order. This plan performs 10,000 seeks, costing you 30,000 random reads.

The second step is to query the Orders table to return information about orders whose keys appear in the set of keys returned by the query implementing the first step, like so:

```
SELECT orderid, orderdate, custid, empid
FROM Sales.Orders
WHERE orderid IN
```

```
(SELECT
    (SELECT TOP (1) orderid
     FROM Sales.Orders AS O
     WHERE O.custid = C.custid
     ORDER BY orderdate DESC, orderid DESC)
 FROM Sales.Customers AS C);
```

The query plan for the complete solution is shown in Figure 3-3.

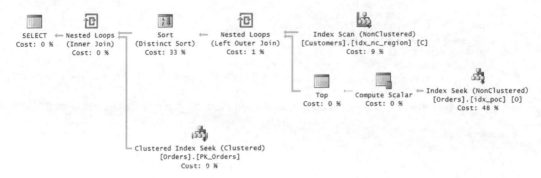

FIGURE 3-3 Complete plan with a seek per customer.

In addition to the work described for the first step of the solution (retrieving the qualifying keys), this plan also performs 10,000 seeks in the index PK_Orders to obtain the desired order attributes for the qualifying orders. That's after sorting the keys to optimize the seeks. This part adds 10,000 more seeks, giving you a total of 20,000 seeks and resulting in 60,000 random reads. That's a factor of 500 compared to the previous solution!

When you're done, run the following code for cleanup:

```
DROP INDEX idx_poc ON Sales.Orders;
```

The EXISTS predicate

The EXISTS predicate accepts a subquery as input and returns *true* or *false*, depending on whether the subquery returns a nonempty set or an empty one, respectively. As a basic example, the following query returns customers who placed orders:

```
SELECT custid, companyname
FROM Sales.Customers AS C
WHERE EXISTS (SELECT * FROM Sales.Orders AS O
              WHERE O.custid = C.custid);
```

The predicate is natural to use because it allows you to express requests like the preceding one in SQL in a manner that is similar to the way you express them in a spoken language.

A curious thing about EXISTS is that, unlike most predicates in SQL, it uses two-valued logic. It returns either *true* or *false*. It cannot return *unknown* because there's no situation where it doesn't know whether the subquery returns at least one row or none. Pardon the triple-negative form of the last sentence, but for the purposes of this chapter, you want to practice this kind of logic. If the inner query involves a filter, the rows for which the filter predicate evaluates to *unknown* because of the presence of NULLs are discarded. Still, the EXISTS predicate always knows with certainty whether the result set is empty or not. In contrast to EXISTS, the IN predicate, for example, uses three-valued logic. Consequently, a query using EXISTS can have a different logical meaning than a query using IN when you negate the predicate and NULLs are possible in the data. I'll demonstrate this later in the chapter.

Another interesting thing about EXISTS is that, from an indexing selection perspective, the optimizer ignores the subquery's SELECT list. For example, the Orders table has an index called idx_nc_custid defined on the custid column as the key with no included columns. Observe the query plan shown in Figure 3-4 for the last EXISTS query.

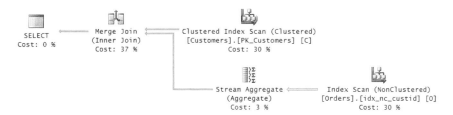

FIGURE 3-4 Plan for EXISTS with SELECT *.

Notice that the only index the plan uses from the Orders table is idx_nc_custid, despite the fact that the subquery uses SELECT *. In other words, this index is considered a covering one for the purposes of this subquery. That's proof that the SELECT list is ignored for index-selection purposes.

Next I'll demonstrate a couple of classic tasks that can be handled using the EXISTS predicate. I'll use a table called T1, which you create and populate by running the following code:

```
SET NOCOUNT ON;
USE tempdb;
IF OBJECT_ID(N'dbo.T1', N'U') IS NOT NULL DROP TABLE dbo.T1;
CREATE TABLE dbo.T1(col1 INT NOT NULL CONSTRAINT PK_T1 PRIMARY KEY);
INSERT INTO dbo.T1(col1) VALUES(1),(2),(3),(7),(8),(9),(11),(15),(16),(17),(28);
```

The key column in the table is *col1*. Suppose you have a key generator that generates consecutive keys starting with 1, but because of deletions you have gaps. One classic challenge is to identify the minimum missing value. To test the correctness of your solution, you can use the small set of sample data that the preceding code generates. For performance purposes, you want to populate the table with a much bigger set. Use the following code to populate it with 10,000,000 rows:

```
TRUNCATE TABLE dbo.T1;
INSERT INTO dbo.T1 WITH (TABLOCK) (col1)
  SELECT n FROM TSQLV3.dbo.GetNums(1, 10000000) AS Nums WHERE n % 10000 <> 0
  OPTION(MAXDOP 1);
```

You can use a CASE expression that returns 1 if 1 doesn't already exist in the table. The trickier part is identifying the minimum missing value when 1 does exist. One way to achieve this is using the following query:

```
SELECT MIN(A.col1) + 1 AS missingval
FROM dbo.T1 AS A
WHERE NOT EXISTS
  (SELECT *
   FROM dbo.T1 AS B
   WHERE B.col1 = A.col1 + 1);
```

The first step in this code is to filter the rows from T1 (aliased as *A*) where the value in A appears before a missing value. That way, you know the value in A appears before a missing value because you cannot find another value in T1 (aliased as *B*) where the B value is greater than the A value by 1. Then, from all remaining values in A, you return the minimum plus one. Perhaps you expected the query to finish instantly; after all, there is an index on *col1* (PK_T1). Theoretically, you should be able to scan the index in order and short-circuit the work as soon as the first point before a missing value is found. But it takes this query a good few seconds to complete against the large set of sample data. On my system, it took it five seconds to complete. To understand why the query is slow, examine the query plan shown in Figure 3-5.

FIGURE 3-5 Plan for a minimum missing value, first attempt.

Observe that the index on *col1* is fully scanned twice. The Merge Join operator is used to apply a right anti semi join to detect nonmatches. The Stream Aggregate operator identifies the minimum. The critical thing in this plan that makes it inefficient is that the input is scanned twice fully. There's no short-circuit even though the scans are ordered.

One attempt to optimize the query is to use the TOP filter instead of the MIN aggregate, like so:

```
SELECT TOP (1) A.col1 + 1 AS missingval
FROM dbo.T1 AS A
WHERE NOT EXISTS
  (SELECT *
   FROM dbo.T1 AS B
   WHERE B.col1 = A.col1 + 1)
ORDER BY A.col1;
```

But again, the query is slow. Examine the execution plan of this query, as shown in Figure 3-6.

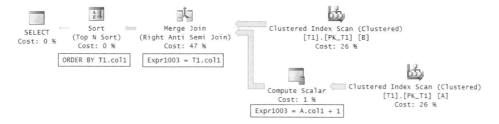

FIGURE 3-6 Plan for a minimum missing value, second attempt.

The Merge Join predicate considers the A input as sorted by *Expr1003 (col1 + 1)* and the B input by *col1 (T1.col1)*. Because the outer query orders the rows by *A.col1* and not by *A.col1 + 1*, the optimizer doesn't realize the rows are already sorted and adds a Sort (Top N Sort) operator that consumes the entire input to determine the top 1 row. To fix this, simply change the outer query's ORDER BY to *A.col1 + 1*, like so:

```
SELECT TOP (1) A.col1 + 1 AS missingval
FROM dbo.T1 AS A
WHERE NOT EXISTS
  (SELECT *
   FROM dbo.T1 AS B
   WHERE B.col1 = A.col1 + 1)
ORDER BY A.col1 + 1;
```

Observe the plan shown in Figure 3-7.

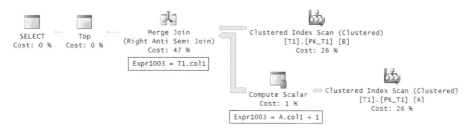

FIGURE 3-7 Plan for a minimum missing value, third attempt.

Now the optimizer realizes that the Merge Join operator returns the rows sorted the same way the TOP filter needs them, so it can short-circuit as soon as the first matching row is found. The query finishes in sub-second time.

Alternatively, you will also get an optimal plan if you change the inner query's WHERE filter from *B.col1 = A.col1 + 1* to *A.col1 = B.col1 − 1*, and the ORDER BY clause from *A.col1 + 1* to *A.col1*, like so:

```
SELECT TOP (1) A.col1 + 1 AS missingval
FROM dbo.T1 AS A
WHERE NOT EXISTS
```

```
    (SELECT *
     FROM dbo.T1 AS B
     WHERE A.col1 = B.col1 - 1)
ORDER BY A.col1;
```

Now add the logic with the CASE expression to return 1 when 1 doesn't exist and to return the result of the subquery (using one of the efficient solutions) otherwise. You get the following complete solution:

```
SELECT
  CASE
    WHEN NOT EXISTS(SELECT * FROM dbo.T1 WHERE col1 = 1) THEN 1
    ELSE (SELECT TOP (1) A.col1 + 1 AS missingval
          FROM dbo.T1 AS A
          WHERE NOT EXISTS
            (SELECT *
             FROM dbo.T1 AS B
             WHERE B.col1 = A.col1 + 1)
          ORDER BY missingval)
  END AS missingval;
```

Another classic task involving a sequence of values is to identify all ranges of missing values. In our case, we'll look for the ones missing between the minimum and maximum that exist in the table. This task is generally known as *identifying gaps*. Here, unlike with the minimum missing-value task, there's no potential for a short circuit. As the first step, you can use the same query you used in the previous task to find all values that appear before a gap:

```
SELECT col1
FROM dbo.T1 AS A
WHERE NOT EXISTS
  (SELECT *
   FROM dbo.T1 AS B
   WHERE B.col1 = A.col1 + 1);
```

You get the following output against the small set of sample data:

```
col1
-----------
3
9
11
17
28
```

Observe that you also get the maximum value in the table (28) because that value plus 1 doesn't exist. But this value doesn't represent a gap you want to return. To exclude it from the output, add the following predicate to the outer query's filter:

```
AND col1 < (SELECT MAX(col1) FROM dbo.T1)
```

Now that you are left with only values that appear before gaps, you need to identify for each current value the related value that appears right after the gap. You can do this in the outer query's

SELECT list with the following subquery, which returns for each current value the minimum value that is greater than the current one:

```
(SELECT MIN(B.col1)
 FROM dbo.T1 AS B
 WHERE B.col1 > A.col1)
```

You might think it's a bit strange to use the alias *B* both here and in the subquery that checks that the value plus 1 doesn't exist. However, because the two subqueries have independent scopes, there's no problem with that.

Last, you add one to the value before the gap and subtract one from the value after the gap to get the actual gap information. Putting it all together, here's the complete solution:

```
SELECT col1 + 1 AS range_from,
  (SELECT MIN(B.col1)
   FROM dbo.T1 AS B
   WHERE B.col1 > A.col1) - 1 AS range_to
FROM dbo.T1 AS A
WHERE NOT EXISTS
  (SELECT *
   FROM dbo.T1 AS B
   WHERE B.col1 = A.col1 + 1)
  AND col1 < (SELECT MAX(col1) FROM dbo.T1);
```

This query generates the following output:

```
range_from  range_to
----------- -----------
4           6
10          10
12          14
18          27
```

The execution plan for this solution is shown in Figure 3-8.

The plan is quite efficient, especially when there's a small number of gaps. The three rightmost operators in the upper branch handle the computation of the maximum *col1* value in the table. The value is obtained from the tail of the index, so the work is negligible. The middle section uses a Merge Join (Right Anti Semi Join) operator to identify the values that appear before gaps. The merge algorithm relies on two ordered scans of the index on *col1*. This strategy is much more efficient than the alternative, which is to apply an index seek per original value in the sequence. Finally, the bottom branch applies an index seek per filtered value (a value that appears before a gap) to identify the respective value after the gap. What's important here is that you get an index seek per filtered value (namely, per gap) and not per original value. So, especially when the number of gaps is small, you get a small number of seeks. For example, the large set of sample data has 10,000,000 rows with 1,000 gaps. With this sample data, the query finishes in five seconds on my system. Chapter 4, "Grouping, pivoting, and windowing," continues the discussion about identifying gaps and shows additional solutions.

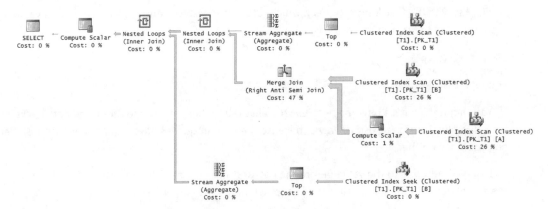

FIGURE 3-8 Plan for the gaps query.

When you're done, run the following code for cleanup:

```
IF OBJECT_ID(N'dbo.T1', N'U') IS NOT NULL DROP TABLE dbo.T1;
```

One of the interesting things about T-SQL querying tasks is that, for any given problem, there are usually many possible solutions. Often, different solutions get different execution plans. So it's important to develop the skill of solving querying tasks in different ways and observing carefully in each case how the optimizer handles things. Later, when you tune a query and need to achieve a certain effect on the plan, it's easier if you already know which change is likely to give you such an effect—for example, by comparing how SQL Server handles a solution based on a subquery versus one that uses a join, how it handles a solution using an aggregate versus one that uses the TOP filter, and so on. Another example for different approaches is applying positive logic versus negative logic. For instance, recall from the beginning of the chapter the task to identify customers for whom all employees handled orders. The solution I presented for the task applied positive logic:

```
USE TSQLV3;

SELECT custid
FROM Sales.Orders
GROUP BY custid
HAVING COUNT(DISTINCT empid) = (SELECT COUNT(*) FROM HR.Employees);
```

Another approach is to apply negative logic, but because what you're after is positive—customers for whom all employees handled orders—you will need two negations to get the same meaning. It's just like saying that something *is common* is the same as saying that it *is not uncommon*. In our case, saying *customers for whom all employees handled orders* is like saying *customers for whom no employees handled no orders*. This translates to the following query with two NOT EXISTS predicates, one nested inside the other:

```
SELECT custid, companyname
FROM Sales.Customers AS C
WHERE NOT EXISTS
  (SELECT * FROM HR.Employees AS E
   WHERE NOT EXISTS
```

```
(SELECT * FROM Sales.Orders AS O
 WHERE O.custid = C.custid
   AND O.empid = E.empid));
```

Perhaps the double-negative form is not very intuitive initially, but the good news is that this kind of thinking can improve with practice.

Now you can examine and compare the plans for the positive solutions versus the negative solutions to learn how the optimizer handles things in the different cases. Note, though, that the tables in the TSQLV3 database are very small, so you can't really do any performance testing with them. You will need much bigger tables to do proper performance analysis and tuning. I demonstrate an example with bigger volumes of data where the double-negative approach enables a very efficient solution in the article "Identifying a Subsequence in a Sequence, Part 2," which you can find here: *http://sqlmag.com/t-sql/identifying-subsequence-in-sequence-part-2*.

I found the double-negative approach to be handy in a number of other cases. For example, suppose you have a character string column called *sn* (for serial number) that is supposed to allow only digits. You want to enforce this rule with a CHECK constraint. You can phrase a predicate that is based on positive logic, but I find the double-negative form to be the most elegant and economic in this case. The positive rule says that *every character in the column is a digit*. The double-negative form is that *no character in the column is not a digit*. In T-SQL, this rule translates to the following predicate:

```
sn NOT LIKE '%[^0-9]%'
```

Nice and simple!

Misbehaving subqueries

There are common tasks that are handled with subqueries for which you can easily get into trouble with bugs when you don't follow certain best practices. I'll describe two such problems: one involving a substitution error in a subquery column name, and another involving unintuitive handling of NULLs in a subquery. I'll also provide best practices that, if followed, can help you avoid getting into such trouble.

Consider the following T1 and T2 tables and the sample data they are populated with:

```
IF OBJECT_ID(N'dbo.T1', N'U') IS NOT NULL DROP TABLE dbo.T1;
IF OBJECT_ID(N'dbo.T2', N'U') IS NOT NULL DROP TABLE dbo.T2;
GO
CREATE TABLE dbo.T1(col1 INT NOT NULL);
CREATE TABLE dbo.T2(col2 INT NOT NULL);

INSERT INTO dbo.T1(col1) VALUES(1);
INSERT INTO dbo.T1(col1) VALUES(2);
INSERT INTO dbo.T1(col1) VALUES(3);

INSERT INTO dbo.T2(col2) VALUES(2);
```

Suppose you need to return the values in T1 that also appear in the set of values in T2. You write the following query (but don't run it yet).

```
SELECT col1 FROM dbo.T1 WHERE col1 IN(SELECT col1 FROM dbo.T2);
```

Before you execute this query, examine the values in both tables and answer the question, which values do you expect to see in the result? Naturally, you expect to see only the value *2* in the result. Now execute the query. You get the following output:

```
col1
-----------
1
2
3
```

Can you explain why you're getting all values from T1 and not just 2?

A close examination of the table definitions and the query code will reveal that the subquery against T2 refers to *col1* by mistake, instead of *col2*. Now the question is, why didn't the code fail? The way SQL resolves which table the column belongs to is it first looks for the column in the table in the immediate query. If it cannot find it there, like in our case, it looks for it in the table in the outer query. In our case, there is a column named *col1* in the outer table; therefore, that one is used. Unintentionally, the inner reference to *col1* became a correlated reference. So when the outer *col1* value is *1*, the inner query selects a *1* for every row in T2. When the outer *col1* value is *2*, the inner query selects a *2* for every row in T2. You realize that as long as there are rows in T2, and the *col1* value is not NULL, you'll always get a match.

Usually, this type of problem happens when you are not consistent in naming attributes the same way in different tables when they represent the same thing. For example, suppose that in a Customers table you name the column holding the customer ID *custid*, and in a related Orders table you name the column *customerid*. Then you write a query similar to the query in our example looking for customers who placed orders, but by mistake you specify *custid* against both tables. You will get all customers back instead of just the ones who truly placed orders. When the outer statement is SELECT, the query returns an incorrect result with all rows, but you realize that when the outer statement is DELETE, you end up deleting all rows.

There are two best practices that can help you avoid such bugs in your code: one is a long-term recommendation, and the other is a short-term one. The long-term best practice is to pay more attention to naming attributes in different tables the same way when they represent the same thing. The short-term recommendation is to simply prefix the column name with the table name (or alias, if you assigned one), and then you're not allowing implied resolution. Apply this practice to our sample query:

```
SELECT col1 FROM dbo.T1 WHERE col1 IN(SELECT T2.col1 FROM dbo.T2);
```

Now the query fails with a resolution error saying there's no column called *col1* in T2:

```
Msg 207, Level 16, State 1, Line 278
Invalid column name 'col1'.
```

Seeing this error, you will of course figure out the problem and fix the query by specifying the right column name, *col2*, in the subquery.

Another classic case where people get into trouble with subqueries has to do with the complexities that are related to the NULL treatment. To see the problem, re-create and repopulate the T1 and T2 tables with the following code:

```
IF OBJECT_ID(N'dbo.T1', N'U') IS NOT NULL DROP TABLE dbo.T1;
IF OBJECT_ID(N'dbo.T2', N'U') IS NOT NULL DROP TABLE dbo.T2;
GO
CREATE TABLE dbo.T1(col1 INT NULL);
CREATE TABLE dbo.T2(col1 INT NOT NULL);

INSERT INTO dbo.T1(col1) VALUES(1);
INSERT INTO dbo.T1(col1) VALUES(2);
INSERT INTO dbo.T1(col1) VALUES(NULL);

INSERT INTO dbo.T2(col1) VALUES(2);
INSERT INTO dbo.T2(col1) VALUES(3);
```

Observe the values in both tables. Suppose you want to return only the values that appear in T2 but not in T1. You write the following code in an attempt to achieve this (but don't run it yet):

```
SELECT col1 FROM dbo.T2 WHERE col1 NOT IN(SELECT col1 FROM dbo.T1);
```

Before you run the code, answer the question, which values do you expect to see in the result? Most people expect to get the value *3* back. Now run the query. You get an empty set back:

```
col1
-----------
```

A key to understanding why you get an empty set is remembering that for a WHERE filter to return a row, the predicate needs to evaluate to *true*; getting *false* or *unknown* causes the row to be discarded. It's clear why you don't get the value *2* back—because the value *2* does appear in T1 (the IN predicate returns *true*), you don't want to see it (the NOT IN is *false*). The trickier part is to figure out why you don't get the value *3* back. The answer to the question whether *3* appears in T1 is unknown because the NULL can represent any value. More technically, the IN predicate translates to *3=1 OR 3=2 OR 3=NULL*, and the result of this disjunction of predicates is the logical value *unknown*. Now apply NOT to the result. When you negate *unknown*, you still get *unknown*. In other words, just like it's unknown that *3* appears in T1, it's also unknown that *3* doesn't appear in T1.

All this means is that when you use NOT IN with a subquery and at least one of the members of the subquery's result is NULL, the query will return an empty set. From a SQL perspective, you don't want to see the values from T2 that appear in T1 exactly, because you know with certainty that they appear in T1, and you don't want to see the rest of the values from T2, because you don't know with certainty that they don't appear in T1. This is one of the absurd implications of NULL handling and the three-valued logic.

You can do certain things to avoid getting into such trouble. For one, if a column is not supposed to allow NULLs, make sure you enforce a NOT NULL constraint. If you don't, chances are that NULLs will find their way into that column. For another, if the column is indeed supposed to allow NULLs, but for example those NULLs represent a missing and inapplicable value, you need to revise your solution to ignore them. You can achieve this behavior in a couple of ways. One option is to explicitly remove the NULLs in the inner query by adding the filter *WHERE col1 IS NOT NULL*, like so:

```
SELECT col1 FROM dbo.T2 WHERE col1 NOT IN(SELECT col1 FROM dbo.T1 WHERE col1 IS NOT NULL);
```

This time, you get the result you probably expected to begin with:

```
col1
-----------
3
```

The other option is to use NOT EXISTS instead of NOT IN, like so:

```
SELECT col1
FROM dbo.T2
WHERE NOT EXISTS(SELECT * FROM dbo.T1 WHERE T1.col1 = T2.col1);
```

Here, when the inner query's filter compares a NULL with anything, the result of the filter predicate is *unknown*, and rows for which the predicate evaluates to *unknown* are discarded. In other words, the implicit removal of the NULLs by the filter in this solution has the same effect as the explicit removal of the NULLs in the previous solution.

Table expressions

Table expressions are named queries you interact with similar to the way you interact with tables. T-SQL supports four kinds of table expressions: derived tables, common table expressions (CTEs), views, and inline table-valued functions (inline TVFs). The first two are visible only in the scope of the statement that defines them. With the last two, the definition of the table expression is stored as a permanent object in the database, and anyone with the right permissions can interact with them.

A query against a table expression involves three parts in the code: the inner query, the name that you assign to the table expression (and when relevant, its columns), and the outer query. The inner query is supposed to generate a table result. This means it needs to satisfy three requirements:

- The inner query cannot have a presentation ORDER BY clause. It can have an ORDER BY clause to support a TOP or OFFSET-FETCH filter, but then the outer query doesn't give you assurance that the rows will be presented in any particular order, unless it has its own ORDER BY clause.

- All columns must have names. So, if you have a column that results from a computation, you must assign it with a name using an alias.

- All column names must be unique. So, if you join tables that have columns with the same name and you need to return the columns with the same name, you'll need to assign them with different aliases. Table names or aliases that are used as prefixes for the column names in intermediate logical-processing phases are removed when a table expression is defined based on the query. Therefore, the column names in the table expression have to be unique as standalone, unqualified, ones.

As long as a query satisfies these three requirements, it can be used as the inner query in a table expression.

From a physical processing perspective, the inner query's result doesn't get persisted anywhere; rather, it is inlined. This means that the outer query and the inner query are merged. When you look at a plan for a query against a table expression, you see the plan interacting with the underlying physical structures directly after the query got inlined. In other words, there's no physical side to table expressions; rather, they are virtual and should be considered to be a logical tool. The one exception to this rule is when using indexed views—in which case, the view result gets persisted in a B-tree. For details see *http://msdn.microsoft.com/en-us/library/ms191432.aspx*).

The following sections describe the different kinds of table expressions.

Derived tables

A *derived table* is probably the type of table expression that most closely resembles a subquery. It is a table subquery that is defined in the FROM clause of the outer query. You use the following form to define and query a derived table:

```
SELECT <col_list> FROM (<inner_query>) AS <table_alias>[(<target_col_list>)];
```

Remember that all columns of a table expression must have names; therefore, you have to assign column aliases to all columns that are results of computations. Derived tables support two different syntaxes for assigning column aliases: inline aliasing and external aliasing. To demonstrate the syntaxes, I'll use a table called T1 that you create and populate by running the following code:

```
IF OBJECT_ID(N'dbo.T1', N'U') IS NOT NULL DROP TABLE dbo.T1;
GO
CREATE TABLE dbo.T1(col1 INT);

INSERT INTO dbo.T1(col1) VALUES(1);
INSERT INTO dbo.T1(col1) VALUES(2);
```

Suppose you need the inner query to define a column alias called *expr1* for the computation *col1 + 1*, and then in the outer query refer to *expr1* in one of the expressions. Using the inline aliasing form, you specify the computation followed by the AS clause followed by the alias, like so:

```
SELECT col1, exp1 + 1 AS exp2
FROM (SELECT col1, col1 + 1 AS exp1
      FROM dbo.T1) AS D;
```

Using the external aliasing form, you specify the target column aliases in parentheses right after the derived table name, like so:

```
SELECT col1, exp1 + 1 AS exp2
FROM (SELECT col1, col1 + 1
      FROM dbo.T1) AS D(col1, exp1);
```

With this syntax, you have to specify names for all columns, even the ones that already have names.

Both syntaxes are standard. Each has its own advantages. What I like about the inline aliasing form is that with long and complex queries it's easy to identify which alias represents which computation. What I like about the external form is that it's easy to see in one place which columns the table expression contains. You need to make a decision about which syntax is more convenient for you to use. If you want, you can combine both, like so:

```
SELECT col1, exp1 + 1 AS exp2
FROM (SELECT col1, col1 + 1 AS exp1
      FROM dbo.T1) AS D(col1, exp1);
```

In case of a conflict, the alias assigned externally is used.

From a language-design perspective, derived tables have two weaknesses. One has to do with nesting and the other with multiple references. Both are results of the derived table being defined in the FROM clause of the outer query. Regarding nesting: if you need to make references from one derived table to another, you need to nest those tables. The problem with nesting is that it can make it hard to follow the logic when you need to review or troubleshoot the code. As an example, consider the following query where derived tables are used to enable the reuse of column aliases:

```
SELECT orderyear, numcusts
FROM (SELECT orderyear, COUNT(DISTINCT custid) AS numcusts
      FROM (SELECT YEAR(orderdate) AS orderyear, custid
            FROM Sales.Orders) AS D1
      GROUP BY orderyear) AS D2
WHERE numcusts > 70;
```

The query returns order years and the distinct number of customers handled in each year for years that had more than 70 distinct customers handled.

Trying to figure out what the code does by reading it from top to bottom is tricky because the outer query is interrupted in the middle by the derived table D2, and then the query defining D2 is interrupted in the middle by the derived table D1. Human brains are not very good at analyzing nested units; they are better at analyzing independent modules where you focus your attention on one unit at a time, from start to end, in an uninterrupted way. So, typically what you do to try and make sense out of such nested code is analyze it from the innermost derived table (D1, in this example), and then gradually work outward, rather than analyzing it in a more natural order.

As for physical processing, as mentioned, table expressions don't get persisted anywhere; instead, they get inlined. This can be seen clearly in the execution plan of the query, as shown in Figure 3-9.

FIGURE 3-9 Table expressions that are inlined.

There are no spool operators representing work tables; rather, the plan interacts with the Orders table directly.

In addition to the nesting aspect, another weakness of derived tables relates to cases where you need multiple references to the same table expression. Take the following query as an example:

```
SELECT CUR.orderyear, CUR.numorders, CUR.numorders - PRV.numorders AS diff
FROM (SELECT YEAR(orderdate) AS orderyear, COUNT(*) AS numorders
      FROM Sales.Orders
      GROUP BY YEAR(orderdate)) AS CUR
  LEFT OUTER JOIN
    (SELECT YEAR(orderdate) AS orderyear, COUNT(*) AS numorders
     FROM Sales.Orders
     GROUP BY YEAR(orderdate)) AS PRV
  ON CUR.orderyear = PRV.orderyear + 1;
```

The query computes the number of orders that were handled in each year, and the difference from the count of the previous year. There are actually simpler and more efficient ways to handle this task—for example, with the LEAD function—but this code is used for illustration purposes. Observe that the outer query joins two derived tables that are based on the exact same query that computes the yearly order counts. SQL doesn't allow you to define and name a derived table once and then refer to it multiple times in the same FROM clause that defines it. Unfortunately, you have to repeat the code. This makes the code longer and harder to maintain. Every time you need to make a change in the derived table query, you need to remember to make it in all copies, which increases the likelihood of errors.

CTEs

Common table expressions (CTEs) are another kind of table expression that, like derived tables, are visible only to the statement that defines them. There are no session-scoped or batch-scoped CTEs. The nice thing about CTEs is that they were designed to resolve the two weaknesses that derived tables have. Here's an example of a CTE definition representing yearly order counts:

```
WITH OrdCount
AS
(
  SELECT
    YEAR(orderdate) AS orderyear,
    COUNT(*) AS numorders
  FROM Sales.Orders
  GROUP BY YEAR(orderdate)
)
SELECT orderyear, numorders
FROM OrdCount;
```

You will find here the same components you have in code interacting with a derived table—namely, there's the CTE name, the inner query, and the outer query. The difference between CTEs and derived tables is in how these three components are arranged with respect to each another. Observe that the code starts with naming the CTE, continues with the inner query expressed from start to end uninterrupted, and then the outer query also is expressed from start to end uninterrupted. This design makes CTEs easier to work with than derived tables.

Recall the example with the nesting of derived tables. Here's the alternative using CTEs:

```
WITH C1 AS
(
  SELECT YEAR(orderdate) AS orderyear, custid
  FROM Sales.Orders
),
C2 AS
(
  SELECT orderyear, COUNT(DISTINCT custid) AS numcusts
  FROM C1
  GROUP BY orderyear
)
SELECT orderyear, numcusts
FROM C2
WHERE numcusts > 70;
```

As you can see, in the same WITH statement you can define multiple CTEs separated by commas. Each can refer in the inner query to all previously defined CTEs. Then the outer query can refer to all CTEs defined by that WITH statement. The nice thing about this approach is that the units are not nested; rather, they are expressed one at a time in an uninterrupted manner. So, if you need to figure out the logic of the code, you analyze it in a more natural order from top to bottom.

The one thing I find a bit tricky when troubleshooting a WITH statement with multiple CTEs is that, if you want to check the result of an intermediate CTE, you cannot just highlight the code down to that part and run it. You need to inject a *SELECT * FROM <ctename>* right after that CTE and then run the code down to that part. Derived tables have an advantage in this respect in the sense that, without any code changes, you can highlight a query against a derived table including all the units you want to test and run it.

From a physical-processing perspective, the treatment of CTEs is the same as that for derived tables. The results of the inner queries don't get persisted anywhere; rather, the code gets inlined. This code generates the same plan as the one shown earlier for derived tables in Figure 3-9.

The other advantage of using CTEs rather than derived tables is that, because you name the CTE before using it, you are allowed to refer to the CTE name multiple times in the outer query without needing to repeat the code. Recall the example shown earlier with two copies of the same derived table to return yearly counts of orders and the difference from the previous yearly count. Here's the CTE-based alternative:

```
WITH OrdCount
AS
(
  SELECT
    YEAR(orderdate) AS orderyear,
      COUNT(*) AS numorders
  FROM Sales.Orders
  GROUP BY YEAR(orderdate)
)
SELECT CUR.orderyear, CUR.numorders,
  CUR.numorders - PRV.numorders AS diff
```

```
FROM OrdCount AS CUR
  LEFT OUTER JOIN OrdCount AS PRV
    ON CUR.orderyear = PRV.orderyear + 1;
```

Clearly, this is a better design.

Note that because SQL Server doesn't persist the table expression's result anywhere, whether you use derived tables or CTEs, all references to the table expression's name will be expanded, and the work will be repeated. This can be seen clearly in the plan shown in Figure 3-10.

FIGURE 3-10 Work that is repeated with multiple references.

You can see the work happening twice. A covering index from the Orders table is scanned twice, and then the rows are sorted, grouped, and aggregated twice. If the table is large and you want to avoid repeating all this work, you should consider using a temporary table or a table variable instead.

Recursive CTEs

T-SQL supports a specialized form of a CTE with recursive syntax. To describe and demonstrate recursive CTEs, I'll use a table called Employees that you create and populate by running the following code:

```
SET NOCOUNT ON;
USE tempdb;

IF OBJECT_ID(N'dbo.Employees', N'U') IS NOT NULL DROP TABLE dbo.Employees;

CREATE TABLE dbo.Employees
(
  empid   INT         NOT NULL
    CONSTRAINT PK_Employees PRIMARY KEY,
  mgrid   INT         NULL
    CONSTRAINT FK_Employees_Employees FOREIGN KEY REFERENCES dbo.Employees(empid),
  empname VARCHAR(25) NOT NULL,
  salary  MONEY       NOT NULL
);

INSERT INTO dbo.Employees(empid, mgrid, empname, salary)
  VALUES(1,   NULL, 'David'  , $10000.00),
        (2,    1, 'Eitan'  ,  $7000.00),
        (3,    1, 'Ina'    ,  $7500.00),
        (4,    2, 'Seraph' ,  $5000.00),
        (5,    2, 'Jiru'   ,  $5500.00),
        (6,    2, 'Steve'  ,  $4500.00),
        (7,    3, 'Aaron'  ,  $5000.00),
        (8,    5, 'Lilach' ,  $3500.00),
        (9,    7, 'Rita'   ,  $3000.00),
```

```
             (10,    5, 'Sean'   ,  $3000.00),
             (11,    7, 'Gabriel',  $3000.00),
             (12,    9, 'Emilia' ,  $2000.00),
             (13,    9, 'Michael',  $2000.00),
             (14,    9, 'Didi'   ,  $1500.00);
```

```
CREATE UNIQUE INDEX idx_nc_mgr_emp_i_name_sal
  ON dbo.Employees(mgrid, empid) INCLUDE(empname, salary);
```

Recursive CTEs have a body with not just one member like regular CTEs, but rather multiple members. Usually, you will have one anchor member and one recursive member, but the syntax certainly allows having multiple anchor members and multiple recursive members. I'll explain the roles of the members through an example. The following code returns all direct and indirect subordinates of employee 3:

```
WITH EmpsCTE AS
(
  SELECT empid, mgrid, empname, salary
  FROM dbo.Employees
  WHERE empid = 3

  UNION ALL

  SELECT C.empid, C.mgrid, C.empname, C.salary
  FROM EmpsCTE AS P
    JOIN dbo.Employees AS C
      ON C.mgrid = P.empid
)
SELECT empid, mgrid, empname, salary
FROM EmpsCTE;
```

The first query you see in the CTE body is the anchor member. The anchor member is a regular query that can run as a self-contained one and executes only once. This query creates the initial result set that is then used by the recursive member. In our case, the anchor query returns the row for employee 3. Then, in the CTE body, the code uses a UNION ALL operator to indicate that the result of the anchor query should be unified with the results of the recursive query that comes next. The recursive member executes repeatedly until it returns an empty set. What makes it recursive is the reference that it has to the CTE name. This reference represents the immediate previous result set. In our case, the recursive query joins the immediate previous result set holding the managers from the previous round with the Employees table to obtain the direct subordinates of those managers. As soon as the recursive query cannot find another level of subordinates, it stops executing. Then the reference to the CTE name in the outer query represents the unified result sets of the anchor and recursive members. Here's the output generated by this code:

```
empid   mgrid   empname   salary
------  ------  --------  --------
3       1       Ina       7500.00
7       3       Aaron     5000.00
9       7       Rita      3000.00
11      7       Gabriel   3000.00
```

12	9	Emilia	2000.00
13	9	Michael	2000.00
14	9	Didi	1500.00

The execution plan for this query is shown in Figure 3-11.

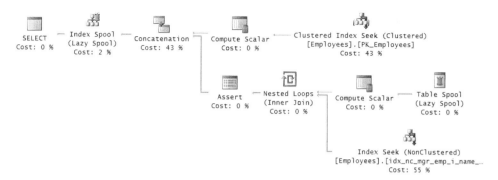

FIGURE 3-11 Plan for a recursive query.

The plan creates a B-tree-based worktable (Index Spool operator) where it stores the intermediate result sets. The plan performs a seek in the clustered index to retrieve the row for employee 3 and writes it to the spool. The plan then repeatedly reads the last round's result from the spool, joining it with the covering index from the Employees table to retrieve the employees from the next level, and it writes those to the spool. The plan keeps a count of how many times the recursive member was executed. It does so by using two Compute Scalar operators. The first initializes a variable with 0, and the second increments the variable by 1 in each iteration. Then the Assert operator fails the query if the counter is greater than 100. In other words, by default the recursive member is allowed to run up to 100 times. You can change the default to the limit you want to set using a query option called MAXRECURSION. To remove the limit, set it to 0. You specify the option in an OPTION clause at the end of the outer query—for example, *OPTION(MAXRECURSION 10)*.

The main benefits I see in recursive queries are the brevity of the code and the ability to traverse graph structures based only on the parent and child IDs (*mgrid* and *empid*, in our example). The main drawback of recursive queries is performance. They tend to perform less efficiently than alternative methods, even your own loop-based solutions. With recursive queries, you don't have any control over the worktable; for example, you can't define your own indexes on it, you can't define how to filter the rows from the previous round, and so on. If you know how to optimize T-SQL code, you can usually get better performance with your own solution.

For more information about recursive queries and handling graph structures, see Chapter 11, "Graphs and recursive queries."

Views

Derived tables and CTEs are available only to the statement that defines them. Once the defining statement finishes, they are gone. If you need the ability to reuse the table expression beyond the single statement, you can use views or inline TVFs. Views and inline TVFs are stored as an object in the database and therefore are reusable by users with the right permissions. What gets stored in the database is the query definition and metadata information, not the data (with the exception of an indexed view as mentioned earlier). When submitting a query or a modification against the table expression, SQL Server inlines the table expression and applies the query or modification to the underlying object.

As an example, suppose you have different branches in your organization. You want users from the USA branch to be able to interact only with customers from the USA. SQL Server doesn't have built-in support for row-level permissions. So you create the following view querying the Customers table and filtering only customers from the USA:

```
USE TSQLV3;
IF OBJECT_ID(N'Sales.USACusts', N'V') IS NOT NULL DROP VIEW Sales.USACusts;
GO
CREATE VIEW Sales.USACusts WITH SCHEMABINDING
AS

SELECT
  custid, companyname, contactname, contacttitle, address,
  city, region, postalcode, country, phone, fax
FROM Sales.Customers
WHERE country = N'USA'
WITH CHECK OPTION;
```

You grant the users from the USA permissions against the view but not against the underlying table.

The SCHEMABINDING option ensures that structural changes against referenced objects and columns will be rejected. This option requires schema-qualifying object names and explicit enumeration of the column list (no *). The CHECK OPTION ensures that modifications against the view that contradict the inner query's filter are rejected. For example, with this option you won't be allowed to insert a customer from the UK through the view. You also won't be allowed to update the country/region to one other than the USA through the view.

Now when you query the view, you interact only with customers from the USA, like in the following example:

```
SELECT custid, companyname
FROM Sales.USACusts
ORDER BY region, city;
```

As mentioned, behind the scenes SQL Server will inline the inner query, so the execution plan you get will be the same as the one you will get for this query:

```
SELECT custid, companyname
FROM Sales.Customers
WHERE country = N'USA'
ORDER BY region, city;
```

Note that despite the fact that the view's inner query gets inlined, sometimes SQL Server cannot avoid doing work even when, intuitively, you think it should. Consider an example where you perform vertical partitioning of a wide table, storing in each narrower table the key and a different subset of the original columns. Then you use a view to join the tables to make it look like one relation. Use the following code to create a basic example for such an arrangement:

```
IF OBJECT_ID(N'dbo.V', N'V') IS NOT NULL DROP VIEW dbo.V;
IF OBJECT_ID(N'dbo.T3', N'U') IS NOT NULL DROP TABLE dbo.T3;
IF OBJECT_ID(N'dbo.T2', N'U') IS NOT NULL DROP TABLE dbo.T2;
IF OBJECT_ID(N'dbo.T1', N'U') IS NOT NULL DROP TABLE dbo.T1;
GO

CREATE TABLE dbo.T1
(
  keycol INT NOT NULL CONSTRAINT PK_T1 PRIMARY KEY,
  col1 INT NOT NULL
);

CREATE TABLE dbo.T2
(
  keycol INT NOT NULL
    CONSTRAINT PK_T2 PRIMARY KEY
    CONSTRAINT FK_T2_T1 REFERENCES dbo.T1,
  col2 INT NOT NULL
);

CREATE TABLE dbo.T3
(
  keycol INT NOT NULL
    CONSTRAINT PK_T3 PRIMARY KEY
    CONSTRAINT FK_T3_T1 REFERENCES dbo.T1,
  col3 INT NOT NULL
);
GO

CREATE VIEW dbo.V WITH SCHEMABINDING
AS

SELECT T1.keycol, T1.col1, T2.col2, T3.col3
FROM dbo.T1
  INNER JOIN dbo.T2
    ON T1.keycol = T2.keycol
  INNER JOIN dbo.T3
    ON T1.keycol = T3.keycol;
GO
```

Note that I'm not getting into a discussion here about whether this is a good design or a bad one—I'm just trying to explain how optimization of code against table expressions works. Suppose you know there's a one-to-one relationship between all tables. Every row in one table has exactly one matching row in each of the other tables. You issue a query against the view requesting columns that originate in only one of the tables:

```
SELECT keycol, col1 FROM dbo.V;
```

Some people intuitively expect the optimizer to be smart enough to know that only T1 should be accessed. The problem is that SQL Server doesn't know what you know—that there's a one-to-one relationship between the tables. As far as SQL Server is concerned, there could be rows in T1 that don't have related rows in the other tables and therefore shouldn't be returned. Also, there could be rows in T1 that have multiple related rows in the other tables and therefore should be returned multiple times. In other words, the optimizer has to create a plan where it joins T1 with T2 and T3 as shown in Figure 3-12.

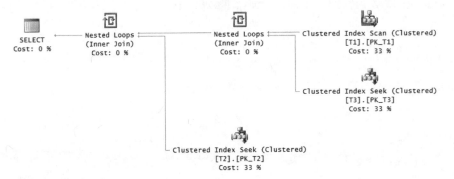

FIGURE 3-12 Plan that shows access to all tables.

To access only T1 to get what you want, you have to query T1 directly and not through the view. I'm using this example to emphasize that sometimes issuing a query through a view (or any other type of table expression) will involve more work than querying only what you think the relevant underlying objects are. That's despite the fact that the inner query gets inlined.

A quick puzzle

Query only *col2* from the view and, before looking at the plan, try to guess which tables should be accessed. Then examine the plan and try to explain what you see. Perhaps you expected all three tables to be accessed based on the previous example, but you will find that T2 and T3 are accessed but not T1. The optimizer realizes that, thanks to the existing foreign-key relationships, every row in T2 and T3 has exactly one matching row in T1. The other way around is not necessarily true; theoretically, a row in T1 can have zero, one, or more matching rows in T2 and T3. Also, inner joins are commutative, meaning that (T1 JOIN T2) JOIN T3 is equivalent to T1 JOIN (T2 JOIN T3). So when asking only for a column from T2, it's enough to join T2 with T3 to get the correct result. The join to T1 becomes redundant. It's nice to see that the optimizer is capable of such tricks. But you do still pay for the join to T3 because, theoretically, this join can affect the result. As mentioned, if you want the optimal plan, you need to access the underlying table directly and not through the view. The same optimization considerations apply to all types of table expressions, not just views.

When you're done, run the following code for cleanup:

```
IF OBJECT_ID(N'dbo.V', N'V') IS NOT NULL DROP VIEW dbo.V;
IF OBJECT_ID(N'dbo.T3', N'U') IS NOT NULL DROP TABLE dbo.T3;
IF OBJECT_ID(N'dbo.T2', N'U') IS NOT NULL DROP TABLE dbo.T2;
IF OBJECT_ID(N'dbo.T1', N'U') IS NOT NULL DROP TABLE dbo.T1;
```

Inline table-valued functions

Suppose you need a reusable table expression like a view, but you also need to be able to pass input parameters to the table expression. Views do not support input parameters. For this purpose, SQL Server provides you with inline table-valued functions (TVFs). As an example, the following code creates an inline TVF called *GetTopOrders* that accepts as inputs a customer ID and a number and returns the requested number of most-recent orders for the input customer:

```
IF OBJECT_ID(N'dbo.GetTopOrders', N'IF') IS NOT NULL DROP FUNCTION dbo.GetTopOrders;
GO
CREATE FUNCTION dbo.GetTopOrders(@custid AS INT, @n AS BIGINT) RETURNS TABLE
AS
RETURN
  SELECT TOP (@n) orderid, orderdate, empid
  FROM Sales.Orders
  WHERE custid = @custid
  ORDER BY orderdate DESC, orderid DESC;
GO
```

The following code queries the function to return the three most recent orders for customer 1:

```
SELECT orderid, orderdate, empid
FROM dbo.GetTopOrders(1, 3) AS O;
```

SQL Server inlines the inner query and performs parameter embedding, meaning that it replaces the parameters with constants. After inlining and embedding, the query that actually gets optimized is the following:

```
SELECT TOP (3) orderid, orderdate, empid
FROM Sales.Orders
WHERE custid = 1
ORDER BY orderdate DESC, orderid DESC;
```

I find inline TVFs to be a great tool, allowing for the encapsulation of the logic and reusability without any performance penalties. I'm afraid I cannot say the same thing about the other types of user-defined functions (UDFs). I elaborate on performance problems of UDFs in Chapter 9, "Programmable objects."

Generating numbers

One of my favorite tools in T-SQL, if not *the* favorite, is a function that returns a sequence of integers in a requested range. Such a function has so many practical uses that I'm surprised SQL Server doesn't provide it as a built-in tool. Fortunately, by employing a few magical tricks, you can create a very efficient version of such a function yourself as an inline TVF.

Before looking at my version, I urge you to try and come up with yours. It's a great challenge. Create a function called *GetNums* that accepts the inputs @low and @high and returns a sequence of integers in the requested range. The goal is best-possible performance. You will use the function to generate millions of rows in some cases, so naturally you will want it to perform well.

There are three critical things I rely on to get a performant solution:

- Generating a large number of rows with cross joins

- Generating row numbers efficiently without sorting

- Short-circuiting the work with TOP when the requested number of rows is reached

The first step is to generate a large number of rows. It doesn't really matter what you will have in those rows because eventually you'll produce the numbers with the ROW_NUMBER function. A great way in T-SQL to generate a large number of rows is to apply cross joins. But you need a table with at least two rows as a starting point. You can create such a table as a virtual one by using the VALUES clause, like so:

```
SELECT c FROM (VALUES(1),(1)) AS D(c);
```

This query generates the following output showing that the virtual table has two rows:

```
c
-----------
1
1
```

The next move is to define a CTE based on the last query (call it *L0*, for *level 0*), and apply a self-cross join between two instances of L0 to get four rows, like so:

```
WITH
  L0 AS (SELECT c FROM (VALUES(1),(1)) AS D(c))
SELECT 1 AS c FROM L0 AS A CROSS JOIN L0 AS B;
```

This query generates the following output:

```
c
-----------
1
1
1
1
```

The next move is to define a CTE called *L1* based on the last query, and then join two instances of L1 to get 16 rows. Repeating this pattern, by the time you get to L5, you have potentially 4,294,967,296 rows! Here's the expression to compute this number:

```
SELECT POWER(2., POWER(2., 5));
```

The next step is to query L5 and compute row numbers (call the column *rownum*) without causing a sort operation to take place. This is done by specifying *ORDER BY (SELECT NULL)*. You define a CTE called Nums based on this query.

Finally, the last step is to query Nums, and with the TOP option filter *@high – @low + 1* rows, ordered by *rownum*. You compute the result number column (call it *n*) as *@low + rownum – 1*.

Here's the complete solution code applied to the sample input range 11 through 20:

```
DECLARE @low AS BIGINT = 11, @high AS BIGINT = 20;

WITH
  L0   AS (SELECT c FROM (VALUES(1),(1)) AS D(c)),
  L1   AS (SELECT 1 AS c FROM L0 AS A CROSS JOIN L0 AS B),
  L2   AS (SELECT 1 AS c FROM L1 AS A CROSS JOIN L1 AS B),
  L3   AS (SELECT 1 AS c FROM L2 AS A CROSS JOIN L2 AS B),
  L4   AS (SELECT 1 AS c FROM L3 AS A CROSS JOIN L3 AS B),
  L5   AS (SELECT 1 AS c FROM L4 AS A CROSS JOIN L4 AS B),
  Nums AS (SELECT ROW_NUMBER() OVER(ORDER BY (SELECT NULL)) AS rownum
              FROM L5)
SELECT TOP(@high - @low + 1) @low + rownum - 1 AS n
FROM Nums
ORDER BY rownum;
```

This code generates the following output:

```
n
--------------------
11
12
13
14
15
16
17
18
19
20
```

For reusability, encapsulate the solution in an inline TVF called *GetNums*, like so:

```
IF OBJECT_ID(N'dbo.GetNums', N'IF') IS NOT NULL DROP FUNCTION dbo.GetNums;
GO
CREATE FUNCTION dbo.GetNums(@low AS BIGINT, @high AS BIGINT) RETURNS TABLE
AS
RETURN
  WITH
    L0   AS (SELECT c FROM (VALUES(1),(1)) AS D(c)),
    L1   AS (SELECT 1 AS c FROM L0 AS A CROSS JOIN L0 AS B),
    L2   AS (SELECT 1 AS c FROM L1 AS A CROSS JOIN L1 AS B),
    L3   AS (SELECT 1 AS c FROM L2 AS A CROSS JOIN L2 AS B),
    L4   AS (SELECT 1 AS c FROM L3 AS A CROSS JOIN L3 AS B),
    L5   AS (SELECT 1 AS c FROM L4 AS A CROSS JOIN L4 AS B),
    Nums AS (SELECT ROW_NUMBER() OVER(ORDER BY (SELECT NULL)) AS rownum
                FROM L5)
  SELECT TOP(@high - @low + 1) @low + rownum - 1 AS n
  FROM Nums
  ORDER BY rownum;
GO
```

Use the following code to test the function:

```
SELECT n FROM dbo.GetNums(11, 20);
```

My friend Laurent Martin refers to this function as the *harp function*. This nickname might seem puzzling until you look at the query plan, which is shown in Figure 3-13.

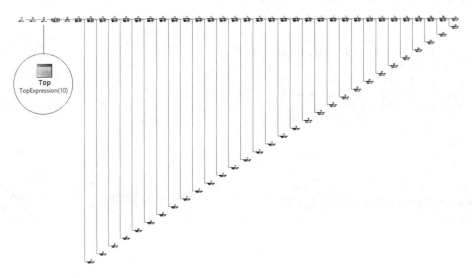

FIGURE 3-13 The harp function.

The beauty of this plan is that the Top operator is the one requesting the rows from the branch to the right of it, and it short-circuits as soon as the requested number of rows is achieved. The Sequence Project and Nested Loops operators, which handle the row-number calculation and cross joins, respectively, respond to the request for rows from the Top operator. As soon as the Top operator stops requesting rows, they stop producing rows. In other words, even though potentially this solution can generate over four billion rows, in practice it generates only the requested number and then short-circuits. Testing the performance of the function on my laptop, it finished generating 10,000,000 numbers in four seconds, with results discarded. That's not so bad.

The APPLY operator

The APPLY operator is one of the most powerful tools I know of in T-SQL, and yet, it seems to be unnoticed by many. Often when I teach about T-SQL, I ask the students who's using APPLY and, in many cases, I get only a small percent saying they do. What's interesting about this operator is that it can be used in very creative ways to solve all kinds of querying tasks.

There are three flavors of APPLY: CROSS APPLY, OUTER APPLY, and implicit APPLY. The following sections describe these flavors.

The CROSS APPLY operator

One way to think of the CROSS APPLY operator is as a hybrid of a cross join and a correlated subquery. Think for a moment of a regular cross join. The inputs can be tables or table expressions, but then the table expressions have to be self-contained. The inner queries are not allowed to be correlated ones. The CROSS APPLY operator is similar to a cross join, only the inner query in the right input is allowed to have correlations to elements from the left input. The left input, like in a cross join, has to be self-contained.

So, *T1 CROSS JOIN T2* is equivalent to *T1 CROSS APPLY T2*. Also, *T1 CROSS JOIN (self_contained_query) AS Q* is equivalent to *T1 CROSS APPLY (self_contained_query) AS Q*. However, unlike a cross join, CROSS APPLY allows the right input to be a correlated table subquery, as in *T1 CROSS APPLY (SELECT ... FROM T2 WHERE T2.col1 = T1.col1) AS Q*. This means that for every row in T1, Q is evaluated separately based on the current value in *T1.col1*.

Interestingly, standard SQL doesn't support the APPLY operator but has a similar feature called a *lateral derived table*. The standard's parallel to T-SQL's CROSS APPLY is a CROSS JOIN with a lateral derived table, allowing the right table expression to be a correlated one. So what in T-SQL is expressed as *T1 CROSS APPLY (SELECT ... FROM T2 WHERE T2.col1 = T1.col1) AS Q*, in standard SQL is expressed as *T1 CROSS JOIN LATERAL (SELECT ... FROM T2 WHERE T2.col1 = T1.col1) AS Q*.

To demonstrate a practical use case for CROSS APPLY, recall the earlier discussion in this chapter about the *top N per group* task. The specific example was filtering the most recent orders per customer. The order for the filter was based on *orderdate* descending with *orderid* descending used as the tiebreaker. I suggested creating the following POC index to support your solution:

```
CREATE UNIQUE INDEX idx_poc
  ON Sales.Orders(custid, orderdate DESC, orderid DESC)
  INCLUDE(empid);
```

I used the following solution based on a regular correlated subquery:

```
SELECT orderid, orderdate, custid, empid
FROM Sales.Orders
WHERE orderid IN
  (SELECT
     (SELECT TOP (1) orderid
      FROM Sales.Orders AS O
      WHERE O.custid = C.custid
      ORDER BY orderdate DESC, orderid DESC)
   FROM Sales.Customers AS C);
```

The problem with a regular subquery is that it's limited to returning only one column. So this solution used a subquery to return the qualifying order ID per customer, but then another layer was needed with a query against Orders to retrieve the rest of the order information per qualifying order ID. So the plan for this solution shown earlier in Figure 3-3 involved a seek in the POC index per customer to retrieve the qualifying order ID, and another seek per customer in the POC index to retrieve the rest of the order information.

Because CROSS APPLY allows you to apply a correlated table expression, you're not limited to returning only one column. So you can simplify the solution by removing the need for the extra layer, and instead of doing two seeks per customer, do only one. Here's what the solution using the CROSS APPLY operator looks like (this time requesting the three most recent orders per customer):

```
SELECT C.custid, A.orderid, A.orderdate, A.empid
FROM Sales.Customers AS C
  CROSS APPLY ( SELECT TOP (3) orderid, orderdate, empid
               FROM Sales.Orders AS O
               WHERE O.custid = C.custid
               ORDER BY orderdate DESC, orderid DESC ) AS A;
```

It's both simpler than the previous one and more efficient, as can be seen in the query plan shown in Figure 3-14.

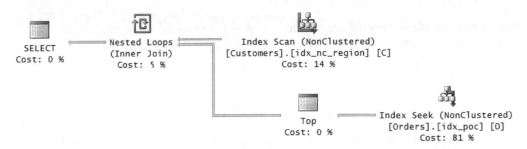

FIGURE 3-14 Plan for a query with the CROSS APPLY operator.

In this example, the inner query is quite simple, so it's no big deal to embed it directly. But in cases where the inner query is more complex, you would probably want to encapsulate it in an inline TVF, like so:

```
IF OBJECT_ID(N'dbo.GetTopOrders', N'IF') IS NOT NULL DROP FUNCTION dbo.GetTopOrders;
GO
CREATE FUNCTION dbo.GetTopOrders(@custid AS INT, @n AS BIGINT)
  RETURNS TABLE
AS
RETURN
  SELECT TOP (@n) orderid, orderdate, empid
  FROM Sales.Orders
  WHERE custid = @custid
  ORDER BY orderdate DESC, orderid DESC;
GO
```

Then you can replace the correlated table expression with a call to the function, passing *C.custid* as the input customer ID (the correlation) and 3 as the number of rows to filter per customer, like so:

```
SELECT C.custid, A.orderid, A.orderdate, A.empid
FROM Sales.Customers AS C
  CROSS APPLY dbo.GetTopOrders( C.custid, 3 ) AS A;
```

You can find a more extensive coverage of efficient handling of the *top N per group* task in Chapter 5.

The OUTER APPLY operator

The CROSS APPLY operator has something in common with an inner join in that left rows that don't have matches on the right side are discarded. So, in the previous query, customers who didn't place orders were discarded. Similar to a left outer join operator, which preserves all left rows, there's an OUTER APPLY operator that preserves all left rows. Like with an outer join, the OUTER APPLY operator uses NULLs as placeholders for nonmatches on the right side.

As an example, to alter the last query to preserve all customers, replace CROSS APPLY with OUTER APPLY, like so:

```
SELECT C.custid, A.orderid, A.orderdate, A.empid
FROM Sales.Customers AS C
  OUTER APPLY dbo.GetTopOrders( C.custid, 3 ) AS A;
```

This time, the output includes customers who didn't place orders:

```
custid      orderid     orderdate   empid
----------- ----------- ----------- -----------
1           11011       2015-04-09  3
1           10952       2015-03-16  1
1           10835       2015-01-15  1
2           10926       2015-03-04  4
2           10759       2014-11-28  3
2           10625       2014-08-08  3
...
22          NULL        NULL        NULL
...
57          NULL        NULL        NULL
58          11073       2015-05-05  2
58          10995       2015-04-02  1
58          10502       2014-04-10  2
...
```

As mentioned, standard SQL's parallel to the T-SQL-specific APPLY operator is called a *lateral derived table*. I described the parallel to the CROSS APPLY operator in the previous section. As for the parallel to OUTER APPLY, what in T-SQL is expressed as *T1 OUTER APPLY (SELECT ... FROM T2 WHERE T2.col1 = T1.col1) AS Q*, in standard SQL is expressed as *T1 LEFT OUTER JOIN LATERAL (SELECT ... FROM T2 WHERE T2.col1 = T1.col1) AS Q ON 1 = 1*.

Implicit APPLY

The documented variations of the APPLY operator are the aforementioned CROSS APPLY and OUTER APPLY ones. There is another variation that involves doing something similar to what you do with the explicit APPLY operator, but without using the APPLY keyword in your code. I refer to this variation as *implicit APPLY*. An implicit APPLY involves using a subquery and, within it, querying a table function to which you pass columns from the outer table as inputs. This is probably best explained through an example.

Consider the *GetTopOrders* function you used in the previous sections to return the requested number of most recent orders for the requested customer. Suppose you want to compute for each customer from the Customers table the distinct count of employees who handled the customer's 10 most recent orders. You want to reuse the logic encapsulated in the *GetTopOrders* function, so you do the following: you query the Customers table; you use a subquery to apply the function to the outer customer to return its 10 most recent orders; finally, you compute the distinct count of employees who handled those orders. Here's the implementation of this logic in T-SQL:

```
SELECT C.custid,
  ( SELECT COUNT(DISTINCT empid) FROM dbo.GetTopOrders( C.custid, 10 ) ) AS numemps
FROM Sales.Customers AS C;
```

Notice that nowhere does the code mention the APPLY keyword explicitly, but clearly the code in the subquery applies the table function to each outer customer. This code generates the following output:

```
custid       numemps
-----------  -----------
1            4
2            3
3            4
4            4
5            6
6            5
7            6
8            2
9            7
11           7
...
```

It's easy to see why the term *implicit APPLY* is appropriate here. Interestingly, before the explicit APPLY operator was added to SQL Server, you couldn't use the implicit APPLY functionality, either. In other words, the implicit functionality was added thanks to the addition of the explicit operator.

Reuse of column aliases

As discussed in Chapter 1, one of the annoying things about SQL is that if you define a column alias in the SELECT clause of a query, you're not allowed to refer to it in most query clauses. The only exception is the ORDER BY clause because it's the only clause that is logically evaluated after the SELECT clause.

There is an elegant trick you can do when using the APPLY operator that solves the problem. Remember that APPLY is a table operator, and table operators are evaluated in the FROM clause of the query. Because the FROM clause is the first clause to be evaluated logically, any aliases you create in it become visible to the rest of the query clauses. Furthermore, because each table operator starts a new series of logical query-processing steps, aliases defined by one table operator are visible to subsequent table operators.

With this in mind, using the APPLY operator you can apply a derived table that defines aliases for expressions based on columns from the left table. The derived table can be based on a SELECT query without a FROM clause, or the VALUES clause, like so:

```
FROM T1 APPLY ( VALUES(<expressions_based_on_columns_in_T1>) ) AS A(<aliases>)
```

As an example, consider the following query:

```
SELECT orderid, orderdate
FROM Sales.Orders
  CROSS APPLY ( VALUES( YEAR(orderdate) ) ) AS A1(orderyear)
  CROSS APPLY ( VALUES( DATEFROMPARTS(orderyear,  1,  1),
                        DATEFROMPARTS(orderyear, 12, 31) )
            ) AS A2(beginningofyear, endofyear)
WHERE orderdate IN (beginningofyear, endofyear);
```

This query is issued against the Orders table. It is supposed to return only orders placed at the beginning or end of the year. The query uses one CROSS APPLY operator to define the alias *orderyear* for the expression *YEAR(orderdate)*. It then uses a second CROSS APPLY operator to define the aliases *beginningofyear* and *endofyear* for the expressions *DATEFROMPARTS(orderyear, 1, 1)* and *DATEFROMPARTS(orderyear, 12, 31)*, respectively. The query then filters only the rows where the *orderdate* value is equal to either the *beginningofyear* value or the *endofyear* value.

This query generates the following output:

```
orderid      orderdate
-----------  ----------
10399        2013-12-31
10400        2014-01-01
10401        2014-01-01
10806        2014-12-31
10807        2014-12-31
10808        2015-01-01
10809        2015-01-01
10810        2015-01-01
```

From an optimization perspective, this trick doesn't have a negative performance impact because the expressions in the derived tables get inlined. Internally, after inlining the expressions, the preceding query becomes equivalent to the following query:

```
SELECT orderid, orderdate
FROM Sales.Orders
WHERE orderdate IN
  (DATEFROMPARTS(YEAR(orderdate),  1,  1), DATEFROMPARTS(YEAR(orderdate), 12, 31));
```

The plans for both queries are the same.

Note that this particular example is pretty simple and is used mainly for illustration purposes. It's so simple that the benefit in reusing column aliases here is questionable. But this trick becomes extremely handy when the computations are much longer and more complex.

As mentioned, you can use the APPLY operator in creative ways to solve a wide variety of problems. You can find examples in the Microsoft Virtual Academy (MVA) seminar "Boost Your T-SQL with the APPLY Operator" here: *http://www.microsoftvirtualacademy.com/training-courses/boost-your-t-sql-with-the-apply-operator.*

When you're done practicing with the APPLY examples, run the following code for cleanup:

```
DROP INDEX idx_poc ON Sales.Orders;
```

Joins

The join is by far the most frequently used type of table operator and one of the most commonly used features in SQL in general. Most queries involve combining data from multiple tables, and one of the main tools used for this purpose is a join.

This section covers the fundamental join types (cross, inner, and outer), self, equi, and nonequi joins. It also covers logical and optimization aspects of multi-join queries, semi joins, and anti semi joins, as well as join algorithms. The section concludes with coverage of a common task called *separating elements* and demonstrates an efficient solution for the task based on joins.

Cross join

Between the three fundamental join types (cross, inner, and outer), the first is the simplest, although it is less commonly used than the others. A cross join produces a Cartesian product of the two input tables. If one table contains *M* rows and the other *N* rows, you get a result with *M* × *N* rows.

In terms of syntax, standard SQL (as well as T-SQL) supports two syntaxes for cross joins. One is an older syntax in which you specify a comma between the table names, like so:

```
SELECT E1.firstname AS firstname1, E1.lastname AS lastname1,
  E2.firstname  AS firstname2, E2.lastname AS lastname2
FROM HR.Employees AS E1, HR.Employees AS E2;
```

Another is a newer syntax that was added in the SQL-92 standard, in which you specify a keyword indicating the join type (CROSS, in our case) followed by the JOIN keyword between the table names, like so:

```
SELECT E1.firstname AS firstname1, E1.lastname AS lastname1,
  E2.firstname  AS firstname2, E2.lastname AS lastname2
FROM HR.Employees AS E1
  CROSS JOIN HR.Employees AS E2;
```

Both syntaxes are standard, and both are supported by T-SQL. There's neither a logical difference nor an optimization difference between the two. You might wonder, then, why did standard SQL bother creating two different syntaxes if they have the same meaning? The reason for this doesn't really have anything to do with cross and inner joins; rather, it is related to outer joins. Recall from the discussions in Chapter 1 that an outer join involves a matching predicate, which has a very different role than a filtering predicate. The former defines only which rows from the nonpreserved side of the join match to rows from the preserved side, but it cannot filter out rows from the preserved side. The latter is used as a basic filter and can certainly discard rows from both sides.

The SQL standards committee decided to add support for outer joins in the SQL-92 standard, but they figured that the traditional comma-based syntax doesn't lend itself to supporting the new type of join. That's because this syntax doesn't allow you to define a matching predicate as part of the join table operator, which as mentioned, is supposed to play a different role than the filtering predicate that you specify in the WHERE clause. So they ended up creating the newer syntax with the JOIN keyword with a designated ON clause where you indicate the matching predicate. This newer syntax with the JOIN keyword is commonly referred to as the *SQL-92 syntax*, and the older comma-based syntax is referred to as the *SQL-89 syntax*.

To allow a consistent coding style for the different types of joins, the SQL-92 standard also added support for a similar JOIN-keyword-based syntax for cross and inner joins. That's the history explaining why you now have two standard syntaxes for cross and inner joins and only one standard syntax for outer joins. It is strongly recommended that you stick to using the JOIN-keyword-based syntax across the board. One reason is that it results in a consistent coding style that is so much easier to maintain than a mixed style. Furthermore, the comma-based syntax is more prone to errors, as I will demonstrate later when discussing inner joins.

I'll demonstrate a couple examples of use cases of cross joins. One is generating sample data, and the other is circumventing an optimization problem related to subqueries.

Suppose you need to generate sample data representing orders. An order has an order ID, was placed on a certain date, was placed by a certain customer, and was handled by a certain employee. You get as inputs the range of order dates as well as the number of distinct customers and employees you need to support. Using the *GetNums* function in the sample database, you can generate sets of dates, customer IDs, and employee IDs. You perform cross joins between those sets to get all possible combinations and, using a ROW_NUMBER function, compute the order IDs, like so:

```
DECLARE @s AS DATE = '20150101', @e AS DATE = '20150131',
  @numcusts AS INT = 50, @numemps AS INT = 10;

SELECT ROW_NUMBER() OVER(ORDER BY (SELECT NULL)) AS orderid,
  DATEADD(day, D.n, @s) AS orderdate, C.n AS custid, E.n AS empid
FROM dbo.GetNums(0, DATEDIFF(day, @s, @e)) AS D
  CROSS JOIN dbo.GetNums(1, @numcusts) AS C
  CROSS JOIN dbo.GetNums(1, @numemps) AS E;
```

The unusual order specification ORDER BY (SELECT NULL) in the ROW_NUMBER function is a trick used to compute row numbers based on an arbitrary order. I use this trick when I need to generate unique values and I don't care about the order in which they are generated.

Note that usually when you generate sample data, you need a more sophisticated solution that results in a more realistic distribution of the data. In reality, you typically don't have even distribution of order dates, customer IDs, and employee IDs. But sometimes you need a very basic form of sample data for certain tests, and this simple technique can be sufficient for you.

Another use case for cross joins has to do with a certain optimization shortcoming in SQL Server related to subqueries. Consider the following query:

```
SELECT orderid, val,
  val / (SELECT SUM(val) FROM Sales.OrderValues) AS pct,
  val - (SELECT AVG(val) FROM Sales.OrderValues) AS diff
FROM Sales.OrderValues;
```

This query is issued against the *OrderValues* view. It returns for each order the percent of the current order value out of the grand total as well as the difference from the grand average. The grand total and grand average are computed by scalar aggregate subqueries. It is true that the query refers to the *OrderValues* view three times, but clearly both subqueries need to operate on the exact same set of values. Unfortunately, currently there's no logic in the optimizer to avoid the duplication of work by collapsing all matching subqueries into one activity that will feed the same set of values to all aggregate calculations. In our case, the problem is even further magnified because *OrderValues* is a view. The view joins the Orders and OrderDetails tables, and it groups and aggregates the data to produce order-level information. All of this work is repeated three times in the execution plan for our query, as you can see in Figure 3-15.

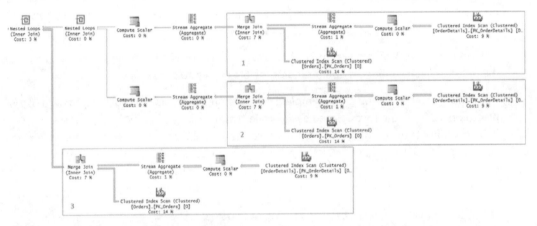

FIGURE 3-15 Work is repeated for every subquery.

The branches marked as *1* and *2* represent the work for the two subqueries feeding the values to the two aggregate calculations. The branch marked as *3* represents the reference to the view in the outer query to obtain the order information—in other words, the detail. As you can imagine, the more aggregates you have, the worse this solution performs. Imagine you had 10 different aggregates to compute. This would require 11 repetitions of the work—10 for the aggregates and one for the detail.

Fortunately, there is a way to avoid the unnecessary repetition of the work. To achieve this, you use one query to compute all aggregates that you need. SQL Server will optimize this query by applying the work only once, feeding the same values to all aggregate calculations. You define a table expression based on that query (call it *Aggs*) and perform a cross join between the *OrderValues* view and *Aggs*. Then, in the SELECT list, you perform all your calculations involving the detail and the aggregates. Here's the complete solution query:

```
SELECT orderid, val,
  val / sumval AS pct,
  val - avgval AS diff
FROM Sales.OrderValues
  CROSS JOIN (SELECT SUM(val) AS sumval, AVG(val) AS avgval
              FROM Sales.OrderValues) AS Aggs;
```

Observe the execution plan for this query shown in Figure 3-16.

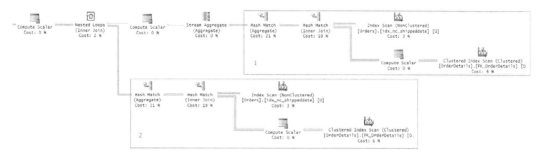

FIGURE 3-16 Avoiding repetition of work with a join.

Notice that this time the work represented by the view happens only once for all aggregates (branch 1) and once for the detail (branch 2). The nice thing with this solution is that it doesn't matter how many aggregates you have—you will still have only one activity that collects the values for all of them.

You will face a similar problem when you need the calculation to be partitioned. For example, suppose that instead of grand aggregates, you need customer aggregates. In other words, you need to compute the percent of the current order value out of the customer total (not the grand total) and the difference from the customer average. Using the subquery approach, you add correlations, like so:

```
SELECT orderid, val,
  val / (SELECT SUM(val) FROM Sales.OrderValues AS I
         WHERE I.custid = O.custid) AS pct,
  val - (SELECT AVG(val) FROM Sales.OrderValues AS I
         WHERE I.custid = O.custid) AS diff
FROM Sales.OrderValues AS O;
```

But again, because you're using subqueries, the work represented by the view will be repeated three times. The solution is similar to the previous one, only instead of using a cross join, you use an inner join and match the customer IDs between the *OrderValues* view and *Aggs*, like so:

```
SELECT orderid, val,
  val / sumval AS pct,
  val - avgval AS diff
FROM Sales.OrderValues AS O
  INNER JOIN (SELECT custid, SUM(val) AS sumval, AVG(val) AS avgval
              FROM Sales.OrderValues
              GROUP BY custid) AS Aggs
  ON O.custid = Aggs.custid;
```

Inner join

From a logical query-processing perspective, an inner join involves two steps. It starts with a Cartesian product between the two input tables, like in a cross join. It then applies a filter that usually involves matching elements from both sides. From a physical query-processing perspective, of course things can be done differently, provided that the output is correct.

Like with cross joins, inner joins currently have two standard syntaxes. One is the SQL-89 syntax, where you specify commas between the table names and then apply all filtering predicates in the WHERE clause, like so:

```
SELECT C.custid, C.companyname, O.orderid
FROM Sales.Customers AS C, Sales.Orders AS O
WHERE C.custid = O.custid
  AND C.country = N'USA';
```

As you can see, the syntax doesn't really distinguish between a cross join and an inner join; rather, it expresses an inner join as a cross join with a filter.

The other syntax is the SQL-92 one, which is more compatible with the standard outer join syntax. You specify the INNER JOIN keywords between the table names (or just JOIN because INNER is the default) and the join predicate in the mandatory ON clause. If you have any additional filters, you can specify them either in the join's ON clause or in the usual WHERE clause, like so:

```
SELECT C.custid, C.companyname, O.orderid
FROM Sales.Customers AS C
  INNER JOIN Sales.Orders AS O
    ON C.custid = O.custid
WHERE C.country = N'USA';
```

Despite the fact that the ON clause is mandatory in the SQL-92 syntax for inner joins, there is no distinction between a matching predicate and a filtering predicate like in outer joins. Both predicates are treated as filtering predicates. So, even though from a logical query-processing perspective, the WHERE clause is supposed to be evaluated after the FROM clause with all of its joins, the optimizer might very well decide to process the predicates from the WHERE clause before it starts processing the joins in the FROM clause. In fact, if you examine the plans for the two queries just shown, you will notice that in both cases the plan starts with a scan of the clustered index on the Customers table and applies the country filter as part of the scan.

I mentioned earlier that it's recommended to stick to the SQL-92 syntax for joins and avoid the SQL-89 syntax even though it's standard for cross and inner joins. I already provided one reason for this recommendation—using one consistent style for all types of joins. Another reason is that the SQL-89 syntax is more prone to errors; specifically, it is more likely you will miss a join predicate and for such a mistake to go unnoticed. With the SQL-92 syntax, you usually specify each join predicate right after the respective join, like so:

```
FROM T1
  INNER JOIN T2
    ON T2.col1 = T1.col1
```

```
INNER JOIN T3
  ON T3.col2 = T2.col2
INNER JOIN T4
  ON T4.col3 = T3.col3
```

With this syntax, the likelihood that you will miss a join predicate is low, and even if you do, the parser will generate an error because the ON clause is mandatory with inner (and outer) joins. Conversely, with the SQL-89 syntax, you specify all table names separated by commas in the FROM clause, and all predicates as a conjunction in the WHERE clause, like so:

```
FROM T1, T2, T3, T4
WHERE T2.col1 = T1.col1 AND T3.col2 = T2.col2 AND T4.col3 = T3.col3
```

Clearly the likelihood that you will miss a predicate by mistake is higher, and if you do, you end up with an unintentional cross join.

A common question I get is whether there's a difference between using the keywords INNER JOIN and just JOIN. There's none. Standard SQL made inner joins the default because it's probably the most commonly used type of join. In a similar way, standard SQL made the keyword OUTER optional in outer joins. For example, LEFT OUTER JOIN and LEFT JOIN are equivalent. As for what's recommended to use, some prefer the full syntax finding it to be clearer. Others prefer the missing syntax because it results in shorter code. I think that what's more important than whether to use the full or missing syntax is to be consistent between the members of the development team. When different people use different styles, it can be hard to maintain each other's code. A good idea is to have meetings to discuss styling choices like full versus missing syntax, indentation, casing, and so on, and to come up with a coding style document that everyone must follow. Sometimes people have strong opinions about certain styling aspects based on their personal preferences, so when conflicts arise you can vote to determine which option will prevail. Once everyone starts using a consistent style, it becomes so much easier for different people to maintain the same code.

Outer join

From a logical query-processing perspective, outer joins start with the same two steps as inner joins. But in addition, they have a third logical step that ensures that all rows from the table or tables that you mark as preserved are returned, even if they don't have any matches in the other table based on the join predicate. Using the keywords LEFT (or LEFT OUTER), RIGHT, or FULL, you mark the left table, right table, or both tables as preserved. Output rows representing nonmatches (aka outer rows) have NULLs used as placeholders in the nonpreserved side's columns.

As an example, the following query returns customers and their orders, including customers with no orders:

```
SELECT C.custid, C.companyname, C.country,
  O.orderid, O.shipcountry
FROM Sales.Customers AS C
  LEFT OUTER JOIN Sales.Orders AS O
    ON C.custid = O.custid;
```

In outer joins, the role of the predicate in the ON clause is different than in inner joins. With the latter, it serves as a simple filtering tool, whereas with the former it serves as a more sophisticated matching tool. All rows from the preserved side will be returned whether they find matching rows based on the predicate or not. If you need any simple filters to be applied, you specify those in the WHERE clause. For example, a classic way to identify only nonmatches is to use an outer join and add a WHERE clause that filters only the rows that have a NULL in a column from the nonpreserved side that doesn't allow NULLs normally. The primary key column is a good choice for this purpose. For example, the following query returns only customers who didn't place orders:

```
SELECT C.custid, C.companyname, O.orderid
FROM Sales.Customers AS C
  LEFT OUTER JOIN Sales.Orders AS O
    ON C.custid = O.custid
WHERE O.orderid IS NULL;
```

It's far more common to see people using left outer joins than right outer ones. It could be because most people tend to specify referenced tables before referencing ones in the query, and usually the referenced table is the one that can have rows with no matches in the referencing one. It's true that in a single join case such as T1 LEFT OUTER JOIN T2 you can express the same thing with a symmetric T2 RIGHT OUTER JOIN T1. However, in certain more complex cases with multiple joins involved, you will find that using a right outer join enables a simpler solution than using left outer joins. I'll demonstrate such a case shortly in the "Multi-join queries" section.

Self join

A *self join* is a join between multiple instances of the same table. As an example, the following query matches employees with their managers, who are also employees:

```
SELECT E.firstname + ' ' + E.lastname AS emp, M.firstname + ' ' + M.lastname AS mgr
FROM HR.Employees AS E
  LEFT OUTER JOIN HR.Employees AS M
    ON E.mgrid = M.empid;
```

What's special about self joins is that it's mandatory to alias the instances of the table differently; otherwise, you end up with duplicate column names, including the table prefixes.

From an optimization perspective, the optimizer looks at the two instances as two different tables. For example, it can use different indexes for each of the instances. In the query plan, you can identify in each physical object that is accessed which instance it represents based on the table alias you assigned to it.

Equi and non-equi joins

The terms *equi joins* and *non-equi joins* refer to the kind of operator you use in the join predicate. When you use an equality operator, like in the vast majority of the queries, the join is referred to as an equi join. When you use an operator other than equality, the join is referred to as a non-equi join.

As an example, the following query uses a non-equi join with a less than (<) operator to identify unique pairs of employees:

```
SELECT E1.empid, E1.lastname, E1.firstname, E2.empid, E2.lastname, E2.firstname
FROM HR.Employees AS E1
  INNER JOIN HR.Employees AS E2
    ON E1.empid < E2.empid;
```

If you're wondering why you should use a non-equi join here rather than a cross join, that's because you don't want to get the self-pairs (same employee *x, x* on both sides) and you don't want to get mirrored pairs (*x, y* and also *y, x*). If you want to produce unique triples, simply add another non-equi join to a third instance of the table (call it *E3*), with the join predicate *E2.empid < E3.empid*.

From an optimization perspective, there's relevance to identifying the join as an equi or non-equi one. Later, the chapter covers the optimization of joins with the join algorithms nested loop, merge, and hash. Nested loops is the only algorithm supported with non-equi joins. Merge and hash require an equi-join or, more precisely, at least one predicate that is based on an equality operator.

Multi-join queries

Multi-join queries are queries with multiple joins (what a surprise). There are a number of interesting considerations concerning such queries, some optimization related and others related to the logical treatment.

As an example, the following query joins five tables to return customer-supplier pairs that had activity together:

```
SELECT DISTINCT C.companyname AS customer, S.companyname AS supplier
FROM Sales.Customers AS C
  INNER JOIN Sales.Orders AS O
    ON O.custid = C.custid
  INNER JOIN Sales.OrderDetails AS OD
    ON OD.orderid = O.orderid
  INNER JOIN Production.Products AS P
    ON P.productid = OD.productid
  INNER JOIN Production.Suppliers AS S
    ON S.supplierid = P.supplierid;
```

The customer company name is obtained from the Customers table. The Customers table is joined with the Orders table to find the headers of the orders that the customers placed. The result is joined with OrderDetails to find the order lines within those orders. The order lines contain the IDs of the products that were ordered. The result is joined with Products, where the IDs of the suppliers of those products are found. Finally, the result is joined with Suppliers to get the supplier company name.

Because the same customer-supplier pair can appear more than once in the result, the query has a DISTINCT clause to eliminate duplicates. Here there was a good reason to use DISTINCT. Note, however, that if you see excessive use of DISTINCT in someone's join queries, it could indicate that they don't correctly understand the relationships in the data model. When joining tables based on incorrect relationships, you can end up with duplicates, and the use of DISTINCT in such a case could be an attempt to hide those.

The following sections discuss aspects of the physical and logical processing of this query.

Controlling the physical-join evaluation order

When discussing logical query processing in Chapter 1, I explained that table operators are evaluated from left to right. That's the case from a logical-processing standpoint. However, from a physical-processing standpoint, under certain conditions the order can be altered without changing the meaning of the query. With outer joins, changing the order can change the meaning, and this is something the optimizer isn't allowed to do. But with inner and cross joins, changing the order doesn't change the meaning. So, with those, the optimizer will apply join-ordering optimization. It will explore different join orders and pick the one from those that according to its estimates is supposed to be the fastest.

As an example, our multi-join query got the plan in Figure 3-17, showing that the physical join order is different than the logical one.

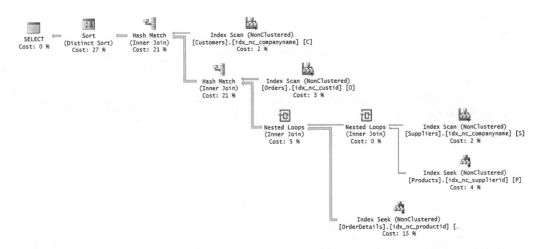

FIGURE 3-17 Plan for a multi-join query.

Observe the order in the plan is as follows: Customers join (Orders join ((Suppliers join Products) join OrderDetails)). For illustration purposes, the following query applies logical join ordering that reflects the physical ordering in Figure 3-17:

```
SELECT DISTINCT C.companyname AS customer, S.companyname AS supplier
FROM Sales.Customers AS C
  INNER JOIN ( Sales.Orders AS O
                INNER JOIN ( Production.Suppliers AS S
                              INNER JOIN Production.Products AS P
                                ON P.supplierid = S.supplierid
                              INNER JOIN Sales.OrderDetails AS OD
                                ON OD.productid = P.productid )
                        ON OD.orderid = O.orderid )
    ON O.custid = C.custid;
```

There are a number of reasons that could lead the optimizer to choose a suboptimal join order. Like with other suboptimal choices, join ordering choices can be affected by inaccurate cardinality estimates.

Furthermore, the theoretical number of possible join orders, or join trees, can be very large even with a small number of tables. Benjamin Nevarez explains this in "Optimizing Join Orders" here: *http://www.benjaminnevarez.com/2010/06/optimizing-join-orders/*. With N tables, the number of possible trees is *(2N – 2)! / (N – 1)!*, where *!* is factorial. As an example, in our case we have 5 tables resulting in 1,680 possible trees. With 10 tables, the number is 17,643,225,600! Here the ! is for amazement, not to represent factorial, thank goodness. As you might realize, if the optimizer actually tried to explore all possible join trees, the optimization process would take too long and become counterproductive. So the optimizer does a number of things to reduce the optimization time. It computes cost-based and time-based thresholds based on the sizes of the tables involved, and if one of them is reached, optimization stops. The optimizer also normally doesn't consider bushy join trees, where results of joins are joined; such trees represent the majority of the trees. What all this means is that the optimizer might not come up with the truly optimal join order.

If you suspect that's the case and want to force the optimizer to use a certain order, you can do so by typing the joins in the order you think is optimal and adding the FORCE ORDER query hint, like so:

```
SELECT DISTINCT C.companyname AS customer, S.companyname AS supplier
FROM Sales.Customers AS C
  INNER JOIN Sales.Orders AS O
    ON O.custid = C.custid
  INNER JOIN Sales.OrderDetails AS OD
    ON OD.orderid = O.orderid
  INNER JOIN Production.Products AS P
    ON P.productid = OD.productid
  INNER JOIN Production.Suppliers AS S
    ON S.supplierid = P.supplierid
OPTION (FORCE ORDER);
```

This hint is certainly good as a troubleshooting tool because you can use it to test the performance of different orders and see if the optimizer, indeed, made a suboptimal choice. The problem with using such a hint in production code is that it makes this part of optimization static. Normally, changes in indexing, data characteristics, and other factors can result in a change in the optimizer's join ordering choice, but obviously not when the hint is used. So the hint is good to use as a troubleshooting tool and sometimes as a short, temporary solution in production in critical cases. However, it's usually not good to use as a long-term solution. For example, suppose the cause for the suboptimal join-ordering choice was a bad cardinality estimate. When you have the time to do more thorough research of the problem, I hope you can find ways to help the optimizer come up with more accurate estimates that naturally lead to a more optimal plan.

Controlling the logical-join evaluation order

You just saw how to control physical join ordering. There are also cases where you need to control logical join ordering to achieve a certain change in the meaning of the query. As an example, consider the query that returns customer-supplier pairs from the previous section:

```
SELECT DISTINCT C.companyname AS customer, S.companyname AS supplier
FROM Sales.Customers AS C
  INNER JOIN Sales.Orders AS O
    ON O.custid = C.custid
  INNER JOIN Sales.OrderDetails AS OD
    ON OD.orderid = O.orderid
  INNER JOIN Production.Products AS P
    ON P.productid = OD.productid
  INNER JOIN Production.Suppliers AS S
    ON S.supplierid = P.supplierid;
```

This query returns 1,236 rows. All joins in the query are inner joins. This means that customers who didn't place any orders aren't returned. There are two such customers in our sample data. Suppose you need to change the solution to include customers without orders. The intuitive thing to do is change the type of join between Customers and Orders to a left outer join, like so:

```
SELECT DISTINCT C.companyname AS customer, S.companyname AS supplier
FROM Sales.Customers AS C
  LEFT OUTER JOIN Sales.Orders AS O
    ON O.custid = C.custid
  INNER JOIN Sales.OrderDetails AS OD
    ON OD.orderid = O.orderid
  INNER JOIN Production.Products AS P
    ON P.productid = OD.productid
  INNER JOIN Production.Suppliers AS S
    ON S.supplierid = P.supplierid;
```

However, if you run the query, you will notice that it still returns the same result as before. Logically, the left outer join between Customers and Orders returns the two customers who didn't place orders with NULLs in the order attributes. Then when joining the result with OrderDetails using an inner join, those outer rows are eliminated. That's because when comparing the NULL marks in the *O.orderid* column in those rows with any *OD.orderid* value, the result is the logical value *unknown*. You can generalize this case and say that any left outer join that is subsequently followed by an inner join or a right outer join causes the left outer join to effectively become an inner join. That's assuming that you compare the NULL elements from the nonpreserved side of the left outer join with elements from another table. In fact, if you look at the execution plan of the query, you will notice that, indeed, the optimizer converted the left outer join to an inner join.

A common way for people to attempt to solve the problem is to make all joins left outer joins, like so:

```
SELECT DISTINCT C.companyname AS customer, S.companyname AS supplier
FROM Sales.Customers AS C
  LEFT OUTER JOIN Sales.Orders AS O
    ON O.custid = C.custid
```

```
    LEFT OUTER JOIN Sales.OrderDetails AS OD
      ON OD.orderid = O.orderid
    LEFT OUTER JOIN Production.Products AS P
      ON P.productid = OD.productid
    LEFT OUTER JOIN Production.Suppliers AS S
      ON S.supplierid = P.supplierid;
```

There are two problems with this solution. One problem is that you actually changed the meaning of the query from the intended one. You were after a left outer join between Customers and the result of the inner joins between the remaining tables. Rows without matches in the remaining tables aren't supposed to be preserved; however, with this solution, if they are left rows, they will be preserved. The other problem is that the optimizer has less flexibility in altering the join order when dealing with outer joins. Pretty much the only flexibility that it does have is to change T1 LEFT OUTER JOIN T2 to T2 RIGHT OUTER JOIN T1.

A better solution is to start with the inner joins between the tables besides Customers and then to apply a right outer join with Customers, like so:

```
SELECT DISTINCT C.companyname AS customer, S.companyname AS supplier
FROM Sales.Orders AS O
  INNER JOIN Sales.OrderDetails AS OD
    ON OD.orderid = O.orderid
  INNER JOIN Production.Products AS P
    ON P.productid = OD.productid
  INNER JOIN Production.Suppliers AS S
    ON S.supplierid = P.supplierid
  RIGHT OUTER JOIN Sales.Customers AS C
    ON C.custid = O.custid;
```

Now the solution is both semantically correct and leaves more flexibility to the optimizer to apply join-ordering optimization. This query returns 1,238 rows, which include the two customers who didn't place orders.

There's an even more elegant solution that allows you to express the joins in a manner similar to the way you think of the task. Remember you want to apply a left outer join between Customers and a unit representing the result of the inner joins between the remaining tables. To define such a unit, simply enclose the inner joins in parentheses and move the join predicate that relates Customers and that unit after the parentheses, like so:

```
SELECT DISTINCT C.companyname AS customer, S.companyname AS supplier
FROM Sales.Customers AS C
  LEFT OUTER JOIN
      (     Sales.Orders AS O
      INNER JOIN Sales.OrderDetails AS OD
        ON OD.orderid = O.orderid
      INNER JOIN Production.Products AS P
        ON P.productid = OD.productid
      INNER JOIN Production.Suppliers AS S
        ON S.supplierid = P.supplierid)
    ON O.custid = C.custid;
```

Curiously, the parentheses are not really required. If you remove them and run the code, you will see it runs successfully and returns the correct result. What really makes the difference is the parentheses-like arrangement of the units and the placement of the ON clauses reflecting this arrangement. Simply make sure that the ON clause that is supposed to relate two units appears right after them; otherwise, the query will not be a valid one. With this in mind, following is another valid arrangement of the units, achieving the desired result for our task:

```
SELECT DISTINCT C.companyname AS customer, S.companyname AS supplier
FROM Sales.Customers AS C
  LEFT OUTER JOIN Sales.Orders AS O
  INNER JOIN Sales.OrderDetails AS OD
  INNER JOIN Production.Products AS P
  INNER JOIN Production.Suppliers AS S
    ON S.supplierid = P.supplierid
    ON P.productid = OD.productid
    ON OD.orderid = O.orderid
    ON O.custid = C.custid;
```

I find that using parentheses accompanied with adequate indentation results in much clearer code, so I recommend using them even though they are not required.

Earlier I mentioned that one of the heuristics the optimizer uses to reduce optimization time is to not consider bushy plans that involve joins between results of joins. If you suspect that such a bushy plan is the most efficient and want the optimizer to use it, you need to force it. The way you achieve this is by defining two units, each based on a join with the respective ON clause, followed by an ON clause that relates the two units. You also need to specify the FORCE ORDER query option.

Following is an example of forcing such a bushy plan:

```
SELECT DISTINCT C.companyname AS customer, S.companyname AS supplier
FROM Sales.Customers AS C
  INNER JOIN
        (Sales.Orders AS O INNER JOIN Sales.OrderDetails AS OD
          ON OD.orderid = O.orderid)
      INNER JOIN
        (Production.Products AS P INNER JOIN Production.Suppliers AS S
          ON S.supplierid = P.supplierid)
        ON P.productid = OD.productid
    ON O.custid = C.custid
OPTION (FORCE ORDER);
```

Here you have one unit (call it *U1*) based on a join between Orders and OrderDetails. You have another unit (call it *U2*) based on a join between Products and Suppliers. Then you have a join between the two units (call the result *U1-2*). Then you have a join between Customers and U1-2. The execution plan for this query is shown in Figure 3-18.

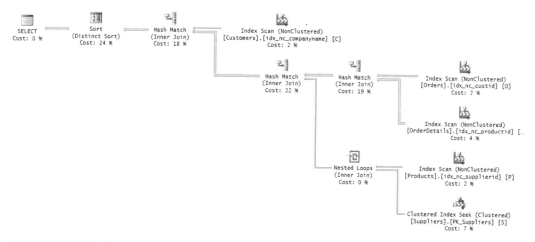

FIGURE 3-18 Bushy plan.

Observe that the desired bushy layout was achieved in the plan.

Semi and anti semi joins

Normally, a join matches rows from two tables and returns elements from both sides. What makes a join a *semi join* is that you return elements from only one of the sides. The side you return the elements from determines whether it's a left or right semi join.

As an example, consider a request to return the customer ID and company name of customers who placed orders. You return information only from the Customers table, provided that a matching row is found in the Orders table. Considering the Customers table as the left table, the operation is a left semi join. There are a number of ways to implement the task. One is to use an inner join and apply a DISTINCT clause to remove duplicate customer info, like so:

```
SELECT DISTINCT C.custid, C.companyname
FROM Sales.Customers AS C
  INNER JOIN Sales.Orders AS O
    ON O.custid = C.custid;
```

Another is to use the EXISTS predicate, like so:

```
SELECT custid, companyname
FROM Sales.Customers AS C
WHERE EXISTS(SELECT *
             FROM Sales.Orders AS O
             WHERE O.custid = C.custid);
```

Both queries get the same plan. Of course, there are more ways to achieve the task.

An anti semi join is one in which you return elements from one table if a matching row cannot be found in a related table. Also here, depending on whether you return information from the left table or the right one, the join is either a left or right anti semi join. As an example, a request to return customers who did not place orders is fulfilled with a left anti semi join operation.

There are a number of classic ways to achieve such an anti semi join. One is to use a left outer join between Customers and Orders and filter only outer rows, like so:

```
SELECT C.custid, C.companyname
FROM Sales.Customers AS C
  LEFT OUTER JOIN Sales.Orders AS O
    ON O.custid = C.custid
WHERE O.orderid IS NULL;
```

Another is to use the NOT EXISTS predicate, like so:

```
SELECT custid, companyname
FROM Sales.Customers AS C
WHERE NOT EXISTS(SELECT *
                 FROM Sales.Orders AS O
                 WHERE O.custid = C.custid);
```

Curiously, it appears that currently the optimizer doesn't have logic to detect the outer join solution as actually applying an anti semi join, but it does with the NOT EXISTS solution. This can be seen in the execution plans for these queries shown in Figure 3-19.

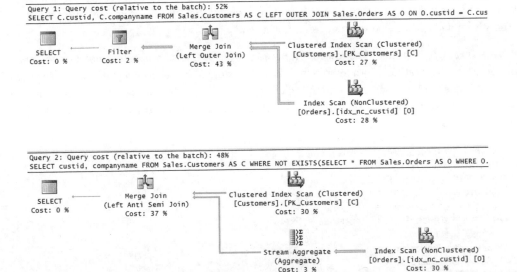

FIGURE 3-19 Plans for anti semi join solutions.

Of course, there are a number of additional ways to implement anti semi joins. The ones I showed are two classic ones.

Join algorithms

Join algorithms are the physical join strategies SQL Server uses to process joins. SQL Server supports three join algorithms: nested loops, merge, and hash. Nested loops is the oldest of the three algorithms and the fallback when the others can't be used. For example, cross join can be processed only with nested loops. Merge and hash require the join to be an equi join or, more precisely, to have at least one join predicate that is based on an equality operator.

In the graphical query plan, the join operator has a distinct icon for each algorithm. In addition, the Physical Operation property indicates the join algorithm (Nested Loops, Hash Match, or Merge Join), and the Logical Operation property indicates the logical join type (Inner Join, Left Outer Join, Left Anti Semi Join, and so on). Also, the physical algorithm name appears right below the operator, and the logical join type appears below the algorithm name in parentheses.

The following sections describe the individual join algorithms, the circumstances in which they tend to be efficient, and indexing guidelines to support them.

Nested loops

The nested loops algorithm is pretty straightforward. It executes the outer (top) input only once and, using a loop, it executes the inner (bottom) input for each row from the outer input to identify matches.

Nested loops tends to perform well when the outer input is small and the inner input has an index with the key list based on the join column plus any additional filtered columns, if relevant. Whether it's critical for the index to be a covering one depends on how many matches you get in total. If the total number of matches is small, a few lookups are not too expensive and therefore the index doesn't have to be a covering one. If the number of matches is large, the lookups become expensive, and then it becomes more critical to avoid them by making the index a covering one.

As an example, consider the following query:

```
USE PerformanceV3;

SELECT C.custid, C.custname, O.orderid, O.empid, O.shipperid, O.orderdate
FROM dbo.Customers AS C
  INNER JOIN dbo.Orders AS O
    ON O.custid = C.custid
WHERE C.custname LIKE 'Cust_1000%'
  AND O.orderdate >= '20140101'
  AND O.orderdate < '20140401';
```

Currently, the tables don't have good indexing to support an efficient nested loops join. Because the smaller side (Customers, in our case) is usually used as the outer input and is executed only once, it's not that critical to support it with a good index. In the worst case, the small table gets fully scanned. The far more critical index here is on the bigger side (Orders, in our case). Nevertheless, if you want to avoid a full scan of the Customers table, you can prepare an index on the filtered column *custname* as the key and include the *custid* column for coverage. As for the ideal index on the Orders table, think of the work involved in a single iteration of the loop for some customer *X*. It's like submitting the following query:

```
SELECT orderid, empid, shipperid, orderdate
FROM dbo.Orders
WHERE custid = X
  AND orderdate >= '20140101'
  AND orderdate < '20140401';
```

Because you have one equality predicate and one range predicate, it's quite straightforward to come up with an ideal index here. You define the index with the key list based on *custid* and *orderdate*, and you include the remaining columns (*orderid, empid,* and *shipperid*) for coverage. Remember the discussions about multiple range predicates in Chapter 2? When you have both an equality predicate and a range predicate, you need to define the index key list with the equality column first. This way, qualifying rows will appear in a consecutive range in the index leaf. That's not going to be the case if you define the key list with the range column first.

Run the following code to create optimal indexing for our query:

```
CREATE INDEX idx_nc_cn_i_cid ON dbo.Customers(custname) INCLUDE(custid);

CREATE INDEX idx_nc_cid_od_i_oid_eid_sid
  ON dbo.Orders(custid, orderdate) INCLUDE(orderid, empid, shipperid);
```

Now run the query and examine the query plan shown in Figure 3-20.

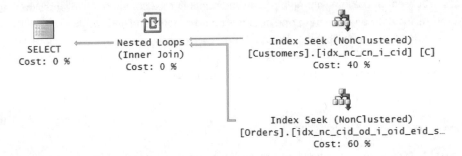

FIGURE 3-20 Plan with a nested loops algorithm.

As you can see, the optimizer chose to use the nested loops algorithm with the smaller table, Customers, as the outer input and the bigger table, Orders, as the inner input. The plan performs a seek and a range scan in the covering index on Customers to retrieve qualifying customers. (There are 11 in our case.) Then, using a loop, the plan performs for each customer a seek and a range scan in the covering index on Orders to retrieve matching orders for the current customer. There are 30 matching orders in total.

Next, I'll discuss the effects that different changes to the query will have on its optimization.

As mentioned, if you have a small number of matches in total, it's not that critical for the index on the inner table to be a covering one. You can test such a case by adding *O.filler* to the query's SELECT list. The plan will still use the nested loops algorithm, but it will add key lookups to retrieve the column *filler* from the clustered index because it's not part of the index idx_nc_cid_od_i_oid_eid_sid. When you're done testing, make sure you remove the column *O.filler* from the query before applying the next change.

When enough rows are returned from the outer input, the optimizer usually applies a prefetch (a read-ahead) to speed up the executions of inner input. Usually, the optimizer considers a prefetch when it estimates that more than a couple of dozen rows will be returned from the outer input. The plan for our current query doesn't involve a prefetch because the optimizer estimates that only a few rows will be returned from Customers. But if you change the query filter against Customers from *C.custname LIKE 'Cust_1000%'* to *C.custname LIKE 'Cust_100%'*, it will use a prefetch. After applying the change, you will find that the Nested Loops operator has a property called *WithUnordered-Prefetch*, which is set to *True*. The reason it's an unordered prefetch is that there's no relevance to returning the rows sorted by the customer IDs. If you add *ORDER BY custid* to the query, the property will change to *WithOrderedPrefetch*. When you're done testing, make sure to revert back to the original query before applying the next change.

I mentioned that the Nested Loops operator is usually efficient when the outer input is small. Change the filter against Customers to *C.custname LIKE 'Cust_10%'*. Now the estimated number of matches from Customers increases from just a few to over a thousand, and the optimizer changes its choice of the join algorithm to hash.

There's an interesting technique the optimizer can use when the plan is a parallel one but there are only a few outer rows. In such a case, without optimizer intervention the work could be unevenly distributed to the different threads. Therefore, when the optimizer detects a case of a few outer rows, it adds a Redistribute Streams operator after obtaining the rows from the outer input. This operator redistributes the rows between the threads more evenly.

Merge

The merge algorithm requires both inputs to be sorted by the join column. It then merges the two like a zipper. If the join is a one-to-many one, as is likely to be the case in most queries, there's only one pass over each input. If the join type is a many-to-many one, one input is scanned once and the other involves rewinds.

Generally, there are two ways for the optimizer to get a sorted input. If the data is already sorted in an index, the optimizer can use an index order scan. The other way is by adding an explicit sort operation to the plan, but then there's the extra cost that is associated with sorting.

Consider the following query as an example of obtaining sorted data from indexes:

```
SELECT C.custid, C.custname, O.orderid, O.empid, O.shipperid, O.orderdate
FROM dbo.Customers AS C
  INNER JOIN dbo.Orders AS O
    ON O.custid = C.custid;
```

The PK_Customers index on the Customers table is a clustered index defined on *custid* as the key. So the data from Customers is covered by the index and sorted like the merge join algorithm requires.

The nonclustered index idx_nc_cid_od_i_oid_eid_sid on Orders that you created for the example in the "Nested loops" section is quite efficient for a merge join. It has the data sorted by *custid* as the leading key, and it covers the elements in the query from Orders. The conditions are optimal for a merge join algorithm; therefore, the optimizer uses this strategy, as you can see in the plan for our query shown in Figure 3-21.

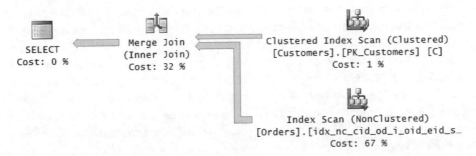

FIGURE 3-21 Plan with a merge algorithm.

As an example for a merge join involving explicit sorting, consider the following query:

```
SELECT C.custid, C.custname, O.orderid, O.empid, O.shipperid, O.orderdate
FROM dbo.Customers AS C
  INNER JOIN dbo.Orders AS O
    ON O.custid = C.custid
WHERE O.orderdate >= '20140101'
  AND O.orderdate < '20140102';
```

The data can be obtained sorted by *custid* from the clustered index on the Customers table. However, with the extra range filter against Orders, it's impossible to create an index that sorts the data primarily by both *orderdate* to support the filter and *custid* to support a merge join. Still, the date range filter is selective—there are only a few hundred qualifying rows. Furthermore, the clustered index on Orders is defined with *orderdate* as the key. So the optimizer figures that it can use a seek and a range scan against the clustered index on Orders to retrieve the qualifying orders, and then with an explicit sort operation order the rows by *custid*. With a small number of rows, the cost of sorting is quite low. The plan for our query, indeed, implements this strategy as you can see in Figure 3-22.

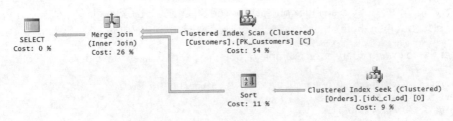

FIGURE 3-22 Plan with a sort operator and merge algorithm.

Observe the small cost percent associated with the sort operation.

Note that such a plan is sensitive to inaccuracies in the cardinality estimate of the activity leading to the Sort operator. That's especially the case when the estimate is for a small number of rows but the actual is a large number, because sorting doesn't scale well. For one, a more accurate estimate could lead the optimizer to use a different join algorithm altogether. For two, the low estimate could result in an insufficient memory grant for the sort activity, and this could result in spills to tempdb. You need to be attentive to such problems and, if you spot one, try to figure out ways to help the optimizer come up with a more accurate estimate.

Hash

The hash algorithm involves the creation of a hash table based on one of the inputs—usually the smaller. The reason that the small side is preferred as the build input is that the memory footprint is usually smaller this way. If the hash table fits in memory, it's ideal. If not, the hash table can be partitioned, but the swapping of partitions in and out of memory makes the algorithm less efficient. The items from the build input are arranged in hash buckets based on the chosen hash function. For illustration purposes, suppose that the join column is an integer one and the optimizer chooses a modulo 50 function as the hash function. Up to 50 hash buckets will be created, with all items that got the same result from the hash function organized in a linked list in the same bucket. Then the other input (known as the *probe input*) is probed, the hash function is applied to the join column values, and based on the result, the algorithm scans the respective hash bucket to look for matches.

The hash algorithm excels in data-warehouse queries, which tend to involve large amounts of data in the fact table and much smaller dimension tables. It tends to scale well with such queries, benefiting greatly from parallelized processing. Note, though, that the hash table requires a memory grant, and hence this algorithm is sensitive to inaccuracies with cardinality estimates. If there's an insufficient memory grant, the hash table will spill to tempdb, and this results in less efficient processing.

When using columnstore indexes, the hash algorithm can use batch-execution mode, which is described in Chapter 2. In SQL Server 2012, only inner joins processed with a hash algorithm could use batch execution. Also, if the operator spilled to tempdb, the execution mode switched to row mode. In SQL Server 2014, outer joins processed with a hash algorithm can use batch execution, and so do operators that spill to tempdb.

Besides the classic data warehouse queries, there's another interesting case where the optimizer tends to choose the hash algorithm—when there aren't good indexes to support the other algorithms. If you think about it, a hash table is an alternative searching structure to a B-tree. When there are no good existing indexes, it is usually more efficient overall to create a hash table, use it, and drop it in every query execution compared to doing the same thing with a B-tree. As an example, run the following code to drop the two indexes you created earlier to support previous examples:

```
DROP INDEX idx_nc_cn_i_cid ON dbo.Customers;
DROP INDEX idx_nc_cid_od_i_oid_eid_sid ON dbo.Orders;
```

Then run the same query you ran earlier in the "Nested loops" section:

```
SELECT C.custid, C.custname, O.orderid, O.empid, O.shipperid, O.orderdate
FROM dbo.Customers AS C
  INNER JOIN dbo.Orders AS O
    ON O.custid = C.custid
WHERE C.custname LIKE 'Cust_1000%'
  AND O.orderdate >= '20140101'
  AND O.orderdate < '20140401';
```

This time, as a result of the absence of efficient indexes to support a nested loops algorithm, the optimizer chooses to use a hash join with a hash table based on the qualifying customers. The plan for this query is shown in Figure 3-23.

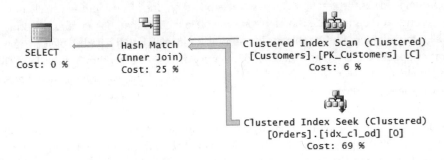

FIGURE 3-23 Plan with a hash algorithm.

So, when you see the optimizer using a hash join in cases where it doesn't seem natural, ask yourself if you're missing important indexes—especially if the query is a frequent one in the system.

Forcing join strategy

If you suspect that the optimizer chose a suboptimal join algorithm, you can try a couple of methods for forcing the one you think is more optimal. One is using a join hint where you specify the join algorithm (LOOP, MERGE, or HASH) right before the JOIN keyword, using the full join syntax (INNER <hint> JOIN, LEFT OUTER <hint> JOIN, and so on). Here's an example for forcing a nested loops algorithm:

```
SELECT C.custid, C.custname, O.orderid, O.empid, O.shipperid, O.orderdate
FROM dbo.Customers AS C
  INNER LOOP JOIN dbo.Orders AS O
    ON O.custid = C.custid;
```

Note that with this method you also force the join order. The left table is used as the outer input, and the right table is used as the inner one.

Another method is to use query hints in the query OPTION clause. The advantage of this method is that you can specify more than one algorithm. Because there are only three supported algorithms, by listing two you are excluding the third. For example, suppose you want to prevent the optimizer from choosing the merge algorithm but you want to leave it with some flexibility to choose between nested loops and hash. You achieve this like so:

```
SELECT C.custid, C.custname, O.orderid, O.empid, O.shipperid, O.orderdate
FROM dbo.Customers AS C
  INNER JOIN dbo.Orders AS O
    ON O.custid = C.custid
OPTION(LOOP JOIN, HASH JOIN);
```

Note, though, that by using this method, all joins in the query are affected. There is no form of a hint that I know of that allows indicating more than one algorithm for a single join. Also note that, unlike the join hint, the query hints for join algorithms don't affect join ordering. If you want to force the join order, you need to add the FORCE ORDER query hint.

Remember the usual disclaimer concerning performance hints. Such hints are handy as a performance troubleshooting tool; however, using them in production queries removes the dynamic nature of optimization that can normally react to changing circumstances by changing optimization choices. If you do find yourself using such hints in production code to solve critical burning problems, you should consider them a temporary solution. When you have the time, you can more thoroughly research the problem and find a fix that will help the optimizer naturally make more optimal choices.

Separating elements

Separating elements is a classic T-SQL challenge. It involves a table called Arrays with strings holding comma-separated lists of values in a column called *arr*. Run the following code to create the Arrays table, and populate it with sample data:

```
SET NOCOUNT ON;
USE tempdb;

IF OBJECT_ID(N'dbo.Arrays', N'U') IS NOT NULL DROP TABLE dbo.Arrays;

CREATE TABLE dbo.Arrays
(
  id  VARCHAR(10)   NOT NULL PRIMARY KEY,
  arr VARCHAR(8000) NOT NULL
);
GO

INSERT INTO dbo.Arrays VALUES('A', '20,223,2544,25567,14');
INSERT INTO dbo.Arrays VALUES('B', '30,-23433,28');
INSERT INTO dbo.Arrays VALUES('C', '12,10,8099,12,1200,13,12,14,10,9');
INSERT INTO dbo.Arrays VALUES('D', '-4,-6,-45678,-2');
```

The challenge is to come up with an efficient solution in T-SQL that splits each string into the individual elements, returned in separate rows along with the id, the position, and the element itself. The desired result looks like the following.

```
id    pos   element
----  ----  --------
A     1     20
A     2     223
A     3     2544
A     4     25567
A     5     14
B     1     30
B     2     -23433
B     3     28
...
```

Note that this task can be solved using .NET more efficiently than with T-SQL—either by using the *System.String.Split* method or by implementing your own iterative solution. However, our challenge is to implement an efficient solution using T-SQL.

One intuitive approach is to implement an iterative solution as a table function operating on a single string and a separator as inputs and returning a table variable. The function would extract one element in each iteration and insert it into the result table variable. The problem with this approach is that iterative solutions in T-SQL tend to be inefficient.

The challenge, therefore, is to find an efficient set-based solution using T-SQL. To implement such a solution, you will want to split the task into three steps:

1. Generate copies.

2. Extract an element.

3. Calculate the position.

The first step is to generate copies from the original rows—as many as the number of elements in the string. The second step is to extract the relevant element from each copy. The third step is to compute the ordinal position of the element within the string.

For the first step, you will find the auxiliary table Nums from the TSQLV3 database very handy. This table has a column called *n* that holds a sequence of integers starting with 1. You can think of the numbers as representing character positions in the string. Namely, $n = 1$ represents character position 1, $n = 2$ represents character position 2, and so on. To generate copies, you join Arrays and Nums. As the join predicate, use the following expression, which says that the *n*th character is a comma: *SUBSTRING(arr, n, 1) = ','*. To avoid extracting a character beyond the end of the string, limit the numbers to the length of the string with the predicate $n <= LEN(arr)$. Here's the code implementing this logic:

```
SELECT id, arr, n
FROM dbo.Arrays
  INNER JOIN TSQLV3.dbo.Nums
    ON n <= LEN(arr)
       AND SUBSTRING(arr, n, 1) = ',';
```

This code generates the following output:

```
id    arr                     n
----- --------------------- ----
A     20,223,2544,25567,14   3
A     20,223,2544,25567,14   7
A     20,223,2544,25567,14   12
A     20,223,2544,25567,14   18
B     30,-23433,28           3
B     30,-23433,28           10
...
```

Observe that the output is missing one copy for each string. The reason is that, for a string with X elements, there are $X - 1$ separators. If you think of the separators as preceding the elements, what's missing is the separator before the first element. To fix this problem, simply plant a separator at the beginning of the string and pass the result as the first input to the SUBSTRING function. Also, make sure you increase the limit of the number of characters you extract by one to account for the extra character. After these two modifications, the query looks like this:

```
SELECT id, arr, n
FROM dbo.Arrays
  INNER JOIN TSQLV3.dbo.Nums
    ON n <= LEN(arr) + 1
      AND SUBSTRING(',' + arr, n, 1) = ',';
```

This query generates the following output:

```
id   arr                     n
---- --------------------- ----
A    20,223,2544,25567,14   1
A    20,223,2544,25567,14   4
A    20,223,2544,25567,14   8
A    20,223,2544,25567,14   13
A    20,223,2544,25567,14   19
B    30,-23433,28           1
B    30,-23433,28           4
B    30,-23433,28           11
...
```

This time, you get the right number of copies. In addition, observe that the modifications to the query had an interesting side effect; the character positions where a separator was found increased by one because the whole string shifted one character to the right. This side effect is actually convenient for us because with respect to the original string (without the separator at the beginning), n actually already represents the starting position of the element. So the first step in the solution for the task is accomplished.

The second step is to extract the element that the current copy represents. For this, you will use the SUBSTRING function. You need to pass the string, the starting position, and the length to extract as inputs. You know that the element starts at position n. For the length, you will need to find the position of the next separator and subtract n from it. You can use the CHARINDEX function for this purpose. The first two inputs are the separator you're looking for and the string where you are looking for it. As the third input, specify *n* as the starting position to look for the separator. You get the following: *CHARINDEX(',', arr, n)*. The tricky thing here is that there's no separator after the last element; in such a case, the function returns a 0. To fix this problem, plant a separator at the end of the string, like so: *CHARINDEX(',', arr + ',', n)*. The complete expression extracting the element then becomes: *SUBSTRING(arr, n, CHARINDEX(',', arr + ',', n) – n)*.

The third and last step in the solution is to compute the ordinal position of the element in the string. For this purpose, use the ROW_NUMBER function, partitioned by *id* and ordered by *n*.

Here's the complete solution query:

```
SELECT id,
  ROW_NUMBER() OVER(PARTITION BY id ORDER BY n) AS pos,
  SUBSTRING(arr, n, CHARINDEX(',', arr + ',', n) - n) AS element
FROM dbo.Arrays
  INNER JOIN TSQLV3.dbo.Nums
    ON n <= LEN(arr) + 1
        AND SUBSTRING(',' + arr, n, 1) = ',';
```

If you need to deal with individual input strings, you can encapsulate this logic in an inline table function, like so:

```
CREATE FUNCTION dbo.Split(@arr AS VARCHAR(8000), @sep AS CHAR(1)) RETURNS TABLE
AS
RETURN
  SELECT
    ROW_NUMBER() OVER(ORDER BY n) AS pos,
    SUBSTRING(@arr, n, CHARINDEX(@sep, @arr + @sep, n) - n) AS element
  FROM TSQLV3.dbo.Nums
  WHERE n <= LEN(@arr) + 1
    AND SUBSTRING(@sep + @arr, n, 1) = @sep;
GO
```

It's the same logic, only it operates on a single string instead of a whole table of strings.

As an example, suppose you have a string holding a comma-separated list of order IDs. To split those into a table of elements, use the *Split* function, like so:

```
SELECT * FROM dbo.Split('10248,10249,10250', ',') AS S;
```

You get the following output:

```
pos   element
----  --------
1     10248
2     10249
3     10250
```

To return further information about the orders in the input string, join the table returned by the function with the Orders table like so:

```
SELECT O.orderid, O.orderdate, O.custid, O.empid
FROM dbo.Split('10248,10249,10250', ',') AS S
  INNER JOIN TSQLV3.Sales.Orders AS O
    ON O.orderid = S.element
ORDER BY S.pos;
```

Observe that the query orders the rows by the ordinal position of the element in the input string. This query generates the following output:

```
orderid     orderdate  custid      empid
----------- ---------- ----------- -----------
10248       2013-07-04 85          5
10249       2013-07-05 79          6
10250       2013-07-08 34          4
```

There's an excellent set of papers written by SQL Server MVP Erland Sommarskog covering the topic of arrays and lists in great depth. You can find those papers here: *http://www.sommarskog.se/ arrays-in-sql.html.*

The UNION, EXCEPT, and INTERSECT operators

The UNION, EXCEPT, and INTERSECT operators are relational operators that combine rows from the result sets of two queries. The general form of code using these operators is shown here:

```
<query 1>
<operator>
<query 2>
[ORDER BY <order_by_list>];
```

The UNION operator unifies the rows from the two inputs. The INTERSECT operator returns only the rows that are common to both inputs. The EXCEPT operator returns the rows that appear in the first input but not the second.

The input queries are not allowed to have an ORDER BY clause because they are supposed to return a relational result. However, an ORDER BY clause is allowed against the result of the operator.

The schemas of the input queries need to be compatible. The number of columns has to be the same, and the types need to be implicitly convertible from the one with the lower data type precedence to the higher. The names of the result columns are defined by the first query.

When comparing rows between the inputs, these operators implicitly use the standard *distinct predicate*. Based on this predicate, one NULL is not distinct from another NULL, and a NULL is distinct from a non-NULL value. Conversely, based on the equality operator, comparing two NULLs results in the logical value *unknown*, and the same applies when comparing a NULL with a non-NULL value. This fact makes these operators simple and intuitive to use, even when NULLs are possible in the data.

When multiple operators are used in a query without parentheses, INTERSECT precedes UNION and EXCEPT. The last two have the same precedence, so they are evaluated based on appearance order. You can always force your desired evaluation order using parentheses.

The following sections provide more details about these operators.

The UNION ALL and UNION operators

The UNION operator unifies the rows from the two inputs. Figure 3-24 illustrates graphically what the operator does. It shows the result of the operator with a darker background.

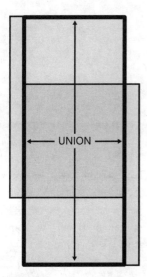

FIGURE 3-24 The UNION operator.

T-SQL supports two variations of the UNION operator: UNION (implied DISTINCT) and UNION ALL. Both unify the rows from the two inputs, but only the former removes duplicates from the result; the latter doesn't. Standard SQL actually supports the explicit form UNION DISTINCT for the former, but T-SQL supports only the implied form.

As an example for UNION, the following code returns distinct unified employee and customer locations:

```
USE TSQLV3;

SELECT country, region, city FROM HR.Employees
UNION
SELECT country, region, city FROM Sales.Customers;
```

This query returns 71 distinct locations.

If you want to keep duplicates, use the UNION ALL variation, like so:

```
SELECT country, region, city FROM HR.Employees
UNION ALL
SELECT country, region, city FROM Sales.Customers;
```

This query returns 100 rows because it unifies 9 employee rows with 91 customer rows. Usually, it's not meaningful to return a result with duplicates, but it could be that you need to apply some further logic against the result. For instance, suppose you need to count how many employees plus customers there are in each location. For this, you define a table expression based on the code with the UNION ALL operator and apply the grouping and aggregation in the outer query.

In terms of performance, UNION is usually more expensive than UNION ALL because it involves an extra step that removes duplicates. Figure 3-25 shows the plans for the last UNION and UNION ALL queries demonstrating this.

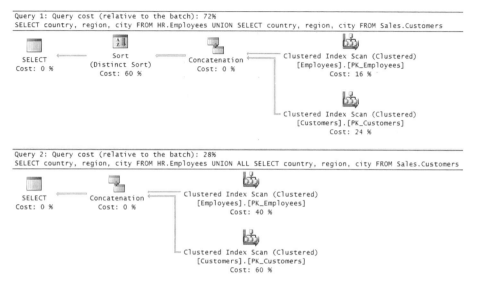

FIGURE 3-25 UNION versus UNION ALL.

The plan for the UNION query uses a Sort (Distinct Sort) operator to remove duplicates. Another option is to use a hash-based algorithm for this purpose. Either way, you can see that there's more work involved than with the UNION ALL query.

When you unify disjoint inputs, such as data for different years that includes a date column, UNION and UNION ALL become logically equivalent. Unfortunately, many use the UNION operator in such a case because the code involves fewer keystrokes, not realizing the unnecessary extra work taking place. So it's important to use the UNION ALL operator as your default and reserve the UNION operator only for cases where the result can have duplicates and you need to remove them.

Interestingly, if you use UNION to unify rows from tables and those tables have CHECK constraints defining disjoint intervals, the optimizer can detect this and help you avoid the extra work of removing duplicates. As an example, the following code creates separate tables to store data for different years, with CHECK constraints enforcing the disjoint year intervals:

```
USE tempdb;
IF OBJECT_ID(N'dbo.T2014', N'U') IS NOT NULL DROP TABLE dbo.T2014;
IF OBJECT_ID(N'dbo.T2015', N'U') IS NOT NULL DROP TABLE dbo.T2015;
GO
CREATE TABLE dbo.T2014
(
  keycol INT NOT NULL CONSTRAINT PK_T2014 PRIMARY KEY,
  dt DATE NOT NULL CONSTRAINT CHK_T2014_dt CHECK(dt >= '20140101' AND dt < '20150101')
);

CREATE TABLE dbo.T2015
(
  keycol INT NOT NULL CONSTRAINT PK_T2015 PRIMARY KEY,
  dt DATE NOT NULL CONSTRAINT CHK_T2015_dt CHECK(dt >= '20150101' AND dt < '20160101')
);
```

Ignoring best practices, you use the following code to unify the rows from the tables with the UNION operator:

```
SELECT keycol, dt FROM dbo.T2014
UNION
SELECT keycol, dt FROM dbo.T2015;
```

Fortunately, thanks to the existence of the constraints, the optimizer figures that duplicates cannot exist in the result and therefore optimizes this query the same as it would UNION ALL. The plan for this query is shown in Figure 3-26.

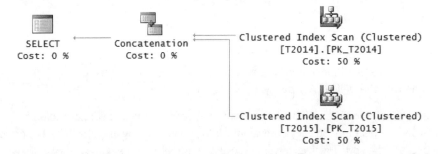

FIGURE 3-26 UNION and CHECK constraints.

It's still recommended to follow the best practice and stick with UNION ALL as your default for the sake of cases where the optimizer won't figure out that the inputs are disjoint.

When you're done testing, run the following code for cleanup:

```
IF OBJECT_ID(N'dbo.T2014', N'U') IS NOT NULL DROP TABLE dbo.T2014;
IF OBJECT_ID(N'dbo.T2015', N'U') IS NOT NULL DROP TABLE dbo.T2015;
```

The INTERSECT operator

The INTERSECT operator returns only distinct rows that are common to both inputs. Figure 3-27 illustrates graphically what this operator returns.

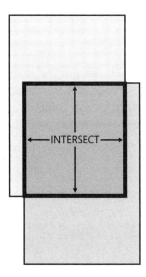

FIGURE 3-27 The INTERSECT operator.

As an example, the following query returns locations that are both employee locations and customer locations:

```
USE TSQLV3;

SELECT country, region, city FROM HR.Employees
INTERSECT
SELECT country, region, city FROM Sales.Customers;
```

This query generates the following output:

```
country          region           city
---------------  ---------------  ---------------
UK               NULL             London
USA              WA               Kirkland
USA              WA               Seattle
```

Observe in the output that the row with UK, NULL, London was returned because there are both employees and customers in this location. Because the operator uses the distinct predicate implicitly to compare rows, when comparing the NULLs on both sides, it got *true* and not *unknown*. If you want to implement the intersection operation with an inner join, you need to add special logic for NULL treatment (with Employees aliased as *E* and Customers as *C*):

```
E.region = C.region OR E.region IS NULL AND C.region IS NULL
```

Like the UNION operator, INTERSECT returns distinct rows. If a row appears at least once in each of the inputs, it's returned once in the output. Interestingly, standard SQL supports an operator called INTERSECT ALL, which returns as many occurrences of a row in the result as the minimum number of occurrences between the two inputs. Say that a row R appears X times in the first input and Y times in the second input, the INTERSECT ALL operator returns the row MIN(X, Y) times in the output. It's as if the operator looks for a separate match for each row. So if you have four occurrences of R in one input and six in the other, you will get R four times in the output.

T-SQL doesn't support the standard INTERSECT ALL operator, but it's quite easy to implement your own solution. You achieve this by adding row numbers to both input queries, marking duplicate numbers. You apply the supported INTERSECT operator to the queries with the row numbers. You then define a CTE based on the intersection code, and then in the outer query return the attributes without the row numbers. Here's the complete solution code:

```
WITH INTERSECT_ALL
AS
(
  SELECT
    ROW_NUMBER()
      OVER(PARTITION BY country, region, city
           ORDER    BY (SELECT 0)) AS rn,
    country, region, city
  FROM HR.Employees

  INTERSECT

  SELECT
    ROW_NUMBER()
      OVER(PARTITION BY country, region, city
           ORDER    BY (SELECT 0)) AS rn,
    country, region, city
  FROM Sales.Customers
)
SELECT country, region, city
FROM INTERSECT_ALL;
```

This code generates the following output:

```
country          region            city
---------------- ----------------- ---------------
UK               NULL              London
USA              WA                Kirkland
USA              WA                Seattle
UK               NULL              London
UK               NULL              London
UK               NULL              London
```

There are four employees from UK, NULL, London and six customers; doing one-to-one matching, four of them intersect. Therefore, the result has four occurrences of the row.

The EXCEPT operator

The EXCEPT operator returns only distinct rows that appear in the first input but not the second. Figure 3-28 illustrates graphically what this operator returns.

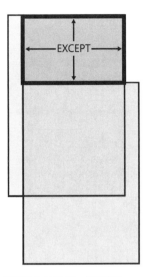

FIGURE 3-28 The EXCEPT operator.

As an example, the following code returns distinct employee locations that are not customer locations:

```
SELECT country, region, city FROM HR.Employees
EXCEPT
SELECT country, region, city FROM Sales.Customers;
```

This query generates the following output:

```
country          region          city
---------------  ---------------  ---------------
USA              WA               Redmond
USA              WA               Tacoma
```

In terms of optimization, like with NOT EXISTS, also with EXCEPT the optimizer can detect that the logical operation is an anti semi join. You can see this if you examine the execution plan for this query.

As it does with INTERSECT ALL, standard SQL supports an operator called EXCEPT ALL, which wasn't implemented in T-SQL. If a row R appears X times in the first input and Y times in the second input, and X is greater than Y, the operator returns the row X – Y times in the output. The logic behind this is that it's as if you're looking for a match for each of the rows and then return only the nonmatches.

To implement your own solution for EXCEPT ALL, you use the same technique you used for INTERSECT ALL. Namely, compute row numbers, marking duplicate numbers in both input queries, and then use the EXCEPT operator. Only the rows from the first input with row numbers that don't have matches in the second input will be returned. You then define a CTE based on the code with the EXCEPT operator, and in the outer query you return the attributes without the row numbers. Here's the complete solution code:

```
WITH EXCEPT_ALL
AS
(
  SELECT
    ROW_NUMBER()
      OVER(PARTITION BY country, region, city
           ORDER    BY (SELECT 0)) AS rn,
    country, region, city
  FROM HR.Employees

  EXCEPT

  SELECT
    ROW_NUMBER()
      OVER(PARTITION BY country, region, city
           ORDER    BY (SELECT 0)) AS rn,
    country, region, city
  FROM Sales.Customers
)
SELECT country, region, city
FROM EXCEPT_ALL;
```

This code generates the following output:

```
country          region           city
---------------- ---------------- ----------------
USA              WA               Redmond
USA              WA               Tacoma
USA              WA               Seattle
```

USA, NULL, Seattle appears twice in Employees and once in Customers; therefore, it is returned once in the output.

As a tip, recall the discussion about finding an efficient solution for the minimum missing value problem earlier in the section "The EXISTS predicate." Here's a much simpler and highly efficient solution for the same task using the EXCEPT operator:

```
SELECT TOP (1) missingval
FROM (SELECT col1 + 1 AS missingval FROM dbo.T1
      EXCEPT
      SELECT col1 FROM dbo.T1) AS D
ORDER BY missingval;
```

As with the previously discussed efficient solutions, here also the optimizer uses a Top operator that short-circuits the scans as soon as the first missing value is found.

Conclusion

This chapter covered a lot of ground discussing different tools you use to combine data from multiple tables. It covered subqueries, table expressions, the powerful APPLY operator, joins, and the relational operators UNION, EXCEPT, and INTERSECT. The chapter described both logical considerations for using these tools as well as how to use them optimally.

Grouping, pivoting, and windowing

This chapter focuses on performing data-analysis calculations with T-SQL for various purposes, such as reporting. A *data-analysis calculation* is one you apply to a set of rows and that returns a single value. For example, aggregate calculations fall into this category.

T-SQL supports numerous features and techniques you can use to perform data-analysis calculations, such as window functions, pivoting and unpivoting, computing custom aggregations, and working with multiple grouping sets. This chapter covers such features and techniques.

Window functions

You use window functions to perform data-analysis calculations elegantly and, in many cases, efficiently. In contrast to group functions, which are applied to groups of rows defined by a grouped query, window functions are applied to windows of rows defined by a windowed query. Where a GROUP BY clause determines groups, an OVER clause determines windows. So think of the window as the set of rows, or the context, for the function to apply to.

The design of window functions is quite profound, enabling you to handle data-analysis calculations in many cases more elegantly and more easily than with other tools. Standard SQL acknowledges the immense power in window functions, providing extensive coverage for those. T-SQL implements a subset of the standard, and I hope Microsoft will continue that investment in the future.

The coverage of window functions in this chapter is organized based on their categories: aggregate, ranking, offset, and statistical. There's also a section with solutions to gaps and islands problems using window functions.

 Note Some of the windowing features described in this section were introduced in Microsoft SQL Server 2012. So if you are using an earlier version of SQL Server, you won't be able to run the related code samples. Those features include frame specification for aggregate window functions (ORDER BY and ROWS or RANGE window frame units), offset window functions (FIRST_VALUE, LAST_VALUE, LAG, and LEAD), and statistical window functions (PERCENT_RANK, CUME_DIST, PERCENTILE_CONT, and PERCENTILE_DISC).

Aggregate window functions

Aggregate window functions are the same functions you know as *grouped functions* (SUM, AVG, and others), only you apply them to a window instead of to a group. To demonstrate aggregate window functions, I'll use a couple of small tables called OrderValues and EmpOrders, and a large table called Transactions. Run the following code to create the tables and fill them with sample data:

```
SET NOCOUNT ON;
USE tempdb;

-- OrderValues table
IF OBJECT_ID(N'dbo.OrderValues', N'U') IS NOT NULL DROP TABLE dbo.OrderValues;

SELECT * INTO dbo.OrderValues FROM TSQLV3.Sales.OrderValues;

ALTER TABLE dbo.OrderValues ADD CONSTRAINT PK_OrderValues PRIMARY KEY(orderid);
GO

-- EmpOrders table
IF OBJECT_ID(N'dbo.EmpOrders', N'U') IS NOT NULL DROP TABLE dbo.EmpOrders;

SELECT empid, ISNULL(ordermonth, CAST('19000101' AS DATE)) AS ordermonth, qty, val, numorders
INTO dbo.EmpOrders
FROM TSQLV3.Sales.EmpOrders;

ALTER TABLE dbo.EmpOrders ADD CONSTRAINT PK_EmpOrders PRIMARY KEY(empid, ordermonth);
GO

-- Transactions table
IF OBJECT_ID('dbo.Transactions', 'U') IS NOT NULL DROP TABLE dbo.Transactions;
IF OBJECT_ID('dbo.Accounts', 'U') IS NOT NULL DROP TABLE dbo.Accounts;

CREATE TABLE dbo.Accounts
(
  actid INT NOT NULL CONSTRAINT PK_Accounts PRIMARY KEY
);

CREATE TABLE dbo.Transactions
(
  actid  INT    NOT NULL,
  tranid INT    NOT NULL,
  val    MONEY NOT NULL,
  CONSTRAINT PK_Transactions PRIMARY KEY(actid, tranid)
);

DECLARE
  @num_partitions     AS INT = 100,
  @rows_per_partition AS INT = 20000;

INSERT INTO dbo.Accounts WITH (TABLOCK) (actid)
  SELECT NP.n
  FROM TSQLV3.dbo.GetNums(1, @num_partitions) AS NP;
```

```
INSERT INTO dbo.Transactions WITH (TABLOCK) (actid, tranid, val)
  SELECT NP.n, RPP.n,
    (ABS(CHECKSUM(NEWID())%2)*2-1) * (1 + ABS(CHECKSUM(NEWID())%5))
  FROM TSQLV3.dbo.GetNums(1, @num_partitions) AS NP
    CROSS JOIN TSQLV3.dbo.GetNums(1, @rows_per_partition) AS RPP;
```

The OrderValues table has a row per order with total order values and quantities. The EmpOrders table keeps track of monthly totals per employee. The Transactions table has 2,000,000 rows with bank account transactions (100 accounts, with 20,000 transactions in each).

Limitations of data analysis calculations without window functions

Before delving into the details of window functions, you first should realize the limitations of alternative tools that perform data-analysis calculations. Knowing those limitations is a good way to appreciate the ingenious design of window functions.

Consider the following grouped query:

```
SELECT custid, SUM(val) AS custtotal
FROM dbo.OrderValues
GROUP BY custid;
```

Compared to analyzing the detail, the grouped query gives you new insights into the data in the form of aggregates. However, the grouped query also hides the detail. For example, the following attempt to return a detail element in a grouped query fails:

```
SELECT custid, val, SUM(val) AS custtotal
FROM dbo.OrderValues
GROUP BY custid;
```

You get the following error:

```
Msg 8120, Level 16, State 1, Line 70
Column 'dbo.OrderValues.val' is invalid in the select list because it is not contained in either
an aggregate function or the GROUP BY clause.
```

The reference to the *val* column in the SELECT list is not allowed because it is not part of the grouping set and not contained in a group aggregate function. But what if you do need to return details and aggregates? For example, suppose you want to query the OrderValues table and return, in addition to the order information, the percent of the current order value out of the grand total and also out of the customer total.

You could achieve this with scalar aggregate subqueries, like so:

```
SELECT orderid, custid, val,
  val / (SELECT SUM(val) FROM dbo.OrderValues) AS pctall,
  val / (SELECT SUM(val) FROM dbo.OrderValues AS O2
        WHERE O2.custid = O1.custid) AS pctcust
FROM dbo.OrderValues AS O1;
```

Or, if you want formatted output:

```
SELECT orderid, custid, val,
  CAST(100. *
    val / (SELECT SUM(val) FROM dbo.OrderValues)
           AS NUMERIC(5, 2)) AS pctall,
  CAST(100. *
    val / (SELECT SUM(val) FROM dbo.OrderValues AS O2
           WHERE O2.custid = O1.custid)
           AS NUMERIC(5, 2)) AS pctcust
FROM dbo.OrderValues AS O1
ORDER BY custid;
```

The problem with this approach is that each subquery gets a fresh view of the data as its starting point. Typically, the desired starting point for the set calculation is the underlying query's result set after most logical query processing phases (table operators, filters, and others) were applied.

For example, suppose you need to filter only orders placed on or after 2015. To achieve this, you add a filter in the underlying query, like so:

```
SELECT orderid, custid, val,
  CAST(100. *
    val / (SELECT SUM(val) FROM dbo.OrderValues)
           AS NUMERIC(5, 2)) AS pctall,
  CAST(100. *
    val / (SELECT SUM(val) FROM dbo.OrderValues AS O2
           WHERE O2.custid = O1.custid)
           AS NUMERIC(5, 2)) AS pctcust
FROM dbo.OrderValues AS O1
WHERE orderdate >= '20150101'
ORDER BY custid;
```

This filter affects only the underlying query, not the subqueries. The subqueries still query all years. This code generates the following output:

```
orderid  custid  val      pctall  pctcust
-------- ------- -------- ------- --------
10835    1       845.80   0.07    19.79
10952    1       471.20   0.04    11.03
11011    1       933.50   0.07    21.85
10926    2       514.40   0.04    36.67
10856    3       660.00   0.05    9.40
10864    4       282.00   0.02    2.11
10953    4       4441.25  0.35    33.17
10920    4       390.00   0.03    2.91
11016    4       491.50   0.04    3.67
10924    5       1835.70  0.15    7.36
...
```

There's a bug in the code. Observe that the percentages per customer don't sum up to 100 like they should, and the same applies to the percentages out of the grand total. To have the subqueries operate on the underlying query's result set, you have to either duplicate code elements or use a table expression.

Window functions were designed with the limitations of grouped queries and subqueries in mind, and that's just the tip of the iceberg in terms of their capabilities!

Unlike grouped queries, windowed queries don't hide the detail. A window function's result is returned in addition to the detail.

Unlike the fresh view of the data exposed to a scalar aggregate in a subquery, an OVER clause exposes the underlying query result as the starting point for the window function. More precisely, in terms of logical query processing, window functions operate on the set of rows exposed to the SELECT phase as input—after the handling of FROM, WHERE, GROUP BY, and HAVING. For this reason, window functions are allowed only in the SELECT and ORDER BY clauses of a query. Using an empty specification in the OVER clause defines a window with the entire underlying query result set. So, *SUM(val) OVER()* gives you the grand total. Adding a window partition clause like *PARTITION BY custid* restricts the window to only the rows that have the same customer ID as in the current row. So *SUM(val) OVER(PARTITION BY custid)* gives you the customer total.

The following query then gives you the detail along with the percent of the current order value out of the grand total as well as out of the customer total:

```
SELECT orderid, custid, val,
  val / SUM(val) OVER() AS pctall,
  val / SUM(val) OVER(PARTITION BY custid) AS pctcust
FROM dbo.OrderValues;
```

Here's a revised version with formatted percentages:

```
SELECT orderid, custid, val,
  CAST(100. * val / SUM(val) OVER()                      AS NUMERIC(5, 2)) AS pctall,
  CAST(100. * val / SUM(val) OVER(PARTITION BY custid) AS NUMERIC(5, 2)) AS pctcust
FROM dbo.OrderValues
ORDER BY custid;
```

Add a filter to the query:

```
SELECT orderid, custid, val,
  CAST(100. * val / SUM(val) OVER()                      AS NUMERIC(5, 2)) AS pctall,
  CAST(100. * val / SUM(val) OVER(PARTITION BY custid) AS NUMERIC(5, 2)) AS pctcust
FROM dbo.OrderValues
WHERE orderdate >= '20150101'
ORDER BY custid;
```

Unlike subqueries, window functions get as their starting point the underlying query result *after* filtering. Observe the query output:

```
orderid  custid  val       pctall  pctcust
-------- ------- --------  ------- --------
10835    1       845.80    0.19    37.58
10952    1       471.20    0.11    20.94
11011    1       933.50    0.21    41.48
10926    2       514.40    0.12    100.00
10856    3       660.00    0.15    100.00
10864    4       282.00    0.06    5.03
10953    4       4441.25   1.01    79.24
10920    4       390.00    0.09    6.96
11016    4       491.50    0.11    8.77
10924    5       1835.70   0.42    27.18
...
```

Notice that this time the percentages per customer (*pctcust*) sum up to 100, and the same goes for the percentages out of the grand total when summing those up in all rows.

Window elements

A window function is conceptually evaluated per row, and the elements in the window specification can implicitly or explicitly relate to the underlying row. Aggregate window functions support a number of elements in their specification, as demonstrated by the following query, which computes a running total quantity per employee and month:

```
SELECT empid, ordermonth, qty,
  SUM(qty) OVER(PARTITION BY empid
                ORDER BY ordermonth
                ROWS BETWEEN UNBOUNDED PRECEDING
                      AND CURRENT ROW) AS runqty
FROM dbo.EmpOrders;
```

The window specification can define a window partition and a window frame. Both elements provide ways to restrict a subset of rows from the underlying query's result set for the function to operate on. The window partition is defined using a window partition clause (PARTITION BY …). The window frame is defined using a window order clause (ORDER BY …) and a window frame clause (ROWS | RANGE …). The following sections describe these window elements in detail.

Window partition   A *window partition* is a subset of the underlying query's result set defined by a window partition clause. The window partition is the subset of rows that have the same values in the window partition elements as in the current row. (Remember, the function is evaluated per row.) For example, *PARTITION BY empid* restricts the rows to only those that have the same *empid* value as in the current row. Similarly, *PARTITION BY custid* restricts the rows to only those that have the same *custid* value as in the current row. Absent a window partition clause, the underlying query result set is considered one big partition. So, for any given row, *OVER()* exposes to the function the underlying query's entire result set. Figure 4-1 illustrates what's considered the qualifying set of rows for the highlighted row with both an empty OVER clause and one containing a window partition clause. The numbers represent customer IDs.

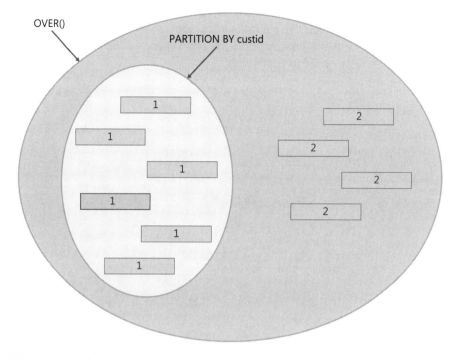

FIGURE 4-1 Window partition.

As an example, the following query computes for each order the percent of the current order value out of the grand total, as well as out of the customer total:

```
SELECT orderid, custid, val,
  CAST(100. * val / SUM(val) OVER()                     AS NUMERIC(5, 2)) AS pctall,
  CAST(100. * val / SUM(val) OVER(PARTITION BY custid) AS NUMERIC(5, 2)) AS pctcust
FROM dbo.OrderValues
ORDER BY custid;
```

This query generates the following output:

```
orderid  custid  val      pctall   pctcust
-------- ------- -------- -------- --------
10643    1       814.50   0.06     19.06
10692    1       878.00   0.07     20.55
10702    1       330.00   0.03     7.72
10835    1       845.80   0.07     19.79
10952    1       471.20   0.04     11.03
11011    1       933.50   0.07     21.85
10926    2       514.40   0.04     36.67
10759    2       320.00   0.03     22.81
10625    2       479.75   0.04     34.20
10308    2       88.80    0.01     6.33
...
```

There are clear advantages in terms of simplicity and elegance to using such a windowed query compared to, say, using multiple grouped queries and joining their results. But what about performance? In this respect, I'm afraid the news is not so good. Before I elaborate, I'd like to stress that the inefficiencies I'm about to describe are limited to window aggregate functions without a frame. As I will explain later, window aggregate functions with a frame, window ranking functions, and window offset functions are optimized differently.

To discuss performance aspects, I'll use the bigger Transactions table, which has 2,000,000 rows. Consider the following query:

```
SELECT actid, tranid, val,
  val / SUM(val) OVER() AS pctall,
  val / SUM(val) OVER(PARTITION BY actid) AS pctact
FROM dbo.Transactions;
```

The execution plan for this query is shown in Figure 4-2.

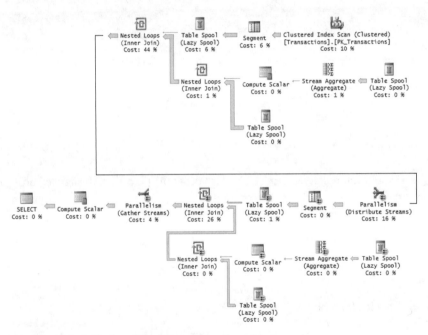

FIGURE 4-2 Optimization with window aggregates.

Recall that the initial set that is exposed to the window function is the underlying query result, after the logical processing phases prior to the SELECT phase have been applied (FROM, WHERE, GROUP BY, and HAVING). Furthermore, the window function's results are returned in addition to the detail, not instead of it. To ensure both requirements, for each of the window functions, the query plan writes the rows to a spool and then reads from the spool twice—once to compute the aggregate and once to read the detail—and then joins the results. Because the query has two unique window specifications, this work happens twice in the plan.

Clearly, there's room for improved optimization, especially in cases like ours where there are no table operators, filters, or grouping involved, and there's an optimal covering index in place (PK_Transactions). Logic can be added to the optimizer to detect cases where there's no need to spool data, and instead the data is read directly from the index.

With the current optimization resulting in the plan shown in Figure 4-2, on my system, it took the query 13.76 seconds to complete, using 16.485 CPU seconds and 10,053,178 logical reads. That's a lot for the amount of data involved!

If you rewrite the solution using grouped queries, you will get much better performance. Here's the version using grouped queries:

```
WITH GrandAgg AS
(
  SELECT SUM(val) AS sumall FROM dbo.Transactions
),
ActAgg AS
(
  SELECT actid, SUM(val) AS sumact
  FROM dbo.Transactions
  GROUP BY actid
)
SELECT T.actid, T.tranid, T.val,
  T.val / GA.sumall AS pctall,
  T.val / AA.sumact AS pctact
FROM dbo.Transactions AS T
  CROSS JOIN GrandAgg AS GA
  INNER JOIN ActAgg AS AA
    ON AA.actid = T.actid;
```

Examine the plan shown in Figure 4-3. Observe that there's no spooling at all, and that efficient order-based aggregates (Stream Aggregate) are computed based on index order.

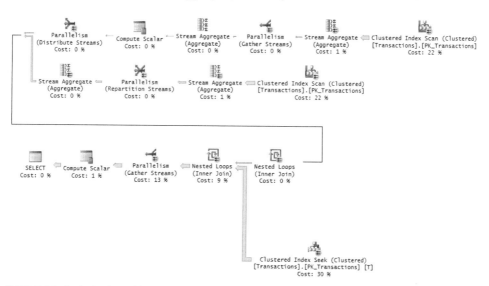

FIGURE 4-3 Optimization with group aggregates.

The performance statistics I got for this solution on my system are as follows:

- Run time: 2.01 seconds

- CPU time: 4.97 seconds

- Logical reads: 19,368

That's quite an improvement.

Because there are great language design benefits in using window functions, we hope to see future investment in better optimization of such functions.

Usually, grouping and windowing are considered different methods to achieve a task, but there are interesting ways to combine them. They are not mutually exclusive. The easiest way to understand this is to think of logical query processing. Remember from Chapter 1, "Logical query processing," that the GROUP BY clause is evaluated in step 3 and the SELECT clause is evaluated in step 5. Therefore, if the query is a grouped query, the SELECT phase operates on the grouped state of the data and not the detailed state. So if you use a window function in the SELECT or ORDER BY phase, the window function also operates on the grouped state.

As an example, consider the following grouped query:

```
SELECT custid, SUM(val) AS custtotal
FROM dbo.OrderValues
GROUP BY custid;
```

The query groups the rows by *custid*, and it returns the total values per customer (*custtotal*).

Before looking at the next query, try to answer the following question: Can you add the *val* column directly to the SELECT list in the preceding query? The answer is, "Of course not." Because the query is a grouped query, a reference to a column name in the SELECT list is allowed only if the column is part of the GROUP BY list or contained in a group aggregate function.

With this in mind, suppose you need to add to the query a calculation returning the percent of the current customer total out of the grand total. The customer total is expressed with the grouped function SUM(val). Normally, to express the grand total in a detailed query you use a windowed function, SUM(val) OVER(). Now try dividing one by the other, like so:

```
SELECT custid, SUM(val) AS custtotal,
  SUM(val) / SUM(val) OVER() AS pct
FROM dbo.OrderValues
GROUP BY custid;
```

You get the same error as when trying to add the *val* column directly to the SELECT list:

```
Msg 8120, Level 16, State 1, Line 229
Column 'dbo.OrderValues.val' is invalid in the select list because it is not contained in either
an aggregate function or the GROUP BY clause.
```

Unlike grouped functions, which operate on the detail rows per group, windowed functions operate on the grouped data. Windowed functions can see what the SELECT phase can see. The error message is a bit misleading in that it says "...because it is not contained in either an aggregate function..." and you're probably thinking that it is. This error message was added to SQL Server well before window functions were introduced. What it means to say is "...because it is not contained in either a group aggregate function...."

If the window function cannot refer to the *val* column directly, what can it refer to? An attempt to refer to the alias *custtotal* also fails because of the *all-at-once* concept in SQL. The answer is that the windowed SUM should be applied to the grouped SUM, like so:

```
SELECT custid, SUM(val) AS custtotal,
  SUM(val) / SUM(SUM(val)) OVER() AS pct
FROM dbo.OrderValues
GROUP BY custid;
```

This idea takes a bit of getting used to, but when thinking in terms of logical query processing, it makes perfect sense.

Window frame   Just as a *partition* is a filtered portion of the underlying query's result set, a *frame* is a filtered portion of the partition. A frame requires ordering specifications using a window order clause. Based on that order, you define two delimiters that frame the rows. Then the window function is applied to that frame of rows. You can use one of two window frame units: ROWS or RANGE.

I'll start with ROWS. Using this unit, you can define three types of delimiters:

- UNBOUNDED PRECEDING | FOLLOWING: First or last row in the partition, respectively.

- CURRENT ROW: Current row.

- N ROWS PRECEDING | FOLLOWING: An offset in terms of the specified number of rows (N) before or after the current row, respectively.

The first delimiter has to be on or before the second delimiter.

Figure 4-4 illustrates the window frame concept. The numbers 1 and 2 represent employee IDs; the values 201307, 201308, and so on represent order months. A sample row is highlighted in bold as the current row.

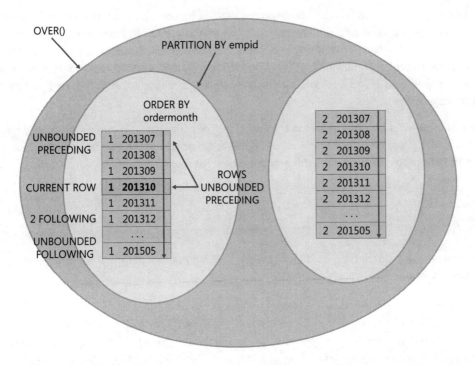

FIGURE 4-4 Window frame.

As an example, suppose you want to query the EmpOrders table and compute for each employee and order month the running total quantity. In other words, you want to see the cumulative performance of the employee over time. You define the window partition clause based on the *empid* column, the window order clause based on the *ordermonth* column, and the window frame clause as *ROWS BETWEEN UNBOUNDED PRECEDING AND CURRENT ROW*, like so:

```
SELECT empid, ordermonth, qty,
  SUM(qty) OVER(PARTITION BY empid
              ORDER BY ordermonth
              ROWS BETWEEN UNBOUNDED PRECEDING
                      AND CURRENT ROW) AS runqty
FROM dbo.EmpOrders;
```

Because this frame specification is so common, the standard defines the equivalent shorter form *ROWS UNBOUNDED PRECEDING*. Here's the shorter form used in our query:

```
SELECT empid, ordermonth, qty,
  SUM(qty) OVER(PARTITION BY empid
              ORDER BY ordermonth
              ROWS UNBOUNDED PRECEDING) AS runqty
FROM dbo.EmpOrders;
```

This query generates the following output:

```
empid   ordermonth qty   runqty
------  ---------- ----- -------
1       2013-07-01 121   121
1       2013-08-01 247   368
1       2013-09-01 255   623
1       2013-10-01 143   766
1       2013-11-01 318   1084
1       2013-12-01 536   1620
...
1       2015-05-01 299   7812
2       2013-07-01 50    50
2       2013-08-01 94    144
2       2013-09-01 137   281
2       2013-10-01 248   529
2       2013-11-01 237   766
2       2013-12-01 319   1085
...
2       2015-04-01 1126  5915
...
```

Using a window function to compute a running total is both elegant and, as you will soon see, very efficient. An alternative technique is to use a query with a join and grouping, like so:

```
SELECT O1.empid, O1.ordermonth, O1.qty,
  SUM(O2.qty) AS runqty
FROM dbo.EmpOrders AS O1
  INNER JOIN dbo.EmpOrders AS O2
    ON O2.empid = O1.empid
       AND O2.ordermonth <= O1.ordermonth
GROUP BY O1.empid, O1.ordermonth, O1.qty;
```

This technique is both more complex and gets optimized extremely inefficiently.

To evaluate the optimization of the different techniques, I'll use the bigger Transactions table. Suppose you need to compute the balance after each transaction for each account. Using a windowed SUM function, you apply the calculation to the *val* column, partitioned by the *actid* column, ordered by the *tranid* column, with the frame *ROWS UNBOUNDED PRECEDING*.

The optimal index for window functions is what I like to think of as a POC index. This acronym stands for Partitioning (*actid,* in our case), Ordering (*tranid*), and Covering (*val*). The P and O parts should make the index key list, and the C part should be included in the index leaf row. The clustered index PK_Orders on the Transactions table is based on this pattern, so we already have the optimal index in place.

The following query computes the aforementioned bank account balances using a window function:

```
SELECT actid, tranid, val,
  SUM(val) OVER(PARTITION BY actid
                ORDER BY tranid
                ROWS UNBOUNDED PRECEDING) AS balance
FROM dbo.Transactions;
```

The plan for this query is shown in Figure 4-5.

FIGURE 4-5 Plan with fast-track optimization of window function for running totals.

The plan starts by scanning the POC index in order. That's a good start. The next pair of Segment and Sequence Project operators are responsible for computing row numbers. The row numbers are used to indicate which rows fit in each underlying row's window frame. The Segment operator flags the next operator when a new partition starts. The Sequence Project operator assigns the row numbers—1 if the row is the first in the partition, and the previous value plus 1 if it is not. The next Segment operator, again, is responsible for flagging the operator to its left when a new partition starts.

Then the next pair of Window Spool and Stream Aggregate operators represent the frame of rows that need to be aggregated and the aggregate applied to the frame, respectively. If it were not for specialized optimization called *fast-track* that the optimizer employs here, for a partition with N rows, the spool would have to store $1 + 2 + ... + N = (N + N^2)/2$ rows. As an example, for an account with just 20,000 transactions, the number would be 200,010,000. Fortunately, when the first delimiter of the frame is the first row in the partition (UNBOUNDED PRECEDING), the optimizer detects the case as a "fast-track" case and uses specialized optimization. For each row, it takes the previous row's accumulation, adds the current row's value, and writes that to the spool.

With this sort of optimization, you would expect the number of rows going out of the spool to be the same as the number of rows going into it (2,000,000 in our case); however, the plan shows that the number of rows going out of the spool is twice the number going in. The reason for this has to do with the fact that the Stream Aggregate operator was designed well before window functions were introduced. Originally, it was used only to compute group functions in grouped queries, which return the aggregates but hide the detail. So the trick Microsoft used to use the operator to compute a window aggregate is that besides the row with the accumulated aggregate, they also add the detail row to the spool so as not to lose it. So, with fast-track optimization, if N rows go into the Window Spool operator, you should see 2N rows going out.

It took four seconds for the query to complete on my system with results discarded.

Here's the alternative solution using a join and grouping:

```
SELECT T1.actid, T1.tranid, T1.val, SUM(T2.val) AS balance
FROM dbo.Transactions AS T1
  INNER JOIN dbo.Transactions AS T2
    ON T2.actid = T1.actid
       AND T2.tranid <= T1.tranid
GROUP BY T1.actid, T1.tranid, T1.val;
```

Running the query and waiting for it to complete is a good exercise in patience. To understand why, examine the query plan shown in Figure 4-6.

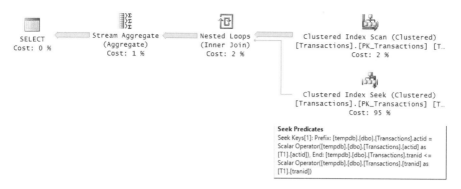

FIGURE 4-6 Plan for running totals with a join and a grouped query.

Here the optimizer doesn't employ any specialized optimization. You see the POC index scanned once for the T1 instance of the table, and then for each row, it performs a seek in the index representing the instance T2 to the beginning of the current account section, and then a range scan of all rows where *T2.actid <= T1.actid*. Besides the cost of the full scan of the index and the cost of the seeks, the range scan processes in total $(N + N^2)/2$ rows per account, where N is the number of transactions per account. (In our sample data, N is equal to 20,000.) It took over an hour and a half for the query to finish on my system.

While the plan for the query with the join and grouping has quadratic scaling (N^2), the plan for the window function has linear scaling. Furthermore, when the optimizer knows that per underlying row there are no more than 10,000 rows in the window frame, it uses a special optimized in-memory spool (as opposed to a more expensive on-disk spool). Remember that when the unit is ROWS and the optimizer uses fast-track optimization, it writes only two rows to the spool per underlying row—one with the aggregate and one with the detail. In such a case, the conditions for using the in-memory spool are satisfied.

Still, with certain frame specifications like *ROWS UNBOUNDED PRECEDING*, which are the more commonly used ones, there's potential for improvements in the optimizer. Theoretically, spooling could be avoided in those cases. Instead, the optimizer could use streaming operators, like the Sequence Project operator it uses to calculate the ROW_NUMBER function. As an example, when replacing the windowed SUM in the query computing balances with the ROW_NUMBER function just to check the performance, the query completes in one second. That's compared to four seconds for the original query. This is the performance improvement potential for calculations like running totals if Microsoft decides to invest further in this area in the future.

As mentioned, you can use the ROWS option to specify delimiters as an offset in terms of a number of rows before (PRECEDING) or after (FOLLOWING) the current row. As an example, the following query computes for each employee and month the moving average quantity of the last three recorded months.

```
SELECT empid, ordermonth,
  AVG(qty) OVER(PARTITION BY empid
                ORDER BY ordermonth
                ROWS BETWEEN 2 PRECEDING AND CURRENT ROW) AS avgqty
FROM dbo.EmpOrders;
```

This query generates the following output:

```
empid  ordermonth avgqty
------ ---------- -------
1      2013-07-01 121
1      2013-08-01 184
1      2013-09-01 207
1      2013-10-01 215
1      2013-11-01 238
1      2013-12-01 332
1      2014-01-01 386
1      2014-02-01 336
1      2014-03-01 249
1      2014-04-01 154
...
```

As another example, the following query computes the moving average value of the last 100 transactions:

```
SELECT actid, tranid, val,
  AVG(val) OVER(PARTITION BY actid
                ORDER BY tranid
                ROWS BETWEEN 99 PRECEDING AND CURRENT ROW) AS avg100
FROM dbo.Transactions;
```

What's interesting about the optimization of frames that don't start at the beginning of the partition is that you would expect the optimizer to create a plan that writes all frame rows to the window spool and aggregates them. In the last example, this would mean 100 × 2,000,000 = 2,000,000,000 rows. However, the optimizer has a trick that it can use under certain conditions to avoid such work. If the frame has more than four rows and the aggregate is a cumulative one like SUM, COUNT, or AVG, the optimizer creates a plan with two fast-track running aggregate computations: one starting at the beginning of the partition and ending with the last row in the desired frame (call it CumulativeBottom) and another starting at the beginning of the partition and ending with the row before the start of the desired frame (call it CumulativeTop). Then it derives the final aggregate as a calculation between the two. You can see this strategy employed in the plan for the last query shown in Figure 4-7.

It took this query 12 seconds to complete on my system. This is not so bad considering the alternative.

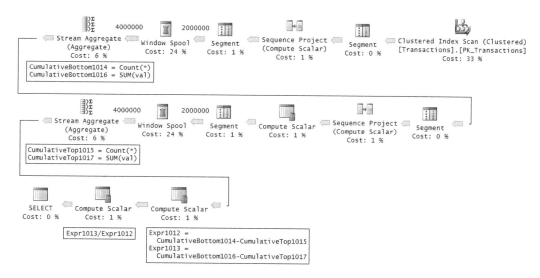

FIGURE 4-7 Plan for moving average.

If the computation is not cumulative—namely, it cannot be derived from bottom and top calculations—the optimizer will not be able to use any tricks and all applicable rows have to be written to the spool and aggregated. Examples of such aggregates are MIN and MAX. To demonstrate this, the following query uses the MAX aggregate to compute the maximum value among the last 100 transactions:

```
SELECT actid, tranid, val,
  MAX(val) OVER(PARTITION BY actid
                ORDER BY tranid
                ROWS BETWEEN 99 PRECEDING AND CURRENT ROW) AS max100
FROM dbo.Transactions;
```

The plan for this query is shown in Figure 4-8.

FIGURE 4-8 Plan for moving maximum.

Observe the number of rows flowing into and from the Window Spool operator. This query took 64 seconds to complete.

Note that even though the plan chosen is a parallel plan, there's a trick developed by Adam Machanic you can use that can improve the treatment of parallelism. When the calculation is partitioned (like in our case, where it is partitioned by *actid*), you can issue a query against the table holding the partitions (Accounts, in our case) and then, with the CROSS APPLY operator, apply a query similar to the original but filtered by the current partition value.

To apply this method to our example, use the following query:

```
SELECT A.actid, D.tranid, D.val, D.max100
FROM dbo.Accounts AS A
  CROSS APPLY (SELECT tranid, val,
                 MAX(val) OVER(ORDER BY tranid
                          ROWS BETWEEN 99 PRECEDING AND CURRENT ROW) AS max100
              FROM dbo.Transactions AS T
              WHERE T.actid = A.actid) AS D;
```

The plan for this query is shown in Figure 4-9.

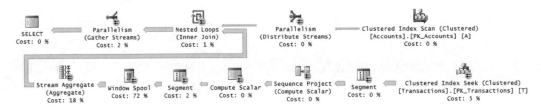

FIGURE 4-9 Optimization with the APPLY operator.

It took this query 30 seconds to complete on my system—half the time of the original query.

Aggregate window functions support another frame unit, called RANGE. Unfortunately though, SQL Server has a limited implementation of this option. In standard SQL, the RANGE option allows you to express the delimiters as an offset from the current row's ordering value. That's in contrast to ROWS, which defines the offset in terms of a number of rows. So with RANGE, the definition of the frame is more dynamic.

As an example, suppose you need to compute for each employee and month the moving average quantity of the last three months—not the last three recorded months. The problem is that you don't have any assurance that every employee had activity in every month. If an employee did not have activity in a certain month, there won't be a row in the EmpOrders table for that employee in that month. For example, employee 9 had activity in July 2013 and then no activity in August and September, activity in October, no activity in November, and then activity in December. If you use the frame *ROWS BETWEEN 2 PRECEDING AND CURRENT ROW* to compute the moving average of the last three recorded months, for employee 9 in December 2013 you will capture a period of half a year. The RANGE option is supposed to help you if you need a period of the last three months, never mind how many rows are included. According to standard SQL, you are supposed to use the following query (don't run it in SQL Server because it's not supported):

```
SELECT empid, ordermonth, qty,
  SUM(qty) OVER(PARTITION BY empid
            ORDER BY ordermonth
            RANGE BETWEEN INTERVAL '2' MONTH PRECEDING
                     AND CURRENT ROW) AS sum3month
FROM dbo.EmpOrders;
```

As a result, you are supposed to get the following output for employee 9:

```
empid       ordermonth qty         sum3month
----------- ---------- ----------- -----------
...
9           2013-07-01 294         294
9           2013-10-01 256         256
9           2013-12-01 25          281
9           2014-01-01 74          99
9           2014-03-01 137         211
9           2014-04-01 52          189
9           2014-05-01 8           197
9           2014-06-01 161         221
9           2014-07-01 4           173
9           2014-08-01 98          263
...
```

Unfortunately, SQL Server is missing two things to allow such a query. One, SQL Server is missing the INTERVAL feature. Two, SQL Server supports only UNBOUNDED and CURRENT ROW as delimiters for the RANGE unit.

To achieve the task in SQL Server, you have a few options. One is to pad the data with missing employee and month entries, and then use the ROWS option, like so:

```
DECLARE
  @frommonth AS DATE = '20130701',
  @tomonth   AS DATE = '20150501';

WITH M AS
(
  SELECT DATEADD(month, N.n, @frommonth) AS ordermonth
  FROM TSQLV3.dbo.GetNums(0, DATEDIFF(month, @frommonth, @tomonth)) AS N
),
R AS
(
  SELECT E.empid, M.ordermonth, EO.qty,
    SUM(EO.qty) OVER(PARTITION BY E.empid
                 ORDER BY M.ordermonth
                 ROWS BETWEEN 2 PRECEDING AND CURRENT ROW) AS sum3month
  FROM TSQLV3.HR.Employees AS E CROSS JOIN M
    LEFT OUTER JOIN dbo.EmpOrders AS EO
      ON E.empid = EO.empid
        AND M.ordermonth = EO.ordermonth
)
SELECT empid, ordermonth, qty, sum3month
FROM R
WHERE qty IS NOT NULL;
```

The other option is to use a query with a join and grouping like the one I showed for the running total example:

```
SELECT O1.empid, O1.ordermonth, O1.qty,
  SUM(O2.qty) AS sum3month
FROM dbo.EmpOrders AS O1
  INNER JOIN dbo.EmpOrders AS O2
    ON O2.empid = O1.empid
    AND O2.ordermonth
      BETWEEN DATEADD(month, -2, O1.ordermonth)
          AND O1.ordermonth
GROUP BY O1.empid, O1.ordermonth, O1.qty
ORDER BY O1.empid, O1.ordermonth;
```

The question is, why even bother supporting RANGE with only UNBOUNDED and CURRENT ROW as delimiters? As it turns out, there is a subtle logical difference between ROWS and RANGE when they use the same frame specification. But that difference manifests itself only when the order is not unique. The ROWS option doesn't include peers (ties in the ordering value), whereas RANGE does. Consider the following query as an example:

```
SELECT orderid, orderdate, val,
  SUM(val) OVER(ORDER BY orderdate ROWS UNBOUNDED PRECEDING) AS sumrows,
  SUM(val) OVER(ORDER BY orderdate RANGE UNBOUNDED PRECEDING) AS sumrange
FROM dbo.OrderValues;
```

This query generates the following output:

```
orderid  orderdate   val       sumrows      sumrange
-------- ----------  --------  -----------  -----------
10248    2013-07-04  440.00    440.00       440.00
10249    2013-07-05  1863.40   2303.40      2303.40
10250    2013-07-08  1552.60   3856.00      4510.06
10251    2013-07-08  654.06    4510.06      4510.06
10252    2013-07-09  3597.90   8107.96      8107.96
...
11070    2015-05-05  1629.98   1257012.06   1263014.56
11071    2015-05-05  484.50    1257496.56   1263014.56
11072    2015-05-05  5218.00   1262714.56   1263014.56
11073    2015-05-05  300.00    1263014.56   1263014.56
11074    2015-05-06  232.09    1263246.65   1265793.22
11075    2015-05-06  498.10    1263744.75   1265793.22
11076    2015-05-06  792.75    1264537.50   1265793.22
11077    2015-05-06  1255.72   1265793.22   1265793.22
```

The *orderdate* column isn't unique. Observe the difference between the results of the functions in orders 10250 and 10251. Notice that in the case of ROWS peers in the *orderdate* values were not included, making the calculation nondeterministic. Access order to the rows determines which values are included in the calculation. With RANGE, peers were included, so both rows get the same results.

While the logical difference between the two options is subtle, the performance difference is not subtle at all. For the Window Spool operator, the optimizer can use either a special optimized in-memory spool or an on-disk spool like the one used for temporary tables with all the I/O and latching overhead. The risk with the in-memory spool is memory consumption. If the optimizer knows that per underlying row there can't be more than 10,000 rows in the frame, it uses the in-memory spool. If it either knows that there could be more or is not certain, it will use the on-disk spool. With ROWS, when the fast-track case is detected you have exactly two rows stored in the spool per underlying row, so you always get the in-memory spool. You have a couple of ways to check what kind of spool was used. One is using an extended event called *window_spool_ondisk_warning*, which is fired when an on-disk spool is used. The other is through STATISTICS IO. The in-memory spool results in zeros in the I/O counters against the worktable, whereas the on-disk spool shows nonzero values.

As an example, run the following query after turning on STATISTICS IO:

```
SELECT actid, tranid, val,
  SUM(val) OVER(PARTITION BY actid
                ORDER BY tranid
                ROWS UNBOUNDED PRECEDING) AS balance
FROM dbo.Transactions;
```

It took this query four seconds to complete on my system. Its plan is similar to the one shown earlier in Figure 4-5. Notice that the I/O statistics reported for the worktable are zeros, telling you that the in-memory spool was used:

```
Table 'Worktable'. Scan count 0, logical reads 0, physical reads 0, read-ahead reads 0,
lob logical reads 0, lob physical reads 0, lob read-ahead reads 0.
Table 'Transactions'. Scan count 1, logical reads 6208, physical reads 168,
read-ahead reads 6200, lob logical reads 0, lob physical reads 0, lob read-ahead reads 0.
```

Remember that RANGE includes peers, so when using this option, the optimizer cannot know ahead how many rows will need to be included. So whenever you use RANGE, the optimizer always chooses the on-disk spool. Here's an example using the RANGE option:

```
SELECT actid, tranid, val,
  SUM(val) OVER(PARTITION BY actid
                ORDER BY tranid
                RANGE UNBOUNDED PRECEDING) AS balance
FROM dbo.Transactions;
```

Observe that the I/O statistics against the worktable are quite significant this time, telling you that the on-disk spool was used:

```
Table 'Worktable'. Scan count 2000100, logical reads 12044701, physical reads 0,
read-ahead reads 0, lob logical reads 0, lob physical reads 0, lob read-ahead reads 0.
Table 'Transactions'. Scan count 1, logical reads 6208, physical reads 0, read-ahead reads 0,
lob logical reads 0, lob physical reads 0, lob read-ahead reads 0.
```

It took this query 37 seconds to complete on my system. That's an order of magnitude slower than with the ROWS option.

> **Important** There are two important things you should make a note of. One is that if you specify a window order clause but do not indicate an explicit frame, the default frame is the much slower *RANGE UNBOUNDED PRECEDING*. The second point is that when the order is unique, ROWS and RANGE that have the same frame specification return the same results, but still the former will be much faster. Unfortunately, the optimizer doesn't internally convert the RANGE option to ROWS when the ordering is unique to allow better optimization. So unless you have a nonunique order and need to include peers, make sure you indicate ROWS explicitly; otherwise, you will just pay for the unnecessary work.

A classic data-analysis calculation called *year-to-date (YTD)* is a variation of a running total calculation. It's just that you need to reset the calculation at the beginning of each year. To achieve this, you specify the expression representing the year, like *YEAR(orderdate)*, in the window partition clause in addition to any other elements you need there.

For example, suppose you need to query the OrderValues table and return for each order the current order info, plus a YTD calculation of the order values per customer based on order date ordering, including peers. This means that your window partition clause will be based on the elements *custid, YEAR(orderdate)*. The window order clause will be based on *orderdate*. The window frame unit will be RANGE because you are requested not to break ties but rather include them. So even though the RANGE option is the more expensive one, that's exactly the special case where you are supposed to use it. Here's the complete query:

```
SELECT custid, orderid, orderdate, val,
  SUM(val) OVER(PARTITION BY custid, YEAR(orderdate)
            ORDER BY orderdate
            RANGE UNBOUNDED PRECEDING) AS YTD_val
FROM dbo.OrderValues;
```

This query generates the following output:

```
custid  orderid  orderdate   val       YTD_val
-------  --------  ----------  --------  --------
1       10643    2014-08-25  814.50    814.50
1       10692    2014-10-03  878.00    1692.50
1       10702    2014-10-13  330.00    2022.50
1       10835    2015-01-15  845.80    845.80
1       10952    2015-03-16  471.20    1317.00
1       11011    2015-04-09  933.50    2250.50
...
10      10389    2013-12-20  1832.80   1832.80
10      10410    2014-01-10  802.00    1768.80
10      10411    2014-01-10  966.80    1768.80
10      10431    2014-01-30  1892.25   3661.05
10      10492    2014-04-01  851.20    4512.25
...
```

Observe that customer 10 placed two orders on January 10, 2014, and that the calculation pro-duces the same YTD values in both rows, as it should.

If you need to return only one row per distinct customer and date, you want to first group the rows by the two, and then apply the windowed SUM function to the grouped SUM function. Now that the combination of partitioning and ordering elements is unique, you should use the ROWS unit. Here's the complete query:

```
SELECT custid, orderdate,
    SUM(SUM(val)) OVER(PARTITION BY custid, YEAR(orderdate)
                    ORDER BY orderdate
                    ROWS UNBOUNDED PRECEDING) AS YTD_val
FROM dbo.OrderValues
GROUP BY custid, orderdate;
```

This query generates the following output:

```
custid  orderdate   YTD_val
-------  ----------  --------
1        2014-08-25  814.50
1        2014-10-03  1692.50
1        2014-10-13  2022.50
1        2015-01-15  845.80
1        2015-03-16  1317.00
1        2015-04-09  2250.50
...
10       2013-12-20  1832.80
10       2014-01-10  1768.80
10       2014-01-30  3661.05
10       2014-04-01  4512.25
10       2014-11-14  7630.25
...
```

Observe that now there's only one row for each unique customer and date, like in the case of cus-tomer 10, on January 10, 2014.

Ranking window functions

Ranking calculations are implemented in T-SQL as window functions. When you rank a value, you don't rank it alone, but rather with respect to some set of values, based on certain order. The windowing concept lends itself to such calculations. The set is defined by the OVER clause. Absent a window partition clause, you rank the current row's value against all rows in the underlying query's result set. With a window partition clause, you rank the row against the rows in the same window partition. A mandatory window order clause defines the order for the ranking.

To demonstrate ranking window functions, I'll use the following Orders table.

```
SET NOCOUNT ON;
USE tempdb;

IF OBJECT_ID(N'dbo.Orders', N'U') IS NOT NULL DROP TABLE dbo.Orders;

CREATE TABLE dbo.Orders
(
  orderid   INT        NOT NULL,
  orderdate DATE       NOT NULL,
  empid     INT        NOT NULL,
  custid    VARCHAR(5) NOT NULL,
  qty       INT        NOT NULL,
  CONSTRAINT PK_Orders PRIMARY KEY (orderid)
);
GO

INSERT INTO dbo.Orders(orderid, orderdate, empid, custid, qty)
  VALUES(30001, '20130802', 3, 'B', 10),
        (10001, '20131224', 1, 'C', 10),
        (10005, '20131224', 1, 'A', 30),
        (40001, '20140109', 4, 'A', 40),
        (10006, '20140118', 1, 'C', 10),
        (20001, '20140212', 2, 'B', 20),
        (40005, '20140212', 4, 'A', 10),
        (20002, '20140216', 2, 'C', 20),
        (30003, '20140418', 3, 'B', 15),
        (30004, '20140418', 3, 'B', 20),
        (30007, '20140907', 3, 'C', 30);
```

T-SQL supports four ranking functions, called ROW_NUMBER, RANK, DENSE_RANK, and NTILE. Here's a query demonstrating all four against the Orders table, without a window partition clause, ordered by the *qty* column:

```
SELECT orderid, qty,
  ROW_NUMBER() OVER(ORDER BY qty) AS rownum,
  RANK()       OVER(ORDER BY qty) AS rnk,
  DENSE_RANK() OVER(ORDER BY qty) AS densernk,
  NTILE(4)     OVER(ORDER BY qty) AS ntile4
FROM dbo.Orders;
```

This query generates the following output:

```
orderid  qty  rownum  rnk  densernk  ntile4
-------- ---- ------- ---- --------- -------
10001    10   1       1    1         1
10006    10   2       1    1         1
30001    10   3       1    1         1
40005    10   4       1    1         2
30003    15   5       5    2         2
30004    20   6       6    3         2
20001    20   7       6    3         3
20002    20   8       6    3         3
10005    30   9       9    4         3
30007    30   10      9    4         4
40001    40   11      11   5         4
```

The ROW_NUMBER function is the most commonly used of the four. It computes unique incrementing integers in the target partition (the entire query result in this example), based on the specified order. When the ordering is not unique within the partition, like in our example, the calculation is nondeterministic. Meaning, if you run the query again, you're not guaranteed to get repeatable results. For example, observe the three rows with the quantity 20. They got the row numbers 6, 7, and 8. What determines which of the three gets which row number is a matter of data layout, optimization, and actual access order. Those things are not guaranteed to be repeatable.

There are cases where you need to guarantee determinism (repeatable results). For example, row numbers can be used for paging purposes, as I will demonstrate in Chapter 5, "TOP and OFFSET-FETCH." For each page, you submit a query filtering only a certain range of row numbers. You do not want the same row to end up in two different pages even though the underlying data didn't change just because in one query it got row number 25 and in the other 26. To force a deterministic calculation of row numbers, add a tiebreaker to the window order clause. In our example, extending it to *qty, orderid* makes the ordering unique, and therefore the calculation deterministic.

RANK and DENSE_RANK differ from ROW_NUMBER in that they produce the same rank value for rows with the same ordering value (quantity, in our case). The difference between RANK and DENSE_RANK is that the former computes one more than the count of rows with lower ordering values than the current, and the latter computes one more than the count of distinct ordering values that are lower than the current. For example, the rows that got row numbers 6, 7, and 8 all got rank values 6 (1 + 5 rows with quantities lower than 20) and dense rank values 3 (1 + 2 distinct quantities that are lower than 20). As a result, rank values can have gaps between them, as is the case between the ranks 1 and 5, whereas dense rank values cannot.

Finally, the NTILE function assigns tile numbers to the rows in the partition based on the specified number of tiles and ordering. In our case, the requested number of tiles is 4 and the ordering is based on the *qty* column. So, based on quantity ordering, the first fourth of the rows in the result is assigned with tile number 1, the next with 2, and so on. If the count of rows doesn't divide evenly by the specified number of tiles, assuming *R* is the remainder, the first R tiles will get an extra row. In our case, we have 11 rows, resulting in a tile size of 2 and a remainder of 3. So the first three tiles will have three rows instead of two. The NTILE calculation is the least commonly used out of the four ranking calculations. Its main use cases are in statistical analysis of data.

Recall that the optional window partition clause is available to all window functions. Here's an example of a computation of row numbers, partitioned by *custid*, and ordered by *orderid*:

```
SELECT custid, orderid, qty,
  ROW_NUMBER() OVER(PARTITION BY custid ORDER BY orderid) AS rownum
FROM dbo.Orders
ORDER BY custid, orderid;
```

This query generates the following output, where you can see the row numbers are independent for each customer:

```
custid orderid      qty       rownum
------ -----------  ----------- --------------------
A      10005        30        1
A      40001        40        2
A      40005        10        3
B      20001        20        1
B      30001        10        2
B      30003        15        3
B      30004        20        4
C      10001        10        1
C      10006        10        2
C      20002        20        3
C      30007        30        4
```

The query defines presentation order by *custid, orderid*. Remember that absent a presentation ORDER BY clause, presentation order is not guaranteed.

From an optimization perspective, like with window aggregate functions, the ideal index for a query with a ranking function like ROW_NUMBER is a POC index. Figure 4-10 has the plan for the query when a POC index does *not* exist.

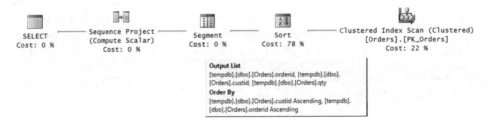

FIGURE 4-10 Optimization of ROW_NUMBER without a POC index.

Because a POC index isn't present in our case, the optimizer chooses a clustered index scan with an Ordered: False property. It then applies a Sort operator to sort the data by *custid, orderid*. This order supports both the calculation of the ROW_NUMBER function and the presentation order, which happen to be aligned. The Segment operator flags the Sequence Project operator when a new segment (partition) starts. In turn, the latter returns 1 when the row is the first in the partition, and adds 1 to the previous value when it isn't.

If you want to avoid the sort, you need to create a POC index, like so:

```
CREATE UNIQUE INDEX idx_cid_oid_i_qty ON dbo.Orders(custid, orderid) INCLUDE(qty);
```

Rerun the query, and you get the plan shown in Figure 4-11.

FIGURE 4-11 Optimization of ROW_NUMBER with a POC index.

This time you get an ordered scan of the POC index, and the sort disappears from the plan.

Compared to the previously described optimization of aggregate window functions, ROW_NUMBER, RANK, and DENSE_RANK are optimized using superfast streaming operators; there's no spooling. It would certainly be great to see in the future similar optimization of aggregate functions that use common specialized frames like *ROWS UNBOUNDED PRECEDING*.

As for NTILE, the optimizer needs to know the count of rows in the query result in order to compute the tile size. For this, it uses optimization similar to adding the window aggregate *COUNT(*) OVER()*, with the spooling technique demonstrated earlier in Figure 4-2.

There's a curious thing about the ROW_NUMBER function and window ordering. A window order clause is mandatory, and it cannot be a constant; though there's no requirement for the window ordering to be unique. These requirements impose a challenge when you want to compute row numbers just for uniqueness purposes and you don't care about order. You also don't want to pay any unnecessary costs that are related to arranging the data in the required order. If you attempt to omit the window order clause, you get an error. If you try to specify a constant like *ORDER BY NULL*, you get an error. Surprisingly, SQL Server is happy when you provide a subquery returning a constant, as in *ORDER BY (SELECT NULL)*. Here's an example for a query using this trick:

```
SELECT orderid, orderdate, custid, empid, qty,
  ROW_NUMBER() OVER(ORDER BY (SELECT NULL)) AS rownum
FROM dbo.Orders;
```

The optimizer realizes that because all rows will have the same ordering value, it doesn't really need the data in any order. So it assigns the row numbers simply based on access order (data layout, optimization).

Offset window functions

You use offset window functions to request an element from a row that is at the beginning or end of the window frame or is in a certain offset from the current row. I'll first describe a pair of offset window functions called FIRST_VALUE and LAST_VALUE, and then I'll describe the pair LAG and LEAD.

FIRST_VALUE and LAST_VALUE

You can use the FIRST_VALUE and LAST_VALUE functions to return an element from the first or last row in the window frame, respectively. The frame specification is the same as what I described in the "Window frame" section in the "Aggregate window functions" topic. This includes the discussion about the critical performance difference between ROWS and RANGE.

You will usually use the FIRST_VALUE and LAST_VALUE functions when you need to return something from the first or last row in the partition. In such a case, you will want to use FIRST_VALUE with the frame *ROWS BETWEEN UNBOUNDED PRECEDING AND CURRENT ROW*, and LAST_VALUE with the frame *ROWS BETWEEN CURRENT ROW AND UNBOUNDED FOLLOWING*.

As an example, the following query against the Orders table returns with each order the quantity of the same customer's first order (*firstqty*) and last order (*lastqty*):

```
SELECT custid, orderid, orderdate, qty,
  FIRST_VALUE(qty) OVER(PARTITION BY custid
                        ORDER BY orderdate, orderid
                        ROWS BETWEEN UNBOUNDED PRECEDING
                              AND CURRENT ROW) AS firstqty,
  LAST_VALUE(qty)  OVER(PARTITION BY custid
                        ORDER BY orderdate, orderid
                        ROWS BETWEEN CURRENT ROW
                              AND UNBOUNDED FOLLOWING) AS lastqty
FROM dbo.Orders
ORDER BY custid, orderdate, orderid;
```

This query generates the following output:

custid	orderid	orderdate	qty	firstqty	lastqty
A	10005	2013-12-24	30	30	10
A	40001	2014-01-09	40	30	10
A	40005	2014-02-12	10	30	10
B	30001	2013-08-02	10	10	20
B	20001	2014-02-12	20	10	20
B	30003	2014-04-18	15	10	20
B	30004	2014-04-18	20	10	20
C	10001	2013-12-24	10	10	30
C	10006	2014-01-18	10	10	30
C	20002	2014-02-16	20	10	30
C	30007	2014-09-07	30	10	30

Typically, you will use these functions combined with other elements in the calculation. For example, compute the difference between the current order quantity and the quantity of the same customer's first order, as in *qty – FIRST_VALUE(qty) OVER(…)*.

As with all window functions, the window partition clause is optional. As you could probably guess, the window order clause is mandatory. An explicit window frame specification is optional, but recall that once you have a window order clause, there is a frame; and the default frame is *RANGE UNBOUNDED PRECEDING*. So you want to make sure you specify the frame explicitly; otherwise, you will have problems with both functions. With the FIRST_VALUE function, the default frame will give you the element from the first row in the partition. However, remember that the default RANGE option is much more expensive than ROWS. As for LAST_VALUE, the last row in the default frame is the current row, and not the last row in the partition.

As for optimization, the FIRST_VALUE and LAST_VALUE functions are optimized like aggregate window functions with the same frame specification.

LAG and LEAD

You can use the LAG and LEAD functions to return an element from the previous or next row, respectively. As you might have guessed, a window order clause is mandatory with these functions. Typical uses for these functions include trend analysis (the difference between the current and previous months' values), recency (the difference between the current and previous orders' supply dates), and so on.

As an example, the following query returns along with order information the quantities of the same customer's previous and next orders:

```
SELECT custid, orderid, orderdate, qty,
  LAG(qty)  OVER(PARTITION BY custid
                 ORDER BY orderdate, orderid) AS prevqty,
  LEAD(qty) OVER(PARTITION BY custid
                 ORDER BY orderdate, orderid) AS nextqty
FROM dbo.Orders
ORDER BY custid, orderdate, orderid;
```

This query generates the following output:

```
custid orderid     orderdate   qty         prevqty     nextqty
------ ----------- ----------- ----------- ----------- -----------
A      10005       2013-12-24  30          NULL        40
A      40001       2014-01-09  40          30          10
A      40005       2014-02-12  10          40          NULL
B      30001       2013-08-02  10          NULL        20
B      20001       2014-02-12  20          10          15
B      30003       2014-04-18  15          20          20
B      30004       2014-04-18  20          15          NULL
C      10001       2013-12-24  10          NULL        10
C      10006       2014-01-18  10          10          20
C      20002       2014-02-16  20          10          30
C      30007       2014-09-07  30          20          NULL
```

As you can see, the LAG function returns a NULL for the first row in the partition and the LEAD function returns a NULL for the last.

These functions support a second parameter indicating the offset in case you want it to be other than NULL, and a third parameter indicating the default instead of a NULL in case a row doesn't exist in the requested offset. For example, the expression *LAG(qty, 3, 0)* returns the quantity from three rows before the current row and 0 if a row doesn't exist in that offset.

As for optimization, the LAG and LEAD functions are internally converted to the LAST_VALUE function with a frame made of one row. In the case of LAG, the frame used is *ROWS BETWEEN 1 PRECEDING AND 1 PRECEDING*; in the case of LEAD, the frame is *ROWS BETWEEN 1 FOLLOWING AND 1 FOLLOWING*.

Statistical window functions

T-SQL supports two pairs of statistical window functions that provide information about distribution of data. One pair of functions provides rank distribution information and another provides inverse distribution information.

Rank distribution functions

Rank distribution functions give you the relative rank of a row expressed as a percent (in the range 0 through 1) in the target partition based on the specified order. T-SQL supports two such functions, called PERCENT_RANK and CUME_DIST. Each of the two computes the rank a bit differently.

Following are the elements involved in the formulas for the two computations:

- rk = Rank of the row based on the same specification as the distribution function.

- nr = Count of rows in the partition.

- np = Number of rows that precede or are peers of the current row.

The formula used to compute PERCENT_RANK is $(rk - 1) / (nr - 1)$.

The formula used to compute CUME_DIST is np / nr.

As an example, the following query uses these functions to compute rank distribution information of student test scores:

```
USE TSQLV3;

SELECT testid, studentid, score,
  CAST( 100.00 *
    PERCENT_RANK() OVER(PARTITION BY testid ORDER BY score)
      AS NUMERIC(5, 2) ) AS percentrank,
  CAST( 100.00 *
    CUME_DIST() OVER(PARTITION BY testid ORDER BY score)
      AS NUMERIC(5, 2) ) AS cumedist
FROM Stats.Scores;
```

This query generates the following output:

testid	studentid	score	percentrank	cumedist
Test ABC	Student E	50	0.00	11.11
Test ABC	Student C	55	12.50	33.33
Test ABC	Student D	55	12.50	33.33
Test ABC	Student H	65	37.50	44.44
Test ABC	Student I	75	50.00	55.56
Test ABC	Student B	80	62.50	77.78
Test ABC	Student F	80	62.50	77.78
Test ABC	Student A	95	87.50	100.00
Test ABC	Student G	95	87.50	100.00
Test XYZ	Student E	50	0.00	10.00
Test XYZ	Student C	55	11.11	30.00
Test XYZ	Student D	55	11.11	30.00

```
Test XYZ    Student H  65    33.33         40.00
Test XYZ    Student I  75    44.44         50.00
Test XYZ    Student B  80    55.56         70.00
Test XYZ    Student F  80    55.56         70.00
Test XYZ    Student A  95    77.78        100.00
Test XYZ    Student G  95    77.78        100.00
Test XYZ    Student J  95    77.78        100.00
```

Inverse distribution functions

Inverse distribution functions compute percentiles. A percentile *N* is the value below which N percent of the observations fall. For example, the 50th percentile (aka *median*) test score is the score below which 50 percent of the scores fall.

There are two distribution models that can be used to compute percentiles: discrete and continuous. When the requested percentile exists as an exact value in the population, both models return that value. For example, when computing the median with an odd number of elements, both models result in the middle element. The two models differ when the requested percentile doesn't exist as an actual value in the population. For example, when computing the median with an even number of elements, there is no middle point. In such a case, the discrete model returns the element closest to the missing one. In the median's case, you get the value just before the missing one. The continuous model interpolates the missing value from the two surrounding it, assuming continuous distribution. In the median's case, it's the average of the two middle values.

T-SQL provides two window functions, called PERCENTILE_DISC and PERCENTILE_CONT, that implement the discrete and continuous models, respectively. You specify the percentile you're after as an input value in the range 0 to 1. Using a clause called WITHIN GROUP, you specify the order. As is usual with window functions, you can apply the calculation against the entire query result set or against a restricted partition using a window partition clause.

As an example, the following query computes the median student test scores within the same test using both models:

```
SELECT testid, studentid, score,
  PERCENTILE_DISC(0.5) WITHIN GROUP(ORDER BY score)
    OVER(PARTITION BY testid) AS mediandisc,
  PERCENTILE_CONT(0.5) WITHIN GROUP(ORDER BY score)
    OVER(PARTITION BY testid) AS mediancont
FROM Stats.Scores;
```

Because a window function is not supposed to hide the detail, you get the results along with the detail rows. The same results get repeated for all rows in the same partition. Here's the output of this query:

```
testid      studentid  score mediandisc mediancont
----------- ---------- ----- ---------- ----------------------
Test ABC    Student E  50    75         75
Test ABC    Student C  55    75         75
Test ABC    Student D  55    75         75
Test ABC    Student H  65    75         75
Test ABC    Student I  75    75         75
```

Test ABC	Student B	80	75	75
Test ABC	Student F	80	75	75
Test ABC	Student A	95	75	75
Test ABC	Student G	95	75	75
Test XYZ	Student E	50	75	77.5
Test XYZ	Student C	55	75	77.5
Test XYZ	Student D	55	75	77.5
Test XYZ	Student H	65	75	77.5
Test XYZ	Student I	75	75	77.5
Test XYZ	Student B	80	75	77.5
Test XYZ	Student F	80	75	77.5
Test XYZ	Student A	95	75	77.5
Test XYZ	Student G	95	75	77.5
Test XYZ	Student J	95	75	77.5

Observe that for Test ABC the two functions return the same results because there's an odd number of rows. For Test XYZ, the results are different because there's an even number of elements. Remember that in the case of median, when there's an even number of elements the two models use different calculations.

Standard SQL supports inverse distribution functions as grouped ordered set functions. That's convenient when you need to return the percentile calculation once per group (test, in our case) and not repeated with all detail rows. Unfortunately, ordered set functions are not supported yet in SQL Server. But just to give you a sense, here's how you would compute the median in both models per test (don't try running this in SQL Server):

```
SELECT testid,
  PERCENTILE_DISC(0.5) WITHIN GROUP(ORDER BY score) AS mediandisc,
  PERCENTILE_CONT(0.5) WITHIN GROUP(ORDER BY score) AS mediancont
FROM Stats.Scores
GROUP BY testid;
```

Note You can find a SQL Server feature enhancement request about ordered set functions here: *https://connect.microsoft.com/SQLServer/feedback/details/728969*. We hope we will see this feature implemented in the future. The concept is applicable not just to inverse-distribution functions but to any set function that has ordering relevance.

The alternative in SQL Server is to use the window functions and eliminate duplicates with a DISTINCT clause, like so:

```
SELECT DISTINCT testid,
  PERCENTILE_DISC(0.5) WITHIN GROUP(ORDER BY score)
    OVER(PARTITION BY testid) AS mediandisc,
  PERCENTILE_CONT(0.5) WITHIN GROUP(ORDER BY score)
    OVER(PARTITION BY testid) AS mediancont
FROM Stats.Scores;
```

This query generates the following output:

```
testid     mediandisc mediancont
---------- ---------- ----------------------
Test ABC   75         75
Test XYZ   75         77.5
```

From an optimization perspective, these functions are optimized very inefficiently. The query plan has a number of rounds where the rows are spooled, and then the spool is read once to compute an aggregate and once for the detail. See Chapter 5 for a discussion about more efficient alternatives.

Gaps and islands

Gaps and islands are classic problems in T-SQL that involve a sequence of values. The type of the values is usually date and time, but sometimes integer and others. The gaps task involves identifying the ranges of missing values, and the islands task involves identifying the ranges of existing values. Examples for gaps and islands tasks are identifying periods of inactivity and periods of activity, respectively. Many gaps and islands tasks can be solved efficiently using window functions.

I'll first demonstrate solutions using a sequence of integers simply because it's much easier to explain the logic with integers. In reality, most gaps and islands tasks involve date and time sequences. Once you figure out a technique to solve the task using a sequence of integers, you need to perform fairly minor adjustments to apply it to a date-and-time sequence.

For sample data, I'll use the following table T1:

```
SET NOCOUNT ON;
USE tempdb;
IF OBJECT_ID('dbo.T1', 'U') IS NOT NULL DROP TABLE dbo.T1;

CREATE TABLE dbo.T1(col1 INT NOT NULL CONSTRAINT PK_T1 PRIMARY KEY);
GO

INSERT INTO dbo.T1(col1) VALUES(1),(2),(3),(7),(8),(9),(11),(15),(16),(17),(28);
```

Gaps

The gaps task is about identifying the ranges of missing values in the sequence as intervals. I'll demonstrate a technique to handle the task against the table T1.

One of the simplest and most efficient techniques involves two steps. The first is to return for each current *col1* value (call it *cur*) the immediate next value using the LEAD function (call it *nxt*). This is achieved with the following query:

```
SELECT col1 AS cur, LEAD(col1) OVER(ORDER BY col1) AS nxt
FROM dbo.T1;
```

This query generates the following output:

```
cur          nxt
-----------  -----------
1            2
2            3
3            7
7            8
8            9
9            11
11           15
15           16
16           17
17           28
28           NULL
```

We have an index on *col1*, so the plan for this query does a single ordered scan of the index to support the LEAD calculation.

Examine the pairs of *cur-nxt* values, and observe that the pairs where the difference is greater than one represent gaps. The second step involves defining a CTE based on the last query, and then filtering the pairs representing gaps, adding one to *cur* and subtracting one from *nxt* to return the actual gap information. Here's the complete solution query:

```
WITH C AS
(
  SELECT col1 AS cur, LEAD(col1) OVER(ORDER BY col1) AS nxt
  FROM dbo.T1
)
SELECT cur + 1 AS range_from, nxt - 1 AS range_to
FROM C
WHERE nxt - cur > 1;
```

This query generates the following output:

```
range_from  range_to
-----------  -----------
4            6
10           10
12           14
18           27
```

Notice also that the pair with the NULL in *nxt* was naturally filtered out because the difference was NULL, NULL > 1 is unknown, and unknown gets filtered out.

Islands

The islands task is the inverse of the gaps task. Identifying islands means returning the ranges of consecutive values. I'll first demonstrate a solution using the generic sequence of integers in *T1.col1*, and then I'll use a more realistic example using a sequence of dates.

One of the most beautiful and efficient techniques to identify islands involves computing row numbers based on the order of the sequence column, and using those to compute an island identifier. To see how this can be achieved, first compute row numbers based on *col1* order, like so:

```
SELECT col1, ROW_NUMBER() OVER(ORDER BY col1) AS rownum
FROM dbo.T1;
```

This query generates the following output:

```
col1         rownum
-----------  --------------------
1            1
2            2
3            3
7            4
8            5
9            6
11           7
15           8
16           9
17           10
28           11
```

Look carefully at the two sequences and see if you can identify an interesting relationship between them that can help you identify islands. For this, focus your attention on one of the islands. If you do enough staring at the output, you will figure it out at some point—within an island, both sequences keep incrementing by a fixed interval of 1 integer; therefore, the difference between the two is the same within the island. Also, when switching from one island to the next *rownum* increases by 1, whereas *col1* increases by more than 1; therefore, the difference keeps growing from one island to the next and hence is unique per island. This means you can use the difference as the island, or group, identifier. Run the following query to compute the group identifier (*grp*) based on this logic:

```
SELECT col1, col1 - ROW_NUMBER() OVER(ORDER BY col1) AS grp
FROM dbo.T1;
```

This query generates the following output:

```
col1         grp
-----------  --------------------
1            0
2            0
3            0
7            3
8            3
9            3
11           4
15           7
16           7
17           7
28           17
```

Because there's an index defined on col1, the computation of the row numbers doesn't require explicit sorting, as can be seen in the plan for this query in Figure 4-12.

FIGURE 4-12 Plan for query computing group identifier.

Most of the cost of this plan is in the ordered scan of the index PK_T1. The rest of the work involving the calculation of the row numbers and the computation of the difference between the sequences is negligible.

Finally, you need to define a CTE based on the last query, and then in the outer query group the rows by *grp*, return the minimum *col1* value as the start of the island, and return the maximum as the end. Here's the complete solution query:

```
WITH C AS
(
  SELECT col1, col1 - ROW_NUMBER() OVER(ORDER BY col1) AS grp
  FROM dbo.T1
)
SELECT MIN(col1) AS range_from, MAX(col1) AS range_to
FROM C
GROUP BY grp;
```

This query generates the following output:

```
range_from  range_to
----------- -----------
1           3
7           9
11          11
15          17
28          28
```

The *col1* sequence in T1 has unique values, but you should be aware that if duplicate values were possible, the solution would not work correctly anymore. That's because the ROW_NUMBER function generates unique values in the target partition, even for rows with the same ordering values. For the logic to be correct, you need a ranking function that assigns the same ranking values for all rows with the same ordering values, with no gaps between distinct ranking values. Fortunately, such a ranking function exists—that's the DENSE_RANK function. Here's the revised solution using DENSE_RANK:

```
WITH C AS
(
  SELECT col1, col1 - DENSE_RANK() OVER(ORDER BY col1) AS grp
  FROM dbo.T1
)
SELECT MIN(col1) AS range_from, MAX(col1) AS range_to
FROM C
GROUP BY grp;
```

Because the DENSE_RANK function works correctly both when the sequence is unique and when it isn't, it makes sense to always use DENSE_RANK and not ROW_NUMBER. It's just easier to explain the logic first with a unique sequence using the ROW_NUMBER function, and then examine a nonunique sequence, and then explain why DENSE_RANK is preferred.

As mentioned, in most cases in reality you will need to identify islands involving date and time sequences. As an example, suppose you need to query the Sales.Orders table in the TSQLV3 database, and identify for each shipper the islands of shipped date values. The shipped date values are stored in the *shippeddate* column. Clearly you can have duplicate values in this column. Also, not all orders recorded in the table are shipped orders; those that were not yet shipped have a NULL shipped date. For the purpose of identifying islands, you should simply ignore those NULLs. To support your solution, you need an index on the partitioning column *shipperid*, sequence column *shippeddate*, and tiebreaker column *orderid* as the keys. Because NULLs are possible and should be ignored, you add a filter that excludes NULLs from the index definition. Run the following code to create the recommended index:

```
USE TSQLV3;

CREATE UNIQUE INDEX idx_sid_sd_oid
  ON Sales.Orders(shipperid, shippeddate, orderid)
WHERE shippeddate IS NOT NULL;
```

When computing the group identifier for the islands in *col1* in T1, both the *col1* values and the dense rank values were integers with the same interval 1. With the *shippeddate* sequence, things are trickier because the shipped date values and the dense rank values are of different types; one is temporal and the other is integer. Still, the interval between consecutive values in each is fixed, only in one case it's the temporal interval 1 day and in the other it's the integer interval 1. So, to apply the logic in this case, you subtract from the temporal shipped date value the dense rank value times the temporal interval (1 day). This way, the group identifier will be a temporal value, but like before it will be the same for all members of the same island.

Here's the complete solution query implementing this logic:

```
WITH C AS
(
  SELECT shipperid, shippeddate,
    DATEADD(
      day,
      -1 * DENSE_RANK() OVER(PARTITION BY shipperid ORDER BY shippeddate),
      shippeddate) AS grp
  FROM Sales.Orders
  WHERE shippeddate IS NOT NULL
)
SELECT shipperid,
  MIN(shippeddate) AS fromdate,
  MAX(shippeddate) AS todate,
  COUNT(*) as numorders
FROM C
GROUP BY shipperid, grp;
```

A good way to understand the logic behind computing the group identifier is to first run the inner query, which defines the CTE C, and examine the result. You will get the following output:

```
shipperid    shippeddate  grp
-----------  -----------  ----------
1            2013-07-10   2013-07-09
1            2013-07-15   2013-07-13
1            2013-07-23   2013-07-20
1            2013-07-29   2013-07-25
1            2013-08-02   2013-07-28
1            2013-08-06   2013-07-31
1            2013-08-09   2013-08-02
1            2013-08-09   2013-08-02
...
1            2014-01-10   2013-12-07
1            2014-01-13   2013-12-09
1            2014-01-14   2013-12-09
1            2014-01-14   2013-12-09
1            2014-01-22   2013-12-16
...
```

You will notice that the dates that belong to the same island get the same group identifier.

The plan for the inner query defining the CTE C can be seen in Figure 4-13.

FIGURE 4-13 Plan for inner query computing group identifier with dates.

This plan is very efficient. It performs an ordered scan of the index you prepared for this solution to support the computation of the dense rank values. The cost of the rest of the work in the plan is negligible.

The complete solution generates the ranges of shipped date values as the following output shows:

```
shipperid    fromdate     todate       numorders
-----------  ----------   ----------   -----------
1            2013-07-10   2013-07-10   1
2            2013-07-11   2013-07-12   2
1            2013-07-15   2013-07-15   1
2            2013-07-16   2013-07-17   2
3            2013-07-15   2013-07-16   2
...
```

There are different variations of islands challenges. A common and interesting one is when you need to identify islands while ignoring gaps of up to a certain size. For example, in our challenge to identify islands of shipped dates per shipper, suppose you need to ignore gaps of up to 7 days.

A very elegant solution to this variation involves the use of two window functions: LAG and SUM. You use LAG to return for each current order the shipped date of the previous order that was shipped by the same shipper. Using a CASE expression, you compute a flag called *startflag* that is set to 0 if the difference between the previous and the current dates is less than or equal to 7 and 1 otherwise. Here's the code implementing this step:

```
SELECT shipperid, shippeddate, orderid,
  CASE WHEN DATEDIFF(day,
    LAG(shippeddate) OVER(PARTITION BY shipperid ORDER BY shippeddate, orderid),
    shippeddate) <= 7 THEN 0 ELSE 1 END AS startflag
FROM Sales.Orders
WHERE shippeddate IS NOT NULL;
```

This query generates the following output:

```
shipperid   shippeddate orderid     startflag
----------- ----------- ----------- -----------
1           2013-07-10  10249       1
1           2013-07-15  10251       0
1           2013-07-23  10258       1
1           2013-07-29  10260       0
1           2013-08-02  10270       0
1           2013-08-06  10267       0
1           2013-08-09  10269       0
1           2013-08-09  10275       0
1           2013-08-12  10265       0
1           2013-08-16  10274       0
1           2013-08-21  10281       0
1           2013-08-21  10282       0
1           2013-08-27  10284       0
1           2013-09-03  10288       0
1           2013-09-03  10290       0
1           2013-09-11  10296       1
1           2013-09-12  10280       0
...
```

As you can see, the *startflag* flag marks the start of each island with a 1 and a nonstart of an island with a 0. Next, using the SUM window aggregate function, you compute the group identifier as the running total of the *startflag* flag over time, like so:

```
WITH C1 AS
(
  SELECT shipperid, shippeddate, orderid,
    CASE WHEN DATEDIFF(day,
      LAG(shippeddate) OVER(PARTITION BY shipperid ORDER BY shippeddate, orderid),
      shippeddate) <= 7 THEN 0 ELSE 1 END AS startflag
  FROM Sales.Orders
  WHERE shippeddate IS NOT NULL
)
SELECT *,
  SUM(startflag) OVER(PARTITION BY shipperid
                      ORDER BY shippeddate, orderid
                      ROWS UNBOUNDED PRECEDING) AS grp
FROM C1;
```

This query generates the following output:

```
shipperid    shippeddate  orderid    startflag  grp
-----------  -----------  ---------  ---------  ---------
1            2013-07-10   10249      1          1
1            2013-07-15   10251      0          1
1            2013-07-23   10258      1          2
1            2013-07-29   10260      0          2
1            2013-08-02   10270      0          2
1            2013-08-06   10267      0          2
1            2013-08-09   10269      0          2
1            2013-08-09   10275      0          2
1            2013-08-12   10265      0          2
1            2013-08-16   10274      0          2
1            2013-08-21   10281      0          2
1            2013-08-21   10282      0          2
1            2013-08-27   10284      0          2
1            2013-09-03   10288      0          2
1            2013-09-03   10290      0          2
1            2013-09-11   10296      1          3
1            2013-09-12   10280      0          3
...
```

Observe that the group identifier, as required, is the same for all members of the same island and is unique per island. The final step is to group the rows by *shipperid* and *grp*, and return the minimum and maximum shipped dates per island, like so:

```
WITH C1 AS
(
  SELECT shipperid, shippeddate, orderid,
    CASE WHEN DATEDIFF(day,
      LAG(shippeddate) OVER(PARTITION BY shipperid ORDER BY shippeddate, orderid),
      shippeddate) <= 7 THEN 0 ELSE 1 END AS startflag
  FROM Sales.Orders
  WHERE shippeddate IS NOT NULL
),
C2 AS
(
  SELECT *,
    SUM(startflag) OVER(PARTITION BY shipperid
                        ORDER BY shippeddate, orderid
                        ROWS UNBOUNDED PRECEDING) AS grp
  FROM C1
)
SELECT shipperid,
  MIN(shippeddate) AS fromdate,
  MAX(shippeddate) AS todate,
  COUNT(*) as numorders
FROM C2
GROUP BY shipperid, grp;
```

This query generates the following output:

```
shipperid    fromdate    todate      numorders
-----------  ----------  ----------  -----------
2            2014-12-31  2015-05-06  118
3            2013-09-11  2013-09-11  1
2            2013-08-26  2013-11-15  33
1            2014-04-04  2014-05-07  11
3            2013-07-15  2013-08-02  8
3            2013-11-18  2014-01-28  31
1            2013-12-13  2014-01-14  12
3            2014-05-12  2014-05-27  5
1            2014-08-06  2014-12-15  57
2            2014-06-18  2014-07-04  8
3            2013-08-12  2013-08-14  3
...
```

Examine the query plan for this solution, which is shown in Figure 4-14.

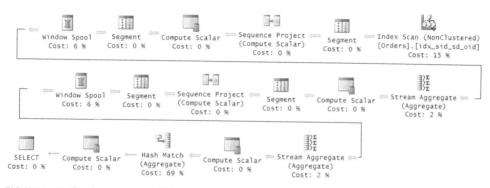

FIGURE 4-14 Plan for query identifying islands ignoring gaps of up to seven days.

Amazingly, not even one sort operation was required throughout the plan. Index order was relied on for the calculation of both the LAG and SUM window functions.

When you're done, run the following code to drop the index you created for this example:

```
DROP INDEX idx_sid_sd_oid ON Sales.Orders;
```

Pivoting

Pivoting is an operation that rotates data from a state of rows to a state of columns. There are different reasons to pivot data. A common reason is related to reporting: you have a certain amount of data to present but a limited space in the web page or printed report. Pivoting helps you fit more data in less space. Also, visually it's often convenient to analyze data presented as the intersection of dimensions represented by rows and columns. Other reasons to use pivoting are to handle custom aggregates (as I will discuss later in the chapter), solve relational division problems, and more.

There are two kinds of pivot operations: one-to-one and many-to-one. I'll describe both in the following sections.

One-to-one pivot

In a one-to-one pivot operation, you return in the result the exact same data you had in the source, only using a different shape. Multiple values from the same column in different source rows are returned as different column values of the same result row. This is best explained through a practical example.

As an example for a scenario where you need to apply a one-to-one pivot operation, I'll use a modeling scheme known as *open schema* and also as *dynamic schema*. You have a table called OpenSchema where you keep track of object attribute values using a model known as *EAV* (for entity, attribute, and value). In this model, you store each object attribute value in a separate row. Each object can have a different set of applicable attributes. Each attribute can be of a different type, so SQL_VARIANT is used as the type for the value column.

Run the following code to create the OpenSchema table and populate it with some sample data:

```
USE tempdb;

IF OBJECT_ID(N'dbo.OpenSchema', N'U') IS NOT NULL DROP TABLE dbo.OpenSchema;

CREATE TABLE dbo.OpenSchema
(
  objectid  INT          NOT NULL,
  attribute NVARCHAR(30) NOT NULL,
  value     SQL_VARIANT  NOT NULL,
  CONSTRAINT PK_OpenSchema PRIMARY KEY (objectid, attribute)
);
GO

INSERT INTO dbo.OpenSchema(objectid, attribute, value) VALUES
  (1, N'attr1', CAST(CAST('ABC'      AS VARCHAR(10)) AS SQL_VARIANT)),
  (1, N'attr2', CAST(CAST(10         AS INT)         AS SQL_VARIANT)),
  (1, N'attr3', CAST(CAST('20130101' AS DATE)        AS SQL_VARIANT)),
  (2, N'attr2', CAST(CAST(12         AS INT)         AS SQL_VARIANT)),
  (2, N'attr3', CAST(CAST('20150101' AS DATE)        AS SQL_VARIANT)),
  (2, N'attr4', CAST(CAST('Y'        AS CHAR(1))     AS SQL_VARIANT)),
  (2, N'attr5', CAST(CAST(13.7       AS NUMERIC(9,3))AS SQL_VARIANT)),
  (3, N'attr1', CAST(CAST('XYZ'      AS VARCHAR(10)) AS SQL_VARIANT)),
  (3, N'attr2', CAST(CAST(20         AS INT)         AS SQL_VARIANT)),
  (3, N'attr3', CAST(CAST('20140101' AS DATE)        AS SQL_VARIANT));
```

Run the following query to show the contents of the table:

```
SELECT objectid, attribute, value FROM dbo.OpenSchema;
```

This query generates the following output:

```
objectid  attribute  value
--------- ---------- ------------------------
1         attr1      ABC
1         attr2      10
1         attr3      2013-01-01 00:00:00.000
2         attr2      12
2         attr3      2015-01-01 00:00:00.000
```

```
2        attr4    Y
2        attr5    13.700
3        attr1    XYZ
3        attr2    20
3        attr3    2014-01-01 00:00:00.000
```

As you can imagine, implementing dynamic schema using the EAV model has advantages and disadvantages compared to alternative models. But that's not your concern—for reasons that have already been debated, this model was chosen. The problem is that attempting to query the data in its current form can be complex. The values of different attributes for the same object are stored in different rows, so even simple requests can result in complex relational division queries. To make reporting simpler, once a night the data needs to be pivoted and the pivoted form should be persisted in a table. Then reports can be issued off of that table, requiring simpler and more efficient queries.

Your task is to write a query that pivots the data into the following form:

```
objectid    attr1   attr2   attr3                     attr4   attr5
----------- ------- ------- ------------------------- ------- -------
1           ABC     10      2013-01-01 00:00:00.000   NULL    NULL
2           NULL    12      2015-01-01 00:00:00.000   Y       13.700
3           XYZ     20      2014-01-01 00:00:00.000   NULL    NULL
```

The result of your query should have a row per distinct object ID, a column per distinct attribute, and the applicable value in the intersection of each object ID and attribute.

A pivot operation involves three steps, described here using the open schema example:

1. **Grouping by *objectid*** Each set of rows that are associated with the same object are going to be represented by a single result row. You achieve this step by grouping the data. In our example, the grouping column is *objectid*. In T-SQL, you simply use *GROUP BY objectid*.

2. **Spreading attribute *IN (attr1, attr2, attr3, attr4, attr5)*** The values in the *value* column should be spread to different result columns based on the attribute that the current row is associated with. The spreading column in our case is the *attribute* column. You need to identify the distinct elements in the spreading column; those become column names in the result. In our case, the distinct elements are *attr1*, *attr2*, *attr3*, *attr4*, and *attr5*. For each such spreading element, you need to write an expression that implements conditional logic to return the value only when it's applicable. For example, for the element *attr1*, the logic should be as follows: if the current row is associated with *attr1*, return the value from the *value* column; otherwise, return a NULL as a placeholder. To implement this logic in T-SQL, you use the expression *CASE WHEN attribute = 'attr1' THEN value END*. When you don't indicate an ELSE clause, *ELSE NULL* is assumed by default. You use such an expression for each distinct spreading element.

3. **Aggregating *MAX(val)*** Remember that the query is implemented as a grouped query and each object is going to be represented by a single result row. With one-to-one pivoting per group, each CASE expression will return at most one applicable value; all the rest will be NULLs. The purpose of the third step is to return that applicable value if it exists and to return NULL otherwise. Because the query is a grouped query, the only tool you are allowed to use for this purpose is an aggregate function applied to the result of the CASE expression. With at

most one applicable value per group, you could use the function MAX (or MIN). The function ignores NULLs and works with most data types. So the aggregate function in our case is MAX, and it is applied to the results of the CASE expression (the *value* column when it's applicable). To summarize, our aggregation element is *MAX(val)*.

The three steps combined give you the following solution query:

```
SELECT objectid,
  MAX(CASE WHEN attribute = 'attr1' THEN value END) AS attr1,
  MAX(CASE WHEN attribute = 'attr2' THEN value END) AS attr2,
  MAX(CASE WHEN attribute = 'attr3' THEN value END) AS attr3,
  MAX(CASE WHEN attribute = 'attr4' THEN value END) AS attr4,
  MAX(CASE WHEN attribute = 'attr5' THEN value END) AS attr5
FROM dbo.OpenSchema
GROUP BY objectid;
```

The execution plan for this query is shown in Figure 4-15.

FIGURE 4-15 Plan for a standard pivot query.

The plan looks like a plan for a normal grouped query with the extra Compute Scalar operator handling the CASE expressions. The index PK_OpenSchema is defined based on the key-list *(objectid, attribute)*, so it has the rows in the desired order, and because it's a clustered index it covers the query. The plan scans the index in order and then provides the rows in that order to the Stream Aggregate operator. As you can see, it's a very efficient plan.

A question that often comes up is how do you deal with a case where you don't know ahead of time what the distinct spreading values are? The answer is that you have to query the distinct values from the data, construct a string with the pivot query based on those values, and then use dynamic SQL to execute it. I will demonstrate how this can be done later in the chapter when discussing specialized solutions for custom aggregations.

The preceding technique to pivot data uses only standard SQL constructs, so it's a very portable technique. Also, as you will see in the section about many-to-one pivoting, you can easily extend it to support multiple aggregates when needed without adding much cost.

T-SQL supports an alternative technique using a proprietary table operator called PIVOT. Like any table operator, you use it in the FROM clause of your query. You use the following syntax:

```
SELECT <col_list>
FROM <source> PIVOT(<agg_func>(<agg_col>) FOR <spreading_col> IN (<spreading_elements>)) AS P;
```

Identifying the elements involved in our pivot task, the solution query looks like this:

```
SELECT objectid, attr1, attr2, attr3, attr4, attr5
FROM dbo.OpenSchema
  PIVOT(MAX(value) FOR attribute IN(attr1, attr2, attr3, attr4, attr5)) AS P;
```

Observe that the spreading elements are specified in this syntax already as identifiers of column names and not the literal character strings they used to be in the source. If the identifier happens to be irregular (starts with a digit, has spaces, is a reserved keyword, and so on), you need to delimit it with double quotes or square brackets, as in "2015".

The plan for this query is shown in Figure 4-16.

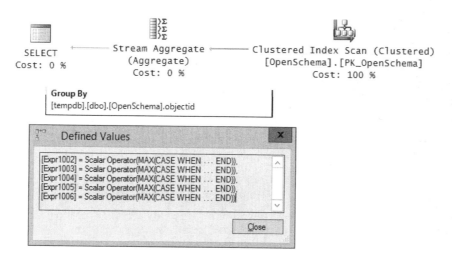

FIGURE 4-16 Plan for a pivot query with the PIVOT operator.

If you look at the properties of the Stream Aggregate operator, you will find a small surprise: SQL Server generated CASE expressions similar to the ones you used in the previous solution. So you realize that from a performance perspective, the two solutions are treated pretty much the same.

A curious thing about the syntax of the PIVOT operator is that while you do indicate the spreading and aggregation parts, you do not indicate the grouping columns. This part is implied; the grouping columns are all columns from the queried table that were not mentioned as the spreading and aggregation columns. In our case, the only column left in the OpenSchema table is *objectid*. But you realize the danger in this syntax; if you add columns to the table in the future, the next time you run the query those columns implicitly also become part of the grouping. For this reason, it is recommended that instead of querying the table directly as the source for the PIVOT operator, you define a table expression like a derived table or CTE, where you project only the columns that need to play a role in the pivot operation. Here's an example for implementing this approach using a derived table:

```
SELECT objectid, attr1, attr2, attr3, attr4, attr5
FROM (SELECT objectid, attribute, value FROM dbo.OpenSchema) AS D
  PIVOT(MAX(value) FOR attribute IN(attr1, attr2, attr3, attr4, attr5)) AS P;
```

This way, your code is safe and you don't need to be concerned about future additions of columns to the table.

This syntax has the advantage that it is less verbose than the previous solution. However, it has a few disadvantages. It is proprietary, so it is less portable. You are limited to only one aggregate function. It might not be apparent why you would want multiple functions when discussing one-to-one pivoting, but with many-to-one pivoting it could be needed. This syntax doesn't allow expressions that manipulate the spreading or aggregation columns. Any needed manipulation has to be done in a table expression that you will use as the input for the PIVOT operator.

In case you were wondering, T-SQL doesn't support providing a subquery as input to the IN clause. Like I explained with the previous solution, if the spreading values are unknown ahead of time, you need to construct the query string yourself and use dynamic SQL to execute it. I will demonstrate an example later in the chapter.

Many-to-one pivot

A many-to-one pivot is a kind of pivot where you can have multiple source rows represented by a single target row-column intersection. Although the aggregate function used in the one-to-one case is artificial, in the many-to-one case it's meaningful. That's pretty much the difference. Otherwise, the techniques used in both cases are the same.

As an example, suppose you need to query the Sales.OrderValues view in the TSQLV3 database. You want to pivot data so that you return a row per customer, a column per order year, and in the intersection of each customer and year, you want to return the sum of applicable values. The grouping column in this case is *custid*. The spreading column is *orderyear* (the result of the YEAR function applied to the *orderdate* column), with the distinct spreading elements currently being 2013, 2014, and 2015. The aggregation function is SUM applied to the column *val*. To allow using the alias *orderyear* in the computations, you can define it in a table expression.

Here's the solution query using the standard method with the grouping and CASE expressions:

```
USE TSQLV3;

SELECT custid,
  SUM(CASE WHEN orderyear = 2013 THEN val END) AS [2013],
  SUM(CASE WHEN orderyear = 2014 THEN val END) AS [2014],
  SUM(CASE WHEN orderyear = 2015 THEN val END) AS [2015]
FROM (SELECT custid, YEAR(orderdate) AS orderyear, val
      FROM Sales.OrderValues) AS D
GROUP BY custid;
```

This query generates the following output:

```
custid  2013      2014       2015
------- --------- ---------- ---------
1       NULL      2022.50    2250.50
2       88.80     799.75     514.40
3       403.20    5960.78    660.00
4       1379.00   6406.90    5604.75
5       4324.40   13849.02   6754.16
6       NULL      1079.80    2160.00
7       9986.20   7817.88    730.00
8       982.00    3026.85    224.00
9       4074.28   11208.36   6680.61
10      1832.80   7630.25    11338.56
...
```

Here's the solution query using the PIVOT operator:

```
SELECT custid, [2013],[2014],[2015]
FROM (SELECT custid, YEAR(orderdate) AS orderyear, val
      FROM Sales.OrderValues) AS D
  PIVOT(SUM(val) FOR orderyear IN([2013],[2014],[2015])) AS P;
```

As mentioned, the advantage of the PIVOT operator is in the brevity of the code, and one of its disadvantages is that it's limited to only one aggregate. So what if you need to support multiple aggregates using the standard solution, and you end up with so many expressions that the length of the code becomes an issue for you? There is a method that can help you shorten the query string.

You create a helper table called Matrix with a row and a column per distinct spreading value. You fill the table with 1s only when the row and column represent the same spreading value. Here's the code to create and populate the Matrix table to support our pivot task, followed by a query that presents its contents:

```
IF OBJECT_ID(N'dbo.Matrix', N'U') IS NOT NULL DROP TABLE dbo.Matrix;

CREATE TABLE dbo.Matrix
(
  orderyear INT NOT NULL PRIMARY KEY,
  y2013 INT NULL,
  y2014 INT NULL,
  y2015 INT NULL
);
GO

INSERT INTO dbo.Matrix(orderyear, y2013) VALUES(2013, 1);
INSERT INTO dbo.Matrix(orderyear, y2014) VALUES(2014, 1);
INSERT INTO dbo.Matrix(orderyear, y2015) VALUES(2015, 1);

SELECT orderyear, y2013, y2014, y2015 FROM dbo.Matrix;
```

The query generates the following output:

```
orderyear   y2013       y2014       y2015
----------- ----------- ----------- -----------
2013        1           NULL        NULL
2014        NULL        1           NULL
2015        NULL        NULL        1
```

Then to shorten the standard solution's length, you do the following:

- Join the source table (D in our case) with the Matrix table, matching rows based on an equality between the *orderyear* values on both sides.

- Instead of the CASE expression form of *SUM(CASE WHEN orderyear = 2015 THEN val END)*, use *SUM(val*y2015)*. The two are equivalent because in both cases, when the year is 2015 the value in the *val* column is returned (*y2015* is 1), and when the year is different a NULL is returned.

Here's the complete solution query:

```
SELECT custid,
   SUM(val*y2013) AS [2013],
   SUM(val*y2014) AS [2014],
   SUM(val*y2015) AS [2015]
FROM (SELECT custid, YEAR(orderdate) AS orderyear, val
      FROM Sales.OrderValues) AS D
   INNER JOIN dbo.Matrix AS M ON D.orderyear = M.orderyear
GROUP BY custid;
```

If you want to compute a count instead of a sum, without the Matrix table you either replace the SUM function with COUNT or use the following trick:

```
SELECT custid,
   SUM(CASE WHEN orderyear = 2013 THEN 1 END) AS [2013],
   SUM(CASE WHEN orderyear = 2014 THEN 1 END) AS [2014],
   SUM(CASE WHEN orderyear = 2015 THEN 1 END) AS [2015]
FROM (SELECT custid, YEAR(orderdate) AS orderyear
      FROM Sales.Orders) AS D
GROUP BY custid;
```

You return a 1 for each applicable order, and therefore the sum of applicable 1s gives you the count. This query generates the following output:

```
custid  2013  2014  2015
-------  -----  -----  -----
1        NULL  3     3
2        1     2     1
3        1     5     1
4        2     7     4
5        3     10    5
6        NULL  4     3
7        3     7     1
8        1     1     1
9        3     8     6
10       1     5     8
...
```

Using the Matrix table, you just apply the SUM function directly to the Matrix column, like so:

```
SELECT custid,
   SUM(y2013) AS [2013],
   SUM(y2014) AS [2014],
   SUM(y2015) AS [2015]
FROM (SELECT custid, YEAR(orderdate) AS orderyear
      FROM Sales.Orders) AS D
   INNER JOIN dbo.Matrix AS M ON D.orderyear = M.orderyear
GROUP BY custid;
```

Because the Matrix column has a 1 only when the order was placed in that year, the SUM function computes a count in practice.

Remember one of the benefits in using the standard method was the fact that it can support multiple aggregate functions without adding significant cost. Here's an example computing the sum, average, and count:

```
SELECT custid,
  SUM(val*y2013) AS sum2013,
  SUM(val*y2014) AS sum2014,
  SUM(val*y2015) AS sum2015,
  AVG(val*y2013) AS avg2013,
  AVG(val*y2014) AS avg2014,
  AVG(val*y2015) AS avg2015,
  SUM(y2013) AS cnt2013,
  SUM(y2014) AS cnt2014,
  SUM(y2015) AS cnt2015
FROM (SELECT custid, YEAR(orderdate) AS orderyear, val
      FROM Sales.OrderValues) AS D
  INNER JOIN dbo.Matrix AS M ON D.orderyear = M.orderyear
GROUP BY custid;
```

Recall the motivation for using the technique with the Matrix table was to shorten the query string. The benefit might not be apparent when you have a small number of expressions, but imagine if you had dozens or hundreds; then the benefit is realized.

Unpivoting

Unpivoting is an operation that rotates data from a state of columns to rows. The starting point for an unpivot task is source data stored in pivoted form. As an example, use the following code to create the table PvtOrders, fill it with sample data, and then query it to present its contents:

```
IF OBJECT_ID(N'dbo.PvtOrders', N'U') IS NOT NULL DROP TABLE dbo.PvtOrders;

SELECT custid, [2013], [2014], [2015]
INTO dbo.PvtOrders
FROM (SELECT custid, YEAR(orderdate) AS orderyear, val
      FROM Sales.OrderValues) AS D
  PIVOT(SUM(val) FOR orderyear IN([2013],[2014],[2015])) AS P;

SELECT custid, [2013], [2014], [2015] FROM dbo.PvtOrders;
```

The query generates the following output:

```
custid   2013     2014      2015
-------  -------  --------  ---------
1        NULL     2022.50   2250.50
2        88.80    799.75    514.40
3        403.20   5960.78   660.00
4        1379.00  6406.90   5604.75
5        4324.40  13849.02  6754.16
6        NULL     1079.80   2160.00
7        9986.20  7817.88   730.00
8        982.00   3026.85   224.00
9        4074.28  11208.36  6680.61
10       1832.80  7630.25   11338.56
...
```

It's common for data to be stored like this in spreadsheets. Imagine you just imported the data from a spreadsheet to the database. It's not very convenient to query the data in its current shape, so you want to unpivot it to a form that has a row per customer and year. In the following sections, I will describe a number of methods to achieve this unpivot task.

Unpivoting with CROSS JOIN and VALUES

You can split an unpivot task into three steps:

1. Generate copies.

2. Extract the element.

3. Remove NULLs.

I will describe these steps applied to our example.

The first step is about generating copies from the source rows. You need as many copies as the number of columns that you need to unpivot. In our case, the columns you need to unpivot represent order years, so you need a copy per order year. You can use the VALUES clause to define a derived table called Y holding order years, like so:

```
(VALUES(2013),(2014),(2015)) AS Y(orderyear)
```

Here's a query against the derived table presenting its contents:

```
SELECT orderyear FROM (VALUES(2013),(2014),(2015)) AS Y(orderyear);
```

This query generates the following output:

```
orderyear
-----------
2013
2014
2015
```

To generate copies, you perform a cross join between the source table PvtOrders and the table Y holding the order years, like so:

```
SELECT custid, [2013], [2014], [2015], orderyear
FROM dbo.PvtOrders
  CROSS JOIN (VALUES(2013),(2014),(2015)) AS Y(orderyear);
```

This query generates the following output:

```
custid  2013    2014      2015      orderyear
------- ------- --------- --------- ----------
1       NULL    2022.50   2250.50   2013
1       NULL    2022.50   2250.50   2014
1       NULL    2022.50   2250.50   2015
2       88.80   799.75    514.40    2013
2       88.80   799.75    514.40    2014
2       88.80   799.75    514.40    2015
3       403.20  5960.78   660.00    2013
3       403.20  5960.78   660.00    2014
3       403.20  5960.78   660.00    2015
...
```

The second step is about extracting the value from the right column in each copy to generate the result *val* column. What determines which column's value to return is the value in the *orderyear* column. When it's 2013, you need to return the value from the column *[2013]*; when it's 2014, you need to return the value from the column *[2014]*, and so on. To implement this step, you can use a simple CASE expression, like so:

```
SELECT custid, orderyear,
  CASE orderyear
    WHEN 2013 THEN [2013]
    WHEN 2014 THEN [2014]
    WHEN 2015 THEN [2015]
  END AS val
FROM dbo.PvtOrders
  CROSS JOIN (VALUES(2013),(2014),(2015)) AS Y(orderyear);
```

This query generates the following output:

```
custid       orderyear    val
----------- ----------- --------
1            2013         NULL
1            2014         2022.50
1            2015         2250.50
2            2013         88.80
2            2014         799.75
2            2015         514.40
3            2013         403.20
3            2014         5960.78
3            2015         660.00
...
```

Finally, the third step is supposed to remove the rows that are inapplicable (representing no activity). Those are the ones with a NULL in the *val* column. You cannot refer to the *val* column alias in the

WHERE clause because it's defined in the SELECT list. As a workaround, you can define the alias in a VALUES clause using the CROSS APPLY operator, and then refer to it in the query's WHERE clause, like so:

```
SELECT custid, orderyear, val
FROM dbo.PvtOrders
  CROSS JOIN (VALUES(2013),(2014),(2015)) AS Y(orderyear)
  CROSS APPLY (VALUES(CASE orderyear
                        WHEN 2013 THEN [2013]
                        WHEN 2014 THEN [2014]
                        WHEN 2015 THEN [2015]
                      END)) AS A(val)
WHERE val IS NOT NULL;
```

This query generates the following output where the rows with a NULL in the *val* column are removed:

```
custid       orderyear    val
-----------  -----------  -------------------------------------
1            2014         2022.50
1            2015         2250.50
2            2013         88.80
2            2014         799.75
2            2015         514.40
3            2013         403.20
3            2014         5960.78
3            2015         660.00
...
```

Unpivoting with CROSS APPLY and VALUES

There's a more elegant way to achieve unpivoting compared to the previous method. You combine the steps that generate the copies and extract the element into one step by using CROSS APPLY and VALUES. The CROSS APPLY operator gives the right table expression visibility to the elements of the left row. The right table expression can use the VALUES clause to produce multiple rows out of each left row. Each row is formed from a constant for the result *orderyear* column, and the corresponding column value for the result *val* column.

Here's the solution query:

```
SELECT custid, orderyear, val
FROM dbo.PvtOrders
  CROSS APPLY (VALUES(2013, [2013]),(2014, [2014]),(2015, [2015])) AS A(orderyear, val)
WHERE val IS NOT NULL;
```

What's interesting about this technique is that it can be used in more complex unpivoting tasks. To demonstrate such a task, I'll use a table called Sales that you create and populate by running the following code:

```
USE tempdb;
IF OBJECT_ID(N'dbo.Sales', N'U') IS NOT NULL DROP TABLE dbo.Sales;
GO
```

```
CREATE TABLE dbo.Sales
(
  custid    VARCHAR(10) NOT NULL,
  qty2013   INT   NULL,
  qty2014   INT   NULL,
  qty2015   INT   NULL,
  val2013   MONEY NULL,
  val2014   MONEY NULL,
  val2015   MONEY NULL,
  CONSTRAINT PK_Sales PRIMARY KEY(custid)
);

INSERT INTO dbo.Sales
    (custid, qty2013, qty2014, qty2015, val2013, val2014, val2015)
  VALUES
    ('A', 606,113,781,4632.00,6877.00,4815.00),
    ('B', 243,861,637,2125.00,8413.00,4476.00),
    ('C', 932,117,202,9068.00,342.00,9083.00),
    ('D', 915,833,138,1131.00,9923.00,4164.00),
    ('E', 822,246,870,1907.00,3860.00,7399.00);
```

Here you need to unpivot not just one, but two sets of columns; one with quantities in different order years, and another with values. To achieve this, you use a solution similar to the last one, only each row in the VALUES clause is formed from three elements: the constant for the order year, the column holding the quantity for that year, and the column holding the value for that year. Here's the complete solution query:

```
SELECT custid, salesyear, qty, val
FROM dbo.Sales
  CROSS APPLY
    (VALUES(2013, qty2013, val2013),
           (2014, qty2014, val2014),
           (2015, qty2015, val2015)) AS A(salesyear, qty, val)
WHERE qty IS NOT NULL OR val IS NOT NULL;
```

This query generates the following output:

```
custid     salesyear   qty         val
---------- ----------- ----------- --------------------
A          2013        606         4632.00
A          2014        113         6877.00
A          2015        781         4815.00
B          2013        243         2125.00
B          2014        861         8413.00
B          2015        637         4476.00
C          2013        932         9068.00
C          2014        117         342.00
C          2015        202         9083.00
D          2013        915         1131.00
D          2014        833         9923.00
D          2015        138         4164.00
E          2013        822         1907.00
E          2014        246         3860.00
E          2015        870         7399.00
```

Using the UNPIVOT operator

Just like with PIVOT, T-SQL supports a table operator called UNPIVOT. It operates on the table provided to it as its left input, and it generates a result table as its output. The design of the UNPIVOT operator is elegant, requiring you to provide the minimal needed information in its specification. Never mind how many columns you need to unpivot, you will always generate two result columns out of them—one to hold the source column values and another to hold the source column names. So the three things you need to provide to the UNPIVOT operator are (specified in order and applied to the PvtOrders table as the input):

1. **Values column** You need to provide the name you want to assign to the column that will hold the source column values. In our case, we want to name this column *val*. The type of this result column is the same as the type of the source columns you're unpivoting. (They all must have the same type.)

2. **Names column** You need to provide the name you want to assign to the column that will hold the source column names. In our case, we want to name this column *orderyear*. The type of this column is NVARCHAR(128).

3. **Source columns** You need to provide the names of the source columns that you want to unpivot. In our case, those are *[2013],[2014],[2015]*.

With the preceding three elements in mind, the syntax for UNPIVOT is as follows:

```
SELECT <col_list>
FROM <source> UNPIVOT(<values_col> FOR <names_col> IN (<source_cols>)) AS U;
```

Applied to our example with the PvtOrders table as input, you get the following query:

```
USE TSQLV3;

SELECT custid, orderyear, val
FROM dbo.PvtOrders
  UNPIVOT(val FOR orderyear IN([2013],[2014],[2015])) AS U;
```

This query generates the following output:

```
custid  orderyear  val
-------  ----------  --------
1        2014        2022.50
1        2015        2250.50
2        2013        88.80
2        2014        799.75
2        2015        514.40
3        2013        403.20
3        2014        5960.78
3        2015        660.00
...
```

The method using the UNPIVOT operator is short and elegant, but it is limited to unpivoting only one set of columns.

From a performance perspective, the method with CROSS JOIN and VALUES is the slowest. The one with CROSS APPLY and VALUES and the one with UNPIVOT get similar plans, although it seems like in more cases the method with CROSS APPLY and VALUES tends to get a parallel plan by default when there's enough data involved.

Custom aggregations

Custom aggregations are aggregate calculations you need to perform but are not provided as built-in aggregate functions. As examples, think of calculations like aggregate string concatenation, aggregate product, and so on.

To demonstrate solutions for custom aggregations, I'll use a table called Groups, which you create and populate by running the following code:

```
USE tempdb;

IF OBJECT_ID(N'dbo.Groups', N'U') IS NOT NULL DROP TABLE dbo.Groups;

CREATE TABLE dbo.Groups
(
  groupid   VARCHAR(10) NOT NULL,
  memberid  INT         NOT NULL,
  string    VARCHAR(10) NOT NULL,
  val       INT         NOT NULL,
  PRIMARY KEY (groupid, memberid)
);
GO

INSERT INTO dbo.Groups(groupid, memberid, string, val) VALUES
  ('a', 3, 'stra1', 6),
  ('a', 9, 'stra2', 7),
  ('b', 2, 'strb1', 3),
  ('b', 4, 'strb2', 7),
  ('b', 5, 'strb3', 3),
  ('b', 9, 'strb4', 11),
  ('c', 3, 'strc1', 8),
  ('c', 7, 'strc2', 10),
  ('c', 9, 'strc3', 12);
```

Run the following code to show the contents of the table:

```
SELECT groupid, memberid, string, val FROM dbo.Groups;
```

This query generates the following output:

```
groupid    memberid    string    val
---------- ----------- --------- -----------
a          3           stra1     6
a          9           stra2     7
b          2           strb1     3
b          4           strb2     7
b          5           strb3     3
b          9           strb4     11
c          3           strc1     8
c          7           strc2     10
c          9           strc3     12
```

Suppose you want to concatenate per group the values in the column *string* based on the order of the values in the column *memberid*. The desired output looks like this:

```
groupid    string
---------- -----------------------------------------
a          stra1,stra2
b          strb1,strb2,strb3,strb4
c          strc1,strc2,strc3
```

There are four main types of solutions you can use:

- Using a cursor

- Using a CLR user-defined aggregate (UDA)

- Using pivoting

- Using a specialized solution

The type using a CLR user-defined aggregate is described in Chapter 9, "Programmable objects." I'll describe the other three types here.

Using a cursor

Recall the discussion in Chapter 2, "Query tuning," comparing iterative and relational solutions. I demonstrated a cursor-based solution for computing a maximum aggregate. In a similar way, you could compute a string concatenation aggregate. You feed the rows to the cursor sorted by the group columns and ordering columns (*groupid* and *memberid* in our example). You keep fetching the cursor records in a loop concatenating the current value to what you have concatenated so far in a variable. If the group changes, you write the result for the last group in a table variable and reset the variable holding the concatenated values. Here's the complete solution code:

```
DECLARE @Result AS TABLE(groupid VARCHAR(10), string VARCHAR(8000));

DECLARE
  @groupid AS VARCHAR(10), @prvgroupid AS VARCHAR(10),
  @string AS VARCHAR(10), @aggstring AS VARCHAR(8000);

DECLARE C CURSOR FAST_FORWARD FOR
  SELECT groupid, string FROM dbo.Groups ORDER BY groupid, memberid;

OPEN C;

FETCH NEXT FROM C INTO @groupid, @string;

WHILE @@FETCH_STATUS = 0
BEGIN
  IF @groupid <> @prvgroupid
  BEGIN
    INSERT INTO @Result VALUES(@prvgroupid, @aggstring);
    SET @aggstring = NULL;
  END;

  SELECT
    @aggstring = COALESCE(@aggstring + ',', '') + @string,
    @prvgroupid = @groupid;

  FETCH NEXT FROM C INTO @groupid, @string;
END

IF @prvgroupid IS NOT NULL
  INSERT INTO @Result VALUES(@prvgroupid, @aggstring);

CLOSE C;
DEALLOCATE C;

SELECT groupid, string FROM @Result;
```

As discussed in Chapter 2, the downsides of a cursor-based solution are that it relies on a nonrelational approach and that iterative constructs in T-SQL are very slow.

The upsides of this solution are that you have control over order and the solution itself doesn't impose any special restrictions on the group size, other than the ones imposed by the data type you use.

Using pivoting

Another approach to handling custom aggregations is using pivoting. This approach is good when the number of elements is small and capped at a certain maximum.

The one tricky thing about using pivoting is that the source table doesn't have all the required elements. Remember that for pivoting you need to identify three things: the grouping column, spreading column, and aggregate function and column. In our example, the grouping column is *groupid* and the aggregate function and column are MAX applied to *string*, but the spreading column is missing. You need the spreading column values to be common across groups. The solution is to compute row numbers that are partitioned by *groupid* and ordered by *memberid*. Assuming there's a maximum number of elements per group (say, four in our example), you can refer to that many row numbers as the spreading values. Here's the solution query using pivoting:

```
SELECT groupid,
    [1]
  + COALESCE(',' + [2], '')
  + COALESCE(',' + [3], '')
  + COALESCE(',' + [4], '') AS string
FROM (SELECT groupid, string,
        ROW_NUMBER() OVER(PARTITION BY groupid ORDER BY memberid) AS rn
      FROM dbo.Groups AS A) AS D
  PIVOT(MAX(string) FOR rn IN([1],[2],[3],[4])) AS P;
```

A group will have at least one element, but it's not guaranteed that there will be more; the rest of the elements could be NULLs in the result of the pivot query. The COALESCE function is used to replace ',' + <element> with an empty string in case that element number doesn't exist. A more elegant way to achieve the same thing is using the CONCAT function, like so:

```
SELECT groupid,
  CONCAT([1], ','+[2], ','+[3], ','+[4]) AS string
FROM (SELECT groupid, string,
        ROW_NUMBER() OVER(PARTITION BY groupid ORDER BY memberid) AS rn
      FROM dbo.Groups AS A) AS D
  PIVOT(MAX(string) FOR rn IN([1],[2],[3],[4])) AS P;
```

The function concatenates its inputs, replacing NULL inputs with empty strings by default.

The advantage of using pivoting to handle custom aggregations is improved performance. Remember that pivot queries are optimized as grouped queries, so you should expect performance like that of a grouped query. The main disadvantage of this approach is that it's most effective when you use it with small groups. With large groups, the query string becomes too long.

Specialized solutions

Solutions for custom aggregations that are based on cursors, pivoting, and CLR UDAs are fairly generic. What I mean by this is that the solution for a string concatenation aggregate looks similar to a product aggregate. But suppose your main priority is efficiency. When aiming at better performance, you usually find yourself using more specialized tools and, as a result, sacrifice the genericness. That's typically the case in life, not just in T-SQL. While specialized tools can give you better performance for a specific task, they are less reusable for other tasks. In the context of custom aggregations, the techniques you use in your fastest solution for a string concatenation aggregate might not be reusable for a product aggregate. So you gain the performance advantage but lose the genericness.

I'll provide specialized solutions for aggregate string concatenation, product, and mode.

String concatenation with FOR XML

One of the fastest methods that exists in T-SQL to apply aggregate string concatenation is based on XML capabilities. I'll first demonstrate the technique for a single group in the Groups table and then apply it to the different groups. Suppose you want to concatenate the strings returned by the following query:

```
SELECT string
FROM dbo.Groups
WHERE groupid = 'b'
ORDER BY memberid;
```

This query generates the following output:

```
String
----------
strb1
strb2
strb3
strb4
```

Using the FOR XML option, you can request to return the result as a single XML instance. Using the PATH mode with an empty string as input and asking to return the nodes as text nodes, you get basic string concatenation without the extra XML tags:

```
SELECT string AS [text()]
FROM dbo.Groups
WHERE groupid = 'b'
ORDER BY membered
FOR XML PATH('');
```

This query generates the following output:

```
strb1strb2strb3strb4
```

Normally, the FOR XML option returns entitized strings. This means that some special characters like <, >, and others are converted to alternatives like &lt, &gt, and similar, respectively. If such special characters are possible in your data and you want to return the strings with the original characters, there is a workaround. You add the TYPE directive and then extract the value from the XML instance as a character string using the *.value* method, like so:

```
SELECT
  (SELECT string AS [text()]
   FROM dbo.Groups
   WHERE groupid = 'b'
   ORDER BY membered
   FOR XML PATH(''), TYPE).value('.[1]', 'VARCHAR(MAX)');
```

To add a separator like a comma between the strings, alter the expression in the SELECT list to ',' + *string*. You will end up with an extra separator at the beginning of the concatenated string. To remove it, you can use the STUFF function, like so:

```
SELECT
  STUFF((SELECT ',' + string AS [text()]
        FROM dbo.Groups
        WHERE groupid = 'b'
        ORDER BY membered
        FOR XML PATH(''), TYPE).value('.[1]', 'VARCHAR(MAX)'), 1, 1, '');
```

The STUFF function operates on the string provided as the first input. It removes from the character position specified as the second input as many characters as specified by the third input. It then inserts the string specified by the fourth input into the position specified by the second input (empty string, in our case). With the inputs provided in the preceding query, the STUFF function simply deletes the first character—the extra separator.

This query does the job for a single group. If you want to apply this logic to all groups, you can implement it as a correlated subquery against the Groups table, like so:

```
SELECT groupid,
  STUFF((SELECT ',' + string AS [text()]
        FROM dbo.Groups AS G2
        WHERE G2.groupid = G1.groupid
        ORDER BY memberid
        FOR XML PATH(''), TYPE).value('.[1]', 'VARCHAR(MAX)'), 1, 1, '') AS string
FROM dbo.Groups AS G1
GROUP BY groupid;
```

Now that you have an efficient specialized technique to concatenate strings, you can employ it to perform dynamic pivoting. Consider the following PIVOT query as an example:

```
USE TSQLV3;

SELECT custid, [2013],[2014],[2015]
FROM (SELECT custid, YEAR(orderdate) AS orderyear, val
      FROM Sales.OrderValues) AS D
  PIVOT(SUM(val) FOR orderyear IN([2013],[2014],[2015])) AS P;
```

You want a solution that doesn't require you to hard-code the order years so that you won't need to change the code at the beginning of every year. Using the specialized technique, you construct the separated list of years, like so:

```
SELECT
  STUFF(
    (SELECT N',' + QUOTENAME(orderyear) AS [text()]
     FROM (SELECT DISTINCT YEAR(orderdate) AS orderyear
           FROM Sales.Orders) AS Years
     ORDER BY orderyear
     FOR XML PATH(''), TYPE).value('.[1]', 'VARCHAR(MAX)'), 1, 1, '');
```

The QUOTENAME function is used to convert the input to a Unicode character string and add square brackets to make it an identifier.

Currently, this query generates the output: [2013],[2014],[2015], but when orders from other years are added to the table, the query will include them the next time you run it.

To complete your solution for dynamic pivoting, construct the entire pivot query from the static and dynamic parts, and then execute the query using *sp_executesql*, like so:

```
DECLARE
  @cols AS NVARCHAR(1000),
  @sql  AS NVARCHAR(4000);

SET @cols =
  STUFF(
    (SELECT N',' + QUOTENAME(orderyear) AS [text()]
     FROM (SELECT DISTINCT YEAR(orderdate) AS orderyear
           FROM Sales.Orders) AS Years
     ORDER BY orderyear
     FOR XML PATH(''), TYPE).value('.[1]', 'VARCHAR(MAX)'), 1, 1, '')

SET @sql = N'SELECT custid, ' + @cols + N'
FROM (SELECT custid, YEAR(orderdate) AS orderyear, val
      FROM Sales.OrderValues) AS D
  PIVOT(SUM(val) FOR orderyear IN(' + @cols + N')) AS P;';

EXEC sys.sp_executesql @stmt = @sql;
```

String concatenation with assignment SELECT

There's another specialized technique that is commonly used to perform aggregate string concatenation. It is based on a syntax where you assign a value to a variable as part of a SELECT query. The problem is that people use this syntax with certain assumptions about how it's supposed to work, but there's no official documentation that provides such guarantees.

Consider the following code:

```
SELECT @local_variable = expression FROM SomeTable;
```

Here's a quote from the official SQL Server documentation indicating what this assignment SELECT does:

> *SELECT @local_variable is typically used to return a single value into the variable. However, when expression is the name of a column, it can return multiple values. If the SELECT statement returns more than one value, the variable is assigned the last value that is returned.*

The term *last* is confusing because there's no order in a set. And if you add an ORDER BY clause to the query, who's to say that ordering will be processed before the assignment? In fact, according to logical query processing, the SELECT clause is supposed to be evaluated before the ORDER BY clause. In short, the documentation simply doesn't provide an explanation as to what it means by *last*.

In practice, if an ORDER BY clause exists in the query, there are no assurances that ordering will be addressed in the query plan before the assignment takes place. I've seen some plans where ordering was addressed before assignment and some after; it's a pure matter of optimization.

An attempt to perform ordered aggregate string concatenation is a good example how this undefined behavior can get you into trouble. To demonstrate this, I'll use a table called T1, which you create and populate by running the following code:

```
USE tempdb;
IF OBJECT_ID(N'dbo.T1', N'U') IS NOT NULL DROP TABLE dbo.T1;

CREATE TABLE dbo.T1
(
  col1   INT NOT NULL IDENTITY,
  col2   VARCHAR(100) NOT NULL,
  filler BINARY(2000) NULL DEFAULT(0x),
  CONSTRAINT PK_T1 PRIMARY KEY(col1)
);

INSERT INTO dbo.T1(col2)
  SELECT 'String ' + CAST(n AS VARCHAR(10))
  FROM TSQLV3.dbo.GetNums(1, 100) AS Nums;
```

Here's an example for a common use of the assignment SELECT syntax with the intention of concatenating the values in col2 based on col1 ordering:

```
DECLARE @s AS VARCHAR(MAX);
SET @s = '';

SELECT @s = @s + col2 + ';'
FROM dbo.T1
ORDER BY col1;

PRINT @s;
```

When I ran this code for the first time, I got the plan shown in Figure 4-17.

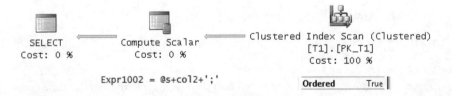

FIGURE 4-17 Plan for test 1 with assignment SELECT.

Observe that this plan scans the clustered index PK_T1, which is defined with col1 as the key, in order. Then the plan handles the assignments using the Compute Scalar operator. The execution of this plan resulted in the following output, which seems to be aligned with the expectation some have that the values will be concatenated based on the specified order:

```
String 1;String 2;String 3;String 4;String 5;String 6;String 7;String 8;String 9;String
10;String 11;String 12;String 13;String 14;String 15;String 16;String 17;String 18;String
19;String 20;String 21;String 22;String 23;String 24;String 25;String 26;String 27;String
28;String 29;String 30;String 31;String 32;String 33;String 34;String 35;String 36;String
37;String 38;String 39;String 40;String 41;String 42;String 43;String 44;String 45;String
46;String 47;String 48;String 49;String 50;String 51;String 52;String 53;String 54;String
55;String 56;String 57;String 58;String 59;String 60;String 61;String 62;String 63;String
64;String 65;String 66;String 67;String 68;String 69;String 70;String 71;String 72;String
73;String 74;String 75;String 76;String 77;String 78;String 79;String 80;String 81;String
82;String 83;String 84;String 85;String 86;String 87;String 88;String 89;String 90;String
91;String 92;String 93;String 94;String 95;String 96;String 97;String 98;String 99;String 100;
```

But as mentioned, there's no documentation that provides you with such a guarantee. It just so happens that the optimizer's choice resulted in such ordered strings.

Next, I added the following nonclustered index to the table and then ran the same assignment SELECT code:

```
CREATE NONCLUSTERED INDEX idx_nc_col2_i_col1 ON dbo.T1(col2, col1);
GO

DECLARE @s AS VARCHAR(MAX);
SET @s = '';

SELECT @s = @s + col2 + ';'
FROM dbo.T1
ORDER BY col1;

PRINT @s;
```

The plan I got for this execution of the query is shown in Figure 4-18.

FIGURE 4-18 Plan for test 2 with assignment SELECT.

Observe that this time the optimizer chose to use the new index. It's narrower than the clustered index because it contains only the interesting columns. But it doesn't sort the rows like the query needs. So the plan performs an unordered scan of the index, and it adds a Sort operator as the last thing it does. The ironic thing is that the plan sorts the rows after the assignments already took place! Not only that, you don't get the concatenated values in the order you need; rather, you get an intermediate state of the concatenation. When I ran this code, I got the following output:

```
String 100;
```

It's sad to see how much production code exists out there that relies on this method, with the authors of it not realizing it's not guaranteed to work the way they expect it to. And then something causes the optimizer to change how it optimizes the code, like a new index, a new service pack, and so on, and they get into trouble. You can save yourself a lot of grief if you stick to supported and well-defined techniques like the one based on the FOR XML PATH option.

Aggregate product

Computing an aggregate product is another classic type of custom aggregate calculation. It is commonly used in financial applications—for example, to compute compound interest rates.

With our Groups table, suppose you need to compute the product of the values in the *val* column per group. There's an efficient solution for this task that is based on mathematics—specifically, logarithmic calculations. There are two sets of equations that are interesting for the solution:

$$logb(y) = x \Leftrightarrow y = bx$$

$$logb(xy) = logb(x) + logb(y) \Leftrightarrow xy = blogb(x) + logb(y)$$

The LOG function in T-SQL computes the logarithm of the first input using the second input as the base. If you don't indicate the base, the function computes the *natural logarithm* of the first input (using *e* as the base, where *e* is an irrational constant approximately equal to 2.718281828).

The EXP function in T-SQL returns the exponent of the input value. That is, it returns e raised to the power of the input. So, EXP(10) is e^{10}. This means that in the following pair of equations, one implies the other:

$$LOG(y) = x \Leftrightarrow EXP(x) = y$$

And therefore in the following pair of equations, one implies the other:

$$LOG(xy) = LOG(x) + LOG(y) \Leftrightarrow EXP(LOG(x) + LOG(y)) = xy$$

Expressed in T-SQL, here's the query that computes the desired product:

```
SELECT groupid, ROUND(EXP(SUM(LOG(val))), 0) AS product
FROM dbo.Groups
GROUP BY groupid;
```

The rounding is required to correct errors caused by the imprecise nature of the floating-point calculations used by the LOG and EXP T-SQL functions. This query generates the following desired output:

```
groupid    product
---------- ----------------------
a          42
b          693
c          960
```

If you want to also support zeros and negative values, things get trickier because the LOG function doesn't support those. To see a demonstration of this, repopulate the Groups table by running the following code:

```
TRUNCATE TABLE dbo.Groups;

INSERT INTO dbo.Groups(groupid, memberid, string, val) VALUES
  ('a', 3, 'stra1', -6),
  ('a', 9, 'stra2', 7),
  ('b', 2, 'strb1', -3),
  ('b', 4, 'strb2', -7),
  ('b', 5, 'strb3', 3),
  ('b', 9, 'strb4', 11),
  ('c', 3, 'strc1', 8),
  ('c', 7, 'strc2', 0),
  ('c', 9, 'strc3', 12);
```

Try running the query against the new data:

```
SELECT groupid, ROUND(EXP(SUM(LOG(val))), 0) AS product
FROM dbo.Groups
GROUP BY groupid;
```

The query fails with the following error:

```
Msg 3623, Level 16, State 1, Line 1049
An invalid floating point operation occurred.
```

To deal with zeros and negatives correctly, you need a few things. Using the ISNULL function, you replace *val* with a NULL if it's zero to avoid an error. You apply the original product calculation against the absolute values. Using the MIN aggregate and a CASE expression, you compute a flag (call it *zero*) that is 1 if you have at least one zero and 0 if you have none. Using the COUNT aggregate and a CASE expression, you compute a flag (call it *negative*) that is –1 if you have an odd number of negative values and 1 otherwise. Here's the code applying these calculations:

```
SELECT groupid,
  -- Replace 0 with NULL using NULLIF, apply product to absolute values
  ROUND(EXP(SUM(LOG(ABS(NULLIF(val, 0))))), 0) AS product,
  -- 0 if a 0 exists, 1 if not
  MIN(CASE WHEN val = 0 THEN 0 ELSE 1 END) AS zero,
  -- -1 if odd, 1 if even
  CASE WHEN COUNT(CASE WHEN val < 0 THEN 1 END) % 2 > 0 THEN -1 ELSE 1 END AS negative
FROM dbo.Groups
GROUP BY groupid;
```

This code generates the following output:

```
groupid  product  zero  negative
-------- -------- ----- ---------
a        42       1     -1
b        693      1     1
c        96       0     1
```

Then to get the correct product, you multiply the product of the absolute values by the *zero* flag and by the *negative* flag, like so:

```
SELECT groupid,
  ROUND(EXP(SUM(LOG(ABS(NULLIF(val, 0))))), 0)
  * MIN(CASE WHEN val = 0 THEN 0 ELSE 1 END)
  * CASE WHEN COUNT(CASE WHEN val < 0 THEN 1 END) % 2 > 0 THEN -1 ELSE 1 END AS product
FROM dbo.Groups
GROUP BY groupid;
```

This query generates the following output:

```
groupid     product
----------  ----------------------
a           -42
b           693
c           0
```

If you like mathematical challenges, try computing the *zero* and *negative* flags mathematically without the use of CASE expressions. This can be done like so:

```
SELECT groupid,
  ROUND(EXP(SUM(LOG(ABS(NULLIF(val, 0))))), 0) AS product,
  MIN(SIGN(ABS(val))) AS zero,
  SUM((1-SIGN(val))/2)%2*-2+1 AS negative
FROM dbo.Groups
GROUP BY groupid;
```

Putting it all together, you get the following query to compute the final product:

```
SELECT groupid,
  ROUND(EXP(SUM(LOG(ABS(NULLIF(val, 0))))), 0)
  * MIN(SIGN(ABS(val)))
  * (SUM((1-SIGN(val))/2)%2*-2+1) AS product
FROM dbo.Groups
GROUP BY groupid;
```

Aggregate mode

Another example of a custom aggregate calculation is computing the mode of the distribution. *Mode* is the most frequently occurring value in a set. As an example, suppose you need to query the Sales.Orders table in the TSQLV3 database and find for each customer the employee who handled the most orders. That's the employee ID that appears the most times in the customer's orders. In case of ties in the count, you're supposed to return the greater employee ID.

One approach to solving the task involves the following steps:

- Write a grouped query computing the count of orders per customer and employee.

- In the same grouped query, also compute a row number that is partitioned by the customer ID and ordered by the count descending and employee ID descending.

- Define a CTE based on the grouped query, and then in the outer query, filter only the rows with the row number 1.

Here's the complete solution code:

```
USE TSQLV3;

WITH C AS
(
  SELECT custid, empid, COUNT(*) AS cnt,
    ROW_NUMBER() OVER(PARTITION BY custid
                      ORDER BY COUNT(*) DESC, empid DESC) AS rn
  FROM Sales.Orders
  GROUP BY custid, empid
)
SELECT custid, empid, cnt
FROM C
WHERE rn = 1;
```

This query generates the following output:

```
custid      empid       cnt
----------- ----------- -----------
1           4           2
2           3           2
3           3           3
4           4           4
5           3           6
...
```

If instead of breaking the ties you want to return all ties, you need to apply two changes to your solution. You need to use the RANK or DENSE_RANK functions (either one will work) and remove the employee ID from the window order clause. Here's the revised code:

```
WITH C AS
(
  SELECT custid, empid, COUNT(*) AS cnt,
    RANK() OVER(PARTITION BY custid
                ORDER BY COUNT(*) DESC) AS rn
  FROM Sales.Orders
  GROUP BY custid, empid
)
SELECT custid, empid, cnt
FROM C
WHERE rn = 1;
```

This code generates the following output:

```
custid      empid       cnt
----------- ----------- -----------
1           1           2
1           4           2
2           3           2
3           3           3
4           4           4
5           3           6
...
```

Observe that for customer 1 there are two employees who handled the maximum number of orders.

Going back to the original task that involves a tiebreaker, consider the optimization of the solution. Because the ROW_NUMBER function's ordering is based in part on the result of the COUNT computation, there will be a sort operation of the entire input set in the query plan even if you create an index on *(custid, empid)*. With a large amount of input, the sort will be expensive. There is a way to avoid the sort with an indexed view (as a challenge, see if you can figure out how), but what if you cannot afford one?

There's an alternative solution that relies on a carry-along-sort concept based on grouping and string concatenation that can efficiently rely on an index on *(custid, empid)*. The solution involves the following steps:

1. Write a grouped query that computes the count of orders per customer and employee.

2. In the same grouped query, compute a binary string made of the count converted to BINARY(4) concatenated with the employee ID, also converted to BINARY(4). Call the concatenated value *binval*.

3. Define a table expression based on the grouped query and name it *D*.

4. Write an outer query against D that groups the rows by customer ID. In that query, the result of the computation *MAX(binval)* contains the maximum count concatenated with the ID of the mode employee (with the maximum employee ID as the tiebreaker). Apply substring logic to extract the two parts and convert them back to the original types.

Here's the complete solution code:

```
SELECT custid,
  CAST(SUBSTRING(MAX(binval), 5, 4) AS INT) AS empid,
  CAST(SUBSTRING(MAX(binval), 1, 4) AS INT) AS cnt
FROM (SELECT custid,
        CAST(COUNT(*) AS BINARY(4)) + CAST(empid AS BINARY(4)) AS binval
      FROM Sales.Orders
      GROUP BY custid, empid) AS D
GROUP BY custid;
```

What's nice about this solution is that both layers of grouping and aggregation can rely on the order of the aforementioned index. To compare the performance of the two solutions, I created a table called OrdersBig with 10,000,000 rows and an index called idx_custid_empid on *(custid, empid)*. Figure 4-19 shows the plans that I got for both solutions against that table. The top plan is for the solution using the ROW_NUMBER function, and the bottom plan is for the solution based on the carry-along-sort concept.

Notice the expensive Sort operator in the first plan before the calculation of the row numbers, and the absence of one in the second plan. The first solution took 15 seconds to complete in my test machine and the second completed in only 5 seconds.

Before concluding the section about custom aggregations, I want to mention that standard SQL defines a type of function called *ordered set function*, which at the date of this writing is not yet available in SQL Server. An ordered set function is a set function with ordering relevance that you can use in a grouped query. The standard defines a clause called WITHIN GROUP where you indicate the function's ordering specification. There are multiple examples for functions that could be implemented as ordered set functions: aggregate string concatenation, percentiles, CLR aggregates, and so on. You can find a feature-enhancement request concerning ordered set functions here: *https://connect.microsoft.com/SQLServer/feedback/details/728969.*

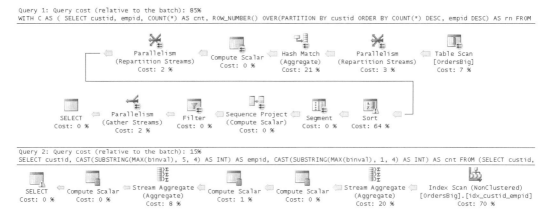

FIGURE 4-19 Plans for solutions to mode.

Grouping sets

T-SQL supports a number of features that are related to the topic of grouping sets and that are useful for data-analysis purposes. Those features are the clauses GROUPING SETS, CUBE, and ROLLUP, as well as the functions GROUPING_ID and GROUPING.

To demonstrate these features, I'll use a table called Orders in my examples. Run the following code to create the Orders table and populate it with sample data:

```
SET NOCOUNT ON;
USE tempdb;

IF OBJECT_ID(N'dbo.Orders', N'U') IS NOT NULL DROP TABLE dbo.Orders;

CREATE TABLE dbo.Orders
(
  orderid    INT        NOT NULL,
  orderdate  DATETIME   NOT NULL,
  empid      INT        NOT NULL,
  custid     VARCHAR(5) NOT NULL,
  qty        INT        NOT NULL,
  CONSTRAINT PK_Orders PRIMARY KEY(orderid)
);
GO
```

```
INSERT INTO dbo.Orders
  (orderid, orderdate, empid, custid, qty)
VALUES
  (30001, '20120802', 3, 'A', 10),
  (10001, '20121224', 1, 'A', 12),
  (10005, '20121224', 1, 'B', 20),
  (40001, '20130109', 4, 'A', 40),
  (10006, '20130118', 1, 'C', 14),
  (20001, '20130212', 2, 'B', 12),
  (40005, '20140212', 4, 'A', 10),
  (20002, '20140216', 2, 'C', 20),
  (30003, '20140418', 3, 'B', 15),
  (30004, '20120418', 3, 'C', 22),
  (30007, '20120907', 3, 'D', 30);
```

Before describing features and functions, I'll start by saying that the term *grouping set* simply describes the set of expressions you group by in a grouped query. For example, if you have a query that groups by *custid, empid, YEAR(orderdate)*, your query defines the grouping set *(custid, empid, YEAR(orderdate))*. Nothing special so far.

Historically, T-SQL supported defining only one grouping set per query. With the features I'm about to describe, you can define multiple grouping sets in one query. The question is, why would you want to do that? There are a couple of reasons. One reason is that there are reports where you need to present more than one level of aggregation—for example, hierarchical time reports where you need to show daily, monthly, yearly, and grand totals. Another reason is to persist aggregates for different grouping sets in a table for fast retrieval. This is a classic need in data warehouses. There are other technologies that help you speed up analytical queries, like columnstore, but this technology requires the Enterprise edition of SQL Server.

The following sections describe the aforementioned features.

GROUPING SETS subclause

You use the GROUPING SETS clause to define multiple grouping sets in one query. You specify this clause as part of the GROUP BY clause. The GROUPING SETS clause has its own pair of parentheses, and each inner pair of parentheses represents a different grouping set. You separate grouping sets with commas. Without an inner pair of parentheses, each expression is considered a separate grouping set. An empty inner pair of parentheses defines only one group from the entire input set; in other words, you use them to compute grand aggregates.

As an example for using the GROUPING SETS clause, the following query defines four grouping sets:

```
SELECT custid, empid, YEAR(orderdate) AS orderyear, SUM(qty) AS qty
FROM dbo.Orders
GROUP BY GROUPING SETS
(
  ( custid, empid, YEAR(orderdate) ),
  ( custid, YEAR(orderdate)        ),
  ( empid, YEAR(orderdate)         ),
  ()
);
```

But then there's the question of how the result sets for the different grouping sets can be combined if they have different structures. The solution is to use NULLs as placeholders in columns that are not part of the grouping set that the result row is associated with. Here's the output of the preceding query:

```
custid empid       orderyear   qty
------ ----------- ----------- -----------
A      1           2012        12
B      1           2012        20
NULL   1           2012        32
C      1           2013        14
NULL   1           2013        14
B      2           2013        12
NULL   2           2013        12
C      2           2014        20
NULL   2           2014        20
A      3           2012        10
C      3           2012        22
D      3           2012        30
NULL   3           2012        62
B      3           2014        15
NULL   3           2014        15
A      4           2013        40
NULL   4           2013        40
A      4           2014        10
NULL   4           2014        10
NULL   NULL        NULL        205
A      NULL        2012        22
B      NULL        2012        20
C      NULL        2012        22
D      NULL        2012        30
A      NULL        2013        40
B      NULL        2013        12
C      NULL        2013        14
A      NULL        2014        10
B      NULL        2014        15
C      NULL        2014        20
```

The rows that have values in *custid*, *empid*, and *orderyear* are related to the grouping set (*custid, empid, YEAR(orderdate)*). Similarly, the rows that have values in *empid* and *orderyear* and NULLs in *custid* are related to the grouping set (*empid, YEAR(orderdate)*), and so on.

If you want to get the same result without the GROUPING SETS clause, you need to write four grouped queries and unify their results, like so:

```
SELECT custid, empid, YEAR(orderdate) AS orderyear, SUM(qty) AS qty
FROM dbo.Orders
GROUP BY custid, empid, YEAR(orderdate)

UNION ALL

SELECT custid, NULL AS empid, YEAR(orderdate) AS orderyear, SUM(qty) AS qty
FROM dbo.Orders
GROUP BY custid, YEAR(orderdate)
```

```
UNION ALL

SELECT NULL AS custid, empid, YEAR(orderdate) AS orderyear, SUM(qty) AS qty
FROM dbo.Orders
GROUP BY empid, YEAR(orderdate)

UNION ALL

SELECT NULL AS custid, NULL AS empid, NULL AS orderyear, SUM(qty) AS qty
FROM dbo.Orders;
```

The GROUPING SETS clause gives you a couple of advantages over multiple queries. Obviously, the code is much shorter. In addition, it gets optimized better. With four queries, the data will be scanned four times. With the GROUPING SETS clause, the optimizer analyzes the grouping sets and tries to minimize the number of scans by rolling up aggregates. To see this optimization technique in action, examine the query plan shown in Figure 4-20 for the query with the GROUPING SETS clause.

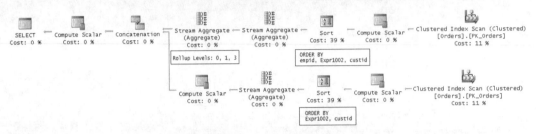

FIGURE 4-20 Plan for a query with GROUPING SETS.

Observe that the data is scanned only twice. The top branch of the plan, from right to left, starts by scanning the clustered index. It then computes a scalar called *Expr1002* representing the result of the computation *YEAR(orderdate)*. Because I did not prepare any indexes to support the grouping and aggregation, the optimizer adds a Sort operator that orders the rows by *empid, YEAR(orderdate), custid*. You can avoid this sort by creating a supporting index, as I'll demonstrate shortly. Based on this order, in a rollup fashion, all grouping sets representing leading combinations can be computed. The rolled-up levels are numbered using a zero-based offset from lower to higher:

- Level 0: *empid, YEAR(orderdate), custid*

- Level 1: *empid, YEAR(orderdate)*

- Level 2: *empid*

- Level 3: *()*

The first aggregate operator to the left of the Sort operator represents the base grouping set (level 0). The second aggregate operator is responsible for the rolling up of the aggregates. If you examine the query, you will notice that the GROUPING SETS clause defines three of the aforementioned grouping sets: the ones with levels 0, 1, and 3, but not 2. So when looking at the properties of the second aggregate operator, the property Rollup Levels will report only the needed levels.

The query defines an additional grouping set *(custid, YEAR(orderdate))* that cannot be computed based on the order in the first branch of the plan. So a second branch in the plan (the bottom one) scans the data again, sorts it by *YEAR(orderdate), custid*, and then computes the aggregates for the remaining grouping set. There's no need for a second aggregate operator because only one grouping set remains; so there's no rolling up to do.

As mentioned, you can avoid explicit sorting in the plan by preparing supporting indexes. In our case, one of the elements is a result of a computation, so you can add a computed column based on that computation and then make it part of your indexes. You want the indexes to be covering, so don't forget to include the aggregated column (*qty* in our case). Here's the code to add the computed column and the supporting indexes:

```
ALTER TABLE dbo.Orders ADD orderyear AS YEAR(orderdate);
GO
CREATE INDEX idx_eid_oy_cid_i_qty ON dbo.Orders(empid, orderyear, custid) INCLUDE(qty);
CREATE INDEX idx_oy_cid_i_qty ON dbo.Orders(orderyear, custid) INCLUDE(qty);
```

Run the query again, and you will get the plan shown in Figure 4-21.

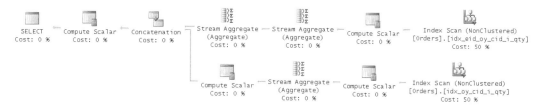

FIGURE 4-21 Plan for a query with GROUPING SETS after adding index.

The supporting indexes are scanned in order, and therefore no sort operation is required this time.

CUBE and ROLLUP clauses

The CUBE and ROLLUP clauses are simply shortcuts for the GROUPING SETS clause. When you need to define a large number of grouping sets (you're allowed to define up to 4,096), it's nice if you can avoid actually listing all of them.

Starting with the CUBE clause, suppose you have a set of expressions and you want to define all possible grouping sets from them. In mathematics, this is what's known as the *power set* of a set. It's the set of all subsets that are formed from the original set's elements. For a set with cardinality N, the power set has cardinality 2^N. For example, for a set with 10 elements you get a power set of 1,024 subsets, including the original set and the empty set. That's pretty much what CUBE is about. You provide it with a set of expressions as inputs, and you get the equivalent of a GROUPING SETS clause with all grouping sets that can be formed from the input expressions. As a simple example, here's a query with a CUBE clause with two input expressions:

```
SELECT custid, empid, SUM(qty) AS qty
FROM dbo.Orders
GROUP BY CUBE(custid, empid);
```

This query is equivalent to the following query, which uses a GROUPING SETS clause with all possible grouping sets:

```
SELECT custid, empid, SUM(qty) AS qty
FROM dbo.Orders
GROUP BY GROUPING SETS
  (
    ( custid, empid ),
    ( custid        ),
    ( empid         ),
    ()
  );
```

With two input elements to the CUBE clause, the power set contains four grouping sets.

As for the ROLLUP clause, it's also a shortcut, but one that assumes that the inputs form a hierarchy like time, location, and so on. You get only grouping sets that are formed by leading combinations of expressions. Consider the following query as an example:

```
SELECT
  YEAR(orderdate) AS orderyear,
  MONTH(orderdate) AS ordermonth,
  DAY(orderdate) AS orderday,
  SUM(qty) AS qty
FROM dbo.Orders
GROUP BY
  ROLLUP(YEAR(orderdate), MONTH(orderdate), DAY(orderdate));
```

For *N* elements, there are *N + 1* leading combinations (including the empty set). The preceding query has a ROLLUP clause with three inputs, and therefore it is equivalent to the following query with a GROUPING SETS clause defining four grouping sets:

```
SELECT
  YEAR(orderdate) AS orderyear,
  MONTH(orderdate) AS ordermonth,
  DAY(orderdate) AS orderday,
  SUM(qty) AS qty
FROM dbo.Orders
GROUP BY
  GROUPING SETS
  (
    ( YEAR(orderdate), MONTH(orderdate), DAY(orderdate) ),
    ( YEAR(orderdate), MONTH(orderdate)                 ),
    ( YEAR(orderdate)                                   ),
    ()
  );
```

What's interesting about the ROLLUP clause is how nicely the optimization of the feature is aligned with its logical design. Recall the rollup concept in the optimization of grouping sets? One ROLLUP clause can be optimized with a single scan based on one order (requiring either an actual sort or an ordered scan of a supporting index). Figure 4-22 has the plan for the preceding ROLLUP query.

FIGURE 4-22 Plan for a query with ROLLUP.

Tip A little known fact about the CUBE and ROLLUP clauses is that their inputs are not limited to only scalar elements; rather, they can be sets. For example, *CUBE((a, b), (x, y))* assumes two input sets: *(a, b)* and *(x, y)*, generating four grouping sets: *(a, b, c, d)*, *(a, b)*, *(x, y)*, *()*.

Grouping sets algebra

One of the interesting aspects in the design of queries with grouping sets is that you can apply algebra-like operations between the clauses that define them (GROUPING SETS, CUBE, and ROLLUP). You have both multiplication and addition operations.

You achieve multiplication simply by putting a comma between the clauses. For example, consider the following query:

```
SELECT
  custid,
  empid,
  YEAR(orderdate) AS orderyear,
  MONTH(orderdate) AS ordermonth,
  SUM(qty) AS qty
FROM dbo.Orders
GROUP BY
  GROUPING SETS
  (
    ( custid, empid ),
    ( custid        ),
    ( empid         )
  ),
  ROLLUP(YEAR(orderdate), MONTH(orderdate), DAY(orderdate));
```

The GROUPING SETS clause defines three grouping sets, and the ROLLUP clause defines four. The multiplication operation results in 12 grouping sets. A typical use case is multiplying a number of ROLLUP clauses, each representing a different dimension hierarchy (time, location, and so on).

To apply addition, you place a ROLLUP or CUBE clause as an additional element within a GROUPING SETS clause, like so:

```
SELECT
  custid,
  empid,
  YEAR(orderdate) AS orderyear,
  MONTH(orderdate) AS ordermonth,
  SUM(qty) AS qty
```

```
FROM dbo.Orders
GROUP BY
  GROUPING SETS
  (
    ( custid, empid ),
    ( custid          ),
    ( empid           ),
    ROLLUP(YEAR(orderdate), MONTH(orderdate), DAY(orderdate))
  );
```

Here you add the four grouping sets that are defined by the ROLLUP clause to the three explicit ones that are defined within the GROUPING SETS clause, getting seven grouping sets in total. So remember, when the comma appears between clauses it behaves like multiplication; when it appears within a GROUPING SETS clause, it behaves like addition.

Materializing grouping sets

As mentioned at the beginning of the section, one of the use cases of the features that allow you to define multiple grouping sets in one query is to persist aggregates that are expensive to compute to speed up retrievals. This is usually done nightly, allowing fast retrievals during the day.

Once persisted, users will typically ask for aggregates that are related to one grouping set at a time. The question is, how do you filter only the rows that are associated with one grouping set? You need a mechanism that identifies a grouping set uniquely. One option is to form a filter with IS NULL and IS NOT NULL predicates against all grouping columns. But there are two problems with this approach. One, it's awkward. Two, if a grouping column allows NULLs in the table, the result will include false positives.

There's an elegant solution in the form of a function called GROUPING_ID. You provide the function with all grouping columns as inputs. The function returns an integer bitmap where each bit represents the respective input, with the rightmost bit representing the rightmost input. The bit is set if the respective column is *not* part of the grouping set (namely, it's an aggregate) and is not set when it is.

As an example, consider the following query:

```
SELECT
  GROUPING_ID( custid, empid, YEAR(orderdate), MONTH(orderdate), DAY(orderdate) ) AS grp_id,
  custid, empid,
  YEAR(orderdate) AS orderyear,
  MONTH(orderdate) AS ordermonth,
  DAY(orderdate) AS orderday,
  SUM(qty) AS qty
FROM dbo.Orders
GROUP BY
  CUBE(custid, empid),
  ROLLUP(YEAR(orderdate), MONTH(orderdate), DAY(orderdate));
```

This query generates the following output, with an extra header with the respective bit values added manually on top for clarity:

```
bit value  16       8      4          2            1
---------- ------  ------ ---------- -----------  --------- ----
grp_id     custid empid  orderyear  ordermonth   orderday  qty
---------- ------  ------ ---------- -----------  --------- -----
...
25         NULL   NULL   2014       4            NULL      15
27         NULL   NULL   2014       NULL         NULL      45
31         NULL   NULL   NULL       NULL         NULL      205
8          A      NULL   2012       8            2         10
...
```

Take, for example, the row where the function returned the value 25. This row is associated with the grouping set (*YEAR(orderdate), MONTH(orderdate)*). The respective bits are the ones with the values 4 and 2, and those are the bits that are not set. The bits for the remaining elements—*custid, empid* and *DAY(orderdate)*—are set. Those are the bits with the bit values 16, 8, and 1, respectively. Sum the values of those bits and you get 25.

You're the one who determines which bit represents which grouping element by providing the elements as inputs to the function in a specific order. Therefore, when the user will request a certain grouping set, you will be able to calculate the integer bitmap value that uniquely identifies that grouping set.

In the query you use to persist the aggregates, you include the computation of the integer bitmap (call the result column *grp_id*) to uniquely identify the grouping set that each result row is associated with. Also, you create a clustered index on the table with the grp_id column as the leading key to support efficient retrieval of aggregates that are related to a single requested grouping set.

Here's code to persist the aggregates for the last query in a table called MyGroupingSets and to create the aforementioned supporting index:

```
USE tempdb;
IF OBJECT_ID(N'dbo.MyGroupingSets', N'U') IS NOT NULL  DROP TABLE dbo.MyGroupingSets;
GO

SELECT
  GROUPING_ID(
    custid, empid,
    YEAR(orderdate), MONTH(orderdate), DAY(orderdate) ) AS grp_id,
  custid, empid,
  YEAR(orderdate) AS orderyear,
  MONTH(orderdate) AS ordermonth,
  DAY(orderdate) AS orderday,
  SUM(qty) AS qty
INTO dbo.MyGroupingSets
FROM dbo.Orders
GROUP BY
  CUBE(custid, empid),
  ROLLUP(YEAR(orderdate), MONTH(orderdate), DAY(orderdate));

CREATE UNIQUE CLUSTERED INDEX idx_cl_groupingsets
  ON dbo.MyGroupingSets(grp_id, custid, empid, orderyear, ordermonth, orderday);
```

Suppose that a user requests the aggregates that are associated with the grouping set (*custid,* *YEAR(orderdate), MONTH(orderdate)*). The bit values of the other grouping elements (*empid* and *DAY(orderdate)*) are 8 and 1, respectively. So you query the table filtering *grp_id* 9, like so:

```
SELECT *
FROM dbo.MyGroupingSets
WHERE grp_id = 9;
```

Because the clustered index on the table has the *grp_id* column as the leading key, you get an efficient plan that performs a seek within that index, as shown in Figure 4-23.

If your source is very large and the full processing of the aggregates takes a long time, you will probably want to avoid doing the full processing every night. You will want to run the full processing once, and then every night run an incremental update process. That's, of course, assuming that the aggregated measures are additive.

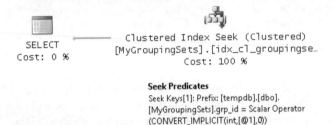

FIGURE 4-23 Plan for a query returning a single grouping.

As an example, suppose that today was April 19, 2014. The persisted aggregates hold data until the 18th, inclusive. Here's code representing new orders added on the 19th:

```
INSERT INTO dbo.Orders
  (orderid, orderdate, empid, custid, qty)
VALUES
  (50001, '20140419', 1, 'A', 10),
  (50002, '20140419', 1, 'B', 30),
  (50003, '20140419', 2, 'A', 20),
  (50004, '20140419', 2, 'B',  5),
  (50005, '20140419', 3, 'A', 15);
```

In the nightly process, you want to merge the aggregates for the last day with the existing ones. You want to update the target row by incrementing the value if the key already exists. You want to insert a new row if the key doesn't exist. To achieve this, you define a CTE called LastDay that computes the aggregates for the last day. You provide the LastDay CTE as the source to the MERGE statement. The MERGE statement will use the EXISTS predicate with an INTERSECT set operator to check if the source key list is matched by a target key list. This will not require you to add special logic for correct NULL treatment. When the EXISTS predicate returns true, the MERGE statement will update the target row by incrementing the value. When the predicate returns false, the MERGE statement will insert a new row. Here's the implementation of such a MERGE statement:

```
WITH LastDay AS
(
  SELECT
    GROUPING_ID(
      custid, empid,
      YEAR(orderdate), MONTH(orderdate), DAY(orderdate) ) AS grp_id,
    custid, empid,
    YEAR(orderdate) AS orderyear,
    MONTH(orderdate) AS ordermonth,
    DAY(orderdate) AS orderday,
    SUM(qty) AS qty
  FROM dbo.Orders
  WHERE orderdate = '20140419'
  GROUP BY
    CUBE(custid, empid),
    ROLLUP(YEAR(orderdate), MONTH(orderdate), DAY(orderdate))
)
MERGE INTO dbo.MyGroupingSets AS TGT
USING LastDay AS SRC
  ON EXISTS(
  SELECT SRC.grp_id, SRC.orderyear, SRC.ordermonth, SRC.orderday, SRC.custid, SRC.empid
  INTERSECT
  SELECT TGT.grp_id, TGT.orderyear, TGT.ordermonth, TGT.orderday, TGT.custid, TGT.empid)
WHEN MATCHED THEN
  UPDATE SET
    TGT.qty += SRC.qty
WHEN NOT MATCHED THEN
  INSERT (grp_id, custid, empid, orderyear, ordermonth, orderday)
  VALUES (SRC.grp_id, SRC.custid, SRC.empid, SRC.orderyear, SRC.ordermonth, SRC.orderday);
```

Chapter 6, "Data modification," has more information about the MERGE statement.

Sorting

Remember that if you don't specify a presentation ORDER BY clause in a query, you don't have any assurances regarding presentation order. Without an ORDER BY clause, even if the rows seem to come back in a certain order, it doesn't mean that you have any guarantees.

For example, suppose you have a query with a ROLLUP clause computing daily, monthly, yearly, and grand aggregates. The optimizer normally optimizes the ROLLUP clause with two Stream Aggregate operators based on the order of the elements in the clause. So there's likelihood that even without an ORDER BY clause you will get the rows presented based on the order of the time hierarchy. But that's not something you want to rely on as guaranteed behavior. Optimization can change. The only way to truly guarantee output order is with an explicit ORDER BY clause.

If you didn't have multiple levels of aggregation, but rather only daily ones, you would simply order the rows by the time vector *YEAR(orderdate), MONTH(orderdate), DAY(orderdate)*. But because you have daily, monthly, yearly, and grand totals, ordering based on the time hierarchy is trickier. A tool that can help you with this is a function called GROUPING. It's similar to the GROUPING_ID function, but it supports only one input. Like GROUPING_ID, the GROUPING function returns a 0 when the element is a detail element (part of the grouping set) and 1 when it's an aggregate (not part of the grouping set). So, to place the rows with a detail year before the row with the grand total, you place *GROUPING(YEAR(orderdate))* before *YEAR(orderdate)* in the ORDER BY clause. The same goes for the month and day elements.

The following query demonstrates how to apply this logic to get the detail sorted before the aggregate in each level (days in the month, then month total; months in the year, then yearly total; years, then grand total):

```
SELECT
  YEAR(orderdate)  AS orderyear,
  MONTH(orderdate) AS ordermonth,
  DAY(orderdate)   AS orderday,
  SUM(qty)         AS totalqty
FROM dbo.Orders
GROUP BY
  ROLLUP(YEAR(orderdate), MONTH(orderdate), DAY(orderdate))
ORDER BY
  GROUPING(YEAR(orderdate)) , YEAR(orderdate),
  GROUPING(MONTH(orderdate)), MONTH(orderdate),
  GROUPING(DAY(orderdate))  , DAY(orderdate);
```

This query generates the following output:

```
orderyear    ordermonth   orderday     totalqty
-----------  -----------  -----------  -----------
2012         4            18           22
2012         4            NULL         22
2012         8            2            10
2012         8            NULL         10
2012         9            7            30
2012         9            NULL         30
2012         12           24           32
2012         12           NULL         32
2012         NULL         NULL         94
2013         1            9            40
2013         1            18           14
2013         1            NULL         54
2013         2            12           12
2013         2            NULL         12
2013         NULL         NULL         66
2014         2            12           10
2014         2            16           20
2014         2            NULL         30
2014         4            18           15
2014         4            19           80
2014         4            NULL         95
2014         NULL         NULL         125
NULL         NULL         NULL         285
```

Now the presentation order is guaranteed, and it does not just happen to be this order because of optimization reasons.

Conclusion

This chapter covered quite a lot of ground concerning data analysis. It started with coverage of the profound window functions, describing the different types, as well as practical uses like handling gaps and islands problems. The chapter continued by covering techniques to handle pivoting and unpivoting tasks, showing both solutions that rely on standard methods and ones based on the proprietary PIVOT and UNPIVOT operators. The chapter then covered different ways to handle custom aggregate calculations like string concatenation and product. Finally, the chapter covered a number of features you can use to compute aggregates for multiple grouping sets in the same query.

TOP and OFFSET-FETCH

Classic filters in SQL like ON, WHERE, and HAVING are based on predicates. TOP and OFFSET-FETCH are filters that are based on a different concept: you indicate order and how many rows to filter based on that order. Many filtering tasks are defined based on order and a required number of rows. It's certainly good to have language support in T-SQL that allows you to phrase the request in a manner that is similar to the way you think about the task.

This chapter starts with the logical design aspects of the filters. It then uses a paging scenario to demonstrate their optimization. The chapter also covers the use of TOP with modification statements. Finally, the chapter demonstrates the use of TOP and OFFSET-FETCH in solving practical problems like *top N per group* and median.

The TOP and OFFSET-FETCH filters

You use the TOP and OFFSET-FETCH filters to implement filtering requirements in your queries in an intuitive manner. The TOP filter is a proprietary feature in T-SQL, whereas the OFFSET-FETCH filter is a standard feature. T-SQL started supporting OFFSET-FETCH with Microsoft SQL Server 2012. As of SQL Server 2014, the implementation of OFFSET-FETCH in T-SQL is still missing a couple of standard elements—interestingly, ones that are available with TOP. With the current implementation, each of the filters has capabilities that are not supported by the other.

I'll start by describing the logical design aspects of TOP and then cover those of OFFSET-FETCH.

The TOP filter

The TOP filter is a commonly used construct in T-SQL. Its popularity probably can be attributed to the fact that its design is so well aligned with the way many filtering requirements are expressed—for example, "Return the three most recent orders." In this request, the order for the filter is based on *orderdate*, descending, and the number of rows you want to filter based on this order is 3.

You specify the TOP option in the SELECT list with an input value typed as BIGINT indicating how many rows you want to filter. You provide the ordering specification in the classic ORDER BY clause. For example, you use the following query to get the three most recent orders.

```
USE TSQLV3;

SELECT TOP (3) orderid, orderdate, custid, empid
FROM Sales.Orders
ORDER BY orderdate DESC;
```

I got the following output from this query:

```
orderid     orderdate  custid      empid
----------- ---------- ----------- -----------
11077       2015-05-06 65          1
11076       2015-05-06 9           4
11075       2015-05-06 68          8
```

Instead of specifying the number of rows you want to filter, you can use TOP to specify the percent (of the total number of rows in the query result). You do so by providing a value in the range 0 through 100 (typed as FLOAT) and add the PERCENT keyword. For example, in the following query you request to filter one percent of the rows:

```
SELECT TOP (1) PERCENT orderid, orderdate, custid, empid
FROM Sales.Orders
ORDER BY orderdate DESC;
```

SQL Server rounds up the number of rows computed based on the input percent. For example, the result of 1 percent applied to 830 rows in the Orders table is 8.3. Rounding up this number, you get 9. Here's the output I got for this query:

```
orderid     orderdate  custid      empid
----------- ---------- ----------- -----------
11074       2015-05-06 73          7
11075       2015-05-06 68          8
11076       2015-05-06 9           4
11077       2015-05-06 65          1
11070       2015-05-05 44          2
11071       2015-05-05 46          1
11072       2015-05-05 20          4
11073       2015-05-05 58          2
11067       2015-05-04 17          1
```

Note that to translate the input percent to a number of rows, SQL Server has to first figure out the count of rows in the query result, and this usually requires extra work.

Interestingly, ordering specification is optional for the TOP filter. For example, consider the following query:

```
SELECT TOP (3) orderid, orderdate, custid, empid
FROM Sales.Orders;
```

I got the following output from this query:

```
orderid      orderdate   custid      empid
-----------  ----------  ----------  -----------
10248        2013-07-04  85          5
10249        2013-07-05  79          6
10250        2013-07-08  34          4
```

The selection of which three rows to return is nondeterministic. This means that if you run the query again, without the underlying data changing, theoretically you could get a different set of three rows. In practice, the row selection will depend on physical conditions like optimization choices, storage engine choices, data layout, and other factors. If you actually run the query multiple times, as long as those physical conditions don't change, there's some likelihood you will keep getting the same results. But it is critical to understand the "physical data independence" principle from the relational model, and remember that at the logical level you do not have a guarantee for repeatable results. Without ordering specification, you should consider the order as being arbitrary, resulting in a nondeterministic row selection.

Even when you do provide ordering specification, it doesn't mean that the query is deterministic. For example, an earlier TOP query used *orderdate, DESC* as the ordering specification. The *orderdate* column is not unique; therefore, the selection between rows with the same order date is nondeterministic. So what do you do in cases where you must guarantee determinism? There are two options: using WITH TIES or unique ordering.

The WITH TIES option causes ties to be included in the result. Here's how you apply it to our example:

```
SELECT TOP (3) WITH TIES orderid, orderdate, custid, empid
FROM Sales.Orders
ORDER BY orderdate DESC;
```

Here's the result I got from this query:

```
orderid      orderdate   custid      empid
-----------  ----------  ----------  -----------
11077        2015-05-06  65          1
11076        2015-05-06  9           4
11075        2015-05-06  68          8
11074        2015-05-06  73          7
```

SQL Server filters the three rows with the most recent order dates, plus it includes all other rows that have the same order date as in the last row. As a result, you can get more rows than the number you specified. In this query, you specified you wanted to filter three rows but ended up getting four. What's interesting to note here is that the row selection is now deterministic, but the presentation order between rows with the same order date is nondeterministic.

The second method to guarantee a deterministic result is to make the ordering specification unique by adding a tiebreaker. For example, you could add *orderid, DESC* as the tiebreaker in our example. This means that, in the case of ties in the order date values, a row with a higher order ID value is preferred to a row with a lower one. Here's our query with the tiebreaker applied:

```
SELECT TOP (3) orderid, orderdate, custid, empid
FROM Sales.Orders
ORDER BY orderdate DESC, orderid DESC;
```

This query generates the following output:

```
orderid     orderdate  custid       empid
----------- ---------- ------------ -----------
11077       2015-05-06 65           1
11076       2015-05-06 9            4
11075       2015-05-06 68           8
```

Use of unique ordering makes both the row selection and presentation ordering deterministic. The result set as well as the presentation ordering of the rows are guaranteed to be repeatable so long as the underlying data doesn't change.

If you have a case where you need to filter a certain number of rows but truly don't care about order, it could be a good idea to specify *ORDER BY (SELECT NULL)*, like so:

```
SELECT TOP (3) orderid, orderdate, custid, empid
FROM Sales.Orders
ORDER BY (SELECT NULL);
```

This way, you let everyone know your choice of arbitrary order is intentional, which helps to avoid confusion and doubt.

As a reminder of what I explained in Chapter 1, "Logical query processing," about the TOP and OFFSET-FETCH filters, presentation order is guaranteed only if the outer query has an ORDER BY clause. For example, in the following query presentation, ordering is not guaranteed:

```
SELECT orderid, orderdate, custid, empid
FROM ( SELECT TOP (3) orderid, orderdate, custid, empid
       FROM Sales.Orders
       ORDER BY orderdate DESC, orderid DESC                ) AS D;
```

To provide a presentation-ordering guarantee, you must specify an ORDER BY clause in the outer query, like so:

```
SELECT orderid, orderdate, custid, empid
FROM ( SELECT TOP (3) orderid, orderdate, custid, empid
       FROM Sales.Orders
       ORDER BY orderdate DESC, orderid DESC            ) AS D
ORDER BY orderdate DESC, orderid DESC;
```

The OFFSET-FETCH filter

The OFFSET-FETCH filter is a standard feature designed similar to TOP but with an extra element. You can specify how many rows you want to skip before specifying how many rows you want to filter.

As you could have guessed, this feature can be handy in implementing paging solutions—that is, returning a result to the user one chunk at a time upon request when the full result set is too long to fit in one screen or web page.

The OFFSET-FETCH filter requires an ORDER BY clause to exist, and it is specified right after it. You start by indicating how many rows to skip in an OFFSET clause, followed by how many rows to filter in a FETCH clause. For example, based on the indicated order, the following query skips the first 50 rows and filters the next 25 rows:

```
SELECT orderid, orderdate, custid, empid
FROM Sales.Orders
ORDER BY orderdate DESC, orderid DESC
OFFSET 50 ROWS FETCH NEXT 25 ROWS ONLY;
```

In other words, the query filters rows 51 through 75. In paging terms, assuming a page size of 25 rows, this query returns the third page.

To allow natural declarative language, you can use the keyword FIRST instead of NEXT if you like, though the meaning is the same. Using FIRST could be more intuitive if you're not skipping any rows. Even if you don't want to skip any rows, T-SQL still makes it mandatory to specify the OFFSET clause (with 0 ROWS) to avoid parsing ambiguity. Similarly, instead of using the plural form of the keyword ROWS, you can use the singular form ROW in both the OFFSET and the FETCH clauses. This is more natural if you need to skip or filter only one row.

If you're curious what the purpose of the keyword ONLY is, it means not to include ties. Standard SQL defines the alternative WITH TIES; however, T-SQL doesn't support it yet. Similarly, standard SQL defines the PERCENT option, but T-SQL doesn't support it yet either. These two missing options are available with the TOP filter.

As mentioned, the OFFSET-FETCH filter requires an ORDER BY clause. If you want to use arbitrary order, like TOP without an ORDER BY clause, you can use the trick with *ORDER BY (SELECT NULL)*, like so:

```
SELECT orderid, orderdate, custid, empid
FROM Sales.Orders
ORDER BY (SELECT NULL)
OFFSET 0 ROWS FETCH NEXT 3 ROWS ONLY;
```

The FETCH clause is optional. If you want to skip a certain number of rows but not limit how many rows to return, simply don't indicate a FETCH clause. For example, the following query skips 50 rows but doesn't limit the number of returned rows:

```
SELECT orderid, orderdate, custid, empid
FROM Sales.Orders
ORDER BY orderdate DESC, orderid DESC
OFFSET 50 ROWS;
```

Concerning presentation ordering, the behavior is the same as with the TOP filter; namely, with OFFSET-FETCH also, presentation ordering is guaranteed only if the outermost query has an ORDER BY clause.

Optimization of filters demonstrated through paging

So far, I described the logical design aspects of the TOP and OFFSET-FETCH filters. In this section, I'm going to cover optimization aspects. I'll do so by looking at different paging solutions. I'll describe two paging solutions using the TOP filter, a solution using the OFFSET-FETCH filter, and a solution using the ROW_NUMBER function.

In all cases, regardless of which filtering option you use for your paging solution, an index on the ordering elements is crucial for good performance. Often you will get good performance even when the index is not a covering one. Curiously, sometimes you will get better performance when the index isn't covering. I'll provide the details in the specific implementations.

I'll use the Orders table from the PerformanceV3 database in my examples. Suppose you need to implement a paging solution returning one page of orders at a time, based on *orderid* as the sort key. The table has a nonclustered index called PK_Orders defined with *orderid* as the key. This index is not a covering one with respect to the paging queries I will demonstrate.

Optimization of TOP

There are a couple of strategies you can use to implement paging solutions with TOP. One is an anchor-based strategy, and the other is TOP over TOP (nested TOP queries).

The anchor-based strategy allows the user to visit adjacent pages progressively. You define a stored procedure that when given the sort key of the last row from the previous page, returns the next page. Here's an implementation of such a procedure:

```
USE PerformanceV3;
IF OBJECT_ID(N'dbo.GetPage', N'P') IS NOT NULL DROP PROC dbo.GetPage;
GO
CREATE PROC dbo.GetPage
  @orderid  AS INT    = 0, -- anchor sort key
  @pagesize AS BIGINT = 25
AS

SELECT TOP (@pagesize) orderid, orderdate, custid, empid
FROM dbo.Orders
WHERE orderid > @orderid
ORDER BY orderid;
GO
```

Here I'm assuming that only positive order IDs are supported. Of course, you can implement such an integrity rule with a CHECK constraint. The query uses the WHERE clause to filter only orders with order IDs that are greater than the input anchor sort key. From the remaining rows, using TOP, the query filters the first @*pagesize* rows based on *orderid* ordering.

Use the following code to request the first page of orders:

```
EXEC dbo.GetPage @pagesize = 25;
```

I got the following result (but yours may vary because of the randomization aspects used in the creation of the sample data):

```
orderid     orderdate  custid      empid
----------- ---------- ----------- -----------
1           2011-01-01 C0000005758 205
2           2011-01-01 C0000015925 251
...
24          2011-01-01 C0000003541 316
25          2011-01-01 C0000005636 256
```

In this example, the last sort key in the first page is 25. Therefore, to request the second page of orders, you pass 25 as the input anchor sort key, like so:

```
EXEC dbo.GetPage @orderid = 25, @pagesize = 25;
```

Of course, in practice the last sort key in the first page could be different than 25, but in my sample data the keys start with 1 and are sequential. I got the following result when running this code:

```
orderid     orderdate  custid      empid
----------- ---------- ----------- -----------
26          2011-01-01 C0000017397 332
27          2011-01-01 C0000012629 27
28          2011-01-01 C0000016429 53
...
49          2011-01-01 C0000015415 95
50          2010-12-06 C0000008667 117
```

To ask for the third page of orders, you pass 50 as the input sort key in the next page request:

```
EXEC dbo.GetPage @orderid = 50, @pagesize = 25;
```

I got the following output for the execution of this code:

```
orderid      orderdate  custid       empid
-----------  ---------- -----------  -----------
51           2011-01-01 C0000000797  438
52           2011-01-01 C0000015945  47
53           2011-01-01 C0000013558  364
...
74           2011-01-01 C0000019720  249
75           2011-01-01 C0000000807  160
```

The execution plan for the query is shown in Figure 5-1. I'll assume the inputs represent the last procedure call with the request for the third page.

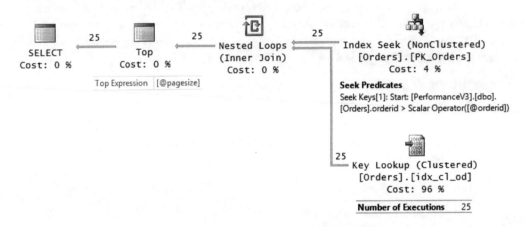

FIGURE 5-1 Plan for TOP with a single anchor sort key.

I'll describe the execution of this plan based on data flow order (right to left). But keep in mind that the API call order is actually left to right, starting with the root node (SELECT). I'll explain why that's important to remember shortly.

The Index Seek operator performs a seek in the index PK_Orders to the first leaf row that satisfies the Start property of the Seek Predicates property: *orderid > @orderid*. In the third execution of the procedure, *@orderid* is 50. Then the Index Seek operator continues with a range scan in the index leaf based on the seek predicate. Absent a Prefix property of the Seek Predicates property, the range scan normally continues until the tail of the index leaf. However, as mentioned, the internal API call order is done from left to right. The Top operator has a property called Top Expression, which is set in the plan to *@pagesize* (25, in our case). This property tells the Top operator how many rows to request from the Nested Loops operator to its right. In turn, the Nested Loops operator requests the specified number of rows (25, in our case) from the Index Seek operator to its right. For each row returned from the Index Seek Operator, Nested Loops executes the Key Lookup operator to collect the remaining elements from the respective data row. This means that the range scan doesn't proceed beyond the 25th row, and this also means that the Key Lookup operator is executed 25 times.

Not only is the range scan in the Index Seek operator cut short because of TOP's row goal (Top Expression property), the query optimizer needs to adjust the costs of the affected operators based on that row goal. This aspect of optimization is described in detail in an excellent article by Paul White: "Inside the Optimizer: Row Goals In Depth." The article can be found here: *http://sqlblog.com/blogs/paul_white/archive/2010/08/18/inside-the-optimiser-row-goals-in-depth.aspx*.

The I/O costs involved in the execution of the query plan are made of the following:

- Seek to the leaf of index: 3 reads (the index has three levels)

- Range scan of 25 rows: 0–1 reads (hundreds of rows fit in a page)

- Nested Loops prefetch used to optimize lookups: 9 reads (measured by disabling prefetch with trace flag 8744)

- 25 key lookups: 75 reads

In total, 87 logical reads were reported for the processing of this query. That's not too bad. Could things be better or worse? Yes on both counts. You could get better performance by creating a covering index. This way, you eliminate the costs of the prefetch and the lookups, resulting in only 3–4 logical reads in total. You could get much worse performance if you don't have any good index with the sort column as the leading key—not even a noncovering index. This results in a plan that performs a full scan of the data, plus a sort. That's a very expensive plan, especially considering that you pay for it for every page request by the user.

With a single sort key, the WHERE predicate identifying the start of the qualifying range is straightforward: *orderid > @orderid*. With multiple sort keys, it gets a bit trickier. For example, suppose that the sort vector is (*orderdate, orderid*), and you get the anchor sort keys *@orderdate* and *@orderid* as inputs to the *GetPage* procedure. Standard SQL has an elegant solution for this in the form of a feature called *row constructor* (aka *vector expression*). Had this feature been implemented in T-SQL, you could have phrased the WHERE predicate as follows: *(orderdate, orderid) > (@orderdate, @orderid)*. This also allows good optimization by using a supporting index on the sort keys similar to the optimization of a single sort key. Sadly, T-SQL doesn't support such a construct yet.

You have two options in terms of how to phrase the predicate. One of them (call it the *first predicate form*) is the following: *orderdate >= @orderdate AND (orderdate > @orderdate OR orderid > @orderid)*. Another one (call it the *second predicate form*) looks like this: *(orderdate = @orderdate AND orderid > @orderid) OR orderdate > @orderdate*. Both are logically equivalent, but they do get handled differently by the query optimizer. In our case, there's a covering index called idx_od_oid_i_cid_eid defined on the Orders table with the key list (*orderdate, orderid*) and the include list (*custid, empid*).

Here's the implementation of the stored procedure with the first predicate form:

```
IF OBJECT_ID(N'dbo.GetPage', N'P') IS NOT NULL DROP PROC dbo.GetPage;
GO
CREATE PROC dbo.GetPage
  @orderdate AS DATE   = '00010101', -- anchor sort key 1 (orderdate)
  @orderid   AS INT    = 0,          -- anchor sort key 2 (orderid)
  @pagesize  AS BIGINT = 25
AS

SELECT TOP (@pagesize) orderid, orderdate, custid, empid
FROM dbo.Orders
WHERE orderdate >= @orderdate
  AND (orderdate > @orderdate OR orderid > @orderid)
ORDER BY orderdate, orderid;
GO
```

Run the following code to get the first page:

```
EXEC dbo.GetPage @pagesize = 25;
```

I got the following output from this execution:

```
orderid     orderdate  custid       empid
----------- ---------- ------------ -----------
310         2010-12-03 C0000014672  218
330         2010-12-03 C0000009594  10
90          2010-12-04 C0000012937  231
...
300         2010-12-07 C0000019961  282
410         2010-12-07 C0000001585  342
```

Run the following code to get the second page:

```
EXEC dbo.GetPage @orderdate = '20101207', @orderid = 410, @pagesize = 25;
```

I got the following output from this execution:

```
orderid     orderdate  custid       empid
----------- ---------- ------------ -----------
1190        2010-12-07 C0000004678  465
1270        2010-12-07 C0000015067  376
1760        2010-12-07 C0000009532  104
...
2470        2010-12-09 C0000008664  205
2830        2010-12-09 C0000010497  221
```

Run the following code to get the third page:

```
EXEC dbo.GetPage @orderdate = '20101209', @orderid = 2830, @pagesize = 25;
```

I got the following output from this execution:

orderid	orderdate	custid	empid
3120	2010-12-09	C0000015659	381
3340	2010-12-09	C0000008708	272
3620	2010-12-09	C0000009367	312
...			
2730	2010-12-10	C0000015630	317
3490	2010-12-10	C0000002887	306

As for optimization, Figure 5-2 shows the plan I got for the implementation using the first predicate form.

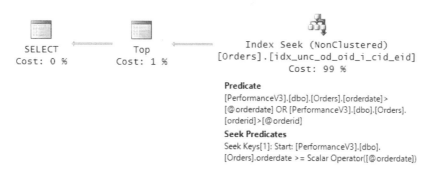

FIGURE 5-2 Plan for TOP with multiple anchor sort keys, first predicate form.

Observe that the Start property of the Seek Predicates property is based only on the predicate *orderdate >= @orderdate*. The residual predicate is *orderdate > @orderdate OR orderid > @orderid*. Such optimization could result in some unnecessary work scanning the pages holding the first part of the range with the first qualifying order date with the nonqualifying order IDs—in other words, the rows where *orderdate = @orderdate AND orderid <= @orderid* are going to be scanned even though they need not be returned. How many unnecessary page reads will be performed mainly depends on the density of the leading sort key—*orderdate*, in our case. The denser it is, the more unnecessary work is likely going to happen. In our case, the density of the *orderdate* column is very low (~1/1500); it is so low that the extra work is negligible. But, when the leading sort key is dense, you could get a noticeable improvement by using the second form of the predicate. Here's an implementation of the stored procedure with the second predicate form:

```
IF OBJECT_ID(N'dbo.GetPage', N'P') IS NOT NULL DROP PROC dbo.GetPage;
GO
CREATE PROC dbo.GetPage
  @orderdate AS DATE   = '00010101', -- anchor sort key 1 (orderdate)
  @orderid   AS INT    = 0,          -- anchor sort key 2 (orderid)
  @pagesize  AS BIGINT = 25
AS

SELECT TOP (@pagesize) orderid, orderdate, custid, empid
FROM dbo.Orders
WHERE (orderdate = @orderdate AND orderid > @orderid)
   OR orderdate > @orderdate
ORDER BY orderdate, orderid;
GO
```

Run the following code to get the third page:

```
EXEC dbo.GetPage @orderdate = '20101209', @orderid = 2830, @pagesize = 25;
```

The query plan for the implementation with the second form of the predicate is shown in Figure 5-3.

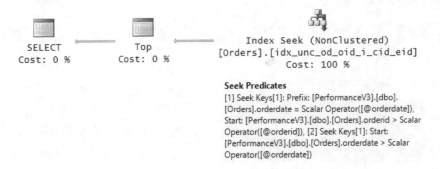

Seek Predicates
[1] Seek Keys[1]: Prefix: [PerformanceV3].[dbo].
[Orders].orderdate = Scalar Operator([@orderdate]),
Start: [PerformanceV3].[dbo].[Orders].orderid > Scalar
Operator([@orderid]), [2] Seek Keys[1]: Start:
[PerformanceV3].[dbo].[Orders].orderdate > Scalar
Operator([@orderdate])

FIGURE 5-3 Plan for TOP with multiple anchor sort keys, second predicate form.

Observe that there's no residual predicate, only Seek Predicates. Curiously, there are two seek predicates. Remember that, generally, the range scan performed by an Index Seek operator starts with the first match for Prefix and Start and ends with the last match for Prefix. In our case, one predicate (marked in the plan as *[1] Seek Keys*...) starts with *orderdate = @orderdate AND orderid > @orderid* and ends with *orderdate = @orderdate*. Another predicate (marked in the plan as *[2] Seek Keys*...) starts with *orderdate = @orderdate* and has no explicit end. What's interesting is that during query execution, if Top Expression rows are found by the first seek, the execution of the operator short-circuits before getting to the second. But if the first seek isn't sufficient, the second will be executed. The fact that in our example the leading sort key (*orderdate*) has low density could mislead you to think that the first predicate form is more efficient. If you test both implementations and compare the number of logical reads, you might see the first one performing 3 or more reads and the second one performing 6 or more reads (when two seeks are used). But if you test the solutions with a dense leading sort key, you will notice a significant difference in favor of the second solution.

There's another method to using TOP to implement paging. You can think of it as the TOP over TOP, or nested TOP, method. You work with *@pagenum* and *@pagesize* as the inputs to the *GetPage* procedure. There's no anchor concept here. You use one query with TOP to filter *@pagenum * @pagesize* rows based on the desired order. You define a table expression based on this query (call it *D1*). You use a second query against D1 with TOP to filter *@pagesize* rows, but in inverse order. You define a table expression based on the second query (call it *D2*). Finally, you write an outer query against D2 to order the rows in the desired order. Run the following code to implement the *GetPage* procedure based on this approach:

```
IF OBJECT_ID(N'dbo.GetPage', N'P') IS NOT NULL DROP PROC dbo.GetPage;
GO
CREATE PROC dbo.GetPage
  @pagenum  AS BIGINT = 1,
  @pagesize AS BIGINT = 25
AS

SELECT orderid, orderdate, custid, empid
FROM ( SELECT TOP (@pagesize) *
       FROM ( SELECT TOP (@pagenum * @pagesize) *
              FROM dbo.Orders
              ORDER BY orderid ) AS D1
       ORDER BY orderid DESC ) AS D2
ORDER BY orderid;
GO
```

Here are three consecutive calls to the procedure requesting the first, second, and third pages:

```
EXEC dbo.GetPage @pagenum = 1, @pagesize = 25;
EXEC dbo.GetPage @pagenum = 2, @pagesize = 25;
EXEC dbo.GetPage @pagenum = 3, @pagesize = 25;
```

The plan for the third procedure call is shown in Figure 5-4.

FIGURE 5-4 Plan for TOP over TOP.

The plan is not very expensive, but there are three aspects to it that are not optimal when compared to the implementation based on the anchor concept. First, the plan scans the data in the index from the beginning of the leaf until the last qualifying row. This means that there's repetition of work—namely, rescanning portions of the data. For the first page requested by the user, the plan will scan *1 * @pagesize* rows, for the second page it will scan *2 * @pagesize* rows, for the *n*th page it will scan *n * @pagesize* rows. Second, notice that the Key Lookup operator is executed 75 times even though only 25 of the lookups are relevant. Third, there are two Sort operators added to the plan: one reversing the original order to get to the last chunk of rows, and the other reversing it back to the original order to present it like this. For the third page request, the execution of this plan performed 241 logical reads. The greater the number of pages you have, the more work there is.

The benefit of this approach compared to the anchor-based strategy is that you don't need to deal with collecting the anchor from the result of the last page request, and the user is not limited to navigating only between adjacent pages. For example, the user can start with page 1, request page 5, and so on.

Optimization of OFFSET-FETCH

The optimization of the OFFSET-FETCH filter is similar to that of TOP. Instead of reinventing the wheel by creating an entirely new plan operator, Microsoft decided to enhance the existing Top operator. Remember the Top operator has a property called Top Expression that indicates how many rows to request from the operator to the right and pass to the operator to the left. The enhanced Top operator used to process OFFSET-FETCH has a new property called OffsetExpression that indicates how many rows to request from the operator to the right and not pass to the operator to the left. The OffsetExpression property is processed before the Top Expression property, as you might have guessed.

To show you the optimization of the OFFSET-FETCH filter, I'll use it in the implementation of the *GetPage* procedure:

```
IF OBJECT_ID(N'dbo.GetPage', N'P') IS NOT NULL DROP PROC dbo.GetPage;
GO
CREATE PROC dbo.GetPage
  @pagenum  AS BIGINT = 1,
  @pagesize AS BIGINT = 25
AS

SELECT orderid, orderdate, custid, empid
FROM dbo.Orders
ORDER BY orderid
OFFSET (@pagenum - 1) * @pagesize ROWS FETCH NEXT @pagesize ROWS ONLY;
GO
```

As you can see, OFFSET-FETCH allows a simple and flexible solution that uses the *@pagenum* and *@pagesize* inputs. Use the following code to request the first three pages:

```
EXEC dbo.GetPage @pagenum = 1, @pagesize = 25;
EXEC dbo.GetPage @pagenum = 2, @pagesize = 25;
EXEC dbo.GetPage @pagenum = 3, @pagesize = 25;
```

Note Remember that under the default isolation level Read Committed, data changes between procedure calls can affect the results you get, causing you to get the same row in different pages or skip some rows. For example, suppose that at point in time T1, you request page 1. You get the rows that according to the paging sort order are positioned 1 through 25. Before you request the next page, at point in time T2, someone adds a new row with a sort key that makes it the 20th row. At point in time T3, you request page 2. You get the rows that, in T1, were positioned 25 through 49 and not 26 through 50. This behavior could be awkward. If you want the entire sequence of page requests to interact with the same state of the data, you need to submit all requests from the same transaction running under the snapshot isolation level.

The plan for the third execution of the procedure is shown in Figure 5-5.

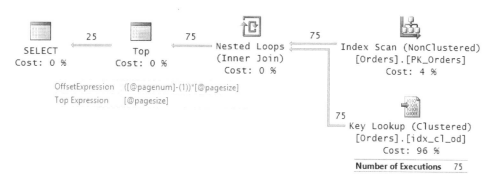

FIGURE 5-5 Plan for OFFSET-FETCH.

As you can see in the plan, the Top operator first requests OffsetExpression rows (50, in our example) from the operator to the right and doesn't pass those to the operator to the left. Then it requests Top Expression rows (25, in our example) from the operator to the right and passes those to the operator to the left. You can see two levels of inefficiency in this plan compared to the plan for the anchor solution. One is that the Index Scan operator ends up scanning 75 rows, but only the last 25 are relevant. This is unavoidable without an input anchor to start after. But the Key Lookup operator is executed 75 times even though, theoretically, the first 50 times could have been avoided. Such logic to avoid applying lookups for the first OffsetExpression rows wasn't added to the optimizer. The number of logical reads required for the third page request is 241. The farther away the page number you request is, the more lookups the plan applies and the more expensive it is.

Arguably, in paging sessions users don't get too far. If users don't find what they are looking for after the first few pages, they usually give up and refine their search. In such cases, the extra work is probably negligible enough to not be a concern. However, the farther you get with the page number you're after, the more the inefficiency increases. For example, run the following code to request page 1000:

```
EXEC dbo.GetPage @pagenum = 1000, @pagesize = 25;
```

This time, the plan involves 25,000 lookups, resulting in a total number of logical reads of 76,644. Unfortunately, because the optimizer doesn't have logic to avoid the unnecessary lookups, you need to figure this out yourself if it's important for you to eliminate unnecessary costs. Fortunately, there is a simple trick you can use to achieve this. Have the query with the OFFSET-FETCH filter return only the sort keys. Define a table expression based on this query (call it *K*, for keys). Then in the outer query, join K with the underlying table to return all the remaining attributes you need. Here's the optimized implementation of *GetPage* based on this strategy:

```
ALTER PROC dbo.GetPage
  @pagenum  AS BIGINT = 1,
  @pagesize AS BIGINT = 25
AS

WITH K AS
(
  SELECT orderid
  FROM dbo.Orders
  ORDER BY orderid
  OFFSET (@pagenum - 1) * @pagesize ROWS FETCH NEXT @pagesize ROWS ONLY
)
SELECT O.orderid, O.orderdate, O.custid, O.empid
FROM dbo.Orders AS O
  INNER JOIN K
    ON O.orderid = K.orderid
ORDER BY O.orderid;
GO
```

Run the following code to get the third page:

```
EXEC dbo.GetPage @pagenum = 3, @pagesize = 25;
```

You will get the plan shown in Figure 5-6.

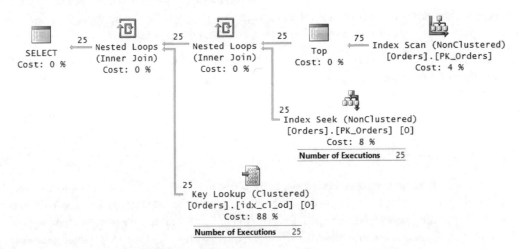

FIGURE 5-6 Plan for OFFSET-FETCH, minimizing lookups.

As you can see, the Top operator is used early in the plan to filter the relevant 25 keys. Then only 25 executions of the Index Seek operator are required, plus 25 executions of the Key Lookup operator (because PK_Orders is not a covering index). The total number of logical reads required for the processing of this plan for the third page request was reduced to 153. This doesn't seem like a dramatic improvement when compared to the 241 logical reads used in the previous implementation. But try running the procedure with a page that's farther out, like 1000:

```
EXEC dbo.GetPage @pagenum = 1000, @pagesize = 25;
```

The optimized implementation uses only 223 logical reads compared to the 76,644 used in the previous implementation. That's a big difference!

Curiously, a noncovering index created only on the sort keys, likè PK_Orders in our case, can be more efficient for the optimized solution than a covering index. That's because with shorter rows, more rows fit in a page. So, in cases where you need to skip a substantial number of rows, you get to do so by scanning fewer pages than you would with a covering index. With a noncovering index, you do have the extra cost of the lookups, but the optimized solution reduces the number of lookups to the minimum.

OFFSET TO | AFTER

As food for thought, if you could change or extend the design of the OFFSET-FETCH filter, what would you do? You might find it useful to support an alternative OFFSET option that is based on an input-anchor sort vector. Imagine syntax such as the following (which shows additions to the standard syntax in bold):

```
OFFSET { <offset row count> { ROW | ROWS } | { TO | AFTER ( <sort vector> ) } }
FETCH { FIRST | NEXT } [ <fetch first quantity> ] { ROW | ROWS } { ONLY | WITH TIES }
[ LAST ROW INTO ( <variables vector> ) ]
```

You would then use a query such as the following in the *GetPage* procedure (but don't try it, because it uses unsupported syntax):

```
SELECT orderid, orderdate, custid, empid
FROM dbo.Orders
ORDER BY orderdate, orderid
OFFSET AFTER (@anchor_orderdate, @anchor_orderid) -- input anchor sort keys
FETCH NEXT @pagesize ROWS ONLY
LAST ROW INTO (@last_orderdate, @last_orderid); -- outputs for next page request
```

The suggested anchor-based offset has a couple of advantages compared to the existing row count–based offset. The former lends itself to good optimization with an index seek directly to the first matching row in the leaf of a supporting index. Also, by using the former, you can see changes in the data gracefully, unlike with the latter.

Optimization of ROW_NUMBER

Another common solution for paging is using the ROW_NUMBER function to compute row numbers based on the desired sort and then filtering the right range of row numbers based on the input @*pagenum* and @*pagesize*.

Here's the implementation of the *GetPage* procedure based on this strategy:

```
IF OBJECT_ID(N'dbo.GetPage', N'P') IS NOT NULL DROP PROC dbo.GetPage;
GO
CREATE PROC dbo.GetPage
  @pagenum  AS BIGINT = 1,
  @pagesize AS BIGINT = 25
AS

WITH C AS
(
  SELECT orderid, orderdate, custid, empid,
    ROW_NUMBER() OVER(ORDER BY orderid) AS rn
  FROM dbo.Orders
)
SELECT orderid, orderdate, custid, empid
FROM C
WHERE rn BETWEEN (@pagenum - 1) * @pagesize + 1 AND @pagenum * @pagesize
ORDER BY rn; -- if order by orderid get sort in plan
GO
```

Run the following code to request the first three pages:

```
EXEC dbo.GetPage @pagenum = 1, @pagesize = 25;
EXEC dbo.GetPage @pagenum = 2, @pagesize = 25;
EXEC dbo.GetPage @pagenum = 3, @pagesize = 25;
```

The plan for the third page request is shown in Figure 5-7.

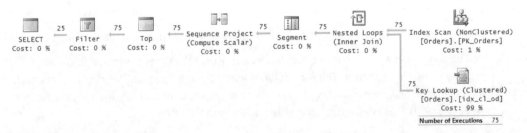

FIGURE 5-7 Plan for ROW_NUMBER.

Interestingly, the optimization of this solution is similar to that of the solution based on the OFFSET-FETCH filter. You will find the same inefficiencies, including the unnecessary lookups. As a result, the costs are virtually the same. For the third page request, the number of logical reads is 241. Run the procedure again asking for page 1000:

```
EXEC dbo.GetPage @pagenum = 1000, @pagesize = 25;
```

The number of logical reads is now 76,644. You can avoid the unnecessary lookups by applying the same optimization principle used in the improved OFFSET-FETCH solution, like so:

```
ALTER PROC dbo.GetPage
  @pagenum  AS BIGINT = 1,
  @pagesize AS BIGINT = 25
AS

WITH C AS
(
  SELECT orderid, ROW_NUMBER() OVER(ORDER BY orderid) AS rn
  FROM dbo.Orders
),
K AS
(
  SELECT orderid, rn
  FROM C
  WHERE rn BETWEEN (@pagenum - 1) * @pagesize + 1 AND @pagenum * @pagesize
)
SELECT O.orderid, O.orderdate, O.custid, O.empid
FROM dbo.Orders AS O
  INNER JOIN K
    ON O.orderid = K.orderid
ORDER BY K.rn;
GO
```

Run the procedure again requesting the third page:

```
EXEC dbo.GetPage @pagenum = 3, @pagesize = 25;
```

The plan for the optimized solution is shown in Figure 5-8.

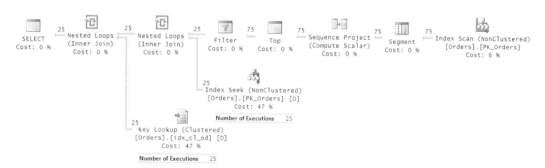

FIGURE 5-8 Plan for ROW_NUMBER, minimizing lookups.

Observe that the Top operator filters the first 75 rows, and then the Filter operator filters the last 25, before applying the seeks and the lookups. As a result, the seeks and lookups are executed only 25 times. The execution of the plan for the third page request involves 153 logical reads, compared to 241 required by the previous solution.

Run the procedure again, this time requesting page 1000:

```
EXEC dbo.GetPage @pagenum = 1000, @pagesize = 25;
```

This execution requires only 223 logical reads, compared to 76,644 required by the previous solution.

Using the TOP option with modifications

T-SQL supports using the TOP filter with modification statements. This section first describes this capability, and then its limitation and a workaround for the limitation. Then it describes a practical use case for this capability when you need to delete a large number of rows.

In my examples, I'll use a table called MyOrders. Run the following code to create this table as an initial copy of the Orders table in the PerformanceV3 database:

```
USE PerformanceV3;
IF OBJECT_ID(N'dbo.MyOrders', N'U') IS NOT NULL DROP TABLE dbo.MyOrders;
GO
SELECT * INTO dbo.MyOrders FROM dbo.Orders;
CREATE UNIQUE CLUSTERED INDEX idx_od_oid ON dbo.MyOrders(orderdate, orderid);
```

TOP with modifications

With T-SQL, you can use TOP with modification statements. Those statements are INSERT TOP, DELETE TOP, UPDATE TOP, and MERGE TOP. This means the statement will stop modifying rows once the requested number of rows are affected. For example, the following statement deletes 50 rows from the table MyOrders:

```
DELETE TOP (50) FROM dbo.MyOrders;
```

When you use TOP in a SELECT statement, you can control which rows get chosen using the ORDER BY clause. But modification statements don't have an ORDER BY clause. This means you can indicate how many rows you want to modify, but not based on what order—at least, not directly. So the preceding statement deletes 50 rows, but you cannot control which 50 rows get deleted. You should consider the order as being arbitrary. In practice, it depends on optimization and data layout.

This limitation is a result of the design choice that the TOP ordering is to be defined by the traditional ORDER BY clause. The traditional ORDER BY clause was originally designed to define presentation order, and it is available only to the SELECT statement. Had the design of TOP been different, with its own ordering specification that is not related to presentation ordering, it would have been natural to use also with modification statements. Here's an example for what such a design might have looked like (but don't run the code, because this syntax isn't supported):

```
DELETE TOP (50) OVER(ORDER BY orderdate, orderid) FROM dbo.MyOrders;
```

Fortunately, when you do need to control which rows get chosen, you can use a simple trick as a workaround. Use a SELECT query with a TOP filter and an ORDER BY clause. Define a table expression based on that query. Then issue the modification against the table expression, like so:

```
WITH C AS
(
  SELECT TOP (50) *
  FROM dbo.MyOrders
  ORDER BY orderdate, orderid
)
DELETE FROM C;
```

In practice, the rows from the underlying table will be affected. You can think of the modification as being defined through the table expression.

The OFFSET-FETCH filter is not supported directly with modification statements, but you can use a similar trick like the one with TOP.

Modifying in chunks

Having TOP supported by modification statements without the ability to indicate order might seem futile, but there is a practical use case involving modifying large volumes of data. As an example, suppose you need to delete all rows from the MyOrders table where the order date is before 2013. The table in our example is fairly small, having about 1,000,000 rows. But imagine there were 100,000,000 rows, and the number of rows to delete was about 50,000,000. If the table was partitioned (say, by year), things would be easy and highly efficient. You switch a partition out to a staging table and then drop the staging table. However, what if the table is currently not partitioned? The intuitive thing to do is to issue a simple DELETE statement to do the job as a single transaction, like so (but don't run this statement):

```
DELETE FROM dbo.MyOrders WHERE orderdate < '20130101';
```

Such an approach can get you into trouble in a number of ways.

A DELETE statement is fully logged, unlike DROP TABLE and TRUNCATE TABLE statements. Log writes are sequential; therefore, log-intensive operations tend to be slow and hard to optimize beyond a certain point. For example, deleting 50,000,000 rows can take many minutes to finish.

There's a section in the log considered to be the active portion, starting with the oldest open transaction and ending with the current pointer in the log. The active portion cannot be recycled. So when you have a long-running transaction, it can cause the transaction log to expand, sometimes well beyond its typical size for your database. This can be an issue if you have limited disk space.

Modification statements acquire exclusive locks on the modified resources (row or page locks, as decided by SQL Server dynamically), and exclusive locks are held until the transaction finishes. Each lock is represented by a memory structure that is approximately 100 bytes in size. Acquiring a large number of locks has two main drawbacks. For one, it requires large amounts of memory. Second, it takes time to allocate the memory structures, which adds to the time it takes the transaction to complete. To reduce the memory footprint and allow a faster process, SQL Server will attempt to escalate from the initial granularity of locks (row or page) to a table lock (or partition, if configured). The first trigger for SQL Server to attempt escalation is when the same transaction reaches 5,000 locks against the same object. If unsuccessful (for example, another transaction is holding locks that the escalated lock would be in conflict with), SQL Server will keep trying to escalate every additional 1,250 locks. When escalation succeeds, the transaction locks the entire table (or partition) until it finishes. This behavior can cause concurrency problems.

If you try to terminate such a large modification that is in progress, you will face the consequences of a rollback. If the transaction was already running for a while, it will take a while for the rollback to finish—typically, more than the original work.

To avoid the aforementioned problems, the recommended approach to apply a large modification is to do it in chunks. For our purge process, you can run a loop that executes a DELETE TOP statement repeatedly until all qualifying rows are deleted. You want to make sure that the chunk size is not too small so that the process will not take forever, but you want it to be small enough not to trigger lock escalation. The tricky part is figuring out the chunk size. It takes 5,000 locks before SQL Server attempts escalation, but how does this translate to the number of rows you're deleting? SQL Server could decide to use row or page locks initially, plus when you delete rows from a table, SQL Server deletes rows from the indexes that are defined on the table. So it's hard to predict what the ideal number of rows is without testing.

A simple solution could be to test different numbers while running a trace or an extended events session with a lock-escalation event. For example, I ran the following extended events session with a Live Data window open, while issuing DELETE TOP statements from a session with session ID 53:

```
CREATE EVENT SESSION [Lock_Escalation] ON SERVER
ADD EVENT sqlserver.lock_escalation(
    WHERE ([sqlserver].[session_id]=(53)));
```

I started with 10,000 rows using the following statement:

```
DELETE TOP (10000) FROM dbo.MyOrders WHERE orderdate < '20130101';
```

Then I adjusted the number, increasing or decreasing it depending on whether an escalation event took place or not. In my case, the first point where escalation happened was somewhere between 6,050 and 6,100 rows. Once you find it, you don't want to use that point minus 1. For example, if you add indexes later on, the point will become lower. To be on the safe side, I take the number that I find in my testing and divide it by two. This should leave enough room for the future addition of indexes. Of course, it's worthwhile to retest from time to time to see if the number needs to be adjusted.

Once you have the chunk size determined (say, 3,000), you implement the purge process as a loop that deletes one chunk of rows at a time using a DELETE TOP statement, like so:

```
SET NOCOUNT ON;

WHILE 1 = 1
BEGIN
  DELETE TOP (3000) FROM dbo.MyOrders WHERE orderdate < '20130101';
  IF @@ROWCOUNT < 3000 BREAK;
END
```

The code uses an infinite loop. Every execution of the DELETE TOP statement deletes up to 3,000 rows and commits. As soon as the number of affected rows is lower than 3,000, you know that you've reached the last chunk, so the code breaks from the loop. If this process is running (and during peak hours), you want to abort it, and it's quite safe to stop it. Only the current chunk will undergo a roll-back. You can then run it again in the next window you have for this and the process will simply pick up where it left off.

Top N per group

The *top N per group* task is a classic task that appears in many shapes in practice. Examples include the following: "Return the latest price for each security," "Return the employee who handled the most orders for each region," "Return the three most recent orders for each customer," and so on. Interestingly, like with many other examples in T-SQL, it's not like there's one solution that is considered the most efficient in all cases. Different solutions work best in different circumstances. For *top N per group* tasks, two main factors determine which solution is most efficient: the availability of a supporting index and the density of the partitioning (group) column.

The task I will use to demonstrate the different solutions is returning the three most recent orders for each customer from the Sales.Orders table in the TSQLV3 database. In any *top N per group* task, you need to identify the elements involved: partitioning, ordering, and covering. The partitioning element defines the groups. The ordering element defines the order—based on which, you filter the first N rows in each group. The covering element simply represents the rest of the columns you need to return. Here are the elements in our sample task:

- Partitioning: *custid*

- Ordering: *orderdate DESC, orderid DESC*

- Covering: *empid*

As mentioned, one of the important factors contributing to the efficiency of solutions is the availability of a supporting index. The recommended index is based on a pattern I like to think of as *POC*—the acronym for the elements involved (partitioning, ordering, and covering). The *PO* elements should form the index key list, and the *C* element should form the index include list. If the index is clustered, only the key list is relevant; all the rest of the columns are included in the leaf row, anyway. Run the following code to create the POC index for our sample task:

```
USE TSQLV3;

CREATE UNIQUE INDEX idx_poc ON Sales.Orders(custid, orderdate DESC, orderid DESC)
  INCLUDE(empid);
```

The other important factor in determining which solution is most efficient is the density of the partitioning element (*custid*, in our case). The Sales.Orders table in our example is very small, but imagine the same structure with a larger volume of data—say, 10,000,000 rows. The row size in our index is quite small (22 bytes), so over 300 rows fit in a page. This means the index will have about 30,000 pages in its leaf level and will be three levels deep. I'll discuss two density scenarios in my examples:

- Low density: 1,000,000 customers, with 10 orders per customer on average

- High density: 10 customers, with 1,000,000 orders per customer on average

I'll start with a solution based on the ROW_NUMBER function that is the most efficient in the low-density case. I'll continue with a solution based on TOP and APPLY that is the most efficient in the high-density case. Finally, I'll describe a solution based on concatenation that performs better than the others when a POC index is not available, regardless of density.

Solution using ROW_NUMBER

Two main optimization strategies can be used to carry out our task. One strategy is to perform a seek for each customer in the POC index to the beginning of that customer's section in the index leaf, and then perform a range scan of the three qualifying rows. Another strategy is to perform a single scan of the index leaf and then filter the interesting rows as part of the scan.

The former strategy is not efficient for low density because it involves a large number of seeks. For 1,000,000 customers, it requires 1,000,000 seeks. With three levels in the index, this approach translates to 3,000,000 random reads. Therefore, with low density, the strategy involving a single full scan and a filter is more efficient. From an I/O perspective, it should cost about 30,000 sequential reads.

To achieve the more efficient strategy for low density, you use the ROW_NUMBER function. You write a query that computes row numbers that are partitioned by *custid* and ordered by *orderdate DESC, orderid DESC*. This query is optimized with a single ordered scan of the POC index, as desired. You then define a CTE based on this query and, in the outer query, filter the rows with a row number that is less than or equal to 3. This part adds a Filter operator to the plan. Here's the complete solution:

```
WITH C AS
(
  SELECT
    ROW_NUMBER() OVER(
      PARTITION BY custid
      ORDER BY orderdate DESC, orderid DESC) AS rownum,
    orderid, orderdate, custid, empid
  FROM Sales.Orders
)
SELECT custid, orderdate, orderid, empid
FROM C
WHERE rownum <= 3;
```

The execution plan for this solution is shown in Figure 5-9.

FIGURE 5-9 Plan for a solution with ROW_NUMBER.

As you can see, the majority of the cost of this plan is associated with the ordered scan of the POC index. As mentioned, if the table had 10,000,000 rows, the I/O cost would be about 30,000 sequential reads.

Solution using TOP and APPLY

If you have high density (10 customers, with 1,000,000 rows each), the strategy with the index scan is not the most efficient. With a small number of partitions (customers), a plan that performs a seek in the POC index for each partition is much more efficient.

If only a single customer is involved in the task, you can achieve a plan with a seek by using the TOP filter, like so:

```
SELECT TOP (3) orderid, orderdate, empid
FROM Sales.Orders
WHERE custid = 1
ORDER BY orderdate DESC, orderid DESC;
```

To apply this logic to each customer, use the APPLY operator with the preceding query against the Customers table, like so:

```
SELECT C.custid, A.orderid, A.orderdate, A.empid
FROM Sales.Customers AS C
  CROSS APPLY ( SELECT TOP (3) orderid, orderdate, empid
                FROM Sales.Orders AS O
                WHERE O.custid = C.custid
                ORDER BY orderdate DESC, orderid DESC ) AS A;
```

The execution plan for this solution is shown in Figure 5-10.

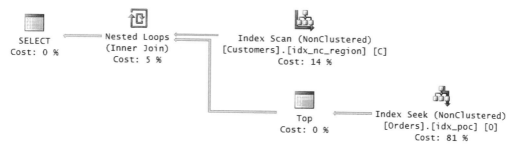

FIGURE 5-10 Plan for a solution with TOP and APPLY.

You get the desired plan for high density. With only 10 customers, this plan requires about 30 logical reads. That's big savings compared to the cost of the scan strategy, which is 30,000 reads.

TOP OVER

Again, as a thought exercise, if you could change or extend the design of the TOP filter, what would you do? In the existing design, the ordering specification for TOP is based on the underlying query's ORDER BY clause. An alternative design is for TOP to use its own ordering specification that is separate from the underlying query's ORDER BY clause. This way, it is clear that the TOP ordering doesn't provide any presentation-ordering guarantees, plus it would allow you to use a different ordering specification for the TOP filter and for presentation purposes. Furthermore, the TOP syntax could benefit from a partitioning element, in that the filter is applied per partition. Because the OVER clause used with window functions already supports partitioning and ordering specifications, there's no need to reinvent the wheel. A similar syntax can be used with TOP, like so:

```
TOP ( < expression > ) [ PERCENT ] [ WITH TIES ]
[ OVER( [ PARTITION BY ( < partition by list > ) ] [ ORDER BY ( <order by list> ) ] ) ]
```

You then use the following query to request the three most recent orders for each customer (but do not run this query, because it relies on unsupported syntax):

```
SELECT TOP (3) OVER ( PARTITION BY custid ORDER BY orderdate, orderid )
  orderid, orderdate, custid, empid
FROM dbo.Orders
ORDER BY custid, orderdate, orderid;
```

You can find a request to Microsoft to improve the TOP filter as described here in the following link: *http://connect.microsoft.com/SQLServer/feedback/details/254390/over-clause-enhancement-request-top-over*. Implementing such a design in SQL Server shouldn't cause compatibility issues. SQL Server could assume the original behavior when an OVER clause isn't present and the new behavior when it is.

Solution using concatenation (a carry-along sort)

Absent a POC index, both solutions I just described become inefficient and have problems scaling. The solution based on the ROW_NUMBER function will require sorting. Sorting has $n \log n$ scaling, becoming more expensive per row as the number of rows increases. The solution with the TOP filter and the APPLY operator might require an Index Spool operator (which involves the creation of an index during the plan) and sorting.

Interestingly, when N equals 1 in the *top N per group* task and a POC index is absent, there's a third solution that performs and scales better than the other two.

Make sure you drop the POC index before proceeding:

```
DROP INDEX idx_poc ON Sales.Orders;
```

The third solution is based on the concatenation of elements. It implements a technique you can think of as a *carry-along sort*. You start by writing a grouped query that groups the rows by the *P* element (*custid*). In the SELECT list, you convert the *O* (*orderdate DESC, orderid DESC*) and *C* (*empid*) elements to strings and concatenate them into one string. What's important here is to convert the original values into string forms that preserve the original ordering behavior of the values. For example, use leading zeros for integers, use the form YYYYMMDD for dates, and so on. It's only important to preserve ordering behavior for the *O* element to filter the right rows. The *C* element should be added just to return it in the output. You apply the MAX aggregate to the concatenated string. This results in returning one row per customer, with a concatenated string holding the elements from the most recent order. Finally, you define a CTE based on the grouped query, and in the outer query you extract the individual columns from the concatenated string and convert them back to the original types. Here's the complete solution query:

```
WITH C AS
(
  SELECT
    custid,
    MAX( (CONVERT(CHAR(8), orderdate, 112)
          + RIGHT('000000000' + CAST(orderid AS VARCHAR(10)), 10)
          + CAST(empid AS CHAR(10)) ) COLLATE Latin1_General_BIN2 ) AS s
  FROM Sales.Orders
  GROUP BY custid
)
SELECT custid,
  CAST( SUBSTRING(s,  1,  8) AS DATE     ) AS orderdate,
  CAST( SUBSTRING(s,  9, 10) AS INT      ) AS orderid,
  CAST( SUBSTRING(s, 19, 10) AS CHAR(10) ) AS empid
FROM C;
```

What's nice about this solution is that it scales much better than the others. With a small input table, the optimizer usually sorts the data and then uses an order-based aggregate (the Stream Aggregate operator). But with a large input table, the optimizer usually uses parallelism, with a local hash-based aggregate for each thread doing the bulk of the work, and a global aggregate that aggregates the local ones. You can see this approach by running the carry-along-sort solution against the Orders table in the PerformanceV3 database:

```
USE PerformanceV3;

WITH C AS
(
  SELECT
    custid,
    MAX( (CONVERT(CHAR(8), orderdate, 112)
          + RIGHT('000000000' + CAST(orderid AS VARCHAR(10)), 10)
          + CAST(empid AS CHAR(10)) ) COLLATE Latin1_General_BIN2 ) AS s
  FROM dbo.Orders
  GROUP BY custid
)
SELECT custid,
  CAST( SUBSTRING(s,  1,  8) AS DATE     ) AS orderdate,
  CAST( SUBSTRING(s,  9, 10) AS INT      ) AS orderid,
  CAST( SUBSTRING(s, 19, 10) AS CHAR(10) ) AS empid
FROM C;
```

The execution plan for this query is shown in Figure 5-11.

FIGURE 5-11 Plan for a solution using concatenation.

This exercise emphasizes again that there are usually multiple ways to solve any given querying task, and it's not like one of the solutions is optimal in all cases. In query tuning, different factors are at play, and under different conditions different solutions are optimal.

Median

Given a set of values, the median is the value below which 50 percent of the values fall. In other words, median is the 50th percentile. Median is such a classic calculation in the statistical analysis of data that many T-SQL solutions were created for it over time. I will focus on three solutions. The first uses the PERCENTILE_CONT window function. The second uses the ROW_NUMBER function. The third uses the OFFSET-FETCH filter and the APPLY operator.

Our calculation of median will be based on the continuous-distribution model. What this translates to is that when you have an odd number of elements involved, you should return the middle element. When you have an even number, you should return the average of the two middle elements. The alternative to the continuous model is the discrete model, which requires the returned value to be an existing value in the input set.

In my examples, I'll use a table called T1 with groups represented by a column called *grp* and values represented by a column called *val*. You're supposed to compute the median value for each group. The optimal index for median solutions is one defined on *(grp, val)* as the key elements. Use the following code to create the table and fill it with a small set of sample data to verify the validity of the solutions:

```
USE tempdb;
IF OBJECT_ID(N'dbo.T1', N'U') IS NOT NULL DROP TABLE dbo.T1;
GO

CREATE TABLE dbo.T1
(
  id  INT NOT NULL IDENTITY
    CONSTRAINT PK_T1 PRIMARY KEY,
  grp INT NOT NULL,
  val INT NOT NULL
);

CREATE INDEX idx_grp_val ON dbo.T1(grp, val);

INSERT INTO dbo.T1(grp, val)
  VALUES(1, 30),(1, 10),(1, 100),
        (2, 65),(2, 60),(2, 65),(2, 10);
```

Use the following code to populate the table with a large set of sample data (10 groups, with 1,000,000 rows each) to check the performance of the solutions:

```
DECLARE
  @numgroups AS INT = 10,
  @rowspergroup AS INT = 1000000;

TRUNCATE TABLE dbo.T1;

DROP INDEX idx_grp_val ON dbo.T1;

INSERT INTO dbo.T1 WITH(TABLOCK) (grp, val)
  SELECT G.n, ABS(CHECKSUM(NEWID())) % 10000000
  FROM TSQLV3.dbo.GetNums(1, @numgroups) AS G
    CROSS JOIN TSQLV3.dbo.GetNums(1, @rowspergroup) AS R;

CREATE INDEX idx_grp_val ON dbo.T1(grp, val);
```

Solution using PERCENTILE_CONT

Starting with SQL Server 2012, T-SQL supports window functions to compute percentiles. PERCENTILE_CONT implements the continuous model, and PERCENTILE_DISC implements the discrete model. The functions are not implemented as grouped, ordered set functions; rather, they are implemented as window functions. This means that instead of grouping the rows by the *grp* column, you will define the window partition based on *grp*. Consequently, the function will return the same result for all rows in the same partition instead of once per group. To get the result only once per group, you need to apply the DISTINCT option. Here's the solution to compute median using the continuous model with PERCENTILE_CONT:

```
SELECT
  DISTINCT grp, PERCENTILE_CONT(0.5) WITHIN GROUP(ORDER BY val) OVER(PARTITION BY grp) AS median
FROM dbo.T1;
```

After you overcome the awkwardness in using a window function instead of a grouped one, you might find the solution agreeable because of its simplicity and brevity. That's until you actually run it and look at its execution plan (which is not for the faint of heart). The plan for the solution is very long and inefficient. It does two rounds of spooling the data in work tables, reading each spool twice—once to get the detail and once to compute aggregates. It took the solution 79 seconds to complete in my system against the big set of sample data. If good performance is important to you, you should consider other solutions.

Solution using ROW_NUMBER

The second solution defines two CTEs. One called Counts is based on a grouped query that computes the count (column *cnt*) of rows per group. Another is called RowNums, and it computes row numbers (column *n*) for the detail rows. The outer query joins Counts with RowNums, and it filters only the relevant values for the median calculation. (Keep in mind that that the relevant values are those where *n* is *(cnt+1)/2* or *(cnt+2)/2*, using integer division.) Finally, the outer query groups the remaining rows by the *grp* column and computes the average of the *val* column as the median. Here's the complete solution:

```
WITH Counts AS
(
  SELECT grp, COUNT(*) AS cnt
  FROM dbo.T1
  GROUP BY grp
),
RowNums AS
(
  SELECT grp, val,
    ROW_NUMBER() OVER(PARTITION BY grp ORDER BY val) AS n
  FROM dbo.T1
)
SELECT C.grp, AVG(1. * R.val) AS median
FROM Counts AS C
  INNER MERGE JOIN RowNums AS R
    on C.grp = R.grp
WHERE R.n IN ( ( C.cnt + 1 ) / 2, ( C.cnt + 2 ) / 2 )
GROUP BY C.grp;
```

The plan for this solution is shown in Figure 5-12.

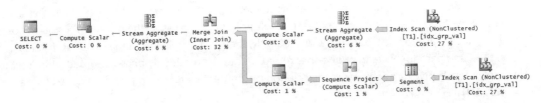

FIGURE 5-12 Plan for a solution using ROW_NUMBER.

SQL Server chose a serial plan that performs two scans of the index, a couple of order-based aggregates, a computation of row numbers, and a merge join. Compared to the previous solution with the PERCENTILE_CONT function, the new solution is quite efficient. It took only 8 seconds to complete in my system. Still, perhaps there's room for further improvements. For example, you could try to come up with a solution that uses a parallel plan, you could try to reduce the number of pages that need to be scanned, and you could try to eliminate the fairly expensive merge join.

Solution using OFFSET-FETCH and APPLY

The third solution I'll present uses the APPLY operator and the OFFSET-FETCH filter. The solution defines a CTE called C, which is based on a grouped query that computes for each group parameters for the OFFSET and FETCH clauses based on the group count. The offset value (call it *ov*) is computed as *(count – 1) / 2*, and the fetch value (call it *fv*) is computed as *2 – count % 2*. For example, if you have a group with 11 rows, *ov* is 5 and *fv* is 1. For a group with 12 rows, *ov* is 5 and *fv* is 2. The outer query applies to each group in C an OFFSET-FETCH query that retrieves the relevant values. Finally, the outer query groups the remaining rows and computes the average of the values as the median.

```
WITH C AS
(
  SELECT grp,
    COUNT(*) AS cnt,
    (COUNT(*) - 1) / 2 AS ov,
    2 - COUNT(*) % 2 AS fv
  FROM dbo.T1
  GROUP BY grp
)
SELECT grp, AVG(1. * val) AS median
FROM C
  CROSS APPLY ( SELECT O.val
                FROM dbo.T1 AS O
                where O.grp = C.grp
                order by O.val
                OFFSET C.ov ROWS FETCH NEXT C.fv ROWS ONLY ) AS A
GROUP BY grp;
```

The plan for this solution is shown in Figure 5-13.

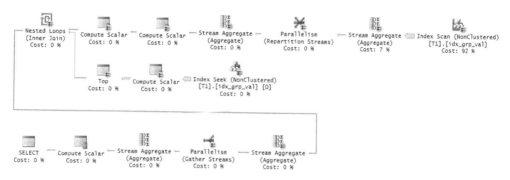

FIGURE 5-13 Plan for a solution using OFFSET-FETCH and APPLY.

The plan for the third solution has three advantages over the plan for the second. One is that it uses parallelism efficiently. The second is that the index is scanned in total one and a half times rather than two. The cost of the seeks is negligible here because the data has dense groups. The third advantage is that there's no merge join in the plan. It took only 1 second for this solution to complete on my system. That's quite impressive for 10,000,000 rows.

Conclusion

This chapter covered the TOP and OFFSET-FETCH filters. It started with a logical description of the filters. It then continued with optimization aspects demonstrated through paging solutions. You saw how critical it is to have an index on the sort columns to get good performance. Even with an index, I gave recommendations how to alter the solutions to avoid unnecessary lookups.

The chapter also covered modifying data with the TOP filter. Finally, the chapter concluded by demonstrating the use of TOP and OFFSET-FETCH to solve common tasks like *top N per group* and using a median value.

Data modification

This chapter covers topics related to data modification. It's not meant to provide exhaustive coverage of all data modification features in Microsoft SQL Server; rather, it focuses on the more pragmatic and perhaps less trivial aspects of some of the features.

The chapter covers data insertion, focusing mainly on bulk-import tools. It discusses the sequence object, comparing and contrasting it with the identity column property. It covers aspects of deleting, updating, and merging data. It also discusses the OUTPUT clause, demonstrating some of its practical uses.

Inserting data

SQL Server supports a number of tools you can use to insert data into your tables. Some of those tools use bulk-load optimizations, and those tools are the focus of this section.

The section starts with a discussion about the SELECT INTO command. It then continues with a discussion about additional bulk-import tools and the requirements they need to meet to be processed with minimal logging. The section then provides examples for using the flexible bulk rowset provider.

SELECT INTO

The SELECT INTO command creates a new table containing the result set of a query. It copies from the source the base definition (column names, types, collation, nullability, and identity property) and the data. It doesn't copy constraints, indexes, triggers, and permissions.

Before I demonstrate the use of SELECT INTO, run the following code to make sure the table MyOrders doesn't exist in the database PerformanceV3:

```
SET NOCOUNT ON;
USE PerformanceV3;
IF OBJECT_ID(N'dbo.MyOrders', N'U') IS NOT NULL DROP TABLE dbo.MyOrders;
```

Run the following SELECT INTO statement to create the MyOrders table with a copy of the rows from the Orders table:

```
SELECT orderid, custid, empid, shipperid, orderdate, filler
INTO dbo.MyOrders
FROM dbo.Orders;
```

The execution plan for this query is shown in Figure 6-1.

FIGURE 6-1 Parallel SELECT INTO.

Observe that the plan handles SELECT INTO with parallelism. This capability was added in SQL Server 2014.

One of the benefits of SELECT INTO is its efficiency, especially when satisfying the requirements for minimal logging. When the target database-recovery model is full, the operation is processed with full logging. The same applies when the recovery model isn't full but transactional replication is enabled. However, when the recovery model is simple or bulk-logged, and transactional replication isn't enabled, the operation is processed with minimal logging. This means that only information required for undo purposes is logged; information for redo and point-in-time recovery purposes is not logged. Because SELECT INTO allocates full extents, changes to allocation bitmaps (GAM, IAM, PFS) are logged, but the actual inserted data is not logged. The difference in the amount of logging between minimal and full logging can be quite dramatic. For example, to populate a table with a gigabyte of data, SQL Server needs to log only a few megabytes under minimal logging versus a whole gigabyte under full logging. See the section "Measuring the amount of logging" for details on how to measure the amount of logging involved in an operation.

If a source column has an identity property, normally the property is copied to the target. If you do not want to copy the property, apply manipulation to the source column, such as *ISNULL(col1, 0) AS col1*.

If you need to create a new target column with an identity property, use the IDENTITY function. Note, though, that even if you specify an ORDER BY clause in the query, there's no assurance that the identity values generated will reflect that order. If you need such a guarantee, use the INSERT SELECT statement instead. For details, see *http://support.microsoft.com/kb/273586*.

If you need a target column to have a different data type than the source column, you can cast the source column to the desired type, as in *CAST(col1 AS BIGINT) AS col1*. Note that such manipulation will make the result column nullable regardless of the nullability of the source column. You can use the ISNULL function to cause the target column to be defined as NOT NULL, as in *ISNULL(CAST(col1 AS BIGINT), 0) AS col1*.

I mentioned and demonstrated that SQL Server 2014 introduced parallel processing of SELECT INTO. Another improvement in SQL Server 2014 (also backported to SQL Server 2012 in Service Pack 1 (SP1) Cumulative Update (CU) 10) is in the way eager writes are handled when the target table is a temporary table. You can find details about the improvement here: *http://blogs.msdn.com/b/psssql/archive/2014/04/09/sql-server-2014-tempdb-hidden-performance-gem.aspx*. *Eager writes* quickly flush dirty pages associated with bulk operations to disk so that SQL Server won't have to wait for the entire operation to finish before writing the pages to disk. This helps prevent bulk operations from flooding the memory with new pages, but then again, it causes physical I/Os. The gist of the improvement is that when performing bulk operations in tempdb, like SELECT INTO against a temporary table, the eager-writing behavior is relaxed, not forcing the flushing of dirty pages as quickly as before. This can be beneficial when creating temporary tables, querying them, and dropping them quickly. Now such work can be done with a reduced number of physical I/Os or none at all.

Compared to INSERT SELECT, the SELECT INTO statement is much simpler to use because you don't need to create the table yourself before copying the data. However, SELECT INTO has its downsides. One drawback is that it doesn't allow you to specify the target filegroup. It uses the target database's default filegroup. Another drawback is that because the statement combines both DDL and DML, until the transaction completes, not only is the target table's data exclusively locked, so is the metadata. This can cause blocking related to metadata access as I will demonstrate.

First, run the following code to drop the MyOrders table if it exists:

```
USE PerformanceV3;
IF OBJECT_ID(N'dbo.MyOrders', N'U') IS NOT NULL DROP TABLE dbo.MyOrders;
```

Open two connections. Run the following code in connection 1 to begin a user transaction and to execute a SELECT INTO statement:

```
USE PerformanceV3;

BEGIN TRAN

SELECT orderid, custid, empid, shipperid, orderdate, filler
INTO dbo.MyOrders
FROM dbo.Orders;
```

Imagine the source table was really big and it took the statement some time to complete. I'm mimicking a long-running SELECT INTO statement by leaving the transaction open. Until the transaction completes, both the data and metadata generated by the operation are exclusively locked.

In connection 2, run the following query against sys.tables to get the set of tables in the database:

```
USE PerformanceV3;
SELECT SCHEMA_NAME(schema_id) AS schemaname, name AS tablename FROM sys.tables;
```

This query is blocked when running under the default isolation level Read Committed. That's because the session needs a shared lock in order to read a resource (the row in sys.tables in this example), and the request is blocked when another session is holding an exclusive lock on the same resource.

Run the following code in connection 1 to commit the transaction:

```
COMMIT TRAN
```

Now that the SELECT INTO transaction committed, it released all locks, so the query in connection 2 completes after the session manages to acquire the shared lock it was waiting for.

The alternative solution is to create the target table in one quick transaction, and then in another transaction use the INSERT SELECT statement to populate it. This way, at least you won't face long blocking situations related to metadata access.

Bulk import

Besides SELECT INTO, SQL Server supports other tools that can insert data into your tables and benefit from bulk optimizations: the bcp.exe utility, the BULK INSERT command, INSERT SELECT with the bulk rowset provider (more on this in a separate section), and INSERT SELECT with a local query. These tools are collectively referred to as *bulk-import* tools.

Like SELECT INTO, the remaining bulk-import tools can be processed with minimal logging, albeit with a longer list of requirements that they need to meet. The requirements are as follows:

- The recovery model of the database has to be simple or bulk-logged. Under full recovery, you get full logging.

- Transactional replication is not enabled. If transactional replication is enabled, you get full logging even when the recovery model is not full.

- If the table is a heap

  - The table doesn't have to be empty.

  - You have to specify the TABLOCK option. Note that for bcp.exe, BULK INSERT, and the bulk rowset provider, this option represents a bulk update lock, which allows multiple processes to bulk load data into the same target table simultaneously. For INSERT SELECT with a local query, this option represents a full-blown exclusive table lock, so only one process can insert data into the table at a time.

- If the table is a B-tree (clustered), any of the following will do:

  - The table is empty, and you specify the TABLOCK option.

  - The table is empty, and trace flag 610 is enabled.

  - The table is nonempty, trace flag 610 is enabled, and you insert a new key range; the new page allocations are minimally logged.

The requirements for minimal logging are summarized with the following logical expression:

```
          non-FULL recovery model AND transactional replicated not enabled
AND (     Heap AND TABLOCK
     OR       B-tree
       AND (    empty AND ( TABLOCK OR TF-610 )
              OR nonempty AND TF-610 AND new key-range ) )
```

When inserting data using the INSERT EXEC and MERGE statements, you get full logging.

For more information about tuning data-loading operations, see "The Data Loading Performance Guide" at: *http://msdn.microsoft.com/en-us/library/dd425070.aspx*.

Measuring the amount of logging

I described the requirements that your bulk-import operation needs to meet in order to be processed with minimal logging. But what if you want to know how much logging is involved? For this purpose, I use the undocumented function *fn_dblog*. This function returns the transaction log records of the current database for the range of log serial numbers (LSNs). If you want to get back all transaction log records, provide two NULLs as inputs.

As an example, the following query returns the count and total size of all log records in the PerformanceV3 database:

```
USE PerformanceV3;

SELECT COUNT(*) AS numrecords, SUM(CAST([Log Record Length] AS BIGINT)) / 1048576. AS sizemb
FROM sys.fn_dblog(null, null);
```

To measure the logging caused by a specific operation, you will want to capture the information before and after the operation and capture it in the same transaction to avoid log truncation, and compute the delta between the captures. I also invoke the CHECKPOINT command manually to force writing dirty pages to disk before and after taking the measurement.

I'll start by demonstrating a fully logged SELECT INTO operation in the PerformanceV3 database. First run the following code to set the database recovery model to full and back up the database to get out of log-truncate mode (make sure the path C:\temp\ exists or alter the path to an existing one on your system):

```
ALTER DATABASE PerformanceV3 SET RECOVERY FULL;
BACKUP DATABASE PerformanceV3 TO DISK = 'C:\temp\PerfV3Data.BAK' WITH INIT;
BACKUP LOG PerformanceV3 TO DISK = 'C:\temp\PerfV3Log.BAK' WITH INIT;
```

Run the following code to measure the logging caused by a SELECT INTO statement:

```
CHECKPOINT;

BEGIN TRAN

DECLARE
  @numrecords AS INT, @sizemb AS NUMERIC(12, 2), @starttime AS DATETIME2, @endtime AS DATETIME2;

-- Drop table if exists
IF OBJECT_ID(N'dbo.MyOrders', N'U') IS NOT NULL DROP TABLE dbo.MyOrders;

-- Stats before import
SELECT
  @numrecords = COUNT(*),
  @sizemb = SUM(CAST([Log Record Length] AS BIGINT)) / 1048576.
FROM sys.fn_dblog(null, null);

SET @starttime = SYSDATETIME();

-- Import data
SELECT orderid, custid, empid, shipperid, orderdate, filler
INTO dbo.MyOrders
FROM dbo.Orders;
```

```
-- Stats after import
SET @endtime = SYSDATETIME();

SELECT
  COUNT(*) - @numrecords AS numrecords,
  SUM(CAST([Log Record Length] AS BIGINT)) / 1048576. - @sizemb AS sizemb,
  DATEDIFF(ms, @starttime, @endtime) AS durationms
FROM sys.fn_dblog(null, null);

COMMIT TRAN

-- Cleanup
IF OBJECT_ID(N'dbo.MyOrders', N'U') IS NOT NULL DROP TABLE dbo.MyOrders;

CHECKPOINT;
```

This code generated the following output in my system:

```
numrecords  sizemb        durationms
----------- ------------- -----------
65627       194.84907745  1109
```

The SELECT INTO statement copied 1,000,000 rows with a length of 195 bytes from the Orders table into the MyOrders table. The size of the data written to the target table is about 195 MB, and as you can see, the size of the data logged is about that much.

To test minimal logging, first set the database recovery model to Simple by running the following code:

```
ALTER DATABASE PerformanceV3 SET RECOVERY SIMPLE;
```

Next, rerun the code that tests the SELECT INTO statement. The code generated the following output in my system:

```
numrecords  sizemb       durationms
----------- ----------- -----------
41208       2.47408676  957
```

Notice the significant reduction in the amount of logging.

BULK rowset provider

The bcp.exe utility and the BULK INSERT command are traditional tools used to import data from a file into a table. They do give you a number of options to control the import (terminators, rows per batch, and so on), but they don't give you the most basic options that a normal query gives you (filter, join, apply calculations, and so on). Fortunately, SQL Server has a feature called *bulk rowset provider* you can use to import file data and that has support for query-manipulation capabilities.

You use the bulk rowset provider via the OPENROWSET function. You specify the input file, a format file like the one you use with bcp.exe and BULK INSERT, and optionally additional bulk options (rows per batch, error file, and others). The beauty of this feature is that the OPENROWSET function is consumed like a table by a query and, as such, allows the usual query-manipulation capabilities.

To demonstrate the feature, I'll query and import data from files I placed in my C:\temp\ folder. If you want to run the examples in your environment, download the book's compressed source code file (available at *http://tsql.solidq.com/books/tq3/*) and place the files from the source temp folder in your C:\temp\ folder.

The file Shippers.txt contains shipper information that I originally exported from the Sales.Shippers table in the TSQLV3 database. To support future imports, I also created a format file called Shippers.fmt by using the bcp.exe utility with the format option, like so (from a command prompt with the right server and instance names):

```
bcp TSQLV3.Sales.Shippers format nul -c -f C:\temp\Shippers.fmt -T -S <server\instance_name>
```

Here's how you use the OPENROWSET function with the bulk rowset provider to query the Shippers.txt file based on the Shippers.fmt format file:

```
SELECT shipperid, companyname, phone
FROM OPENROWSET(BULK 'C:\temp\Shippers.txt',
               FORMATFILE = 'C:\temp\Shippers.fmt') AS F;
```

This code generates the following output:

```
shipperid  companyname        phone
---------- ------------------ ---------------
1          Shipper GVSUA      (503) 555-9831
2          Shipper ETYNR      (503) 555-3199
3          Shipper ZHISN      (503) 555-9931
```

That's just amazingly simple!

Because you consume the OPENROWSET function in the FROM clause like a table, you can apply the usual query-manipulation capabilities. For example, suppose you had a table called TargetTable in your database, and you wanted to import into it only shippers from the file that have a phone number that starts with *(503) 555-9*. You filter the data using the normal query WHERE clause, like so:

```
INSERT INTO TargetTable WITH (TABLOCK) (shipperid, companyname, phone)
  SELECT shipperid, companyname, phone
  FROM OPENROWSET(BULK 'C:\temp\Shippers.txt',
       FORMATFILE = 'C:\temp\Shippers.fmt') AS F
  WHERE phone LIKE '(503) 555-9%';
```

Notice the use of the TABLOCK option to enable minimal logging.

You can also use the bulk rowset provider in a single mode to query and return the contents of a file as a rowset with a single row and a single large-object-typed column. You specify one of three options: SINGLE_NCLOB for Unicode character data, SINGLE_CLOB for regular character data, and SINGLE_BLOB for binary data. Placing such a query in parentheses makes it a scalar self-contained subquery; as such, it can be used as a scalar expression in INSERT and UPDATE statements.

To demonstrate the use of the bulk rowset provider in a single mode, I'll import data from files in the C:\temp\ folder into a table called T1 in the tempdb database. First run the following code to create the table T1:

```
USE tempdb;

IF OBJECT_ID(N'dbo.T1', N'U') IS NOT NULL DROP TABLE dbo.T1;

CREATE TABLE dbo.T1
(
  id        INT          NOT NULL PRIMARY KEY,
  xmlval    XML          NULL,
  textval   VARCHAR(MAX) NULL,
  ntextval  NVARCHAR(MAX) NULL,
  binval    VARBINARY(MAX) NULL
);
```

As you can see, the table has a key column, and four large-object-typed columns.

The following code inserts a new row into the table with the key 1, and the value for the XML column *xmlval* obtained from the XML file xmlfile.xml using the bulk rowset provider:

```
INSERT INTO dbo.T1(id, xmlval)
  VALUES( 1,
    (SELECT xmlval FROM OPENROWSET(
      BULK 'C:\temp\xmlfile.xml', SINGLE_NCLOB) AS F(xmlval)) );
```

The SINGLE_NCLOB option was used because xmlfile.xml is a Unicode file.

As mentioned, you can use a similar scalar subquery to set the value of a column in an UPDATE statement. As an example, the following UPDATE statement sets the values of the remaining three columns in the new row to values obtained from three files:

```
UPDATE dbo.T1
  SET textval = (SELECT textval FROM OPENROWSET(
    BULK 'C:\temp\textfile.txt', SINGLE_CLOB) AS F(textval)),
      ntextval = (SELECT ntextval FROM OPENROWSET(
    BULK 'C:\temp\ntextfile.txt', SINGLE_NCLOB) AS F(ntextval)),
      binval  = (SELECT binval FROM OPENROWSET(
    BULK 'C:\temp\binfile.jpg', SINGLE_BLOB) AS F(binval))
WHERE id = 1;
```

Query the table to see the data that was imported:

```
SELECT id, xmlval, textval, ntextval, binval
FROM dbo.T1
WHERE id = 1;
```

You will get the following output (shown here in abbreviated form):

```
id  xmlval      textval      ntextval     binval
--- ----------- ------------ ------------ ----------
1   <ShowPl...  This fil...  This fil...  0xFFD8F...
```

Sequences

SQL Server gives you two main built-in tools that help you generate surrogate keys. One is the long-standing identity column property, which you're probably familiar with, and the other is the sequence object, which was added in SQL Server 2012. The focus of this section is the sequence object and its advantages and disadvantages compared to identity.

Microsoft implemented the sequence object in SQL Server based on standard SQL with a few extensions. The main benefits of the sequence object are realized when you compare it with identity. I'll start by reminding you of the characteristics and inflexibilities of the identity property; I'll continue by introducing the sequence object and compare and contrast it with identity; I'll then discuss performance considerations concerning both features.

Characteristics and inflexibilities of the identity property

The identity property is inflexible in a number of ways. It is a property of a column in a table specified as part of the column definition, as in *orderid INT NOT NULL IDENTITY(1, 1)*. It's not an independent object in the database. This can be a problem when you need to generate surrogate keys for use across multiple tables—for example, in a custom table-partitioning solution.

You cannot associate an identity property with or disassociate it from an already existing column. The property has to be defined when creating the table or altering it to add a new column. Therefore, achieving such a change might involve significant downtime for the table.

Identity cannot be used with a nullable column.

Sometimes you need to generate a surrogate key before using it. Identity doesn't support this capability. You have to insert a new row into the target table and then request the newly generated key using the SCOPE_IDENTITY function.

You cannot use identity to generate new keys in a regular SELECT query. You can use the IDENTITY function in a SELECT INTO statement to generate a column with an identity property in the target table. In such a case, there's no assurance that the identity values will be generated in a particular order, even if the query has an ORDER BY clause. If you need the keys to be generated in a particular order, use an INSERT SELECT statement with an ORDER BY clause. For details, see the following Knowledge Base article: *http://support.microsoft.com/kb/273586*.

A column with an identity property cannot be updated.

You cannot define minimum and maximum values for the identity property. The workaround is to constrain the column itself using a CHECK constraint.

The identity property cannot be defined to cycle automatically after it reaches the maximum value based on the column's type. In such a case, an attempt to generate the next value causes an overflow error. You can change the current value manually using the DBCC CHECKIDENT command.

Once defined, you cannot alter the increment of an identity property.

You cannot define your own cache value for the identity property. Prior to SQL Server 2012, identity had no cache; rather, every value generation caused a disk write that was also logged. In SQL Server 2012 and 2014, identity has a predefined cache value that depends on the data type of the target column. Microsoft doesn't document what cache value it uses because it wants to reserve the right to change it as it sees fit. But you can figure it out through testing, as I will demonstrate later. The caching feature gives you a performance benefit, but it means that if there's an unclean termination of the SQL Server process—such as in a power failure or a failover in an AlwaysOn availability group—the next identity value generated might be at a gap of up to the cache value compared to the previous value. You can disable caching for identity to get pre-2012 behavior using trace flag 272.

Regardless of caching, identity doesn't guarantee you won't have gaps between values. An identity value change isn't undone if the INSERT statement that caused the change fails or the transaction rolls back. If you need to guarantee no gaps between keys, you have to roll your own solution for generating those.

Identity doesn't support obtaining a range of sequence values in one request. This could be needed when, in the application, you want to assign an entire range of keys for some purpose and know ahead of time how many keys you are after.

The sequence object

Unlike identity, the sequence object is an independent object in the database. You create it using the CREATE SEQUENCE command, alter its properties using the ALTER SEQUENCE command, and retrieve a new value from it using the NEXT VALUE FOR function. Following is the syntax for creating a sequence:

```
CREATE SEQUENCE <schema_name>.<sequence_name> AS <type>
  START WITH <constant>
  INCREMENT BY <constant>
  MINVALUE <constant> | NO MINVALUE
  MAXVALUE <constant> | NO MAXVALUE
  NO CYCLE | CYCLE
  CACHE <constant> | NO CACHE;
```

Like any other object in the database, you place the sequence in a schema. Similar to identity, it supports all numeric types with a scale of zero: TINYINT, SMALLINT, INT, BIGINT, NUMERIC(p, 0)/ DECIMAL(p, 0). If you don't indicate a type, BIGINT is used by default. If the target column where you will eventually store the values has a type different than BIGINT, you want to make sure to create the sequence with the right type. Otherwise, you will pay extra for type conversion. The data type is the one aspect of the sequence that cannot be altered once defined. To change the type, you will basically need to drop and re-create the sequence.

Using the MINVALUE and MAXVALUE properties, you can define the range of values supported by the sequence. The defaults are the minimum and maximum values supported by the type. For example, using the INT type, the sequence will default to MINVALUE –2147483648—not to 1 like many expect.

By default, the sequence is defined not to cycle; however, if you need to support cycling, specify the CYCLE option.

Use the START WITH property to define the first value that the sequence will generate. If unspecified, the START WITH property defaults to MINVALUE when the INCREMENT BY property is positive and to MAXVALUE when it's negative. Be aware that if the sequence is defined to cycle, after it reaches the MAXVALUE property, it cycles to the value defined by the MINVALUE property (assuming the increment is 1) and not to the original START WITH property. It's a common mistake when you need to create a cycling sequence that supports only the positive range of values to specify START WITH 1 CYCLE. After reaching the maximum value, the sequence will cycle to the minimum value (for example, –2147483648 for INT) and not 1. The correct thing to do is set MINVALUE to 1, not START WITH; upon sequence creation, the latter is set to the former by default and not the other way around.

Use the INCREMENT BY property to specify the step value. As you might have guessed, it is set to 1 by default.

You can use the CACHE property to control how often a request for a new value will cause a disk write and to use logging rather than a memory-only write. The bigger the value is, the better performance you will get. However, upon an unclean termination of the SQL Server process, the next value generated might be at a gap of up to the cache value compared to the previous value. I discuss performance considerations with the caching feature in the next section.

As an example, the following code creates a sequence called *Seqorderids* for generating order IDs in the PerformanceV3 database:

```
USE PerformanceV3;

IF OBJECT_ID(N'dbo.Seqorderids', N'SO') IS NOT NULL DROP SEQUENCE dbo.Seqorderids;

CREATE SEQUENCE dbo.Seqorderids AS INT
  MINVALUE 1
  CYCLE
  CACHE 1000;
```

The sequence is defined as INT, supports only the positive range of values in the type, allows cycling, and uses a cache value of 1000.

To get a new value from the sequence, invoke the NEXT VALUE FOR function, like so:

```
SELECT NEXT VALUE FOR dbo.Seqorderids;
```

You can use the function in many places, such as a DEFAULT constraint, variable assignment, UPDATE and MERGE assignments, single-row and multi-row SELECT statements, single-row and multi-row INSERT VALUES statements, and the INSERT SELECT statement. You cannot use the function in a subquery.

You can alter all sequence properties other than the data type with the ALTER SEQUENCE command using the following syntax:

```
ALTER SEQUENCE dbo.Seqorderids
  RESTART WITH <constant>
  INCREMENT BY <constant>
  MINVALUE <constant> | NO MINVALUE
  MAXVALUE <constant> | NO MAXVALUE
  NO CYCLE | CYCLE
  CACHE <constant> | NO CACHE;
```

To get metadata information about existing sequences, query the sys.Sequences view. For example, the following query retrieves the properties of the *Seqorderids* sequence:

```
SELECT current_value, start_value, increment, minimum_value, maximum_value, is_cycling,
  is_cached, cache_size
FROM sys.Sequences
WHERE object_id = OBJECT_ID(N'dbo.Seqorderids', N'SO');
```

This query generates the following output:

```
current_value start_value increment minimum_value maximum_value is_cycling is_cached cache_size
------------- ----------- --------- ------------- ------------- ---------- --------- -----------
1             1           1         1             2147483647    1          1         1000
```

Recall the inflexibilities of the identity property. In contrast, the sequence object is much more flexible. Interestingly, identity and sequence are internally implemented using the same physical object, but the language surface makes sequence much more flexible. There's also a critical performance difference between the two that you should be aware of. I'll discuss it in the next section.

Because sequence is an independent object in the database, you can use the keys you generate with a sequence anywhere you like—for example, across multiple tables in a custom table partitioning solution.

Note that neither sequence nor identity by themselves guarantee uniqueness. Remember that, at any point, you can change the current value, as well as insert values of your own. You want to make sure to use integrity enforcement tools like constraints to guarantee uniqueness in some column.

If you want to automate the creation of keys in some column using a sequence, you can invoke the NEXT VALUE FOR function in a DEFAULT constraint. That's an extension to the standard. Unlike with the identity property, a DEFAULT constraint can be added to an existing column or removed from one. Say you have a table called Orders with a column called orderid and you want to automate the creation of order IDs using the sequence *Seqorderids*. Here's the code to add such a constraint:

```
ALTER TABLE dbo.Orders
  ADD CONSTRAINT DFT_Orders_orderid
    DEFAULT(NEXT VALUE FOR dbo.Seqorderids) FOR orderid;
```

If at any point you want to stop the automation of the generation of order IDs, you drop the constraint, like so:

```
ALTER TABLE dbo.Orders DROP CONSTRAINT DFT_Orders_orderid;
```

Because the sequence object is independent of the target table and the column where you store the values generated, nothing prevents you from allowing NULLs in the target column if you want.

If you need to generate a sequence value before using it, you can simply store it somewhere temporarily and use it later when you're ready. For example, you could store it in a variable, like so:

```
DECLARE @newkey AS INT = NEXT VALUE FOR dbo.Seqorderids;
SELECT @newkey;
```

You can even use a sequence to overwrite existing keys with new ones using the UPDATE and MERGE statements. To demonstrate this, I'll use a table called MyOrders that you create and populate by running the following code:

```
IF OBJECT_ID(N'dbo.MyOrders', N'U') IS NOT NULL DROP TABLE dbo.MyOrders;

SELECT orderid, custid, empid, shipperid, orderdate, filler
INTO dbo.MyOrders
FROM dbo.Orders
WHERE empid = 1;

ALTER TABLE dbo.MyOrders ADD CONSTRAINT PK_MyOrders PRIMARY KEY(orderid);
```

Run the following UPDATE statement to overwrite the existing keys with new ones from the *Seqorderids* sequence:

```
UPDATE dbo.MyOrders
  SET orderid = NEXT VALUE FOR dbo.Seqorderids;
```

SQL Server supports an extension to the standard NEXT VALUE FOR function in the form of an OVER clause you use to control the order in which sequence values are generated in a multi-row insert. This capability is needed, for example, when you want target keys to be generated based on the order of the source keys. Here's an example for using this feature when copying orders from the Orders table to the MyOrders table, generating new order IDs from the sequence, while preserving the order of the original keys:

```
INSERT INTO dbo.MyOrders(orderid, custid, empid, shipperid, orderdate, filler)
  SELECT NEXT VALUE FOR dbo.Seqorderids OVER(ORDER BY orderid) AS orderid,
    custid, empid, shipperid, orderdate, filler
  FROM dbo.Orders
  WHERE empid = 2;
```

Suppose you need your application to request an entire range of keys in one shot and you know ahead of time what the range size is. SQL Server provides you with a stored procedure called *sp_sequence_get_range* for this purpose. The point is to update the sequence only once and assign the values in the range that you get as you see fit. You provide as inputs the sequence name and the range size. You collect as output the first value in the range and, optionally, the last value, cycle count, increment, minimum, and maximum. Here's an example for requesting a range of 1000000 values from the sequence *Seqorderids*:

```
DECLARE @first AS SQL_VARIANT;

EXEC sys.sp_sequence_get_range
  @sequence_name     = N'dbo.Seqorderids',
  @range_size        = 1000000,
  @range_first_value = @first OUTPUT ;

SELECT @first;
```

The last sequence value generated in my system before issuing this code was 3973, so the range that was just allocated by the command is 3974 through 1003973. The variable *@first* was assigned with the value 3974, and the current sequence value is 1003973. The next time someone requests a value from the sequence, he will get 1003974.

Remember that, just like with identity, the sequence object doesn't guarantee you won't have gaps between values, regardless of the cache size you define. If you request a value from a sequence in a transaction and the transaction is rolled back, the sequence value change is not undone. Here's a test demonstrating this:

```
SELECT NEXT VALUE FOR dbo.Seqorderids;
BEGIN TRAN
  SELECT NEXT VALUE FOR dbo.Seqorderids;
ROLLBACK TRAN
SELECT NEXT VALUE FOR dbo.Seqorderids;
```

When I ran this code on my system, I got the following output:

```
-----------
1003974


-----------
1003975


-----------
1003976
```

As you can see, the value generated in the transaction that rolled back was not reused. If you need to guarantee no gaps between keys, you shouldn't use identity or sequence; instead, roll your own custom key generator. I'll demonstrate how to implement one in the section "Updating data."

Performance considerations

As mentioned, sequence and identity are implemented internally based on the same physical object. However, there are important differences in the implementation of the two features that could have different performance implications. These differences are especially important when you change an implementation using one feature with an implementation using the other.

The main aspect that affects the performance of identity and sequence is caching. The cache value dictates how often SQL Server writes to disk. For example, say you define a cache value of 1000 for a sequence object. The first time you request a value, SQL Server writes *1000* to disk and, in two memory members, stores the current value 1 and the number of values left, *999*. After 999 more requests, the member holding the current value is *1000* and the one holding the number of values left is *0*. The next request will write to disk *2000*, and to the memory members it will write *1001* as the current value and *999* as the number of values left. And so on. If there's an unclean termination of the SQL Server process—such as a power failure, crash (you can mimic this by ending the SQL Server process from Task Manager), or failover in an AlwaysOn availability group—upon restart, the current value is set to the on-disk value. So you can lose up to the cache size value in one go. In choosing the cache value, you need to decide how many values you are willing to lose in such an event in favor of improved performance. I'll provide specific performance numbers shortly. But don't forget what I mentioned and demonstrated earlier: that neither sequence nor identity give you a guarantee you won't have gaps, regardless of the cache size.

The first interesting thing about the cache is what SQL Server uses by default. Microsoft doesn't document this information. More precisely, there's a note in the documentation explicitly saying the company doesn't want to publish this information:

> *"If the cache option is enabled without specifying a cache size, the Database Engine will select a size. However, users should not rely upon the selection being consistent. Microsoft might change the method of calculating the cache size without notice."*

Despite this, you can figure out what the current cache size is through testing. Prior to SQL Server 2012, identity had no cache (tested on SQL Server 2008 R2 SP3). In SQL Server 2012 SP2 and 2014 RTM, sequence has a default cache of 50, regardless of data type, and identity has a cache value that depends on the type, as shown in Table 6-1.

TABLE 6-1 Relationship between type and cache size

Type	Cache size
TINYINT	10
SMALLINT	100
INT	1000
BIGINT, NUMERIC	10000

You can enable trace flag 272 if you want to disable caching for identity, but other than that you have no control over the cache size.

If you're running your tests on a different build than the one I used in my testing, be aware, as the documentation says, that the default cache values in your system could be different.

To figure out the default cache values, use the following test. In preparation, you create sequences of different types as well as tables with columns of different types with an identity property. You generate a few values, and then query the current values. You do so by running the following code:

```
IF DB_ID(N'testdb') IS NULL CREATE DATABASE testdb;
USE testdb;

IF OBJECT_ID(N'dbo.SeqTINYINT'  , N'SO') IS NOT NULL DROP SEQUENCE dbo.SeqTINYINT;
IF OBJECT_ID(N'dbo.SeqSMALLINT' , N'SO') IS NOT NULL DROP SEQUENCE dbo.SeqSMALLINT;
IF OBJECT_ID(N'dbo.SeqINT'      , N'SO') IS NOT NULL DROP SEQUENCE dbo.SeqINT;
IF OBJECT_ID(N'dbo.SeqBIGINT'   , N'SO') IS NOT NULL DROP SEQUENCE dbo.SeqBIGINT;
IF OBJECT_ID(N'dbo.SeqNUMERIC9' , N'SO') IS NOT NULL DROP SEQUENCE dbo.SeqNUMERIC9;
IF OBJECT_ID(N'dbo.SeqNUMERIC38', N'SO') IS NOT NULL DROP SEQUENCE dbo.SeqNUMERIC38;

IF OBJECT_ID(N'dbo.TTINYINT'  , N'U') IS NOT NULL DROP TABLE dbo.TTINYINT;
IF OBJECT_ID(N'dbo.TSMALLINT' , N'U') IS NOT NULL DROP TABLE dbo.TSMALLINT;
IF OBJECT_ID(N'dbo.TINT'      , N'U') IS NOT NULL DROP TABLE dbo.TINT;
IF OBJECT_ID(N'dbo.TBIGINT'   , N'U') IS NOT NULL DROP TABLE dbo.TBIGINT;
IF OBJECT_ID(N'dbo.TNUMERIC9' , N'U') IS NOT NULL DROP TABLE dbo.TNUMERIC9;
IF OBJECT_ID(N'dbo.TNUMERIC38', N'U') IS NOT NULL DROP TABLE dbo.TNUMERIC38;

CREATE SEQUENCE dbo.SeqTINYINT   AS TINYINT       MINVALUE 1;
CREATE SEQUENCE dbo.SeqSMALLINT  AS SMALLINT      MINVALUE 1;
CREATE SEQUENCE dbo.SeqINT       AS INT           MINVALUE 1;
CREATE SEQUENCE dbo.SeqBIGINT    AS BIGINT        MINVALUE 1;
CREATE SEQUENCE dbo.SeqNUMERIC9  AS NUMERIC( 9, 0) MINVALUE 1;
CREATE SEQUENCE dbo.SeqNUMERIC38 AS NUMERIC(38, 0) MINVALUE 1;

CREATE TABLE dbo.TTINYINT  (keycol TINYINT       IDENTITY);
CREATE TABLE dbo.TSMALLINT (keycol SMALLINT      IDENTITY);
CREATE TABLE dbo.TINT      (keycol INT           IDENTITY);
CREATE TABLE dbo.TBIGINT   (keycol BIGINT        IDENTITY);
CREATE TABLE dbo.TNUMERIC9 (keycol NUMERIC( 9, 0) IDENTITY);
CREATE TABLE dbo.TNUMERIC38(keycol NUMERIC(38, 0) IDENTITY);
GO

SELECT
  NEXT VALUE FOR dbo.SeqTINYINT   ,
  NEXT VALUE FOR dbo.SeqSMALLINT  ,
  NEXT VALUE FOR dbo.SeqINT       ,
  NEXT VALUE FOR dbo.SeqBIGINT    ,
  NEXT VALUE FOR dbo.SeqNUMERIC9  ,
  NEXT VALUE FOR dbo.SeqNUMERIC38;
GO 5

INSERT INTO dbo.TTINYINT   DEFAULT VALUES;
INSERT INTO dbo.TSMALLINT  DEFAULT VALUES;
INSERT INTO dbo.TINT       DEFAULT VALUES;
INSERT INTO dbo.TBIGINT    DEFAULT VALUES;
INSERT INTO dbo.TNUMERIC9  DEFAULT VALUES;
INSERT INTO dbo.TNUMERIC38 DEFAULT VALUES;
GO 5
```

```
SELECT name, current_value FROM sys.Sequences
WHERE object_id IN
  ( OBJECT_ID(N'dbo.SeqTINYINT  '),
    OBJECT_ID(N'dbo.SeqSMALLINT '),
    OBJECT_ID(N'dbo.SeqINT      '),
    OBJECT_ID(N'dbo.SeqBIGINT   '),
    OBJECT_ID(N'dbo.SeqNUMERIC9 '),
    OBJECT_ID(N'dbo.SeqNUMERIC38') );

SELECT
  IDENT_CURRENT(N'dbo.TTINYINT  ') AS TTINYINT  ,
  IDENT_CURRENT(N'dbo.TSMALLINT ') AS TSMALLINT ,
  IDENT_CURRENT(N'dbo.TINT      ') AS TINT      ,
  IDENT_CURRENT(N'dbo.TBIGINT   ') AS TBIGINT   ,
  IDENT_CURRENT(N'dbo.TNUMERIC9 ') AS TNUMERIC9 ,
  IDENT_CURRENT(N'dbo.TNUMERIC38') AS TNUMERIC38;
```

Having generated five values, I get the output *5* in all cases:

```
name          current_value
------------- --------------
SeqTINYINT    5
SeqSMALLINT   5
SeqINT        5
SeqBIGINT     5
SeqNUMERIC9   5
SeqNUMERIC38  5


TTINYINT  TSMALLINT  TINT  TBIGINT  TNUMERIC9  TNUMERIC38
--------- ---------- ----- -------- ---------- -----------
5         5          5     5        5          5
```

Next you end the SQL Server service from Task Manager (using Shift+Ctrl+Esc to load it), you restart it, and then you query the current sequence and identity values by running the following code:

```
USE testdb;

SELECT name, current_value FROM sys.Sequences
WHERE object_id IN
  ( OBJECT_ID(N'dbo.SeqTINYINT  '),
    OBJECT_ID(N'dbo.SeqSMALLINT '),
    OBJECT_ID(N'dbo.SeqINT      '),
    OBJECT_ID(N'dbo.SeqBIGINT   '),
    OBJECT_ID(N'dbo.SeqNUMERIC9 '),
    OBJECT_ID(N'dbo.SeqNUMERIC38') );

SELECT
  IDENT_CURRENT(N'dbo.TTINYINT  ') AS TTINYINT  ,
  IDENT_CURRENT(N'dbo.TSMALLINT ') AS TSMALLINT ,
  IDENT_CURRENT(N'dbo.TINT      ') AS TINT      ,
  IDENT_CURRENT(N'dbo.TBIGINT   ') AS TBIGINT   ,
  IDENT_CURRENT(N'dbo.TNUMERIC9 ') AS TNUMERIC9 ,
  IDENT_CURRENT(N'dbo.TNUMERIC38') AS TNUMERIC38;
```

Here's the output I got on my system:

```
name            current_value
-------------   --------------
SeqTINYINT      50
SeqSMALLINT     50
SeqINT          50
SeqBIGINT       50
SeqNUMERIC9     50
SeqNUMERIC38    50


TTINYINT   TSMALLINT   TINT   TBIGINT   TNUMERIC9   TNUMERIC38
--------   ---------   -----  -------   ----------  -----------
11         101         1001   10001     10001       10001
```

There's the obvious difference between identity and sequence in the cache sizes. There's also the curious fact that, in identity's case, the recovered value is off by 1 from the cache size and in the sequence case it isn't. From testing, it seems that with identity the first write of the current-plus-cache-size-minus-one value to disk happened after the second request, whereas with sequence it was after the first one.

When I request the next value from the sequence *SeqINT*, I get *51*:

```
SELECT NEXT VALUE FOR dbo.SeqINT;
```

When I insert a new row to TINT, the identity value generated is *1002*:

```
INSERT INTO dbo.TINT OUTPUT inserted.$identity DEFAULT VALUES;
```

When you're done testing, run the following code for cleanup:

```
IF OBJECT_ID(N'dbo.SeqTINYINT'  , N'SO') IS NOT NULL DROP SEQUENCE dbo.SeqTINYINT;
IF OBJECT_ID(N'dbo.SeqSMALLINT' , N'SO') IS NOT NULL DROP SEQUENCE dbo.SeqSMALLINT;
IF OBJECT_ID(N'dbo.SeqINT'      , N'SO') IS NOT NULL DROP SEQUENCE dbo.SeqINT;
IF OBJECT_ID(N'dbo.SeqBIGINT'   , N'SO') IS NOT NULL DROP SEQUENCE dbo.SeqBIGINT;
IF OBJECT_ID(N'dbo.SeqNUMERIC9' , N'SO') IS NOT NULL DROP SEQUENCE dbo.SeqNUMERIC9;
IF OBJECT_ID(N'dbo.SeqNUMERIC38', N'SO') IS NOT NULL DROP SEQUENCE dbo.SeqNUMERIC38;

IF OBJECT_ID(N'dbo.TTINYINT'  , N'U') IS NOT NULL DROP TABLE dbo.TTINYINT;
IF OBJECT_ID(N'dbo.TSMALLINT' , N'U') IS NOT NULL DROP TABLE dbo.TSMALLINT;
IF OBJECT_ID(N'dbo.TINT'      , N'U') IS NOT NULL DROP TABLE dbo.TINT;
IF OBJECT_ID(N'dbo.TBIGINT'   , N'U') IS NOT NULL DROP TABLE dbo.TBIGINT;
IF OBJECT_ID(N'dbo.TNUMERIC9' , N'U') IS NOT NULL DROP TABLE dbo.TNUMERIC9;
IF OBJECT_ID(N'dbo.TNUMERIC38', N'U') IS NOT NULL DROP TABLE dbo.TNUMERIC38;
```

Next I'll describe the test I used to measure the performance of identity and sequence with different cache values. The test results are eye-opening, showing significant performance differences when generating values in a user database versus tempdb, as well as a very interesting difference between identity and sequence with regards to log buffer flushes.

In preparation for the test, you create a database called testdb and set its recovery model to Simple. You create a sequence called *Seq1* in both testdb and tempdb. Here's the code that handles the preparation part:

```
IF DB_ID(N'testdb') IS NULL CREATE DATABASE testdb;
ALTER DATABASE testdb SET RECOVERY SIMPLE;

USE testdb;
IF OBJECT_ID(N'dbo.Seq1', N'SO') IS NOT NULL DROP SEQUENCE dbo.Seq1;
CREATE SEQUENCE dbo.Seq1 AS INT MINVALUE 1;

USE tempdb;
IF OBJECT_ID(N'dbo.Seq1', N'SO') IS NOT NULL DROP SEQUENCE dbo.Seq1;
CREATE SEQUENCE dbo.Seq1 AS INT MINVALUE 1;
```

The actual performance test generates 10,000,000 identity/sequence values by querying the *TSQLV3.dbo.GetNums* function, and it collects information about logging (the number of log records, their total size in megabytes, the number of log flushes), the duration in milliseconds, and normalized duration (duration minus the duration of the query without generating identity/sequence values). The collection of the statistics about logging and the actual work are done in the same transaction to prevent the log from recycling itself until the statistics are collected. Here's the code to conduct the test:

```
-- To enable TF 272: DBCC TRACEON(272, -1), to disable: DBCC TRACEOFF(272, -1)
SET NOCOUNT ON;
--USE tempdb; -- to test in tempdb
USE testdb; -- to test in user database testdb

DECLARE @numrecords AS INT, @sizemb AS NUMERIC(12, 2), @logflushes AS INT,
  @starttime AS DATETIME2, @endtime AS DATETIME2;

CHECKPOINT;

BEGIN TRAN

  ALTER SEQUENCE dbo.Seq1 CACHE 50; -- try with CACHE 10, 50, 10000, NO CACHE
  IF OBJECT_ID(N'dbo.T', N'U') IS NOT NULL DROP TABLE dbo.T;

  -- Stats before
  SELECT @numrecords = COUNT(*), @sizemb = SUM(CAST([Log Record Length] AS BIGINT)) / 1048576.,
    @logflushes = (SELECT cntr_value FROM sys.dm_os_performance_counters
                   WHERE counter_name = 'Log Flushes/sec'
                       AND instance_name = 'testdb' -- to test in testdb
--                     AND instance_name = 'tempdb' -- to test in tempdb
                  )
  FROM sys.fn_dblog(null, null);

  SET @starttime = SYSDATETIME();

  -- Actual work
  SELECT
--    n -- to test without seq or identity
    NEXT VALUE FOR dbo.Seq1 AS n -- to test sequence
--    IDENTITY(INT, 1, 1) AS n -- to test identity
  INTO dbo.T
  FROM TSQLV3.dbo.GetNums(1, 10000000) AS N
  OPTION(MAXDOP 1);

  -- Stats after
  SET @endtime = SYSDATETIME();
```

```
SELECT
    COUNT(*) - @numrecords AS numrecords,
    SUM(CAST([Log Record Length] AS BIGINT)) / 1048576. - @sizemb AS sizemb,
    (SELECT cntr_value FROM sys.dm_os_performance_counters
     WHERE counter_name = 'Log Flushes/sec'
       AND instance_name = 'testdb' -- to test in testdb
--         AND instance_name = 'tempdb' -- to test in tempdb
     ) - @logflushes AS logflushes,
    DATEDIFF(ms, @starttime, @endtime) AS durationms
  FROM sys.fn_dblog(null, null);

COMMIT TRAN

CHECKPOINT;
```

The code can be customized by commenting and uncommenting sections to test it with the different databases, cache sizes, and features. As is, the code tests the sequence object with a cache size of 50 in testdb.

Here are the results of my performance test on a machine running SQL Server 2014 RTM:

database	object	cache	numrecords	sizemb	logflushes	durationms	normdurms
tempdb	none		8717	0.58334350	42	4468	
tempdb	identity	DFT	6563	0.43955993	13	5969	1501
tempdb	identity	TF272	6563	0.43945693	9	93933	89465
tempdb	sequence	10000	6562	0.43933868	33	4710	242
tempdb	sequence	1000	6562	0.43933868	34	4889	421
tempdb	sequence	DFT- 50	6562	0.43933868	34	6177	1709
tempdb	sequence	10	6562	0.43933868	48	11625	7157
tempdb	sequence	NO CACHE	6562	0.43933868	34	70367	65899
testdb	none		29868	1.75932121	32	4743	
testdb	identity	DFT	32751	2.06301689	38	6013	1270
testdb	identity	TF272	10022862	726.15297889	13444	105341	100598
testdb	sequence	10000	23801	1.41382026	1000	5254	511
testdb	sequence	1000	32759	2.06282615	10000	10489	5746
testdb	sequence	DFT- 50	222863	15.85624122	200002	68390	63647
testdb	sequence	10	1022872	73.83788490	1000008	292110	287367
testdb	sequence	NO CACHE	10031030	726.87624200	10000050	2812090	2807347

There are quite a few interesting things to observe in the results, to explain, and to infer best practices from.

Observe that with both identity and sequence, when the target object is in tempdb there's no correlation between cache size and logging. That's because there's no need to log any cache-related disk writes because objects in tempdb do not survive restarts. The minimal numbers you do see for log records, total size, and log flushes are because of the actual insertion to support a rollback if needed. The duration does increase with smaller cache sizes, but that's not due to logging. You can see that, especially with smaller cache sizes, the performance in tempdb is significantly better than in testdb.

The other interesting observation is that in the user database (testdb), with the same cache value, the number of log records and their total size is similar for identity and sequence, but the number of log flushes and actual performance are quite different. Here's a subset of the performance results to allow you to more easily see this:

database	object	cache	numrecords	sizemb	logflushes	durationms	normdurms
tempdb	identity	DFT	6563	0.43955993	13	5969	1501
tempdb	sequence	1000	6562	0.43933868	34	4889	421
testdb	identity	DFT	32751	2.06301689	38	6013	1270 <--
testdb	sequence	1000	32759	2.06282615	10000	10489	5746 <--
tempdb	identity	TF272	6563	0.43945693	9	93933	89465
tempdb	sequence	NO CACHE	6562	0.43933868	34	70367	65899
testdb	identity	TF272	10022862	726.15297889	13444	105341	100598 <--
testdb	sequence	NO CACHE	10031030	726.87624200	10000050	2812090	2807347 <--

You also have the run time comparison between identity and sequence for some of the cache sizes shown graphically in Figure 6-2.

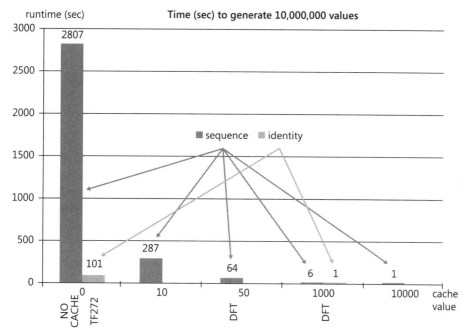

FIGURE 6-2 Sequence and identity performance test.

It's clear why the number of log records and their total size should be similar for identity and sequence with the same cache sizes—after all, they're both implemented based on the same object internally. So why the difference in the number of log buffer flushes?

This has to do with the fact that identity is table-specific and sequence isn't. Say you insert a new row into a table with identity. It so happens that this insert triggers a cache-related disk write. A log record is written to the log buffer, but suppose that the buffer is not full yet. Then there's a power failure before the log buffer is flushed. It's not a big deal if the recovered identity value will be an earlier one, because the recovery process will also undo the insert. So it's not a problem to reuse an older identity value that was generated by an insert that didn't commit. For this reason, SQL Server doesn't need to force flushing the log buffer for every identity cache-related disk write.

With the sequence object, the situation is different. An application can request a sequence value and use it for any purpose—not necessarily store it in a row in the database. If SQL Server crashes and then the application asks for a new value, what gives it the guarantee that an older value that it already used won't be produced again? To guarantee this, SQL Server forces the flushing of the log buffer for every sequence cache-related disk write.

You can see the correlation between the sequence cache size and the number of log flushes in the results of the performance test in the user database. For example, with no cache, when generating 10,000,000 values, the sequence gets about 10,000,000 flushes, whereas identity gets a fraction of those (about 13,000). The performance difference is quite dramatic: almost an hour for sequence and about a couple of minutes for identity.

Another important thing to keep in mind is the default cache sizes and the fact that they are not guaranteed to remain the same. In the versions and builds I tested, with an INT type, identity defaults to a cache size of 1000 and takes about a second to create 10,000,000 values. A sequence object defaults to a cache size of 50 and takes about a minute to create 10,000,000 values. This is especially important to remember when switching from one feature to another. First, you want to make sure that you do some testing. Second, consider using an explicit cache size that is big enough to give you similar performance to what you're used to.

Summarizing the comparison of identity with sequence

The section about sequences in this chapter compared and contrasted the sequence object with the identity column property. A lot of aspects were discussed. For your convenience and for reference, the information is provided in a summarized form in Table 6-2.

TABLE 6-2 Comparing identity with sequence

Aspect	Identity	Sequence
Table-independent	No	Yes
Can associate/disassociate with an existing column	No	Yes
Used with a nullable column	No	Yes
Obtain value before use	No	Yes
Used in SELECT	No The * IDENTITY() function can be used in SELECT INTO	Yes
Control order	Not in SELECT INTO Yes in INSERT SELECT	Yes
Used in UPDATE	No	Yes
Can define minimum and maximum values	No	Yes

Aspect	Identity	Sequence
Can cycle	No	Yes
Can change the current value	Yes	Yes
Can change the increment	No	Yes
Supports a user-defined cache value	No, can disable the cache with TF272	Yes
Default cache value (as of SQL Server 2014 RTM and SQL Server 2012 SP2)	Depends on type (TINYINT – 10, SMALLINT – 100, INT – 1000, BIGINT and NUMERIC – 10000)	50
Affected by rollback	No	No
Requires log flush on write to disk	No	Yes
Obtain range of values	No	Yes

Deleting data

This section covers two main aspects of data deletion: the TRUNCATE TABLE statement and deleting duplicates. You can find additional coverage of data deletion in Chapter 5, "TOP and OFFSET-FETCH," which describes how to split large deletes into chunks in the section "Modifying in chunks."

TRUNCATE TABLE

The TRUNCATE TABLE statement is a highly efficient statement that deletes all rows from a table and resets an identity property if one exists, but leaves the table definition in place.

The statement has basic syntax. For example, if you had a table called T1, you would truncate it like this:

```
TRUNCATE TABLE dbo.T1;
```

Regardless of the database recovery model, the TRUNCATE TABLE statement involves substantially less logging than the DELETE statement; hence, it is significantly faster than it. The former needs to log only which extents or pages were deallocated to support roll-back and roll-forward capabilities. The latter needs to log every row that is deleted.

Because of the significant performance difference, it is generally preferred that you use the TRUNCATE TABLE statement over the DELETE statement. But you should be aware of a few differences besides performance.

The TRUNCATE TABLE statement requires stronger permissions. You need at minimum the ALTER permission on the target table. If you don't want to grant such permission to the executing user, you can incorporate the statement in a stored procedure that is defined with the EXECUTE AS clause, and ensure that the impersonated user has the right permissions.

As mentioned, unlike the DELETE statement, the TRUNCATE TABLE statement resets an identity property if one exists. If you want to clear a table but leave the current identity value unchanged, you need to take care of this yourself. You do so by applying the following steps:

1. Open a transaction.

2. Lock the table.

3. Capture the current identity value plus 1 in a variable.

4. Issue the TRUNCATE TABLE statement.

5. Reseed the identity property with the value stored in the variable.

6. Commit the transaction.

I'll use the following sample data to demonstrate this solution:

```
IF OBJECT_ID(N'dbo.T1', N'U') IS NOT NULL DROP TABLE dbo.T1;
GO

CREATE TABLE dbo.T1
(
  keycol  INT NOT NULL IDENTITY,
  datacol VARCHAR(10) NOT NULL
);

INSERT INTO dbo.T1(datacol) VALUES('A'),('B'),('C');

SELECT keycol, datacol FROM dbo.T1;
```

Here's the output of the last query showing the contents of the table T1:

```
keycol       datacol
-----------  ----------
1            A
2            B
3            C
```

The current identity value is 3.

The following code truncates the table and manually reseeds the identity property to the current value plus 1:

```
IF EXISTS(SELECT * FROM dbo.T1)
BEGIN
  BEGIN TRAN
    DECLARE @tmp AS INT = (SELECT TOP (1) keycol FROM dbo.T1 WITH (TABLOCKX)); -- lock
    DECLARE @reseedval AS INT = IDENT_CURRENT(N'dbo.T1') + 1;                  -- save
    TRUNCATE TABLE dbo.T1;                                                      -- truncate
    DBCC CHECKIDENT(N'dbo.T1', RESEED, @reseedval);                            -- reseed
    PRINT 'Identity reseeded to ' + CAST(@reseedval AS VARCHAR(10)) + '.';
  COMMIT TRAN
END
ELSE
  PRINT 'Table is empty, no need to truncate.' ;
```

This code generates the following output:

```
Identity reseeded to 4.
```

Now add new rows into the table and query it:

```
INSERT INTO dbo.T1(datacol) VALUES('X'),('Y'),('Z');
SELECT keycol, datacol FROM dbo.T1;
```

You will get the following output, which shows the first identity value generated was *4*:

```
keycol      datacol
----------- ----------
4           X
5           Y
6           Z
```

A table cannot be truncated if there are foreign keys pointing to it, even if the referencing tables are empty. You will have to drop the foreign keys before truncating the table and re-create them after you're done.

Similarly, a table cannot be truncated if there are indexed views based on the table. Like with foreign keys, one option is to drop the indexed views before truncating the table and re-create them after you're done.

Another option is to rely on partition switching. With partition switching, you don't need to drop and re-create the indexed view. SQL Server supports partition switching even when there's an indexed view based on the table, so long as the partitioning of the indexed view is aligned with the table partition. If you didn't explicitly partition the table and the indexed view, you satisfy this requirement by definition. The solution involves the following steps:

1. Create a staging table with the same structure as the source.

2. Switch the source table to the stage table.

3. Drop the stage table.

I'll use the following sample data to demonstrate this solution:

```
SET NOCOUNT ON;
USE tempdb;

IF OBJECT_ID(N'dbo.V1', N'V') IS NOT NULL DROP VIEW dbo.V1;
IF OBJECT_ID(N'dbo.T1', N'U') IS NOT NULL DROP TABLE dbo.T1;
GO

CREATE TABLE dbo.T1
(
  col1 INT NOT NULL PRIMARY KEY,
  col2 INT NOT NULL,
  col3 NUMERIC(12, 2) NOT NULL
);
```

```
INSERT INTO dbo.T1(col1, col2, col3) VALUES
  ( 2, 10,  200.00),
  ( 3, 10,  800.00),
  ( 5, 10,  100.00),
  ( 7, 20,  300.00),
  (11, 20,  500.00),
  (13, 20, 1300.00);
GO

CREATE VIEW dbo.V1 WITH SCHEMABINDING
AS

SELECT col2, SUM(col3) AS total , COUNT_BIG(*) AS cnt
FROM dbo.T1
GROUP BY col2;
GO

CREATE UNIQUE CLUSTERED INDEX idx_col2 ON dbo.V1(col2);
GO

SELECT col2, total, cnt FROM dbo.V1;
```

The sample data has a table called T1 and an indexed view based on it. The last query in the code produces the following output showing the current contents of the table:

```
col2  total     cnt
----- --------- ----
10    1100.00   3
20    2100.00   3
```

Now attempt to clear the table by truncating it:

```
TRUNCATE TABLE dbo.T1;
```

You get the following error saying you cannot truncate the table because it's referenced by the indexed view:

```
Msg 3729, Level 16, State 2, Line 1
Cannot TRUNCATE TABLE 'dbo.T1' because it is being referenced by object 'V1'.
```

Here's the solution for clearing the table based on partition switching without the need to drop and re-create the indexed view:

```
CREATE TABLE dbo.T1_STAGE
(
  col1 INT NOT NULL PRIMARY KEY,
  col2 INT NOT NULL,
  col3 NUMERIC(12, 2) NOT NULL
);

ALTER TABLE dbo.T1 SWITCH TO dbo.T1_STAGE;

DROP TABLE dbo.T1_STAGE;
```

When you're done testing, run the following code for cleanup:

```
IF OBJECT_ID(N'dbo.V1', N'V') IS NOT NULL DROP VIEW dbo.V1;
IF OBJECT_ID(N'dbo.T1', N'U') IS NOT NULL DROP TABLE dbo.T1;
```

It's common for people to consider the TRUNCATE TABLE statement as a DDL statement and not as a DML one. You can understand the confusion when you consider that, in SQL Server, you need ALTER permissions on the table and not just DELETE permissions, and that the statement resets the identity property. Also, some think of the TRUNCATE TABLE statement as DDL when thinking of the physical processing of the data. Indeed, in physical terms, TRUNCATE TABLE is processed similarly to DROP TABLE in how it deallocates extents or pages and in what it logs. But according to standard SQL, the TRUNCATE TABLE statement is considered a DML statement. That's because standard SQL isn't concerned with the physical layer; rather, it is concerned only with the logical one. Logically, the statement deletes all rows from the table—it doesn't change the table definition.

Deleting duplicates

Suppose you have data that contains duplicate rows and you need to deduplicate the data, keeping only one occurrence of each logical key. This could be a result of not enforcing integrity in your data or importing data from a source that did not enforce integrity.

As an example for a table with duplicates, the following code creates a table called Orders and fills it with duplicate rows:

```
USE tempdb;
IF OBJECT_ID(N'dbo.Orders', N'U') IS NOT NULL DROP TABLE dbo.Orders;
GO

SELECT
  orderid, custid, empid, orderdate, requireddate, shippeddate,
  shipperid, freight, shipname, shipaddress, shipcity, shipregion,
  shippostalcode, shipcountry
INTO dbo.Orders
FROM TSQLV3.Sales.Orders
  CROSS JOIN TSQLV3.dbo.Nums
WHERE n <= 3;
```

The *orderid* column is supposed to be unique but currently isn't. You need to deduplicate the data, resulting in a set that has only one occurrence of each distinct order ID. After deduplicating the data, it is a good idea to enforce uniqueness with a constraint.

The recommended method to use for deduplicating the data varies depending on the number of rows that need to be deleted and on the percentage out of the entire set that the number represents. Suppose that there are 50,000,000 rows in the table. If the number of rows to be deleted is small—for example, 10,000—it's quite alright to use a single DELETE statement that is fully logged. Here's the solution you can use in such a case to implement the task:

```
WITH C AS
(
  SELECT *,
    ROW_NUMBER()
      OVER(PARTITION BY orderid ORDER BY (SELECT NULL)) AS n
  FROM dbo.Orders
)
DELETE FROM C
WHERE n > 1;
```

The inner query computes a row number (call it *n*) that is partitioned by the logical key (*orderid* in our case). If it doesn't matter to you which row you keep as long as you keep only one occurrence of each distinct order ID, use arbitrary ordering in the window order clause as our query does—namely, *ORDER BY (SELECT NULL)*. If different rows with the same order ID value can be distinct from each other and you do have attributes that determine which to prefer, make sure to specify those attributes in the window order clause. The column *n* represents the duplicate number. So say you have three rows with the order ID 10248; they will get the distinct *n* values 1, 2, and 3. The code defines a CTE called *C* based on the query that computes *n*. The outer query then deletes the rows where *n* is greater than 1 through the CTE C. The underlying table Orders is the one that is actually affected by the DELETE statement.

If the percentage of rows that need to be deleted is small, but still the number of rows is large—for example, 5,000,000—the preceding solution might not be good. It might cause the log to significantly expand, and it might result in lock escalation. To avoid both, you can split the large delete to a delete in chunks as described in Chapter 5 in the section "Modifying in chunks." Here's the implementation of this approach in our case:

```
WHILE 1 = 1
BEGIN
  WITH C AS
  (
    SELECT *,
      ROW_NUMBER()
        OVER(PARTITION BY orderid ORDER BY (SELECT NULL)) AS n
    FROM dbo.Orders
  )
  DELETE TOP (3000) FROM C
  WHERE n > 1;

  IF @@ROWCOUNT < 3000 BREAK;
END;
```

If both the percentage and number of rows that need to be deleted are large—for example, 25,000,000 rows—a third solution might be optimal. You copy the rows where *n* equals 1 to a staging table using a minimally logged bulk operation like SELECT INTO. After copying, you drop the original table, rename the staging table to the original table name, and then create anything you need on that table (constraints, indexes, triggers, permissions). Here's the code implementing this approach:

```
-- Copy distinct rows to staging table
WITH C AS
(
  SELECT *,
    ROW_NUMBER()
      OVER(PARTITION BY orderid ORDER BY (SELECT NULL)) AS n
  FROM dbo.Orders
)
SELECT orderid, custid, empid, orderdate, requireddate, shippeddate, shipperid,
  freight, shipname, shipaddress, shipcity, shipregion, shippostalcode, shipcountry
INTO dbo.Orders_Stage
FROM C
WHERE n = 1;

-- Drop original table
DROP TABLE dbo.Orders;

-- Rename staging table to original table name
EXEC sp_rename N'dbo.Orders_Stage', N'Orders';

-- Create constraints, indexes, triggers and permissions on Orders
ALTER TABLE dbo.Orders ADD CONSTRAINT PK_Orders PRIMARY KEY(orderid);
```

Updating data

This section covers two specialized update capabilities in T-SQL: updating data through table expressions and updating data using variables.

As sample data for use in both the section on updating data and the subsequent section on merging data, I'll use the tables Customers and CustomersStage, which you create and populate in tempdb using the following code:

```
USE tempdb;

IF OBJECT_ID(N'dbo.Customers', N'U') IS NOT NULL DROP TABLE dbo.Customers;

CREATE TABLE dbo.Customers
(
  custid      INT        NOT NULL,
  companyname VARCHAR(25) NOT NULL,
  phone       VARCHAR(20) NULL,
  address     VARCHAR(50) NOT NULL,
  CONSTRAINT PK_Customers PRIMARY KEY(custid)
);
GO

INSERT INTO dbo.Customers(custid, companyname, phone, address)
  VALUES(1, 'cust 1', '(111) 111-1111', 'address 1'),
        (2, 'cust 2', '(222) 222-2222', 'address 2'),
        (3, 'cust 3', '(333) 333-3333', 'address 3'),
        (4, 'cust 4', '(444) 444-4444', 'address 4'),
        (5, 'cust 5', '(555) 555-5555', 'address 5');
GO
```

```
IF OBJECT_ID(N'dbo.CustomersStage', N'U') IS NOT NULL DROP TABLE dbo.CustomersStage;

CREATE TABLE dbo.CustomersStage
(
  custid      INT         NOT NULL,
  companyname VARCHAR(25) NOT NULL,
  phone       VARCHAR(20) NULL,
  address     VARCHAR(50) NOT NULL,
  CONSTRAINT PK_CustomersStage PRIMARY KEY(custid)
);
GO

INSERT INTO dbo.CustomersStage(custid, companyname, phone, address)
  VALUES(2, 'AAAAA', '(222) 222-2222', 'address 2'),
        (3, 'cust 3', '(333) 333-3333', 'address 3'),
        (5, 'BBBBB', 'CCCCC', 'DDDDD'),
        (6, 'cust 6 (new)', '(666) 666-6666', 'address 6'),
        (7, 'cust 7 (new)', '(777) 777-7777', 'address 7');
```

Update using table expressions

Suppose you need to update the information of existing customers in the Customers table with more recent information from the CustomersStage table. Normally, you do this with an UPDATE statement that is based on a join. Sometimes, though, you need to be able to see what's supposed to be modified before you actually modify the data.

One solution people use for this purpose is to comment out the UPDATE clause and run the statement with a SELECT clause instead. Then, to run the actual modification, you comment out the SELECT clause and uncomment the UPDATE clause. But this solution is a bit awkward and prone to errors. A more elegant solution is to rely on the fact that T-SQL allows you to modify data in tables through table expressions. You join Customers and CustomersStage using a SELECT statement, returning the pairs of source and target columns that are involved in the modification. You define a CTE based on the SELECT statement, and then modify the data through the CTE, like so:

```
WITH C AS
(
  SELECT
    TGT.custid,
    SRC.companyname AS src_companyname,
    TGT.companyname AS tgt_companyname,
    SRC.phone       AS src_phone,
    TGT.phone       AS tgt_phone,
    SRC.address     AS src_address,
    TGT.address     AS tgt_address
  FROM dbo.Customers AS TGT
    INNER JOIN dbo.CustomersStage AS SRC
      ON TGT.custid = SRC.custid
)
UPDATE C
  SET tgt_companyname = src_companyname,
      tgt_phone       = src_phone,
      tgt_address     = src_address;
```

With this solution, when you just want to see which rows are supposed to be modified and with what, you highlight only the inner query and run it independently. When you're ready to run the actual modification, you simply run the entire thing.

The rules for modifying data through CTEs that are based on joins are similar to the rules for modifying data through views that are based on joins. You can insert and update data through the CTE, but you're allowed to modify only one target table at a time.

Update using variables

T-SQL supports a proprietary, specialized, UPDATE syntax you can use to modify data in a table and perform variable assignment at the same time. This capability is handy when you need to roll your own solution for generating surrogate keys with a guarantee that you won't have a gap between the values. Recall that neither the sequence object nor the identity column property guarantee that you won't have gaps between values, regardless of the cache value that you use.

An example where you need a custom sequence generator that guarantees no gaps is for invoicing systems. In many countries/regions, legally you're not allowed to have gaps between invoice numbers.

The typical solution people use for this purpose is to store the last-used value in a table. The following code creates such a table, called MySequence, and populates it with the value *0*, assuming that the first value you will need to generate is 1:

```
USE tempdb;
IF OBJECT_ID(N'dbo.MySequence', N'U') IS NOT NULL DROP TABLE dbo.MySequence;
CREATE TABLE dbo.MySequence(val INT NOT NULL);
INSERT INTO dbo.MySequence(val) VALUES(0);
```

The natural way to generate a new value is to use separate UPDATE and SELECT statements in an explicit transaction to ensure that no one else uses the value you generated. But this approach results in two visits to the row for every key you generate. A more efficient method is to use the specialized UPDATE syntax to both update the value and assign the updated value to a variable in one visit to the row, like so:

```
DECLARE @newval AS INT;
UPDATE dbo.MySequence SET @newval = val += 1;
SELECT @newval;
```

Run this code three times, and notice that the values returned are 1, 2, and 3.

The UPDATE statement requires an exclusive lock on the target row, and an exclusive lock is held until the end of the transaction. So once a transaction generates a key, until it finishes, no other transaction can obtain a new key. If the transaction ends up rolling back, the key change is undone. That's how you guarantee no gaps.

To demonstrate this approach, open two connections. Run the following code in connection 1 to open a transaction and request a new key, leaving the transaction open:

```
BEGIN TRAN

  DECLARE @newval AS INT;
  UPDATE dbo.MySequence SET @newval = val += 1;
  SELECT @newval;
```

You get the new key *4* back, but the row is still exclusively locked. Run the following code in connection 2 to try and obtain a new key:

```
BEGIN TRAN

  DECLARE @newval AS INT;
  UPDATE dbo.MySequence SET @newval = val += 1;
  SELECT @newval;
```

Connection 2 is blocked.

Back in connection 1, run the following code to roll back the transaction:

```
ROLLBACK TRAN
```

The value in the table is undone to 3, and the lock is released by connection 1. Connection 2 manages to get the exclusive lock it was waiting for, updates the value from 3 to 4, and returns it.

Run the following code in connection 2 to commit the transaction:

```
COMMIT TRAN
```

Now that the value change to 4 is committed, the exclusive lock on the row is released by connection 2, and another transaction can request the next value.

You see how this solution guarantees you will not have gaps between values using the normal locking and blocking mechanism that SQL Server uses when updating data.

Merging data

You use the MERGE statement to merge data into some target table using data from some source table. It can be used in data-warehouse scenarios for merging data into summary tables, handling slowly changing dimensions, and more. It can also be used in online transaction processing (OLTP) scenarios when your system is not the one generating the data; instead, you periodically get updates from an external source that you need to merge into a table in your database.

T-SQL implements the MERGE statement based on standard SQL with an extension in the form of a clause called WHEN NOT MATCHED BY SOURCE, which handles a case that the standard statement doesn't.

To demonstrate the MERGE statement, I'll use the same Customers and CustomersStage tables you created earlier in the section "Updating data."

MERGE examples

I'll explain the MERGE statement through examples. I'll start with the fundamental clauses that the statement supports.

Suppose you need to merge the data you have in the source CustomersStage table into the target Customers table. For source customers that are matched by a target customer, you want to update the target row with the more recent information from the source row. For source customers that are not matched by a target customer, you want to insert the source customer as a new customer row into the target. Finally, for target customers that are not matched by a source customer, you want to delete the target customer row. You implement such a merge task with the following MERGE statement:

```
MERGE INTO dbo.Customers AS TGT
USING dbo.CustomersStage AS SRC
  ON TGT.custid = SRC.custid
WHEN MATCHED THEN
  UPDATE SET
    TGT.companyname = SRC.companyname,
    TGT.phone = SRC.phone,
    TGT.address = SRC.address
WHEN NOT MATCHED THEN
  INSERT (custid, companyname, phone, address)
  VALUES (SRC.custid, SRC.companyname, SRC.phone, SRC.address)
WHEN NOT MATCHED BY SOURCE THEN
  DELETE;
```

The MERGE INTO clause is where you define the target table and, optionally, alias it. In our case, the target is the Customers table, and it's aliased as TGT.

The USING clause is where you define the source for the merge task and, optionally, alias it. In our case, the source is the CustomersStage table, and it's aliased as SRC. An interesting thing about the USING clause is that it's designed similar to the FROM clause in a SELECT statement. You are not limited to querying a table as the source; rather, you can use sources like table operators, table expressions, and table functions. I'll say more about this capability shortly.

The next part to define in the MERGE statement is the merge ON predicate. The purpose of the merge predicate is to determine whether a source row is matched by a target row or not, as well as whether a target row is matched by a source row. For us, making such a determination is intuitive, but not for the MERGE statement. Remember the statement doesn't require the source and target tables to have keys defined in order to work. So, in our case, the merge predicate is *TGT.custid = SRC.custid*.

With the target and source identified and the merge predicate defined, the remaining clauses define which actions to take against the target in the different cases (INSERT, UPDATE, or DELETE). Using the WHEN MATCHED clause, you define what to do against the target when a source row is matched by a target row. With our sample data, customers 2, 3, and 5 qualify. There are two possible actions you can take against the target row when you have a match: UPDATE and DELETE. If you think about it, an INSERT action doesn't make sense here because the target row exists. In fact, the MERGE statement doesn't support an INSERT action in this case. In our MERGE statement example, the action taken in this clause is UPDATE; you update the target row with the more recent information from the source row.

Unlike an UPDATE statement based on a join, if a MERGE statement detects that multiple source rows match one target row, it generates an error. An UPDATE statement simply does a nondeterministic update in such a case; namely, one of the source rows will be used to update the target. The MERGE statement is more robust in such cases, protecting you from bugs. You need to figure out how to prepare the source data to ensure that no more than one source row matches a target row.

Technically, the MERGE statement supports as many occurrences of a clause as the number of valid actions. Because the WHEN MATCHED clause supports two valid actions—UPDATE and DELETE—you are allowed two such clauses. You can specify an additional predicate after an AND operator that indicates the condition in which to apply the action that is associated with that clause. This way, based on different additional conditions, you can apply the different actions. For example, suppose the source table has a column called *actiontype* that holds the string 'UPDATE' or 'DELETE' that tells you which action you are supposed to take. In your MERGE statement, you use two WHEN MATCHED clauses with extra predicates that specify when to apply each action, like so:

```
WHEN MATCHED AND actiontype = 'UPDATE' THEN
    UPDATE SET
      TGT.companyname = SRC.companyname,
      TGT.phone = SRC.phone,
      TGT.address = SRC.address
WHEN MATCHED AND actiontype = 'DELETE' THEN
    DELETE
```

If you indicate an additional predicate in the first clause but none in the second clause, the rows that satisfy the additional predicate in the first clause will cause the action associated with the first clause to be activated, and those that don't will cause the action associated with the second clause to be activated.

The WHEN NOT MATCHED clause (short for WHEN NOT MATCHED BY TARGET) gives you a way to define the action to take when the source row is not matched by a target row. In our sample data, customers 6 and 7 qualify. The only valid action in this clause is INSERT, for an obvious reason—there is no respective target row. You can still add an extra predicate after an AND operator so that the insert takes place only if the extra predicate is true.

The WHEN MATCHED and WHEN NOT MATCHED clauses are standard. But that's where the standard stops. Microsoft reckoned that there's a case that the standard doesn't deal with but which might be important for you to deal with—when a target row is not matched by a source row. Such is the case in our sample data, with customers 1 and 4. So Microsoft introduced an extension to the standard in the form of a clause called WHEN NOT MATCHED BY SOURCE. You can use this clause to define the action to take against the target row when there's no matching source row. Because the target row exists, the valid actions you can apply are DELETE and UPDATE; INSERT is not supported. In our example MERGE statement, the action taken in this clause is DELETE.

Just like with the WHEN MATCHED clause, because there are two valid actions in the WHEN NOT MATCHED BY SOURCE clause, you are allowed two occurrences of the clause. And by using extra predicates you can control when to apply each action. As an example, suppose that if the current date is an end-of-month date, you need to update an *isdeleted* flag in the target row to 1; if the current date is not an end-of-month date, you need to actually delete the target row. You achieve this with the following two WHEN NOT MATCHED BY SOURCE clauses:

```
WHEN NOT MATCHED BY SOURCE AND CAST(SYSDATETIME() AS DATE) = EOMONTH(SYSDATETIME()) THEN
  UPDATE SET
    TGT.isdeleted = 1
WHEN NOT MATCHED BY SOURCE THEN
  DELETE
```

Back to the WHEN MATCHED clause, suppose you want to apply the update only if at least one of the column values is different between the source rows and the target rows. You do not want to apply the update if they are identical. For one, you don't want to pay the cost of the update, and two, perhaps you have additional processes triggered when rows are updated and you don't want those processes to run if there's no actual change. You can use the extra predicate in the clause to check that at least one column value is different. For columns that do not allow NULLs, you can simply use the predicate *TGT.colname <> SRC.colname*. But for columns that allow NULLs, you need to use the longer form *TGT.colname <> SRC.colname OR TGT.colname IS NULL AND SRC.colname IS NOT NULL OR TGT.colname IS NOT NULL AND SRC.colname IS NULL*. In our merge example, the *phone* column allows NULLs, so for this column you need the longer predicate form. Here's the last merge example, which is modified to apply the update only if at least one of the column values is different:

```
MERGE INTO dbo.Customers AS TGT
USING dbo.CustomersStage AS SRC
  ON TGT.custid = SRC.custid
WHEN MATCHED AND
      (   TGT.companyname <> SRC.companyname
       OR TGT.phone <> SRC.phone
          OR TGT.phone IS NULL AND SRC.phone IS NOT NULL
          OR TGT.phone IS NOT NULL AND SRC.phone IS NULL
       OR TGT.address <> SRC.address) THEN
  UPDATE SET
    TGT.companyname = SRC.companyname,
    TGT.phone = SRC.phone,
    TGT.address = SRC.address
WHEN NOT MATCHED THEN
  INSERT (custid, companyname, phone, address)
  VALUES (SRC.custid, SRC.companyname, SRC.phone, SRC.address)
WHEN NOT MATCHED BY SOURCE THEN
  DELETE;
```

A much more concise alternative is to use the EXCEPT set operator, like so:

```
WHEN MATCHED AND EXISTS ( SELECT TGT.* EXCEPT SELECT SRC.* ) THEN
```

The thing about set operators is that, when comparing rows, they implicitly use the *distinct predicate* as opposed to the *different than* (<>) operator. When checking whether a NULL is distinct from a non-NULL, you get *true*. When checking whether a NULL is different than a non-NULL, you get *unknown*. This makes it much simpler to compare rows using set operators, because you don't need special treatment for NULLs. Of course, the assumption here is that the structures of both tables are the same. If they are not, you can always define views to get compatible structures and use the views as the source and target for the MERGE statement.

What could make it easier to phrase conditions that consider a NULL versus non-NULL as different, and NULL versus NULL as the same, is if T-SQL supported the standard *distinct predicate*. You can find a request to add support for the distinct predicate in SQL Server here: *https://connect.microsoft.com/ SQLServer/feedback/details/286422/.*

Preventing MERGE conflicts

When multiple MERGE statements handle overlapping keys and are executed concurrently, they can run into conflicts that result in primary key violations. That's because under the default Read Committed isolation level, you are not guaranteed to get serialized access to the data throughout the transaction. It could happen that two or more statements check whether a certain key exists at the same time, all getting *false*; therefore, all try to insert a new row with that key. One will succeed, and the rest will fail with a primary key violation.

For example, consider the following stored procedure called *AddCustomer*:

```
IF OBJECT_ID(N'dbo.AddCustomer', N'P') IS NOT NULL DROP PROC dbo.AddCustomer;
GO
CREATE PROC dbo.AddCustomer
  @custid INT, @companyname VARCHAR(25), @phone VARCHAR(20), @address VARCHAR(50)
AS

MERGE INTO dbo.Customers /* WITH (SERIALIZABLE) */ AS TGT
USING (VALUES(@custid, @companyname, @phone, @address))
        AS SRC(custid, companyname, phone, address)
  ON TGT.custid = SRC.custid
WHEN MATCHED THEN
  UPDATE SET
    TGT.companyname = SRC.companyname,
    TGT.phone = SRC.phone,
    TGT.address = SRC.address
WHEN NOT MATCHED THEN
  INSERT (custid, companyname, phone, address)
  VALUES (SRC.custid, SRC.companyname, SRC.phone, SRC.address);
GO
```

The procedure accepts information about a customer as input. If the customer ID already exists, it updates the existing customer with the new information; otherwise, it adds a new customer. If multiple sessions execute the procedure concurrently with the same customer ID, and that customer doesn't exist, one will succeed and the others will get a primary key violation. To demonstrate this, run the following code from multiple sessions:

```
SET NOCOUNT ON;
USE tempdb;

WHILE 1 = 1
BEGIN
  DECLARE @curcustid AS INT = CHECKSUM(CAST(SYSDATETIME() AS DATETIME2(2)));
  EXEC dbo.AddCustomer @custid = @curcustid, @companyname = 'A', @phone = 'B', @address = 'C';
END;
```

After a few iterations, you'll start getting primary key violations like the following:

```
Msg 2627, Level 14, State 1, Procedure AddCustomer, Line 5
Violation of PRIMARY KEY constraint 'PK_Customers'. Cannot insert duplicate key in object
'dbo.Customers'. The duplicate key value is (1777624945).
```

To avoid the conflict, you need to serialize access to the data throughout the transaction. To achieve this, you use the SERIALIZABLE isolation level. In our procedure, remove the block comment delimiters in the MERGE INTO clause after the table name to specify the SERIALIZABLE isolation as a table hint. You can also use the HOLDLOCK hint, which is equivalent. You can then try the test again and see that you don't get any primary key violation errors anymore.

ON isn't a filter

It's a common mistake to think of the MERGE ON predicate as a filter and end up with a bug. The ON predicate defines whether a source row is matched by a target row or not, and then accordingly directs the row to the right clause to apply the respective action. As an example, suppose you need to merge only the source row for customer 2 into the target, updating the existing row if the customer exists and inserting a new row if it doesn't. Thinking (incorrectly) of the ON predicate as a filter, you write the following MERGE statement:

```
MERGE INTO dbo.Customers AS TGT
USING dbo.CustomersStage AS SRC
  ON TGT.custid = SRC.custid
  AND SRC.custid = 2
WHEN MATCHED THEN
  UPDATE SET
    TGT.companyname = SRC.companyname,
    TGT.phone = SRC.phone,
    TGT.address = SRC.address
WHEN NOT MATCHED THEN
  INSERT (custid, companyname, phone, address)
  VALUES (SRC.custid, SRC.companyname, SRC.phone, SRC.address);
```

What happens in practice is that for all source rows with a customer ID other than 2, the ON predicate evaluates to *false*; in such a case, the row is directed to the WHEN NOT MATCHED clause, resulting in an insert action. Instead of ignoring all source customers other than 2, the statement applies an insert action for them. If any of those customer IDs exist in the target, you will get a primary key violation. Worse, if none already exist, you will insert them into the target even though you were not supposed to. For example, when I ran this statement, I got the following primary key violation related to customer 3:

```
Msg 2627, Level 14, State 1, Line 805
Violation of PRIMARY KEY constraint 'PK_Customers'. Cannot insert duplicate key in object
'dbo.Customers'. The duplicate key value is (3).
The statement has been terminated.
```

The correct solution is to prepare a table expression where you filter only the source row for customer 2 and use that table expression as the source for the MERGE statement, like so:

```
MERGE INTO dbo.Customers AS TGT
USING (SELECT * FROM dbo.CustomersStage WHERE custid = 2) AS SRC
  ON TGT.custid = SRC.custid
WHEN MATCHED THEN
  UPDATE SET
    TGT.companyname = SRC.companyname,
    TGT.phone = SRC.phone,
    TGT.address = SRC.address
WHEN NOT MATCHED THEN
  INSERT (custid, companyname, phone, address)
  VALUES (SRC.custid, SRC.companyname, SRC.phone, SRC.address);
```

USING is similar to FROM

An interesting fact about the MERGE statement is that the USING clause is designed like the SELECT statement's FROM clause. This means you're not limited to referring to a table as the source; rather, you can apply table operators like JOIN, APPLY, PIVOT, and UNPIVOT, as well as refer to table functions.

An example where this capability can be handy is when the source data for a merge process is in a file. You don't have to first import the data to a staging table and then use the staging table as the source. Instead, you can use the file as the direct source for the MERGE statement by specifying the OPENROWSET function with the BULK provider in the USING clause.

To demonstrate this, I'll export the data from the Customers table to a file called C:\temp\Customers.txt, and then use that file as the source for a merge example. First run the following *bcp* command from a command prompt to create a format file called CustomersFmt.xml based on the structure of the Customers table (making sure the folder c:\temp\ exists and changing the server and instance names to yours):

```
bcp tempdb.dbo.Customers format nul -c -x -f C:\temp\CustomersFmt.xml -T -S <server\instance>
```

Then run the following *bcp* command to export the data from the Customers table to the file Customers.txt:

```
bcp tempdb.dbo.Customers out C:\temp\Customers.txt -c -T -S <server\instance>
```

Now, suppose you need to merge the data from the Customers.txt file into your existing Customers table, updating customers that exist with the new info and inserting customers that don't exist. You specify the OPENROWSET function in the USING clause to use the file as the source for the MERGE statement directly, like so:

```
MERGE INTO dbo.Customers AS TGT
USING OPENROWSET(BULK 'C:\temp\Customers.txt',
                 FORMATFILE = 'C:\temp\CustomersFmt.xml') AS SRC
  ON TGT.custid = SRC.custid
WHEN MATCHED THEN
  UPDATE SET
    TGT.companyname = SRC.companyname,
    TGT.phone = SRC.phone,
    TGT.address = SRC.address
WHEN NOT MATCHED THEN
  INSERT (custid, companyname, phone, address)
  VALUES (SRC.custid, SRC.companyname, SRC.phone, SRC.address);
```

The OUTPUT clause

The OUTPUT clause is a powerful feature that allows modification statements to return information from the modified rows. You can use it for purposes like auditing, archiving, and others. The syntax for using the clause is

```
OUTPUT <output_list> [INTO <output_table>]
```

Without an INTO clause, the output rows are returned to the caller as a result set just like with a SELECT statement. With an INTO clause, they are written to a table. When using INTO, *output_table* must exist. It cannot have triggers, foreign keys, or check constraints. You are allowed to have two OUTPUT clauses if you like—one with INTO, directing the output rows to a table, and another without INTO, directing the rows to the caller.

When referring to columns from the modified rows, you need to prefix them with the keywords *inserted* or *deleted*, depending on whether you need the column from the inserted or deleted row. In INSERT statements, naturally you refer to *inserted*, and in DELETE statements you refer to *deleted*. In UPDATE and MERGE statements, you might want to refer to both to get the old and new states of an updated row. In the OUTPUT clause of an INSERT statement, you can refer to elements from the inserted row but not from the source table. Interestingly, in the OUTPUT clause of a MERGE statement you are allowed to refer to elements from the source table. I will demonstrate this capability shortly.

The beauty of the OUTPUT clause is that it's designed similar to the SELECT clause. You're not limited to just referring to columns directly; rather, you can apply calculations, call functions, and assign aliases to the result columns. For example, suppose that in an UPDATE statement you wanted to capture the difference between the new and old values of a column called *qty*; in the OUTPUT clause, you can specify *inserted.qty – deleted.qty AS qtydiff*.

In the following sections, I'll provide practical examples for using the OUTPUT clause with different modification statements.

Example with INSERT and identity

Suppose you have a multi-row insert into a table with an identity column and you need to capture the newly generated identity values for further use. SQL Server provides you with the SCOPE_IDENTITY function to capture the last identity value generated in your session and scope, but it doesn't provide you with a tool to capture multiple generated identity values. The solution is to use the OUTPUT clause.

To demonstrate this, first run the following code, which creates a table called T1 with an identity column:

```
USE tempdb;
IF OBJECT_ID(N'dbo.T1', N'U') IS NOT NULL DROP TABLE dbo.T1;
GO

CREATE TABLE dbo.T1
(
  keycol   INT           NOT NULL IDENTITY(1, 1) CONSTRAINT PK_T1 PRIMARY KEY,
  datacol  NVARCHAR(40) NOT NULL
);
```

The following INSERT statement copies five rows from the table TSQLV3.HR.Employees into the table T1, causing five identity values to be generated:

```
INSERT INTO dbo.T1(datacol)
  OUTPUT inserted.$identity, inserted.datacol
    SELECT lastname
    FROM TSQLV3.HR.Employees
    WHERE country = N'USA';
```

Using the OUTPUT clause, the statement returns the newly generated identity values along with other information from the inserted rows. Observe the reference to the identity column using the generalized form *$identity*. SQL Server supports this generalized form because only one identity column is allowed per table. Of course, you can refer to the original column name *inserted.keycol* directly if you want.

This code generates the following output:

```
keycol  datacol
------- --------
1       Davis
2       Funk
3       Lew
4       Peled
5       Cameron
```

To direct the output rows to a table variable for further use, add the INTO clause. To demonstrate this, first truncate the table T1:

```
TRUNCATE TABLE dbo.T1;
```

Then add to the previous example a declaration of a table variable and an INTO clause, like so:

```
DECLARE @NewRows TABLE(keycol INT, datacol NVARCHAR(40));

INSERT INTO dbo.T1(datacol)
  OUTPUT inserted.$identity, inserted.datacol
  INTO @NewRows(keycol, datacol)
    SELECT lastname
    FROM TSQLV3.HR.Employees
    WHERE country = N'USA';

SELECT keycol, datacol FROM @NewRows;
```

You get the following output showing the contents of the table variable:

```
keycol  datacol
-------  --------
1        Davis
2        Funk
3        Lew
4        Peled
5        Cameron
```

Example for archiving deleted data

To better understand the OUTPUT clause with a DELETE statement, consider a task involving data deletion and a requirement to also archive the rows you're deleting. The archiving can be achieved using the OUTPUT clause in the DELETE statement.

To demonstrate this, first run the following code, which creates a table called Orders with some sample data in tempdb, as well as a table called Orders in a database called Archive to absorb archived orders:

```
IF DB_ID(N'Archive') IS NULL CREATE DATABASE Archive;
GO

USE Archive;
IF OBJECT_ID(N'dbo.Orders', N'U') IS NOT NULL DROP TABLE dbo.Orders;

SELECT ISNULL(orderid, 0) AS orderid, orderdate, empid, custid
INTO dbo.Orders
FROM TSQLV3.Sales.Orders WHERE 1 = 2;

ALTER TABLE dbo.Orders ADD CONSTRAINT PK_Orders PRIMARY KEY(orderid);

USE tempdb;
IF OBJECT_ID(N'dbo.Orders', N'U') IS NOT NULL DROP TABLE dbo.Orders;

SELECT orderid, orderdate, empid, custid INTO dbo.Orders FROM TSQLV3.Sales.Orders;

ALTER TABLE dbo.Orders ADD CONSTRAINT PK_Orders PRIMARY KEY(orderid);

-- Before delete
SELECT orderid, orderdate, empid, custid FROM dbo.Orders;
SELECT orderid, orderdate, empid, custid FROM Archive.dbo.Orders;
```

The last two queries show the contents of the active and archived Orders tables before the deletion.

Suppose you need to delete orders placed prior to 2014 from the active Orders table in tempdb and archive the deleted orders in the Orders table in Archive. You do this with the OUTPUT clause, like so:

```
DELETE FROM dbo.Orders
  OUTPUT
    deleted.orderid,
    deleted.orderdate,
    deleted.empid,
    deleted.custid
  INTO Archive.dbo.Orders
WHERE orderdate < '20140101';
```

If the number of rows you need to delete is large, you can apply the modification-in-chunks technique demonstrated earlier, only this time with the added OUTPUT INTO clause, like so:

```
WHILE 1 = 1
BEGIN
  DELETE TOP (3000) FROM dbo.Orders
    OUTPUT
      deleted.orderid,
      deleted.orderdate,
      deleted.empid,
      deleted.custid
    INTO Archive.dbo.Orders
  WHERE orderdate < '20140101';

  IF @@ROWCOUNT < 3000 BREAK;
END;
```

Run the following queries to show the contents of the active and archived Orders tables after the deletion:

```
SELECT orderid, orderdate, empid, custid FROM dbo.Orders;
SELECT orderid, orderdate, empid, custid FROM Archive.dbo.Orders;
```

Example with the MERGE statement

With the MERGE statement, you have complexity that you don't have with the other statements: how do you know which action affected each output row? For this, SQL Server provides you with the function *$action*, which returns a string with the action 'INSERT', 'UPDATE', or 'DELETE'.

To demonstrate using this function, first repopulate the Customers and CustomersStage tables with new sample data by running the following code:

```
TRUNCATE TABLE dbo.Customers;
TRUNCATE TABLE dbo.CustomersStage;
```

```
INSERT INTO dbo.Customers(custid, companyname, phone, address)
  VALUES(1, 'cust 1', '(111) 111-1111', 'address 1'),
        (2, 'cust 2', '(222) 222-2222', 'address 2'),
        (3, 'cust 3', '(333) 333-3333', 'address 3'),
        (4, 'cust 4', '(444) 444-4444', 'address 4'),
        (5, 'cust 5', '(555) 555-5555', 'address 5');

INSERT INTO dbo.CustomersStage(custid, companyname, phone, address)
  VALUES(2, 'AAAAA', '(222) 222-2222', 'address 2'),
        (3, 'cust 3', '(333) 333-3333', 'address 3'),
        (5, 'BBBBB', 'CCCCC', 'DDDDD'),
        (6, 'cust 6 (new)', '(666) 666-6666', 'address 6'),
        (7, 'cust 7 (new)', '(777) 777-7777', 'address 7');
```

Then run the following MERGE statement using the OUTPUT clause with the *$action* function, also returning the old and new keys of the modified rows:

```
MERGE INTO dbo.Customers AS TGT
USING dbo.CustomersStage AS SRC
  ON TGT.custid = SRC.custid
WHEN MATCHED THEN
  UPDATE SET
    TGT.companyname = SRC.companyname,
    TGT.phone = SRC.phone,
    TGT.address = SRC.address
WHEN NOT MATCHED THEN
  INSERT (custid, companyname, phone, address)
  VALUES (SRC.custid, SRC.companyname, SRC.phone, SRC.address)
WHEN NOT MATCHED BY SOURCE THEN
  DELETE
OUTPUT
  $action AS the_action, deleted.custid AS del_custid, inserted.custid AS ins_custid;
```

This statement generates the following output:

```
the_action del_custid  ins_custid
---------- -----------  -----------
DELETE     1            NULL
UPDATE     2            2
UPDATE     3            3
DELETE     4            NULL
UPDATE     5            5
INSERT     NULL         6
INSERT     NULL         7
```

You can clearly see which action affected the output row. Also observe that with inserted rows deleted columns are NULLs, and with deleted rows inserted columns are NULLs. With updated rows, both inserted and deleted columns have values.

As mentioned earlier, unlike with the INSERT statement, the MERGE statement allows you to refer to the source elements. This capability is beneficial when you need to return elements from the source that were not inserted into the target in the output. To demonstrate this, I'll use the table T1 from the previous INSERT example. First run the following code to truncate the table:

```
TRUNCATE TABLE dbo.T1;
```

Suppose you need to query from the TSQLV3.HR.Employees table *lastname* values of employees from the US and insert those into T1 as *datacol* values. You need to return output rows showing the target *keycol* and *datacol* values, but you also need to return the source keys (*empid* values). Try to accomplish the task using an INSERT statement by running the following code:

```
INSERT INTO dbo.T1(datacol)
  OUTPUT SRC.empid AS sourcekey, inserted.keycol AS targetkey, inserted.datacol AS targetdatacol
    SELECT lastname
    FROM TSQLV3.HR.Employees AS SRC
    WHERE country = N'USA';
```

You get the following error:

```
Msg 4104, Level 16, State 1, Line 1056
The multi-part identifier "SRC.empid" could not be bound.
```

The attempt fails because the INSERT statement doesn't support referring to the source table's elements in the OUTPUT clause. Conversely, the MERGE statement does. So you could implement the task with MERGE by applying an INSERT action; however, an INSERT action is allowed only in the WHEN NOT MATCHED clause, and this clause is applied when the merge predicate is *false*. So the trick is to use a condition that is always *false*, like so:

```
MERGE INTO dbo.T1 AS TGT
USING (SELECT * FROM TSQLV3.HR.Employees WHERE country = N'USA') AS SRC
  ON 1 = 2
WHEN NOT MATCHED THEN
  INSERT (datacol) VALUES(SRC.lastname)
OUTPUT SRC.empid AS sourcekey, inserted.keycol AS targetkey, inserted.datacol AS targetdatacol;
```

This statement succeeds, generating the following output:

```
sourcekey   targetkey   targetdatacol
---------   ---------   -------------
1           1           Davis
2           2           Funk
3           3           Lew
4           4           Peled
8           5           Cameron
```

You can find an example for a practical application of this technique in the article "Copying Data with Dependencies" at *http://sqlmag.com/t-sql/copying-data-dependencies*.

Composable DML

Suppose you need to modify rows in some table and write output information from the modified rows into some target table. Normally, you simply use the OUTPUT INTO clause. But you need to capture only a subset of the output rows—not all of them. As an example, suppose you want to delete all rows representing orders placed prior to 2014 from the Orders table in the tempdb database. You need to archive deleted rows in the Orders table in the Archive database, but only for customers 11 and 42. You don't want to write the entire set of output rows into a stage and then copy only the interesting subset of rows from the stage because this could represent a lot of unnecessary work.

T-SQL supports nesting a DML statement with an OUTPUT clause in an INSERT SELECT statement—a feature known in some platforms as *composable DML*. With this feature, you can achieve tasks such as our *delete with archive* without an intermediate stage, like so:

```
INSERT INTO Archive.dbo.Orders (orderid, orderdate, empid, custid)
  SELECT orderid, orderdate, empid, custid
  FROM ( DELETE FROM dbo.Orders
           OUTPUT
             deleted.orderid,
             deleted.orderdate,
             deleted.empid,
             deleted.custid
         WHERE orderdate < '20140101' ) AS D
  WHERE custid IN (11, 42);
```

Composable DML can also be useful to handle *slowly changing dimensions* (SCD) type 2 in a data warehouse. You can define a derived table based on a MERGE statement that has an OUTPUT clause with a call to the *$action* function. Then, in the outer query, you can filter the output rows that were updated (the action is 'UPDATE'), and insert those into the table as the new version of the rows.

Composable DML is implemented currently in T-SQL in a limited form. You can use this feature only in an INSERT SELECT statement. You can specify a WHERE filter, but you cannot apply any further manipulations like joins or other table operators, grouping, and so on.

Finally, this feature has restrictions similar to those for the OUTPUT clause. The target table can be a permanent table, temporary table, or table variable. The target cannot be a table expression (such as a view), have triggers, or participate in primary key–foreign key relationships.

Conclusion

This chapter covered a number of topics related to data modification. It described some of the bulk-import tools SQL Server supports and the requirements they need to meet in order to be processed with minimal logging. It covered the sequence object, comparing and contrasting it with the identity column property and providing important performance considerations. The chapter covered data deletion and updating topics. It also provided a number of tips for working correctly with the MERGE statement and avoiding possible pitfalls. Finally, the chapter covered the OUTPUT clause, describing practical use cases of the feature.

Working with date and time

Working with date and time is one of the more critical topics that anyone who deals with T-SQL at any level needs to know well. That's because almost every piece of data you store in the database has some kind of date and time element related to it. There are many pitfalls you need to be aware of that can lead to buggy and poorly performing code.

This chapter starts by covering the date and time types Microsoft SQL Server supports, followed by coverage of built-in functions that operate on the inputs of those types. It then covers challenges you face when working with date and time data and provides best practices to handle those. Finally, the chapter covers date and time querying tasks, the inefficiencies in some of the common solutions to those tasks, and creative well-performing solutions.

Date and time data types

The latest version of SQL Server at the date of this writing (SQL Server 2014) supports six date and time data types. The DATETIME and SMALLDATETIME types are longstanding features in the product. The rest of the types—DATE, TIME, DATETIME2, and DATETIMEOFFSET—are later additions that were introduced in SQL Server 2008. Table 7-1 provides the specifications of the supported date and time types.

The rule of thumb in choosing a type is to use the smallest one that covers your needs in terms of date range, precision, functionality, and API support. The smaller the type is, the less storage it uses. With large tables, the saving add up, resulting in fewer reads to process queries, which in turn translates to faster queries.

The more veteran types, DATETIME and SMALLDATETIME, are still quite widely used, especially the former. That's mainly because of legacy data, code, and habits. People usually don't rush to alter types of columns and related code because of the complexities involved, unless there's a compelling reason to do so. Also, when you need to store both date and time and don't need precision finer than a minute, SMALLDATETIME is still the most economic choice.

In terms of the supported range of dates, for the types DATE, DATETIME2, and DATETIMEOFFSET, SQL Server uses the proleptic Gregorian calendar. This calendar extends support for dates that precede those that are supported by the Gregorian calendar, which was introduced in 1582. For details, see *http://en.wikipedia.org/wiki/Proleptic_Gregorian_calendar*.

TABLE 7-1 Date and time data types

Data type	Storage (in bytes)	Date range	Precision	Recommended entry format and example
DATETIME	8	January 1, 1753 through December 31, 9999	3 1/3 milliseconds	'YYYYMMDD hh:mm:ss.nnn' '20090212 12:30:15.123'
SMALLDATETIME	4	January 1, 1900 through June 6, 2079	1 minute	'YYYYMMDD hh:mm' '20090212 12:30'
DATE	3	January 1, 0001 through December 31, 9999	1 day	'YYYYMMDD' '20090212'
TIME(p)	3 to 5		100 nanoseconds	'hh:mm:ss.nnnnnnn' '12:30:15.1234567'
DATETIME2(p)	6 to 8	January 1, 0001 through December 31, 9999	100 nanoseconds	'YYYY-MM-DD hh:mm:ss.nnnnnnn' '2009-02-12 2:30:15.1234567'
DATETIMEOFFSET(p)	8 to 10	January 1, 0001 through December 31, 9999	100 nanoseconds	'YYYY-MM-DD hh:mm:ss.nnnnnnn [+|-]hh:mm' '2009-02-12 12:30:15.1234567 +02:00'

If you do need a separation between date and time, you should use DATE and TIME, respectively. It's more common to need to store date-only information, like order date, shipped date, invoice date, and so on. The DATE type is the most economic choice for such information. If you need to store time-only information, like business opening and closing times, the TIME type is the most economic option.

One of the trickier parts of working with the DATETIME type is its limited and awkward precision of 3 1/3 milliseconds, rounded to the nearest tick (for example, 0, 3, 7, 10, 13, 17, and so on). If this precision is not sufficient for you, you will have to use one of the other types. For example, DATETIME2 supports a level of precision of up to 100 nanoseconds. Also, the rounding treatment of this type can create problems, as I will describe later in the "Rounding issues" section.

The types TIME, DATETIME2, and DATETIMEOFFSET all support a level of precision of up to 100 nanoseconds. If you don't need such fine precision, you can specify the level of precision in parentheses as a fraction of a second: 0 means one-second precision, and 7 (the default) means 100-nanosecond precision. Make sure you specify the lowest precision you need explicitly because this can save you up to two bytes of storage per value. For example, DATETIME(3) gives you one-millisecond precision and 7 bytes of storage instead of the maximum of 8 bytes.

As for DATETIMEOFFSET, this type is similar to DATETIME2 in that it stores the combined date and time values with up to 100-nanosecond precision. In addition, it stores the offset from UTC. This is the only type that captures the true meaning of the time *when* and *where* it was collected. With all other types, to know the true meaning of the value, you need extra information recorded such as time zone and daylight saving time state. Even though the DATETIMEOFFSET type doesn't store the actual time zone and daylight saving time state, the value stored does take those into consideration. For example, suppose you need to store the date and time value November 1, 2015 at 1:30 AM, Pacific Daylight Time. The Pacific Time Zone (PTZ) switches from Pacific Daylight Time (PDT) to Pacific

Standard Time (PST) on November 1, 2015 at 2:00 AM, setting the clock one hour backward to 1:00 AM. So, November 1, 2015, 1:30 AM, PDT is at an offset of –7 hours from UTC, which at that point is November 1, 2015, 8:30 AM. An hour later, November 1, 2015, 1:30 AM, PST is at an offset of –8 hours from UTC, which at that point is November 1, 2015, 9:30 AM. With the DATETIMEOFFSET type, you can correctly capture the two date and time values collected in PTZ as '20151101 01:30:00.0000000 –07:00' and '20151101 01:30:00.0000000 –08:00'. You can also capture the current date and time as a DATETIMEOFFSET value using the SYSDATETIMEOFFSET function. (You'll read more on date and time functions shortly.) Suppose you ran the following code in 2015 a few seconds before the switch from PDT to PST and a few seconds after:

```
SELECT SYSDATETIMEOFFSET();
```

I actually changed my computer clock to a few seconds before the switch and then ran the code before and after the switch. I got the following output before the switch:

```
-----------------------------------
2015-11-01 01:59:43.8788709 -07:00
```

I got the following output after the switch:

```
-----------------------------------
2015-11-01 01:00:03.4339354 -08:00
```

As you can see, the true meaning of the date and time values are correctly captured.

As mentioned, if you store a value in one of the other types, like DATETIME2, you need to record extra information to capture the value's true meaning.

Some people would like to see more time zone–related capabilities in the product, like capturing the time zone name, daylight saving time state, and more.

The date and time types and functions that are supported by SQL Server do not support leap seconds. A *leap second* is a one-second adjustment that is occasionally applied to UTC to keep it close to mean solar time (the time as reckoned by the sun's position in the sky). The adjustment compensates for a drift in mean solar time from atomic time as a result of irregularities in the earth's rotation. For example, on June 30, 2012, UTC inserted a positive leap second to the last minute of the day, so the time in the last second of the day was 23:59:60, followed by midnight. In a similar way, UTC also supports the concept of a *negative leap second*, where the last second of the day would be 23:59:58, followed by midnight. The date and time types and functions in SQL Server ignore the concept of leap seconds. So you can neither represent a date and time value such as '20120630 23:59:60', nor account for the leap seconds by using functions like DATEADD and DATEDIFF.

As for functions that return the current date and time values like SYSDATETIME, they return the values based on Microsoft Windows time, which also ignores leap seconds. The Windows Time service does receive a packet that includes a leap second from the time server, but in a sense, it ignores it. It doesn't add or remove a second to the last minute of the day like UTC does; rather, it resolves the one-second time difference created between the local computer's clock and the correct time in the next time synchronization. This is pretty much like correcting a time difference between the local computer's clock and the correct time for any other reason, like for the inaccuracies of the internal computer's clock rate. If the time difference is small, the local clock is adjusted gradually to allow it to converge toward the correct time; if the time difference is larger, it is adjusted immediately. If you need to take leap seconds into consideration in your calculations (for example, if you want to determine the difference in seconds between two UTC date and time values), you need to maintain a leap-seconds table and consult it when making your calculation.

All six supported date and time types represent a point in time. A big missing piece in SQL Server is native support for intervals of date and time in the form of a data type, related functionality, and optimization. Later in the chapter in the "Intervals" section, I will cover the current challenges in creating efficient solutions for common tasks involving date and time intervals.

Date and time functions

This section covers date and time functions supported by SQL Server. I'm going to only briefly go over the available functions and their purpose and spend more time on less trivial aspects. For full details on the functions, consult books online using the following URL: *http://msdn.microsoft.com/en-us/ library/ms186724(v=sql.120).aspx.*

SQL Server supports six functions that return the current date and time:

```
SELECT
    GETDATE()           AS [GETDATE],
    CURRENT_TIMESTAMP   AS [CURRENT_TIMESTAMP],
    GETUTCDATE()        AS [GETUTCDATE],
    SYSDATETIME()       AS [SYSDATETIME],
    SYSUTCDATETIME()    AS [SYSUTCDATETIME],
    SYSDATETIMEOFFSET() AS [SYSDATETIMEOFFSET];
```

GETDATE returns the current date and time of the machine on which the SQL Server instance is installed as a DATETIME value. CURRENT_TIMESTAMP (observe the lack of parentheses) is the same as GETDATE, but it is the standard version of the function. GETUTCDATE returns the current UTC date and time as a DATETIME value. SYSDATETIME and SYSUTCDATETIME are higher-precision versions of GETDATE and GETUTCDATE, respectively, returning the results as DATETIME2 values. Finally, SYSDATETIMEOFFSET returns the current date and time value including the current offset from UTC, taking daylight saving time state into consideration. As an example, in a system set to the Pacific Time Zone, during Pacific Standard Time (PST) the function will return the offset –08:00, whereas during Pacific Daylight Time (PDT) it will return the offset –07:00. Using the SYSDATETIMEOFFSET function is the best way in SQL Server to capture the true meaning of the current date and time where and when the value was collected.

There are no built-in functions returning the current date and the current time. To get those, simply cast the SYSDATETIME function's result to the DATE and TIME types, respectively, like so:

```
SELECT
  CAST(SYSDATETIME() AS DATE) AS [current_date],
  CAST(SYSDATETIME() AS TIME) AS [current_time];
```

The DATEPART function extracts the specified part of the input date and time value. For example, the following code extracts the month number and the weekday number of the input date:

```
SELECT
  DATEPART(month,   '20150212')   AS monthnum,
  DATEPART(weekday, '20150212') AS weekdaynum;
```

Note that the weekday number that the function will return depends on the effective language for the connected login. For example, the input date February 12, 2015, is a Thursday. Under *us_english*, the function will return the weekday number 5, and under British, it will return 4. Later in the chapter in the "Identifying weekdays" section I will provide techniques to control when the week starts as part of the calculation.

The DATEPART function supports a part called *TZoffset*, which you use to extract the offset of an input DATETIMEOFFSET value from UTC. There's no part you can use to extract the daylight saving time state, because this information is not stored with the value. There's no built-in function to get the current daylight saving time state, but there are a number of ways to achieve this.

One option is to store in a table the current system's time zone offset from UTC. For example, in a system configured with the Pacific Time Zone, you store the value –480 (for 480 minutes behind UTC) regardless of the current daylight saving time state. Then, to get the current daylight saving time state, compare the stored value with the result of the expression *DATEPART(TZoffset, SYSDATE-TIMEOFFSET())*. If they are the same, daylight saving time is off; otherwise, it's on.

Getting the current daylight saving time state without storing time zone info in a table is trickier. You can compute this information by querying the registry, but in SQL Server this requires you to use the undocumented and unsupported extended procedure *xp_regread*. The registry key *Bias* in the hive SYSTEM\CurrentControlSet\Control\TimeZoneInformation holds the time bias for the configured time zone. It is specified as the offset in minutes UTC is from the configured time zone. For example, UTC is +480 minutes from Pacific Time, not taking daylight saving time state into consideration. Using the expression *DATEPART(TZoffset, SYSDATETIMEOFFSET())*, you get the active offset of the local time from UTC, taking daylight saving time states into consideration. So under PST, you get –480 and under PDT you get –420. To get the current daylight saving time state, collect the value of the *Bias* key into a local variable (call it *@bias*), and return the result of the computation *SIGN(DATEPART(TZoffset, SYSDATETIMEOFFSET()) + @bias)*. Here's the code required to achieve this:

```
DECLARE @bias AS INT;

EXEC master.dbo.xp_regread
  'HKEY_LOCAL_MACHINE',
  'SYSTEM\CurrentControlSet\Control\TimeZoneInformation',
  'Bias',
  @bias OUTPUT;

SELECT
  SYSDATETIMEOFFSET() currentdatetimeoffset,
  DATEPART(TZoffset, SYSDATETIMEOFFSET()) AS currenttzoffset,
  SIGN(DATEPART(TZoffset, SYSDATETIMEOFFSET()) + @bias) AS currentdst;
```

Suppose you ran this code in a system configured with the Pacific Time Zone on May 5, 2015 at noon. Your output would look like this:

```
currentdatetimeoffset                 currenttzoffset currentdst
------------------------------------- --------------- -----------
2015-05-05 12:00:00.0000000 -07:00    -420            1
```

If you're looking for a supported way to get the current daylight saving time state, you can use a CLR function. Return the result of the *IsDaylightSavingTime* method, applied to the property *Now* of the *DateTime* class. (*DateTime.Now* returns a *DateTime* object that is set to the current date and time on this computer.) Here's the CLR C# code defining such a function called *IsDST*:

```
using System;
using System.Data.SqlTypes;
using Microsoft.SqlServer.Server;

public partial class TimeZone
{
    [SqlFunction(IsDeterministic = false, DataAccess = DataAccessKind.None)]
    public static SqlBoolean IsDST()
    {
        return DateTime.Now.IsDaylightSavingTime();
    }
}
```

If you're not familiar with developing and deploying CLR code, see Chapter 9, "Programmable objects," for details.

Assuming you created a .dll file called C:\Temp\TimeZone\TimeZone\bin\Debug\TimeZone.dll with the assembly, use the following code to deploy it in SQL Server:

```
USE TSQLV3;

EXEC sys.sp_configure 'CLR Enabled', 1;
RECONFIGURE WITH OVERRIDE;

IF OBJECT_ID(N'dbo.IsDST', N'FS') IS NOT NULL DROP FUNCTION dbo.IsDST;
IF EXISTS(SELECT * FROM sys.assemblies WHERE name = N'TimeZone') DROP ASSEMBLY TimeZone;

CREATE ASSEMBLY TimeZone FROM 'C:\Temp\TimeZone\TimeZone\bin\Debug\TimeZone.dll';
GO
CREATE FUNCTION dbo.IsDST() RETURNS BIT EXTERNAL NAME TimeZone.TimeZone.IsDST;
```

Once the function is deployed, test it by running the following code:

```
SELECT
  SYSDATETIMEOFFSET() currentdatetimeoffset,
  DATEPART(TZoffset, SYSDATETIMEOFFSET()) AS currenttzoffset,
  dbo.IsDST() AS currentdst;
```

Assuming you ran the code on May 5, 2015 and your system's time zone is configured to Pacific Time, you will get the following output:

```
currentdatetimeoffset              currenttzoffset currentdst
---------------------------------- --------------- ----------
2015-05-05 12:00:00.0000000 -07:00 -420               1
```

 Note If you manually change the time zone in the system to one with a different day-light saving time state (for example, from Pacific Time to Coordinate Universal Time), the function might not return the correct daylight saving time state because of the caching of the old value. Any of the following actions will flush the cached value: invoking the method *System.Globalization.CultureInfo.CurrentCulture.ClearCachedData()*, dropping and re-creating the assembly, and recycling the SQL Server service.

The functions DAY, MONTH, and YEAR are simply abbreviations of the DATEPART function for extracting the respective parts of the input value. Here's an example for using these functions:

```
SELECT
    DAY('20150212') AS theday,
    MONTH('20150212') AS themonth,
    YEAR('20150212') AS theyear;
```

The DATENAME function extracts the requested part name from the input value, returning it as a character string. For some parts, the function is language-dependent. For example, the expression *DATENAME(month, '20150212')* returns February when the effective language is *us_english* and *febbraio* when it's Italian.

The ISDATE function accepts an input character string and indicates whether it's convertible to the DATETIME type. If for whatever reason you need to store date and time values in a character string column in a table, you can use the ISDATE function in a CHECK constraint to allow only valid values. The following example validates two input values:

```
SELECT
    ISDATE('20150212') AS isdate20150212,
    ISDATE('20150230') AS isdate20150230;
```

This code generates the following output showing that the first input represents a valid date and the second doesn't:

```
isdate20150212 isdate20150230
-------------- --------------
1              0
```

You use the SWITCHOFFSET function to switch the offset of an input DATETIMEOFFSET value to a desired offset. For example, the following code returns the current date and time value in both offset –05:00 and –08:00, adjusted from the current date and time value with the system's active offset:

```
SELECT
    SWITCHOFFSET(SYSDATETIMEOFFSET(), '-05:00') AS [now as -05:00],
    SWITCHOFFSET(SYSDATETIMEOFFSET(), '-08:00') AS [now as -08:00];
```

For example, if the offset of the input value is +02:00, to return the value with offset −05:00, the function will subtract seven hours from the local time.

The TODATETIMEOFFSET function helps you construct a DATETIMEOFFSET value using a local date and time value and an offset that you provide as inputs. Think of it as a helper function that saves you from messing with the conversion of the inputs to character strings, concatenating them using the right format, and then converting them to DATETIMEOFFSET. Here's an example for using the function:

```
SELECT TODATETIMEOFFSET('20150212 00:00:00.0000000', '-08:00');
```

You can also use the function to merge information from two columns that separately hold the local date and time value and the offset into one DATETIMEOFFSET value, say, as a computed column. For example, suppose you have a table *T1* with columns *dt* holding the local date and time value and *offset* holding the offset from UTC. The following code will add a computed column called *dto* that merges those:

```
ALTER TABLE dbo.T1 ADD dto AS TODATETIMEOFFSET(dt, offset);
```

The DATEADD function adds or subtracts a number of units of a specified part from a given date and time value. For example, the following expression adds one year to the input date:

```
SELECT DATEADD(year, 1, '20150212');
```

There's no DATESUBTRACT function; to achieve subtraction, simply use a negative number of units.

The DATEDIFF function computes the difference between two date and time values in terms of the specified part. For example, the following expression returns the difference in terms of days between two dates:

```
SELECT DATEDIFF(day, '20150212', '20150213');
```

Note that the function ignores any parts in the inputs with a lower level of precision than the specified part. For example, consider the following expression that looks for the difference in years between the two inputs:

```
SELECT DATEDIFF(year, '20151231 23:59:59.9999999', '20160101 00:00:00.0000000');
```

The function ignores the parts of the inputs below the year and therefore concludes that the difference is 1 year, even though in practice the difference is only 100 nanoseconds.

Also note that if the inputs are DATETIMEOFFSET values, the difference is always computed in UTC terms, not in local terms, based on the stored source or target offsets. It can certainly be surprising if you're not aware of this. For example, before you run the following code, try to answer what the result of the calculation should be:

```
DECLARE
  @dto1 AS DATETIMEOFFSET = '20150212 10:30:00.0000000 -08:00',
  @dto2 AS DATETIMEOFFSET = '20150213 22:30:00.0000000 -08:00';

SELECT DATEDIFF(day, @dto1, @dto2);
```

Most people would say the result should be 1, but in practice it is 2. That's because the difference is done between the UTC values, which are 8 hours ahead of the local values. When adjusted to UTC, @dto1 doesn't cross a date boundary, but @dto2 does.

If you want the calculation to be done differently, you first need to determine what you're after exactly. One option is to do the calculation locally when the offsets are the same and return a NULL when they are not. This method is achieved like so:

```
DECLARE
  @dto1 AS DATETIMEOFFSET = '20150212 10:30:00.0000000 -08:00',
  @dto2 AS DATETIMEOFFSET = '20150213 22:30:00.0000000 -08:00';

SELECT
  CASE
    WHEN DATEPART(TZoffset, @dto1) = DATEPART(TZoffset, @dto2)
      THEN DATEDIFF(day, CAST(@dto1 AS DATETIME2), CAST(@dto2 AS DATETIME2))
  END;
```

Keep in mind, however, that under the same configured time zone, values can have different off-sets at different times depending on the daylight saving time state. As mentioned earlier, during PST they will have the offset –08:00 and during PDT they will have –07:00. So another approach is to use either the source or target offset. Here's an example using the target's offset:

```
DECLARE
  @dto1 AS DATETIMEOFFSET = '20150301 23:30:00.0000000 -08:00',
  @dto2 AS DATETIMEOFFSET = '20150401 11:30:00.0000000 -07:00'; -- try also with -08:00

SELECT
  DATEDIFF(day,
    CAST(SWITCHOFFSET(@dto1, DATEPART(TZoffset, @dto2)) AS DATETIME2),
    CAST(@dto2 AS DATETIME2));
```

One of the tricky things about working with the DATEADD and DATEDIFF functions is that they work with four-byte integers, not eight-byte ones. This means that with DATEADD you are limited in the number of units you can add, and with DATEDIFF you are limited in the number of units you can return as the difference. This limitation becomes a problem when you need to express a date and time value as an offset from a certain starting point at some level of precision, and the offset doesn't fit in a four-byte integer. You have a similar problem when you need to apply the inverse calculation.

As an example, suppose you need to express any DATETIME2 value as an offset in multiples of 100 nanoseconds from January 1, in the year 1. The maximum offset you will need to represent is for the date and time value '99991231 23:59:59.9999999', and it is the integer 3155378975999999999. Clearly, a four-byte integer isn't sufficient here; rather, you need an eight-byte one (the BIGINT type). What would have been nice is if SQL Server supported BIGDATEADD and BIGDATEDIFF functions (or DATEADD_BIG and DATEDIFF_BIG, similar to COUNT_BIG) that worked with the BIGINT type as well as a 100-nanosecond part for such purposes. You can find and vote for such feature enhancement requests submitted to Microsoft at the following URLs: *https://connect.microsoft.com/SQLServer/feedback/details/320998* and *https://connect.microsoft.com/SQLServer/feedback/details/783293/*.

Meanwhile, you have to resort to awkward and convoluted alternatives of your own, such as the following DATEDIFF_NS100 inline table-valued function (TVF):

```
USE TSQLV3;

IF OBJECT_ID(N'dbo.DATEDIFF_NS100', N'IF') IS NOT NULL
  DROP FUNCTION dbo.DATEDIFF_NS100;
GO
CREATE FUNCTION dbo.DATEDIFF_NS100(@dt1 AS DATETIME2, @dt2 AS DATETIME2) RETURNS TABLE
AS
RETURN
  SELECT
    CAST(864000000000 AS BIGINT) * (dddiff - subdd) + ns100diff as ns100
  FROM ( VALUES( CAST(@dt1 AS TIME), CAST(@dt2 AS TIME),
                 DATEDIFF(dd, @dt1, @dt2)
               ) )
        AS D(t1, t2, dddiff)
    CROSS APPLY ( VALUES( CASE WHEN t1 > t2 THEN 1 ELSE 0 END ) )
      AS A1(subdd)
    CROSS APPLY ( VALUES( CAST(864000000000 AS BIGINT) * subdd
        + (CAST(10000000 AS BIGINT) * DATEDIFF(ss, '00:00', t2) + DATEPART(ns, t2)/100)
        - (CAST(10000000 AS BIGINT) * DATEDIFF(ss, '00:00', t1) + DATEPART(ns, t1)/100) ) )
      AS A2(ns100diff);
GO
```

The function splits the calculation into differences expressed in terms of days, seconds within the day, and remaining nanoseconds—converting each difference to the corresponding multiple of 100 nanoseconds. The reason I use an inline TVF and not a scalar one is performance related. I explain this in Chapter 9 in the section "User-defined functions."

Use the following code to test the function:

```
SELECT ns100
FROM dbo.DATEDIFF_NS100('20150212 00:00:00.0000001', '20160212 00:00:00.0000000');
```

You will get the output 315359999999999.

Sometimes you need to compute the difference not based on just one part, and rather go gradually from the less precise parts to the more precise parts. For example, suppose you want to express the difference between '20150212 00:00:00.0000001' and '20160212 00:00:00.0000000' as 11 months, 30 days, 23 hours, 59 minutes, 59 seconds, and 999999900 nanoseconds. You can achieve this using the following inline TVF DATEDIFFPARTS:

```
IF OBJECT_ID(N'dbo.DATEDIFFPARTS', N'IF') IS NOT NULL DROP FUNCTION dbo.DATEDIFFPARTS;
GO
CREATE FUNCTION dbo.DATEDIFFPARTS(@dt1 AS DATETIME2, @dt2 AS DATETIME2) RETURNS TABLE
/* The function works correctly provided that @dt2 >= @dt1 */
AS
RETURN
  SELECT
    yydiff - subyy AS yy,
    (mmdiff - submm) % 12 AS mm,
    DATEDIFF(day, DATEADD(mm, mmdiff - submm, dt1), dt2) - subdd AS dd,
    nsdiff / CAST(3600000000000 AS BIGINT) % 60 AS hh,
```

```
      nsdiff / CAST(60000000000 AS BIGINT) % 60 AS mi,
      nsdiff / 1000000000 % 60 AS ss,
      nsdiff % 1000000000 AS ns
   FROM ( VALUES( @dt1, @dt2,
                   CAST(@dt1 AS TIME), CAST(@dt2 AS TIME),
                   DATEDIFF(yy, @dt1, @dt2),
                   DATEDIFF(mm, @dt1, @dt2),
                   DATEDIFF(dd, @dt1, @dt2)
                 ) )
         AS D(dt1, dt2, t1, t2, yydiff, mmdiff, dddiff)
      CROSS APPLY ( VALUES( CASE WHEN DATEADD(yy, yydiff, dt1) > dt2 THEN 1 ELSE 0 END,
                            CASE WHEN DATEADD(mm, mmdiff, dt1) > dt2 THEN 1 ELSE 0 END,
                            CASE WHEN DATEADD(dd, dddiff, dt1) > dt2 THEN 1 ELSE 0 END ) )
         AS A1(subyy, submm, subdd)
      CROSS APPLY ( VALUES( CAST(86400000000000 AS BIGINT) * subdd
         + (CAST(1000000000 AS BIGINT) * DATEDIFF(ss, '00:00', t2) + DATEPART(ns, t2))
         - (CAST(1000000000 AS BIGINT) * DATEDIFF(ss, '00:00', t1) + DATEPART(ns, t1)) ) )
         AS A2(nsdiff);
GO
```

The function computes the year, remaining month, and remaining day differences as *yy*, *mm*, and *dd*, respectively. Those take into consideration a case where one unit of the part needs to be subtracted; this is required when adding the original difference in terms of that part to the source value exceeds the target value (handled in the table expression *A1*). The difference in terms of the remaining parts (hours, minutes, seconds, and nanoseconds) is computed based on the nanosecond difference (*nsdiff*) between the time portions of the source and the target (handled in the table expression *A2*).

Run the following code to test the function:

```
SELECT yy, mm, dd, hh, mi, ss, ns
FROM dbo.DATEDIFFPARTS('20150212 00:00:00.0000001', '20160212 00:00:00.0000000');
```

You will get the following output:

```
yy  mm  dd  hh  mi  ss  ns
--- --- --- --- --- --- ----------
0   11  30  23  59  59  999999900
```

Recall that earlier I mentioned that the DATEDIFF function ignores the parts in the inputs with a lower level of precision than the specified part. As an example, I explained that the expression *DATEDIFF(year, '20151231 23:59:59.9999999', '20160101 00:00:00.0000000')* returns a 1-year difference even though in practice the difference is only 100 nanoseconds. You can use the DATEDIFFPARTS function to compute a more precise difference, like so:

```
SELECT yy, mm, dd, hh, mi, ss, ns
FROM dbo.DATEDIFFPARTS('20151231 23:59:59.9999999', '20160101 00:00:00.0000000');
```

You will get the following output:

```
yy  mm  dd  hh  mi  ss  ns
--- --- --- --- --- --- ----------
0   0   0   0   0   0   100
```

Note that, as the comment in the function's definition says, the function works correctly provided that *@dt2* >= *@dt1*, assuming you have a way to enforce this using a constraint or by other means. If you can't guarantee this and need the function to be more generic and robust, you can swap the inputs when *@dt2* < *@dt1* and add to the output a column called *sgn* with the sign of the result, like so:

```
IF OBJECT_ID(N'dbo.DATEDIFFPARTS', N'IF') IS NOT NULL DROP FUNCTION dbo.DATEDIFFPARTS;
GO
CREATE FUNCTION dbo.DATEDIFFPARTS(@dt1 AS DATETIME2, @dt2 AS DATETIME2) RETURNS TABLE
AS
RETURN
  SELECT
    sgn,
    yydiff - subyy AS yy,
    (mmdiff - submm) % 12 AS mm,
    DATEDIFF(day, DATEADD(mm, mmdiff - submm, dt1), dt2) - subdd AS dd,
    nsdiff / CAST(3600000000000 AS BIGINT) % 60 AS hh,
    nsdiff / CAST(60000000000 AS BIGINT) % 60 AS mi,
    nsdiff / 1000000000 % 60 AS ss,
    nsdiff % 1000000000 AS ns
  FROM ( VALUES( CASE WHEN @dt1 > @dt2 THEN @dt2 ELSE @dt1 END,
                 CASE WHEN @dt1 > @dt2 THEN @dt1 ELSE @dt2 END,
                 CASE WHEN @dt1 < @dt2 THEN 1
                      WHEN @dt1 = @dt2 THEN 0
                      WHEN @dt1 > @dt2 THEN -1 END ) ) AS D(dt1, dt2, sgn)
    CROSS APPLY ( VALUES( CAST(dt1 AS TIME), CAST(dt2 AS TIME),
                          DATEDIFF(yy, dt1, dt2),
                          DATEDIFF(mm, dt1, dt2),
                          DATEDIFF(dd, dt1, dt2) ) )
      AS A1(t1, t2, yydiff, mmdiff, dddiff)
    CROSS APPLY ( VALUES( CASE WHEN DATEADD(yy, yydiff, dt1) > dt2 THEN 1 ELSE 0 END,
                          CASE WHEN DATEADD(mm, mmdiff, dt1) > dt2 THEN 1 ELSE 0 END,
                          CASE WHEN DATEADD(dd, dddiff, dt1) > dt2 THEN 1 ELSE 0 END ) )
      AS A2(subyy, submm, subdd)
    CROSS APPLY ( VALUES( CAST(86400000000000 AS BIGINT) * subdd
        + (CAST(1000000000 AS BIGINT) * DATEDIFF(ss, '00:00', t2) + DATEPART(ns, t2))
        - (CAST(1000000000 AS BIGINT) * DATEDIFF(ss, '00:00', t1) + DATEPART(ns, t1)) ) )
      AS A3(nsdiff);
GO
```

Use the following code to test the function:

```
SELECT sgn, yy, mm, dd, hh, mi, ss, ns
FROM dbo.DATEDIFFPARTS('20160212 00:00:00.0000000', '20150212 00:00:00.0000001');
```

You will get the following output:

```
sgn  yy  mm  dd  hh  mi  ss  ns
---- --- --- --- --- --- --- ----------
-1   0   11  30  23  59  59  999999900
```

Of course, life would have been much easier had SQL Server supported an INTERVAL type like some of the other relational database management systems (RDBMSs) do. (I am holding my breath in hope of seeing such support in SQL Server in the future.)

SQL Server 2012 added support for a few more date and time functions, which I will describe next.

You get six helper functions that help you construct date and time values of the six types from their numeric components, like so:

```
SELECT
  DATEFROMPARTS(2015, 02, 12),
  DATETIME2FROMPARTS(2015, 02, 12, 13, 30, 5, 1, 7),
  DATETIMEFROMPARTS(2015, 02, 12, 13, 30, 5, 997),
  DATETIMEOFFSETFROMPARTS(2015, 02, 12, 13, 30, 5, 1, -8, 0, 7),
  SMALLDATETIMEFROMPARTS(2015, 02, 12, 13, 30),
  TIMEFROMPARTS(13, 30, 5, 1, 7);
```

These functions help you avoid the need to mess with constructing character-string representations of the date and time value. Without these functions, you need to worry about using the right style so that when you convert the character string to the target date and time type, it converts correctly.

The EOMONTH function returns for the given input the respective end-of-month date, typed as DATE. For example, the following code returns the last date of the current month:

```
SELECT EOMONTH(SYSDATETIME());
```

This function supports a second optional parameter you use to indicate a month offset. For example, the following code returns the last date of the previous month:

```
SELECT EOMONTH(SYSDATETIME(), -1);
```

You use the PARSE function to parse an input string as a specified target type, optionally providing a .NET culture name for the conversion. It actually uses .NET behind the scenes. This function can be used as an alternative to the CONVERT function; you can use it to provide a user-friendly culture name as opposed to the more cryptic style number used with the CONVERT function. For example, suppose you need to convert the character-string value '01/02/15' to a DATE type. With CONVERT, you need to specify style 1 to get US English–based conversion (MDY) and style 3 to get British-based conversion (DMY). Using PARSE, you specify the more user-friendly culture names 'en-US' and 'en-GB', respectively, like so:

```
SELECT
  PARSE('01/02/15' AS DATE USING 'en-US') AS [US English],
  PARSE('01/02/15' AS DATE USING 'en-GB') AS [British];
```

However, you should be aware that while the PARSE function might be more user friendly to use than CONVERT, it's significantly more expensive, as I will demonstrate shortly.

One of the tricky parts with all conversion functions (CAST, CONVERT, and PARSE) is that if the conversion fails, the whole query fails. There are cases where you have bad source data and you're not certain that all inputs will successfully convert to the target type. Suppose that for inputs that don't convert successfully you want to return a NULL as opposed to letting the entire query fail. It's not always simple to come up with a CASE expression that applies logic that covers all potential causes for conversion failure. To address this, SQL Server provides you with TRY_ versions of the three conversion functions (TRY_CONVERT, TRY_CAST, and TRY_PARSE). These functions simply return a NULL if the conversion isn't successful.

As an example, the following code issues two attempts to convert a character string to a DATE:

```
SELECT TRY_CONVERT(DATE, '20150212', 112) AS try1, TRY_CONVERT(DATE, '20150230', 112) AS try2;
```

The first conversion is successful, but the second one isn't. This code doesn't fail; rather, it returns the following output:

```
try1       try2
---------- ----------
2015-02-12 NULL
```

The TRY_ functions seem to perform similarly to their original counterparts.

You use the FORMAT function to convert an input value to a character string based on a .NET format string, optionally specifying a .NET culture name. Like PARSE, it uses .NET behind the scenes and performs badly, as I will demonstrate shortly. As an example, the following code formats the current date and time value as short date ('d') using US English and British cultures:

```
SELECT
  FORMAT(SYSDATETIME(), 'd', 'en-US') AS [US English],
  FORMAT(SYSDATETIME(), 'd', 'en-GB') AS [British];
```

Assuming you ran this code on May 8, 2015, you get the following output:

```
US English  British
----------- -----------
5/8/2015    08/05/2015
```

Here's an example for formatting the current date and time using the explicit format 'MM/dd/yyyy':

```
SELECT FORMAT(SYSDATETIME(), 'MM/dd/yyyy') AS dt;
```

As mentioned, the PARSE and FORMAT functions are quite inefficient, especially when compared to using more native functions, which were internally developed with a low-level language and not .NET. I'll demonstrate this with a performance test. Run the following code to create a temporary table called #T, and fill it with 1,000,000 rows:

```
SELECT orderdate AS dt, CONVERT(CHAR(10), orderdate, 101) AS strdt
INTO #T
FROM PerformanceV3.dbo.Orders;
```

The table #T has two columns: dt holds dates as DATE-typed values, and strdt holds dates as CHAR(10)-typed values using US English format.

The first test compares the performance of PARSE with that of CONVERT to parse the values in the column strdt as DATE. To exclude the time it takes to present the values in SQL Server Management Studio (SSMS), I ran the test with results discarded (after enabling the Discard Results After Execution option under Results, Grid, in the Query Options dialog box). Here's the code testing the PARSE function:

```
SELECT PARSE(strdt AS DATE USING 'en-US') AS mydt
FROM #T;
```

It took this code with the PARSE function over three minutes to complete on my system.

Here's the code testing the CONVERT function to achieve the same task:

```
SELECT CONVERT(DATE, strdt, 101) AS mydt
FROM #T;
```

It took this code with the CONVERT function under a second to complete.

The second test compares FORMAT with CONVERT to format the values in *dt* as character strings using the format '*MM/dd/yyyy*'.

Here's the code to achieve the task using the FORMAT function, which took 28 seconds to complete:

```
SELECT FORMAT(dt, 'MM/dd/yyyy') AS mystrdt
FROM #T;
```

Here's the code to achieve the task using the CONVERT function, which took under a second to complete:

```
SELECT CONVERT(CHAR(10), dt, 101) AS mystrdt
FROM #T;
```

What's interesting is that you can achieve much better performance than the supplied FORMAT function by implementing your own CLR-based date and time formatting function. You simply invoke the *ToString* method against the input date and time value, and provide the input format string as input to the method, as in *(SqlString)dt.Value.ToString(formatstring.Value)*. In my test, the query with the user-defined CLR function finished in three seconds; that's 10 times faster than with the supplied FORMAT function. In short, you better stay away from the supplied PARSE and FORMAT functions and use the suggested alternatives.

When you're done, run the following code for cleanup:

```
DROP TABLE #T;
```

SQL Server 2014 doesn't add support for any new date and time functions.

Challenges working with date and time

You will encounter many challenges when working with date and time data, and they are related to writing both correct and efficient code. This section covers challenges like working with literals; identifying the weekday of a date; handling date-only and time-only data; handling first, last, previous, and next date calculations; handling search arguments; and dealing with rounding issues.

Literals

Handling date and time literals is an area that tends to cause quite a lot of trouble, often leading to bugs in the code. This section describes the complexities involved with handling date and time literals and provides recommendations and best practices to help you avoid getting into trouble.

For starters, note that although standard SQL defines date and time literals, T-SQL doesn't support those. The practice in T-SQL is to express those as character strings. Then, based on SQL Server's implicit conversion rules, which take into consideration things like context and date type precedence, the character string gets converted to the target date and time type. For example, suppose that in the filter *WHERE dt = '20150212'*, the column *dt* is of a DATE type. SQL Server sees a DATE type of the column on the left side and a VARCHAR type of the literal on the right side, and its implicit conversion rules tell it to convert the literal to DATE.

The part where this conversion gets tricky is in how SQL Server interprets the value. With time literals, there's no ambiguity, but some date literal formats are ambiguous, with their interpretation being language dependent. That is, their interpretation depends on the effective language of the login running the code (which is set as the login's default language and can be overwritten at the session level with the SET LANGUAGE and SET DATEFORMAT options). Take the following query as an example:

```
USE TSQLV3;

SELECT orderid, custid, empid, orderdate
FROM Sales.Orders
WHERE orderdate = '02/12/2015';
```

Whether SQL Server will interpret the date as February 12, 2015 or December 2, 2015 depends on your effective language. For example, under British your session's DATEFORMAT setting is set to *dmy*, and hence the value will be interpreted as December 2, 2015. You can verify this by overwriting the current session's language using the SET LANGUAGE command, like so:

```
SET LANGUAGE British;

SELECT orderid, custid, empid, orderdate
FROM Sales.Orders
WHERE orderdate = '02/12/2015';
```

Apparently, no orders were placed on December 2, 2015, so the output is an empty set:

```
orderid     custid      empid       orderdate
----------- ----------- ----------- ----------
```

Try the same query under US English (where DATEFORMAT is set to *mdy*):

```
SET LANGUAGE us_english;

SELECT orderid, custid, empid, orderdate
FROM Sales.Orders
WHERE orderdate = '02/12/2015';
```

This time, the interpretation is February 12, 2015, and the query returns the following output:

```
orderid      custid       empid        orderdate
-----------  -----------  -----------  ----------
10883        48           8            2015-02-12
10884        45           4            2015-02-12
10885        76           6            2015-02-12
```

As you can see, using an ambiguous format is a bad idea. Different logins running the same code can get different interpretations. Fortunately, a number of formats are considered language neutral, or unambiguous, such as 'YYYYMMDD'. Try this format under both British and US English:

```
SET LANGUAGE British;

SELECT orderid, custid, empid, orderdate
FROM Sales.Orders
WHERE orderdate = '20150212';

SET LANGUAGE us_english;

SELECT orderid, custid, empid, orderdate
FROM Sales.Orders
WHERE orderdate = '20150212';
```

In both cases, you get the same interpretation of February 12, 2015.

If you insist on using a style that, in its raw form, is considered ambiguous, you can get an unambiguous interpretation by applying explicit conversion and providing information about the style you use. You can use the CONVERT function with a style number or the PARSE function with a culture name. For example, the following expressions will give you an *mdy* interpretation:

```
SELECT CONVERT(DATE, '02/12/2015', 101);
SELECT PARSE('02/12/2015' AS DATE USING 'en-US');
```

The following conversions will give you *dmy* interpretation:

```
SELECT CONVERT(DATE, '12/02/2015', 103);
SELECT PARSE('12/02/2015' AS DATE USING 'en-GB');
```

Using the CONVERT function doesn't incur any extra cost compared to implicit conversion because conversion happens one way or the other. But keep in mind the earlier discussion about the inefficiency of the PARSE function. Using PARSE *is* going to cost you more.

For your convenience, Table 7-2 provides the formats that are considered unambiguous for the different date and time types.

TABLE 7-2 Date and time data type formats

Data type	Language-neutral formats	Examples
DATETIME	'YYYYMMDD hh:mm:ss.nnn' 'YYYY-MM-DDThh:mm:ss.nnn' 'YYYYMMDD'	'20090212 12:30:15.123' '2009-02-12T12:30:15.123' '20090212'
SMALLDATETIME	'YYYYMMDD hh:mm' 'YYYY-MM-DDThh:mm' 'YYYYMMDD'	'20090212 12:30' '2009-02-12T12:30' '20090212'
DATE	'YYYYMMDD' 'YYYY-MM-DD'	'20090212' '2009-02-12'
DATETIME2	'YYYYMMDD hh:mm:ss.nnnnnnn' 'YYYY-MM-DD hh:mm:ss.nnnnnnn' 'YYYY-MM-DDThh:mm:ss.nnnnnnn' 'YYYYMMDD' 'YYYY-MM-DD'	'20090212 12:30:15.1234567' '2009-02-12 12:30:15.1234567' '2009-02-12T12:30:15.1234567' '20090212' '2009-02-12'
DATETIMEOFFSET	'YYYYMMDD hh:mm:ss.nnnnnnn [+|-]hh:mm' 'YYYY-MM-DD hh:mm:ss.nnnnnnn [+|-]hh:mm' 'YYYY-MM-DDThh:mm:ss.nnnnnnn' 'YYYYMMDD' 'YYYY-MM-DD'	'20090212 12:30:15.1234567 +02:00' '2009-02-12 12:30:15.1234567 +02:00' '2009-02-12T12:30:15.1234567' '20090212' '2009-02-12'

Important The format 'YYYY-MM-DD' is considered unambiguous for the types DATE, DATETIME2, and DATETIMEOFFSET in accordance with the standard. However, for backward-compatibility reasons, it *is* considered ambiguous for the more veteran types DATETIME and SMALLDATETIME. For example, with the more veteran types, the value '2015-02-12' will be interpreted as December 2, 2015 under British and February 12, 2015 under US English. With the newer types, it's always going to be interpreted as February 12, 2015. This can lead to trouble if you're using one of the veteran types and assuming you'll get a British-like interpretation, and at some point alter the type of the column to one of the newer types, getting a different interpretation. For this reason, I prefer to stick to the format 'YYYYMMDD'. It's unambiguous across all types—with and without a time portion added. Generally, it's recommended to stick to coding habits that give you correct and unambiguous interpretation in all cases.

Identifying weekdays

Suppose that in your application you need to identify the weekday number of an input date. You need to be aware of some complexities involved in such a calculation, and this section provides the details.

To calculate the weekday number of a given date, you can use the DATEPART function with the weekday part (or *dw* for short), as in DATEPART(weekday, SYSDATETIME()) for today's weekday number. You need to be aware that this calculation is language dependent. In the previous section, I explained that your effective language determines a related session option called DATEFORMAT, which in turn determines how date literals are interpreted. In a similar way, your language determines a session option called DATEFIRST, which in turn determines what's considered the first day of the week (*1* means Monday, *2* means Tuesday, ..., *7* means Sunday). You can query the effective setting using the @@DATEFIRST function and overwrite it using the SET DATEFIRST command. However, generally changing such language settings is not recommended because there could be calculations in the session that depend on the login's language perspective. Plus, a cached query plan created with certain language settings cannot be reused by a session with different language settings.

Suppose today is a Thursday and you are computing today's weekday number using the expression *DATEPART(weekday, SYSDATETIME())*. If you are connected with US English as your language, SQL Server sets your session's DATEFIRST setting to *7* (indicating Sunday is the first day of the week); therefore, the expression returns the weekday number *5*. If you are connected with British, SQL Server sets DATEFIRST to *1* (indicating Monday is the first day of the week); therefore, the expression returns the weekday number *4*. If you explicitly set DATEFIRST to, say, *2* (indicating Tuesday is the first day of the week), the expression returns *3*. This is illustrated in Figure 7-1, with the arrow marking the DATEFIRST setting and *x* being the 1-based ordinal representing the result of the expression.

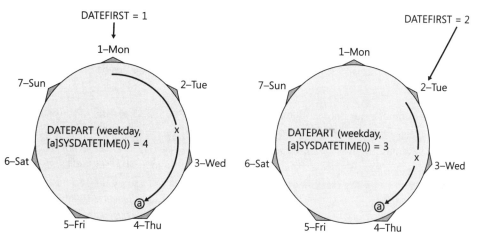

FIGURE 7-1 Language-dependent weekday.

You might run into cases where you need the weekday-number computation to assume *your* chosen first day of the week, ignoring the effective one. You do not want to overwrite any of the existing session's language-related settings; rather, you want to somehow control this in the calculation itself. I can suggest a couple of methods to achieve this. I'll refer to one method as the *diff and modulo* method and the other as the *compensation* method. For the sake of the example, suppose you want to consider Monday as the first day of the week in your calculation.

With the diff and modulo method you choose a date from the past that falls on the same weekday as the one you want to consider as the first day of the week. For this purpose, it's convenient to use dates from the week of the base date (starting with January 1, 1900). That's because the day parts and respective weekdays during this week are nicely aligned with the numbers and respective weekdays that DATEFIRST uses (*1* for Monday, *2* for Tuesday, and so on). As an aside, curiously, for January 1, *1* was also a Monday. So, to consider Monday as the first day of the week, use the date January 1, 1900. Compute the difference in terms of days between that date and the target date (call this difference *diff*). The computation *diff % 7* (% is modulo in T-SQL) will give you *0* for a target date whose weekday is a Monday (because *diff* is a multiplication of 7 in such a case), *1* for a Tuesday, and so on. Because you want to get *1* for the first day of the week, *2* for the second, and so on, simply add 1 to the computation. Here's the complete expression in T-SQL giving you the weekday number of today's date when considering Monday as the first day of the week:

```
SELECT DATEDIFF(day, '19000101', SYSDATETIME()) % 7 + 1;
```

To consider Sunday as the first day of the week, use the value *'19000107'* as the starting point. If there's some reason for you to consider Tuesday as the first day of the week, use the value *'19000102'* as the starting point, and so on.

Another method to compute the weekday number with control over when the week starts is what I refer to as the *compensation* method. You use the DATEPART function with the weekday part, but instead of applying the function to the original input date, you apply it to an adjusted input date to compensate for the effect of changes in the DATEFIRST setting. Adjusting the input date by moving it @@DATEFIRST days forward neutralizes the effect of direct or indirect changes to the DATEFIRST setting.

To understand how this works, first make sure you have some coffee beside you, and then consider the following.

Let *a* be the original input date, and let *b* be the effective DATEFIRST setting (also the output of @@DATEFIRST). Let *x* be the original computation *DATEPART(weekday, a)*, which is language dependent. To get a language-neutral computation, use *DATEPART(weekday, DATEADD(day, b, a))*. If *b* changes by a certain delta (such as a different language resulting in a different DATEFIRST setting), both the starting point for the calculation and the adjusted date change by the same delta, meaning that the calculation's result remains the same. In other words, adding *b* (@@DATEFIRST) days to the date you're checking compensates for any direct or indirect changes to DATEFIRST.

Now you know that regardless of the login's language and the effective DATEFIRST setting, the computation *DATEPART(weekday, DATEADD(day, @@DATEFIRST, @input))* will always return the same output for the same input. By default, the calculation behaves as if Sunday is the first day of the week. This means it will always return *1* for a Sunday, *2* for a Monday, and so on. Try it. If you want to consider a different weekday as the first day of the week, you need to further adjust the input by subtracting a constant number of days (call it *c*). Luckily, *c* and the weekday it represents are aligned with the numbers and respective weekdays DATEFIRST uses (*1* for Monday, *2* for Tuesday, and so on). So, if you want to consider Monday as the first day of the week, use the expression *DATEPART(weekday, DATEADD(day, @@DATEFIRST – 1, @input))*. You can test the calculation with today's date as input by using the following code:

```
SELECT DATEPART(weekday, DATEADD(day, @@DATEFIRST - 1, SYSDATETIME()));
```

The compensation method is illustrated in Figure 7-2, using today's date as input, assuming today is a Thursday. Remember *a* is the input date, *b* is @@DATEFIRST, *c* is the constant you need to subtract (*1* for Monday), and *x* is the result of the original computation *DATEPART(weekday, a)*.

The illustration to the left represents an environment with DATEFIRST set to *1* (where normally Monday is the first day of the week), and the illustration to the right represents an environment with DATEFIRST set to *2* (Tuesday is the first day of the week). Observe how in both cases the result is *4* assuming Monday is the first day of the week for the calculation.

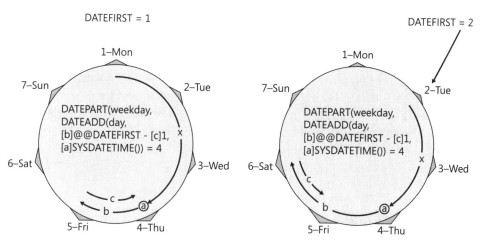

FIGURE 7-2 Language-neutral weekday.

Handling date-only or time-only data with DATETIME and SMALLDATETIME

As mentioned earlier, the more veteran types DATETIME and SMALLDATETIME are still quite widely used, especially the former, for historic and other reasons. The question is, how do you handle date-only and time-only data with these types, considering that they contain both elements? The recommended practice is that when you need to store the date only, you store the date with midnight as the time; and when you need to store time only, you store the time with the base date (January 1, 1900) as the date.

If you're wondering why you specifically use midnight and the base date and not other choices, there's a reason for this. When SQL Server converts a character string that contains the date only to a date and time type, it assumes midnight as the time. As an example, say you have a query with the filter *WHERE dt = '20150212'*, and the *dt* column is of a DATETIME type. SQL Server will implicitly convert the literal character string to DATETIME, assuming midnight as the time. If you stored all values in the *dt* column with midnight as the time, this filter will correctly return the rows where the date is February 12, 2015.

As an example for time-only data, say you have a query with the filter *WHERE tm = '12:00:00.000'* and the *tm* column is of a DATETIME type. SQL Server will implicitly convert the literal character string to DATETIME, assuming the base date as the date. If you stored all values in the *tm* column with the base date as the date, this filter will correctly return the rows where the time is midnight.

Based on the recommended practice, you need to be able to take an input date and time value, like the SYSDATETIME function, and convert it to DATETIME or SMALLDATETIME, setting the time to midnight to capture date-only data or setting the date to the base date to capture time-only data. To capture date-only data, simply convert the input to DATE and then to DATETIME (or SMALLDATETIME), like so:

```
SELECT CAST(CAST(SYSDATETIME() AS DATE) AS DATETIME);
```

There's a slightly more complex way to set the time part of the input to midnight, but it's worthwhile to know it because the concept can be used in other calculations, as I will demonstrate in the next section. The method involves using a starting point that is a date from the past with midnight as the time. I like to use January 1, 1900 at midnight for this purpose. You compute the difference in terms of days between that starting point and the input value (call that difference *diff*). Then you add *diff* days to the same starting point you used to compute the difference, and you get the target date at midnight as the result. Here's the complete calculation applied to SYSDATETIME as the input:

```
SELECT DATEADD(day, DATEDIFF(day, '19000101', SYSDATETIME()), '19000101');
```

To capture time-only data, convert the input to TIME and then to DATETIME (or SMALLDATETIME), like so:

```
SELECT CAST(CAST(SYSDATETIME() AS TIME) AS DATETIME);
```

First, last, previous, and next date calculations

This section covers calculations such as finding the date of the first or last day in a period, the date of the last or next occurrence of a certain weekday, and so on. All calculations that I'll cover are with respect to some given date and time value. I'll use the SYSDATETIME function as the given value, but you can change SYSDATETIME to any date and time value.

First or last day of a period

This section covers calculations of the first and last date in a period, such as the month or year, with respect to some given reference date and time value.

Earlier I provided the following expression to set the time part of a given date and time value to midnight:

```
SELECT DATEADD(day, DATEDIFF(day, '19000101', SYSDATETIME()), '19000101');
```

You can use similar logic to calculate the date of the first day of the month. You need to make sure you use an anchor date that is a first day of a month and use the *month* part instead of the *day* part, like so:

```
SELECT DATEADD(month, DATEDIFF(month, '19000101', SYSDATETIME()), '19000101');
```

This expression calculates the difference in terms of whole months between some first day of a month and the reference date. Call that difference *diff*. The expression then adds *diff* months to the anchor date, producing the date of the first day of the month corresponding to the given reference date.

An alternative method to compute the first day of the month is to use the DATEFROMPARTS function, like so:

```
SELECT DATEFROMPARTS(YEAR(SYSDATETIME()), MONTH(SYSDATETIME()), 1);
```

To return the date of the last day of the month, you can use the previous calculation I showed for beginning of month, but with an anchor date that is an end of a month, like so:

```
SELECT DATEADD(month, DATEDIFF(month, '18991231', SYSDATETIME()), '18991231');
```

Note that it's important to use an anchor date that is a 31st of some month, such as December, so that if the target month has 31 days the calculation works correctly.

Specifically with the end of month calculation, you don't need to work that hard because T-SQL supports the EOMONTH function described earlier:

```
SELECT EOMONTH(SYSDATETIME());
```

To calculate the date of the first day of the year, use an anchor that is a first day of some year, and specify the year part, like so:

```
SELECT DATEADD(year, DATEDIFF(year, '19000101', SYSDATETIME()), '19000101');
```

Or you could use the DATEFROMPARTS function, like so:

```
SELECT DATEFROMPARTS(YEAR(SYSDATETIME()), 1, 1);
```

To calculate the date of the last day of the year, use an anchor date that is the last day of some year:

```
SELECT DATEADD(year, DATEDIFF(year, '18991231', SYSDATETIME()), '18991231');
```

Or, again, you could use the DATEFROMPARTS function, like so:

```
SELECT DATEFROMPARTS(YEAR(SYSDATETIME()), 12, 31);
```

Previous or next weekday

This section covers calculations that return a next or previous weekday with respect to a given date and time value. I use the word *respective* to describe this sort of calculation.

Suppose you need to calculate the latest Monday before or on a given reference date and time. The calculation needs to be *inclusive* of the reference date. That is, if the reference date is a Monday, return the reference date; otherwise, return the latest Monday before the reference date. You can use the following expression to achieve this:

```
SELECT DATEADD(
       day,
       DATEDIFF(
         day,
         '19000101', -- Base Monday date
         SYSDATETIME()) /7*7,
       '19000101'); -- Base Monday date
```

The expression calculates the difference in terms of days between some anchor date that is a Monday and the reference date. Call that difference *diff*.

As I mentioned earlier, it's convenient to use dates in the range January 1, 1900, and January 7, 1900, as anchor dates because they represent the weekdays Monday through Sunday, respectively. The day parts of the suggested anchor dates (1 through 7) are aligned with the integers used in SQL Server to represent the first day of the week; therefore, it's easy to remember which day of the week each date in the range represents.

The expression then rounds the value down to the nearest multiple of 7 by dividing *diff* by 7 using integer division, and then multiplying it by 7. Call the result *floor_diff*. Note that the calculation of *floor_diff* will work correctly only when the result of DATEDIFF is nonnegative. So make sure you use an anchor date that is earlier than the reference date. The expression then adds *floor_diff* days to the anchor date, producing the latest occurrence of a Monday, inclusive. Remember that by *inclusive* I mean that if the reference date is a Monday, the calculation is supposed to return the reference date.

Here's the expression formatted in one line of code:

```
SELECT DATEADD(day, DATEDIFF(day, '19000101', SYSDATETIME()) /7*7, '19000101');
```

Similarly, to return the date of the last Tuesday, use an anchor date that is a Tuesday:

```
SELECT DATEADD(day, DATEDIFF(day, '19000102', SYSDATETIME()) /7*7, '19000102');
```

And to return the date of the last Sunday, use an anchor date that is a Sunday:

```
SELECT DATEADD(day, DATEDIFF(day, '19000107', SYSDATETIME()) /7*7, '19000107');
```

To make the calculation exclusive of the reference date—meaning that you're after the last occurrence of a weekday before the reference date (as opposed to on or before)—simply subtract a day from the reference date. For example, the following expression returns the date of the last occurrence of a Monday before the reference date:

```
SELECT DATEADD(day, DATEDIFF(day, '19000101', DATEADD(day, -1, SYSDATETIME())) /7*7,
       '19000101');
```

To return the next occurrence of a weekday in an inclusive manner (on or after the reference date), subtract a day from the reference date and add 7 days to *floor_diff*. For example, the following expression returns the next occurrence of a Monday on or after the reference date:

```
SELECT DATEADD(day, DATEDIFF(day, '19000101', DATEADD(day, -1, SYSDATETIME()))) /7*7 + 7,
    '19000101');
```

Like before, replace the anchor date if you need to handle a different weekday—for example, Tuesday:

```
SELECT DATEADD(day, DATEDIFF(day, '19000102', DATEADD(day, -1, SYSDATETIME()))) /7*7 + 7,
    '19000102');
```

Or Sunday:

```
SELECT DATEADD(day, DATEDIFF(day, '19000107', DATEADD(day, -1, SYSDATETIME()))) /7*7 + 7,
    '19000107');
```

To make the calculation exclusive, meaning the next occurrence of a weekday after the reference date (as opposed to on or after), simply skip the step of subtracting a day from the anchor date. For example, the following expression returns the next occurrence of a Monday after the reference date:

```
SELECT DATEADD(day, DATEDIFF(day, '19000101', SYSDATETIME()) /7*7 + 7, '19000101');
```

This calculation is for the next occurrence of a Tuesday, exclusive:

```
SELECT DATEADD(day, DATEDIFF(day, '19000102', SYSDATETIME()) /7*7 + 7, '19000102');
```

This calculation is for the next occurrence of a Sunday, exclusive:

```
SELECT DATEADD(day, DATEDIFF(day, '19000107', SYSDATETIME()) /7*7 + 7, '19000107');
```

First or last weekday

In this section, I'll describe calculations that return the first and last occurrences of a certain weekday in a period such as a month or year. To calculate the first occurrence of a certain weekday in a month, you need to combine two types of calculations I described earlier. One is the calculation of the first day of the month:

```
SELECT DATEADD(month, DATEDIFF(month, '19000101', SYSDATETIME()), '19000101');
```

The other is the calculation of the next occurrence of a weekday, inclusive—Monday, in this example:

```
SELECT DATEADD(day, DATEDIFF(day, '19000101', DATEADD(day, -1, SYSDATETIME()))) /7*7 + 7,
    '19000101');
```

The trick is to simply use the first day of the month calculation as the reference date within the next-weekday-occurrence calculation. For example, the following expression returns the first occurrence of a Monday in the reference month:

```
SELECT DATEADD(day, DATEDIFF(day, '19000101',
  -- first day of month
  DATEADD(month, DATEDIFF(month, '19000101', SYSDATETIME()), '19000101')
    -1) /7*7 + 7, '19000101');
```

To handle a different weekday, replace the anchor date in the part of the expression that calculates the next occurrence of a weekday—not in the part that calculates the first month day. The following expression returns the date of the first occurrence of a Tuesday in the reference month:

```
SELECT DATEADD(day, DATEDIFF(day, '19000102',
  -- first day of month
  DATEADD(month, DATEDIFF(month, '19000101', SYSDATETIME()), '19000101')
    -1) /7*7 + 7, '19000102');
```

To calculate the date of the last occurrence of a weekday in the reference month, you need to combine two calculations as well. One is the calculation of the last day of the reference month:

```
SELECT DATEADD(month, DATEDIFF(month, '18991231', SYSDATETIME()), '18991231');
```

The other is the calculation of the previous occurrence of a weekday, inclusive—Monday, in this example:

```
SELECT DATEADD(day, DATEDIFF(day, '19000101', SYSDATETIME()) /7*7, '19000101');
```

Simply use the last day of the month calculation as the reference date in the last-weekday calculation. For example, the following expression returns the last occurrence of a Monday in the reference month:

```
SELECT DATEADD(day, DATEDIFF(day, '19000101',
  -- last day of month
  DATEADD(month, DATEDIFF(month, '18991231', SYSDATETIME()), '18991231')
  ) /7*7, '19000101');
```

To address a different weekday, substitute the anchor date in the last weekday calculation with the applicable one. For example, the following expression returns the last occurrence of a Tuesday in the reference month:

```
SELECT DATEADD(day, DATEDIFF(day, '19000102',
  -- last day of month
  DATEADD(month, DATEDIFF(month, '18991231', SYSDATETIME()), '18991231')
  ) /7*7, '19000102');
```

In a manner similar to calculating the first and last occurrences of a weekday in the reference month, you can calculate the first and last occurrence of a weekday in the reference year. Simply substitute the first-month-day or last-month-day calculation with the first-year-day or last-year-day calculation. Following are a few examples.

The first occurrence of a Monday in the reference year:

```
SELECT DATEADD(day, DATEDIFF(day, '19000101',
  -- first day of year
  DATEADD(year, DATEDIFF(year, '19000101', SYSDATETIME()), '19000101')
    -1) /7*7 + 7, '19000101');
```

The first occurrence of a Tuesday in the reference year:

```
SELECT DATEADD(day, DATEDIFF(day, '19000102',
  -- first day of year
  DATEADD(year, DATEDIFF(year, '19000101', SYSDATETIME()), '19000101')
    -1) /7*7 + 7, '19000102');
```

The last occurrence of a Monday in the reference year:

```
SELECT DATEADD(day, DATEDIFF(day, '19000101',
  -- last day of year
  DATEADD(year, DATEDIFF(year, '18991231', SYSDATETIME()), '18991231')
) /7*7, '19000101');
```

The last occurrence of a Tuesday in the reference year:

```
SELECT DATEADD(day, DATEDIFF(day, '19000102',
  -- last day of year
  DATEADD(year, DATEDIFF(year, '18991231', SYSDATETIME()), '18991231')
) /7*7, '19000102');
```

Search argument

One of the most fundamental concepts in query tuning is that of a *search argument* (SARG). It's not really unique to working with date and time data, but it is very common with such data. Suppose that you have a query with a filter in the form *WHERE <column> <operator> <value>* and a supporting index on the filtered column. As long as you don't apply manipulation to the filtered column, SQL Server can rely on the index order—for example, to consider performing a seek followed by a range scan in the index. If the index is not a covering one, of course there would be the question of whether the selectivity of the filter is high enough to justify using the index, but the point is that the potential is there. If you do apply manipulation to the column, besides some exceptional cases, this might result in SQL Server not relying on the index order and using less optimal access methods like full scans.

As mentioned, the issue of SARGablility is not really unique to date and time data but is quite common in that scenario, because you often filter data based on date and time. A classic example is filtering range-of-date and time values like a whole day, week, month, quarter, year, and so on. To allow optimal index usage, you should get into the habit of expressing the range filter without manipulating the filtered column. As an example, the following two queries are logically equivalent—both filtering the entire order year 2014:

```
USE PerformanceV3;

SELECT orderid, orderdate, filler
FROM dbo.Orders
WHERE YEAR(orderdate) = 2014;

SELECT orderid, orderdate, filler
FROM dbo.Orders
WHERE orderdate >= '20140101'
  AND orderdate < '20150101';
```

There's a clustered index defined on the *orderdate* column, so clearly the optimal plan here is to perform a seek followed by a range scan of the qualifying rows in the index. Figure 7-3 shows the actual plans you do get for these queries.

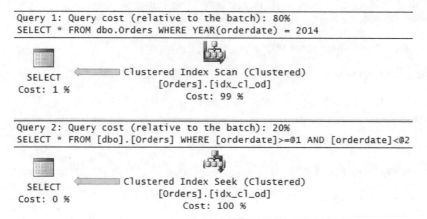

```
Query 1: Query cost (relative to the batch): 80%
SELECT * FROM dbo.Orders WHERE YEAR(orderdate) = 2014
```

SELECT
Cost: 1 %

Clustered Index Scan (Clustered)
[Orders].[idx_cl_od]
Cost: 99 %

```
Query 2: Query cost (relative to the batch): 20%
SELECT * FROM [dbo].[Orders] WHERE [orderdate]>=@1 AND [orderdate]<@2
```

SELECT
Cost: 0 %

Clustered Index Seek (Clustered)
[Orders].[idx_cl_od]
Cost: 100 %

FIGURE 7-3 Non-SARG versus SARG.

The predicate in the first query is non SARGable. The optimizer doesn't try to be smart and understand the meaning of what you're doing; rather, it just resorts to a full scan. With the second query, the predicate is SARGable, allowing an efficient seek and partial scan in the index.

As mentioned, there are exceptions where SQL Server will consider a predicate that applies manipulation to the filtered column as SARGable. An example for such an exception is when the predicate converts the column to the DATE type, as in the following query:

```
SELECT orderid, orderdate, filler
FROM dbo.Orders
WHERE CAST(orderdate AS DATE) = '20140212';
```

Microsoft added logic to the optimizer to consider such a predicate as SARGable, and hence it chooses here to perform a seek and a range scan in the index. The problem is, this example is the exception and not the norm.

If you're an experienced database practitioner, it's likely that other people mimic your coding practices without always fully understanding them. For this reason, as a general rule, you should prefer the form without manipulation whenever possible because that's the one that is more likely to be SARGable. So instead of using the predicate form in the preceding query, it's recommended to use the following form:

```
SELECT orderid, orderdate, filler
FROM dbo.Orders
WHERE orderdate >= '20140212'
  AND orderdate < '20140213';
```

Rounding issues

When you convert a character-string value to a date and time type, or convert one from a higher level of precision to a lower one, you need to be aware of how SQL Server handles such conversions. Some find SQL Server's treatment surprising.

One of the common pitfalls occurs when converting a character-string value to the DATETIME type. To demonstrate this, I'll use the following sample data:

```
USE TSQLV3;
IF OBJECT_ID(N'Sales.MyOrders', N'U') IS NOT NULL DROP TABLE Sales.MyOrders;
GO

SELECT * INTO Sales.MyOrders FROM Sales.Orders;
ALTER TABLE Sales.MyOrders ALTER COLUMN orderdate DATETIME NOT NULL;
CREATE CLUSTERED INDEX idx_cl_od ON Sales.MyOrders(orderdate);
```

Suppose you need to filter the orders where the order date falls within a certain date and time range. Imagine that the time part in the stored values wasn't necessarily midnight and you want to filter a range like a whole day, month, year, and so on. For example, filter only the orders placed on January 1, 2015. A common yet incorrect way for people to express the filter is using the BETWEEN predicate, like so:

```
SELECT orderid, orderdate, custid, empid
FROM Sales.MyOrders
WHERE orderdate BETWEEN '20150101' AND '20150101 23:59:59.999';
```

When using this form, people think that 999 is the last expressible millisecond part of the second. However, recall that the precision of the DATETIME type is 3 1/3 milliseconds, rounded to the nearest tick. So the only valid values for the last digit of the milliseconds part are 0, 3, and 7. Any other value gets rounded to the closest supported one. This means that the value specified as the end delimiter in the preceding query is rounded up to midnight in the next day. This causes the query to return the following output:

```
orderid     orderdate               custid      empid
----------- ----------------------- ----------- -----------
10808       2015-01-01 00:00:00.000 55          2
10809       2015-01-01 00:00:00.000 88          7
10810       2015-01-01 00:00:00.000 42          2
10811       2015-01-02 00:00:00.000 47          8
10812       2015-01-02 00:00:00.000 66          5
```

Observe that even though you were looking for only orders placed on January 1, 2015, you're also getting the ones from the 2nd. For this reason, the recommended practice is to express your range as greater than or equal to midnight of the first date in the range and less than midnight of the date immediately following the last date in the range. In our example, you should change your filter like so:

```
SELECT orderid, orderdate, custid, empid
FROM Sales.MyOrders
WHERE orderdate >= '20150101'
  AND orderdate < '20150102';
```

And this time you get the correct result:

```
orderid     orderdate  custid      empid
----------- ---------- ----------- -----------
10808       2015-01-01 55          2
10809       2015-01-01 88          7
10810       2015-01-01 42          2
```

If you follow this practice, your code will work correctly with all date and time types, whether the values include a relevant time portion or not. It's always good to get used to forms that work correctly in all cases.

Back to our example with the DATETIME column, to return orders placed today manipulate the result of the SYSDATETIME function to compute today at midnight and tomorrow at midnight as the delimiters of the closed-open interval, like so:

```
SELECT orderid, orderdate, custid, empid
FROM Sales.MyOrders
WHERE orderdate >= CAST(CAST(SYSDATETIME() AS DATE) AS DATETIME)
  AND orderdate < DATEADD(day, 1, CAST(CAST(SYSDATETIME() AS DATE) AS DATETIME));
```

When you're done, run the following code for cleanup:

```
IF OBJECT_ID(N'Sales.MyOrders', N'U') IS NOT NULL DROP TABLE Sales.MyOrders;
```

You might not be aware that SQL Server applies similar rounding logic also when converting from a higher precision date and time value to a lower precision one. For example, when you convert the result of the SYSDATETIME function (returns a DATETIME2 value) to SMALLDATETIME (minute precision), SQL Server doesn't floor the value to the bottom of the minute; rather, it rounds the value to the closest minute. This means the value is rounded to the beginning of the minute before the half-minute point and to the next minute on or beyond that point. If you want to apply flooring instead of rounding logic, subtract 30 seconds before converting the value. The following code returns the result of the SYSDATETIME function, demonstrating both the rounding and flooring of the value:

```
SELECT
  SYSDATETIME() AS currentdatetime,
  CAST(SYSDATETIME() AS SMALLDATETIME) AS roundedtominute,
  CAST(DATEADD(ss, -30, SYSDATETIME()) AS SMALLDATETIME) AS flooredtominute;
```

Suppose you ran this code when SYSDATETIME returns '2015-02-12 13:47:53.7996475'. You will get the following output:

```
currentdatetime            roundedtominute         flooredtominute
-------------------------- ----------------------- -----------------------
2015-02-12 13:47:53.7996475 2015-02-12 13:48:00     2015-02-12 13:47:00
```

The same rounding logic applies with any conversion from a higher precision date and time value to a lower one. For example, convert the result of SYSDATETIME to DATETIME(0), and you get rounding to the closest second. If you want to floor the value to the beginning of the second, subtract 500 milliseconds before converting. Here's the code demonstrating both rounding and flooring with a granularity of a second:

```
SELECT
  SYSDATETIME() AS currentdatetime,
  CAST(SYSDATETIME() AS DATETIME2(0)) AS roundedtosecond,
  CAST(DATEADD(ms, -500, SYSDATETIME()) AS DATETIME2(0)) AS flooredtosecond;
```

Again, assume you ran this code when SYSDATETIME returns '*2015-02-12 13:47:53.7996475*'. You will get the following output:

```
currentdatetime               roundedtosecond            flooredtosecond
---------------------------   ------------------------   ------------------------
2015-02-12 13:47:53.7996475   2015-02-12 13:47:54        2015-02-12 13:47:53
```

Querying date and time data

This section covers the handling of querying tasks involving date and time data. It starts by providing a method to group data by week, and then provides solutions to various querying tasks involving date and time intervals.

Grouping by the week

Suppose you need to query the Sales.OrderValues view, group the rows by the order week (based on the order date), and return for each group the count of orders and total order values. As it turns out, the task is not as trivial as it might have seemed at the beginning. The main challenge is to compute a common week identifier for all dates that are associated with the same week. If you're thinking of the DATEPART function with the *week* part (or *wk* or *ww* for short), this part gives you the week number in the year. If a week starts in one year and ends in another, the first few days will give you a different week number than the last few days. You need a different solution.

The solution I like to use is to compute for each date the respective start-of-week date, and then use that as my week identifier. The first step in the calculation is to compute the weekday number of the input date (call it *wd*). This is done using the DATEPART function with the weekday part: *DATEPART(weekday, orderdate)*. Remember that this calculation is language dependent; it reflects the effective DATEFIRST setting based on the language of the login running the code. If you want the login's perspective to determine when the week starts, you have your final *wd* value and therefore you're done with the first step. If you need the calculation itself to control where the week starts, you have two different methods to achieve this as I explained earlier—the diff and modulo method, and the compensation method. For example, using the compensation method and considering Monday as the first day of the week, use the expression *DATEPART(weekday, DATEADD(day, @@DATEFIRST −1, orderdate))*.

Now that you have *wd*, the second step is to compute the distance of the input date from the respective start-of-week date (call it *dist*). Fortunately, that's a simple calculation: a date with *wd* = N is at a distance of N − 1 days from the respective start-of-week date. For example, a date with *wd* = 3 is 2 days away from the respective start-of-week date. So the expression to compute *dist* is *wd* – *1*.

The third and last step is to compute the respective start-of-week date (call it *startofweek*). That's done by subtracting *dist* days from *orderdate* using the following expression: *DATEADD(day, −dist, orderdate)*. You now have your week identifier and can use it as the only element in the grouping set of your grouped query.

Here's the complete solution code:

```
USE TSQLV3;

SELECT
  startofweek,
  DATEADD(day, 6, startofweek) AS endofweek,
  SUM(val) AS totalval,
  COUNT(*) AS numorders
FROM Sales.OrderValues
  CROSS APPLY ( VALUES( DATEPART(weekday, DATEADD(day, @@DATEFIRST -1, orderdate)) ) ) AS A1(wd)
  CROSS APPLY ( VALUES( wd - 1 ) ) AS A2(dist)
  CROSS APPLY ( VALUES( DATEADD(day, -dist, orderdate) ) ) AS A3(startofweek)
GROUP BY startofweek;
```

Observe that to also return the end-of-week date (call it *endofweek*), you simply add six days to *startofweek*. This query generates the following output:

```
startofweek endofweek   totalval  numorders
----------- ----------  --------- -----------
2013-07-01  2013-07-07  2303.40   2
2013-07-08  2013-07-14  10296.48  6
2013-07-15  2013-07-21  5306.03   6
2013-07-22  2013-07-28  4675.99   5
2013-07-29  2013-08-04  8160.00   6
...
2015-04-06  2015-04-12  21074.05  17
2015-04-13  2015-04-19  52976.83  17
2015-04-20  2015-04-26  15460.63  16
2015-04-27  2015-05-03  21720.42  17
2015-05-04  2015-05-10  12885.07  11
```

Intervals

An *interval* in mathematics is the set of values between some lower and upper values. A date and time interval is, therefore, the set of date and time values between some lower and upper values, with the granularity being based on the data type's precision. The need to store and manipulate date and time intervals in databases is quite common. They represent things like sessions, chats, phone calls, validity periods, appointments, contracts, projects, patients' visits to hospitals, and so on.

Common querying tasks related to intervals include identifying intervals that intersect with an input one, computing the maximum number of concurrent intervals, packing intervals, and others. Creating correct solutions for such tasks is not all that difficult. There are fairly simple classic solutions. But as it turns out, creating solutions that are both correct and perform well is far from being trivial. Achieving good performance is tricky mainly because of the fundamental optimization challenges I described in Chapter 2, "Query tuning," concerning filters with multiple range predicates. Here you will see practical examples where this problem manifests itself. Fortunately, there are efficient solutions, although they are not as simple as the classic ones.

To demonstrate how to solve common tasks involving date and time intervals, I will use sample data representing mobile phone accounts and phone call sessions. Run the following code to create and populate the Accounts and Sessions tables in tempdb with a small set of sample data:

```
SET NOCOUNT ON;
USE tempdb;

IF OBJECT_ID('dbo.Sessions') IS NOT NULL DROP TABLE dbo.Sessions;
IF OBJECT_ID('dbo.Accounts') IS NOT NULL DROP TABLE dbo.Accounts;

CREATE TABLE dbo.Accounts
(
  actid INT NOT NULL,
  CONSTRAINT PK_Accounts PRIMARY KEY(actid)
);
GO

INSERT INTO dbo.Accounts(actid) VALUES(1), (2), (3);

CREATE TABLE dbo.Sessions
(
  sessionid INT          NOT NULL IDENTITY(1, 1),
  actid     INT          NOT NULL,
  starttime DATETIME2(0) NOT NULL,
  endtime   DATETIME2(0) NOT NULL,
  CONSTRAINT PK_Sessions PRIMARY KEY(sessionid),
  CONSTRAINT CHK_endtime_gteq_starttime
    CHECK (endtime >= starttime)
);
GO

INSERT INTO dbo.Sessions(actid, starttime, endtime) VALUES
  (1, '20151231 08:00:00', '20151231 08:30:00'),
  (1, '20151231 08:30:00', '20151231 09:00:00'),
  (1, '20151231 09:00:00', '20151231 09:30:00'),
  (1, '20151231 10:00:00', '20151231 11:00:00'),
  (1, '20151231 10:30:00', '20151231 12:00:00'),
  (1, '20151231 11:30:00', '20151231 12:30:00'),
  (2, '20151231 08:00:00', '20151231 10:30:00'),
  (2, '20151231 08:30:00', '20151231 10:00:00'),
  (2, '20151231 09:00:00', '20151231 09:30:00'),
  (2, '20151231 11:00:00', '20151231 11:30:00'),
  (2, '20151231 11:32:00', '20151231 12:00:00'),
  (2, '20151231 12:04:00', '20151231 12:30:00'),
  (3, '20151231 08:00:00', '20151231 09:00:00'),
  (3, '20151231 08:00:00', '20151231 08:30:00'),
  (3, '20151231 08:30:00', '20151231 09:00:00'),
  (3, '20151231 09:30:00', '20151231 09:30:00');
```

A phone call session is an interval defined by the delimiters *starttime* and *endtime* with a granularity of a second using the type DATETIME2(0). I will leave the aspect of whether each of the delimiters is an open (exclusive) or closed (inclusive) one undefined so that you can define it on a case-by-case basis, depending on what real-life scenario you need the sample data to represent for you.

Use the small set of sample data created by the preceding code to verify the correctness of the solutions. For performance testing, you can use the following code, which creates a large set of sample data with 50 accounts and 10,000,000 intervals:

```
-- 10,000,000 intervals
DECLARE
  @num_accounts            AS INT          = 50,
  @sessions_per_account    AS INT          = 200000,
  @start_period            AS DATETIME2(3) = '20120101',
  @end_period              AS DATETIME2(3) = '20160101',
  @max_duration_in_seconds AS INT          = 3600; -- 1 hour

TRUNCATE TABLE dbo.Sessions;
TRUNCATE TABLE dbo.Accounts;

INSERT INTO dbo.Accounts(actid)
  SELECT A.n AS actid
  FROM TSQLV3.dbo.GetNums(1, @num_accounts) AS A;

WITH C AS
(
  SELECT A.n AS actid,
    DATEADD(second,
      ABS(CHECKSUM(NEWID())) %
        (DATEDIFF(s, @start_period, @end_period) - @max_duration_in_seconds),
      @start_period) AS starttime
  FROM TSQLV3.dbo.GetNums(1, @num_accounts) AS A
    CROSS JOIN TSQLV3.dbo.GetNums(1, @sessions_per_account) AS I
)
INSERT INTO dbo.Sessions WITH (TABLOCK) (actid, starttime, endtime)
  SELECT actid, starttime,
    DATEADD(second,
      ABS(CHECKSUM(NEWID())) % (@max_duration_in_seconds + 1),
      starttime) AS endtime
  FROM C;
```

Feel free to change the parameters for the sample data if you want to test the solutions with different data characteristics.

Intersection

An interval *intersection* test checks whether two intervals have any form of intersection. James F. Allen defines 13 relations between intervals, which are known as *Allen's interval algebra*. (For details, see *http://www.ics.uci.edu/~alspaugh/cls/shr/allen.html*.) Out of the 13, 11 relations represent different forms of intersection. Those are all of Allen's relations except *before* and *after*.

As an example, suppose you get as inputs an account id (*@actid*) and a closed interval [*@s, @e*] (with *@s* for start and *@e* for end), and your task is to return all account intervals from the Sessions table that intersect with the input one. The classic way in SQL to identify intersection is actually quite straightforward, using the predicates *starttime <= @e AND endtime >= @s*. These two range predicates are specified in addition to the equality predicate *actid* = *@actid*. The problem is that this classic method is often very inefficient in T-SQL. Recall the discussion about multiple range predicates in Chapter 2. Whether you create an index on the key list (*actid*, *starttime*, *endtime*) or (*actid*, *endtime*, *starttime*), only one range predicate can be used as a seek predicate (in addition to any equality predicates against leading keys). All rows that satisfy the seek predicates are scanned, and then the remaining range predicates are applied to the scanned rows as residual predicates.

You could be lucky if most queries target a limited period at the edge of the entire period covered by your data, constituting a small percentage of it. For example, usually for billing purposes you need to look for intervals that intersect only with a very recent period (last month/week). But then it's very easy to fall into a trap from an indexing standpoint. The intuitive key order for most people to define in the index is (*starttime*, *endtime*); that's following the equality column *actid*, of course. Remember that when you have multiple range predicates in your filter, you want the more selective one to appear first so that the range scan in the index leaf needs to scan a smaller range. Now think about it; which of the predicates is more selective when querying a recent period: *starttime* <= *@e* or *endtime* >= *@s*? Clearly, it's the latter. But with an index on (*starttime*, *endtime*), your leading range key is the far less selective one, so the range scan will end up scanning most rows for the account in question.

To demonstrate this, first create the intuitive but less efficient index by running the following code:

```
CREATE UNIQUE INDEX idx_start_end ON dbo.Sessions(actid, starttime, endtime, sessionid);
```

Suppose you need to look for active sessions for account ID 1, during the hour between 11:00 AM and noon in the last day recorded (December 31, 2015). You issue the following query (RECOMPILE is used to apply parameter embedding):

```
DECLARE
  @actid AS INT = 1,
  @s     AS DATETIME2(0) = '20151231 11:00:00',
  @e     AS DATETIME2(0) = '20151231 12:00:00';

SELECT sessionid, actid, starttime, endtime
FROM dbo.Sessions
WHERE actid = @actid
  AND starttime <= @e
  AND endtime >= @s
OPTION(RECOMPILE);
```

Here's the output you get with the small set of sample data just to verify the validity of the code:

```
sessionid  actid  starttime            endtime
---------- ------ -------------------- --------------------
4          1      2015-12-31 10:00:00  2015-12-31 11:00:00
5          1      2015-12-31 10:30:00  2015-12-31 12:00:00
6          1      2015-12-31 11:30:00  2015-12-31 12:30:00
```

Figure 7-4 illustrates how much data needs to be scanned in the leaf of the intuitive yet less efficient index (to the left) versus the less intuitive but more efficient one (to the right).

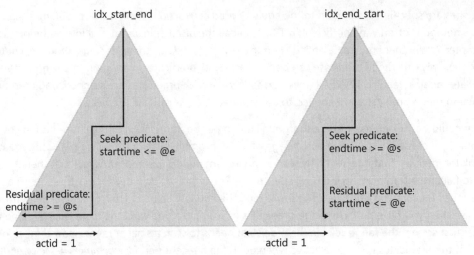

FIGURE 7-4 Indexing strategies for interval intersection queries.

The figure shows which range predicate is applied as a seek predicate for determining how many rows need to be scanned in the index leaf, and which predicate is applied as a residual predicate and evaluated against all remaining rows. As you can see, with an index on (*starttime*, *endtime*) most rows for account ID 1 need to be scanned, whereas with an index on (*endtime*, *starttime*) only a small percentage needs to be scanned.

Figure 7-5 shows the actual plan I got for the query against the large set of sample data.

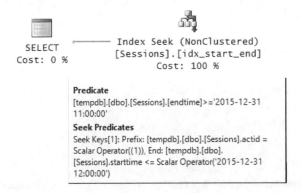

SELECT
Cost: 0 %

Index Seek (NonClustered)
[Sessions].[idx_start_end]
Cost: 100 %

Predicate
[tempdb].[dbo].[Sessions].[endtime]>='2015-12-31
11:00:00'
Seek Predicates
Seek Keys[1]: Prefix: [tempdb].[dbo].[Sessions].actid =
Scalar Operator((1)), End: [tempdb].[dbo].
[Sessions].starttime <= Scalar Operator('2015-12-31
12:00:00')

FIGURE 7-5 Interval intersection with index idx_start_end.

Observe that the less selective predicate *starttime <= '2015-12-31 12:00:00'* appears as a seek predicate and the more selective one *endtime >= '2015-12-31 11:00:00'* appears as a residual predicate. I populated the table with 200,000 rows per account, and with about 300 rows fitting in a page, you get about 650 pages used per account. With the current index idx_start_end, most of those pages need to be scanned. When I ran this intersection query against the large set of sample data, it performed 648 logical reads.

The conclusion is that you're better off creating the index with the more selective column *endtime* appearing before the less selective column *starttime*, like so:

```
CREATE UNIQUE INDEX idx_end_start ON dbo.Sessions(actid, endtime, starttime, sessionid);
```

Rerun the query:

```
DECLARE
  @actid AS INT = 1,
  @s      AS DATETIME2(0) = '20151231 11:00:00',
  @e      AS DATETIME2(0) = '20151231 12:00:00';

SELECT sessionid, actid, starttime, endtime
FROM dbo.Sessions
WHERE actid = @actid
  AND starttime <= @e
  AND endtime >= @s
OPTION(RECOMPILE);
```

This time, you get the plan in Figure 7-6, showing the more selective column used as a seek predicate and the less selective one used as a residual predicate.

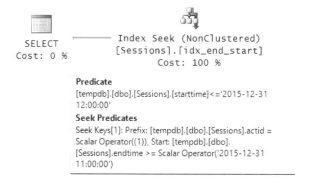

FIGURE 7-6 Interval intersection with index idx_end_start.

When I ran this query on my system, it performed only four logical reads!

When you're done testing intersection queries, run the following code to drop the index idx_end_start (and keep the index idx_start_end for later examples):

```
DROP INDEX idx_end_start ON dbo.Sessions;
```

So, when you're lucky enough to have most intersection queries applied to recent periods in your data, it's easy to get good performance as long as you create the right index. However, if in your environment intersection queries can be applied to any period, you're in trouble. Whether you create the index with *starttime* before *endtime* or the other way around, on average, every query will result in scanning half the rows for the account. The sample data I use has 200,000 rows per partition (account), so scanning half the rows is not necessarily a disaster, but what if you have millions per partition?

There's a solution for intersection queries that works well in the more general cases. It is based on an ingenious model called the Relational Interval Tree (RI-tree) model. It was crafted by Hans-Peter Kriegel, Marco Pötke, and Thomas Seidl from the University of Munich, with further optimizations by Laurent Martin. The implementation of this model involves: (1) adding a column to the table representing what's called the *fork node* in the model, (2) two B-tree-based indexes based on (*forknode, starttime, key*) and (*forknode, endtime, key*), and (3) new intersection queries that unify three disjoint sets of intersecting intervals, each using no more than one range predicate. This model and the improvements are downright beautiful and quite an impressive accomplishment. If you have the need to perform intersection queries in your application and you currently suffer from performance problems, it is certainly worthwhile getting familiar with it. You can find the details about the model, improvements, and implementation in SQL Server in the following resources:

- "Interval Queries in SQL Server" by Itzik Ben-Gan (*http://sqlmag.com/t-sql/ sql-server-interval-queries*)

- "Managing Intervals Efficiently in Object-Relational Databases" by Hans-Peter Kriegel, Marco Pötke, and Thomas Seidl (*http://www.dbs.ifi.lmu.de/Publikationen/Papers/VLDB2000.pdf*)

- "A Static Relational Interval Tree" by Laurent Martin (*http://www.solidq.com/ static-relational-interval-tree/*)

- "Advanced interval queries with the Static Relational Interval Tree" by Laurent Martin (*http:// www.solidq.com/advanced-interval-queries-static-relational-interval-tree/*)

- "Using the Static Relational Interval Tree with time intervals" by Laurent Martin (*http://www. solidq.com/using-static-relational-interval-tree-time-intervals/*)

Max concurrent intervals

Finding the maximum number of concurrent intervals is a classic task. With our Sessions table, you need to compute for each account the maximum number of sessions that were active concurrently. Such calculations are usually done for reasons like figuring out peak use for capacity planning, billing purposes, and so on.

As usual, you need to know whether the interval delimiters are closed (exclusive) or open (inclusive). You need to know this to tell which intervals are considered active during any given point in time *ts*. For example, for a closed, closed interval [*starttime, endtime*] the interval is active during *ts* if *ts* >= *starttime* AND *ts* <= *endtime*. For a closed, open interval [*starttime, endtime*] the interval is active during *ts* if *ts* >= *starttime* AND *ts* < *endtime*. For the sake of this example, I'll assume the latter (closed, open intervals).

For the small set of sample data, your solution should generate the following output:

```
actid       mx
----------- -----------
1           2
2           3
3           2
```

I'll start with a traditional yet inefficient set-based solution that is based on a subquery, and then I'll continue with much more efficient solutions that are based on window functions.

The traditional subquery-based solution will benefit from the index idx_start_end you created earlier. If your Sessions table currently doesn't have this index, create it by running the following code:

```
CREATE UNIQUE INDEX idx_start_end ON dbo.Sessions(actid, starttime, endtime, sessionid);
```

The solution starts by identifying the points in time when the maximum number of intervals potentially falls. If you follow the arrow of time, the count of active intervals changes only when an interval starts or ends. In between events, the count remains the same. Furthermore, every time an interval starts, the count increases; whereas every time an interval ends, the count decreases. Therefore, the maximum count has to fall on one of the start events. So the solution starts by defining a CTE called P that returns start-event time stamps (call the column *ts*) when the maximum count potentially falls:

```
WITH P AS -- time points
(
  SELECT actid, starttime AS ts FROM dbo.Sessions
)
SELECT actid, ts FROM P;
```

The second step is to define a CTE called C with a query against P. The query uses a subquery to count the number of active intervals at *ts* for the same account based on the predicate I provided earlier. Here's the code implementing this step:

```
WITH P AS -- time points
(
  SELECT actid, starttime AS ts FROM dbo.Sessions
),
C AS -- counts
(
  SELECT actid, ts,
    (SELECT COUNT(*)
      FROM dbo.Sessions AS S
     WHERE P.actid = S.actid
       AND P.ts >= S.starttime
       AND P.ts < S.endtime) AS cnt
  FROM P
)
SELECT actid, ts, cnt FROM C;
```

This code generates the following output using the small set of sample data:

```
actid   ts                    cnt
------  --------------------  ----
1       2015-12-31 08:00:00   1
1       2015-12-31 08:30:00   1
1       2015-12-31 09:00:00   1
1       2015-12-31 10:00:00   1
1       2015-12-31 10:30:00   2
1       2015-12-31 11:30:00   2
2       2015-12-31 09:00:00   3
```

2	2015-12-31 08:30:00	2
2	2015-12-31 08:00:00	1
2	2015-12-31 11:00:00	1
2	2015-12-31 11:32:00	1
2	2015-12-31 12:04:00	1
3	2015-12-31 08:00:00	2
3	2015-12-31 08:00:00	2
3	2015-12-31 08:30:00	2
3	2015-12-31 09:30:00	0

Note If you're wondering how it can be that there are 0 active intervals at the last time stamp for account 3, that's because the sample data has a degenerate interval with the same start time and end time. I wanted to include such an interval for examples involving closed, closed intervals like with the intersection test I discussed in the previous section. Currently, there's a CHECK constraint that enforces the predicate *endtime >= starttime* to allow degenerate intervals. In practice, when your table will represent closed, open intervals and you won't want to allow empty ones, your constraint will enforce this with the predicate *endtime > starttime*.

The third and final step is to group the rows from C by account and return the maximum count per account, like so:

```
WITH P AS -- time points
(
  SELECT actid, starttime AS ts FROM dbo.Sessions
),
C AS -- counts
(
  SELECT actid, ts,
    (SELECT COUNT(*)
     FROM dbo.Sessions AS S
     WHERE P.actid = S.actid
       AND P.ts >= S.starttime
       AND P.ts < S.endtime) AS cnt
  FROM P
)
SELECT actid, MAX(cnt) AS mx
FROM C
GROUP BY actid;
```

This solution is pretty simple and straightforward, so from a logical standpoint it's alright. The problem is that it gets optimized very inefficiently even with the optimal index idx_start_end in place. The plan for this solution is shown in Figure 7-7.

The outer branch of the Nested Loops join scans the index to get the time stamps against which you will compute the counts. You have as many time stamps as the number of intervals because those time stamps are the start points of all intervals. For each time stamp, the inner branch of the Nested Loops join performs a seek and a range scan in the index based on the predicate in the subquery:

P.actid = S.actid AND P.ts >= S.starttime AND P.ts < S.endtime. Therein lies the problem. Thinking of the predicates from the perspective of the interval delimiters, you have two range predicates: *S.starttime <= P.ts AND S.endtime > P.ts.* On average, per time stamp, the Index Seek operator will scan about half the number of rows for the current account in the index leaf. With N rows per account, this means $N^2/2$ rows are going to be scanned in total. Our table has 200,000 rows per account. This translates to 20,000,000,000 rows processed per account. On my system, it took about 11 minutes and 30 seconds to process one account. With 50 accounts, it takes the query about 10 hours to complete. What's misleading in the plan that prevents you from seeing the excessive work is that the Index Seek operator doesn't tell you how many rows it scanned; rather, it tells you how many rows it returned after applying all predicates.

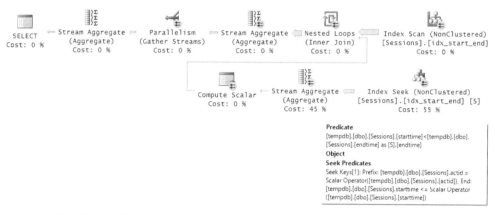

FIGURE 7-7 Plan for a traditional solution to the Max Concurrent Intervals task.

When you're done testing this solution, drop the index idx_start_end:

```
DROP INDEX idx_start_end ON dbo.Sessions;
```

There are much more efficient solutions to the Max Concurrent Intervals task, based on window functions. I'll first provide a solution that is based on a window aggregate function with a frame, so it is supported only in SQL Server 2012 and later. I'll then show a solution that is based on the ROW_NUMBER function, which is supported in earlier versions. Both solutions will benefit from the following indexes, which hold separate start and end events:

```
CREATE UNIQUE INDEX idx_start ON dbo.Sessions(actid, starttime, sessionid);
CREATE UNIQUE INDEX idx_end ON dbo.Sessions(actid, endtime, sessionid);
```

The first step in the solution is to generate the chronological sequence of events based on the order in which they happened. You mark start events with a +1 event type, meaning that the event increases the count of active intervals, and end events with a –1 because it decreases the count. Because the intervals in our example are open, closed ones, in cases where end and start events happen at the same time, you position end events before start events so that the count first drops before increasing. You achieve this by using *type* (ascending) as the tiebreaker after *ts* when you order the events. The following code implements the first step as a CTE called C1.

```
WITH C1 AS
(
  SELECT actid, starttime AS ts, +1 AS type
  FROM dbo.Sessions

  UNION ALL

  SELECT actid, endtime AS ts, -1 AS type
  FROM dbo.Sessions
)
SELECT actid, ts, type
FROM C1
ORDER BY actid, ts, type;
```

This code generates the following output (only events for account 2 are shown):

```
actid       ts                          type
----------- --------------------------- -----------
...
2           2015-12-31 08:00:00         1
2           2015-12-31 08:30:00         1
2           2015-12-31 09:00:00         1
2           2015-12-31 09:30:00         -1
2           2015-12-31 10:00:00         -1
2           2015-12-31 10:30:00         -1
2           2015-12-31 11:00:00         1
2           2015-12-31 11:30:00         -1
2           2015-12-31 11:32:00         1
2           2015-12-31 12:00:00         -1
2           2015-12-31 12:04:00         1
2           2015-12-31 12:30:00         -1
...
```

The second step computes the count of active intervals after each event simply as the running total *type* over time. Here's the code implementing the second step as a CTE called C2:

```
WITH C1 AS
(
  SELECT actid, starttime AS ts, +1 AS type
  FROM dbo.Sessions

  UNION ALL

  SELECT actid, endtime AS ts, -1 AS type
  FROM dbo.Sessions
),
C2 AS
(
  SELECT *,
    SUM(type) OVER(PARTITION BY actid
                   ORDER BY ts, type
                   ROWS UNBOUNDED PRECEDING) AS cnt
  FROM C1
)
SELECT actid, ts, type, cnt FROM C2;
```

This step generates the following output (for account 2):

```
actid   ts                      type   cnt
------  -------------------     -----  ----
...
2       2015-12-31 08:00:00     1      1
2       2015-12-31 08:30:00     1      2
2       2015-12-31 09:00:00     1      3
2       2015-12-31 09:30:00     -1     2
2       2015-12-31 10:00:00     -1     1
2       2015-12-31 10:30:00     -1     0
2       2015-12-31 11:00:00     1      1
2       2015-12-31 11:30:00     -1     0
2       2015-12-31 11:32:00     1      1
2       2015-12-31 12:00:00     -1     0
2       2015-12-31 12:04:00     1      1
2       2015-12-31 12:30:00     -1     0
...
```

Then the final step is just to group the rows from C2 by account and return the maximum count for each group, like so:

```
WITH C1 AS
(
  SELECT actid, starttime AS ts, +1 AS type
  FROM dbo.Sessions

  UNION ALL

  SELECT actid, endtime AS ts, -1 AS type
  FROM dbo.Sessions
),
C2 AS
(
  SELECT *,
    SUM(type) OVER(PARTITION BY actid
                   ORDER BY ts, type
                   ROWS UNBOUNDED PRECEDING) AS cnt
  FROM C1
)
SELECT actid, MAX(cnt) AS mx
FROM C2
GROUP BY actid;
```

The execution plan for this query is shown in Figure 7-8.

The plan is quite efficient. The indexes idx_start and idx_end are both scanned in order; the rows are merged, preserving the order. Then both the window aggregate and the group aggregate are computed based on that order. No sort operations are applied in the plan. The query took 44 seconds to complete on my system and has linear scaling. That's not too bad considering that the traditional solution with the subquery took 10 hours to complete.

Another solution to the task is based on the ROW_NUMBER function. It has two advantages over the solution with the window aggregate. Remember that window aggregates with a frame option are available only in SQL Server 2012 and later, whereas window ranking functions were available earlier.

Also, window aggregate functions use the Window Spool operator to spool the frame of rows, which is extra work. The ROW_NUMBER function uses streaming operators to handle the computation with no spooling. So handling the task with the ROW_NUMBER function results in better performance.

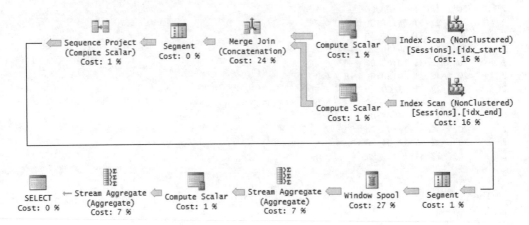

FIGURE 7-8 Plan for a solution with a window aggregate function to the Max Concurrent Intervals task.

The solution based on the ROW_NUMBER function starts similarly to the solution based on the window aggregate. It generates the chronological sequence of events by unifying start and end events. In addition, it computes two row numbers: one that counts how many start events happened until the current start event (call it *s*), and another computing how many start and end events happened until the current start or end event (call it *se*). You compute the ordinal *s* in the query that returns start events, and you return a NULL as a placeholder in the parallel column in the query that returns end events. You define a CTE called C1 representing the unified chronological sequence of events including the ordinal *s*. Then you query C1 and compute the ordinal *se* against the unified events. You define a CTE called C2 based on this query, giving you the unified chronological sequence of events, including both ordinals *s* and *se*. Here's the code implementing the first step:

```
WITH C1 AS
(
  SELECT actid, starttime AS ts, +1 AS type, sessionid,
    ROW_NUMBER() OVER(PARTITION BY actid ORDER BY starttime, sessionid) AS s
  FROM dbo.Sessions

  UNION ALL

  SELECT actid, endtime AS ts, -1 AS type, sessionid, NULL AS s
  FROM dbo.Sessions
),
C2 AS
(
  SELECT *,
    ROW_NUMBER() OVER(PARTITION BY actid ORDER BY ts, type, sessionid) AS se
  FROM C1
)
SELECT sessionid, actid, ts, type, s, se FROM C2;
```

This code generates the following output (only events for account 2 are shown here):

```
sessionid  actid  ts                    type  s     se
---------- ------ --------------------- ----- ----- ---
...
7          2      2015-12-31 08:00:00   1     1     1
8          2      2015-12-31 08:30:00   1     2     2
9          2      2015-12-31 09:00:00   1     3     3
9          2      2015-12-31 09:30:00   -1    NULL  4
8          2      2015-12-31 10:00:00   -1    NULL  5
7          2      2015-12-31 10:30:00   -1    NULL  6
10         2      2015-12-31 11:00:00   1     4     7
10         2      2015-12-31 11:30:00   -1    NULL  8
11         2      2015-12-31 11:32:00   1     5     9
11         2      2015-12-31 12:00:00   -1    NULL  10
12         2      2015-12-31 12:04:00   1     6     11
12         2      2015-12-31 12:30:00   -1    NULL  12
...
```

Recall that the maximum count necessarily falls on one of the start events; that's why it's not interesting to compute counts near end events. You now know for each start event how many start events happened so far (*s*) and how many start and end events happened so far (*se*). Based on these two, you compute how many end events happened so far simply as *se − s*. Then the count of active intervals is the count of start events so far (*s*) minus the count of end events so far (*se − s*), namely *s − (se − s)*. You compute this count (call it *cnt*) in a query against the CTE C2. Then the final step is to group the rows by account and compute the maximum count per group, like so:

```
WITH C1 AS
(
  SELECT actid, starttime AS ts, +1 AS type, sessionid,
    ROW_NUMBER() OVER(PARTITION BY actid ORDER BY starttime, sessionid) AS s
  FROM dbo.Sessions

  UNION ALL

  SELECT actid, endtime AS ts, -1 AS type, sessionid, NULL AS s
  FROM dbo.Sessions
),
C2 AS
(
  SELECT *,
    ROW_NUMBER() OVER(PARTITION BY actid ORDER BY ts, type, sessionid) AS se
  FROM C1
)
SELECT actid, MAX(cnt) AS mx
FROM C2
  CROSS APPLY ( VALUES( s - (se - s) ) ) AS A(cnt)
GROUP BY actid;
```

The plan for this query is shown in Figure 7-9.

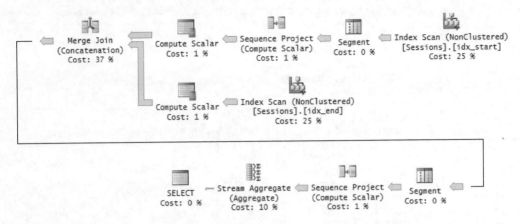

FIGURE 7-9 Plan for a solution with a ROW_NUMBER function to the Max Concurrent Intervals task.

The two indexes idx_start and idx_end are scanned in order. The ordinal *s* is computed by the Segment and Sequence Project operators based on the order of the start events. The start and end events are merged, preserving the order. Another pair of Segment and Sequence Project operators compute the ordinal *se* based on that order. Finally, a Stream Aggregate operator handles the group count, still relying on that order. No explicit sort operations are required. The advantage of this plan is that there's no spooling, unlike in the plan for the previous solution. The Sequence Project operator, which computes the row numbers, is a streaming operator. It would certainly be nice to see future improvements in SQL Server's optimization of aggregate window functions handling common calculations like running totals with streaming operators instead of spooling ones. This plan completed in 17 seconds on my system.

You can further improve the performance of the solution by enabling parallel treatment for different accounts. Encapsulate the logic for a single account in an inline TVF, like so:

```
IF OBJECT_ID(N'dbo.MaxConcurrent', N'IF') IS NOT NULL
  DROP FUNCTION dbo.MaxConcurrent;
GO
CREATE FUNCTION dbo.MaxConcurrent( @actid AS INT ) RETURNS TABLE
AS
RETURN
WITH C1 AS
(
  SELECT starttime AS ts, +1 AS type, sessionid,
    ROW_NUMBER() OVER(ORDER BY starttime, sessionid) AS s
  FROM dbo.Sessions
  WHERE actid = @actid

  UNION ALL

  SELECT endtime AS ts, -1 AS type, sessionid, NULL AS s
  FROM dbo.Sessions
  WHERE actid = @actid
),
```

```
C2 AS
(
  SELECT *,
    ROW_NUMBER() OVER(ORDER BY ts, type, sessionid) AS se
  FROM C1
)
SELECT MAX(cnt) AS mx
FROM C2
  CROSS APPLY ( VALUES( s - (se - s) ) ) AS A(cnt);
GO
```

Query the Accounts table, and using the CROSS APPLY operator apply the inline TVF to each account, like so (trace flag 8649 is used to get a parallel plan for demonstration purposes):

```
SELECT A.actid, C.mx
FROM dbo.Accounts AS A
  CROSS APPLY dbo.MaxConcurrent(A.actid) AS C
OPTION(QUERYTRACEON 8649);
```

I got the plan shown in Figure 7-10 for this query.

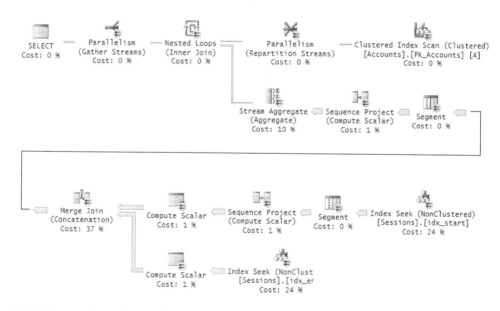

FIGURE 7-10 Solution to the Max Concurrent Intervals task with improved parallelism.

The outer branch of the Nested Loops join scans the Accounts table with a parallel scan, and then it uses the Repartition Streams operator to distribute the work to the different threads using a round-robin algorithm. This results in the inner branch of the Nested Loops join doing work for one account per thread from the outer branch. So even though each account is handled by one thread, multiple accounts are handled in parallel. This plan took eight seconds to complete on my system. That's quite amazing compared to the 10-hour run time of the first solution.

Packing intervals

Packing is another classic task involving intervals. The idea is to merge all intervals that intersect into one packed interval. With our sample data, you're supposed to pack the intervals in the Sessions table per account so that you get the contiguous intervals in which each account had active sessions, never mind how many.

For example, suppose a certain account has the following intervals: [p1, p4), [p2, p3), [p4, p7), [p9, p12), and [p12, p14). The packed intervals are [p1, p7) and [p9, p14). Observe that if one interval starts when another ends, the two are packed together. Following is the desired result for packing the intervals represented by the small set of sample data in the Sessions table:

```
actid        starttime                    endtime
-----------  ---------------------------  ---------------------------
1            2015-12-31 08:00:00          2015-12-31 09:30:00
1            2015-12-31 10:00:00          2015-12-31 12:30:00
2            2015-12-31 08:00:00          2015-12-31 10:30:00
2            2015-12-31 11:00:00          2015-12-31 11:30:00
2            2015-12-31 11:32:00          2015-12-31 12:00:00
2            2015-12-31 12:04:00          2015-12-31 12:30:00
3            2015-12-31 08:00:00          2015-12-31 09:00:00
3            2015-12-31 09:30:00          2015-12-31 09:30:00
```

Like with the Max Concurrent Intervals task, the Packing task also has older, traditional solutions that perform very badly and much faster, newer solutions based on window functions. I'll spare you from going over the traditional solutions and jump straight to the efficient ones. Indexing guidelines are the same as before—namely, create separate indexes for start and end events. If you currently don't have the indexes idx_start and idx_end defined on the Sessions table, run the following code to create those:

```
CREATE UNIQUE INDEX idx_start ON dbo.Sessions(actid, starttime, sessionid);
CREATE UNIQUE INDEX idx_end ON dbo.Sessions(actid, endtime, sessionid);
```

You handle the Packing task based on concepts similar to the ones used in the solutions for the Max Concurrent Intervals task, but with a few extra complexities on top. Also, with packing you rely on computing counts of active intervals, and you can compute those counts either using a window aggregate function or using the ROW_NUMBER function. I'll first describe the solution using a window aggregate.

The first step is to generate a unified chronological sequence of events with a +1 type marking start events and a –1 type marking end events. You define a CTE called C1 based on the query that implements this step.

The second step is to compute the count of active intervals by applying a running sum of the *type* column. However, there are two things that are different about the running sum calculation in the Packing task compared to the Max Concurrent Intervals task. One is that in the window order clause you use *type DESC* as the tiebreaker after *ts* for start and end events that happen at the same time. That's because when packing intervals, you want such events to be part of the same packed interval, and by placing start events before end events, you ensure that the count doesn't drop to zero during a packed interval. The second thing that is different is that when the event is a start event, you need to subtract 1 from the count because for packing purposes, it needs to reflect how many intervals were active before the event was applied. With end events, you actually do need the count to reflect the state after the event was applied, so there's no need to subtract anything in such a case. The subtraction logic can be handled with a CASE expression. You define a CTE called *C2* based on the query that implements the second step. Here's the code handling the first two steps:

```
WITH C1 AS
(
  SELECT sessionid, actid, starttime AS ts, +1 AS type
  FROM dbo.Sessions

  UNION ALL

  SELECT sessionid, actid, endtime AS ts, -1 AS type
  FROM dbo.Sessions
),
C2 AS
(
  SELECT *,
    SUM(type) OVER(PARTITION BY actid
                   ORDER BY ts, type DESC
                   ROWS UNBOUNDED PRECEDING)
      - CASE WHEN type = 1 THEN 1 ELSE 0 END AS cnt
  FROM C1
)
SELECT sessionid, actid, ts, type, cnt FROM C2;
```

This code generates the following output for account 2:

```
sessionid  actid  ts                   type         cnt
---------- ------ -------------------- ------------ -----------
...
7          2      2015-12-31 08:00:00  1            0
8          2      2015-12-31 08:30:00  1            1
9          2      2015-12-31 09:00:00  1            2
9          2      2015-12-31 09:30:00  -1           2
8          2      2015-12-31 10:00:00  -1           1
7          2      2015-12-31 10:30:00  -1           0
10         2      2015-12-31 11:00:00  1            0
10         2      2015-12-31 11:30:00  -1           0
11         2      2015-12-31 11:32:00  1            0
11         2      2015-12-31 12:00:00  -1           0
12         2      2015-12-31 12:04:00  1            0
12         2      2015-12-31 12:30:00  -1           0
...
```

The third step is to filter only events that represent start and end points of a packed interval. Those are the events where *cnt* is zero. Once filtered, each consecutive pair of events represents a packed interval. You need to compute a pair identifier (call it *p*) so that you can handle each pair as a group. For this purpose, you compute a row number (call it *rn*), and then *p* is computed as *FLOOR((rn + 1) / 2)*.

> **Note** In T-SQL, you don't need to explicitly floor the result of the calculation because with integer inputs, you will get integer division. But in other platforms, like Oracle, you get numeric division by default, and the FLOOR function is required for the calculation to be correct. Because I wanted the solution to be more portable, I used this form even though in SQL Server the FLOOR function is unnecessary.

You define a CTE called *C3* based on the query that implements this step.

Finally, you query C3, group the rows by the account and pair identifier, and then return the minimum time stamp as the start of the packed interval and the maximum time stamp as the end. Here's the complete solution code:

```
WITH C1 AS
(
  SELECT sessionid, actid, starttime AS ts, +1 AS type
  FROM dbo.Sessions

  UNION ALL

  SELECT sessionid, actid, endtime AS ts, -1 AS type
  FROM dbo.Sessions
),
C2 AS
(
  SELECT *,
    SUM(type) OVER(PARTITION BY actid
                   ORDER BY ts, type DESC
                   ROWS UNBOUNDED PRECEDING)
      - CASE WHEN type = 1 THEN 1 ELSE 0 END AS cnt
  FROM C1
),
C3 AS
(
  SELECT *,
    FLOOR((ROW_NUMBER() OVER(PARTITION BY actid ORDER BY ts) + 1) / 2) AS p
  FROM C2
  WHERE cnt = 0
)
SELECT actid, MIN(ts) AS starttime, max(ts) AS endtime
FROM C3
GROUP BY actid, p;
```

This query took 54 seconds to complete on my system.

Just like with the Max Concurrent Intervals task, with the Packing task you can compute the count of concurrent intervals using the ROW_NUMBER function more efficiently than using a window aggregate function. For packing purposes, you will need to apply a few adjustments to the previous calculations, but the general idea is pretty similar.

One adjustment is to the calculation of the ordinal *se*, which counts start and end events. Remember that for packing purposes, in case start and end events happen at the same time, they are considered part of the same packed interval. For this reason, in the window order clause of the ROW_NUMBER function computing *se*, you specify *type DESC* (as opposed to the ascending direction used before) as the tiebreaker after *ts*, not allowing the count to drop to zero during a packed interval.

Another adjustment is to the calculation of the counts near start events (what was called *cnt* before and will now be referred to as *cs*). For packing purposes, you need the count to reflect the state before the start event was applied. So you need to subtract 1 from the previous calculation, giving you $s - (se - s) - 1$.

Another adjustment is that, unlike in the previous task where you needed counts only near start events, with packing you also need the counts near end events (call the column *ce*). For this purpose, you will apply a symmetric calculation to *cs*. This means you will compute a row number counting end events (call it *e*) in the query retrieving end events, and you will use a NULL as a placeholder in the query retrieving start events. Then you will compute *ce* based on *e* and *se* as $(se - e) - e$.

Once you have *cs* and *ce* computed, you handle the filtering of only events representing start and end points of packed intervals by using the predicate $cs = 0$ OR $ce = 0$. The rest of the solution is the same as in the solution based on the window aggregate function; namely, you compute the pair identifier (*p*), group the rows by account and pair identifier, and return the minimum and maximum time stamps as the start and end of the packed interval.

Here's the complete solution code:

```
WITH C1 AS
(
  SELECT sessionid, actid, starttime AS ts, +1 AS type,
    ROW_NUMBER() OVER(PARTITION BY actid ORDER BY starttime, sessionid) AS s,
    NULL AS e
  FROM dbo.Sessions

  UNION ALL

  SELECT sessionid, actid, endtime AS ts, -1 AS type,
    NULL AS s,
    ROW_NUMBER() OVER(PARTITION BY actid ORDER BY endtime, sessionid) AS e
  FROM dbo.Sessions
),
C2 AS
(
  SELECT *,
    ROW_NUMBER() OVER(PARTITION BY actid ORDER BY ts, type DESC, sessionid) AS se
  FROM C1
),
C3 AS
(
  SELECT *,
    FLOOR((ROW_NUMBER() OVER(PARTITION BY actid ORDER BY ts) + 1) / 2) AS p
  FROM C2
    CROSS APPLY ( VALUES(s - (se - s) - 1, (se - e) - e) ) AS A(cs, ce)
  WHERE cs = 0 OR ce = 0
)
SELECT actid, MIN(ts) AS starttime, MAX(ts) AS endtime
FROM C3
GROUP BY actid, p;
```

The plan for this solution is shown in Figure 7-11.

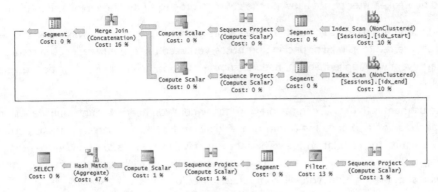

FIGURE 7-11 Plan for a solution based on ROW_NUMBER to the Packing task.

This solution completed in 26 seconds on my system.

Just like with the previous task, with the Packing task you can further improve parallelism handling by encapsulating the work for a single account in an inline TVF and then applying the TVF to the Accounts table using the APPLY operator. Run the following code to define the inline TVF:

```
IF OBJECT_ID(N'dbo.PackedIntervals', N'IF') IS NOT NULL DROP FUNCTION dbo.PackedIntervals;
GO
CREATE FUNCTION dbo.PackedIntervals( @actid AS INT ) RETURNS TABLE
AS
RETURN
WITH C1 AS
(
  SELECT sessionid, starttime AS ts, +1 AS type,
    ROW_NUMBER() OVER(ORDER BY starttime, sessionid) AS s,
    NULL AS e
  FROM dbo.Sessions
  WHERE actid = @actid

  UNION ALL

  SELECT sessionid, endtime AS ts, -1 AS type,
    NULL AS s,
    ROW_NUMBER() OVER(ORDER BY endtime, sessionid) AS e
  FROM dbo.Sessions
  WHERE actid = @actid
),
C2 AS
(
  SELECT *,
    ROW_NUMBER() OVER(ORDER BY ts, type DESC, sessionid) AS se
  FROM C1
),
```

```
C3 AS
(
  SELECT *,
    FLOOR((ROW_NUMBER() OVER(ORDER BY ts) + 1) / 2) AS p
  FROM C2
    CROSS APPLY ( VALUES(s - (se - s) - 1, (se - e) - e ) ) AS A(cs, ce)
  WHERE cs = 0 OR ce = 0
)
SELECT MIN(ts) AS starttime, MAX(ts) AS endtime
FROM C3
GROUP BY p;
GO
```

Then use the following query to apply the TVF to the Accounts table (again, TF 8649 is used to force parallelism for demonstration purposes):

```
SELECT A.actid, P.starttime, P.endtime
FROM dbo.Accounts AS A
  CROSS APPLY dbo.PackedIntervals(A.actid) AS P
OPTION(QUERYTRACEON 8649);
```

Figure 7-12 has the plan that I got for this query on my system.

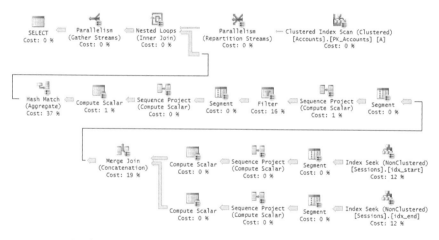

FIGURE 7-12 Plan for a solution to the Packing task with improved parallelism.

This query took only 10 seconds to complete on my system.

Conclusion

As you can see, there's a lot of trickiness in dealing with date and time data. There are pitfalls related to different language conventions, rounding problems, nonSARGable filters, and limitations of the implementation. Fortunately, there are solutions you can use to handle date and time related tasks correctly and efficiently, even though some of those solutions are more complex and require some creativity. This chapter gave you an appreciation of the importance of following best practices and the tools to do your job well as far as handling of date and time data is concerned.

T-SQL for BI practitioners

Huge amounts of data already exist in transactional databases worldwide. There is more and more need to analyze this data. Database and business intelligence (BI) developers need to create thousands, if not millions, of reports on a daily basis. Many of these reports include statistical analyses. Statistical analysis of data is useful for data overview and data quality assessment, which are two typical initial stages of more in-depth analyses. However, there are not many statistical functions in Microsoft SQL Server. In addition, a good understanding of statistics is not common among T-SQL practitioners.

This chapter explains the basics of statistical analysis. It introduces many ways to calculate different statistics with T-SQL and Common Language Runtime (CLR) code. The code is based on real-life experience. I developed the code for myself because I am dealing with BI projects, especially with data mining, and I needed to create a lot of statistical queries in the initial state of many projects. Of course, there are many statistical packages available for purchase. However, many of my clients do not permit installing any additional software on their systems. Therefore, the only software I can rely upon is SQL Server.

Optimizing statistical queries is different than optimizing transactional queries. To calculate statistics, the query typically scans all the data. If the query is too slow, you can prepare a random sample of your data and then scan the sample data. However, if the queries follow the formulas blindly, many times they finish with multiple scans of the data. Optimizing such queries means minimizing the number of passes through the data. To achieve this task, you often need to develop an algorithm that uses additional mathematics to convert the formulas to equivalent ones that can be better optimized in SQL Server. You also need to understand T-SQL in depth. For example, you need a really good understanding of window functions and calculations. Besides teaching you about statistics and statistical queries, this chapter will help you with query optimization for efficiently writing nonstatistical queries too.

Data preparation

Before starting any statistical analysis, you need to understand what you are analyzing. In statistics, you analyze cases using their variables. To put it in SQL Server terminology, you can think of a *case* as a row in a table, and you can think of a *variable* as a column in the same table. For most statistical analyses, you prepare a single table or view. It is not always easy to define your case. For example, for a credit-risk analysis, you might define a family as a case, rather than defining it as a single customer. When you prepare the data for statistical analyses, you have to transform the source data accordingly. For each case, you need to encapsulate all available information in the columns of the table you are going to analyze.

Before starting a serious data overview, you need to understand how data values are measured in your data set. You might need to check this with a subject matter expert and analyze the business system that is the source for your data. There are different ways to measure data values and different types of columns:

- **Discrete variables**   These variables can take a value only from a limited domain of possible values. Discrete values include categorical or nominal variables that have no natural order. Examples include states, status codes, and colors. *Ranks* can also take a value only from a discrete set of values. They have an order but do not permit any arithmetic. Examples include opinion ranks and binned (grouped, discretized) true numeric values.

  There are also some specific types of categorical variables. Single-valued variables, or *constants*, are not very interesting for analysis because they do not contribute any information. Two-valued, or *dichotomous*, variables have two values, which is the minimum needed for any analysis. Binary variables are specific dichotomous variables that take on only the values 0 and 1.

- **Continuous variables**   These variables can take any of an unlimited number of possible values; however, the domain itself can have a lower boundary, upper boundary, or both. Intervals have one or two boundaries, have an order, and allow some arithmetic-like subtraction, but they do not always have a summation. Examples include dates, times, and temperatures. True numeric variables support all arithmetic. Examples include amounts and values. Monotonic variables are a specific type of continuous variables, which increase monotonously without bound. If they are simply IDs, they might not be interesting. Still, they can be transformed (binned into categories) if the ever-growing ID contains time order information (lower IDs are older than higher IDs).

Sales analysis view

In this chapter, I will perform all the statistical queries on a view for sales analysis. In this view, I join the OrderDetails table with the Orders, Customers, Products, Categories, and Employees tables to get some interesting variables to analyze. I am not using all the columns in the following code. However, you can use them for further investigation and tests of the statistical queries.

To create the SalesAnalysis view, run the code in Listing 8-1. Partial contents (a selection of columns and rows) of the SalesAnalysis view are shown in Table 8-1.

LISTING 8-1 Data-definition language for the SalesAnalysis view.

```
SET NOCOUNT ON;
USE TSQLV3;
IF OBJECT_ID(N'dbo.SalesAnalysis', N'V') IS NOT NULL DROP VIEW dbo.SalesAnalysis;
GO
CREATE VIEW dbo.SalesAnalysis
AS
SELECT O.orderid, P.productid, C.country AS customercountry,
  CASE
    WHEN c.country IN
      (N'Argentina', N'Brazil', N'Canada', N'Mexico',
       N'USA', N'Venezuela') THEN 'Americas'
    ELSE 'Europe'
  END AS 'customercontinent',
  e.country AS employeecountry, PC.categoryname,
  YEAR(O.orderdate) AS orderyear,
  DATEDIFF(day, O.requireddate, o.shippeddate) AS requiredvsshipped,
  OD.unitprice, OD.qty, OD.discount,
  CAST(OD.unitprice * OD.qty AS NUMERIC(10,2)) AS salesamount,
  CAST(OD.unitprice * OD.qty * OD.discount AS NUMERIC(10,2)) AS discountamount
FROM Sales.OrderDetails AS OD
  INNER JOIN Sales.Orders AS O
  ON OD.orderid = O.orderid
  INNER JOIN Sales.Customers AS C
  ON O.custid = C.custid
  INNER JOIN Production.Products AS P
  ON OD.productid = P.productid
  INNER JOIN Production.Categories AS PC
  ON P.categoryid = PC.categoryid
  INNER JOIN HR.Employees AS E
  ON O.empid = E.empid;
GO
```

TABLE 8-1 Partial contents of the SalesAnalysis view

orderid	productid	categoryname	salesamount	discountamount
10643	28	Produce	684	171
10643	39	Beverages	378	94.5
10643	46	Seafood	24	6
10692	63	Condiments	878	0
10702	3	Condiments	60	0
10702	76	Beverages	270	0
10835	59	Dairy Products	825	0
10835	77	Condiments	26	5.2
10952	6	Condiments	400	20
10952	28	Produce	91.2	0

Frequencies

For a quick overview of discrete variables, use frequency tables. In a frequency table, you can show values, absolute frequency of those values, absolute percentage, cumulative frequency, cumulative percentage, and the histogram of the absolute percentage.

Frequencies without window functions

Calculating the absolute frequency and absolute percentage is a straightforward aggregation. However, calculating the cumulative frequency and cumulative percentage means calculating running totals. Before SQL Server 2012 added support for window aggregate functions with a frame, you needed to use either correlated subqueries or non-equi self joins for this task. Both methods are pretty inefficient.

Run the following code to analyze the frequency distribution of the *categoryname* variable, which implements a solution with correlated subqueries:

```
WITH FreqCTE AS
(
SELECT categoryname,
  COUNT(categoryname) AS absfreq,
  ROUND(100. * (COUNT(categoryname)) /
    (SELECT COUNT(*) FROM dbo.SalesAnalysis), 4) AS absperc
FROM dbo.SalesAnalysis
GROUP BY categoryname
)
SELECT C1.categoryname,
  C1.absfreq,
  (SELECT SUM(C2.absfreq)
   FROM FreqCTE AS C2
   WHERE C2.categoryname <= C1.categoryname) AS cumfreq,
  CAST(ROUND(C1.absperc, 0) AS INT) AS absperc,
  CAST(ROUND((SELECT SUM(C2.absperc)
   FROM FreqCTE AS C2
   WHERE C2.categoryname <= C1.categoryname), 0) AS INT) AS cumperc,
  CAST(REPLICATE('*',C1.absPerc) AS VARCHAR(100)) AS histogram
FROM FreqCTE AS C1
ORDER BY C1.categoryname;
```

The preceding code generates the following output:

```
categoryname     absfreq     cumfreq     absperc     cumperc     histogram
---------------  ----------  ----------  ----------  ----------  --------------------
Beverages        404         404         19          19          *******************
Condiments       216         620         10          29          **********
Confections      334         954         15          44          ***************
Dairy Products   366         1320        17          61          *****************
Grains/Cereals   196         1516        9           70          *********
Meat/Poultry     173         1689        8           78          ********
Produce          136         1825        6           84          ******
Seafood          330         2155        15          100         ***************
```

Frequencies with window functions

A much more efficient solution uses the window aggregate functions with a frame available in SQL Server versions 2012 and newer. The first part of the query, the common table expression query that calculates the absolute numbers, is the same as in the previous query. However, the cumulative values, also known as the *running totals*, are calculated with the help of the window aggregate functions.

```
WITH FreqCTE AS
(
SELECT categoryname,
  COUNT(categoryname) AS absfreq,
  ROUND(100. * (COUNT(categoryname)) /
    (SELECT COUNT(*) FROM dbo.SalesAnalysis), 4) AS absperc
FROM dbo.SalesAnalysis
GROUP BY categoryname
)
SELECT categoryname,
  absfreq,
  SUM(absfreq)
   OVER(ORDER BY categoryname
        ROWS BETWEEN UNBOUNDED PRECEDING
         AND CURRENT ROW) AS cumfreq,
  CAST(ROUND(absperc, 0) AS INT) AS absperc,
  CAST(ROUND(SUM(absperc)
   OVER(ORDER BY categoryname
        ROWS BETWEEN UNBOUNDED PRECEDING
         AND CURRENT ROW), 0) AS INT) AS CumPerc,
  CAST(REPLICATE('*',absperc) AS VARCHAR(50)) AS histogram
FROM FreqCTE
ORDER BY categoryname;
```

Of course, the output of this query is the same as the output of the previous query.

I found another interesting solution with window analytic functions. The CUME_DIST function calculates the cumulative distribution of a value in a group of values. That is, CUME_DIST computes the relative position of a specified value in a group of values. For a row *r*, assuming ascending ordering, the CUME_DIST of *r* is the number of rows with values lower than or equal to the value of *r*, divided by the number of rows evaluated in the partition or query result set. The PERCENT_RANK function calculates the relative rank of a row within a group of rows. Use PERCENT_RANK to evaluate the relative standing of a value within a query result set or partition.

The following query calculates the row number once partitioned over the *categoryname* column and once over the entire input set. It also calculates the percent rank and the cumulative distribution over the complete input set:

```
SELECT categoryname,
  ROW_NUMBER() OVER(PARTITION BY categoryname
   ORDER BY categoryname, orderid, productid) AS rn_absfreq,
  ROW_NUMBER() OVER(
   ORDER BY categoryname, orderid, productid) AS rn_cumfreq,
  PERCENT_RANK()
   OVER(ORDER BY categoryname) AS pr_absperc,
  CUME_DIST()
   OVER(ORDER BY categoryname, orderid, productid) AS cd_cumperc
FROM dbo.SalesAnalysis;
```

Partial output with rows is interesting for showing the algorithm for calculating frequencies:

```
categoryname     rn_absfreq rn_cumfreq pr_absperc           cd_cumperc
---------------- ---------- ---------- -------------------- ----------------------
Beverages        1          1          0                    0.000464037122969838
Beverages        2          2          0                    0.000928074245939675
...              ...
Beverages        404        404        0                    0.187470997679814
Condiments       1          405        0.187558031569174    0.187935034802784
...              ...
Condiments       216        620        0.187558031569174    0.287703016241299
Confections      1          621        0.287836583101207    0.288167053364269
```

As you can see, the last row number in a category actually represents the absolute frequency of the values in that category. The last unpartitioned row number in a category represents the cumulative frequency up to and including the current category. For example, the absolute frequency for beverages is 404 and the cumulative frequency is 404; for condiments, the absolute frequency is 216 and the cumulative frequency is 620. The CUME_DIST function (the *cd_cumperc* column in the output) for the last row in a category returns the cumulative percentage up to and including the category. If you subtract the PERCENT_RANK (the *pr_absperc* column in the output) for the last row in a category from the CUME_DIST of the last row in a category, you get the absolute percentage for the category. For example, the absolute percentage for condiments is around 10 percent (0.287703016241299 – 0.187558031569174).

The following query calculates the frequency distribution using the observations from the results of the previous query:

```
WITH FreqCTE AS
(
SELECT categoryname,
  ROW_NUMBER() OVER(PARTITION BY categoryname
   ORDER BY categoryname, orderid, productid) AS rn_absfreq,
  ROW_NUMBER() OVER(
   ORDER BY categoryname, orderid, productid) AS rn_cumfreq,
  ROUND(100 * PERCENT_RANK()
   OVER(ORDER BY categoryname), 4) AS pr_absperc,
  ROUND(100 * CUME_DIST()
   OVER(ORDER BY categoryname, orderid, productid), 4) AS cd_cumperc
FROM dbo.SalesAnalysis
)
SELECT categoryname,
  MAX(rn_absfreq) AS absfreq,
  MAX(rn_cumfreq) AS cumfreq,
  ROUND(MAX(cd_cumperc) - MAX(pr_absperc), 0) AS absperc,
  ROUND(MAX(cd_cumperc), 0) AS cumperc,
  CAST(REPLICATE('*',ROUND(MAX(cd_cumperc) - MAX(pr_absperc),0)) AS VARCHAR(100)) AS histogram
FROM FreqCTE
GROUP BY categoryname
ORDER BY categoryname;
GO
```

Although the concept of the last query is interesting, it is not as efficient as one using the window aggregate function. Therefore, the second query from these three solutions for calculating the frequency distribution is the recommended one.

Descriptive statistics for continuous variables

Frequencies are useful for analyzing the distribution of discrete variables. You describe continuous variables with *population moments*, which are measures that give you some insight into the distribution. These measures give you an insight into the distribution of the values of the continuous variables. The first four population moments include center, spread, skewness, and peakedness of a distribution.

Centers of a distribution

There are many measures for a center of a distribution. Here are three of the most popular ones:

- The *mode* is the most frequent (that is, the most popular) value. This is the number that appears most often in a set of numbers. It is not necessarily unique—a distribution can have the same maximum frequency at different values.

- The *median* is the middle value in your distribution. When the number of cases is odd, the median is the middle entry in the data after you sort your variable data points in increasing order. When the number of cases is even, the median is equal to the sum of the two middle numbers (sorted in increasing order) divided by two. Note that there are other definitions of median, as I will show with the T-SQL PERCENTILE_CONT and PERCENTILE_DISC functions.

- The *mean* is the average value of your distribution. This is actually the arithmetic mean. There are other types of means, such as a geometric mean or harmonic mean. To avoid confusion, you should use the term *arithmetic mean*. However, for the sake of simplicity, I will use the term *mean* in the following text when discussing the arithmetic mean.

You'll find it useful to calculate more than one measure—more than one center of a distribution. You get some idea of the distribution just by comparing the values of the mode, median, and mean. If the distribution is symmetrical and has only a single peak, the mode, median, and mean all coincide. If not, the distribution is skewed in some way. Perhaps it has a long tail to the right. Then the *mode* would stay on the value with the highest relative frequency, while the *median* would move to the right to pick up half the observations. Half of the observations lie on either side of the median, but the cases on the right are farther out and exert more downward leverage. To balance them out, the mean must move even further to the right. If the distribution of data is skewed to the left, the mean is less than the median, which is often less than the mode. If the distribution of data is skewed to the right, the mode is often less than the median, which is less than the mean. However, calculating how much the distribution is skewed means calculating the third population moment, the *skewness*, which is explained later in this chapter.

Mode

The mode is the most fashionable value of a distribution—*mode* is actually the French word for *fashion*. Calculating the mode is simple and straightforward. In the following query, I use the TOP (1) WITH TIES expression to get the most frequent values in the distribution of the *salesamount* variable.

```
SELECT TOP (1) WITH TIES salesamount, COUNT(*) AS number
FROM dbo.SalesAnalysis
GROUP BY salesamount
ORDER BY COUNT(*) DESC;
```

The result is

```
salesamount                              number
---------------------------------------- -----------
360.00                                   29
```

The WITH TIES clause is needed because there could be more than one value with the same number of occurrences in the distribution. We call distributions with more than one mode *bi-modal distribution*, *three-modal distribution*, and so on.

Median

The median is the value that splits the distribution into two halves. The number of rows with a value lower than the median must be equal to the number of rows with a value greater than the median for a selected variable. If there is an odd number of rows, the median is the middle row. If the number of rows is even, the median can be defined as the average value of the two middle rows (the financial median), the smaller of them (the lower statistical median), or the larger of them (the upper statistical median).

The PERCENTILE_DISC function computes a specific percentile for sorted values in an entire rowset or within distinct partitions of a rowset. For a given percentile value P, PERCENTILE_DISC sorts the values of the expression in the ORDER BY clause and returns the value with the smallest CUME_DIST value (with respect to the same sort specification) that is greater than or equal to P. PERCENTILE_DISC calculates the percentile based on a discrete distribution of the column values; the result is equal to a specific value in the column. Therefore, the PERCENTILE_DISC (0.5) function calculates the lower statistical median.

The PERCENTILE_CONT function calculates a percentile based on a continuous distribution of the column value in SQL Server. The result is interpolated and might not be equal to any specific values in the column. Therefore, this function calculates the financial median. The financial median is by far the most-used median.

The following code shows the difference between the PERCENTILE_DISC and PERCENTILE_CONT functions. It creates a simple table and inserts four rows with the values 1, 2, 3, and 4 for the only column in the table. Then it calculates the lower statistical and financial medians:

```
IF OBJECT_ID(N'dbo.TestMedian',N'U') IS NOT NULL
  DROP TABLE dbo.TestMedian;
GO
CREATE TABLE dbo.TestMedian
(
 val INT    NOT NULL
);
GO
INSERT INTO dbo.TestMedian (val)
VALUES (1), (2), (3), (4);
SELECT DISTINCT            -- can also use TOP (1)
  PERCENTILE_DISC(0.5) WITHIN GROUP (ORDER BY val) OVER () AS mediandisc,
  PERCENTILE_CONT(0.5) WITHIN GROUP (ORDER BY val) OVER () AS mediancont
FROM dbo.TestMedian;
GO
```

The result of the code is

```
mediandisc  mediancont
----------- ----------------------
2           2.5
```

You can clearly see the difference between the two percentile functions. I calculate the financial median for the *salesamount* column of the SalesAnalysis view in the following query:

```
SELECT DISTINCT
  PERCENTILE_CONT(0.5) WITHIN GROUP (ORDER BY salesamount) OVER () AS median
FROM dbo.SalesAnalysis;
```

The query returns the following result:

```
median
----------------------
360
```

In this case, for the *salesamount* column, the mode and the median are equal. However, this does not mean that the distribution is not skewed. I need to calculate the mean as well before making any conclusion about the skewness.

Mean

The mean is the most common measure for determining the center of a distribution. It is also probably the most abused statistical measure. The mean does not *mean* anything without the standard deviation (explained later in the chapter), and it should never be used alone. Let me give you an example. Imagine there are two pairs of people. In the first pair, both people earn the same wage—let's say, $80,000 per year. In the second pair, one person earns $30,000 per year, while the other earns $270,000 per year. The mean wage for the first pair is $80,000, while the mean for the second pair is $150,000 per year. By just listing the mean, you could conclude that each person from the second pair earns more than either of the people in the first pair. However, you can clearly see that this would be a seriously incorrect conclusion.

The definition of the mean is simple: it is the sum of all values of a continuous variable divided by the number of cases, as shown in the following formula:

$$\mu = \frac{1}{n} * \sum_{i=1}^{n} v_i$$

Because of the great importance of the mean, the T-SQL language has included the AVG aggregate function. The following query uses it to calculate the mean value for the *salesamount* variable:

```
SELECT AVG(salesamount) AS mean
FROM dbo.SalesAnalysis;
```

The result of the query is

```
mean
-----------
628.519067
```

Compare this value to the value for the median and the mode, which is 360. Apparently, the mean is much higher; this means that the distribution is skewed to the right, having a long tail of infrequent, but high values on the right side—that is, on the side with bigger values.

The mean is the first population moment. It is also called the *estimated value* or the *estimator*, because you can use it to estimate the value of a variable for an unknown case. However, you have already seen that the mean alone can be a very bad estimator.

Spread of a distribution

As mentioned, you need to know how spread out or varied the observations are—are you dealing with a very uniform or a very spread population? Similar to the center, the spread can be measured in several ways as well.

From among the many different definitions for the spread of the distribution, I will discuss the most popular ones: the range, the inter-quartile range, the mean absolute and mean squared deviation, the variance, and the standard deviation. I will also introduce the term *degrees of freedom* and explain the difference between *variance* and *standard deviation* for samples and for population.

Range

The range is the simplest measure of the spread; it is the plain distance between the maximal value and the minimal value that the variable takes. (A quick review: a variable is an attribute of an observation, represented as a column in a table.) The first formula for the range is

$$R = v_{max} - v_{min}$$

Of course, you use the MAX and MIN T-SQL aggregate functions to calculate the range of a variable:

```
SELECT MAX(salesamount) - MIN(salesamount) AS range
FROM dbo.SalesAnalysis;
```

You get the following output:

```
range
-----------
15805.20
```

Inter-Quartile range

The median is the value that splits the distribution into two halves. You can split the distribution more—for example, you can split each half into two halves. This way, you get quartiles as three values that split the distribution into quarters. Let's generalize this splitting process. You start with sorting rows (cases, observations) on a selected column (attribute, variable). You define the rank as the absolute position of a row in your sequence of sorted rows. The percentile rank of a value is a relative measure that tells you how many percent of all (*n*) observations have a lower value than the selected value.

By splitting the observations into quarters, you get three percentiles (at 25%, 50%, and 75% of all rows), and you can read the values at those positions that are important enough to have their own names: the quartiles. The second quartile is, of course, the median. The first one is called the *lower quartile* and the third one is known as the *upper quartile*. If you subtract the lower quartile (the first one) from the upper quartile (the third one), you get the formula for the Inter-Quartile Range (IQR):

$$IQR = Q_3 - Q_1$$

Calculating the IQR is simple with the window analytic function PERCENTILE_CONT:

```
SELECT DISTINCT
  PERCENTILE_CONT(0.75) WITHIN GROUP (ORDER BY salesamount) OVER () -
  PERCENTILE_CONT(0.25) WITHIN GROUP (ORDER BY salesamount) OVER () AS IQR
FROM dbo.SalesAnalysis;
```

This query returns the following result:

```
IQR
---------
568.25
```

The IQR is resistant to a change just like the median. This means it is not sensitive to a wild swing in a single observation. (Let's quickly review: a single observation is a single case, represented as a row in a table.) The resistance is logical, because you use only two key observations. When you see a big difference between the range and the inter-quartile range of the same variable, like in the *salesamount* variable in the example, some values in the distribution are quite far away from the mean value.

Mean absolute deviation

For the IQR, you use only two key observations: the lower and upper quartiles. Is there a measure that would take both observations into account? You can measure the distance between each value and the mean value and call it the *deviation*. The sum of all distances gives you a measure of how spread out your population is. But you must consider that some of the distances are positive while others are negative; actually, they mutually cancel themselves out, so the total gives you exactly zero. The same is true for the average of the deviations, so this would be a useless measure of spread. You solve this problem by ignoring the signs, and instead using the absolute values of the distances. Calculating the average of the absolute deviations, you get the formula for the Mean Absolute Deviation (MAD):

$$MAD = \frac{1}{n} * \sum_{i=1}^{n} |v_i - \mu|$$

From the formula for the MAD, you can see that you need to calculate the mean with the AVG T-SQL aggregate function and then use this aggregation in the SUM T-SQL aggregate function. However, SQL Server cannot perform an aggregate function on an expression containing an aggregate or a subquery; therefore, I am going to do it by storing the mean value to a variable:

```
DECLARE @mean AS NUMERIC(10,2);
SET @mean = (SELECT AVG(salesamount) FROM dbo.SalesAnalysis);
SELECT SUM(ABS(salesamount - @mean))/COUNT(*) AS MAD
FROM dbo.SalesAnalysis;
```

You get the following output:

```
MAD
----------------------------------------
527.048886
```

Mean squared deviation

Another way of avoiding the problems of the signs of the deviations is to square each deviation. With a slight modification of the MAD formula—specifically, calculating the average of the squared deviations instead of the absolute deviations—you get the formula for the Mean Squared Deviation (MSD):

$$MSD = \frac{1}{n} * \sum_{i=1}^{n} (v_i - \mu)^2$$

To calculate the MSD, you need to change the query for the MAD slightly:

```
DECLARE @mean AS NUMERIC(10,2);
SET @mean = (SELECT AVG(salesamount) FROM dbo.SalesAnalysis);
SELECT SUM(SQUARE(salesamount - @mean))/COUNT(*) AS MSD
FROM dbo.SalesAnalysis;
```

The query returns the following result for the MSD:

MSD

1073765.30181991

Degrees of freedom and variance

Let's suppose for a moment you have only one observation ($n=1$). This observation is also your sample mean, but there is no spread at all. You can calculate the spread only if you have the n that exceeds 1. Only the ($n–1$) pieces of information help you calculate the spread, considering that the first observation is your mean. These pieces of information are called *degrees of freedom*. You can also think of degrees of freedom as of the number of pieces of information that can vary. For example, imagine a variable that can take five different discrete states. You need to calculate the frequencies of four states only to know the distribution of the variable; the frequency of the last state is determined by the frequencies of the first four states you calculated, and they cannot vary, because the cumulative percentage of all states must equal 100.

Remember that the sum of all deviations, without canceling out the sign, always gives you zero. So there are only (n–1) deviations free; the last one is strictly determined by the requirement just stated. The definition of the Variance (*Var*) is similar to the definition of the MSD; you just replace the number of cases n with the degrees of freedom ($n–1$):

$$Var = \frac{1}{n-1} * \sum_{i=1}^{n} (v_i - \mu)^2$$

This is the formula for the variance of a sample, used as an estimator for the variance of the population. Now imagine that your data represents the complete population, and the mean value is unknown. Then all the observations contribute to the variance calculation equally, and the degrees of freedom make no sense. The variance of a population is defined, then, with the same formula as the MSD:

$$Var = \frac{1}{n} * \sum_{i=1}^{n} (v_i - \mu)^2$$

Transact-SQL includes an aggregate function that calculates the variance for a sample as an estimator for the variance of the population (the VARP function) and a function that calculates the variance for the population (the VAR function). A query that uses them is very simple. The following query calculates both variances and also compares them in two ways: by dividing them, and by dividing the number of cases minus one with the number of cases, to show that the difference is only a result of the degrees of freedom used in calculating the variance of a sample as an estimator for the variance of the population:

```
SELECT VAR(salesamount) AS populationvariance,
  VARP(salesamount) AS samplevariance,
  VARP(salesamount) / VAR(salesamount) AS samplevspopulation1,
  (1.0 * COUNT(*) - 1) / COUNT(*) AS samplevspopulation2
FROM dbo.SalesAnalysis;
```

The query returns the following result:

```
populationvariance samplevariance     samplevspopulation1 samplevspopulation2
------------------ ------------------  ------------------- -------------------
1074263.80010215   1073765.30181904   0.99953596287703    0.999535962877
```

If your sample is big enough, the difference is negligible. In the example I am using when analyzing the sales, the data represents the complete sales—that is, the population. Therefore, using the variance for the population is more appropriate for a correct analysis here.

Standard deviation and the coefficient of the variation

To compensate for having the deviations squared, you can take the square root of the variance. This is the definition of the standard deviation (σ):

$$\sigma = \sqrt{Var}$$

Of course, you can use the same formula to calculate the standard deviation of the population, and the standard deviation of a sample as an estimator of the standard deviation for the population; just use the appropriate variance in the formula.

I derived the absolute measures of the spread, the interpretation of which is quite evident for a single variable—the bigger the values of the measures are, the more spread out the variable in the observations is. But the absolute measures cannot be used to compare the spread between two or more variables. Therefore, I need to derive relative measures. I can derive the relative measures of the spread for any of the absolute measures mentioned, but I will limit myself to only the most popular one: the standard deviation. The definition of the relative standard deviation or the Coefficient of the Variation (CV) is a simple division of the standard deviation with the mean value:

$$CV = \frac{\sigma}{\mu}$$

T-SQL includes two aggregate functions to calculate the standard deviation for the population (STDEVP) and to calculate the standard deviation for a sample (STDEV) as an estimator for the standard deviation for the population. Calculating standard deviation and the coefficient of the variation, therefore, is simple and straightforward. The following query calculates both standard deviations for the *salesamount* column and the coefficient of the variation for the *salesamount* and *discountamount* columns:

```sql
SELECT STDEV(salesamount) AS populationstdev,
  STDEVP(salesamount) AS samplestdev,
  STDEV(salesamount) / AVG(salesamount) AS CVsalesamount,
  STDEV(discountamount) / AVG(discountamount) AS CVdiscountamount
FROM dbo.SalesAnalysis;
```

The query returns the following result:

```
populationstdev    samplestdev        CVsalesamount       CVdiscountamount
------------------ ------------------  ------------------- -------------------
1036.46697974521   1036.2264722632    1.64906211150028    3.25668651182147
```

You can see that the *discountamount* variable varies more than the *salesamount* variable.

Higher population moments

By comparing the mean and the median, you can determine whether your distribution is skewed. Can you also measure this skewness? Of course, the answer is yes. However, before defining and calculating this measure, you need to define the normal and standard-normal distributions.

Normal and standard normal distributions

Normal distributions are a family of distributions that have the same general shape. Normal distributions are symmetric, with scores more concentrated in the middle than in the tails. Normal distributions are described as *bell shaped*. The bell curve is also called a *Gaussian curve*, in honor of Karl Friedrich Gauss.

The height of a normal distribution is specified mathematically with two parameters: the mean (μ) and the standard deviation (σ). Constants in the formula are π (3.14159) and e (the base of natural logarithms = 2.718282). The formula for the normal distribution is

$$f(x,\mu,\sigma) = \frac{1}{\sqrt{2\pi\sigma}} * e^{-(x-\mu)^2/2\sigma^2}$$

The normal distribution is a commonly occurring, continuous probability distribution. It is a function that tells the probability that any real observation will fall between any two real limits or real numbers, as the curve approaches zero on either side. Normal distributions are extremely important in statistics and are often used in the natural and social sciences for real-valued random variables whose distributions are not known. Simply said, if you do not know the distribution of a continuous variable in advance, you assume that it follows the normal distribution.

The standard normal distribution (Z distribution) is a normal distribution with a mean of 0 and a standard deviation of 1. You can easily calculate the *z* values of the standard normal distribution by normalizing the *x* values of the normal distribution:

$$z = \frac{x - \mu}{\sigma}$$

Figure 8-1 shows the standard normal distribution curve.

You can see that the probability that a value lies more than couple of standard deviations away from the mean gets low very quickly. The figure shows the probability function calculated only to four standard deviations from the mean on both sides. Later in this chapter, I will show you how to calculate this probability.

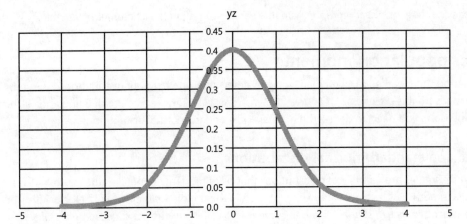

FIGURE 8-1 Standard normal distribution.

Skewness

Skewness is a parameter that describes asymmetry in a random variable's probability distribution. Skewness characterizes the degree of asymmetry of a distribution around its mean. Positive skewness indicates a distribution with an asymmetric tail extending toward more positive values. Negative skewness indicates a distribution with an asymmetric tail extending toward more negative values.

Skewness tells you that values in the tail on one side of the mean (depending on whether the skewness is positive or negative) might still be valid and you don't want to deal with them as outliers. Outliers are rare and far out-of-bounds values that might be erroneous. Therefore, knowing the skewness of a variable does not give you only information about the variable distribution; it also can help you when you cleanse your data.

The formula for the skewness is

$$\text{Skew} = \frac{n}{(n-1)*(n-2)} * \sum_{i=1}^{n} \left(\frac{v_i - \mu}{\sigma}\right)^3$$

Similar to the mean-absolute-deviation and the mean-squared-deviation formulas, the formula for the skewness uses the mean value. In addition, there is also the standard deviation in the formula. I calculated the MAD and MSD with inefficient code; I calculated the mean in advance, and then the MAD and MSD. This means I scanned all the data twice. I did not bother to optimize the code for the MAD and MSD, because I used these two measures of a spread only to lead you slowly to the variance and the standard deviation, which are commonly used. For the variance and the standard deviation, aggregate functions are included in T-SQL. There is no skewness aggregate function; therefore, you need to optimize the code. I want to calculate the skewness by scanning the data only once.

I use a bit of mathematics for this optimization. First, I expand the formula for the subtraction of the mean from the *i*th value cubed.

$$(v_i - \mu)^3 = v_i^3 - 3v_i^2\mu + 3v_i\mu^2 - \mu^3$$

Then I use the fact that the sum is distributive over the product, as shown in the formula for two values only:

$$3v_1\mu^2 + 3v_2\mu^2 = 3\mu^2(v_1 + v_2)$$

This formula can be generalized for all values:

$$\sum_{i=1}^{n}(3v_i\mu^2) = 3\mu^2 \sum_{i=1}^{n}(v_i)$$

Of course, I can do the same mathematics for the remaining elements of the expanded formula for the subtraction and calculate all the aggregates I need with a single pass through the data in a common table expression (CTE), and then calculate the skewness with these aggregates, like the following query shows:

```
WITH SkewCTE AS
(
SELECT SUM(salesamount) AS rx,
  SUM(POWER(salesamount,2)) AS rx2,
  SUM(POWER(salesamount,3)) AS rx3,
  COUNT(salesamount) AS rn,
  STDEV(salesamount) AS stdv,
  AVG(salesamount) AS av
FROM dbo.SalesAnalysis
)
SELECT
  (rx3 - 3*rx2*av + 3*rx*av*av - rn*av*av*av)
  / (stdv*stdv*stdv) * rn / (rn-1) / (rn-2) AS skewness
FROM SkewCTE;
```

The query returns the following result:

```
skewness
----------------------
6.78219500069942
```

Positive skewness means that the distribution of the *salesamount* variable has a longer tail on the right side, extending more toward the positive values.

Kurtosis

Kurtosis characterizes the relative peakedness or flatness of a distribution compared with the normal distribution. A positive kurtosis means a higher peak around the mean and some extreme values on any side tail. A negative kurtosis indicates a relatively flat distribution. For a peaked distribution, consider that values far from the mean in any direction might be correct. The formula for the kurtosis is

$$\text{Kurt} = \frac{n*(n+1)}{(n-1)*(n-2)*(n-3)} * \sum_{i=1}^{n}(\frac{v_i - \mu}{\sigma})^4 - \frac{3*(n-1)^2}{(n-2)*(n-3)}$$

As with the skewness, you can see that the formula for the kurtosis also includes the mean and the standard deviation. To get an efficient query, I start with expanding the subtraction again:

$$(v_i - \mu)^4 = v_i{}^4 - 4v_i{}^3\mu + 6v_i{}^2\mu^2 - 4v_i\mu^3 + \mu^4$$

After that, I can use the fact that the sum is distributive over the product again, and calculate the kurtosis with a single scan of the data, as the following query shows:

```
WITH KurtCTE AS
(
SELECT SUM(salesamount) AS rx,
   SUM(POWER(salesamount,2)) AS rx2,
   SUM(POWER(salesamount,3)) AS rx3,
   SUM(POWER(salesamount,4)) AS rx4,
   COUNT(salesamount) AS rn,
   STDEV(salesamount) AS stdv,
   AVG(salesamount) AS av
FROM dbo.SalesAnalysis
)
SELECT
   (rx4 - 4*rx3*av + 6*rx2*av*av - 4*rx*av*av*av + rn*av*av*av*av)
   / (stdv*stdv*stdv*stdv) * rn * (rn+1) / (rn-1) / (rn-2) / (rn-3)
   - 3.0 * (rn-1) * (rn-1) / (rn-2) / (rn-3) AS kurtosis
FROM KurtCTE;
```

The result for the kurtosis of the *salesamount* variable is

```
kurtosis
----------------------
68.7756494703992
```

The value for the kurtosis tells you that there are many values of the *salesamount* variable around the mean, because there is a high peak in the distribution around the mean; however, the variable has quite a few values far away from the mean in either or both of the tails as well.

Mean, standard deviation, skewness, and kurtosis are also called the *four population moments*. Mean uses the values on the first degree in the calculation; therefore, it is the first population moment. Standard deviation uses the squared values and is therefore the second population moment. Skewness is the third, and kurtosis is the fourth population moment. All together, they give you a very good estimation of the population distribution.

Skewness and kurtosis with CLR UDAs

The queries for calculating skewness and kurtosis are more complex than the queries earlier in the chapter. Now imagine you need to calculate these two values in groups. Calculating mean and standard deviation in groups is simple, because you have appropriate T-SQL aggregate functions, which can be used together with the GROUP BY clause. However, calculating skewness and kurtosis in groups with T-SQL expressions only leads to more complex queries.

Calculating skewness and kurtosis in groups would be simple if there were appropriate T-SQL aggregate functions. You can actually expand the list of the T-SQL aggregate functions with user-defined aggregate functions. However, you can't define a user-defined aggregate (UDA) in T-SQL. You need a Common Language Runtime (CLR) language for this—for example, Visual C#. You can use either a SQL Server Database Project template or a simple Class Library template in Microsoft Visual Studio with the appropriate programming languages installed. Refer to books online for details on how to create such a project. Then you can simply copy the following C# code for the skewness and kurtosis UDAs, which uses the same mathematics as the T-SQL solutions for an efficient calculation with a single scan of the data:

```
using System;
using System.Data;
using System.Data.SqlClient;
using System.Data.SqlTypes;
using Microsoft.SqlServer.Server;

[Serializable]
[SqlUserDefinedAggregate(
    Format.Native,
    IsInvariantToDuplicates = false,
    IsInvariantToNulls = true,
    IsInvariantToOrder = true,
    IsNullIfEmpty = false)]
public struct Skew
{
    private double rx;    // running sum of current values (x)
    private double rx2;   // running sum of squared current values (x^2)
    private double r2x;   // running sum of doubled current values (2x)
    private double rx3;   // running sum of current values raised to power 3 (x^3)
    private double r3x2;  // running sum of tripled squared current values (3x^2)
    private double r3x;   // running sum of tripled current values (3x)
    private Int64 rn;     // running count of rows

    public void Init()
    {
        rx = 0;
        rx2 = 0;
        r2x = 0;
        rx3 = 0;
        r3x2 = 0;
        r3x = 0;
        rn = 0;
    }

    public void Accumulate(SqlDouble inpVal)
    {
        if (inpVal.IsNull)
        {
            return;
        }
        rx = rx + inpVal.Value;
        rx2 = rx2 + Math.Pow(inpVal.Value, 2);
        r2x = r2x + 2 * inpVal.Value;
        rx3 = rx3 + Math.Pow(inpVal.Value, 3);
        r3x2 = r3x2 + 3 * Math.Pow(inpVal.Value, 2);
        r3x = r3x + 3 * inpVal.Value;
        rn = rn + 1;
```

```csharp
        }

        public void Merge(Skew Group)
        {
            this.rx = this.rx + Group.rx;
            this.rx2 = this.rx2 + Group.rx2;
            this.r2x = this.r2x + Group.r2x;
            this.rx3 = this.rx3 + Group.rx3;
            this.r3x2 = this.r3x2 + Group.r3x2;
            this.r3x = this.r3x + Group.r3x;
            this.rn = this.rn + Group.rn;
        }

        public SqlDouble Terminate()
        {
            double myAvg = (rx / rn);
            double myStDev = Math.Pow((rx2 - r2x * myAvg + rn * Math.Pow(myAvg, 2))
                            / (rn - 1), 1d / 2d);
            double mySkew = (rx3 - r3x2 * myAvg + r3x * Math.Pow(myAvg, 2) -
                            rn * Math.Pow(myAvg, 3)) /
                        Math.Pow(myStDev,3) * rn / (rn - 1) / (rn - 2);
            return (SqlDouble)mySkew;
        }

    }


[Serializable]
[SqlUserDefinedAggregate(
    Format.Native,
    IsInvariantToDuplicates = false,
    IsInvariantToNulls = true,
    IsInvariantToOrder = true,
    IsNullIfEmpty = false)]
public struct Kurt
{
    private double rx;    // running sum of current values (x)
    private double rx2;   // running sum of squared current values (x^2)
    private double r2x;   // running sum of doubled current values (2x)
    private double rx4;   // running sum of current values raised to power 4 (x^4)
    private double r4x3;  // running sum of quadrupled current values raised to power 3 (4x^3)
    private double r6x2;  // running sum of squared current values multiplied by 6 (6x^2)
    private double r4x;   // running sum of quadrupled current values (4x)
    private Int64 rn;     // running count of rows

    public void Init()
    {
        rx = 0;
        rx2 = 0;
        r2x = 0;
        rx4 = 0;
        r4x3 = 0;
        r4x = 0;
        rn = 0;
    }

    public void Accumulate(SqlDouble inpVal)
```

```
        {
            if (inpVal.IsNull)
            {
                return;
            }
            rx = rx + inpVal.Value;
            rx2 = rx2 + Math.Pow(inpVal.Value, 2);
            r2x = r2x + 2 * inpVal.Value;
            rx4 = rx4 + Math.Pow(inpVal.Value, 4);
            r4x3 = r4x3 + 4 * Math.Pow(inpVal.Value, 3);
            r6x2 = r6x2 + 6 * Math.Pow(inpVal.Value, 2);
            r4x = r4x + 4 * inpVal.Value;
            rn = rn + 1;
        }

        public void Merge(Kurt Group)
        {
            this.rx = this.rx + Group.rx;
            this.rx2 = this.rx2 + Group.rx2;
            this.r2x = this.r2x + Group.r2x;
            this.rx4 = this.rx4 + Group.rx4;
            this.r4x3 = this.r4x3 + Group.r4x3;
            this.r6x2 = this.r6x2 + Group.r6x2;
            this.r4x = this.r4x + Group.r4x;
            this.rn = this.rn + Group.rn;
        }

        public SqlDouble Terminate()
        {
            double myAvg = (rx / rn);
            double myStDev = Math.Pow((rx2 - r2x * myAvg + rn * Math.Pow(myAvg, 2))
                            / (rn - 1), 1d / 2d);
            double myKurt = (rx4 - r4x3 * myAvg + r6x2 * Math.Pow(myAvg, 2)
                            - r4x * Math.Pow(myAvg, 3) + rn * Math.Pow(myAvg, 4)) /
                        Math.Pow(myStDev, 4) * rn * (rn + 1)
                            / (rn - 1) / (rn - 2) / (rn - 3) -
                        3 * Math.Pow((rn - 1), 2) / (rn - 2) / (rn - 3);
            return (SqlDouble)myKurt;
        }
    }

}
```

Then you can build the project and later deploy the assembly (the .dll file) to your SQL Server instance. Of course, you can also use the project with the source code or the pre-built assembly provided with the accompanying code for the book.

Once your assembly is built, you need to deploy it. The first step is to enable the CLR in your SQL Server instance:

```
EXEC sp_configure 'clr enabled', 1;
RECONFIGURE WITH OVERRIDE;
```

Then you deploy the assembly. Deploying an assembly means importing it into a database. SQL Server does not rely on .dll files on disk. You can deploy an assembly from Visual Studio directly, or you can use the T-SQL CREATE ASSEMBLY command. The following command assumes that the DescriptiveStatistics.dll file exists in the C:\temp folder.

```
CREATE ASSEMBLY DescriptiveStatistics
FROM 'C:\temp\DescriptiveStatistics.dll'
WITH PERMISSION_SET = SAFE;
```

After you import the assembly to your database, you can create the user-defined aggregates with the CREATE AGGREGATE command. The following two commands create the skewness and the kurtosis UDAs:

```
-- Skewness UDA
CREATE AGGREGATE dbo.Skew(@s float)
RETURNS float
EXTERNAL NAME DescriptiveStatistics.Skew;
GO
-- Kurtosis UDA
CREATE AGGREGATE dbo.Kurt(@s float)
RETURNS float
EXTERNAL NAME DescriptiveStatistics.Kurt;
GO
```

After you deploy the UDAs, you can use them in the same way as you do standard T-SQL aggregate functions. For example, the following query calculates the skewness and the kurtosis for the *salesamount* variable:

```
SELECT dbo.Skew(salesamount) AS skewness,
  dbo.Kurt(salesamount) AS kurtosis
FROM dbo.SalesAnalysis;
```

The result of the query is

```
skewness                kurtosis
--------------------    --------------------
6.78219499972001        68.7756494631014
```

Of course, now when you have the UDAs, you can use them to calculate the skewness and the kurtosis in groups as well. The following query calculates the four population moments for the *salesamount* continuous variable in groups of the *employeecountry* discrete variable:

```
SELECT employeecountry,
  AVG(salesamount) AS mean,
  STDEV(salesamount) AS standarddeviation,
  dbo.Skew(salesamount) AS skewness,
  dbo.Kurt(salesamount) AS kurtosis
FROM dbo.SalesAnalysis
GROUP BY employeecountry;
```

The result is

employeecountry	mean	standarddeviation	skewness	kurtosis
UK	665.538450	1151.18458127003	5.25006816518545	34.9789294559445
USA	615.269533	992.247411594278	7.56357332529894	88.6908404800727

You can see from the higher values for the skewness and the kurtosis that the *salesamount* variable has a more important right tail for the USA employees. You can probably conclude that there are some big customers from the USA that placed quite bigger orders than the average customers.

Linear dependencies

I dealt with analyses of a single variable so far in this chapter. Now it is time to check whether two selected variables are independent or somehow related. In statistics, you start with the *null hypothesis*. The null hypothesis is a general statement or default position that there is no relationship between two measured variables. Then you try to prove or reject the hypothesis with statistical analyses. I am going to analyze linear relationships only.

As you already know, there are discrete and continuous variables. I will explain and develop code for analyzing relationships between two continuous variables, between two discrete variables, and between one continuous variable and one discrete variable.

Analyzing relationships between pairs of variables many times is the goal of doing an analysis. In addition, analyzing these relationships is useful as a first step to prepare for some deeper analysis—for example, an analysis that uses data-mining methods. Relationships found between pairs of variables help you select variables for more complex methods. For example, imagine you have one target variable and you want to explain its states with a couple of input variables. If you find a strong relationship between a pair of input variables, you can omit one and consider only the other one in your further, more complex analytical process. Thus, you reduce the complexity of the problem.

Two continuous variables

I will start by measuring the strength of the relationship of two continuous variables. I will define three measures: the covariance, the correlation coefficient, and the coefficient of determination. Finally, I will express one variable as a function of the other, using the linear regression formula.

Covariance

Imagine you are dealing with two variables with a distribution of values as shown (for the sake of brevity, in a single table) in Table 8-2.

TABLE 8-2 Distribution of two variables

Value Xi	Probability Xi	Value Yi	Probability Yi
0	0.14	1	0.25
1	0.39	2	0.50
2	0.36	3	0.25
3	0.11		

The first variable can have four different states, and the second variable can have three. Of course, these two variables actually represent two continuous variables with many more possible states; however, for the sake of providing a simpler explanation, I limited the number of possible states.

If the variables are truly independent, you can expect the same distribution of Y over every value of X and vice versa. You can easily compute the probability of each possible combination of the values of both variables: the probability of each combination of values of two independent variables is simply a product of the separate probabilities of each value:

$$P(X_i, Y_i) = P(X_i) * P(Y_i)$$

According to the formula, you can calculate an example as follows:

```
P(X=1, Y=2): P(1,2) = P(X1) * P(Y2) = 0.39 * 0.50 = 0.195
```

This is the expected probability for independent variables. But you have a different situation now, as shown in Table 8-3. There you see a cross-tabulation of X and Y with distributions of X and Y shown on the margins (the rightmost column and the bottommost row) and measured distributions of combined probabilities in the middle cells.

TABLE 8-3 Combined and marginal probabilities

X/Y	1	2	3	P(X)
0	0.14	0	0	0.14
1	0	0.26	0.13	0.39
2	0	0.24	0.12	0.36
3	0.11	0	0	0.11
P(Y)	0.25	0.50	0.25	1/1

I want to measure the deviation of the actual from the expected probabilities in the intersection cells. Remember the formula for the variance of one variable? Let's write the formula once again, this time for both variables, X and Y:

$$Var(X) = \frac{1}{n} * \sum_{i=1}^{n} (X_i - \mu(X))^2$$

$$Var(Y) = \frac{1}{n} * \sum_{i=1}^{n} (Y_i - \mu(Y))^2$$

I will start measuring the covariance of a variable with itself. Let's take an example of variable Z, which has only three states (1, 2, and 3), and for each state it has one value only. You can imagine a SQL Server table with three rows, one column Z, and a different value in each row. The probability of each value is 0.33, or exactly *1 / (number of rows)*—that is, 1 divided by 3. Table 8-4 shows this variable cross-tabulated with itself. To distinguish between vertical and horizontal representations of the same variable Z, let's call the variable "Z vertical" and "Z horizontal."

TABLE 8-4 A variable cross-tabulated with itself

Zv/Zh	1	2	3	P(Zv)
1	0.33	0	0	0.33
2	0	0.33	0	0.33
3	0	0	0.33	0.33
P(Zh)	0.33	0.33	0.33	1/1

The formula for the variance of a single variable can be expanded to a formula that measures how the variable covaries with itself:

$$Var(Z) = CoVar(Z, Z) = \sum_{i=1}^{n}(Z_{hi} - \mu(Z_h)) * (Z_{vi} - \mu(Z_v)) * P(Z_{hi}, Z_{vi})$$

This formula seems suitable for two variables as well. Of course, it was my intention to develop a formula to measure the spread of combined probabilities of two variables. I simply replace one variable—for example, the "horizontal" Z with X, and the other one (the "vertical" Z) with Y— and get the formula for the covariance:

$$CoVar(X, Y) = \sum_{i=1}^{n}(X_i - \mu(X)) * (Y_i - \mu(Y)) * P(X, Y)$$

Now I can calculate the covariance for two continuous variables from my sales analysis view. I can replace the probability for the combination of the variables P(X, Y) with probability for each of the n rows combined with itself—that is, with 1 / n2—and the sum of these probabilities for n rows with 1 / n, because each row has an equal probability. Here is the query that calculates the covariance of the variables *salesamount* and *discountamount*:

```
WITH CoVarCTE AS
(
SELECT salesamount as val1,
  AVG(salesamount) OVER () AS mean1,
  discountamount AS val2,
  AVG(discountamount) OVER() AS mean2
FROM dbo.SalesAnalysis
)
SELECT
  SUM((val1-mean1)*(val2-mean2)) / COUNT(*) AS covar
FROM CoVarCTE;
```

The result of this query is

```
covar
-------------------
76375.801912
```

Covariance indicates how two variables, X and Y, are related to each other. When large values of both variables occur together, the deviations are both positive (because *Xi – Mean(X)* > 0 and *Yi – Mean(Y)* > 0), and their product is therefore positive. Similarly, when small values occur together, the product is positive as well. When one deviation is negative and one is positive, the product is negative. This can happen when a small value of X occurs with a large value of Y and the other way around. If positive products are absolutely larger than negative products, the covariance is positive; otherwise, it is negative. If negative and positive products cancel each other out, the covariance is zero. And when do they cancel each other out? Well, you can imagine such a situation quickly—when two variables are really independent. So the covariance evidently summarizes the relation between variables:

- If the covariance is positive, when the values of one variable are large, the values of the other one tend to be large as well.

- If the covariance is negative, when the values of one variable are large, the values of the other one tend to be small.

- If the covariance is zero, the variables are independent.

Correlation and coefficient of determination

When I derived formulas for the spread of the distribution of a single variable, I wanted to have the possibility of comparing the spread of two or more variables. I had to derive a relative measurement formula—the *coefficient of the variation* (CV):

$$CV = \frac{\sigma}{\mu}$$

Now I want to compare the two covariances computed for two pairs of the variables. Let's again try to find a similar formula—let's divide the covariance with something. It turns out that a perfect denominator is a product of the standard deviations of both variables. This is the formula for the correlation coefficient:

$$Correl(X, Y) = \frac{Covar(X, Y)}{\sigma(X) * \sigma(Y)}$$

The reason that the correlation coefficient is a useful measure of the relation between two variables is that it is always bounded: $-1 <= Correl <= 1$. Of course, if the variables are independent, the correlation is zero, because the covariance is zero. The correlation can take the value 1 if the variables have a perfect positive linear relation (if you correlate a variable with itself, for example). Similarly, the correlation would be -1 for the perfect negative linear relation. The larger the absolute value of the coefficient is, the more the variables are related. But the significance depends on the size of the sample. A coefficient over 0.50 is generally considered to be significant. However, there could be a casual link between variables as well. To correct the too-large value of the correlation coefficient, it is often squared and thus diminished. The squared coefficient is called the *coefficient of determination* (CD):

$$CD(X, Y) = Correl(X, Y)^2$$

In statistics, when the coefficient of determination is above 0.20, you typically can reject the null hypothesis, meaning you can say that the two continuous variables are not independent and that, instead, they are correlated. The following query calculates the covariance, the correlation coefficient, and the coefficient of determination for the *salesamount* and *discountamount* variables:

```
WITH CoVarCTE AS
(
SELECT salesamount as val1,
  AVG(salesamount) OVER () AS mean1,
  discountamount AS val2,
  AVG(discountamount) OVER() AS mean2
FROM dbo.SalesAnalysis
)
SELECT
  SUM((val1-mean1)*(val2-mean2)) / COUNT(*) AS covar,
  (SUM((val1-mean1)*(val2-mean2)) / COUNT(*)) /
  (STDEVP(val1) * STDEVP(val2)) AS correl,
  SQUARE((SUM((val1-mean1)*(val2-mean2)) / COUNT(*)) /
  (STDEVP(val1) * STDEVP(val2))) AS CD
FROM CoVarCTE;
```

The result is

```
covar          correl                CD
-------------  --------------------  -----------------------
76375.801912   0.550195368441261     0.302714943454215
```

From the result, you can see that you can safely reject the null hypothesis for these two variables. The *salesamount* and *discountamount* variables are positively correlated: the higher the *salesamount* is, the higher the *discountamount* is. Of course, this is what you could expect.

Before concluding this part, let me point out the common misuse of the correlation coefficient. Correlation does not mean causation. This is a very frequent error. When people see high correlation, they incorrectly infer that one variable causes or influences the values of the other one. Again, this is not true. Correlation has no direction. In addition, remember that I measure linear dependencies only. Even if the correlation coefficient is zero, it still does not mean that the variables are independent (or not related at all). You can say that, if the two variables are independent, they are also uncorrelated, but if they are uncorrelated, they are not necessarily independent.

Linear regression

If the correlation coefficient is significant, you know there is some linear relation between the two variables. I would like to express this relation in a functional way—that is, one variable as a function of the other one. The linear function between two variables is a line determined by its slope and its intercept. Logically, the goal is to calculate the slope and the intercept. You can quickly imagine that the slope is somehow connected with the covariance.

But I start to develop the formula for the slope from another perspective. I start with the formula for the line, where the slope is denoted with b and the intercept with a:

$$Y' = a + b * X$$

You can imagine that the two variables you are analyzing form a two-dimensional plane. Their values define coordinates of the points in the plane. You are searching for a line that fits all the points best. Actually, it means that you want the points to fall as close to the line as possible. You need the deviations from the line—that is, the difference between the actual value for Yi and the line value

Y'. If you use simple deviations, some are going to be positive and others negative, so the sum of all deviations is going to be zero for the best-fit line. A simple sum of deviations, therefore, is not a good measure. You can square the deviations, like they are squared to calculate the mean squared deviation. To find the best-fit line, you have to find the minimal possible sum of squared deviations. I am not going to do the complete derivation of the formula here; after this brief explanation, I am just showing the final formulas for the slope and the intercept:

$$Slope(Y) = \frac{\sum_{i=1}^{n}(X_i - \mu(X)) * (Y_i - \mu(Y))}{\sum_{i=1}^{n}(X_i - \mu(X))^2}$$

$$Intercept(Y) = \mu(Y) - Slope(Y) * \mu(X)$$

If you look back at the formulas for the covariance and the mean squared deviation, you can see that the numerator of the slope is really connected with the covariance, while the denominator closely resembles the mean squared deviation of the independent variable.

As I go along, I have nonchalantly started to use terms like "independent" and implicitly "dependent" variables. How do I know which one is the cause and which one is the effect? Well, in real life it is usually easy to qualify the roles of the variables. In statistics, just for the overview, I can calculate both combinations, Y as a function of X and X as a function of Y, as well. So I get two lines, which are called the *first regression line* and the *second regression line*.

After I have the formulas, it is easy to write the queries in T-SQL, as shown in the following query:

```
WITH CoVarCTE AS
(
SELECT salesamount as val1,
  AVG(salesamount) OVER () AS mean1,
  discountamount AS val2,
  AVG(discountamount) OVER() AS mean2
FROM dbo.SalesAnalysis
)
SELECT Slope1=
        SUM((val1 - mean1) * (val2 - mean2))
        /SUM(SQUARE((val1 - mean1))),
      Intercept1=
        MIN(mean2) - MIN(mean1) *
          (SUM((val1 - mean1)*(val2 - mean2))
          /SUM(SQUARE((val1 - mean1)))),
      Slope2=
        SUM((val1 - mean1) * (val2 - mean2))
        /SUM(SQUARE((val2 - mean2))),
      Intercept2=
        MIN(mean1) - MIN(mean2) *
          (SUM((val1 - mean1)*(val2 - mean2))
          /SUM(SQUARE((val2 - mean2))))
  FROM CoVarCTE;
```

The result is

```
Slope1                 Intercept1             Slope2                 Intercept2
---------------------  ---------------------  ---------------------  ---------------------
0.0711289532105013     -3.56166730855091      4.25586107754898       453.41491444211
```

Contingency tables and chi-squared

Covariance and correlation measure dependencies between two continuous variables. During the calculation, they both use the means of the two variables involved. (Correlation also uses standard deviation.) Mean values and other population moments make no sense for categorical (nominal) variables.

If you denote "Clerical" as 1 and "Professional" as 2 for the variable occupation, what does the average of 1.5 mean? You have to find another test for dependencies—a test that does not rely on the numeric values. You can use contingency tables and the *chi-squared test*.

Contingency tables are used to examine the relationship between subjects' scores on two qualitative or categorical variables. They show the actual and expected distribution of cases in a cross-tabulated (pivoted) format for the two variables. Table 8-5 is an example of the actual (or observed) and expected distribution of cases over the occupation column (on rows) and the maritalstatus column (or columns):

TABLE 8-5 A contingency table example

Occupation/marital status		Married	Single	Totals
Clerical	Actual	4745	4388	9133
	Expected	4946	4187	9133
Professional	Actual	5266	4085	9351
	Expected	5065	4286	9351
Total	Actual	10011	8473	18484
	Expected	10011	8473	18484

If the columns are not contingent on the rows, the row and column frequencies are independent. The test of whether the columns are contingent on the rows is called the *chi-squared test of independence*. The null hypothesis is that there is no relationship between row and column frequencies. Therefore, there should be no difference between the observed (O) and expected (E) frequencies.

Chi-squared is simply a sum of normalized squared frequencies' deviations (that is, the sum of squares of differences between observed and expected frequencies divided by expected frequencies). This formula is also called the *Pearson chi-squared formula*.

$$\chi^2 = \frac{1}{n} * \sum_{i=1}^{n} \frac{(O-E)^2}{E}$$

There are already prepared tables with critical points for the chi-squared distribution. If the calculated chi-squared value is greater than a critical value in the table for the defined degrees of freedom and for a specific confidence level, you can reject the null hypothesis with that confidence (which means the variables are interdependent). The degrees of freedom is the product of the degrees of freedom for columns (C) and rows (R):

$$DF = (C - 1) * (R - 1)$$

Table 8-6 is an example of a chi-squared critical-points table. Greater differences between expected and actual data produce a larger chi-squared value. The larger the chi-squared value is, the greater the probability is that there really is a significant difference. The Probability row in the table shows you the maximal probability that the null hypothesis holds when the chi-squared value is greater than or equal to the value in the table for the specific degrees of freedom.

TABLE 8-6 Chi-squared critical points

DF	Chi-squared value										
1	0.004	0.02	0.06	0.15	0.46	1.07	1.64	2.71	3.84	6.64	10.83
2	0.10	0.21	0.45	0.71	1.39	2.41	3.22	4.60	5.99	9.21	13.82
3	0.35	0.58	1.01	1.42	2.37	3.66	4.64	6.25	7.82	11.34	16.27
4	0.71	1.06	1.65	2.20	3.36	4.88	5.99	7.78	9.49	13.28	18.47
5	1.14	1.61	2.34	3.00	4.35	6.06	7.29	9.24	11.07	15.09	20.52
6	1.63	2.20	3.07	3.83	5.35	7.23	8.56	10.64	12.59	16.81	22.46
7	2.17	2.83	3.82	4.67	6.35	8.38	9.80	12.02	14.07	18.48	24.32
8	2.73	3.49	4.59	5.53	7.34	9.52	11.03	13.56	15.51	20.09	26.12
9	3.32	4.17	5.38	6.39	8.34	10.66	12.24	14.68	16.92	21.67	27.88
10	3.94	4.86	6.18	7.27	9.34	11.78	13.44	15.99	18.31	23.21	29.59
Probability	**0.95**	**0.90**	**0.80**	**0.70**	**0.50**	**0.30**	**0.20**	**0.10**	**0.05**	**0.01**	**0.001**
	Not significant								**Significant**		

For example, you have calculated chi-squared for two discrete variables. The value is 16, and the degrees of freedom are 7. Search for the first smaller and first bigger value for the chi-squared in the row for degrees of freedom 7 in Table 8-6. The values are 14.07 and 18.48. Check the appropriate probability for these two values, which are 0.05 and 0.01. This means there is less than a 5% probability that the two variables are independent, and more than a 1% probability that they are independent. This is a significant percentage, meaning you can say the variables are dependent with more than a 95% probability.

Calculating chi-squared is not that simple with T-SQL. It is not a problem to get the actual (observed) frequencies; the problem is getting the expected frequencies. For example, the following query uses the PIVOT operator to get the actual frequencies of combinations of states of the *categoryname* and *employeecountry* variables from the sales analysis view:

```
SELECT categoryname, [USA],[UK]
FROM (SELECT categoryname, employeecountry, orderid FROM dbo.SalesAnalysis) AS S
  PIVOT(COUNT(orderid) FOR employeecountry
    IN([USA],[UK])) AS P
ORDER BY categoryname;
```

The query produces the following result:

```
categoryname      USA          UK
---------------   -----------  -----------
Beverages         294          110
Condiments        158          58
Confections       256          78
Dairy Products    240          126
Grains/Cereals    157          39
Meat/Poultry      131          42
Produce           96           40
Seafood           255          75
```

You can calculate expected frequencies from the marginal frequencies, or from the totals over rows and columns. The following query does this step by step, by calculating the observed frequencies for the combination of both variables' states, and then observed frequencies for the first and second variables, and then observed total frequencies (total number of cases), and only after that the expected frequencies for the combination of both variables' states, and finally it joins together the observed and expected frequencies:

```
WITH
ObservedCombination_CTE AS
(
SELECT categoryname, employeecountry, COUNT(*) AS observed
FROM dbo.SalesAnalysis
GROUP BY categoryname, employeecountry
),
ObservedFirst_CTE AS
(
SELECT categoryname, NULL AS employeecountry, COUNT(*) AS observed
FROM dbo.SalesAnalysis
GROUP BY categoryname
),
ObservedSecond_CTE AS
(
SELECT NULL AS categoryname, employeecountry, COUNT(*) AS observed
FROM dbo.SalesAnalysis
GROUP BY employeecountry
),
ObservedTotal_CTE AS
(
SELECT NULL AS categoryname, NULL AS employeecountry, COUNT(*) AS observed
FROM dbo.SalesAnalysis
),
```

```
ExpectedCombination_CTE AS
(
SELECT F.categoryname, S.employeecountry,
  CAST(ROUND(1.0 * F.observed * S.observed / T.observed, 0) AS INT) AS expected
FROM ObservedFirst_CTE AS F
  CROSS JOIN ObservedSecond_CTE AS S
  CROSS JOIN ObservedTotal_CTE AS T
),
ObservedExpected_CTE AS
(
SELECT O.categoryname, O.employeecountry, O.observed, E.expected
FROM ObservedCombination_CTE AS O
  INNER JOIN ExpectedCombination_CTE AS E
  ON O.categoryname = E.categoryname
    AND O.employeecountry = E.employeecountry
)
SELECT * FROM ObservedExpected_CTE;
```

It produces the following result:

```
categoryname      employeecountry  observed     expected
---------------   ---------------  ----------   ----------
Condiments        UK               58           57
Produce           UK               40           36
Dairy Products    USA              240          270
Grains/Cereals    UK               39           52
Seafood           USA              255          243
Seafood           UK               75           87
Confections       USA              256          246
Meat/Poultry      USA              131          127
Dairy Products    UK               126          96
Beverages         USA              294          298
Confections       UK               78           88
Meat/Poultry      UK               42           46
Beverages         UK               110          106
Produce           USA              96           100
Condiments        USA              158          159
Grains/Cereals    USA              157          144
```

Of course, the query is pretty inefficient. It scans the data many times. I am showing the query to help you more easily understand the process of calculating the expected frequencies. Alternatively, you can use window aggregate functions, which make this calculation much simpler. The following query uses only two common table expressions: the first one calculates just the observed frequencies for the combination of both variables' states, and the second one uses the window aggregate functions to calculate the marginal and total frequencies and the expected frequencies for the combination of both variables' states, while the outer query calculates the chi-squared and the degrees of freedom.

```
WITH ObservedCombination_CTE AS
(
SELECT categoryname AS onrows,
  employeecountry AS oncols,
  COUNT(*) AS observedcombination
FROM dbo.SalesAnalysis
```

```
GROUP BY categoryname, employeecountry
),
ExpectedCombination_CTE AS
(
SELECT onrows, oncols, observedcombination,
  SUM(observedcombination) OVER (PARTITION BY onrows) AS observedonrows,
  SUM(observedcombination) OVER (PARTITION BY oncols) AS observedoncols,
  SUM(observedcombination) OVER () AS observedtotal,
  CAST(ROUND(SUM(1.0 * observedcombination) OVER (PARTITION BY onrows)
    * SUM(1.0 * observedcombination) OVER (PARTITION BY oncols)
    / SUM(1.0 * observedcombination) OVER (), 0) AS INT) AS expectedcombination
FROM ObservedCombination_CTE
)
SELECT SUM(SQUARE(observedcombination - expectedcombination)
  / expectedcombination) AS chisquared,
 (COUNT(DISTINCT onrows) - 1) * (COUNT(DISTINCT oncols) - 1) AS degreesoffreedom
FROM ExpectedCombination_CTE;
```

Here is the result:

```
chisquared              degreesoffreedom
----------------------  ----------------
22.2292997748233        7
```

Now you can read Table 8-6, which is the chi-squared critical-points table shown earlier. For 7 degrees of freedom, you can read the first lower and first higher values, which you can find in the last two columns: 18.48 and 24.32. Read the probability for the lower value—it is 0.01. You can say with more than a 99% probability that the *categoryname* and *employeecountry* variables are dependent. Apparently, employees from the USA sell more items in some product categories, while employees from the UK sell more items in other product categories.

Analysis of variance

Finally, it is time to check for linear dependencies between a continuous and a discrete variable. You can do this by measuring the variance between means of the continuous variable in different groups of the discrete variable. The null hypothesis here is that all variance between means is a result of the variance within each group. If you reject it, this means that there is some significant variance of the means between groups. This is also known as the *residual*, or unexplained, variance. You are analyzing the variance of the means, so this analysis is called the *analysis of variance*, or ANOVA.

You calculate the variance between groups MS_A as the sum of squares of deviations of the group mean from the total mean times the number of cases in each group, with the degrees of freedom equal to the number of groups minus one. The formula is

$$MS_A = \frac{SS_A}{DF_A}, where\ SS_A = \sum_{i=1}^{a} n_i * (\mu_i - \mu), and\ DF_A = (a - 1)$$

The discrete variable has discrete states, μ is the overall mean of the continuous variable, and μ_i is the mean in the continuous variable in the *i*th group of the discrete variable.

You calculate the variance within groups MS_E as the sum over groups of the sum of squares of deviations of individual values from the group mean, with the degrees of freedom equal to the sum of the number of rows in each group minus one:

$$MS_E = \frac{SS_E}{DF_E}, where\ SS_E = \sum_{i=1}^{a}\sum_{j=1}^{ni}(v_{ij} - \mu_i)\ , and\ DF_E = \sum_{i=1}^{a}(n_i - 1)$$

The individual value of the continuous variable is denoted as v_{ij}, μ_i is the mean in the continuous variable in the ith group of the discrete variable, and n_i is the number of cases in the ith group of the discrete variable.

Once you have both variances, you calculate the so-called F ratio as the ratio between the variance between groups and the variance within groups:

$$F = \frac{MS_A}{MS_E}$$

A large F value means you can reject the null hypothesis. Tables for the cumulative distribution under the tails of F distributions for different degrees of freedom are already calculated. For a specific F value with degrees of freedom between groups and degrees of freedom within groups, you can get critical points where there is, for example, less than a 5% distribution under the F distribution curve up to the F point. This means that there is less than a 5% probability that the null hypothesis is correct (that is, there is an association between the means and the groups). If you get a large F value when splitting or sampling your data, the splitting or sampling was not random.

As I mentioned, you could now use the F value to search the F distribution tables. However, I want to show you how you can calculate the F probability on the fly. It is quite simple to calculate the cumulative F distribution using CLR code (for example, with a C# application). Unfortunately, the CLR *FDistribution* method, which performs the task, is implemented in a class that is not supported inside SQL Server. However, you can create a console application and then call it from SQL Server Management Studio using the SQLCMD mode. Here is the C# code for the console application that calculates the cumulative F distribution:

```
using System;
using System.Collections.Generic;
using System.Linq;
using System.Text;
using System.Windows.Forms.DataVisualization.Charting;

class FDistribution
{
    static void Main(string[] args)
    {
        // Test input arguments
        if (args.Length != 3)
        {
            Console.WriteLine("Please use three arguments: double FValue, int DF1, int DF2.");
            //Console.ReadLine();
            return;
        }
    }
```

```
// Try to convert the input arguments to numbers.
// FValue
double FValue;
bool test = double.TryParse(args[0], System.Globalization.NumberStyles.Float,
    System.Globalization.CultureInfo.InvariantCulture.NumberFormat, out FValue);
if (test == false)
{
    Console.WriteLine("First argument must be double (nnn.n).");
    return;
}

// DF1
int DF1;
test = int.TryParse(args[1], out DF1);
if (test == false)
{
    Console.WriteLine("Second argument must be int.");
    return;
}

// DF2
int DF2;
test = int.TryParse(args[2], out DF2);
if (test == false)
{
    Console.WriteLine("Third argument must be int.");
    return;
}

// Calculate the cumulative F distribution function probability
Chart c = new Chart();
double result = c.DataManipulator.Statistics.FDistribution(FValue, DF1, DF2);
Console.WriteLine("Input parameters: " +
    FValue.ToString(System.Globalization.CultureInfo.InvariantCulture.NumberFormat)
    + " " + DF1.ToString() + " " + DF2.ToString());
Console.WriteLine("Cumulative F distribution function probability: " +
    result.ToString("P"));
    }
}
```

The following query performs the one-way ANOVA, the analysis of variance using one input discrete variable, the *categoryname* variable, and the *salesamount* continuous variable:

```
WITH Anova_CTE AS
(
SELECT categoryname, salesamount,
  COUNT(*) OVER (PARTITION BY categoryname) AS gr_casescount,
  DENSE_RANK() OVER (ORDER BY categoryname) AS gr_denserank,
  SQUARE(AVG(salesamount) OVER (PARTITION BY categoryname) -
        AVG(salesamount) OVER ()) AS between_gr_SS,
  SQUARE(salesamount -
        AVG(salesamount) OVER (PARTITION BY categoryname))
        AS within_gr_SS
FROM dbo.SalesAnalysis
)
```

```
SELECT N'Between groups' AS [Source of Variation],
  SUM(between_gr_SS) AS SS,
  (MAX(gr_denserank) - 1) AS df,
  SUM(between_gr_SS) / (MAX(gr_denserank) - 1) AS MS,
  (SUM(between_gr_SS) / (MAX(gr_denserank) - 1)) /
  (SUM(within_gr_SS) / (COUNT(*) - MAX(gr_denserank))) AS F
FROM Anova_CTE
UNION
SELECT N'Within groups' AS [Source of Variation],
  SUM(within_gr_SS) AS SS,
  (COUNT(*) - MAX(gr_denserank)) AS df,
  SUM(within_gr_SS) / (COUNT(*) - MAX(gr_denserank)) AS MS,
  NULL AS F
FROM Anova_CTE;
```

The query uses a bit of creativity to calculate the degrees of freedom. It calculates the degrees of freedom between groups by calculating the dense rank of the groups and subtracting 1. Dense rank has the same value for all groups. By finding the maximal dense rank, you can find the number of groups. The query also calculates the degrees of freedom within groups as the total number of cases minus the number of groups. This way, everything can be calculated with a single scan of the data in the common table expression and in the outer query that refers to the common table expression. The outer query actually consists of two queries with unioned result sets. This is not necessary from the query perspective, and it might be even less efficient than a single query. However, I decided on the approach with the two unioned result sets to get the output that follows the standard statistical way of presenting the ANOVA results. Here is the output of the query:

```
Source of Variation SS                  df         MS                 F
------------------- ------------------  ---------- -----------------  ----------------------
Between groups      55804413.9792925    7          7972059.13989894   7.57962783966074
Within groups       2258159811.46234    2147       1051774.48135181   NULL
```

The last thing to do is check the significance level of the F value for the specified degrees of freedom. I deployed the FDistribution.exe console application to the C:\temp folder. In SQL Server Management Studio, you can enable the SQLCMD mode in the Query menu. Then you can execute the following command:

```
!!C:\temp\FDistribution 7.57962783966074 7 2147
```

With these input parameters, which are the result of the analysis-of-variance query, you get the following result:

```
Input parameters: 7.57962783966074 7 2147
Cumulative F distribution function probability: 0.00 %
```

The result means that there is less than a 0.01% probability that the two variables would be independent. Of course, some product categories include cheaper products while others include more expensive products; thus, the difference in the mean of the sales amount is the result of the variability between groups.

Definite integration

When checking whether I could prove or reject the null hypothesis, I used statistical tables—for example, for chi-squared distribution with specific degrees of freedom. For the F distribution, I used a CLR application instead of a statistical table. In addition, I kind of arbitrarily selected the threshold where I defined that the relationship between two variables is significant. The threshold was at 95% (or at 5% from the different angle of view), meaning that I could reject the null hypothesis with a 95% probability. The question is where do these tables come from, or how does the CLR application calculate the values ad hoc, and why did I select a threshold at 95%.

The tables are calculated from a distribution function. For example, there is a set of distribution functions for the chi-squared values: one function for each degree of freedom. You can calculate the area under the function for all possible values, the total area, and the area for a specific interval of values, which can be closed or open for one side—this would be the tail area. If you know the distribution function, you can calculate the area under the function with a definite integration. Then you can compare the specific area with the total area to find out the percentage of cases in the specific area.

Of course, there is no definite integration function in T-SQL. However, there are many ways for performing numerical integration and for calculating the numerical value of a definite integral. The trapezoidal rule can be implemented in a simple and efficient way in T-SQL code. You define a trapezium for the curve f(x) and then calculate the surface of the trapezium, like Figure 8-2 shows.

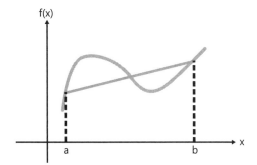

FIGURE 8-2 Trapezoidal rule for a definite integration.

The formula for the trapezoidal rule is

$$\int_a^b f(x)dx \approx \frac{(b-a)}{2} * (f(a) + f(b))$$

In the formula, *a* and *b* denote the values of the variable *x*, which defines the area for which the definite integral is approximately calculated.

By splitting the area under a curve into a bigger number of small trapeziums and then calculating and summing the area of these smaller trapeziums, you can get an accurate approximation for the numerical value of a definite integral.

By specifying *n* points in equal distance *h*, thus having a uniform grid for *n–1* trapeziums, the formula becomes

$$\int_{a}^{b} f(x)dx \approx \frac{h}{2} * (f(x_1) + 2 * f(x_2) + 2 * f(x_3) + \cdots + 2 * f(x_{n-1}) + f(x_n))$$

From here, it is simple to implement definite integration in T-SQL. I will show it in an example where I will use the standard normal distribution, for which I already defined the distribution function. I am creating a temporary table that has two columns only—the z0 column, denoting the *Z* value, and yz, denoting the *f(z0)* value, the standard normal distribution function value. Then I populate the table with *Z* values between –4 and 4, with distance *h* equal to 0.01. The following code creates and populates the table:

```
-- Standard normal distribution table
CREATE TABLE #StdNormDist
(z0 DECIMAL(3,2)  NOT NULL,
 yz DECIMAL(10,9) NOT NULL);
GO
-- Insert the data
DECLARE @z0 DECIMAL(3,2), @yz DECIMAL(10,9);
SET @z0=-4.00;
WHILE @z0 <= 4.00
  BEGIN
    SET @yz=1.00/SQRT(2.00*PI())*EXP((-1.00/2.00)*SQUARE(@z0));
    INSERT INTO #StdNormDist(z0,yz) VALUES(@z0, @yz);
    SET @z0=@z0+0.01;
END
GO
```

Here are a few rows from the table:

z0	yz
-4.00	0.000133830
-3.99	0.000139285
-3.98	0.000144948
-3.97	0.000150825
...	
-0.03	0.398762797
-0.02	0.398862500
-0.01	0.398922334
0.00	0.398942280
0.01	0.398922334
0.02	0.398862500
0.03	0.398762797
...	
3.97	0.000150825
3.98	0.000144948
3.99	0.000139285
4.00	0.000133830

According to the trapezoidal rule for the definite integration, I have to take the first and last distribution function values of an interval for which I am calculating the area for only once, and all other distribution function values in the interval twice. I can also reverse the logic and calculate the double sum of all distribution function values, and then subtract the first and last values. I can get the first and last values in a range with the FIRST_VALUE and LAST_VALUE window analytic functions. For example, the following query calculates the percentage of the area below the standard normal distribution function between Z values of 0 (which is the mean value of the standard normal distribution) and 1 (which is the standard deviation of the standard normal distribution):

```
WITH ZvaluesCTE AS
(
SELECT z0, yz,
  FIRST_VALUE(yz) OVER(ORDER BY z0 ROWS UNBOUNDED PRECEDING) AS fyz,
  LAST_VALUE(yz)
   OVER(ORDER BY z0
        ROWS BETWEEN CURRENT ROW
         AND UNBOUNDED FOLLOWING) AS lyz
FROM #StdNormDist
WHERE z0 >= 0 AND z0 <= 1
)
SELECT 100.0 * ((0.01 / 2.0) * (SUM(2 * yz) - MIN(fyz) - MAX(lyz))) AS pctdistribution
FROM ZvaluesCTE;
```

The result is

```
pctdistribution
---------------
34.134270
```

Now let me calculate the percentage of the area in the right tail from 1.96 standard deviations away from the mean. Because the standard normal distribution function is symmetric, I know that the area on the right side of the mean is exactly 50% of the total area. I use this fact in the following query:

```
WITH ZvaluesCTE AS
(
SELECT z0, yz,
  FIRST_VALUE(yz) OVER(ORDER BY z0 ROWS UNBOUNDED PRECEDING) AS fyz,
  LAST_VALUE(yz)
   OVER(ORDER BY z0
        ROWS BETWEEN CURRENT ROW
         AND UNBOUNDED FOLLOWING) AS lyz
FROM #StdNormDist
WHERE z0 >= 0 AND z0 <= 1.96
)
SELECT 50 - 100.0 * ((0.01 / 2.0) * (SUM(2 * yz) - MIN(fyz) - MAX(lyz))) AS pctdistribution
FROM ZvaluesCTE;
```

The result is

```
pctdistribution
---------------
2.499885
```

This means that if you go approximately two standard deviations away from the mean in the standard normal distribution, the cumulative area under the distribution function under both left and right tails covers approximately 5% of the total area under the function. This number influenced the decision that the threshold for deciding whether the null hypothesis can be rejected or not is commonly set at 5%.

Moving averages and entropy

I have already shown in this chapter how to calculate the linear regression formula. You can use the linear regression for estimating unknown values for predictions. Even the mean itself is called an *estimator*; you can use it for simple estimations as well. However, both mean and linear regression include all values. When you deal with time-series data, you many times don't want to do the prediction based on all past values, because older data might be completely irrelevant for current predictions. Or you might decide to put more stress on the recent values and less on the older values when estimating an unknown or new value. Moving averages can help you with this task.

I mentioned that you might want to check the linear dependencies of pairs of variables in the data overview stage, before doing some in-depth analysis. In addition, you also might want to check which variables can contribute to the analysis, which variables can give you some information, and which variables don't give much information. I will show you how you can measure the amount of the information in a discrete variable.

Moving averages

In addition to being useful for estimation and prediction, moving averages are useful for data preparation as well. Moving averages smooth extreme values. Extreme values can influence a lot on all four population moments. If you smooth them, you can spot the trend in a much easier way than with the original values. Figure 8-3 shows a graph of the original values and two different moving averages, one that follows the original line better (WMA) and one that does more smoothing (SMA).

You probably already met moving averages in this book—they were mentioned, together with the query optimization techniques, in Chapter 4, "Grouping, pivoting, and windowing." I am expanding the topic here to add different moving averages and to explain them more from the mathematical perspective than the query-optimization perspective.

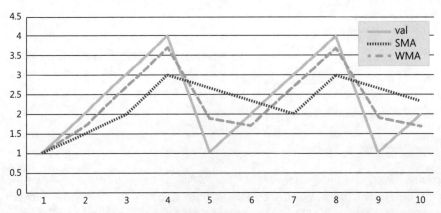

FIGURE 8-3 Moving-averages smoothing.

The following code creates and populates a simple table I will use for explaining the moving averages:

```
CREATE TABLE dbo.MAvg
(id  INT   NOT NULL IDENTITY(1,1),
 val FLOAT NULL);
GO
INSERT INTO dbo.MAvg(val) VALUES
(1), (2), (3), (4), (1), (2), (3), (4), (1), (2);
GO
```

This is the data from this demo table:

```
id          val
----------- ------------
1           1
2           2
3           3
4           4
5           1
6           2
7           3
8           4
9           1
10          2
```

I also used this data for the graph in Figure 8-3.

Simple moving average

In financial applications, a *simple moving average* (SMA) is the unweighted mean of the previous *n* data. This is the moving average you learned about in Chapter 4. The formula for a simple moving average calculated over the last three values is

$$SMA_i = \frac{\sum_{i-2}^{i} v_i}{3}$$

The following query calculates an SMA over last three values:

```
SELECT id, val,
 ROUND
 (AVG(val)
  OVER (ORDER BY id
        ROWS BETWEEN 2 PRECEDING
            AND CURRENT ROW)
 ,2) AS SMA
FROM dbo.MAvg
ORDER BY id;
```

The query produces the following result:

id	val	SMA
1	1	1
2	2	1.5
3	3	2
4	4	3
5	1	2.67
6	2	2.33
7	3	2
8	4	3
9	1	2.67
10	2	2.33

Weighted moving average

A *weighted moving average* (WMA) is any average that has multiplying factors to give different weights to data at different positions in the sample window. The sum of all weights must be equal to 1. With WMA, you can give more importance to the recent values and less importance to the older values. Here is the formula for a weighted moving average over the last two values:

$$WMA_i = \frac{\sum_{i-1}^{i}(v_i * w_i)}{3}, where \sum_{i-1}^{i} w_i = 1$$

The following query calculates the WMA over the last two values, giving the weight 0.7 to the current value and weight 0.3 to the previous value:

```
DECLARE  @A AS FLOAT;
SET @A = 0.7;
SELECT id, val,
 LAG(val, 1, val) OVER (ORDER BY id) AS prevval,
 @A * val + (1 - @A) *
   (LAG(val, 1, val) OVER (ORDER BY id))  AS WMA
FROM dbo.MAvg
ORDER BY id;
```

The result of the query is

id	val	prevval	WMA
1	1	1	1
2	2	1	1.7
3	3	2	2.7
4	4	3	3.7
5	1	4	1.9
6	2	1	1.7
7	3	2	2.7
8	4	3	3.7
9	1	4	1.9
10	2	1	1.7

Exponential moving average

An *exponential moving average* (EMA) is a moving average that includes an unlimited list of previous values, meaning all previous values. It is also weighted, so again you typically put more importance on the more recent values. EMA is frequently used in economics for forecasting. The formula for EMA is

$$EMA_i = \alpha * v_i + (1 - \alpha) * EMA_{i-1}, where\ EMA_1 = v_1$$

The problem with calculating the EMA is that the calculation for the current EMA uses the previous EMA. With window functions, SQL Server doesn't expose the running calculation. You can't refer to it in a query like you can do with a cursor. The following query shows an example of an EMA calculation with a cursor, where the weight (parameter) α is equal to 0.7:

```
DECLARE @CurrentEMA AS FLOAT, @PreviousEMA AS FLOAT,
 @Id AS INT, @Val AS FLOAT,
 @A AS FLOAT;
DECLARE @Results AS TABLE(id INT, val FLOAT, EMA FLOAT);
SET @A = 0.7;

DECLARE EMACursor CURSOR FOR
SELECT id, val
FROM dbo.MAvg
ORDER BY id;

OPEN EMACursor;

FETCH NEXT FROM EMACursor
 INTO @Id, @Val;
SET @CurrentEMA = @Val;
SET @PreviousEMA = @CurrentEMA;

WHILE @@FETCH_STATUS = 0
BEGIN
 SET @CurrentEMA = ROUND(@A * @Val + (1-@A) * @PreviousEMA, 2);
 INSERT INTO @Results (id, val, EMA)
  VALUES(@Id, @Val, @CurrentEMA);
  SET @PreviousEMA = @CurrentEMA;
 FETCH NEXT FROM EMACursor
  INTO @Id, @Val;
END;

CLOSE EMACursor;
DEALLOCATE EMACursor;

SELECT id, val, EMA
FROM @Results;
GO
```

The query produces the following result:

```
id          val        EMA
----------- ---------- -----------
1           1          1
2           2          1.7
3           3          2.61
4           4          3.58
5           1          1.77
6           2          1.93
7           3          2.68
8           4          3.6
9           1          1.78
10          2          1.93
```

Of course, you know that using cursors does not produce the most efficient T-SQL code. Can you avoid the cursor? One option is to use a recursive common table expression, like the following query:

```
DECLARE  @A AS FLOAT;
SET @A = 0.7;
WITH RnCTE AS
(
SELECT id, val,
 ROW_NUMBER() OVER(ORDER BY id) AS rn
FROM dbo.MAvg
),
EMACTE AS
(
  SELECT id, rn, val, val AS EMA
  FROM RnCTE
  WHERE id = 1

  UNION ALL

  SELECT C.id, C.rn, C.val,
   ROUND (@A * C.val + (1 - @A) * P.EMA, 2) AS EMA
  FROM EMACTE AS P
   INNER JOIN RnCTE AS C
     ON C.rn = P.rn + 1
)
SELECT id, val, EMA
FROM EMACTE;
```

Of course, this query is still not efficient, although it looks more set-oriented. A recursive CTE means a loop. Mimicking a recursive CTE with a WHILE loop also does not help much in optimizing the EMA calculation. I tried to convert the EMA formula to an equivalent formula that would use values only, and not the previous EMA in the formula. I started with expanding the EMA formula by replacing the previous EMA with the formula. Here is the process for expanding the EMA formula for five values:

$$EMA_5 = \alpha * v_5 + (1 - \alpha) * EMA_4$$

$$EMA_5 = \alpha * v_5 + (1 - \alpha) * (\alpha * v_4 + (1 - \alpha) * EMA_3)$$

$$EMA_5 = \alpha * v_5 + (1 - \alpha) * (\alpha * v_4 + (1 - \alpha) * (\alpha * v_3 + (1 - \alpha) * EMA_2))$$

$$EMA_5 = \alpha * v_5 + (1 - \alpha) * \left(\alpha * v_4 + (1 - \alpha) * \left(\alpha * v_3 + (1 - \alpha) * (\alpha * v_2 + (1 - \alpha) * EMA_1)\right)\right)$$

Because EMA_1 is equal to the value 1, the formula uses the values only. After rearranging the equation, I found the generalized formula for calculating the EMA with values only:

$$EMA_i = \sum_{j=2}^{i} (\alpha * (1 - \alpha)^{i-j} * v_j) + (1 - \alpha)^{i-1} * v_1$$

Now I am able to start searching for more efficient set-oriented solutions for calculating the EMA. I came up with the following query:

```
DECLARE  @A AS FLOAT;
SET @A = 0.7;
WITH RnCTE AS
(
SELECT id, val,
 ROW_NUMBER() OVER(ORDER BY id) AS rn,
 FIRST_VALUE(val) OVER (ORDER BY id ROWS UNBOUNDED PRECEDING) AS v1
FROM dbo.MAvg
),
MaCTE AS
(
SELECT RN1.id AS id, Rn1.rn AS rn1, Rn2.rn AS rn2,
 Rn1.v1, Rn1.val AS YI1, Rn2.val AS YI2,
 MAX(RN2.rn) OVER (PARTITION BY RN1.rn) AS TRC
FROM RnCTE AS Rn1
 INNER JOIN RnCTE AS Rn2
  ON Rn1.rn >= Rn2.rn
)
SELECT id, MAX(YI1) AS val,
 ROUND(
 SUM(@A * POWER((1 - @A), (rn1 - rn2)) * YI2)
 +
 MAX(POWER((1 - @A), (TRC - 1)))
 ,2) AS EMA
FROM MaCTE
WHERE rn2 > 1
GROUP BY ID
UNION
SELECT 1, 1, 1
ORDER BY Id;
```

Unfortunately, although it is pretty complex, the query is still not efficient. It uses a non-equi join in the second common table expression, and this is a quadratic complexity. Therefore, with larger data sets, this query would quickly become much less efficient than the cursor. After many tries, I nearly gave up, and I started to think that the only reasonable way to calculate the EMA would be by using the cursor. I wrote a blog about this problem. After a couple of days, there was a comment on my blog. Quintin du Bruyn, a distinguished member of the SQL Server community, found the solution for an efficient set-oriented query for the EMA using the modified formula that uses the values only. Here is his query:

```
DECLARE @A AS FLOAT = 0.7, @B AS FLOAT;
SET @B = 1 - @A;
WITH cte_cnt AS
(
SELECT id, val,
  ROW_NUMBER() OVER (ORDER BY id) - 1 as exponent
FROM dbo.MAvg
)
SELECT id, val,
 ROUND(
  SUM(CASE WHEN exponent=0 THEN 1
          ELSE @A
      END * val * POWER(@B, -exponent))
  OVER (ORDER BY id) * POWER(@B, exponent)
 , 2) AS EMA
FROM cte_cnt;
```

Therefore, you should never give up, and you should keep in mind that more people know more.

Entropy

Information theory is a branch of applied mathematics, electrical engineering, and computer science involving the quantification of information, developed by Claude E. Shannon. He wanted to find fundamental limits on signal-processing operations such as compressing data and on reliably storing and communicating data.

In a data set, you have a finite number of possible system states. If you have one binary variable, you have two possible states. Shannon defined information content in bits as a logarithm with a base two of the number of system states. For a discrete variable, the number of system states is the number of discrete values. Before performing some in-depth analysis, it is frequently useful to measure the amount of information in different variables. Variables with low information content—that is, with just very little info—might not be useful in the analysis. In information theory, information is the same thing as a surprise.

Introduction to entropy

Surprise measures the "unexpectedness" of a particular state. In a data set, surprise is quantified in terms of the probability (that is, relative frequency) of a particular state. If a system state has a lower probability, you are more surprised when it happens. So you get more information. Imagine that you buy five lottery tickets out of the 10 issued. How surprised are you if you win? How surprised are you if you buy only one ticket and win?

Information of a particular state i of the variable x is thus defined as a probability multiplied with the logarithm with base two of the probability:

$$I(x) = -P(x_i) * LOG_2(P(x_i))$$

A negative sign is added because probability can take a value in an interval between 0 and 1, and a logarithm function returns negative values for this interval.

The total amount of information of a variable is a sum of all information of all its states. This total amount of information is called *entropy*. Therefore, the formula for the entropy of the variable *x* is:

$$H(x) = -\sum_{i=1}^{n} P(x_i) * LOG_2(P(x_i))$$

What is the maximal entropy for a specific variable? Suppose you have a variable with two states only. In one case, the distribution of the values between the two states is pretty unequal, one state probability is 0.9, and the other state probability is 0.1. In another case, both states have the same probability 0.5. The following query calculates the entropy for these two examples:

```
SELECT (-1) * (0.1*LOG(0.1,2) + 0.9*LOG(0.9,2)) AS unequaldistribution,
  (-1) * (0.5*LOG(0.5,2) + 0.5*LOG(0.5,2)) AS equaldistribution;
```

The result is

```
unequaldistribution     equaldistribution
---------------------   ---------------------
0.468995593589281       1
```

What you can see is that a more equal distribution means higher entropy. In a uniform distribution, where only one state is represented (that is, all values are equal to one constant value), the entropy is 0. Such a variable is useless for analysis. The entropy of a discrete variable is the highest when the values are distributed equally.

Let me test now the highest possible entropy for variables with a different number of possible states. The following query calculates the maximal possible entropy for variables with two, three, and four states, using the equal distribution of the values over the states:

```
SELECT (-1)*(2)*(1.0/2)*LOG(1.0/2,2) AS TwoStatesMax,
  (-1)*(3)*(1.0/3)*LOG(1.0/3,2) AS ThreeStatesMax,
  (-1)*(4)*(1.0/4)*LOG(1.0/4,2) AS FourStatesMax;
```

The result of the query is

```
TwoStatesMax            ThreeStatesMax          FourStatesMax
---------------------   ---------------------   ---------------------
1                       1.58496235845298        2
```

From the mathematics, you can learn that

$$LOG\left(\frac{x}{y}\right) = LOG(x) - LOG(y)$$

Therefore, the former query that calculates the maximal possible entropy for a different number of states can be simplified to

```
SELECT LOG(2,2) AS TwoStatesMax,
 LOG(3,2) AS ThreeStatesMax,
 LOG(4,2) AS FourStatesMax;
```

What you can see from the results is that with more states, the maximal possible entropy increases. For continuous variables, you can calculate the entropy by discretizing or binning them. Fewer bins means lower maximal possible entropy. Discretizing into bins with an equal number of cases means that you retain as much entropy as possible for the specified number of bins. This fact can also explain why SQL Server uses this equal area distribution for the statistics of the values of a column.

Calculating the entropy

It is quite simple to follow the entropy formula in T-SQL to calculate it. Besides calculating the entropy of a variable, you can also calculate the maximal possible entropy of the variable, and the percentage of the actual entropy from the maximal possible entropy for the variable. The following query does this calculation for the *customercountry* variable:

```
WITH ProbabilityCTE AS
(
SELECT customercountry,
 COUNT(customercountry) AS StateFreq
FROM dbo.SalesAnalysis
WHERE customercountry IS NOT NULL
GROUP BY customercountry
),
StateEntropyCTE AS
(
SELECT customercountry,
 1.0*StateFreq / SUM(StateFreq) OVER () AS StateProbability
FROM ProbabilityCTE
)
SELECT (-1)*SUM(StateProbability * LOG(StateProbability,2)) AS TotalEntropy,
 LOG(COUNT(*),2) AS MaxPossibleEntropy,
 100 * ((-1)*SUM(StateProbability * LOG(StateProbability,2))) /
 (LOG(COUNT(*),2)) AS PctOfMaxPossibleEntropy
FROM StateEntropyCTE;
```

The result is

TotalEntropy	MaxPossibleEntropy	PctOfMaxPossibleEntropy
3.91977859896801	4.39231742277876	89.2416968464042

Let me repeat the same query for the *productcategory* variable:

```
WITH ProbabilityCTE AS
(
SELECT categoryname,
 COUNT(categoryname) AS StateFreq
FROM dbo.SalesAnalysis
WHERE categoryname IS NOT NULL
GROUP BY categoryname
),
StateEntropyCTE AS
(
SELECT categoryname,
 1.0*StateFreq / SUM(StateFreq) OVER () AS StateProbability
FROM ProbabilityCTE
)
SELECT (-1)*SUM(StateProbability * LOG(StateProbability,2)) AS TotalEntropy,
 LOG(COUNT(*),2) AS MaxPossibleEntropy,
 100 * ((-1)*SUM(StateProbability * LOG(StateProbability,2))) /
 (LOG(COUNT(*),2)) AS PctOfMaxPossibleEntropy
FROM StateEntropyCTE;
```

The result for the *productcategory* variable is

TotalEntropy	MaxPossibleEntropy	PctOfMaxPossibleEntropy
2.90951317302341	3	96.9837724341137

You can see that the *customercountry* variable has a bigger maximal possible entropy, because it can occupy a value from a bigger amount of possible states, while the values of the *productcategory* variable are more equally distributed, and the actual entropy is closer to the maximal possible entropy.

Because this was the last query in this chapter, I have to clean my database:

```
DROP TABLE dbo.TestMedian;
DROP AGGREGATE dbo.Skew;
DROP AGGREGATE dbo.Kurt;
DROP ASSEMBLY DescriptiveStatistics;
EXEC sp_configure 'clr enabled', 0;
RECONFIGURE WITH OVERRIDE;
DROP TABLE #StdNormDist;
DROP TABLE dbo.MAvg;
```

Conclusion

In this chapter, you learned how to write many different queries that can help you when you have to develop a business intelligence application. You can extend your SQL Server toolset and your analytical queries a lot with the code from this chapter.

In addition, you also learned how to properly use the results of the queries and to understand the statistics behind them. Finally, I hope you also learned that optimizing a query does not always involve just finding the best possible execution plan. Analytical queries typically scan huge amounts of data, and optimizing with the classical nonclustered indexes does not bring any improvements. Of course, columnstore indexes can help with lowering disk IO. However, the real optimization technique you learned in this chapter is optimization with an algorithm. I showed many times how you can minimize the number of scans through the data by finding a different algorithm for some calculation and then rewriting the query to follow that algorithm.

For the queries in this chapter, I prepared a sales analysis view. In the introduction part, I also discussed the difference between discrete and continuous variables. Then I showed how to calculate the frequency distribution of a discrete variable efficiently and thus quickly get an overview of this distribution.

Then a big portion of this chapter dealt with continuous variables. I defined and showed how you can calculate the different measures of the descriptive statistics, from the measures for the center of distribution (including mode, median, and mean) through the measures for the spread of the distribution (including range, inter-quartile range, mean absolute deviation, mean squared deviation, variance, and standard deviation) to higher population moments (including skewness and kurtosis). I also explained and defined standard normal distribution and the statistical concept of degrees of freedom.

Another big portion of this chapter covered checking for linear dependencies. I developed queries that calculate the strength of the relationship for pairs of two continuous variables (including covariance, correlation coefficient, and coefficient of determination), two discrete variables (including contingency tables and a chi-squared test), and one discrete and one continuous variable with an analysis of variance. I also developed the calculations needed for the linear regression formula. On the fly, I also defined the statistical significance and showed how you can calculate the definite integration with T-SQL.

In the last part of this chapter, I covered a few unrelated topics useful for business-intelligence developers. From this material, you can learn about different moving averages, including simple, weighted, and exponential moving averages. You also can learn the basics of information theory and calculate the entropy of a variable to check whether, based on the information content, it can be used in further analysis.

Table 8-7 summarizes the statistical measures introduced in this chapter with a short definition.

TABLE 8-7 Summary of the statistical measures introduced in this chapter

Measure	Short definition
Frequencies	The frequency (or absolute frequency) of an event is the number of times the event occurred in an experiment or study.
Mode	Center of a distribution—the most fashionable value of a distribution.
Median	Center of a distribution—the value that splits the distribution into two halves.
Mean	Center of a distribution—the average value.
Range	Spread of a distribution—the distance between the maximal value and the minimal value.
Inter-quartile range	Spread of a distribution—the distance between the upper quartile (the third one) and the lower quartile (the first one).
Mean absolute deviation	Spread of a distribution—the sum of absolute values of the distances between each value and the mean.
Mean squared deviation	Spread of a distribution—the sum of squared values of the distances between each value and the mean, population measure.
Variance	Spread of a distribution—the sum of squared values of the distances between each value and the mean, population or sample measure.
Standard deviation	Spread of a distribution—the square root of the variance.
Coefficient of the variation	Spread of a distribution—the relative standard deviation.
Degrees of freedom	The number of values in the final calculation of a statistic that are free to vary.
Skewness	A measure of the asymmetry of the probability distribution of a real-valued random variable about its mean.
Kurtosis	A measure of the peakedness of the probability distribution of a real-valued random variable.
Covariance	Linear dependencies (continuous variables)—a measure of how much two random variables change together.
Correlation	Linear dependencies (continuous variables)—the relative strength of the linear relation.
Coefficient of determination	Linear dependencies (continuous variables)—correlation squared.
Linear regression	A model for the relationship between a scalar dependent variable and one or more explanatory variables.
Contingency table	Linear dependencies (discrete variables)—a table in a matrix format that displays the (multivariate) frequency distribution of the variables.
Chi-squared test	Linear dependencies (discrete variables)—a test for dependency of two discrete variables.
Analysis of variance	Linear dependencies (discrete and continuous variable)—a test of whether or not the means of several groups are equal.
F-test	Linear dependencies (discrete and continuous variable)—a test for dependency of a continuous and a discrete variable.
Definite integral	The signed area of the region in the xy plane under a function that is bounded by the graph of the function, the x-axis, and the vertical lines x = lower boundary and x = upper boundary
Moving average	A calculation to analyze data points by creating a series of averages of different subsets of the full data set.
Entropy	A measure of the unpredictability of information content.

Programmable objects

This chapter focuses on the programmatic constructs in T-SQL. It covers dynamic SQL, user-defined functions, stored procedures, triggers, SQLCLR programming, transactions and concurrency, and exception handling. Because the book's focus is on querying, most of the discussions involving programmatic constructs will tend to center on their use to support querying, with emphasis on the performance of the code.

Dynamic SQL

Dynamic SQL is, in essence, T-SQL code that constructs and executes T-SQL code. You usually build the batch of code as a character string that you store in a variable, and then you execute the code stored in the variable using one of two tools: the EXEC command (short for EXECUTE) or the *sp_executesql* stored procedure. The latter is the more flexible tool and, therefore, the recommended one to use.

The code you execute dynamically operates in a batch that is considered separate from the calling batch. That's important to keep in mind because the batch is the unit for a number of things in Microsoft SQL Server. It's the unit of parsing, binding, and optimization. The batch is also the scope for variables and parameters. You cannot access a variable declared in one batch within another. This means that if you have a variable in the calling batch, it is not visible to the code in the dynamic batch, and the other way around. So if you need to be able to pass variable values between the batches, and you want to avoid writing to and reading from tables for this purpose, you will need an interface in the form of input and output parameters. Between the EXEC and *sp_executesql* tools, only the latter supports such an interface; therefore, it is the recommended tool to use. I'll demonstrate using both tools.

Using the EXEC command

As mentioned, the EXEC command doesn't support an interface. You pass the character string holding the batch of code that you want to run as input, and the command executes the code within it. The lack of support for an interface introduces a challenge if in the dynamic batch you need to refer to a value in a variable or a parameter from the calling batch.

For example, suppose that the calling batch has a variable called *@s* that holds the last name of an employee. You need to construct a dynamic batch that, among other things, queries the

HR.Employees table in the TSQLV3 database and returns the employee or employees with that last name. What some do in such a case is concatenate the content of the variable (the actual last name) as a literal in the code and then execute the constructed code with the EXEC command, like so:

```
SET NOCOUNT ON;
USE TSQLV3;

DECLARE @s AS NVARCHAR(200);
SET @s = N'Davis'; -- originates in user input

DECLARE @sql AS NVARCHAR(1000);
SET @sql = N'SELECT empid, firstname, lastname, hiredate
FROM HR.Employees WHERE lastname = N''' + @s + N'''';';

PRINT @sql; -- for debug purposes
EXEC (@sql);
```

Running this code produces the following output, starting with the generated batch of code for troubleshooting purposes:

```
SELECT empid, firstname, lastname, hiredate
FROM HR.Employees WHERE lastname = N'Davis';

empid       firstname  lastname             hiredate
----------- ---------- -------------------- ----------
1           Sara       Davis                2012-05-01
```

There are two problems with this approach—one related to performance and the other to security. The performance-related problem is that for each distinct last name, the generated query string will be different. This means that unless SQL Server decides to parameterize the code—and it's quite conservative about the cases that it automatically parameterizes—it will end up creating and caching a separate plan for each distinct string. This behavior can result in flooding the memory with all those ad hoc plans, which will rarely get reused.

As for the security-related problem, concatenating user inputs as constants directly into the code exposes your environment to SQL injection attacks. Imagine that the user providing the last name that ends up in your code is a hacker. Imagine that instead of providing just a last name, they pass the following (by running the preceding code and replacing just the variable assignment with the following one):

```
SET @s = N'abc''; PRINT ''SQL injection!''; --';
```

Observe the query string and the outputs that are generated:

```
SELECT empid, firstname, lastname, hiredate
FROM HR.Employees WHERE lastname = N'abc'; PRINT 'SQL injection!'; --';
empid       firstname  lastname             hiredate
----------- ---------- -------------------- ----------

SQL injection!
```

Notice the last bit of output. It tells you that you ended up running code in your system that the hacker injected and you didn't intend to run. In this example, the injected code is a harmless PRINT command, but it could have been code with much worse implications, as the following comic strip will attest: *http://xkcd.com/327/*.

Often hackers will not try to inject code that does direct damage, because such an attempt is likely to be discovered quickly. Instead, they will try to steal information from your environment. Using the employee-name example to demonstrate, a hacker will first pass any last name just to see the structure of the result. The hacker will see that it contains four columns: the first is an integer, the second and third are character strings, and the fourth is a date. The hacker then submits the following "last name" to collect information about the objects in the database:

```
SET @s = N'abc'' UNION ALL SELECT object_id, SCHEMA_NAME(schema_id), name, NULL
FROM sys.objects WHERE type IN (''U'', ''V''); --';
```

Instead of getting employee information, the hacker gets the following information about the object IDs, schema, and object names of all objects in the database (the object IDs in your case will be different, of course):

```
SELECT empid, firstname, lastname, hiredate
FROM HR.Employees WHERE lastname = N'abc' UNION ALL
SELECT object_id, SCHEMA_NAME(schema_id), name, NULL
FROM sys.objects WHERE type IN ('U', 'V'); --';
```

empid	firstname	lastname	hiredate
245575913	HR	Employees	NULL
309576141	Production	Suppliers	NULL
341576255	Production	Categories	NULL
373576369	Production	Products	NULL
485576768	Sales	Customers	NULL
517576882	Sales	Shippers	NULL
549576996	Sales	Orders	NULL
645577338	Sales	OrderDetails	NULL
805577908	Stats	Tests	NULL
837578022	Stats	Scores	NULL
901578250	dbo	Nums	NULL
933578364	Sales	OrderValues	NULL
949578421	Sales	OrderTotalsByYear	NULL
965578478	Sales	CustOrders	NULL
981578535	Sales	EmpOrders	NULL

Because the hacker is interested in stealing customer information, his next move is to query *sys.columns* to ask for the metadata information about the columns in the Customers table. (Again, the hacker will need to use the object ID representing the Customers table in your database.) Here's the query he will use:

```
SET @s = N'abc'' UNION ALL
SELECT NULL, name, NULL, NULL FROM sys.columns WHERE object_id = 485576768; --';
```

The hacker gets the following output:

```
SELECT empid, firstname, lastname, hiredate
FROM HR.Employees WHERE lastname = N'abc' UNION ALL
SELECT NULL, name, NULL, NULL FROM sys.columns WHERE object_id = 485576768; --';
```

```
empid        firstname     lastname   hiredate
-----------  ------------- ---------  ----------
NULL         custid        NULL       NULL
NULL         companyname   NULL       NULL
NULL         contactname   NULL       NULL
NULL         contacttitle  NULL       NULL
NULL         address       NULL       NULL
NULL         city          NULL       NULL
NULL         region        NULL       NULL
NULL         postalcode    NULL       NULL
NULL         country       NULL       NULL
NULL         phone         NULL       NULL
NULL         fax           NULL       NULL
```

Then the hacker's next move is to collect the phone numbers of the customers by using the following code:

```
SET @s = N'abc'' UNION ALL SELECT NULL, companyname, phone, NULL FROM Sales.Customers; --';
```

He gets the following output:

```
SELECT empid, firstname, lastname, hiredate
FROM HR.Employees WHERE lastname = N'abc' UNION ALL
SELECT NULL, companyname, phone, NULL FROM Sales.Customers; --';
```

```
empid        firstname       lastname         hiredate
-----------  --------------- ---------------  ----------
NULL         Customer NRZBB  030-3456789      NULL
NULL         Customer MLTDN  (5) 789-0123     NULL
NULL         Customer KBUDE  (5) 123-4567     NULL
NULL         Customer HFBZG  (171) 456-7890   NULL
NULL         Customer HGVLZ  0921-67 89 01    NULL
...
```

All of this was possible because you concatenated the user input straight into the code. If you're thinking you can check the inputs by looking for common elements used in injection, you need to be aware that it's hard to cover all possible injection methods. Hackers keep reinventing themselves. Like my friend and colleague Richard Waymire once said, "They're not necessarily smarter than you, but they have more time than you." The only real way to avoid injection is not to concatenate user inputs into your code; rather, pass them as parameters. However, to do this, you need a tool that supports an interface, and unfortunately the EXEC command doesn't. Fortunately, the *sp_executesql* procedure does support such an interface, as I will demonstrate shortly.

The EXEC command has an interesting capability you can use to concatenate multiple variables within the parentheses, like so:

```
EXEC(@v1 + @v2 + @v2);
```

Even if the inputs are character strings with a limited size—for example, VARCHAR(8000)—you are allowed to exceed 8,000 characters in the combined string. With legacy versions of SQL Server prior to the support for VARCHAR(MAX) and NVARCHAR(MAX), this used to be an important capability. But with these types, you can pass an input batch that is up to 2 GB in size. EXEC supports both regular character strings and Unicode ones as inputs, unlike *sp_executesql*, which supports only the latter kind.

Using EXEC AT

In addition to supporting an EXEC command that executes a dynamic batch locally, SQL Server also supports a command called EXEC AT that executes a dynamic batch against a linked server. What's interesting about this tool is that if the provider you use to connect to the linked server supports parameters, you can pass inputs to the dynamic batch through parameters.

As an example, assuming you have access to another SQL Server instance called YourServer, run the following code to create a linked server:

```
EXEC sp_addlinkedserver
  @server = N'YourServer',
  @srvproduct = N'SQL Server';
```

Assuming you installed the sample database TSQLV3 in that instance, run the following code to test the EXEC AT command:

```
DECLARE @sql AS NVARCHAR(1000), @pid AS INT;

SET @sql =
N'SELECT productid, productname, unitprice
FROM TSQLV3.Production.Products
WHERE productid = ?;';

SET @pid = 3;

EXEC(@sql, @pid) AT [YourServer];
```

The code constructs a batch that queries the Production.Products table, filters a product ID that is provided as a parameter, and then executes the batch against the linked server, passing the value *3* as the input. This code generates the following output:

```
productid    productname     unitprice
-----------  --------------  ----------
3            Product IMEHJ   10.00
```

Using the *sp_executesql* procedure

Unlike the EXEC command, the *sp_executesql* procedure supports defining input and output parameters, much like a stored procedure does. This tool accepts three parts as its inputs. The first part, called *@stmt*, is the input batch of code you want to run (with the references to the input and output parameters). The second part, called *@params*, is where you provide the declaration of your parameters. The third part is where you assign values to the dynamic batch's input parameters and collect values from the output parameters into variables.

Back to the original task of querying the Employees table based on a last name that originated in user input, here's how you achieve it with a parameterized query using *sp_executesql*:

```
DECLARE @s AS NVARCHAR(200);
SET @s = N'Davis';

DECLARE @sql AS NVARCHAR(1000);
SET @sql = 'SELECT empid, firstname, lastname, hiredate
FROM HR.Employees WHERE lastname = @lastname;';

PRINT @sql; -- For debug purposes

EXEC sp_executesql
  @stmt = @sql,
  @params = N'@lastname AS NVARCHAR(200)',
  @lastname = @s;
```

The code generates the following query string and output:

```
SELECT empid, firstname, lastname, hiredate
FROM HR.Employees WHERE lastname = @lastname;
```

empid	firstname	lastname	hiredate
1	Sara	Davis	2012-05-01

This solution doesn't have the performance and security problems you had with EXEC. Regarding performance, the query gets optimized in the first execution of the code and the plan is cached. Subsequent executions of the code can potentially reuse the cached plan regardless of which last name is passed. This behavior is quite similar to the way plans for parameterized queries in stored procedures are cached and reused.

Regarding security, because the actual user input is not embedded in the code, there's absolutely no exposure to SQL injection. The user input is always considered as a value in the parameter and is never made an actual part of the code.

Dynamic pivot

In Chapter 4, "Grouping, pivoting, and windowing," I covered pivoting methods and provided the following example demonstrating how to handle pivoting dynamically:

```
USE TSQLV3;

DECLARE
  @cols AS NVARCHAR(1000),
  @sql  AS NVARCHAR(4000);
```

```
SET @cols =
  STUFF(
    (SELECT N',' + QUOTENAME(orderyear) AS [text()]
      FROM (SELECT DISTINCT YEAR(orderdate) AS orderyear
            FROM Sales.Orders) AS Years
    ORDER BY orderyear
    FOR XML PATH(''), TYPE).value('.[1]', 'VARCHAR(MAX)'), 1, 1, '')

SET @sql = N'SELECT custid, ' + @cols + N'
FROM (SELECT custid, YEAR(orderdate) AS orderyear, val
      FROM Sales.OrderValues) AS D
  PIVOT(SUM(val) FOR orderyear IN(' + @cols + N')) AS P;';

EXEC sys.sp_executesql @stmt = @sql;
```

This example constructs a pivot query that returns a row per customer, a column per order year, and the sum of all order values for each intersection of customer and year. The code returns the following output:

```
custid  2013      2014       2015
-------  --------  ---------  ---------
1        NULL      2022.50    2250.50
2        88.80     799.75     514.40
3        403.20    5960.78    660.00
4        1379.00   6406.90    5604.75
5        4324.40   13849.02   6754.16
6        NULL      1079.80    2160.00
7        9986.20   7817.88    730.00
8        982.00    3026.85    224.00
9        4074.28   11208.36   6680.61
10       1832.80   7630.25    11338.56
...
```

Dynamic SQL is used here to avoid the need to hard code the years into the query. Instead, you query the distinct years from the data. Using an aggregate string concatenation method that is based on the FOR XML PATH option, you construct the comma-separated list of years for the pivot query's IN clause. This way, when orders are recorded from a new year, the next time you execute the code that year is automatically included. If you're reading the book's chapters out of order and are not familiar with pivoting and aggregate string concatenation methods, you can find those in Chapter 4 in the sections "Pivoting" and "Custom aggregations," respectively. In the next section, I'll assume you are familiar with both.

The dynamic pivot example from Chapter 4 handled a specific pivoting task. If you need a similar solution for a different pivot task, you need to duplicate the code and change the pivoting elements to the new ones. The following *sp_pivot* stored procedure provides a more generalized solution for dynamic pivoting:

```
USE master;
GO
IF OBJECT_ID(N'dbo.sp_pivot', N'P') IS NOT NULL DROP PROC dbo.sp_pivot;
GO
```

```
CREATE PROC dbo.sp_pivot
  @query    AS NVARCHAR(MAX),
  @on_rows  AS NVARCHAR(MAX),
  @on_cols  AS NVARCHAR(MAX),
  @agg_func AS NVARCHAR(257) = N'MAX',
  @agg_col  AS NVARCHAR(MAX)
AS
BEGIN TRY
  -- Input validation
  IF @query IS NULL OR @on_rows IS NULL OR @on_cols IS NULL
     OR @agg_func IS NULL OR @agg_col IS NULL
    THROW 50001, 'Invalid input parameters.', 1;

  -- Additional input validation goes here (SQL injection attempts, etc.)

  DECLARE
    @sql     AS NVARCHAR(MAX),
    @cols    AS NVARCHAR(MAX),
    @newline AS NVARCHAR(2) = NCHAR(13) + NCHAR(10);

  -- If input is a valid table or view
  -- construct a SELECT statement against it
  IF COALESCE(OBJECT_ID(@query, N'U'), OBJECT_ID(@query, N'V')) IS NOT NULL
    SET @query = N'SELECT * FROM ' + @query;

  -- Make the query a derived table
  SET @query = N'(' + @query + N') AS Query';

  -- Handle * input in @agg_col
  IF @agg_col = N'*' SET @agg_col = N'1';

  -- Construct column list
  SET @sql =
    N'SET @result = '                                + @newline +
    N'  STUFF('                                      + @newline +
    N'    (SELECT N'',['' + '
          + 'CAST(pivot_col AS sysname) + '
          + 'N'']'''' AS [text()]'                   + @newline +
    N'     FROM (SELECT DISTINCT('
          + @on_cols + N') AS pivot_col'             + @newline +
    N'           FROM' + @query + N') AS DistinctCols'  + @newline +
    N'     ORDER BY pivot_col'+ @newline +
    N'     FOR XML PATH('''')),'+ @newline +
    N'    1, 1, N'''''');'

  EXEC sp_executesql
    @stmt   = @sql,
    @params = N'@result AS NVARCHAR(MAX) OUTPUT',
    @result = @cols OUTPUT;
```

```
-- Create the PIVOT query
SET @sql =
  N'SELECT *'                                     + @newline +
  N'FROM (SELECT '
          + @on_rows
          + N', ' + @on_cols + N' AS pivot_col'
          + N', ' + @agg_col + N' AS agg_col'    + @newline +
  N'       FROM ' + @query + N')' +
          + N' AS PivotInput'                     + @newline +
  N'  PIVOT(' + @agg_func + N'(agg_col)'          + @newline +
  N'    FOR pivot_col IN(' + @cols + N')) AS PivotOutput;'

  EXEC sp_executesql @sql;

END TRY
BEGIN CATCH
  ;THROW;
END CATCH;
GO
```

The stored procedure accepts the following input parameters:

- The *@query* parameter is either a table or view name or an entire query whose result you want to pivot—for example, *N'Sales.OrderValues'*.

- The *@on_rows* parameter is the pivot grouping element—for example, *N'custid'*.

- The *@on_cols* parameter is the pivot spreading element—for example, *N'YEAR(orderdate)'*.

- The *@agg_func* parameter is the pivot aggregate function—for example, *N'SUM'*.

- The *@agg_col* parameter is the input expression to the pivot aggregate function—for example, *N'val'*.

> **Important** This stored procedure supports SQL injection by definition. The input parameters are injected directly into the code to form the pivot query. For this reason, you want to be extremely careful with how and for what purpose you use it. For example, it could be a good idea to restrict the use of this procedure only to developers to aid in constructing pivot queries. Having an application invoke this procedure after collecting user inputs puts your environment at risk.

Because the stored procedure is created in the master database with the *sp_* prefix, it can be executed in the context of any database. This is done either by calling it without the database prefix while connected to the desired database or by invoking it using the three-part name with the desired database as the database prefix, as in *mydb.dbo.sp_pivot*.

The stored procedure performs some basic input validation to ensure all inputs were provided. The procedure then checks if the input *@query* contains an existing table or view name in the target database. If it does, the procedure replaces the content of *@query* with a query against the object; if it does not, the procedure assumes that *@query* already contains a query. Then the procedure replaces the contents of *@query* with the definition of a derived table called Query based on the input query. This derived table will be considered as the input for finding both the distinct spreading values and the final pivot query.

The next step in the procedure is to check if the input *@agg_col* is *. It's common for people to use * as the input to the aggregate function COUNT to count rows. However, the PIVOT operator doesn't support * as an input to COUNT. So the code replaces * with the constant *1*, and it will later define a column called *agg_col* based on what's stored in *@agg_col*. This column will eventually be used as the input to the aggregate function stored in *@agg_func*.

The next two steps represent the heart of the stored procedure. These steps construct two different dynamic batches. The first creates a string with the comma-separated list of distinct spreading values that will eventually appear in the PIVOT operator's IN clause. This batch is executed with *sp_executesql* and, using an output parameter called *@result*, the result string is stored in a local variable called *@cols*.

The second dynamic batch holds the final pivot query. The code constructs a derived table called PivotInput from a query against the derived table stored in *@query*. All pivoting elements (grouping, spreading, and aggregation) are injected into the inner query's SELECT list. Then the PIVOT operator's specification is constructed from the input aggregate function applied to *agg_col* and the IN clause with the comma-separated list of spreading values stored in *@cols*. The final pivot query is then executed using *sp_executesql*.

As an example of using the procedure, the following code computes the count of orders per employee and order year pivoted by order month:

```
EXEC TSQLV3.dbo.sp_pivot
  @query    = N'Sales.Orders',
  @on_rows  = N'empid, YEAR(orderdate) AS orderyear',
  @on_cols  = N'MONTH(orderdate)',
  @agg_func = N'COUNT',
  @agg_col  = N'*';
```

This code generates the following output:

empid	orderyear	1	2	3	4	5	6	7	8	9	10	11	12
1	2014	3	2	5	1	5	4	7	3	8	7	3	7
5	2013	0	0	0	0	0	0	3	0	1	2	2	3
2	2015	7	3	9	18	2	0	0	0	0	0	0	0
6	2014	2	2	2	4	2	2	2	2	1	4	5	5
8	2014	5	8	6	2	4	3	6	5	3	7	2	3
9	2015	5	4	6	4	0	0	0	0	0	0	0	0
2	2013	0	0	0	0	0	0	1	2	5	2	2	4
3	2014	7	9	3	5	5	6	2	4	4	7	8	11
7	2013	0	0	0	0	0	0	0	1	2	5	3	0
4	2015	6	14	12	10	2	0	0	0	0	0	0	0

...

As another example, the following code computes the sum of order values (*quantity * unit price*) per employee pivoted by order year:

```
EXEC TSQLV3.dbo.sp_pivot
  @query    = N'SELECT O.orderid, empid, orderdate, qty, unitprice
FROM Sales.Orders AS O
  INNER JOIN Sales.OrderDetails AS OD
    ON OD.orderid = O.orderid',
  @on_rows  = N'empid',
  @on_cols  = N'YEAR(orderdate)',
  @agg_func = N'SUM',
  @agg_col  = N'qty * unitprice';
```

This code generates the following output:

```
empid  2013       2014        2015
------ ---------- ----------- ---------
9      11365.70   29577.55    42020.75
3      19231.80   111788.61   82030.89
6      17731.10   45992.00    14475.00
7      18104.80   66689.14    56502.05
1      38789.00   97533.58    65821.13
4      53114.80   139477.70   57594.95
5      21965.20   32595.05    21007.50
2      22834.70   74958.60    79955.96
8      23161.40   59776.52    50363.11
```

When you're done, run the following code for cleanup:

```
USE master;
IF OBJECT_ID(N'dbo.sp_pivot', N'P') IS NOT NULL DROP PROC dbo.sp_pivot;
```

Dynamic search conditions

Dynamic search conditions, also known as *dynamic filtering*, are a common need in applications. The idea is that the application provides the user with an interface to filter data by various attributes, and the user chooses which attributes to filter by with each request. To demonstrate techniques to handle dynamic search conditions, I'll use a table called Orders in my examples. Run the following code to create the Orders table in tempdb as a copy of TSQLV3.Sales.Orders, along with a few indexes to support common filters:

```
SET NOCOUNT ON;
USE tempdb;

IF OBJECT_ID(N'dbo.GetOrders', N'P') IS NOT NULL DROP PROC dbo.GetOrders;
IF OBJECT_ID(N'dbo.Orders', N'U') IS NOT NULL DROP TABLE dbo.Orders;
GO

SELECT orderid, custid, empid, orderdate,
  CAST('A' AS CHAR(200)) AS filler
INTO dbo.Orders
FROM TSQLV3.Sales.Orders;
```

```
CREATE CLUSTERED INDEX idx_orderdate ON dbo.Orders(orderdate);
CREATE UNIQUE INDEX idx_orderid ON dbo.Orders(orderid);
CREATE INDEX idx_custid_empid ON dbo.Orders(custid, empid) INCLUDE(orderid, orderdate, filler);
```

Your task is to create a stored procedure called *dbo.GetOrders* that accepts four optional inputs, called *@orderid*, *@custid*, *@empid*, and *@orderdate*. The procedure is supposed to query the Orders table and filter the rows based only on the parameters that get non-NULL input values.

The following implementation of the stored procedure represents one of the most commonly used techniques to handle the task:

```
IF OBJECT_ID(N'dbo.GetOrders', N'P') IS NOT NULL DROP PROC dbo.GetOrders;
GO
CREATE PROC dbo.GetOrders
  @orderid   AS INT  = NULL,
  @custid    AS INT  = NULL,
  @empid     AS INT  = NULL,
  @orderdate AS DATE = NULL
AS

SELECT orderid, custid, empid, orderdate, filler
FROM dbo.Orders
WHERE (orderid   = @orderid   OR @orderid   IS NULL)
  AND (custid    = @custid    OR @custid    IS NULL)
  AND (empid     = @empid     OR @empid     IS NULL)
  AND (orderdate = @orderdate OR @orderdate IS NULL);
GO
```

The procedure uses a static query that, for each parameter, uses the following disjunction of predicates (OR'd predicates): *column = @parameter OR @parameter IS NULL*. If a value isn't provided for the parameter, the right predicate is *true*. With a disjunction of predicates when one of the operands is *true*, the whole thing is *true*, so no filtering happens based on this column. If a value is specified, the right predicate is *false*; therefore, the left predicate is the only one that counts for determining which rows to filter.

This solution is simple and easy to maintain; however, absent an extra element, it tends to result in suboptimal query plans. The reason for this is that when you execute the procedure for the first time, the optimizer optimizes the parameterized form of the code, including all predicates from the query. This means that both the predicates that are relevant for the current execution of the query and the ones that aren't relevant are included in the plan. This approach is used to promote plan reuse behavior to save the time and resources that would have been associated with the creation of a new plan with every execution. This topic is covered in detail later in the chapter in the "Compilations, recompilations, and reuse of execution plans" section. This approach guarantees that if the procedure is called again with a different set of relevant parameters, the cached plan would still be valid and therefore can be reused. But if the plan has to be correct while taking into consideration all predicates in the query, including the irrelevant ones for the current execution, you realize that it's unlikely to be efficient.

As an example, run the following code to execute the procedure with an input value provided only to the *@orderdate* parameter:

```
EXEC dbo.GetOrders @orderdate = '20140101';
```

Observe the plan that the optimizer created for the query as shown in Figure 9-1.

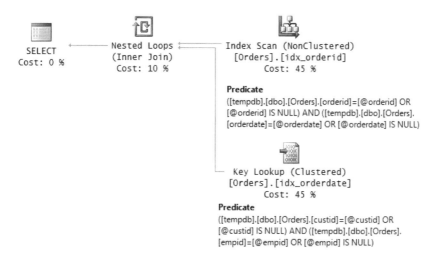

FIGURE 9-1 Plan for a solution using a static query.

There are different places in the plan where the different predicates are processed, but the point is that all predicates are processed. With a filter based only on the *orderdate* column, the most efficient plan would be one that performs a seek and a range scan in the clustered index. But what you see here is an entirely different plan that is very inefficient for this execution.

You can do a number of things to get efficient plans. If you are willing to forgo the benefits of plan reuse, add OPTION(RECOMPILE) at the end of the query, which forces SQL Server to create a new plan with every execution. It's critical, though, to use the statement-level RECOMPILE option and not the procedure-level one. With the former, the parser performs parameter embedding, where it replaces the parameters with the constants and removes the redundant parts of the query before passing it to the optimizer. As a result, the query that gets optimized contains only the predicates that are relevant to the current execution, so the likelihood of getting an efficient plan is quite high.

Run the following code to re-create the *GetOrders* procedure, adding the RECOMPILE option to the query:

```
IF OBJECT_ID(N'dbo.GetOrders', N'P') IS NOT NULL DROP PROC dbo.GetOrders;
GO
CREATE PROC dbo.GetOrders
  @orderid   AS INT  = NULL,
  @custid    AS INT  = NULL,
  @empid     AS INT  = NULL,
  @orderdate AS DATE = NULL
AS
```

```
SELECT orderid, custid, empid, orderdate, filler
FROM dbo.Orders
WHERE (orderid   = @orderid   OR @orderid   IS NULL)
  AND (custid    = @custid    OR @custid    IS NULL)
  AND (empid     = @empid     OR @empid     IS NULL)
  AND (orderdate = @orderdate OR @orderdate IS NULL)
OPTION (RECOMPILE);
GO
```

Run the following code to test the procedure with a filter based on the *orderdate* column:

```
EXEC dbo.GetOrders @orderdate = '20140101';
```

The plan for this execution is shown in Figure 9-2.

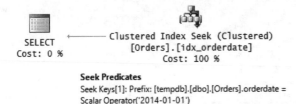

Seek Predicates
Seek Keys[1]: Prefix: [tempdb].[dbo].[Orders].orderdate =
Scalar Operator('2014-01-01')

FIGURE 9-2 Plan for a query with RECOMPILE filtering by *orderdate*.

The plan is optimal, with a seek in the clustered index, which is defined with *orderdate* as the key. Observe that only the predicate involving the *orderdate* column appears in the plan, and that the reference to the parameter was replaced with the constant.

Execute the procedure again, this time with a filter based on the *orderid* column:

```
EXEC dbo.GetOrders @orderid    = 10248;
```

The plan for this execution is shown in Figure 9-3.

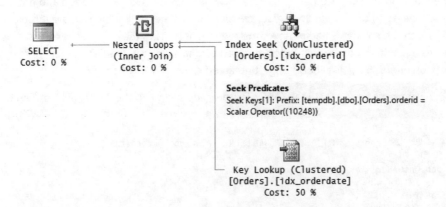

FIGURE 9-3 Plan for a query with RECOMPILE filtering by *orderid*.

The plan is, again, optimal, performing a seek in the index on *orderid*, followed by a lookup. The only predicate appearing in this plan is the one based on the *orderid* column—again, with the parameter replaced with the constant.

Because of the forced recompiles and parameter embedding that takes place, you get very efficient plans. The solution uses static SQL, so it's not exposed to SQL injection attacks. It's simple and easy to maintain. The one drawback of this solution is that, by definition, it doesn't reuse plans. But what if the procedure is called frequently with common combinations of input parameters and you would like to get both efficient plans and efficient plan reuse? There are a couple of ways to achieve this goal.

You could create a separate procedure for each unique combination of parameters and have the *GetOrders* procedure use nested IF-ELSE IF statements to invoke the right procedure based on which parameters are specified. Each procedure will have a unique query with only the relevant predicates, without the RECOMPILE option. With this solution, the likelihood of getting efficient plans is high. Also, the plans can be cached and reused. Because the solution uses static SQL, it has no exposure to SQL injection. However, as you can imagine, it can be a maintenance nightmare. With P parameters, the number of procedures you will need is 2^P. For example, with 8 parameters, you will have 256 procedures. Imagine that whenever you need to make a change, you will need to apply it to all procedures. Not a picnic.

Another strategy is to use dynamic SQL, but with a parameterized form of the code to promote efficient plan reuse behavior and avoid exposure to SQL injection. You construct the query string starting with the known SELECT and FROM clauses of the query. You start the WHERE clause with *WHERE 1 = 1*. This way, you don't need to maintain a flag to know whether you need a WHERE clause and whether you need an AND operator before concatenating a predicate. The parser will eliminate this redundant predicate. Then, for each procedure parameter whose value was specified, you concatenate a parameterized predicate to the WHERE clause. Then you execute the parameterized query using *sp_executesql*, passing the query string to the *@stmt* input, declaring the four dynamic batch parameters in the *@params* input, and assigning the procedure parameters to the respective dynamic batch parameters.

Here's the code to re-create the procedure based on the new strategy:

```
IF OBJECT_ID(N'dbo.GetOrders', N'P') IS NOT NULL DROP PROC dbo.GetOrders;
GO
CREATE PROC dbo.GetOrders
  @orderid   AS INT  = NULL,
  @custid    AS INT  = NULL,
  @empid     AS INT  = NULL,
  @orderdate AS DATE = NULL
AS

DECLARE @sql AS NVARCHAR(1000);
```

```
SET @sql =
    N'SELECT orderid, custid, empid, orderdate, filler'
  + N' /* 27702431-107C-478C-8157-6DFCECC148DD */'
  + N' FROM dbo.Orders'
  + N' WHERE 1 = 1'
  + CASE WHEN @orderid IS NOT NULL THEN
      N' AND orderid = @oid' ELSE N'' END
  + CASE WHEN @custid IS NOT NULL THEN
      N' AND custid = @cid' ELSE N'' END
  + CASE WHEN @empid IS NOT NULL THEN
      N' AND empid = @eid' ELSE N'' END
  + CASE WHEN @orderdate IS NOT NULL THEN
      N' AND orderdate = @dt' ELSE N'' END;

EXEC sp_executesql
  @stmt = @sql,
  @params = N'@oid AS INT, @cid AS INT, @eid AS INT, @dt AS DATE',
  @oid = @orderid,
  @cid = @custid,
  @eid = @empid,
  @dt  = @orderdate;
GO
```

Observe the GUID that I planted in a comment in the query. I created it by invoking the NEWID function. The point is to make it easy later to track down the cached plans that are executed by the procedure to demonstrate plan caching and reuse behavior. I'll demonstrate this shortly.

Run the following code to execute the procedure twice with a filter based on the *orderdate* column, but with two different dates:

```
EXEC dbo.GetOrders @orderdate = '20140101';
EXEC dbo.GetOrders @orderdate = '20140102';
```

The plan for these executions is shown in Figure 9-4.

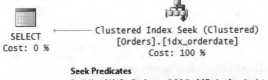

```
SELECT                 ┌────────── Clustered Index Seek (Clustered)
Cost: 0 %                             [Orders].[idx_orderdate]
                                              Cost: 100 %

                Seek Predicates
                Seek Keys[1]: Prefix: [tempdb].[dbo].[Orders].orderdate =
                Scalar Operator([@dt])
```

FIGURE 9-4 Plan for a dynamic query filtering by *orderdate*.

The plan is very efficient because the query that was optimized contains only the relevant predicates. Furthermore, unlike when using the RECOMPILE query option, there's no parameter embedding here, which is good in this case. The parameterized form of the query gets optimized and cached, allowing plan reuse when the procedure is executed with the same combination of parameters. In the first execution of the procedure with a filter based on *orderdate*, SQL Server couldn't find an existing plan in cache, so it optimized the query and cached the plan. For the second execution, it found a cached plan for the same query string and therefore reused it.

Execute the procedure again, this time with a filter based on the *orderid* column:

```
EXEC dbo.GetOrders @orderid   = 10248;
```

This time the constructed query string contains a parameterized filter based on the *orderid* column. Because there was no plan in cache for this query string, SQL Server created a new plan and cached it too. Figure 9-5 shows the plan that SQL Server created for this query string.

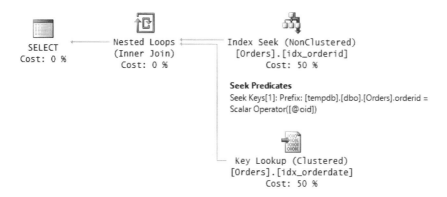

FIGURE 9-5 Plan for a dynamic query filtering by *orderid*.

Again, you get a highly efficient plan for this query string, with only the relevant predicates in a parameterized form. Now you have two plans in cache for the two unique query strings that were executed by the stored procedure. Use the following query to examine the cached plans and their reuse behavior, filtering only plans for queries that contain the GUID you planted in the code:

```
SELECT usecounts, text
FROM sys.dm_exec_cached_plans AS CP
  CROSS APPLY sys.dm_exec_sql_text(cp.plan_handle) AS ST
WHERE ST.text LIKE '%27702431-107C-478C-8157-6DFCECC148DD%'
  AND ST.text NOT LIKE '%sys.dm_exec_cached_plans%'
  AND CP.objtype = 'Prepared';
```

This code generates the following output:

```
usecounts    text
-----------  ---------------------------------------------------
1            (@oid AS INT, @cid AS INT, @eid AS INT, @dt AS DATE)
             SELECT orderid, custid, empid, orderdate, filler
             /* 27702431-107C-478C-8157-6DFCECC148DD */
             FROM dbo.Orders WHERE 1 = 1 AND orderid = @oid
2            (@oid AS INT, @cid AS INT, @eid AS INT, @dt AS DATE)
             SELECT orderid, custid, empid, orderdate, filler
             /* 27702431-107C 478C-8157-6DFCECC148DD */
             FROM dbo.Orders WHERE 1 = 1 AND orderdate = @dt
```

Observe that two plans were created because there were two unique query strings—one with a filter on *orderid*, so far used once, and another with a filter on *orderdate*, so far used twice.

This solution supports efficient plans and efficient plan reuse. Because the dynamic code uses parameters rather than injecting the constants into the code, it is not exposed to SQL injection attacks. Compared to the solution with the multiple procedures, this one is much easier to maintain. It certainly seems like this solution has strong advantages compared to the others.

There's an excellent paper written on the topic of dynamic search conditions by my friend and fellow SQL Server MVP Erland Sommarskog. If this topic is important to you, be sure to check out Erland's paper. You can find it at his website: *http://www.sommarskog.se/dyn-search.html*.

Dynamic sorting

Similar to dynamic search conditions, *dynamic sorting* is another common application need. As an example, suppose you need to develop a stored procedure called *dbo.GetSortedShippers* in the TSQLV3 database. The procedure accepts an input parameter called *@colname*, and it is supposed to return the rows from the Sales.Shippers table sorted by the input column name.

One of the most common first attempts at a solution for the task is to use a static query with an ORDER BY clause based on a CASE expression that looks like this:

```
ORDER BY
  CASE @colname
    WHEN N'shipperid'   THEN shipperid
    WHEN N'companyname' THEN companyname
    WHEN N'phone'       THEN phone
  END
```

If you try running the procedure passing *N'companyname'* as input, you get a type-conversion error. The reason for the error is that CASE is an expression, and as such, the type of the result is determined by the data type precedence among the expression's operands (the possible returned values in this case). Among the types of the three operands, INT is the one with the highest data type precedence; hence, it's predetermined that the CASE expression's type is INT. So when you pass *N'companyname'* as input, SQL Server tries to convert the *companyname* values to integers and, of course, fails.

One possible workaround is to add the following ELSE clause to the expression:

```
ORDER BY
  CASE @colname
    WHEN N'shipperid'   THEN shipperid
    WHEN N'companyname' THEN companyname
    WHEN N'phone'       THEN phone
    ELSE CAST(NULL AS SQL_VARIANT)
  END
```

This clause is not supposed to be activated because the procedure will be called by the application with names of columns that exist in the table; however, from SQL Server's perspective, it theoretically could be activated. The SQL_VARIANT type is considered stronger than the other types; therefore, it's chosen as the CASE expression's type. The thing with the SQL_VARIANT type is that it can hold within it most other base types, including all those that participate in our expression, while preserving the information about the base type and its ordering semantics. So when the user calls the procedure with, say, *N'companyname'* as input, the CASE expression returns the *companyname* values as SQL_ VARIANT values with NVARCHAR as the base type. So you get correct NVARCHAR-based ordering semantics.

With this trick, you get a solution that is correct. However, similar to non SARGable filters, because you're applying manipulation to the ordering element, the optimizer will not rely on index order even if you have a supporting covering index. Curiously, as described by Paul White in the article "Parameter Sniffing, Embedding, and the RECOMPILE Options" (*http://sqlperformance.com/2013/08/ t-sql-queries/parameter-sniffing-embedding-and-the-recompile-options*), as long as you use a separate CASE expression for each input and add the RECOMPILE query option, you get a plan that can rely on index order. That's thanks to the parameter embedding employed by the parser that's similar to what I explained in the discussion about dynamic search conditions. So, instead of using one CASE expression, you will use multiple expressions, like so:

```
ORDER BY
  CASE WHEN @colname = N'shipperid'   THEN shipperid   END,
  CASE WHEN @colname = N'companyname' THEN companyname END,
  CASE WHEN @colname = N'phone'       THEN phone       END
OPTION(RECOMPILE)
```

Say the user executes the procedure passing *N'companyname'* as input; after parsing, the ORDER BY clause becomes the following (although NULL constants are normally not allowed in the ORDER BY directly): ORDER BY NULL, companyname, NULL. As long as you have a covering index in place, the optimizer can certainly rely on its order and avoid explicit sorting in the plan.

For the procedure to be more flexible, you might also want to support a second parameter called *@sortdir* to allow the user to specify the sort direction (*'A'* for ascending and *'D'* for descending). Supporting this second parameter will require you to double the number of CASE expressions in the query.

Run the following code to create the *GetSortedShippers* procedure based on this strategy:

```
USE TSQLV3;

IF OBJECT_ID(N'dbo.GetSortedShippers', N'P') IS NOT NULL DROP PROC dbo.GetSortedShippers;
GO
CREATE PROC dbo.GetSortedShippers
  @colname AS sysname, @sortdir AS CHAR(1) = 'A'
AS

SELECT shipperid, companyname, phone
FROM Sales.Shippers
ORDER BY
  CASE WHEN @colname = N'shipperid'   AND @sortdir = 'A' THEN shipperid   END,
  CASE WHEN @colname = N'companyname' AND @sortdir = 'A' THEN companyname END,
  CASE WHEN @colname = N'phone'       AND @sortdir = 'A' THEN phone       END,
  CASE WHEN @colname = N'shipperid'   AND @sortdir = 'D' THEN shipperid   END DESC,
  CASE WHEN @colname = N'companyname' AND @sortdir = 'D' THEN companyname END DESC,
  CASE WHEN @colname = N'phone'       AND @sortdir = 'D' THEN phone       END DESC
OPTION (RECOMPILE);
GO
```

Run the following code to test the procedure:

```
EXEC dbo.GetSortedShippers N'shipperid', N'D';
```

After parsing, the ORDER BY clause became the following:

```
ORDER BY NULL, NULL, NULL, shipperid DESC, NULL DESC, NULL DESC
```

The plan for this execution is shown in Figure 9-6.

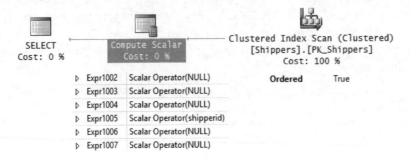

FIGURE 9-6 Plan for a query with multiple CASE expressions and RECOMPILE.

Observe that the plan performs an ordered scan of the clustered index on *shipperid*, avoiding the need for explicit sorting.

This solution produces efficient plans. Because it uses a static query, it's not exposed to SQL injection attacks. However, it has two drawbacks. First, by definition, it does not reuse query plans. Second, it doesn't lend itself to supporting multiple sort columns as inputs; you'd just end up with many CASE expressions.

A solution that doesn't have these drawbacks is one based on dynamic SQL. You construct a query string with an ORDER BY clause with an injected sort column and direction. The obvious challenge with this solution is the exposure to SQL injection. Then, again, table structures tend to be pretty stable. So you could incorporate a test to ensure that the input column name appears in the hard-coded set of sort columns you want to support from the table. If the column doesn't appear in the set, you abort the query, suspecting an attempted SQL injection. If the set of supported sort columns needs to change, you alter the procedure definition. Most likely, such changes will be infrequent enough to make this approach viable.

Use the following code to re-create the procedure based on this strategy:

```
IF OBJECT_ID(N'dbo.GetSortedShippers', N'P') IS NOT NULL DROP PROC dbo.GetSortedShippers;
GO
CREATE PROC dbo.GetSortedShippers
  @colname AS sysname, @sortdir AS CHAR(1) = 'A'
AS

IF @colname NOT IN(N'shipperid', N'companyname', N'phone')
  THROW 50001, 'Column name not supported. Possibly a SQL injection attempt.', 1;
```

```
DECLARE @sql AS NVARCHAR(1000);

SET @sql = N'SELECT shipperid, companyname, phone
FROM Sales.Shippers
ORDER BY '
  + QUOTENAME(@colname) + CASE @sortdir WHEN 'D' THEN N' DESC' ELSE '' END + ';';

EXEC sys.sp_executesql @stmt = @sql;
GO
```

The QUOTENAME function is used to delimit the sort column name with square brackets. In our specific example, delimiters aren't required, but in case you need to support column names that are considered irregular identifiers, you will need the delimiters.

Use the following code to test the procedure:

```
EXEC dbo.GetSortedShippers N'shipperid', N'D';
```

The plan for this execution is shown in Figure 9-7.

FIGURE 9-7 Plan for a dynamic query.

It's an efficient plan that relies on index order. Unlike the previous solution, this one can efficiently reuse previously cached plans. This solution can also be easily extended if you need to support multiple input sort columns, as the following revised definition demonstrates:

```
IF OBJECT_ID(N'dbo.GetSortedShippers', N'P') IS NOT NULL DROP PROC dbo.GetSortedShippers;
GO
CREATE PROC dbo.GetSortedShippers
  @colname1 AS sysname, @sortdir1 AS CHAR(1) = 'A',
  @colname2 AS sysname = NULL, @sortdir2 AS CHAR(1) = 'A',
  @colname3 AS sysname = NULL, @sortdir3 AS CHAR(1) = 'A'
AS

IF @colname1 NOT IN(N'shipperid', N'companyname', N'phone')
   OR @colname2 IS NOT NULL AND @colname2 NOT IN(N'shipperid', N'companyname', N'phone')
   OR @colname3 IS NOT NULL AND @colname3 NOT IN(N'shipperid', N'companyname', N'phone')
   THROW 50001, 'Column name not supported. Possibly a SQL injection attempt.', 1;

DECLARE @sql AS NVARCHAR(1000);
```

```
SET @sql = N'SELECT shipperid, companyname, phone
FROM Sales.Shippers
ORDER BY '
  + QUOTENAME(@colname1) + CASE @sortdir1 WHEN 'D' THEN N' DESC' ELSE '' END
  + ISNULL(N',' + QUOTENAME(@colname2) + CASE @sortdir2 WHEN 'D' THEN N' DESC' ELSE '' END, N'')
  + ISNULL(N',' + QUOTENAME(@colname3) + CASE @sortdir3 WHEN 'D' THEN N' DESC' ELSE '' END, N'')
  + ';';

EXEC sys.sp_executesql @stmt = @sql;
GO
```

Regarding security, it's important to know that normally the user executing the stored procedure will need direct permissions to run the code that executes dynamically. If you don't want to grant such direct permissions, you can use the EXECUTE AS clause to impersonate the security context of the user specified in that clause. You can find the details about how to do this in Books Online: *http://msdn.microsoft.com/en-us/library/ms188354.aspx*.

As an extra resource, you can find excellent coverage of dynamic SQL in the paper "The Curse and Blessings of Dynamic SQL" by Erland Sommarskog: *http://www.sommarskog.se/dynamic_sql.html*.

User-defined functions

User-defined functions (UDFs) give you powerful encapsulation and reusability capabilities. They are convenient to use because they can be embedded in queries. However, they also incur certain performance-related penalties you should be aware of. For this purpose, I'm referring to scalar UDFs and multistatement, table-valued functions (TVFs). I'm not referring to inline TVFs, which I covered in Chapter 3, "Multi-table queries." Inline TVFs, by definition, get inlined, so they don't incur any performance penalties.

This section covers T-SQL UDFs. Later, the chapter covers CLR UDFs in the "SQLCLR programming" section.

Scalar UDFs

Scalar UDFs accept arguments and return a scalar value. They can be incorporated where single-valued expressions are allowed—for example, in queries, constraints, and computed columns.

T-SQL UDFs (not just scalar) are limited in a number of ways. They are not allowed to have side effects on the database or the system. Therefore, you are not allowed to apply data or structural changes to database objects other than variables (including table variables) defined within the function. You're also not allowed to invoke activities that have indirect side effects, like when invoking the RAND and NEWID functions. For example, one invocation of the RAND function will determine the seed that will be used in a subsequent seedless invocation of RAND. You're not allowed to use dynamic SQL, and you're not allowed to include exception handling with the TRY-CATCH construct.

Scalar T-SQL UDFs are implemented in two main ways. In one, the function invokes a single expression that returns a scalar result. In the other, the function invokes multiple statements and eventually returns a scalar result. Either way, you need to be aware that there are performance penalties associated with the use of scalar UDFs. I'll start with an example for a scalar UDF that is based on a single expression. I'll compare the performance of a query that contains the expression directly to one where you encapsulate the expression in a UDF.

The following query filters only orders that were placed on the last day of the year:

```
USE PerformanceV3;

SELECT orderid, custid, empid, shipperid, orderdate, filler
FROM dbo.Orders
WHERE orderdate = DATEADD(year, DATEDIFF(year, '19001231', orderdate), '19001231');
```

If you're not familiar with the method used here to compute the last day of the year, you can find the details in Chapter 7, "Working with date and time."

On my system, this query got the execution plan shown in Figure 9-8.

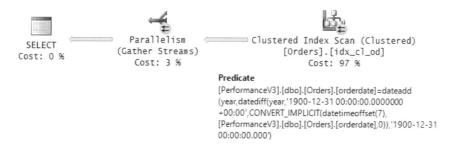

FIGURE 9-8 Plan for a query without a function.

Observe that the plan uses a parallel scan of the clustered index, mainly to process the filter using multiple threads. When running this query against hot cache in my system, the query took 281 milliseconds to complete, and it used 704 milliseconds of CPU time.

To check the impact of parallelism here, I forced a serial plan by specifying the hint MAXDOP 1, like so:

```
SELECT orderid, custid, empid, shipperid, orderdate, filler
FROM dbo.Orders
WHERE orderdate = DATEADD(year, DATEDIFF(year, '19001231', orderdate), '19001231')
OPTION(MAXDOP 1);
```

This time, it took the query 511 milliseconds to complete. So, on my system, the execution time of the parallel plan was half the execution time of the serial plan.

Without a doubt, from a programming perspective, it's beneficial to encapsulate the expression that computes the end-of-year date in a scalar UDF. This encapsulation helps you hide the complexity and enables reusability. Run the following code to encapsulate the expression in the *EndOfYear* UDF.

```
IF OBJECT_ID(N'dbo.EndOfYear') IS NOT NULL DROP FUNCTION dbo.EndOfYear;
GO
CREATE FUNCTION dbo.EndOfYear(@dt AS DATE) RETURNS DATE
AS
BEGIN
  RETURN DATEADD(year, DATEDIFF(year, '19001231', @dt), '19001231');
END;
GO
```

Now run the query after you replace the direct expression with a call to the UDF, like so:

```
SELECT orderid, custid, empid, shipperid, orderdate, filler
FROM dbo.Orders
WHERE orderdate = dbo.EndOfYear(orderdate);
```

There's no question about the programmability benefits you get here compared to not using the UDF. The code is clearer and more concise. However, the impact of the use of the UDF on performance is quite severe. Observe the plan for this query shown in Figure 9-9.

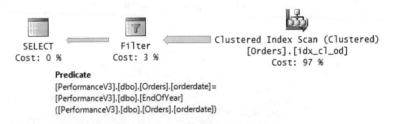

FIGURE 9-9 Plan for a query with a scalar UDF.

Unfortunately, even when the UDF is based on a single expression, SQL Server doesn't inline it. This means that the UDF is invoked per row in the underlying table, as you can see in the Filter operator's Predicate property in the plan. In our case, the UDF gets invoked 1,000,000 times. There's overhead in each invocation, and with a million invocations this overhead amounts to something substantial. Also, observe that the query plan is serial. Any use of T-SQL scalar UDFs prevents parallelism.

It took this query over four seconds to complete on my system, with a total CPU cost of over four seconds. That's about 16 times more than the query without the UDF (with the default parallel plan), and 8 times more than when I forced the serial plan. Either way, as you can see, the penalty for using the UDF is quite high.

Curiously, there's a workaround that will allow you to encapsulate your logic in a function while not incurring the performance penalty. Instead of using a scalar UDF, use an inline TVF. The tricky part is that an inline TVF has to return a query. So specify the expression along with a column alias in a FROM-less SELECT query, and return that query from the function. Here's the code to drop the scalar UDF and create an inline TVF instead:

```
IF OBJECT_ID(N'dbo.EndOfYear') IS NOT NULL DROP FUNCTION dbo.EndOfYear;
GO
CREATE FUNCTION dbo.EndOfYear(@dt AS DATE) RETURNS TABLE
AS
RETURN
  SELECT DATEADD(year, DATEDIFF(year, '19001231', @dt), '19001231') AS endofyear;
GO
```

To invoke a table function in a query and pass a column from the outer table as input, you need to use either the explicit APPLY operator or an implicit one in a subquery. Here's an example using the implicit form:

```
SELECT orderid, custid, empid, shipperid, orderdate, filler
FROM dbo.Orders
WHERE orderdate = (SELECT endofyear FROM dbo.EndOfYear(orderdate));
```

This time, the expression in the function does get inlined. SQL Server creates the same plan as the one I showed earlier in Figure 9-8 for the original query without the UDF. Thus, there's no performance penalty for using the inline TVF.

As for scalar UDFs that are based on multiple statements, those are usually used to implement iterative logic. As discussed earlier in the book in Chapter 2, "Query tuning," T-SQL iterations are slow. So, especially when you need to apply many iterations, you'll tend to get better performance using a CLR UDF instead of a T-SQL one. Furthermore, as long as a CLR UDF isn't marked as applying data access, it doesn't prevent parallelism.

As an example for a T-SQL UDF that uses iterative logic, consider the following definition of the *RemoveChars* UDF:

```
USE TSQLV3;
IF OBJECT_ID(N'dbo.RemoveChars', N'FN') IS NOT NULL DROP FUNCTION dbo.RemoveChars;
GO
CREATE FUNCTION dbo.RemoveChars(@string AS NVARCHAR(4000), @pattern AS NVARCHAR(4000))
  RETURNS NVARCHAR(4000)
AS
BEGIN
  DECLARE @pos AS INT;
  SET @pos = PATINDEX(@pattern, @string);

  WHILE @pos > 0
  BEGIN
    SET @string = STUFF(@string, @pos, 1, N'');
    SET @pos = PATINDEX(@pattern, @string);
  END;

  RETURN @string;
END;
GO
```

This function accepts two parameters as inputs. One is *@string*, representing an input string. Another is *@pattern*, representing the pattern of a single character. The UDF's purpose is to return a string representing the input string after the removal of all occurrences of the input character pattern.

The function's code starts by using the PATINDEX function to compute the first position of the character pattern in *@string* and stores it in *@pos*. The code then enters a loop that keeps running while there are still occurrences of the character pattern in the string. In each iteration, the code uses the STUFF function to remove the first occurrence from the string and then looks for the position of the next occurrence. Once the loop is done, the code returns what's left in *@string*.

Here's an example for using the UDF in a query against the Sales.Customers table to return clean phone numbers (by removing all nonmeaningful characters):

```
SELECT custid, phone, dbo.RemoveChars(phone, N'%[^0-9]%') AS cleanphone
FROM Sales.Customers;
```

This function returns the following output:

```
custid  phone             cleanphone
-------  ----------------  -----------
1        030-3456789       0303456789
2        (5) 789-0123      57890123
3        (5) 123-4567      51234567
4        (171) 456-7890    1714567890
5        0921-67 89 01     0921678901
6        0621-67890        062167890
7        67.89.01.23       67890123
8        (91) 345 67 89    913456789
9        23.45.67.89       23456789
10       (604) 901-2345    6049012345
...
```

You will find coverage of CLR UDFs later in the chapter in the "SQLCLR programming" section. In that section, you will find the definition of a CLR UDF called *RegExReplace*. This UDF applies regex-based replacement to the input string based on the input regex pattern. With this UDF, you handle the task using the following code:

```
SELECT custid, phone, dbo.RegExReplace(N'[^0-9]', phone, N'') AS cleanphone
FROM Sales.Customers;
```

You get two main advantages by using the CLR-based solution rather than the T-SQL solution. First, regular expressions are much richer compared to the primitive patterns you can use with the PATINDEX function and the LIKE predicate. Second, you get better performance. I tested the query against a table with 1,000,000 rows. Even though there aren't many iterations required to clean phone numbers, the query ran for 16 seconds with the T-SQL UDF and 8 seconds with the CLR one.

Multistatement TVFs

Multistatement TVFs have multiple statements in their body, and they return a table variable as their output. The returned table variable is defined in the function's header. The purpose of the body is to fill the table variable with data. When you query such a function, SQL Server declares the table variable, runs the flow to fill it with data, and then hands it to the calling query.

To demonstrate using multistatement TVFs, I'll use a table called Employees that you create and populate by running the following code:

```
SET NOCOUNT ON;
USE tempdb;
GO
IF OBJECT_ID(N'dbo.Employees', N'U') IS NOT NULL DROP TABLE dbo.Employees;
GO
CREATE TABLE dbo.Employees
(
  empid    INT         NOT NULL CONSTRAINT PK_Employees PRIMARY KEY,
  mgrid    INT         NULL     CONSTRAINT FK_Employees_Employees REFERENCES dbo.Employees,
  empname VARCHAR(25) NOT NULL,
  salary  MONEY       NOT NULL,
  CHECK (empid <> mgrid)
);

INSERT INTO dbo.Employees(empid, mgrid, empname, salary)
  VALUES(1, NULL, 'David', $10000.00),
        (2, 1, 'Eitan', $7000.00),
        (3, 1, 'Ina', $7500.00),
        (4, 2, 'Seraph', $5000.00),
        (5, 2, 'Jiru', $5500.00),
        (6, 2, 'Steve', $4500.00),
        (7, 3, 'Aaron', $5000.00),
        (8, 5, 'Lilach', $3500.00),
        (9, 7, 'Rita', $3000.00),
        (10, 5, 'Sean', $3000.00),
        (11, 7, 'Gabriel', $3000.00),
        (12, 9, 'Emilia' , $2000.00),
        (13, 9, 'Michael', $2000.00),
        (14, 9, 'Didi', $1500.00);

CREATE UNIQUE INDEX idx_unc_mgr_emp_i_name_sal ON dbo.Employees(mgrid, empid)
  INCLUDE(empname, salary);
```

Following is the definition of a function called *GetSubtree*:

```
IF OBJECT_ID(N'dbo.GetSubtree', N'TF') IS NOT NULL DROP FUNCTION dbo.GetSubtree;
GO
CREATE FUNCTION dbo.GetSubtree (@mgrid AS INT, @maxlevels AS INT = NULL)
RETURNS @Tree TABLE
(
  empid    INT         NOT NULL PRIMARY KEY,
  mgrid    INT         NULL,
  empname VARCHAR(25) NOT NULL,
  salary  MONEY       NOT NULL,
  lvl      INT         NOT NULL
)
AS
BEGIN
  DECLARE @lvl AS INT = 0;
```

```
-- Insert subtree root node into @Tree
INSERT INTO @Tree
  SELECT empid, mgrid, empname, salary, @lvl
  FROM dbo.Employees
  WHERE empid = @mgrid;

WHILE @@ROWCOUNT > 0 AND (@lvl < @maxlevels OR @maxlevels IS NULL)
BEGIN
  SET @lvl += 1;

  -- Insert children of nodes from prev level into @Tree
  INSERT INTO @Tree
    SELECT E.empid, E.mgrid, E.empname, E.salary, @lvl
    FROM dbo.Employees AS E
      INNER JOIN @Tree AS T
        ON E.mgrid = T.empid AND T.lvl = @lvl - 1;
END;

  RETURN;
END;
GO
```

The function returns a subtree of employees below an input manager (@*mgrid*), with an optional input level limit (@*maxlevels*). The function defines a table variable called @*Tree* as the returned output. The variable holds employee information as well as a column called *lvl* representing the distance in levels from the input subtree root manager (*0* for the root, *1* for the level below, and so on).

The code in the function's body starts by declaring a level counter called @*lvl* and initializes it with zero. The code then inserts the row for the input manager into the table variable along with the just-initialized level zero. The code then runs a loop that keeps iterating as long as the last insert has at least one row and, if the user provided a level limit, that limit wasn't exceeded. In each iteration, the code increments the level counter and then inserts into @*Tree* the next level of subordinates. Once the loop is done, the code returns. At that point, the function hands the table variable @*Tree* to the calling query.

As an example of using the function, the following code requests the subtree of manager 3 without a level limit:

```
SELECT empid, empname, mgrid, salary, lvl
FROM GetSubtree(3, NULL);
```

This code generates the following output:

```
empid  empname  mgrid  salary    lvl
------ -------- ------ --------- ----
3      Ina      1      7500.00   0
7      Aaron    3      5000.00   1
9      Rita     7      3000.00   2
11     Gabriel  7      3000.00   2
12     Emilia   9      2000.00   3
13     Michael  9      2000.00   3
14     Didi     9      1500.00   3
```

One thing to remember about the use of multistatement TVFs is that they return a table variable. Remember that, unlike it does with temporary tables, SQL Server doesn't maintain histograms for table variables. As a result, when the optimizer needs to make cardinality estimates related to the table variable, it is more limited in the tools that it can use. The lack of histograms can result in suboptimal choices. This is true both for the queries against the table variable within the function's body and for the outer queries against the table function. If you identify performance problems that you connect to the lack of histograms, you'll need to reevaluate your solution.

An alternative option is to use a stored procedure with temporary tables. The downside with this approach is that it's not as convenient to interact with the result of a stored procedure as querying the result of a table function. You will need to figure out your priorities and do some testing to see if there's a performance difference and how big it is.

Stored procedures

In this section, I cover the use of T-SQL stored procedures. As mentioned, because the focus of the book is querying, I will cover mainly how to use stored procedures to execute queries and the tuning aspects of the code. I'll first describe the advantages stored procedures have over ad hoc code. I'll then cover the way SQL Server handles compilations, recompilations, and the reuse of execution plans. I'll also cover the use of table types and table-valued parameters, as well as the EXECUTE WITH RESULT SETS clause.

Stored procedures are an important programming tool that gives you a number of benefits compared to implementing your solutions with ad hoc code. Like in other programming environments, encapsulating the logic in a routine enables reusability and allows you to hide the complexity.

Compared to deploying changes in the application, deploying changes in a stored procedure is much simpler. Whether you have a bug to fix or a more efficient way to achieve the task, you issue an ALTER PROC command, and everyone immediately starts using the altered version.

With stored procedures, you tend to reduce a lot of the network traffic. All you pass through the network is the procedure name and the input parameters. The logic is executed in the database engine, and only the final outcome needs to be transmitted back to the caller. Implementing the logic in the application tends to result in more round trips between the application and the database, causing more network traffic.

The use of parameterized queries in stored procedures promotes efficient plan caching and reuse behavior. That's the focus of the next section. I should note, though, that this capability is not exclusive to queries in stored procedures. You can get similar benefits when using *sp_executesql* with parameterized queries.

Compilations, recompilations, and reuse of execution plans

When you need to tune stored procedures that have performance problems, you should focus your efforts on two main areas. One is tuning the queries within the procedure based on what you've learned so far in the book. For this purpose, it doesn't matter if the query resides in a stored procedure or not. Another is related to plan caching, reuse, parameter sniffing, variable sniffing, and recompilations.

> **Note** The examples in this section assume you have a clean copy of the sample database PerformanceV3. If you don't, run the script PerformanceV3.sql from the book's source code first.

Reuse of execution plans and parameter sniffing

When you create a stored procedure, SQL Server doesn't optimize the queries within it. It does so the first time you execute the procedure. The initial compilation, which mainly involves optimization of the queries, takes place at the entire batch (procedure) level. SQL Server caches the query plans to enable reuse in subsequent executions of the procedure. When SQL Server triggers a recompilation, it does so at the statement level.

The reason for plan caching and reuse is to save the time, CPU, and memory resources that are involved in the creation of a new plan. How long it takes SQL Server to create a new plan varies. I've seen plans that took a few milliseconds to create and also plans that took minutes to create. SQL Server takes the sizes of the tables involved into consideration to determine time and cost thresholds for the optimization process. You can find details about the compilation in the properties of the root node (in a SELECT query, it's the SELECT node) in a graphical or XML query plan. You will find the following properties: CompileTime (in ms), CompileCPU (in ms), CompileMemory (in KB), Optimization Level (TRIVIAL or FULL), Reason For Early Termination (Good Enough Plan Found if a plan with a cost below the cost threshold is found, or Time Out if the time threshold is reached), and others.

The assumption that SQL Server makes is that if a valid cached plan exists, normally it's beneficial to reuse it. So, by default, it will try to. Under certain conditions, SQL Server will trigger a recompilation, causing a new plan to be created. I'll discuss this topic in the section "Recompilations."

I'll use a stored procedure called *GetOrders* to demonstrate plan caching and reuse behavior. Run the following code to create the procedure in the PerformanceV3 database:

```
USE PerformanceV3;
IF OBJECT_ID(N'dbo.GetOrders', N'P') IS NOT NULL DROP PROC dbo.GetOrders;
GO

CREATE PROC dbo.GetOrders( @orderid AS INT )
AS

SELECT orderid, custid, empid, orderdate, filler
/* 703FCFF2-970F-4777-A8B7-8A87B8BE0A4D */
FROM dbo.Orders
WHERE orderid >= @orderid;
GO
```

The procedure accepts an order ID as input and returns information about all orders that have an order ID that is greater than or equal to the input one. I planted a GUID as a comment in the code to easily track down the plans in cache that are associated with this query.

There is a nonclustered, noncovering index called PK_Orders defined on the *orderid* column as the key. Depending on the selectivity of the filter, different plans are considered optimal. For a filter with high selectivity, the optimal plan is one that uses the PK_Orders index and applies lookups. For low selectivity, a serial plan that scans the clustered index is optimal. For a filter with medium selectivity, a parallel plan that scans the clustered index is optimal. (There needs to be few enough filtered rows that when the gather streams cost is added to the scan cost it does not exceed the serial plan cost.)

Say you execute the procedure and currently there's no reusable cached plan for the query. SQL Server sniffs the current parameter value (also known as the *parameter compiled value*) and optimizes the plan accordingly. SQL Server then caches the plan and will reuse it for subsequent executions of the procedure until the conditions for a recompilation are met. This strategy assumes that the sniffed value represents the typical input.

To see a demonstration of this behavior, enable the inclusion of the actual execution plan in SQL Server Management Studio (SSMS) and execute the procedure for the first time with a selective input, like so:

```
EXEC dbo.GetOrders @orderid = 999991;
```

The plan for this execution is shown in Figure 9-10.

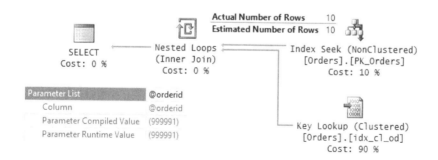

FIGURE 9-10 Plan for the first execution of the procedure.

Observe in the properties of the root node that both the compiled value and the run-time value of the *@orderid* parameter is 999991. Based on this sniffed value, the cardinality estimate for the filter is 10 rows. Consequently, the optimizer chose a plan that performs a seek and a range scan in the index PK_Orders and applies lookups for the qualifying rows. With 10 lookups, the execution of this plan performed only 33 logical reads in total.

If, indeed, subsequent executions of the procedure will be done with high selectivity, the default plan reuse behavior will be beneficial to you. To see an example, execute the procedure again providing another value with high selectivity:

```
EXEC dbo.GetOrders @orderid = 999996;
```

Figure 9-11 shows the graphical execution plan for this execution.

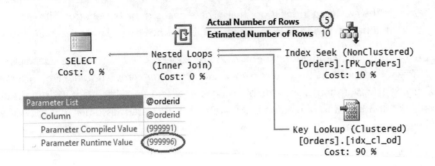

FIGURE 9-11 Plan for the second execution of the procedure.

Observe that the parameter compiled value and, hence, the estimated number of rows returned by the Index Seek operation are unchanged because they reflect the compile-time information. After all, SQL Server reused the cached plan. The parameter run-time value this time is 999996, and the actual number of rows returned is 5. With 5 matches, the execution of this plan performs only 18 reads.

You can analyze plan reuse behavior by querying the plan cache, filtering only plans for the query containing our planted GUID, like so:

```
SELECT CP.usecounts, CP.cacheobjtype, CP.objtype, CP.plan_handle, ST.text
FROM sys.dm_exec_cached_plans AS CP
  CROSS APPLY sys.dm_exec_sql_text(CP.plan_handle) AS ST
WHERE ST.text LIKE '%703FCFF2-970F-4777-A8B7-8A87B8BE0A4D%'
  AND ST.text NOT LIKE '%sys.dm_exec_cached_plans%';
```

At this point, the *usecounts* column should show a use count of 2 for our query plan.

Note In an active system with lots of cached query plans, this query can be expensive because it needs to scan the text to look for the GUID. Starting with SQL Server 2012, you can label your queries using the query hint *OPTION(LABEL = 'some label')*. Unfortunately, though, this label is not exposed in dynamic management views (DMVs) like *sys.dm_exec_cached_plans* as a separate column. I hope this capability will be added in the future to allow interesting queries to be filtered in a less expensive way. See the following Microsoft Connect item with such a feature enhancement request to Microsoft: *https://connect. microsoft.com/SQLServer/feedback/details/833055*.

As you can see, plan reuse is beneficial when the different executions of the procedure provide inputs of a similar nature. But what if that's not the case? For example, execute the procedure with an input parameter that has medium selectivity:

```
EXEC dbo.GetOrders @orderid = 800001;
```

Normally, this query would benefit from a plan that performs a full scan of the clustered index. But because there's a plan in cache, it's reused, as you can see in Figure 9-12.

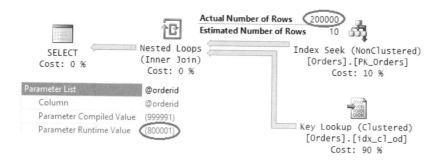

FIGURE 9-12 Plan for the third execution of the procedure.

The parameter compiled value is the one provided when the plan was created (999991), but the run-time value is 800001. The cost percentages of the operators and estimated row counts are the same as when the plan was created because they reflect the parameter compiled value. But the arrows are much thicker than before because they reflect the actual row counts in this execution. The Index Seek operator returns 200,000 rows, and therefore the plan performs that many key lookups. This plan execution performed 600,524 logical reads on my system. That's a lot compared to how much a clustered index scan would cost you!

The query in our stored procedure is pretty simple; all it has is just a filter and a SELECT list with a few columns. Still, this simple example helps illustrate the concept of inaccurate cardinality estimates and some of its possible implications, like choosing an index seek and lookups versus an index scan, and choosing a serial plan versus a parallel one. You can feel free to experiment with more query elements to demonstrate other implications. For example, if you add grouping and aggregation, you will also be able to observe the implications of inaccurate cardinality estimates on choosing the aggregate algorithm, as well as on computing the required memory grant (for sort and hash operators). Use the following code to alter the procedure, adding grouping and aggregation to the query:

```
ALTER PROC dbo.GetOrders( @orderid AS INT )
AS

SELECT empid, COUNT(*) AS numorders
/* 703FCFF2-970F-4777-A8B7-8A87B8BE0A4D */
FROM dbo.Orders
WHERE orderid >= @orderid
GROUP BY empid;
GO
```

Normally, with high selectivity (for example, with the input *@orderid = 999991*) the optimal plan is a serial plan with an index seek and key lookups, a sort operator, and an order-based aggregate (Stream Aggregate). With medium selectivity (for example, with the input *@orderid = 800001*), the optimal plan is a parallel plan with an index scan, a local hash aggregate, and a global order aggregate.

Which plan you will get in practice depends on the input you provide in the first execution. For example, execute the procedure first with high selectivity. You will get a serial plan with an index seek and key lookups, a sort operator, and an order-based aggregate. Also, the query will request a small memory grant for the sort activity. (See the properties of the root SELECT node of the actual query plan.) This plan will be cached. Then execute the procedure again with medium selectivity. The cached plan will be reused. Not only that, the cached plan will be inefficient for the second execution, very likely the memory grant for the sort operation won't be sufficient, and it will have to spill to tempdb. (The Sort operator in the actual query plan will show a warning to that effect.)

Adding grouping and aggregation to the query is just one idea of how you can experiment with different query elements to observe the implications of inaccurate cardinality estimates. Of course, there are many other things you can try, like joins, ordering, and so on.

Preventing reuse of execution plans

When facing situations like in the previous section, where plan reuse is not beneficial to you, you usually can do a number of things. If all you have is just the query with the filter (no grouping and aggregation or other elements), one option is to create a covering index, causing the plan for the query to be a trivial one. The optimizer will choose a plan that performs a seek and a range scan in the covering index regardless of the cardinality estimate. Regardless of the selectivity of the input, the same plan is always the optimal one. But you might not be able to create such an index. Also, if your query does involve additional activities like grouping and aggregating, joining, and so on, even with a covering index an accurate cardinality estimate might still be important to determine things like which algorithms to use and how much of a memory grant is required.

Another option is to force SQL Server to recompile the query in every execution by adding the RECOMPILE query hint, like so:

```
ALTER PROC dbo.GetOrders( @orderid AS INT )
AS

SELECT orderid, custid, empid, orderdate, filler
/* 703FCFF2-970F-4777-A8B7-8A87B8BE0A4D */
FROM dbo.Orders
WHERE orderid >= @orderid
OPTION(RECOMPILE);
GO
```

The tradeoff between using the RECOMPILE query option and reusing plans is that you're likely to get efficient plans at the cost of compiling the query in every execution. You should be able to tell whether it makes sense for you to use this approach based on the benefit versus cost in your case.

Tip In case you are familiar with the procedure-level RECOMPILE option, I should point out that it's less recommended to use. For one, it will affect all queries in the procedure, and perhaps you want to prevent reuse only for particular queries. For another, it doesn't benefit from parameter embedding (replacing the parameters with constants) like the statement option does. I described this capability earlier in the chapter in the section "Dynamic search conditions."

In terms of caching, an interesting difference between the two is that when using the procedure-level option, SQL Server doesn't cache the plan. When using the statement-level option, SQL Server does cache the last plan, but it doesn't reuse that plan. So you will find information about the last plan in DMVs like *sys.dm_exec_cached_plans* and *sys.dm_exec_query_stats*.

To test the revised procedure, execute it with both high and medium selectivity:

```
EXEC dbo.GetOrders @orderid = 999991;
EXEC dbo.GetOrders @orderid = 800001;
```

The plans for the two executions are shown in Figure 9-13.

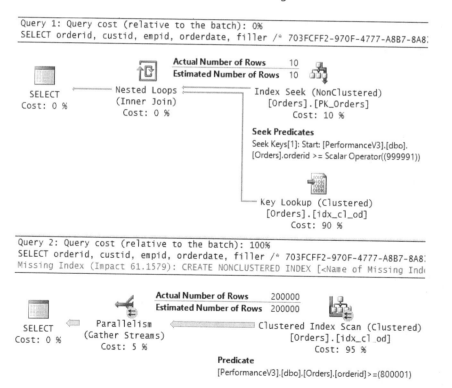

FIGURE 9-13 Plans for executions with a query using RECOMPILE.

As you can see, the plans are different. Each is optimal for its respective input, thanks to the recompiles and the accurate cardinality estimates. The first plan performs a seek in the nonclustered index PK_Orders and key lookups. The execution of this plan performed 33 logical reads on my system. The second plan is a parallel plan that performs a clustered index scan. The execution of this plan performed 25,331 logical reads on my system. There's no Parameter List property in the root node of these plans because SQL Server applied parameter embedding due to the use of the RECOMPILE option.

Lack of variable sniffing

There's a curious difference between how SQL Server handles parameters you pass to a procedure and variables you declare within the procedure. Remember that the initial compilation unit is the entire batch (procedure). SQL Server sniffs the parameter values before it optimizes the queries in the procedure. Therefore, the optimizer can apply cardinality estimates based on the sniffed values. You saw this behavior in previous examples. With variables, the situation is different because the optimizer isn't supposed to run the code that assigns values to the variables as part of the optimization process. So, unlike it can with parameter values, SQL Server cannot normally sniff variable values. It has to resort to alternative cardinality-estimation methods that do not rely on known sniffed values.

As an example, consider the following revised procedure:

```
ALTER PROC dbo.GetOrders( @orderid AS INT )
AS

DECLARE @i AS INT = @orderid - 1;

SELECT orderid, custid, empid, orderdate, filler
/* 703FCFF2-970F-4777-A8B7-8A87B8BE0A4D */
FROM dbo.Orders
WHERE orderid >= @i;
GO
```

The first time you execute the procedure, the optimizer gets the batch for optimization with no information about what the value of the variable @i is. It doesn't make sense here to use the histogram on the *orderid* column because there's no value to look for. In such a case, the optimizer applies a cardinality estimation using predefined hard-coded percentages. The estimate depends on things like the operator you use, the size of the input set, whether density information is available, and whether the column is unique. Table 9-1 shows the hard-coded estimates.

Our query uses the >= operator, so the hard-coded percentage used is 30. When you apply this percentage to the cardinality of the input set, which is 1,000,000 rows, you get 300,000 rows. With such an estimate, the optimizer will choose a clustered index scan. As you might realize, this choice is suboptimal if the typical input has high selectivity. To see a demonstration of this, execute the procedure with an input value that results in only five matching rows:

```
EXEC dbo.GetOrders @orderid = 999997;
```

TABLE 9-1 Hardcoded estimates

Operator	Estimate
>, >=, <, <=	30%
BETWEEN/LIKE	9% Exception: in 2014 BETWEEN with variables/parameters with sniffing disabled the estimate is 16.4317%
= with a unique column	1 row
= with a nonunique column prior to SQL Server 2014	$C^{3/4}$ (C = table cardinality)
= with a nonunique column in SQL Server 2014	$C^{1/2}$

The plan for this execution is shown in Figure 9-14.

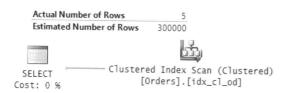

FIGURE 9-14 Plan for a query using a variable.

The execution of this plan performed 25,072 reads on my system. That's inefficient, considering the small number of matches. Here, a plan that applies a seek in the nonclustered index PK_Orders and key lookups would have been much more efficient.

There are two main solutions to the "lack of variable sniffing" problem. Which solution you should use depends on whether plan reuse is desirable or not. Plan reuse is desirable when typically the values stored in the variable are of the same nature. In such a case, you can use the query hint OPTIMIZE FOR and provide a value for the variable for optimization purposes. In our case, the variable in question is @orderid, so you will use the following form: *<query>OPTION(OPTIMIZE FOR (@i = <value>))*. Because the optimizer cannot sniff the variable value, you're telling it what value to optimize for. The optimizer will use that value to make cardinality estimates.

It's a bit tricky to figure out which value to provide because you have to provide a constant. In our case, you want the optimizer to assume high selectivity. If you provide a value like 1000000, the estimate will be for high selectivity with the current state of the data, but after sufficiently more data is added, it won't be anymore. It would have been handy if SQL Server supported specifying a hint with a percentage of matches from the input set, but unfortunately it doesn't. So you need to provide a constant value that will keep getting a high-selectivity estimate even though the data keeps changing. You can achieve this by providing the maximum supported value in the type. For INT, the value is 2147483647. The cardinality estimate in such a case is 1 (the minimum amount the optimizer can estimate), and consequently the optimal plan is one that uses the nonclustered index PK_Orders and applies key lookups.

Alter the stored procedure by running the following code to implement this solution:

```
ALTER PROC dbo.GetOrders( @orderid AS INT )
AS

DECLARE @i AS INT = @orderid - 1;

SELECT orderid, custid, empid, orderdate, filler
/* 703FCFF2-970F-4777-A8B7-8A87B8BE0A4D */
FROM dbo.Orders
WHERE orderid >= @i
OPTION (OPTIMIZE FOR(@i = 2147483647));
GO
```

Run the following code to test the procedure:

```
EXEC dbo.GetOrders @orderid = 999997;
```

The plan for this execution is shown in Figure 9-15.

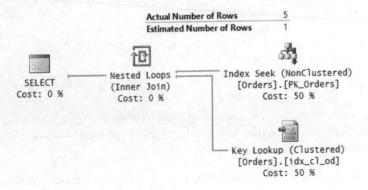

FIGURE 9-15 Plan for a query using OPTIMIZE FOR.

As you can see, the plan is the optimal one for high selectivity. Observe that the estimated number of rows returned after applying the filter is 1 and the actual number is 5. The estimate is good enough for the optimizer to choose the optimal plan. The execution of this plan performed 18 logical reads on my system.

If the typical case in your system is that the filter has low selectivity, you can specify the "optimize for" value 0. However, if the typical case is that the filter has medium selectivity, there's no way with this hint that you can get such an estimate both with the current and future states of the data. This hint definitely has its limitations.

If you do not desire plan reuse—for example, when the different executions of the procedure store values of different natures in the variable—you're in luck. You specify the query hint RECOMPILE to prevent reuse, and by doing so at the statement level you get an interesting side effect. The statement is optimized after the variable value is assigned. In other words, you get variable sniffing.

Alter the procedure to implement this solution:

```
ALTER PROC dbo.GetOrders( @orderid AS INT )
AS

DECLARE @i AS INT = @orderid - 1;

SELECT orderid, custid, empid, orderdate, filler
/* 703FCFF2-970F-4777-A8B7-8A87B8BE0A4D */
FROM dbo.Orders
WHERE orderid >= @i
OPTION (RECOMPILE);
GO
```

Run the following code to test the procedure with high selectivity:

```
EXEC dbo.GetOrders @orderid = 999997;
```

The plan for this execution is shown in Figure 9-16.

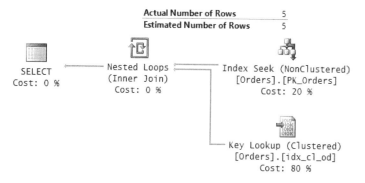

FIGURE 9-16 Plan for a query using RECOMPILE with high selectivity.

Notice the accuracy of the cardinality estimate in this plan, thanks to the fact that the optimizer was able to sniff the variable value. It chose the optimal plan for high selectivity with a seek in the index PK_Orders and key lookups. This plan performed 18 logical reads on my system.

Run the following code to test the procedure with medium selectivity:

```
EXEC dbo.GetOrders @orderid = 800002;
```

The plan for this execution is shown in Figure 9-17.

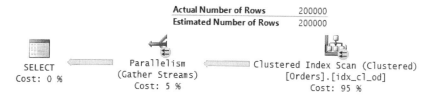

FIGURE 9-17 Plan for a query using RECOMPILE with medium selectivity.

SQL Server created a new plan that is suitable for the new cardinality estimate of 200,000 rows. On my system, it chose a parallel plan that scans the clustered index. The execution of this plan performed 25,322 reads on my system.

Preventing parameter sniffing

You saw cases where parameter sniffing is a beneficial feature. However, you might face cases where this feature is counterproductive. Oddly, in some of those cases, you might get a more optimal plan by disabling parameter sniffing.

As an example, consider a classic challenge with cardinality estimates that involves a column with ascending keys. The *orderid* column in the Orders table falls into this category because order IDs normally keep increasing. Suppose that the typical execution of the *GetOrders* procedure is with medium selectivity—say, five to ten percent matches. With such selectivity, the optimal plan is one that performs a clustered index scan. Furthermore, with eight logical CPUs on my system, the optimal plan is a parallel one. The question is, will the optimizer manage to figure this out?

The challenge is that histograms normally get refreshed after 500 plus 20 percent changes have occurred. In the procedure, you are querying the top range of the keys. If a large percentage of rows is added, but not a large enough number to trigger a refresh of the histogram, the new range of keys is not represented in the histogram. If, at that point, SQL Server creates a new plan and relies on the histogram alone to make a cardinality estimate, it will likely result in an underestimation.

Microsoft took measures to address this problem in SQL Server 2014. When the predicate's interval exceeds the maximum value in the histogram, as is the case with the >= operator, the cardinality estimator takes into consideration both the existing histogram and the count of changes that took place since the last refresh. It interpolates the estimate assuming the new range has distribution that is based on the average distribution in the existing data. You can find coverage of this technique in Chapter 2 as part of the discussion about the improvements in the cardinality estimator. So, in SQL Server 2014, there's high likelihood that in our situation you will get a decent estimate and, in turn, an optimal plan. However, prior to SQL Server 2014, by default you will likely get an underestimation. This is one case where you might be better off disabling parameter sniffing and letting SQL Server rely on the cardinality-estimation techniques it uses when the parameter value is unknown.

At the moment, the Orders table contains 1,000,000 rows with the order IDs 1 through 1000000. The statistics are up to date because the source code that creates and populates the database creates the indexes after it populates the table. Run the following code to add 100,000 rows (10 percent) to the table:

```
INSERT INTO dbo.Orders(orderid, custid, empid, shipperid, orderdate, filler)
  SELECT 2000000 + orderid, custid, empid, shipperid, orderdate, filler
  FROM dbo.Orders
  WHERE orderid <= 100000;
```

Run the following code to show the histogram:

```
DBCC SHOW_STATISTICS (N'dbo.Orders', N'PK_Orders') WITH HISTOGRAM;
```

This code generates the following output:

RANGE_HI_KEY	RANGE_ROWS	EQ_ROWS	DISTINCT_RANGE_ROWS	AVG_RANGE_ROWS
1	0	1	0	1
1000000	999998	1	999998	1

Observe that the maximum value recorded in the histogram is 1000000. The histogram doesn't have a representation of the rows you just added to the table.

Next, I'll demonstrate an underestimation of cardinality that you get prior to SQL Server 2014. Because I'm running the code in SQL Server 2014, I'll use the query trace flag 9481 to force SQL Server to use the legacy cardinality estimator. Execute the following query:

```
SELECT orderid, custid, empid, orderdate, filler
/* 703FCFF2-970F-4777-A8B7-8A87B8BE0A4D */
FROM dbo.Orders
WHERE orderid >= 1000001
OPTION(QUERYTRACEON 9481);
```

The plan for this query is shown in Figure 9-18.

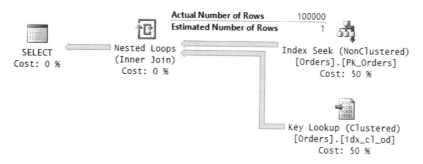

FIGURE 9-18 Plan for a query based on a cardinality estimate prior to SQL Server 2014.

The legacy cardinality estimator found that the range you are filtering is after the maximum value in the histogram. As far as it's concerned, there are supposed to be zero matches, but the minimum it can estimate is 1. Based on the estimate of 1, the optimizer chose a plan suitable for high selectivity. In practice, the actual number of matches is 100,000. Consequently, the execution of this plan performed 300,264 logical reads on my system. That's clearly excessive compared to what the optimal plan should cost you (about 25,000 reads for a clustered index scan).

Prior to SQL Server 2014, Microsoft provided trace flag 2389 as a possible tool to deal with the ascending-key problem. When the trace flag is enabled, if in three consecutive refreshes of a histogram SQL Server observes that the keys keep increasing, it brands the column as ascending. Then, at query compile time, SQL Server updates statistics and adds a ministep at the end of the histogram to model the recently added data.

But what if you're using a pre-2014 version of SQL Server and you'd rather not enable this trace flag? Another option is to disable parameter sniffing. If you choose to do this, you're forcing SQL

Server to rely on cardinality-estimation methods that assume the parameter value is unknown. You can find the estimates that SQL Server uses in such a case in Table 9-1 shown earlier.

There are two main ways to disable parameter sniffing locally at the query/procedure level. The less recommended one is to store the parameter value in a variable and then refer to the variable in the query, like so:

```
ALTER PROC dbo.GetOrders( @orderid AS INT )
AS

DECLARE @i AS INT = @orderid;

SELECT orderid, custid, empid, orderdate, filler
/* 703FCFF2-970F-4777-A8B7-8A87B8BE0A4D */
FROM dbo.Orders
WHERE orderid >= @i;
GO
```

Remember, normally SQL Server cannot sniff variable values.

Test the procedure by running the following code:

```
EXEC dbo.GetOrders @orderid = 1000001;
```

The execution of this procedure generates the plan shown in Figure 9-19.

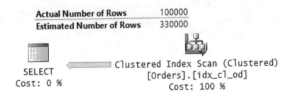

| Actual Number of Rows | 100000 |
| Estimated Number of Rows | 330000 |

```
SELECT          ◄───────── Clustered Index Scan (Clustered)
Cost: 0 %                  [Orders].[idx_cl_od]
                              Cost: 100 %
```

FIGURE 9-19 Plan for a query preventing sniffing with a variable.

If you examine the hard-coded estimates in Table 9-1, you will find that with the >= operator the estimate is 30 percent. Apply this percentage to the table's cardinality (1,100,000 rows) and you get 330,000 rows. Observe in the query plan that, indeed, the estimated number of rows is 330,000 versus an actual of 100,000. Perhaps it's not a perfect estimate, but it's certainly better than an estimate of 1. The optimizer chose a clustered index scan, albeit a serial one, involving 27,871 logical reads on my system. With medium to low selectivity, this plan is certainly better than the one that applies a seek in the PK_Orders index and key lookups.

This method seems to do the trick, but there are a couple of problems with it. First, it's awkward. Second, if a recompile happens, it happens at the statement level, and then SQL Server can suddenly sniff the variable value. The recommended way to disable parameter sniffing is with a designated query hint. To disable the sniffing of a particular parameter, use the hint *OPTIMIZE FOR (@orderid UNKNOWN)*. To disable the sniffing of all parameters, use *OPTIMIZE FOR UNKNOWN*.

Apply this solution to our procedure:

```
ALTER PROC dbo.GetOrders( @orderid AS INT )
AS

SELECT orderid, custid, empid, orderdate, filler
/* 703FCFF2-970F-4777-A8B7-8A87B8BE0A4D */
FROM dbo.Orders
WHERE orderid >= @orderid
OPTION(OPTIMIZE FOR (@orderid UNKNOWN));
GO
```

Run the following code to test the procedure:

```
EXEC dbo.GetOrders @orderid = 1000001;
```

You will get the same plan shown earlier in Figure 9-19.

As mentioned, in SQL Server 2014 (thanks to the improvements in the cardinality estimator), you don't really need to disable parameter sniffing to get a good estimate in our scenario. Run the following code to alter the procedure so that it uses the original form of the code without any hints:

```
ALTER PROC dbo.GetOrders( @orderid AS INT )
AS

SELECT orderid, custid, empid, orderdate, filler
/* 703FCFF2-970F-4777-A8B7-8A87B8BE0A4D */
FROM dbo.Orders
WHERE orderid >= @orderid;
GO
```

Run the following code to test the procedure:

```
EXEC dbo.GetOrders @orderid = 1000001;
```

The plan for this execution is shown in Figure 9-20.

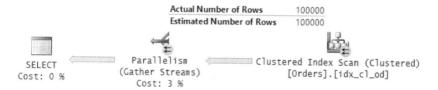

FIGURE 9-20 Plan for a query based on a SQL Server 2014 cardinality estimate.

The new cardinality estimator took into consideration both the histogram and the count of changes since the last refresh. As you can see in the plan, the interpolated cardinality estimate is accurate. This resulted in an optimal plan for the medium selectivity of our filter—namely, a parallel clustered index scan.

The ascending-key problem is just one case where you might want to disable parameter sniffing. You might stumble onto other cases. In those cases, remember, the *OPTIMIZE FOR (@parameter UNKNOWN) / OPTIMIZE FOR UNKNOWN* hints are the preferred tool compared to using a variable.

When you're done testing, run the following code for cleanup:

```
DELETE FROM dbo.Orders WHERE orderid > 1000000;
UPDATE STATISTICS dbo.Orders WITH FULLSCAN;
```

Recompilations

In some situations, SQL Server will not reuse a previously cached plan; rather, it will create a new one. The creation of a new plan instead of reusing an existing one is known as a *recompilation*. Generally, recompilations fall into two categories: plan correctness (also known as *plan stability*) and plan optimality.

SQL Server performs plan correctness recompilations when the correctness, or stability, of the cached plan is in doubt. An example for an event that triggers such recompilations is a data-definition language (DDL) change, like dropping an index or a table that the plan uses. Such an event causes the cached plans that refer to the affected object to be invalidated. The next time you run the stored procedure, the affected queries will be recompiled.

Another example of a cause of plan-correctness recompilations is when any set option that is considered plan-affecting is in a different state in the environment where you're executing the procedure than the environment where the cached plan was created. The set options that are considered plan-affecting are these:

- ANSI_NULL_DFLT_OFF

- ANSI_NULL_DFLT_ON

- ANSI_NULLS

- ANSI_PADDING

- ANSI_WARNINGS

- ARITHABORT

- CONCAT_NULL_YIELDS_NULL

- DATEFIRST

- DATEFORMAT

- FORCEPLAN

- LANGUAGE

- NO_BROWSETABLE

- NUMERIC_ROUNDABORT

- QUOTED_IDENTIFIER

The reasoning behind such recompilations is that the same query can have different meanings when any of these set options is in a different state. SQL Server stores with the cached plans the state of the plan-affecting set options in attributes called *set_options* (as a bitmap), *language_id*, *date_format*, and *date_first*. Recall that DDL changes cause SQL Server to invalidate existing cached plans. If SQL Server doesn't find a cached plan with a state of set options matching the state in the current environment, it handles the situation differently. SQL Server creates a new plan and caches it without invalidating the existing plans. This way, unique environments can keep reusing their respective cached plans.

Before I demonstrate recompilations related to plan-affecting set options, run the following code to force SQL Server to recompile the *GetOrders* procedure next time you execute it:

```
EXEC sp_recompile N'dbo.GetOrders';
```

Next, run the following code to execute the stored procedure twice—once with the default state of the option CONCAT_NULL_YIELDS_NULL (on), and again after setting it to off:

```
EXEC dbo.GetOrders @orderid = 1000000;
SET CONCAT_NULL_YIELDS_NULL OFF;
EXEC dbo.GetOrders @orderid = 1000000;
SET CONCAT_NULL_YIELDS_NULL ON;
```

This option controls what happens when you concatenate something with a NULL. When the option is on, the result is a NULL; when the option is off, a NULL is treated like an empty string. In the *GetOrders* procedure, there's no string concatenation taking place. Still, because the two executions have different environments, the plan created for the first execution cannot be reused by the second.

Run the following code to request information about the plans that are associated with the query in our procedure:

```
SELECT CP.usecounts, PA.attribute, PA.value
FROM sys.dm_exec_cached_plans AS CP
  CROSS APPLY sys.dm_exec_sql_text(CP.plan_handle) AS ST
  CROSS APPLY sys.dm_exec_plan_attributes(CP.plan_handle) AS PA
WHERE ST.text LIKE '%703FCFF2-970F-4777-A8B7-8A87B8BE0A4D%'
  AND ST.text NOT LIKE '%sys.dm_exec_cached_plans%'
  AND attribute = 'set_options';
```

You get the following output:

```
usecounts    attribute    value
-----------  -----------  ------
1            set_options  4339
1            set_options  4347
```

Observe that the *set_options* bitmap is different for the two plans that the query found in cache. As you probably gathered, the bit value 8 represents the CONCAT_NULL_YIELDS_NULL option in this bitmap.

The conclusion based on this behavior is that you should strive to use consistent environments to connect to SQL Server to promote efficient plan reuse behavior.

The other category of recompilations is called *plan optimality*. SQL Server applies such recompilations when the optimality of the cached plan is in doubt—not its correctness. As an example, a sufficient amount of data changes is considered a plan-optimality cause for a recompilation. The thinking is that, with enough data changes, the existing cached plan might not be optimal anymore.

SQL Server keeps track of changes at the column level. When SQL Server considers reusing a cached plan, for every histogram that was used during the optimization process, it checks how many changes took place in the respective column since the last statistics refresh. If a recompilation threshold is reached, SQL Server will update the statistics and trigger a recompilation. The recompilation threshold changes gradually based on the number of rows you add. The steps are a bit different for regular tables and for temporary tables. For regular tables, the steps are as follows: after 1 row is added, after 500 more are added, and then after every 500 plus 20 percent are added. With temporary tables, the steps are after 1 row is added, after 6 are added, after 500 are added, and then after every 500 plus 20 percent are added.

With large tables, 500 plus 20 percent can represent a very large number of rows. This can result in automatic statistics updates that are not frequent enough to support optimal plans. SQL Server supports trace flag 2371, which causes the percentage to be reduced as the table grows. You can find details about this trace flag here: *http://blogs.msdn.com/b/saponsqlserver/archive/2011/09/07/ changes-to-automatic-update-statistics-in-sql-server-traceflag-2371.aspx.*

In SQL Server 2014, Microsoft introduced incremental statistics for partitioned tables. Normally, SQL Server maintains statistics at the table level. It uses up to 200 steps in the histogram for the entire table, and it applies the calculation of 500 + 20 percent to the table's cardinality. With incremental statistics, SQL Server maintains statistics at the partition level. It uses up to 200 steps in the histogram per partition, and it applies the calculation of 500 + 20 percent to the partition's cardinality. For details about this feature, see the INCREMENTAL option in the CREATE STATISTICS command here: *http://msdn.microsoft.com/en-us/library/ms188038.aspx.*

You might encounter cases where the plan SQL Server creates the first time the procedure executes keeps being the optimal one even after significant data changes. For example, suppose the typical use case for the *GetOrders* procedure is to query the last few orders. In such a case, the plan optimality recompilations are pointless. Every time a new plan is created, it's going to be the same plan. To prevent such recompilations, you can add the query hint KEEPFIXED PLAN. This hint cannot prevent SQL Server from applying plan-stability recompilations, because you can't force it to use a plan that is considered invalid. With optimality recompilations, the cached plan is known to be valid. Therefore, SQL Server has no problem accommodating a request to not recompile if you take responsibility for the performance implications of such a choice.

Use the following code to alter the *GetOrders* procedure with the KEEPFIXED PLAN query hint:

```
ALTER PROC dbo.GetOrders( @orderid AS INT )
AS

SELECT orderid, custid, empid, orderdate, filler
/* 703FCFF2-970F-4777-A8B7-8A87B8BE0A4D */
FROM dbo.Orders
WHERE orderid >= @orderid
OPTION(KEEPFIXED PLAN);
GO
```

When you're done testing the code, make sure to rerun the PerformanceV3.sql script to re-create the sample database.

Table type and table-valued parameters

A *table type* is a table definition you store as an object in the database. You can use it as the type for table variables and for table-valued parameters in stored procedures and user-defined functions.

A table type can have the usual elements that are allowed in a table-variable definition. These elements include an identity property, computed columns, and CHECK, DEFAULT, PRIMARY KEY, and UNIQUE constraints. Starting with SQL Server 2014, a table type can even have inline index definitions. It cannot have foreign-key constraints.

As a type for table variables, it gives you reusability. If you have different places in the code where you need to declare table variables based on the same structure, with a table type you avoid repeating the definition. As an example, suppose you have multiple places in the code where you use a table variable holding order IDs and sort positions for presentation-ordering purposes. You define a table type called *OrderIDs* with the CREATE TYPE command, like so:

```
USE TSQLV3;
IF TYPE_ID('dbo.OrderIDs') IS NOT NULL DROP TYPE dbo.OrderIDs;
GO
CREATE TYPE dbo.OrderIDs AS TABLE
(
  pos INT NOT NULL PRIMARY KEY,
  orderid INT NOT NULL UNIQUE
);
```

Then, to declare a table variable of this type, use the DECLARE statement and, instead of specifying the table definition, specify *AS dbo.OrderIDs*. As an example, the following code declares a table variable called *@T* based on this type, fills it with a few rows, and queries it:

```
DECLARE @T AS dbo.OrderIDs;
INSERT INTO @T(pos, orderid) VALUES(1, 10248),(2, 10250),(3, 10249);
SELECT * FROM @T;
```

Such reusability is nice. But the real power in this feature is that you can define table-valued parameters (TVPs) in stored procedures and user-defined functions based on table types. Note, though, that as of SQL Server 2014 TVPs are read-only and have to be marked as such with the READONLY attribute. You're not allowed to issue modifications against a TVP in a stored procedure.

To see an example of using a TVP, run the following code to create the stored procedure *GetOrders*:

```
IF OBJECT_ID(N'dbo.GetOrders', N'P') IS NOT NULL DROP PROC dbo.GetOrders;
GO
CREATE PROC dbo.GetOrders( @T AS dbo.OrderIDs READONLY )
AS

SELECT O.orderid, O.orderdate, O.custid, O.empid
FROM Sales.Orders AS O
  INNER JOIN @T AS K
    ON O.orderid = K.orderid
ORDER BY K.pos;
GO
```

The procedure accepts a TVP called *@T* of the *OrderIDs* table type. The procedure's query joins *@T* with the Sales.Orders table to filter orders with order IDs that appear in *@T*. The query returns the filtered orders sorted by *pos*.

To execute the procedure from T-SQL, declare a table variable of the *OrderIDs* table type, fill it with rows, and then pass the variable to the TVP, like so:

```
DECLARE @MyOrderIDs AS dbo.orderids;
INSERT INTO @MyOrderIDs (pos, orderid) VALUES(1, 10248),(2, 10250),(3, 10249);
EXEC dbo.GetOrders @T = @MyOrderIDs;
```

This code generates the following output:

```
orderid      orderdate   custid       empid
-----------  ----------  -----------  -----------
10248        2013-07-04  85           5
10250        2013-07-08  34           4
10249        2013-07-05  79           6
```

Just like with table variables, SQL Server doesn't maintain distribution statistics on columns in TVPs. However, SQL Server does maintain cardinality information. With table variables, often cardinality information isn't visible to the optimizer due to the inability to sniff variable values, because the initial optimization unit is the entire batch. I described this limitation earlier in the section "Lack of variable sniffing." But recall that parameter values can be sniffed. So, when you pass a TVP to a stored procedure, you do so after filling it with data. And then at least the cardinality information is visible to the optimizer. So, even though TVPs don't have histograms, sometimes cardinality information can go a long way in helping the optimizer with cardinality estimates.

 Tip Starting with SQL Server 2014, you can define a table type based on a memory-optimized table definition. You add the table option WITH (MEMORY_OPTIMIZED = ON). This way, table variables and TVPs based on this type use the In-Memory OLTP technology. You can find details about this technology in Chapter 10, "In-Memory OLTP."

If you're looking for extra reading material about TVPs, you can find an excellent article written by Erland Sommarskog here: *http://www.sommarskog.se/arrays-in-sql-2008.html*.

When you're done testing, run the following code for cleanup.

```
IF OBJECT_ID(N'dbo.GetOrders', N'P') IS NOT NULL DROP PROC dbo.GetOrders;
IF TYPE_ID('dbo.OrderIDs') IS NOT NULL DROP TYPE dbo.OrderIDs;
```

EXECUTE WITH RESULT SETS

You can use the WITH RESULT SETS clause to define the expected shapes of the query result sets that a stored procedure or a dynamic batch returns. You can think of it as a contract between you and the procedure. If the procedure returns results that are compatible with the specified shapes, the procedure runs successfully. If it returns results that are not compatible, depending on what's different, the execution of the procedure either fails or compensates for the difference by changing the results.

An example where this feature can be handy is when you're the user of a procedure that you're not responsible for maintaining. You want to make sure you execute it only when it returns the expected shapes of the query result sets. If the author changes the queries in the procedure, you don't want your code to execute it. The exception is when the difference is what you can consider to be cosmetic.

Consider the following *GetOrderInfo* procedure definition:

```
IF OBJECT_ID(N'dbo.GetOrderInfo', N'P') IS NOT NULL DROP PROC dbo.GetOrderInfo;
GO
CREATE PROC dbo.GetOrderInfo( @orderid AS INT )
AS

SELECT orderid, orderdate, custid, empid
FROM Sales.Orders
WHERE orderid = @orderid;

SELECT orderid, productid, qty, unitprice
FROM Sales.OrderDetails
WHERE orderid = @orderid;
GO
```

The procedure accepts an order ID as input and executes two queries: one that returns the header of the input order, and another that returns the related order lines. Here's how you execute the procedure and add the WITH RESULT SETS clause to define the expected shapes of the query result sets:

```
EXEC dbo.GetOrderInfo @orderid = 10248
WITH RESULT SETS
(
  (
    orderid   INT  NOT NULL,
    orderdate DATE NOT NULL,
    custid    INT  NOT NULL,
    empid     INT      NULL
  ),
```

```
    (
      orderid   INT            NOT NULL,
      productid INT            NOT NULL,
      qty       SMALLINT       NOT NULL,
      unitprice NUMERIC(19, 3) NOT NULL
    )
);
```

In this case, the specified shapes and the returned ones match, so the procedure runs successfully.

If you want to apply cosmetic changes like assigning your names to columns, changing types (assuming the values are convertible), or changing NULLability (assuming it's possible), you can achieve this using the WITH RESULT SETS clause. For example, the following execution changes the name of the *orderid* column in both result sets to *id*:

```
EXEC dbo.GetOrderInfo @orderid = 10248
WITH RESULT SETS
(
  (
    id        INT  NOT NULL,
    orderdate DATE NOT NULL,
    custid    INT  NOT NULL,
    empid     INT      NULL
  ),
  (
    id        INT            NOT NULL,
    productid INT            NOT NULL,
    qty       SMALLINT       NOT NULL,
    unitprice NUMERIC(19, 3) NOT NULL
  )
);
```

This execution generates the following output:

```
id      orderdate    custid  empid
------  -----------  -------  ------
10248   2013-07-04   85       5

id      productid  qty  unitprice
------  ---------- ----  ----------
10248   11         12   14.000
10248   42         10   9.800
10248   72         5    34.800
```

This is similar to assigning column aliases. If you change the type of a column, SQL Server will try to convert the values. If any value doesn't convert, execution will stop at run time with an error. Similarly, if you change a column's NULLability from NULL to NOT NULL, SQL Server will check the values at run time, and if a NULL is found, it will stop the execution and generate an error. The ability to apply such changes as part of the execution of the code is handy when you're not allowed to change the stored procedure's definition.

If there's a difference in the number of columns, the attempt to execute the procedure fails immediately. For example, run the following code indicating that you expect three columns in the first query result set:

```
EXEC dbo.GetOrderInfo @orderid = 10248
WITH RESULT SETS
(
  (
    orderid   INT  NOT NULL,
    orderdate DATE NOT NULL,
    custid    INT  NOT NULL
  ),
  (
    orderid   INT            NOT NULL,
    productid INT            NOT NULL,
    qty       SMALLINT       NOT NULL,
    unitprice NUMERIC(19, 3) NOT NULL
  )
);
```

You get the following error indicating that you expected three columns in the first result set but got four:

```
Msg 11537, Level 16, State 1, Procedure GetOrderInfo, Line 1175
EXECUTE statement failed because its WITH RESULT SETS clause specified 3 column(s)
for result set number 1, but the statement sent 4 column(s) at run time.
```

When you're done testing, run the following code for cleanup:

```
IF OBJECT_ID(N'dbo.GetOrderInfo', N'P') IS NOT NULL DROP PROC dbo.GetOrderInfo;
```

Triggers

A *trigger* is a special kind of stored procedure. It's a routine you attach to an event, and when the event happens, SQL Server executes the trigger's code. This section starts with a description of the different types of triggers SQL Server supports. It then continues with a discussion about efficient trigger programming.

Trigger types and uses

SQL Server supports different types of triggers. These include AFTER DML triggers, INSTEAD OF DML triggers and AFTER DDL triggers.

AFTER DML triggers

An AFTER DML trigger is attached to INSERT, UPDATE, and DELETE actions against a table. SQL Server doesn't support AFTER DML triggers on views. When a user submits such an action against the target table, the trigger code executes after the action already changed the table but before the transaction commits. If you issue a ROLLBACK TRAN command within the trigger, you roll back all the work you performed within the trigger as well as all work you performed in the transaction that caused the trigger to fire.

DML triggers in SQL Server are statement-level triggers and not row-level ones. This means that one trigger instance fires per statement regardless of how many rows were affected, even zero. Within the trigger, you have access to tables called inserted and deleted, which hold the pre-modification and post-modification state of the modified rows. In INSERT triggers, only inserted has rows. In DELETE triggers, only deleted has rows. In UPDATE triggers, deleted holds the pre-modification state of the updated rows and inserted holds their post-modification state. There are no MERGE triggers. You can define INSERT, UPDATE, and DELETE triggers to handle respective actions submitted by a MERGE statement.

Typical use cases of AFTER DML triggers include auditing, maintaining denormalized data, and keeping track of the last modification date and time of a row. To see a demonstration of the last-use case, first create a table called T1 by running the following code:

```
SET NOCOUNT ON;
USE tempdb;
IF OBJECT_ID('dbo.T1', 'U') IS NOT NULL DROP TABLE dbo.T1;

CREATE TABLE dbo.T1
(
  keycol       INT         NOT NULL IDENTITY
    CONSTRAINT PK_T1 PRIMARY KEY,
  datacol      VARCHAR(10) NOT NULL,
  lastmodified DATETIME2   NOT NULL
    CONSTRAINT DFT_T1_lastmodified DEFAULT(SYSDATETIME())
);
```

You need to create an AFTER UPDATE trigger that writes the current date and time value in the *lastmodified* column of the updated rows. Use the following code to create such a trigger:

```
CREATE TRIGGER trg_T1_u ON T1 AFTER UPDATE
AS

UPDATE T1
  SET lastmodified = SYSDATETIME()
FROM dbo.T1
  INNER JOIN inserted AS I
    ON I.keycol = T1.keycol;
GO
```

Figure 9-21 illustrates the trigger you just created.

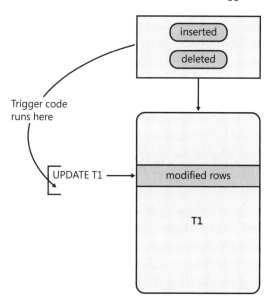

AFTER UPDATE trigger

Trigger code
runs here

inserted

deleted

UPDATE T1 → modified rows

T1

FIGURE 9-21 Trigger that updates the *lastmodified* value.

If you need to check whether a column was updated within an UPDATE trigger, you can use the UPDATE(*<col_name>*) and COLUMNS_UPDATED() functions. The former accepts a column name as input and returns true or false depending on whether the column was updated or not, respectively. This function is convenient to use when you need to check a small number of columns. The latter returns a bitmap with a different bit representing each column in the table. It requires you to use predicates with bitwise operators to figure out whether the columns of interest were updated. This function is convenient to use when you need to check a large number of columns. Note that the functions don't tell you whether a column value changed; rather, they tell you only whether the column was the target of an assignment in the UPDATE statement.

SQL Server supports nesting and recursion of AFTER DML triggers. *Nesting* means that an action submitted from one trigger against some table causes another trigger to fire. *Recursion* means that an action submitted from one trigger against some table causes the same trigger to fire, directly or indirectly. Either way, the maximum number of allowed nesting levels is 32. The nesting of triggers is enabled by default and is controlled at the instance level with a server configuration option called '*nested triggers*'. The following code will disable nesting in your instance (but don't run it unless you're actually interested in this behavior):

```
EXEC sp_configure 'nested triggers', 0;
RECONFIGURE;
```

Change the setting back to *1* if you want to enable nesting in an environment where it's currently disabled.

Trigger recursion is disabled by default and is controlled at the database level using a database option called RECURSIVE_TRIGGERS. For example, say you want to enable recursive triggers in a database called MyDB. You do so by running the following code:

```
ALTER DATABASE MyDB SET RECURSIVE_TRIGGERS ON;
```

In SQL Server, you can define multiple AFTER triggers based on the same action against the same table. It will run those one at a time. You can mark which one you want to run first and last using a stored procedure called *sp_settriggerorder*, but you don't have control over order beyond that.

INSTEAD OF DML triggers

INSTEAD OF DML triggers are similar to AFTER DML triggers, except that the trigger fires instead of the original statement and not after it. You still have the inserted and deleted tables available in the trigger, but they represent the before and after states of the rows that were supposed to be modified. If you need the trigger to do some work and then have the original change take place, it's now your responsibility to generate the change against the target based on what you have in inserted and deleted. If you don't, nothing really happens to the target.

In terms of syntax, INSTEAD OF triggers are defined similarly to AFTER triggers. In the header of the CREATE TRIGGER command specify CREATE TRIGGER ... INSTEAD OF *<action>* rather than specifying CREATE TRIGGER ... AFTER *<action>*. As mentioned, within the trigger you interact with inserted and deleted just like you do in AFTER triggers.

Unlike AFTER triggers, INSTEAD OF triggers are allowed on views. One of the interesting use cases of such triggers is to substitute an unsupported kind of modification against a view with your own logic. For example, suppose one of the columns in the view is a result of a calculation. In such a case, SQL Server will not support inserts and updates against the view. Assuming that the computation is reversible, you can intercept INSERT and UPDATE statements against the view with an INSTEAD OF trigger. In the trigger, you reverse engineer the computation based on the data in inserted and submit the change against the underlying table.

With AFTER triggers, constraints are evaluated before the trigger has a chance to execute. So, if the statement violates a constraint, the trigger doesn't get a chance to run. With INSTEAD OF triggers, remember that the trigger substitutes the original modification. It executes before constraints are validated. This allows you to substitute actions that normally would violate constraints with your alternative actions that do not violate any constraints.

SQL Server supports nesting of INSTEAD OF triggers but doesn't support recursion.

AFTER DDL triggers

SQL Server supports AFTER DDL triggers. Depending on the scope of the event in question, you create the trigger either as a database-level trigger or as a server-level one. As an example, a CREATE_TABLE event is obviously a database-scoped event, whereas a CREATE_DATABASE event is a server-scoped event.

You can attach DDL triggers to individual events, like CREATE_TABLE and ALTER_TABLE, or to event groups, like DDL_TABLE_EVENTS (for CREATE_TABLE, ALTER_TABLE, and DROP TABLE) and DDL_DATABASE_LEVEL_EVENTS (for all database-level events). You can find the events and event groups that DDL triggers support here: *http://msdn.microsoft.com/en-us/library/bb510452.aspx*.

Typical use cases for DDL triggers include auditing DDL changes, enforcing policies, and change management.

In DML triggers, you access the data that is related to the event through the inserted and deleted tables. With DDL triggers, Microsoft made an interesting choice to expose the event information through a function called EVENTDATA as XML. This information includes the login of the person who submitted the change, the post time, the affected object, and even the T-SQL statement. As you might have guessed, different events can have different associated event information. The use of XML allowed Microsoft to provide a simple and flexible solution that accommodates such differences easily. You will need to use the XML type's *value()* method to extract the information from the XML instance you get from the function.

I'll demonstrate using a DDL trigger to audit all DDL changes submitted against a database called testdb. Run the following code to create the database:

```
USE master;
IF DB_ID(N'testdb') IS NOT NULL DROP DATABASE testdb;
CREATE DATABASE testdb;
GO
USE testdb;
```

Run the following code to create the table AuditDDLEvents, where the trigger will store the audit information:

```
IF OBJECT_ID(N'dbo.AuditDDLEvents', N'U') IS NOT NULL
  DROP TABLE dbo.AuditDDLEvents;

CREATE TABLE dbo.AuditDDLEvents
(
  auditlsn         INT      NOT NULL IDENTITY,
  posttime         DATETIME NOT NULL,
  eventtype        sysname  NOT NULL,
  loginname        sysname  NOT NULL,
  schemaname       sysname  NOT NULL,
  objectname       sysname  NOT NULL,
  targetobjectname sysname  NULL,
  eventdata        XML      NOT NULL,
  CONSTRAINT PK_AuditDDLEvents PRIMARY KEY(auditlsn)
);
```

Finally, run the following code to create the audit trigger:

```
CREATE TRIGGER trg_audit_ddl_events ON DATABASE FOR DDL_DATABASE_LEVEL_EVENTS
AS
SET NOCOUNT ON;

DECLARE @eventdata AS XML = eventdata();

INSERT INTO dbo.AuditDDLEvents(
  posttime, eventtype, loginname, schemaname, objectname, targetobjectname, eventdata)
  VALUES( @eventdata.value('(/EVENT_INSTANCE/PostTime)[1]',          'VARCHAR(23)'),
          @eventdata.value('(/EVENT_INSTANCE/EventType)[1]',          'sysname'),
          @eventdata.value('(/EVENT_INSTANCE/LoginName)[1]',          'sysname'),
          @eventdata.value('(/EVENT_INSTANCE/SchemaName)[1]',          'sysname'),
          @eventdata.value('(/EVENT_INSTANCE/ObjectName)[1]',          'sysname'),
          @eventdata.value('(/EVENT_INSTANCE/TargetObjectName)[1]', 'sysname'),
          @eventdata );
GO
```

Observe that the trigger first stores the XML instance that the function returns in a variable. The trigger then inserts an audit row into the audit table. The VALUES clause has calls to the *value()* method to extract values you want to store in relational form in separate columns. In addition, the VALUES clause has the XML variable with the complete event information for the target XML column *eventdata*. That's just in case someone needs event information you didn't store in separate columns.

Run the following four DDL statements to test the trigger:

```
CREATE TABLE dbo.T1(col1 INT NOT NULL PRIMARY KEY);
ALTER TABLE dbo.T1 ADD col2 INT NULL;
ALTER TABLE dbo.T1 ALTER COLUMN col2 INT NOT NULL;
CREATE NONCLUSTERED INDEX idx1 ON dbo.T1(col2);
```

Run the following code to query the audit table:

```
SELECT * FROM dbo.AuditDDLEvents;
```

I got the following output when I ran this query on my system (with XML shown here in abbreviated form):

auditlsn	posttime	eventtype	loginname
1	2015-02-12 15:23:29.627	CREATE_TABLE	K2\Gandalf
2	2015-02-12 15:23:29.713	ALTER_TABLE	K2\Gandalf
3	2015-02-12 15:23:29.720	ALTER_TABLE	K2\Gandalf
4	2015-02-12 15:23:29.723	CREATE_INDEX	K2\Gandalf

auditlsn	schemaname	objectname	targetobjectname	eventdata
1	dbo	T1	NULL	<EVENT_INSTANCE>...
2	dbo	T1	NULL	<EVENT_INSTANCE>...
3	dbo	T1	NULL	<EVENT_INSTANCE>...
4	dbo	idx1	T1	<EVENT_INSTANCE>...

To create a server-level trigger, specify ON ALL SERVER instead of ON DATABASE.

You want to make sure to remember that SQL Server supports only AFTER DDL triggers. It doesn't support INSTEAD OF or BEFORE DDL triggers. With this in mind, you don't want to use DDL triggers to prevent expensive activities like creating and rebuilding indexes on large tables from being submitted. That's because the trigger will fire after the event finishes, just a moment before SQL Server commits the transaction. If you issue a rollback at that point, you'll just cause SQL Server to perform extra work to undo the operation.

When you're done testing, run the following code for cleanup:

```
USE master;
IF DB_ID(N'testdb') IS NOT NULL DROP DATABASE testdb;
```

Efficient trigger programming

Triggers are one of those tools that, if you don't understand them well, you can end up with performance problems. This section explains what the performance pitfalls are and provides recommendations for efficient trigger programming.

One of the most important things to understand about triggers is how to interact with the inserted and deleted tables. The rows in these tables are constructed from row versions, which are maintained in tempdb. These tables are structured just like the underlying table, but they are not indexed. You should be especially mindful of this fact when you need to access these tables repeatedly. As an example, suppose you need to define an AFTER INSERT trigger, and the task you need to implement requires you to process the rows from inserted one at a time. The first thing you need to ask yourself is whether there is a possible set-based solution you can use to achieve the task without iterations by accessing inserted only once.

Assuming the task truly mandates an iterative solution, the next thing to consider is the method to use to process the rows individually. People hear so many bad things about cursors, such as that they are evil and you should never use them, that they think any alternative is better. One of the common alternatives is to use a WHILE loop with a TOP (1) query based on key order. This solution is worse than using a cursor when you don't have an index on the key column. Every execution of the TOP query requires a full scan of the inserted table and a Sort (Top N Sort) operation. Using a cursor involves only one pass over the data. So, despite the overhead of fetching the records from the cursor, it is a more efficient tool than the alternative.

Furthermore, within the trigger you can check how many rows were affected by the INSERT statement and determine which method to use to handle the rows accordingly. If zero rows were affected, you simply return from the trigger. If one row was affected, you don't need a cursor. You can collect the elements from the row in the inserted table using an assignment SELECT statement. If more than one row was affected, you can use a cursor.

Note Be careful not to rely on the *@@rowcount* function to figure out how many rows were affected by the statement that caused the trigger to fire. That's because if the trigger fires as a result of a MERGE statement, the function will indicate how many rows were affected by the statement in total (inserted, updated, and deleted), and not just how many rows were inserted.

In our case, we just need to know if the number of affected rows is zero, one, or more. So it's enough to use the following code for this purpose:

```
DECLARE @rc AS INT = (SELECT COUNT(*) FROM (SELECT TOP (2) * FROM inserted) AS D);
```

This way, you scan at most two rows in inserted.

Using the same T1 table you used earlier for the AFTER UPDATE trigger example, the following AFTER INSERT trigger implements this strategy:

```
USE tempdb;
GO
CREATE TRIGGER trg_T1_i ON T1 AFTER INSERT
AS

DECLARE @rc AS INT = (SELECT COUNT(*) FROM (SELECT TOP (2) * FROM inserted) AS D);

IF @rc = 0 RETURN;

DECLARE @keycol AS INT, @datacol AS VARCHAR(10);

IF @rc = 1 -- single row
BEGIN
  SELECT @keycol = keycol, @datacol = datacol FROM inserted;

  PRINT 'Handling keycol: ' + CAST(@keycol AS VARCHAR(10))
    + ', datacol: ' + @datacol;
END;
ELSE -- multi row
BEGIN

  DECLARE @C AS CURSOR;

  SET @C = CURSOR FAST_FORWARD FOR SELECT keycol, datacol FROM inserted;

  OPEN @C;

  FETCH NEXT FROM @C INTO @keycol, @datacol;

  WHILE @@FETCH_STATUS = 0
  BEGIN
    PRINT 'Handling keycol: ' + CAST(@keycol AS VARCHAR(10))
      + ', datacol: ' + @datacol;
```

```
        FETCH NEXT FROM @C INTO @keycol, @datacol;
    END;

END;
GO
```

For every row in inserted, the trigger prints a message that contains the elements from the row. Normally, you would do something with those elements based on the task your trigger is supposed to fulfill.

Run the following code to test the trigger with zero affected rows:

```
INSERT INTO dbo.T1(datacol) SELECT 'A' WHERE 1 = 0;
```

The trigger returns without doing any work.

Run the following code to test the trigger with one affected row:

```
INSERT INTO dbo.T1(datacol) VALUES('A');
```

The trigger uses an assignment SELECT statement to process the row and generates the following output:

```
Handling keycol: 1, datacol: A
```

Run the following code to test the trigger with multiple affected rows:

```
INSERT INTO dbo.T1(datacol) VALUES('B'), ('C'), ('D');
```

The trigger uses a cursor to process the rows and generates the following output:

```
Handling keycol: 4, datacol: D
Handling keycol: 3, datacol: C
Handling keycol: 2, datacol: B
```

When you're done, run the following code for cleanup:

```
IF OBJECT_ID(N'dbo.T1', N'U') IS NOT NULL DROP TABLE dbo.T1;
```

Another thing to consider in terms of efficiency is how to enforce integrity rules on data that is inserted or updated in a table. Generally, if you can enforce a rule with a constraint, you will tend to get better performance than with a trigger. That's because the constraint rejects the change before it happens, whereas a trigger lets the change happen and then rolls it back. There are cases, though, in which a constraint cannot do what you need it to do. For example, if you need to enforce referential integrity between tables that reside in different databases, you cannot use foreign-key constraints. Triggers can be used in such a case. The point I'm trying to make is that you should consider constraints first and resort to triggers only if you can't achieve the integrity enforcement with constraints.

You might face cases where you need to apply a modification but you don't want a related trigger to fire. Perhaps the trigger does some further processing of new data, but you're about to insert data that has already been processed. You don't want to disable the trigger using the ALTER TABLE DISABLE TRIGGER command because this command will disable it globally. You just want to prevent it from firing for the specific statement you're about to issue.

One of the tools people use for such a purpose is called *session context*. It's a BINARY(128) value that is associated with your session. You can modify and query it from any point in the call stack. You overwrite the value using the SET CONTEXT_INFO command and query it using the CONTEXT_INFO function. To prevent the trigger from running the usual code, you can plant a signal in your session context before you issue the modification. You add logic to the trigger that queries the session context and returns if it finds that the signal was set. Otherwise, the trigger continues running its original code. This sounds like a good solution, but if you ever tried working with the session context you know that it can be very awkward. There's just one such value per session. If different developers want to use it, you need to coordinate which segment of the value each developer will use. Then, to write to your segment, you need to query the current value, merge the part you want to add, and write it back. You can see that there's great potential for problems with this solution.

The solution I like to use is simpler and has less potential for errors. It uses an empty local temporary table as the signaling mechanism. A local temporary table you create in one level in the call stack is visible throughout that level as well as in all inner levels in the call stack. This means that if you create the temporary table before you issue your statement, it's visible inside the trigger that fired as a result of that statement. Also, if you create a temporary table but don't insert any rows, no page allocations take place, making it a cheap tool to use for such a purpose. So, as your signaling mechanism, create a temporary table with a specific name before you issue your modification, and drop it after the modification. Have the trigger check if a temporary table with that name exists, and if so, return; otherwise, continue normally.

To see a demonstration of this strategy, first create a table called T1 by running the following code:

```
IF OBJECT_ID(N'dbo.T1', N'U') IS NOT NULL DROP TABLE dbo.T1;
CREATE TABLE dbo.T1(col1 INT);
```

Then create the following AFTER INSERT trigger on the table:

```
CREATE TRIGGER trg_T1_i ON dbo.T1 AFTER INSERT
AS

IF OBJECT_ID(N'tempdb..#do_not_fire_trg_T1_i', N'U') IS NOT NULL RETURN;

PRINT 'trg_T1_i in action...';
GO
```

The PRINT statement represents the usual code you have in your trigger. I use it to show when the usual code gets to run. The IF statement is the addition related to the signaling mechanism that returns if a temporary table named #do_not_fire_trg_T1_i exists. Notice that the table name is qualified with the tempdb database name. Without this qualifier, the OBJECT_ID function will look for it in the current database, which usually will be a user database.

To make sure the trigger keeps running as usual when you don't create the signal, run the following code to insert a new row into T1:

```
INSERT INTO dbo.T1(col1) VALUES(1);
```

The temporary table doesn't exist, so the trigger continues by running the usual code. The trigger generates the following output:

```
trg_T1_i in action...
```

Suppose you want to inset a new row, but this time you don't want the trigger to run its usual code. You create a temporary table called #do_not_fire_trg_T1_i, issue the INSERT statement, and then drop the temporary table, like so:

```
-- Setting signal
CREATE TABLE #do_not_fire_trg_T1_i(col1 INT);
INSERT INTO T1(col1) VALUES(2);
-- Clearing signal
DROP TABLE #do_not_fire_trg_T1_i;
```

This time the trigger executes, finds that the temporary table does exist, and therefore returns without running its usual code.

SQLCLR programming

Although T-SQL is no doubt the premier programming language of SQL Server, it can sometimes be tricky to arrive at simple solutions when faced with certain types of problems. Complex algorithms, ordered computations, and interoperability with other systems are some of the challenges for which T-SQL isn't always the best choice.

Starting with SQL Server 2005, developers were given a new option: an integrated .NET runtime engine known as SQLCLR. Make no mistake, SQLCLR is tied into and exposed within T-SQL, and it cannot be leveraged without T-SQL. It is not a stand-alone data language, and it certainly is not a replacement for your existing T-SQL skills. However, it can be used to enhance T-SQL and brings immense flexibility and power, allowing developers to more easily solve problems that would otherwise be extremely difficult to tackle in a database environment. Because SQLCLR is based on the Microsoft .NET Framework, it can leverage the framework's rich library of built-in functionality, in addition to the ease of programming afforded by languages like Microsoft C# and Visual Basic .NET.

This section covers how SQLCLR works, the types of objects and routines that can be created with it (types, aggregates, functions, triggers, and procedures), as well as some guidelines for its use in practice.

 Note The text and examples in this section assume you have a basic understanding of C# and the .NET Framework. For more information on these topics, consult the Microsoft Developer Network at *http://msdn.microsoft.com*.

SQLCLR architecture

SQL Server, at its core, is intended to act as an enterprise-grade data store. The term *enterprise* can mean different things to different people, but at its heart are the ideas of scalability and availability. The system must be able to grow to service the demands of the largest companies and applications, and the system must provide mechanisms for ensuring it will respond when requests are made.

As a pure development platform—and not a database product itself—the .NET Framework has no particular concern with either of these qualities. Therefore, when introducing it into the SQL Server ecosystem, special care was taken to ensure both that the runtime would be able to comply with a demanding environment and that it would not reduce the ability of SQL Server to perform as an enterprise-grade system.

In-process hosting model

SQL Server leverages .NET via an in-process runtime model. This means that the runtime shares the same virtual memory and thread space as everything else running within SQL Server. This key design decision has a few pros and cons:

- Moving data into .NET routines, or back out into T-SQL, is computationally inexpensive because the data does not need to cross process boundaries.

- Resource utilization by hosted .NET code can potentially directly interfere with resource utilization by other SQL Server elements as a result of the shared resources.

- The runtime inherits the security privileges granted to the SQL Server process, with no additional administrative work.

- The core SQL Server operating system management component (SQLOS) has full access to control the runtime, without requiring special permissions or crossing process boundaries.

This final point is the most important and the key to the in-process model. SQLCLR is hosted within SQL Server, but it is also a true SQL Server component in that it is completely integrated with SQLOS. Like all other SQL Server components, SQLCLR receives both memory allocations and CPU time from SQLOS, and SQLOS is able to withhold or reallocate these resources as necessary to keep the entire SQL Server system balanced and responsive.

In addition to controlling resources, SQLOS is also responsible for top-level monitoring of the hosted runtime to ensure that overallocation or overuse of resources does not threaten the availability of the SQL Server instance. The runtime is monitored for such conditions as memory leaks and scheduler monopolization, and SQLOS is able to either dynamically unload an AppDomain (as in the case of a memory leak) or force a nonyielding thread to back off of a busy scheduler to give other queries a chance to run (which is referred to as *quantum punishment*).

Important Before you can start running custom SQLCLR code, you must first enable the functionality at the instance level. This is done by first running "*EXEC sp_configure 'clr enabled', 1*" and then committing the change using the "RECONFIGURE" statement. This reconfiguration is not required to use built-in SQLCLR features like the *HIERARCHYID* and *geospatial* data types.

Assemblies hosted in the database

Although the runtime itself is globally (and automatically) managed at the SQL Server instance level, .NET assemblies—the modules that encapsulate our custom SQLCLR routines—are both managed and secured within individual databases. At the database level, each assembly is granted a set of permissions via one of three possible buckets. In addition, AppDomains are dynamically managed and scoped by the runtime not globally, but rather within each database that hosts assemblies.

.NET assemblies are compiled DLL or EXE files, and applications generally rely on either physical copies of these compiled files or versions loaded into a Global Assembly Cache (GAC). SQL Server, on the other hand, follows a different model. When an assembly DLL is needed within a SQL Server database, it is first loaded into the database via the CREATE ASSEMBLY statement. This statement reads and copies the DLL into the database. From this point forward, the physical file is no longer used or accessed in any way by SQL Server. This eliminates management overhead; because the assembly is literally part of the database, it moves with the database everywhere that the database goes—including replication, backups, log shipping, availability replicas, and so on.

One of the key options when bringing an assembly into SQL Server using the CREATE ASSEMBLY statement is the PERMISSION_SET. This option restricts the assembly's operations, giving the database administrator (DBA) or database developer an element of trust that even if the assembly contains rogue (or merely buggy) code, it will not be able to go beyond certain limits. There are three available permission sets:

- **SAFE** This permission set is the most restrictive, allowing the assembly to use basic .NET Framework classes, including those necessary for math and string operations. In addition, the assembly is allowed to connect back to the hosting database, using a special type of ADO.NET connection type called the *Context Connection*.

- **EXTERNAL_ACCESS** This permission set includes everything allowed by the SAFE permission set, plus the ability for the assembly to access resources outside of the hosting database. For example, in this permission set the assembly can access another database on the same server, another database on another server, or a file somewhere else on the network.

- **UNSAFE** This permission set includes everything allowed by the EXTERNAL_ACCESS permission set, plus the ability to take actions that can potentially destabilize the SQL Server instance. Examples include threading, synchronization, and even the ability to shut down SQL Server via code.

These three permission sets are implemented using two different types of checks. When the assembly is just-in-time compiled (JITed), checks are made against an attribute called *HostProtection*. Various .NET Framework classes and methods are decorated with this attribute, and referencing them in an assembly with insufficient permissions will result in an exception during the JIT process. Security limitations, on the other hand, are enforced at run time via .NET's Code Access Security (CAS) infrastructure. Generally speaking, granting the EXTERNAL_ACCESS set involves easing security permissions (and limiting CAS enforcement), whereas granting the UNSAFE set involves allowing potential reliability-impacting code, as enforced by *HostProtection* checks.

Another option specified when creating an assembly is the AUTHORIZATION, or specifying the owner of the assembly. Aside from basic database object security—the ability to ALTER or DROP the assembly—the owner has an important impact on the way the assembly is handled. Specifically, all assemblies in a given database that are owned by the same database principal will be loaded into the same AppDomain. This separation gives each set of assemblies its own memory *sandbox*, completely isolated from other sets of assemblies.

The main benefit of this design decision is to give SQLOS the ability to selectively spin up and tear down AppDomains on a targeted basis, without affecting other parts of the system. For example, if your database has two functional sets of assemblies, each owned by different principals, and SQL Server detects that one of your assemblies has code that is leaking memory, only the affected one of the two AppDomains will need to be recycled. Users of the other AppDomain will not be affected in any way. This design also means that if you have two or more assemblies that should closely interact with one another, they must be owned by the same principal. Developers should carefully design assembly ownership schemes bearing in mind both of these considerations.

CLR scalar functions and creating your first assembly

There are several types of SQLCLR objects and routines that can be created, but the simplest and perhaps most useful type is the scalar user-defined function (UDF). Scalar functions are useful for encapsulating complex logic or operations; mathematical algorithms, string-manipulation logic, and even data compression are all common use cases for CLR scalar functions.

Compared with T-SQL scalar functions, the CLR variety will almost always yield better performance and simpler query plans. The reason for this is that CLR functions are treated as compiled and encapsulated code, and they are referenced in Compute Scalar operators within a query plan, much the same as any built-in function. Figure 9-22 shows the query plan for a simple CLR scalar function that returns an empty string.

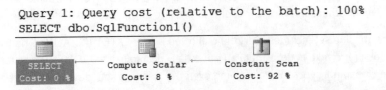

```
Query 1: Query cost (relative to the batch): 100%
SELECT dbo.SqlFunction1()
```

FIGURE 9-22 Query plan for a CLR scalar function.

T-SQL scalar functions, on the other hand, are treated like special stored procedures and are both logically and physically accessed and reevaluated on every iteration. Figure 9-23 shows the query plan for a T-SQL scalar UDF with the same logic as the CLR UDF (simply returning an empty string). The T-SQL version actually produces two query plans: an outer plan for the SELECT, and a second inner plan for row-by-row invocation of the UDF. This is where performance issues come into play.

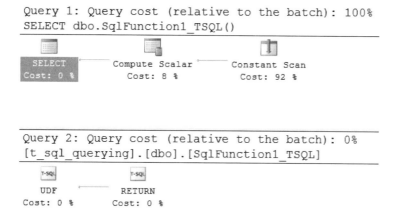

FIGURE 9-23 Query plan for a T-SQL scalar function; note the extra second plan.

One of the key aspects of CLR functions is that they look and feel—to the end user—exactly the same as T-SQL functions. So, if you have an algorithm that is not performing well in a T-SQL function, it can be migrated to a CLR function without changing any downstream code. Likewise, if you decide that a CLR function would be better as a T-SQL function, you can migrate back again. This flexibility is one of the things that makes SQLCLR a powerful tool for performance-tuning exercises.

Visual Studio and SQL Server Data Tools

Before you can create an assembly, you need to decide on an environment in which to work. Although you can easily create C# code with any text editor and compile it using csc.exe (the C# compiler), most developers prefer to use an Integrated Development Environment (IDE). The usual choice is Microsoft Visual Studio, which includes a SQL Server development add-in called SQL Server Data Tools (SSDT). This add-in is designed to help ease many of the pains of full-cycle database development, including various features that assist with refactoring, deployment, and debugging. It also includes specific templates to help with the creation of SQLCLR assemblies.

The remainder of this section assumes you are working in Visual Studio with SSDT. However, the techniques discussed herein should be easily transferrable to any .NET development environment.

SSDT projects and creating a CLR function

SSDT projects in Visual Studio are nested under the SQL Server template category. Once you have created a project in which to work, you can add a user-defined function by right-clicking on the project in Solution Explorer, selecting Add, and then clicking New Item. This will bring up a dialog box with various item types. The SQL CLR C# category contains the correct templates for creating new

SQLCLR objects. Choose the SQL CLR C# User Defined Function category to bring up a generic function definition like the one shown in Listing 9-1.

LISTING 9-1 Generic template for a user-defined function

```
public partial class UserDefinedFunctions
{
    [Microsoft.SqlServer.Server.SqlFunction]
    public static SqlString SqlFunction1()
    {
        // Put your code here
        return new SqlString (string.Empty);
    }
}
```

The most important thing to note about this code is that it implements a complete and working scalar user-defined function. A SQLCLR scalar UDF is, in fact, nothing more than a scalar-valued static method, specially exposed to T-SQL via the CREATE FUNCTION statement. (In this case, the *SqlFunction* attribute that decorates the method is used to tell Visual Studio to do this work on your behalf. But that attribute is entirely optional.) That's it; whatever type of logic, algorithm, or .NET Framework functionality you decide to put between the curly braces is fair game.

Note Although the *SqlFunction* attribute is optional for scalar functions, it does have some important options. If you want to create an index on a function (for example, by using the function in a computed column), you must use it and you must set the *IsDeterministic* property to *true*. This is a rare use case, so it won't be covered here. For more information, refer to the *SqlFunctionAttribute* documentation in the Microsoft Developer Network (*http://msdn.microsoft.com*).

SqlTypes namespace

One thing you might have noticed about the code in Listing 9-1 is that instead of returning a standard .NET *System.String*, the code returns a type called *SqlString*. This type, along with several others, is found in the *System.Data.SqlTypes* namespace. Each of the types mirrors a SQL Server built-in type and implements both proper NULL behavior (via an interface called *INullable*) and behavior similar to that of the base SQL Server type.

These behaviors include value ranges that follow the SQL Server data-type rules, along with actions that mimic those of SQL Server. For example, by default in .NET, adding 1 to an integer variable with a value of 2147483647 results in the variable having a value of –2147483648. In SQL Server, on the other hand, this same operation results in an arithmetic overflow exception. The *SqlInt32* data type—which is designed to mirror the behavior of SQL Server's INTEGER type—also throws an exception when this operation is attempted.

Use of the *SqlTypes* data types is not required for SQLCLR methods. SQL Server can internally map similar types, such as a *System.String* to an NVARCHAR. However, using the *SqlTypes* for method inputs and outputs is highly recommended, because it guarantees appropriate behaviors and capabilities and ensures that your CLR modules will respond in ways that T-SQL consumers expect—whether or not they know that they're working with a CLR module instead of a T-SQL one.

Publishing the assembly

Once the function has been added, the assembly is just about ready for "publication" (deployment) to the target database. Prior to publishing a real assembly, you might first want to visit the project properties tab—specifically, the SQLCLR section—and configure both the Permission Level and Assembly Owner options to your liking. But given the simplicity of this example, that is probably not necessary.

To publish the assembly, right-click on the project in Solution Explorer and click Publish. You will need to first specify a target database. If this is a database that holds other objects or data you care about, you might want to visit the Advanced options dialog box and make sure to clear any options that could overwrite your prior work. Once you've configured things, it is recommended that you save your settings (by clicking Save Profile), because SSDT does not automatically remember them for subsequent publications.

Clicking the Publish button will deploy the function to the database. Under the hood, this is done via a series of T-SQL scripts, starting with something like the following:

```
CREATE ASSEMBLY [t_sql_querying_project]
    AUTHORIZATION [dbo]
    FROM 0x4D5A9000030000004000000FFFF0000B800000000 ... (truncated for brevity)
```

This code uses the CREATE ASSEMBLY statement to load the assembly into the target database. The FROM clause supports either a physical file path to a compiled dynamic-link library (DLL) or a binary string that represents the actual bytes of the DLL. In this case, Visual Studio compiles the DLL (which you can find in the build folder), reads the bytes, and represents them in string form so that they can be more easily scripted and deployed to remote locations without concern for network permissions. The AUTHORIZATION clause sets the assembly owner to *dbo* (the default). This statement lacks a WITH PERMISSION_SET clause, which means that the default SAFE permission set will be used.

At this point, the assembly has been loaded into the database, but the scalar function is not available to be called via T-SQL. Before that can happen, a T-SQL stub function must be created that points to the internal method. The SSDT publication does this using a script like this one:

```
CREATE FUNCTION [dbo].[SqlFunction1]
( )
RETURNS NVARCHAR (4000)
AS
 EXTERNAL NAME [t_sql_querying_project].[UserDefinedFunctions].[SqlFunction1]
```

This T-SQL function has the same set of input parameters (none) and the same output parameter type as the generated C# method. Visual Studio has automatically mapped the *SqlString* type to NVARCHAR(4000). (Remember that .NET strings are always Unicode.) Beyond that, there is no function body, because any logic would have been implemented in C#. Instead, the EXTERNAL NAME clause is used to map this T-SQL stub to the method exposed by the assembly that has already been created. Note the class and method names are case sensitive and must exactly match the case as defined in the C# code.

Once the function has been exposed, it can be called in T-SQL just like any other scalar function:

```
SELECT dbo.SqlFunction1() AS result;
```

```
---

result
------



(1 row(s) affected)
```

Because the function does nothing more than return an empty string, the output is not especially exciting. However, again, the actual body of this method can be virtually any C# code; the important thing to notice is the ease with which .NET can be leveraged within T-SQL.

SqlTypes pitfalls and the *SqlFacet* attribute

Although the *SqlTypes* data types are key interfaces for emulating proper SQL Server data-type behaviors in .NET, and although Visual Studio automatically maps the two during its publication process, sometimes things don't work as expected. Many SQLCLR developers have been shocked to discover that some Visual Studio behaviors are less than ideal for their given scenarios. Cases that are particularly problematic are the SQL Server NUMERIC (also known as DECIMAL) type, large strings, and some of SQL Server's newer temporal data types.

To see the basic issue with the NUMERIC type, modify the basic function template into the following form:

```
public partial class UserDefinedFunctions
{
    [Microsoft.SqlServer.Server.SqlFunction]
    public static SqlDecimal DecimalFunction1()
    {
        return new SqlDecimal (123.4567);
    }
}
```

This seems relatively straightforward: return the decimal value 123.4567. But when you publish and run it, something different happens:

```
SELECT dbo.DecimalFunction1() AS decimalValue;
```

```
---

decimalValue
------------
123

(1 row(s) affected)
```

The decimal part of the value has been truncated, effectively yielding an integer. This is probably not desired behavior if you're explicitly using the decimal data type! The root cause becomes immediately apparent upon examining Visual Studio's generated script:

```
CREATE FUNCTION [dbo].[DecimalFunction1]
( )
RETURNS NUMERIC (18)
AS
 EXTERNAL NAME [t_sql_querying_project].[UserDefinedFunctions].[DecimalFunction1]
```

SQL Server's NUMERIC type has fixed precision and scale. Because you haven't told Visual Studio what precision or scale you're looking for, a default was used: a precision of 18, with a scale of 0 (18 total digits, with zero digits after the decimal point). Neither the .NET *System.Decimal* type, nor the *SqlDecimal* type have fixed precision or scale, so a fix for this issue must be done purely on the SQL Server side. To change this behavior, you can either manually create your own stub function definition—specifying the correct precision and scale in the RETURNS clause—or give Visual Studio more information by using an attribute called *SqlFacet*:

```
public partial class UserDefinedFunctions
{
    [Microsoft.SqlServer.Server.SqlFunction]
    [return: SqlFacet(Precision=24, Scale=12)]
    public static SqlDecimal DecimalFunction2()
    {
        return new SqlDecimal (123.4567);
    }
}
```

Here you are telling Visual Studio to generate its script using a return precision of 24 and a scale of 12. Thanks to the attribute, this version of the function behaves as expected:

```
SELECT dbo.DecimalFunction2() AS decimalValue;

---

decimalValue
------------
123.456700000000

(1 row(s) affected)
```

> **Note** The behavior described in this section depends on the version of Visual Studio and SSDT. Most versions will reproduce these issues, but as of the time of this writing the November 2014 SSDT build along with Visual Studio 2013 treats all non-overridden string types as NVARCHAR(MAX).

Another issue is related to string types. As shown with the *SqlFunction1* example, Visual Studio scripts *SqlString* as NVARCHAR(4000). This can cause larger strings to truncate, as illustrated by the following function.

```
public partial class UserDefinedFunctions
{
    [Microsoft.SqlServer.Server.SqlFunction]
    public static SqlInt32 ReturnStringLength1(
        SqlString theString)
    {
        return new SqlInt32 (theString.Value.Length);
    }
}
```

This function illustrates an important point regarding the *SqlTypes*: each of the data types in the namespace implements a property called *Value*, which maps back to the base .NET type. Using this property is the recommended way to work with the type in your C# code, rather than using a static cast.

Once the function is published, it can be tested against the built-in LEN function:

```
DECLARE @bigString NVARCHAR(MAX) =
    REPLICATE(CONVERT(NVARCHAR(MAX), 'a'), 12345);

SELECT
    LEN(@bigString) AS SQL_Length,
    dbo.ReturnStringLength1(@bigString) AS CLR_Length;

---

SQL_Length           CLR_Length
-------------------- -----------
12345                4000

(1 row(s) affected)
```

Once again, the problem can be mitigated by using the *SqlFacet* attribute—this time applied to the input value (and, therefore, without the "return" declaration):

```
public partial class UserDefinedFunctions
{
    [Microsoft.SqlServer.Server.SqlFunction]
    public static SqlInt32 ReturnStringLength2(
        [SqlFacet(MaxSize=-1)]
        SqlString theString)
    {
        return new SqlInt32 (theString.Value.Length);
    }
}
```

After publication, the previous script now works as expected:

```
DECLARE @bigString NVARCHAR(MAX) =
    REPLICATE(CONVERT(NVARCHAR(MAX), 'a'), 12345);

SELECT
    LEN(@bigString) AS SQL_Length,
    dbo.ReturnStringLength2(@bigString) AS CLR_Length;
```

```
---

SQL_Length           CLR_Length
-------------------- -----------
12345                12345
```

(1 row(s) affected)

The final major *SqlTypes* pitfall has to do with some of SQL Server's newer temporal data types. The *SqlTypes* namespace was initially released in 2005, and it has not received an update in the meantime. Therefore, although it includes a *SqlDateTime* type that maps to DATETIME, it has no support for the DATE, TIME, DATETIME2, and DATETIMEOFFSET that first shipped in SQL Server 2008. The solution, in these cases, unfortunately requires manual intervention.

Visual Studio will automatically map *System.TimeSpan* to TIME and *System.DateTimeOffset* to DATETIMEOFFSET, but if support for NULLs is desired you will have to resort to using .NET *nullable* versions of the types (*System.TimeSpan?* and *System.DateTimeOffset?*). Unfortunately, these types, although fully supported for SQLCLR assemblies, cause script-generation errors in all current versions of SSDT as of the time of this writing.

The DATE and DATETIME2 classes have no corresponding .NET classes, but both are compatible with *System.DateTime* (and *System.DateTime?* for NULL support). Unfortunately, there is no way to tell Visual Studio to script these relationships via *SqlFacet*. So, once again, a manual step is required.

In both of these cases, the best current workaround, at least for scalar functions, is to leave the *SqlFunction* attribute off of the function's C# method definition. This will cause Visual Studio to not attempt to script a T-SQL stub for the function, which will avoid the scripting errors. You can create your own stub script and include it in a post-build .SQL file, which can be added to your SSDT project from the User Scripts category.

String types and case sensitivity

When writing T-SQL, case-sensitivity concerns—or lack thereof—are dictated by the collations of the strings involved in the operation. Collations can be inherited from the database or from an individual column of a table, depending on how things are set up and what, exactly, you're doing.

In .NET, things are a bit different. By default, all operations on strings use binary comparisons—which means that all operations are case sensitive. This behavior can be easily changed on a case-by-case basis by using flags that are available on almost all the string methods in the .NET Base Class Library (BCL). However, hardcoding a selection might not be a great option when working in SQLCLR, because an assembly might need to be used in both case-sensitive and case-insensitive contexts, and you might not want to maintain two versions of the same code with only a single modified flag.

The solution to this problem is to take advantage of the *SqlCompareOptions* enumeration exposed as a property of the *SqlString* class. This enumeration contains information about the collation of the hosting database, which can be used to infer whether or not string comparisons in SQLCLR modules should be done using case sensitivity.

Having access to this information opens the door to many useful cases. For example, the following are two regular expression functions that can be deployed to any SQL Server database and will automatically pick up the correct case-sensitivity settings.

```
[Microsoft.SqlServer.Server.SqlFunction]
 public static SqlBoolean RegExMatch(
     SqlString pattern,
     [SqlFacet(MaxSize=-1)]
     SqlString input)
 {
     //handle NULLs
     if (pattern.IsNull || input.IsNull)
         return (SqlBoolean.Null);

     //does the hosting database use a case-sensitive collation?
     var options =
         (0 != (input.SqlCompareOptions & SqlCompareOptions.IgnoreCase)) ?
             System.Text.RegularExpressions.RegexOptions.IgnoreCase :
             System.Text.RegularExpressions.RegexOptions.None;

     //instantiate a regEx object with the options
     var regEx =
         new System.Text.RegularExpressions.Regex(pattern.Value, options);

     //do we have a match?
     return new SqlBoolean (regEx.IsMatch(input.Value));
 }

[Microsoft.SqlServer.Server.SqlFunction]
 [return: SqlFacet(MaxSize = -1)]
 public static SqlString RegExReplace(
     SqlString pattern,
     [SqlFacet(MaxSize = -1)]
     SqlString input,
     SqlString replacement)
 {
     //handle NULLs
     if (pattern.IsNull || input.IsNull || replacement.IsNull)
         return (SqlString.Null);

     //does the hosting database use a case-sensitive collation?
     var options =
         (0 != (input.SqlCompareOptions & SqlCompareOptions.IgnoreCase)) ?
             System.Text.RegularExpressions.RegexOptions.IgnoreCase :
             System.Text.RegularExpressions.RegexOptions.None;

     //instantiate a regEx object with the options
     var regEx =
         new System.Text.RegularExpressions.Regex(pattern.Value, options);

     //do we have a match?
     return new SqlString(regEx.Replace(input.Value, replacement.Value));
 }
```

These functions illustrate various techniques: *SqlFacet* is used for setting input and return sizes as appropriate, the *IsNull* property is checked to handle NULL inputs, and the *SqlCompareOptions* enumeration is verified. This final check is done by doing a binary *and* operation and checking to see whether the output is not equal to zero. If the *IgnoreCase* bit is set, the result will be nonzero. (It will actually be equal to the value of the *IgnoreCase* bit.) If, on the other hand, that bit is not set, the *and* operation will return zero and the code will not use *RegexOptions.IgnoreCase* to do its work.

SQLCLR scalar function use cases

The preceding examples are designed to show as simply as possible how to work with and develop SQLCLR functions. As such, they don't illustrate actual cases where these functions can add value to your development tasks. These cases tend to fall into one (or more) of the following three categories:

- SQLCLR functions provide excellent performance compared to T-SQL functions. For complex math algorithms, it is not uncommon for a SQLCLR function to achieve performance gains of 1,000 percent or more compared with T-SQL functions. Surprisingly, SQLCLR functions can also outperform built-in SQL Server functions in some cases. A test of the built-in REPLACE function compared with a SQLCLR function that leveraged *String.Replace* showed a 700 percent performance improvement for very large strings (up to 50,000 characters).

- Another case for SQLCLR scalar functions is situations where logic is simply too difficult to represent in T-SQL. As a data-access language, T-SQL is not really designed for complex iterative tasks. Imperative languages such as C# and Visual Basic .NET, on the other hand, have numerous forms of flow control, advanced collection classes, and powerful debuggers.

- The final case has to do with leveraging the power of the .NET Base Class Library (BCL). This library has numerous features that are otherwise simply not available in SQL Server, such as the ability to perform disk I/O, network operations, data compression, and advanced XML manipulation.

As a SQL Server developer considering SQLCLR, it is important to question whether doing a given task in SQL Server is a good idea. The same .NET code you can leverage in a SQLCLR function is also available in your application, so you should always question whether the task might be better offloaded to a different server. (Remember that SQL Server is much more expensive, from a licensing standpoint, than an application server.)

If the logic is data intensive (rather than process intensive), shared (that is, data logic that might be leveraged by numerous downstream applications), if the logic is used to filter or aggregate large amounts of data and can save network bandwidth, or any combination of these scenarios apply, doing the work in SQL Server and perhaps SQLCLR might be a good fit.

Streaming table-valued functions

Much like in T-SQL, SQLCLR functions come in two varieties: scalar and table-valued. Although the scalar-valued functions are behaviorally similar to their T-SQL counterparts, SQLCLR table-valued functions (TVFs) aren't quite the same as either the T-SQL inline or multistatement versions. SQLCLR table-valued functions, although they're closest in essence to T-SQL multistatement functions, do not use tempdb to store intermediate data. Rather, they are based on a streaming methodology that uses the .NET *IEnumerable* interface to send one row at a time back to SQL Server.

SQLCLR table-valued function life cycle

Table-valued functions are created using the same basic methods as those used for scalar functions. The core difference between the two is that a scalar function returns a single value and table-valued functions return a collection of values cast as *IEnumerable*. This interface is implemented by every built-in collection type in .NET, and it can easily be leveraged in your own code through either a custom implementation or via the *yield* statement, which tells the compiler to build an *IEnumerable* implementation on your behalf.

SQLCLR table-valued functions have two primary components: the *IEnumerable*-valued entry method, and a secondary method known as the "fill row method." When the table-valued function is invoked from SQL Server, the query processor first calls the entry method. It is this method's job to prepare an *IEnumerable* instance representing the rows to be sent back. Once the query processor gets a reference to the *IEnumerable* instance, it creates an instance of *IEnumerator* and begins calling *MoveNext*. Each time this method returns *true*, the query processor calls *Current*, passing the returned object to the "fill row" method. This second method's job is to map the object (or its properties) to output columns, which will then be consumed by the query processor in the form of a row.

 Note The *IEnumerable* interface intentionally lacks any kind of property indicating how many elements exist to be enumerated. This means that elements can be dynamically accessed from a source, without holding references in memory. For example, if some code were reading a file line by line, only the current line would ever have to be in memory, along with a pointer to the next line in the file. This is why *IEnumerable* is referred to as a *streaming interface*, and this is what makes it especially nice within SQL Server, where memory is often at a premium.

Creating a SQLCLR table-valued function

Creating a table-valued function can start with the same template as that used for scalar functions. However, the return type must be modified, so we will revisit the *SqlFunction* attribute. Following is an example entry point method that implements a simple string split for comma-separated values:

```
[Microsoft.SqlServer.Server.SqlFunction(
    TableDefinition="value NVARCHAR(MAX)",
    FillRowMethodName="StringSplit_fill")]
public static System.Collections.IEnumerable StringSplit(
    [SqlFacet(MaxSize=-1)]
    SqlString input)
{
    if (input.IsNull)
        return (new string[] {});
    else
        return (input.Value.Split(','));
}
```

This method internally leverages *System.String.Split*, which returns a collection of strings split on whatever delimiter is provided—a comma in this case. (Of course, the delimiter can be passed to the method instead, but it is hard coded here for simplicity.) Because it doesn't make sense to attempt to split a NULL string, a check is made against the *IsNull* property, which is implemented on all the *SqlTypes* data types for just such a purpose. If the string is NULL, you return an empty collection, which will result in no rows getting returned to the caller, which is exactly how someone might expect the function to behave if it was implemented in T-SQL.

Much like scalar functions, this method is decorated with the *SqlFunction* attribute, but this time it uses a couple of new options. The *TableDefinition* tells Visual Studio how to script the T-SQL stub. In this case, a single output column is specified, but the definition can include as many as are supported by the TDS protocol—65,535, which is probably not recommended. The other option used is *FillRow-MethodName*, which specifies the name of the "fill row" method that will be called for each element returned by the enumerator. A common convention is to name the "fill row" method *[entry method name]_fill*.

The next step is to create the "fill row" method itself, which in this case would be as follows:

```
public static void StringSplit_fill(
    object o,
    out SqlString value)
{
    value = (string)o;
}
```

The "fill row" method is always a void-valued static method. Its first parameter must be of type *object*, because that is what the enumerator will return. (SQLCLR does not currently use generic enumerators.) Aside from the *object* parameter, it must have one *out* parameter per column as defined in the *TableDefinition* option of the *SqlFunction* attribute on the *entry* method. In this case, the column is a *SqlString*, to match the NVARCHAR(MAX) definition. Note that the *SqlFacet* attribute is not required here, because the *TableDefinition* takes care of the mapping.

The job of the "fill row" method, again, is to map the input object to one or more output columns, and in this case that task is simple. The collection returned by the *entry* method consists of strings, and the enumerator returns one string at a time typed as an object. To map it back to a string, the "fill row" method must simply use a static cast.

Once both methods are written and compiled, Visual Studio produces the following T-SQL stub for publication:

```
CREATE FUNCTION [dbo].[StringSplit]
(@input NVARCHAR (MAX))
RETURNS
    TABLE (
        [value] NVARCHAR (MAX) NULL)
AS
 EXTERNAL NAME [t_sql_querying_project].[UserDefinedFunctions].[StringSplit]
```

This function can be referenced just like any other table-valued function, and it is quite useful in a number of scenarios. It also happens to be significantly faster than any T-SQL-based method of splitting comma-separated values (CSVs). Following is an example call:

```
SELECT
    *
FROM dbo.StringSplit('abc,def,ghi');


---

value
-----
abc
def
ghi

(3 row(s) affected)
```

> **Note** An optional ORDER BY clause is available for the CREATE FUNCTION statement when it's used for SQLCLR table-valued functions. This clause tells SQL Server that the table returned by the function is guaranteed to be ordered as specified in the ORDER BY clause. This allows the query optimizer to generate better plans in some cases, and it is recommended if your function, in fact, does return its data ordered. Note that the ordering is verified at run time, and an exception will occur if the output doesn't match the specification. More information on this feature is available in SQL Server Books Online at *http://msdn.microsoft.com/en-us/library/ms186755.aspx.*

Memory utilization and a faster, more scalable string splitter

It is vitally important, when leveraging SQLCLR routines in active environments, to remember that memory is always at a premium in SQL Server. Most DBAs like to see the server's memory used for central purposes like the buffer and procedure caches, and not taken over by large allocations in the CLR space.

The string splitter created in the prior section, although functionally sound, does not do a great job of keeping its memory use to a minimum. Its behavior is, in fact, almost the opposite of what might be desirable: it uses *String.Split* to populate a collection of all possible substrings, and then holds onto the collection until all the elements have been returned to the caller. This means that memory will be used not only for each of the substrings, but also for references to each of those substrings. When splitting large strings, this overhead can really add up, creating a significant amount of pressure on memory resources.

Problems like this are often not simple to solve, and this case is no exception. To fix the situation, you need to stop using the simple—and built-in—*String.Split* method and instead roll your own string-split algorithm. The following code was developed over the course of several days, in a forum thread, in conjunction with several top SQL Server developers. (If you would like to see the thread, visit *http://www.sqlservercentral.com/Forums/Topic695508-338-1.aspx.*)

```
[Microsoft.SqlServer.Server.SqlFunction(
    FillRowMethodName = "FillRow_Multi",
    TableDefinition = "item nvarchar(4000)"
    )
]
public static IEnumerator SplitString_Multi(
    [SqlFacet(MaxSize = -1)]
    SqlChars Input,
    [SqlFacet(MaxSize = 255)]
    SqlChars Delimiter
    )
{
    return (
        (Input.IsNull || Delimiter.IsNull) ?
        new SplitStringMulti(new char[0], new char[0]) :
        new SplitStringMulti(Input.Value, Delimiter.Value));
}

public static void FillRow_Multi(object obj, out SqlString item)
{
    item = new SqlString((string)obj);
}

public class SplitStringMulti : IEnumerator
{
    public SplitStringMulti(char[] TheString, char[] Delimiter)
    {
        theString = TheString;
        stringLen = TheString.Length;
        delimiter = Delimiter;
        delimiterLen = (byte)(Delimiter.Length);
        isSingleCharDelim = (delimiterLen == 1);

        lastPos = 0;
        nextPos = delimiterLen * -1;
    }

    #region IEnumerator Members

    public object Current
    {
        get
        {
            return new string(theString, lastPos, nextPos - lastPos)
        }
    }

    public bool MoveNext()
    {
        if (nextPos >= stringLen)
            return false;
        else
        {
            lastPos = nextPos + delimiterLen;
```

```csharp
                for (int i = lastPos; i < stringLen; i++)
                {
                    bool matches = true;

                    //Optimize for single-character delimiters
                    if (isSingleCharDelim)
                    {
                        if (theString[i] != delimiter[0])
                            matches = false;
                    }
                    else
                    {
                        for (byte j = 0; j < delimiterLen; j++)
                        {
                            if (((i + j) >= stringLen) || (theString[i + j] != delimiter[j]))
                            {
                                matches = false;
                                break;
                            }
                        }
                    }

                    if (matches)
                    {
                        nextPos = i;

                        //Deal with consecutive delimiters
                        if ((nextPos - lastPos) > 0)
                            return true;
                        else
                        {
                            i += (delimiterLen-1);
                            lastPos += delimiterLen;
                        }
                    }
                }

                lastPos = nextPos + delimiterLen;
                nextPos = stringLen;

                if ((nextPos - lastPos) > 0)
                    return true;
                else
                    return false;
            }
        }

        public void Reset()
        {
            lastPos = 0;
            nextPos = delimiterLen * -1;
        }

        #endregion
```

```
    private int lastPos;
     private int nextPos;

    private readonly char[] theString;
     private readonly char[] delimiter;
     private readonly int stringLen;
     private readonly byte delimiterLen;
     private readonly bool isSingleCharDelim;
 }
```

This code solves the memory issue by finding and streaming back one substring at a time, rather than doing all the work up front. This means that the input string must be held in memory, but because only a single reference is needed, this generally consumes significantly less memory than holding references to each of the substrings. As a bonus, the algorithm used in this code is actually faster than that used by *String.Split*. So this string splitter both performs well and keeps memory utilization to a minimum.

Data access and the context connection

So far, all the examples shown have relied on the data being passed into the functions by the caller. However, both table-valued and scalar functions—as well as other SQLCLR module types—can access data from the hosting database, even if the assembly is cataloged as SAFE. This is done using standard ADO.NET access methods in conjunction with a special connection string called the *context connection*.

The context connection gives code running in SQLCLR the ability to access data with the same visibility and privileges as normal T-SQL code being run by the caller. This means that the CLR code will be able to see the same data that the caller can see, with no escalation of privilege. Visibility includes anything available at a nested level of scope, including local temporary tables created prior to invoking the SQLCLR routine.

The following example entry function selects and returns rows from a temporary table with a well-known shape:

```
[Microsoft.SqlServer.Server.SqlFunction(
    DataAccess=DataAccessKind.Read,
    TableDefinition="col1 INT, col2 FLOAT",
    FillRowMethodName="GetTempValues_fill")]
public static System.Collections.IEnumerable GetTempValues()
{
    var build = new SqlConnectionStringBuilder();
    build.ContextConnection = true;

    using (var conn = new SqlConnection(build.ConnectionString))
    {
        var comm = conn.CreateCommand();
        comm.CommandText = "SELECT * FROM #values";

        var adapter = new SqlDataAdapter(comm);
```

```
        var dt = new DataTable();
        adapter.Fill(dt);

        return (dt.Rows);
    }
}
```

This function first creates a context connection string by using the *SqlConnectionStringBuilder* class. The connection string is passed to a *SqlConnection* object, which is used to invoke a *SqlCommand* that selects from the temporary table. After that, a *SqlDataAdapter* is used to fill a *DataTable* with the rows from the query. The same rows are returned as a collection, which naturally implements *IEnumerable*. Aside from the connection string, all of this is standard ADO.NET code, making it easy to migrate code into or out of SQL Server as necessary. The only other element worth noting is the *DataAccess* option specified in the *SqlFunction* attribute, which must be set in order to access data.

 Note The only choices available for the *DataAccess* are *None* (the default) and *ReadOnly*. This is a significant point; just like with T-SQL functions, SQLCLR functions cannot cause side effects. That is, they are designed to only read data, not alter it. If you would like to alter data, a stored procedure is the recommended approach.

You also need to create a "fill row" method, which follows:

```
public static void GetTempValues_fill(
    object o,
    out SqlInt32 col1,
    out SqlDouble col2)
{
    var dr = (DataRow)o;
    col1 = new SqlInt32((int)dr[0]);
    col2 = new SqlDouble((double)dr[1]);
}
```

This method casts the *object* parameter as a *DataRow*, which is what the *entry* method returned a collection of. The *DataRow* is known to contain two columns: the first typed as an integer, and the second typed as a double-precision floating point. These are assigned to their respective *out* parameters—which map the types specified in the *SqlFunction* attribute on the *entry* method—and that is a complete implementation.

Calling the function, after creating a temporary table of the correct shape, does exactly what you might expect—the rows flow through the CLR method and back to the caller:

```
CREATE TABLE #values
(col1 INT, col2 FLOAT);

INSERT #values VALUES
(1, 1.123),
(2, 2.234),
(3, 3.345);
```

```
SELECT
    *
FROM dbo.GetTempValues();

---

(3 row(s) affected)
col1        col2
----------- ----------------------
1           1.123
2           2.234
3           3.345

(3 row(s) affected)
```

Other data access—to remote servers, for example—is also possible, and that access uses the same style of ADO.NET code but requires elevated privileges. Any remote access requires that the assembly is cataloged using the EXTERNAL_ACCESS permission set. Naturally, there might also be network or database permissions issues, but those are beyond the scope of this book.

> **Important** The EXTERNAL_ACCESS and UNSAFE permission sets require either setting the database to a mode called TRUSTWORTHY or setting up a security scheme based on certificates. Both of these concepts go far beyond what can be covered here. Because these are important considerations, I highly recommended you take a look at the "Module Signing (Database Engine)" topic in SQL Server Books Online for thorough coverage. This is available at *http://technet.microsoft.com/en-us/library/ms345102%28v=sql.105%29.aspx*.

SQLCLR stored procedures and triggers

Compared to functions, stored procedures are much more flexible, but much less interface-driven, programmatic modules. Just like their T-SQL counterparts, SQLCLR stored procedures can have a large number of both input and output parameters, can return one or more table-valued results (or not), and can set a return value. And just like T-SQL stored procedures—but much different than T-SQL or SQLCLR functions—SQLCLR stored procedures can change their output behaviors dynamically, at run time. (Whether or not this is recommended is another topic entirely.)

Thanks to their extreme flexibility, stored procedures are the workhorses of the T-SQL world, usually by far the most common type of module in most databases. In the SQLCLR world, they are not nearly as ubiquitous thanks to the ease with which functions can be created. Nonetheless, they are handy tools and well worth understanding, especially given that unlike functions, they are designed to both read and modify data in the database.

In addition to stored procedures, this part of the chapter will also cover SQLCLR triggers. Just like in the T-SQL world, a SQLCLR trigger is nothing more than a special variant of a SQLCLR stored procedure. The coding style and patterns are almost identical.

Creating a SQLCLR stored procedure

As with the functions already discussed, SSDT includes a template for stored procedures that is available in the SQL CLR C# items list. Applying this template will create a C# program similar to that shown in Listing 9-2.

LISTING 9-2 Template for a SQLCLR stored procedure

```
public partial class StoredProcedures
{
    [Microsoft.SqlServer.Server.SqlProcedure]
    public static void SqlStoredProcedure1 ()
    {
        // Put your code here
    }
}
```

Much like a function, a SQLCLR stored procedure is a static method, usually inside of a class. A big difference is that because a stored procedure does not require an explicit output type (and, in fact, most never set a return value), the template defaults to void output—which will actually set a 0 when the stored procedure is called from T-SQL. If you want to set an explicit return value, any integer type can be used rather than the void shown in the listing.

This stored procedure is also, like a function created from the template, decorated with an attribute to help SSDT with deployment. Unlike the *SqlFunction* attribute, the procedure attribute has no options that are required for any more advanced purposes; the attribute's only use case is for SSDT.

Although there is no body to this stored procedure, it is still considered to be a complete implementation and can be both published and executed. Publication of a stored procedure is similar to publication of a function, in which a T-SQL stub is scripted to match the signature of the C# method. In the case of a stored procedure, only the parameter signature and return value (if any) must match; there is no output signature. Following is the script created by SSDT for *SqlStoredProcedure1*:

```
CREATE PROCEDURE [dbo].[SqlStoredProcedure1]
AS EXTERNAL NAME [t_sql_querying_project].[StoredProcedures].[SqlStoredProcedure1]
```

Once deployed, the procedure can be executed—although the results are not especially riveting:

```
EXEC SqlStoredProcedure1;

---

Command(s) completed successfully.
```

The procedure did nothing, but this should serve to illustrate the flexibility available to you as a programmer working with these types of modules. The body of the stored procedure can be populated with virtually any C# (or none at all), and it can do any action allowed by the permission set in which you have cataloged the assembly.

Most stored procedures will deal with data inside the host database, and for this, just like in a function, you can use standard ADO.NET via the context connection. Unlike a function, there is no *DataAccess* option in the attribute used to mark stored procedures; your stored procedure is free to insert, update, or delete data in any table that the calling context has access to.

For returning simple scalar values to the caller, a series of one or more output parameters can be added to a stored procedure, as in the following code block:

```
[Microsoft.SqlServer.Server.SqlProcedure]
public static void AddToInput(
    SqlInt32 input,
    out SqlInt32 inputPlusOne,
    out SqlInt32 inputPlusTwo)
{
    inputPlusOne = input + 1;
    inputPlusTwo = input + 2;
}
```

After this procedure is published, it can be executed just like a T-SQL stored procedure, using the OUTPUT clause to access the values returned in the output variables:

```
DECLARE @out1 INT, @out2 INT;

EXEC dbo.AddToInput
    @input = 123,
    @inputPlusOne = @out1 OUTPUT,
    @inputPlusTwo = @out2 OUTPUT;

SELECT @out1 AS out1, @out2 AS out2;

---

out1        out2
----------- -----------
124         125

(1 row(s) affected)
```

It is also common to return data from a stored procedure in the form of a table (or sometimes as a message). For that, you will need a slightly different set of tools.

The SQL pipe

ADO.NET, although great for reading data, has no obvious mechanism that can be exploited within a SQLCLR stored procedure to send data back to a caller. For this purpose, Microsoft introduced a class called *SqlPipe*, which gives developers the ability to create messages and return tabular results from within the body of a SQLCLR stored procedure.

The key method on the *SqlPipe* class is called *Send*, and it is overloaded to accept a *String*, *SqlDataRecord*, or *SqlDataReader*—each of which has a slightly different behavior. Sending a string, as in the following method, returns a message to the caller, similar to the following T-SQL PRINT statement.

```
[Microsoft.SqlServer.Server.SqlProcedure]
public static void SendMessage (SqlString message)
{
    var pipe = Microsoft.SqlServer.Server.SqlContext.Pipe;
    pipe.Send("The message is: " + message.Value);
}
```

Here a reference to a *SqlPipe* object was obtained via another class, *SqlContext*, which provides access to the *SqlPipe* via a static property. This class also provides access to a few other useful static properties that can help with tying your SQLCLR routines back to the calling context. These are covered later in this section.

When executed, the stored procedure sends a message but not a result set. In SQL Server Management Studio, this manifests as a message in the Messages pane, as shown in Figure 9-24.

FIGURE 9-24 Calling *SqlPipe.Send* with a string returns a message to the caller.

The other two overloads send back tabular results. If you would like to return a table of only a single row, a formatted *SqlDataRecord* can be passed to the send method. It is probably advisable, in most cases, to use output parameters instead whenever possible. If you have a reference to a *SqlDataReader*—for example, from reading data from a remote data source—that can also be passed directly to *Send* to return the data to SQL Server as a table.

The much more interesting variation of this theme is the ability to construct your own tabular result with an arbitrary number of rows, as might be derived from runtime calculations. To accomplish this, a trio of *SqlPipe* methods are required: *SendResultsStart*, *SendResultsRow*, and *SendResultsEnd*. Each of these serves a purpose, as illustrated in this method, which returns a sequence of integers:

```
[Microsoft.SqlServer.Server.SqlProcedure]
public static void SendRows(SqlInt32 numRows)
{
    //set up the output shape
    var col = new SqlMetaData("col", SqlDbType.Int);
    var rec = new SqlDataRecord(col);

    var pipe = Microsoft.SqlServer.Server.SqlContext.Pipe;

    //start the output stream -- this doesn't actually send anything
    pipe.SendResultsStart(rec);

    //send the rows
    for (int i = 1; i <= numRows.Value; i++)
```

```
    {
        //set field 0 (col) to the value
        r.SetInt32(0, i);
        pipe.SendResultsRow(rec);
    }

    pipe.SendResultsEnd();
}
```

Starting at the top of the method, the first task is to describe the output shape by creating one instance of *SqlMetaData* per output column—in this case, a single integer called *"col"*. This column is passed to the *SqlDataRecord* constructor, creating a record that will be used throughout the remainder of the method.

From there, a reference is obtained to the *SqlPipe*, and *SendResultsStart* is called for the record. This call does not actually send the record; rather, it sets up the output stream for the tabular shape that the record defines. To actually send back some rows, a local variable is initialized and looped based on how many rows were requested. For each row, its value is set on the appropriate *SqlDataRecord* column (0, in this case), and the row is returned using the *SendResultsRow* method. Finally, the stream is terminated using *SendResultsEnd*.

The result, once published, looks like this:

```
EXEC dbo.SendRows
    @numRows = 3;


---


col
-----------
1
2
3


(3 row(s) affected)
```

Using this pattern allows for a large amount of flexibility when it comes to sending data back from a CLR stored procedure. Neither the number of rows, nor the output shape, are fixed or predetermined in any way. That said, it is generally a good idea to try to fix and document expected results from stored procedures to make it easier to write solid data-access code.

CLR exceptions and T-SQL exception handling

As mentioned previously, one of the key benefits of CLR integration is the flexibility it brings to the world of SQL Server development. Most types of CLR routines can be used, when needed, as seamless replacements for existing T-SQL routines. This allows developers to fix problems without creating any downstream consequences or even needing to tell users that something has changed.

One area in which this breaks down a bit is when dealing with exceptions. Users are accustomed to seeing T-SQL exceptions that look and feel a certain way, and CLR exceptions simply don't meet the same standard. Consider the following stored procedure.

```
[Microsoft.SqlServer.Server.SqlProcedure]
public static void DivideByZero ()
{
    int i = 1;
    int j = 0;
    int k = i / j;
}
```

When compared with a standard T-SQL divide-by-zero exception, the .NET counterpart is wordy and confusing to users who aren't used to looking at stack traces:

```
SELECT 1/0;
GO
```

```
Msg 8134, Level 16, State 1, Line 1
Divide by zero error encountered.
```

```
EXEC dbo.DivideByZero;
GO
```

```
Msg 6522, Level 16, State 1, Procedure DivideByZero, Line 2
A .NET Framework error occurred during execution of user-defined routine or aggregate
"DivideByZero":
System.DivideByZeroException: Attempted to divide by zero.
System.DivideByZeroException:
   at StoredProcedures.DivideByZero()
```

.

If you're dealing with SQLCLR user-defined functions or methods on SQLCLR user-defined types (covered later in this chapter), your options are quite limited. But for SQLCLR stored procedures, there are ways to emulate T-SQL-style exceptions—albeit with some consequences.

The key to producing nicer looking exceptions from SQLCLR stored procedures is to leverage yet another method of the *SqlPipe* class: *ExecuteAndSend*. This method takes as its input a T-SQL statement (in the form of a .NET *SqlCommand* object), which is routed to the calling context and called there, with the results sent to the client—just as though an application had directly invoked the statement. In the following stored procedure, *ExecuteAndSend* is used to invoke a SELECT:

```
[Microsoft.SqlServer.Server.SqlProcedure]
public static void ExecuteASelect()
{
    var pipe = Microsoft.SqlServer.Server.SqlContext.Pipe;
    var comm = new SqlCommand("SELECT 'this is the result' AS theResult");
    pipe.ExecuteAndSend(comm);
}
```

After publication, the stored procedure is run and the results are returned directly, as though the caller executed the query directly from SSMS:

```
EXEC dbo.ExecuteASelect;
GO

---

theResult
-----------------
this is the result

(1 row(s) affected)
```

This method is of limited utility except when writing dynamic SQL within a SQLCLR stored procedure, but it can be useful for creating custom errors in your stored procedures that feel a bit more like T-SQL errors than .NET errors.

An initial attempt at using *ExecuteAndSend* can be to simply send back a RAISERROR call, as needed:

```
[Microsoft.SqlServer.Server.SqlProcedure]
public static void ThrowAnException_v1()
{
    var pipe = Microsoft.SqlServer.Server.SqlContext.Pipe;
    var comm = new SqlCommand("RAISERROR('test exception', 16, 1)");
    pipe.ExecuteAndSend(comm);
}
```

This code causes RAISERROR to execute, and the results (the exception) are immediately sent to the calling application. Unfortunately, a nasty side effect occurs; as soon as the exception is thrown, control returns to the .NET method and *ExecuteAndSend* reports that it encountered an exception. Now a second exception is thrown, this time from .NET. The result is even uglier than the normal state of affairs:

```
EXEC dbo.ThrowAnException_v1;

---

Msg 50000, Level 16, State 1, Line 16
test exception
Msg 6522, Level 16, State 1, Procedure ThrowAnException_v1, Line 15
A .NET Framework error occurred during execution of user-defined routine or aggregate
"ThrowAnException_v1":
System.Data.SqlClient.SqlException: test exception
System.Data.SqlClient.SqlException:
   at System.Data.SqlClient.SqlConnection.OnError(SqlException exception, Boolean
   breakConnection,
Action`1 wrapCloseInAction)
   at System.Data.SqlClient.SqlCommand.RunExecuteNonQuerySmi(Boolean sendToPipe)
   at System.Data.SqlClient.SqlCommand.InternalExecuteNonQuery(TaskCompletionSource`1
   completion,
String methodName, Boolean sendToPipe, Int32 timeout, Boolean asyncWrite)
   at System.Data.SqlClient.SqlCommand.ExecuteToPipe(SmiContext pipeContext)
   at Microsoft.SqlServer.Server.SqlPipe.ExecuteAndSend(SqlCommand command)
   at StoredProcedures.ThrowAnException_v1()
.
```

The solution? Notice that the nicely formatted (that is, T-SQL-style) exception is returned to the client prior to the .NET exception. So getting only the nicely formatted exception means stopping the .NET exception—and that means using *try-catch*:

```
[Microsoft.SqlServer.Server.SqlProcedure]
public static void ThrowAnException_v2()
{
    var pipe = Microsoft.SqlServer.Server.SqlContext.Pipe;
    var comm = new SqlCommand("RAISERROR('test exception', 16, 1)");

    try
    {
        pipe.ExecuteAndSend(comm);
    }
    catch
    { }
}
```

Because the *ExecuteAndSend* call is expected to cause an exception, there is no reason to handle anything in the *catch* block; it can simply return control. The result of this addition is that the caller sees only the simple T-SQL-style error message:

```
EXEC dbo.ThrowAnException_v2;

---

Msg 50000, Level 16, State 1, Line 16
test exception
```

Taking this technique one step further, it can be applied to unknown and unexpected exceptions by using nested *try-catch* blocks:

```
[Microsoft.SqlServer.Server.SqlProcedure]
public static void DivideByZero_Nicer()
{
    try
    {
        int i = 1;
        int j = 0;
        int k = i / j;
    }
    catch (Exception e)
    {
        var pipe = Microsoft.SqlServer.Server.SqlContext.Pipe;
        var tsqlThrow = String.Format("RAISERROR('{0}', 16, 1)", e.Message);
        var comm = new SqlCommand(tsqlThrow);

        try
        {
            pipe.ExecuteAndSend(comm);
        }
        catch
        { }
    }
}
```

Here the potentially exception-prone code—the math—is wrapped in an outer *try* block. Inside the *catch* block, the error message from the outer block is stripped (using the *Message* property of the *System.Exception* object), and a RAISERROR call is formatted. The result is a nicely formatted message even for a noncustom exception:

```
EXEC dbo.DivideByZero_Nicer;

---

Msg 50000, Level 16, State 1, Line 15
Attempted to divide by zero.
```

Although this technique does make for a better user experience when nondevelopers are involved, there are two important tradeoffs. First of all, the element of the standard .NET exceptions that many less-technical users find to be confusing is the stack trace. This information, for someone who does know how to read it, is invaluable for debugging purposes. So it might be a good idea to use preprocessor directives in your C# code to ensure that the well-formatted exceptions are only used in release builds, and never in debug builds.

The second tradeoff is a bit more subtle, and also somewhat shocking:

```
BEGIN TRY
    EXEC dbo.DivideByZero_Nicer;
END TRY
BEGIN CATCH
    SELECT 'you will never see this';
END CATCH;

---

Msg 50000, Level 16, State 1, Line 14
Attempted to divide by zero.
```

Here the stored procedure call was wrapped in TRY-CATCH on the T-SQL side and an exception was thrown, yet the CATCH block was completely ignored. The reason is that this exception was already caught—in the .NET code.

There is, alas, no great solution for this particular tradeoff. Note that the @@ERROR function will return a nonzero value if checked immediately after the invocation of the stored procedure, but TRY-CATCH was added to T-SQL to eliminate the various pains and annoyances associated with checking @@ERROR. So the fact that it works here doesn't provide much satisfaction. In the end, the best ideas are either to use this technique only when outer exception handling is not required or to educate users how to read stack traces.

> **Note** The examples in this section used RAISERROR rather than the newer T-SQL THROW statement. This was done purposefully, because THROW does not seem to interact well with the SQLCLR exception-handling mechanisms, and it causes two exceptions to be thrown either with or without the C# *try-catch* blocks.

Identity and impersonation

As you work with SQLCLR routines, you might hit upon cases where your method will have to reach outside of SQL Server to a remote resource. In this case—especially when dealing with file-level and other network permissions—it can be important to know under whose security credentials the request is being made.

By default, SQL Server will use the credentials of its service account when making outbound requests. However, if your users are connecting via Integrated Authentication, you might want to use their credentials instead—and, therefore, their access rights. This is accomplished by leveraging the *WindowsIdentity* object that is available from the *SqlContext* class. This object represents—when Integrated Authentication is being used—the identity of the caller (that is, the login used to authenticate to SQL Server). And the *WindowsIdentity* class implements an *Impersonate* method, which makes your SQLCLR code act on behalf of the caller's credentials.

Setting this up in a SQLCLR stored procedure is simple:

```
[Microsoft.SqlServer.Server.SqlProcedure]
public static void Impersonation ()
{
    var pipe = Microsoft.SqlServer.Server.SqlContext.Pipe;
    var ident = Microsoft.SqlServer.Server.SqlContext.WindowsIdentity;

    //if the user logged in with SQL authentication the object will be NULL
    if (ident == null)
    {
        pipe.Send("Could not impersonate");
    }
    else
    {
        //otherwise, try to impersonate
        using (var context = ident.Impersonate())
        {
            pipe.Send(String.Format("Successfully impersonated as: {0}", ident.Name));
        }
    }
}
```

This stored procedure attempts to impersonate only if the *WindowsIdentity* object is not null. This is a good check to put in place, because the property is not set on the *SqlContext* class when the caller has logged in using SQL authentication. If your code expects a valid security context—other than that of the SQL Server service account—such a check will make sure that everything is in order.

Once the presence of a valid object is confirmed, the code calls the *Impersonate* method of the *WindowsIdentity* class, which does the actual impersonation. This method returns an instance of a class called *WindowsImpersonationContext*, which is primarily used to revert the impersonation via a method called *Undo*. The class also implements *IDisposable*, so in this stored procedure *Impersonate* is invoked in a *using* block, which automatically calls the *Dispose* method after executing. You should take care to ensure that your impersonation code always calls either the *Undo* or *Dispose* method once the code is finished using the network resource for which you have impersonated. This keeps things as secure as possible.

SQLCLR triggers

Triggers—in either T-SQL or SQLCLR—are effectively stored procedures bound to table DML actions, with access to the special *inserted* and *deleted* virtual tables. There are also DDL triggers, which are stored procedures bound to DDL operations. Beyond what has already been discussed regarding stored procedures, there is not much to say about SQLCLR triggers; they offer the same features and functionality as stored procedures. The SSDT template for a SQLCLR trigger is shown in Listing 9-3.

LISTING 9-3 Generic template for a SQLCLR trigger

```
public partial class Triggers
{
    // Enter existing table or view for the target and uncomment the attribute line
    // [Microsoft.SqlServer.Server.SqlTrigger (Name="SqlTrigger1", Target="Table1",
       Event="FOR UPDATE")]
    public static void SqlTrigger1 ()
    {
        // Replace with your own code
        SqlContext.Pipe.Send("Trigger FIRED");
    }
}
```

Like stored procedures, the *SqlContext* class is available with a *SqlPipe* object that can be used to send messages or table-valued results back to the calling context. A SQLCLR trigger, unlike a stored procedure, is always void valued and does not support either input or output parameters; there is no syntax in T-SQL to input arguments or collect return values from a trigger.

SQLCLR triggers use an attribute called *SqlTrigger*, which specifies a target table as well as one or more events for which to fire. The attribute is commented out in the SSDT template so that the code will compile and pass the SSDT validation rules. To get things working, you will have to add your table to the SSDT project. For the sake of this section, the table's DDL is

```
CREATE TABLE [dbo].[MyTable]
(
    [i] INT NOT NULL PRIMARY KEY
);
```

Once the table has been added to the project, creating a functional SQLCLR trigger is a simple exercise:

```
[Microsoft.SqlServer.Server.SqlTrigger (
    Name="SqlTrigger1", Target="MyTable", Event="FOR INSERT, UPDATE")]
public static void SqlTrigger1 ()
{
    var build = new SqlConnectionStringBuilder();
    build.ContextConnection = true;
```

```
    using (var conn = new SqlConnection(build.ConnectionString))
    {
        var comm = conn.CreateCommand();
        comm.CommandText = "SELECT COUNT(*) FROM inserted";

        conn.Open();

        int rowCount = (int)(comm.ExecuteScalar());

        SqlContext.Pipe.Send(String.Format("Rows affected: {0}", rowCount));
    }
}
```

This trigger fires after rows are either inserted or updated in *MyTable*. To get access to the inserted or deleted virtual tables, a query needs to be run, and just like in a stored procedure this is done by using ADO.NET in conjunction with the context connection. Here the trigger counts the rows in the inserted virtual table, returning a message with the count:

```
INSERT MyTable
VALUES (123), (456);
GO

---

Rows affected: 2

(2 row(s) affected)
```

The *SqlContext* class has a property called *TriggerContext*, which returns an instance of a class called *SqlTriggerContext*. This class has some useful properties and methods for various cases:

- The *TriggerAction* property identifies which action caused the trigger to fire, without having to query the inserted and deleted tables to make that determination, as you would in T-SQL.

- The *IsUpdatedColumn* method allows you to identify whether or not a certain column was updated in the action that caused the trigger to fire.

- The *EventData* property is quite possibly the most useful, because it returns the event data XML for a DDL action formatted as a *SqlXml* object. This class can expose the data via an *XmlReader*, which makes processing both easier and faster than in T-SQL.

The primary use cases for SQLCLR triggers include advanced logging and data transmission. Unfortunately, because each SQLCLR trigger must specify a specific table in the *SqlTrigger* attribute, a new method must be created for every targeted table. This means that it is difficult to create generic triggers (for example, for logging), and the potential for reuse is lower than it could be. It is therefore often a better idea, if you require .NET functionality in a trigger, to call either SQLCLR stored procedures or user-defined functions, as required, from a T-SQL trigger.

SQLCLR user-defined types

Of the various types of SQLCLR modules that are available, user-defined types and user-defined aggregates are the two that provide the most functionality not available within T-SQL. User-defined types allow a developer to create a complex data type that can include static or instance methods, properties, data-validation logic, or all of these things. This functionality has been successfully used by Microsoft to implement the T-SQL *HIERARCHYID*, *GEOGRAPHY*, and *GEOMETRY* data types, although you should be aware that these types are integrated into the query-optimization process. User types will not have quite as much flexibility, but they still have a lot of potential.

Creating a user-defined type

Much like functions and stored procedures, user-defined types can be created using SSDT. Listing 9-4 shows the template for a SQLCLR user-defined type.

LISTING 9-4 Generic template for a user-defined type

```
[Serializable]
[Microsoft.SqlServer.Server.SqlUserDefinedType(Format.Native)]
public struct SqlUserDefinedType1: INullable
{
    public override string ToString()
    {
        // Replace with your own code
        return string.Empty;
    }

    public bool IsNull
    {
        get
        {
            // Put your code here
            return _null;
        }
    }

    public static SqlUserDefinedType1 Null
    {
        get
        {
            SqlUserDefinedType1 h = new SqlUserDefinedType1();
            h._null = true;
            return h;
        }
    }
}
```

```
public static SqlUserDefinedType1 Parse(SqlString s)
{
    if (s.IsNull)
        return Null;
    SqlUserDefinedType1 u = new SqlUserDefinedType1();
    // Put your code here
    return u;
}

// This is a place-holder method
public string Method1()
{
    // Put your code here
    return string.Empty;
}

// This is a place-holder static method
public static SqlString Method2()
{
    // Put your code here
    return new SqlString("");
}

// This is a place-holder member field
public int _var1;

//  Private member
private bool _null;
}
```

SQLCLR user-defined types can be either structs or classes. They must implement the *INullable* interface, which includes the *IsNull* property. Unlike stored procedures and functions, user-defined types must be decorated with the appropriate attributes: both *SqlUserDefinedType*, which controls various behaviors of the type, and *Serializable*, which allows SQL Server to store an instance of the type in a binary format.

User-defined types have a few required methods and properties outside those defined by *INullable* (these methods and properties are verified during deployment):

- *Null* is a static property that must return a null instance of the type. Nullability is implemented in the template using a Boolean member, *_null*, and it is generally not worthwhile to modify the template's logic of either the *Null* or *IsNull* properties.

- *Parse* is a static method that creates an instance of the type from a string. This method is overridden via T-SQL so that the type can be initialized by using syntax like *DECLARE @t dbo.YourType = 'value'*.

- *ToString* is an instance-level method that is effectively the opposite of *Parse*; its job is to output a string representing the instance of the type. Ideally, *ToString* and *Parse* should be fully compatible with one another; any string output by *ToString* should be able to be turned into a new instance of the type via a call to *Parse*.

Deploying and using a user-defined type

Publication via SSDT is the same for user-defined types as it is for other SQLCLR routines. The assembly in which the type has been defined is pushed into the target database, after which a stub T-SQL CREATE is used to map and expose the type for use within your scripts.

Prior to publishing, a few modifications can be made to the base template to provide some basic functionality:

```
[Serializable]
[Microsoft.SqlServer.Server.SqlUserDefinedType(Format.Native)]
public struct SqlUserDefinedType1: INullable
{
    public override string ToString()
    {
        return _var1.ToString();
    }

    public bool IsNull
    {
        get
        {
            // Put your code here
            return _null;
        }
    }

    public static SqlUserDefinedType1 Null
    {
        get
        {
            SqlUserDefinedType1 h = new SqlUserDefinedType1();
            h._null = true;
            return h;
        }
    }

    public static SqlUserDefinedType1 Parse(SqlString s)
    {
        if (s.IsNull)
            return Null;
        SqlUserDefinedType1 u = new SqlUserDefinedType1();
        u._var1 = Convert.ToInt32(s.Value);
        return u;
    }

    private int _var1;
    private bool _null;
}
```

The type now implements a basic container to store an integer. *Parse* casts the input string as an integer and stores it in *_var1*, and *ToString* reverses the operation. It is not a useful type, to be sure, but it has enough functionality to illustrate the basic behaviors of a user-defined type.

Publication from SSDT produces the following T-SQL stub:

```
CREATE TYPE [dbo].[SqlUserDefinedType1]
    EXTERNAL NAME [t_sql_querying_project].[SqlUserDefinedType1];
```

Once published, the type can be instantiated much like any other type:

```
DECLARE @t dbo.SqlUserDefinedType1 = '123';
GO
```

There are two important things to note in this example. First of all, notice that the type is schema qualified; it is referenced as part of the *dbo* schema. Types are bound not directly to the database, but rather to schemas within a database. Unfortunately, SSDT cannot create a type in any schema except *dbo*. Putting a type into a different schema will require a post-deployment step. The second thing to notice is that although this type deals only with an integer, the value must be specified as a string when initializing an instance of the type.

Naturally, once the type has been defined, it can be used in virtually any way that a built-in type can be used. It can be passed to a stored procedure or function, stored in a table, or used in a query. One caveat is that because types are stored in individual databases, stored procedures and functions in other databases are not able to reference them.

The first time you use a user-defined type in a query, you might be a bit surprised by what happens:

```
DECLARE @t dbo.SqlUserDefinedType1 = '123';

SELECT @t AS typeValue;
GO

---

typeValue
------------
0x8000007B00

(1 row(s) affected)
```

Rather than returning the integer value 123 formatted as a string, as might be expected, this query returned a binary string. This string is the binary-formatted representation of the type, which is used internally by SQL Server to store and rehydrate instances of the type as needed. Each time a new instance of a given type is created, it is binary formatted and kept in that form for most of its life cycle. Only when instance methods or properties on the type are called is the binary converted back into an in-memory instance of the type.

The binary in this case was automatically generated by SQL Server, as was specified at type creation time in the *SqlUserDefinedType* attribute: the format for the type is *Native*, which means that SQL Server will automatically discover and encode the various member variables. *Native* formatting is available only if all the member variables are simple value types (for example, integers). Reference types such as strings and collections require a more involved user-defined process.

To actually get back the string representation of the type, you must explicitly call the *ToString* method to do the conversion work. This is done as follows:

```
DECLARE @t dbo.SqlUserDefinedType1 = '123';

SELECT @t.ToString() AS typeValue;
GO

---

typeValue
-----------
123

(1 row(s) affected)
```

> **Important** Method and property names on SQLCLR user-defined types are case sensitive. Failing to use the proper casing will result in a confusing "could not find method" error.

Working with more complex types

As a developer working with user-defined types, you will not get especially far without requiring more advanced functionality in the form of either reference types or difficult parsing scenarios. Strings, collections, and classes are used throughout the .NET BCL and most other libraries, and because these types are not compatible with *Native* formatting, a second and more advanced option is exposed. Furthermore, the *Parse* method might not be the best choice for every scenario.

To illustrate the kind of type that might need different techniques, consider addresses as stored in a database. It is common to see these modeled—at least for the United States—as one column for city, one for state, one for postal code, and a column or two for address lines. An example of an address line is "546 W. Contoso St." This address line, although usually treated as a single scalar value, actually has various constituent parts. US addresses are composed of some combination of the following:

- A building number, which might or might not include non-numeric characters—for example, 546 or 546B.

- A pre-directional for the street, such as the "W." in "W. Contoso." Not all streets use these, so they are optional when defining the parts of an address line.

- The name of the street.

- The type of the street, which might be "street," "way," "boulevard," and so on. These are generally abbreviated.

- A post-directional, which like the pre-directional is not used for all streets. An example is "Contoso ST SW."

Imagine you want to develop a database and store address lines in the usual way—as columns in addition to *city*, *state*, and *postal code*—but you also want to both validate and extract the constituent parts for certain reporting requirements. In this case, a user-defined type might be an ideal choice.

This type—which will be named *USAddressLine*—will have to store five different strings, one for each part defined in the preceding list. This will require the following five member variables:

```
private SqlString _buildingNumber;
private SqlString _streetName;
private SqlString _streetType;
private SqlString _preDirectional;
private SqlString _postDirectional;
```

The type is intended for verification, so each of these members is defined as private, with a public *getter/setter* property. The building number, street name, and street type are not optional and can be verified to be both non-null and not composed entirely of white space. This can be done using the following helper method:

```
private SqlString validateNull(SqlString input)
{
    if (input.IsNull ||
        input.Value.Trim() == "")
        throw new Exception("Attempted to use NULL or an empty string in a non-nullable field");

    return (input);
}
```

Aside from being non-null, the street type can also be verified as a correct and supported type of street. For this purpose, the following method is used:

```
private SqlString validateType(SqlString type)
{
    if (!(
        type == "ST" ||
        type == "LN" ||
        type == "RD" ||
        type == "WAY" ||
        type == "BLVD" ||
        type == "HWY"))
        throw new ArgumentException(String.Format("Invalid type: {0}", type.Value));

    return (type);
}
```

The final validation method required is for the pre-directional and post-directional values:

```
private SqlString validateDirection(SqlString direction)
{
    if (!(
        direction.IsNull ||
        direction == "N" ||
        direction == "NE" ||
        direction == "NW" ||
        direction == "E" ||
        direction == "S" ||
        direction == "SE" ||
        direction == "SW" ||
        direction == "W"))
        throw new ArgumentException(String.Format("Invalid direction: {0}", direction.Value));

    return (direction);
}
```

Once each of these methods is defined, public accessor properties can be created as follows:

```
public SqlString BuildingNumber
{
    get { return (_buildingNumber); }
    set { _buildingNumber = validateNull(value); }
}

public SqlString StreetName
{
    get { return (_streetName); }
    set { _streetName = validateNull(value); }
}

public SqlString StreetType
{
    get { return (_streetType); }
    set { _streetType = validateType(validateNull(value)); }
}

public SqlString PreDirectional
{
    get { return (_preDirectional); }
    set { _preDirectional = validateDirection(value); }
}

public SqlString PostDirectional
{
    get { return (_postDirectional); }
    set { _postDirectional = validateDirection(value); }
}
```

As long as these methods are used for both public and internal manipulation of the values, verification will be built-in and guaranteed.

Generally, the first task after defining member variables is to implement a *Parse* routine, but in this case it is a fairly difficult task. Figuring out which parts are and are not present—especially when dealing with street names with two, three, or four words—can be an arduous task. Rather than attempting this, you can use the simpler option of disabling the *Parse* method altogether by marking it as not implemented and, instead, introducing one or more static *factory* methods that return a fully-formed instance of the type.

Parse is disabled using the .NET convention of throwing a *NotImplementedException*:

```
public static USAddressLine Parse(SqlString s)
{
    throw new NotImplementedException("Parse not supported.");
}
```

The method is still required by the user-defined type specifications, but once this code is in place a run-time exception will be thrown whenever someone tries to initialize the type using a string. Instead of doing that, the user can use one of the factory methods:

```
public static USAddressLine StandardLine(
    SqlString BuildingNumber,
    SqlString StreetName,
    SqlString StreetType)
{
    var addressLine = new USAddressLine();

    addressLine.BuildingNumber = BuildingNumber;
    addressLine.StreetName = StreetName;
    addressLine.StreetType = StreetType;

    return (addressLine);
}

public static USAddressLine PreDirectionalLine(
    SqlString BuildingNumber,
    SqlString PreDirectional,
    SqlString StreetName,
    SqlString StreetType)
{
    var addressLine = StandardLine(
        BuildingNumber,
        StreetName,
        StreetType);

    addressLine.PreDirectional = PreDirectional;

    return (addressLine);
}
```

It is common to have address lines without any kind of directional, so implementation of the *StandardLine* method returns an address based only on a building number, street name, and street type. The public accessors are used, so everything is verified. It is also common to see an address line that includes a pre-directional, so a second method has been implemented to handle that case. Because post-directionals are not especially common, no explicit method has been created; the user would have to call one of these two methods first, and then set the post-directional property separately. Note that two methods are required, because inheritance is not supported for public SQLCLR methods, properties, or types.

Using these factory methods requires a special referencing syntax that applies only to static methods. The following example instantiates the type using a factory method and then sets the post-directional value using the SET keyword:

```
DECLARE @t dbo.USAddressLine =
    dbo.USAddressLine::StandardLine('123', 'Contoso', 'ST');

SET @t.PostDirectional = 'SW';
GO
```

Prior to the type actually being able to function on this level, it needs to be able to be binary serialized. Because it internally uses reference types, several options will have to be set on the *SqlUserDefinedType* attribute:

```
[Microsoft.SqlServer.Server.SqlUserDefinedType(
    Format.UserDefined,
    MaxByteSize = 82,
    IsFixedLength = false,
    IsByteOrdered = true)]
```

The format is set to *UserDefined*, which will require an explicit binary-formatting implementation. As part of this implementation, a developer must define the maximum size the type's binary might reach, in bytes, from 1 to 8,000, or –1 for up to 2 GB. In this case, 82 is used, based on the following assumptions (keeping in mind that all strings in .NET are Unicode and consume two bytes):

- Building numbers will be at most eight characters.

- Pre-directionals will be at most two characters.

- Street names will be at most 25 characters.

- Street types will be at most four characters.

- Post-directionals will be at most two characters.

The type is not a fixed length; in other words, the binary format will have a different length depending on various instances of the types and the values of the various parts of the address line. And the type is to be considered byte ordered.

This last option is, perhaps, not especially useful on the *USAddressLine* type, but it is key for many others. *Byte ordered* means that instances of the type can be compared to one another using a greater-than or less-than operation, by comparing the types' binary formats. If this property is set to *true*, a type can participate—for example, as a key in indexes or as an ORDER BY column. However, you must be careful to implement the binary format so that instances are actually properly compared, lest you introduce subtle bugs into your data.

To do the actual binary-formatting work, the type must implement an interface called *IBinarySerialize*:

```
public struct USAddressLine : INullable, IBinarySerialize
```

This interface specifies two methods, *Read* and *Write*. *Write* outputs a binary representation of the type, while *Read* reconstitutes the type from binary. Following is the *Write* method for the *USAddressLine* type:

```
public void Write(System.IO.BinaryWriter w)
{
    w.Write(_null);

    if (!_null)
    {
        w.Write(BuildingNumber.Value);

        if (!PreDirectional.IsNull)
            w.Write(PreDirectional.Value);
        else
            //represent NULL as an empty string
            w.Write("");

        w.Write(StreetName.Value);
        w.Write(StreetType.Value);

        if (!PostDirectional.IsNull)
            w.Write(PostDirectional.Value);
        else
            w.Write("");
    }
}
```

This method first writes the value of the _null member, which controls whether or not the instance is null. If it is not null, processing continues. The building number is written first, followed by the pre-directional. Each *Write* call must have a corresponding *Read* call. So, even if one of the values is null, something must be written—in this case, an empty string. The street name and street type are also written, followed by a similar null check against the post-directional. It is because everything is written in a specific order that this type can call itself "byte ordered," whether or not that is useful in practice.

Read follows the same patterns as *Write*:

```
public void Read(System.IO.BinaryReader r)
{
    _null = r.ReadBoolean();

    if (!_null)
    {
        BuildingNumber = new SqlString(r.ReadString());

        var preDir = r.ReadString();
        if (preDir != "")
            PreDirectional = new SqlString(preDir);

        StreetName = r.ReadString();
        StreetType = r.ReadString();
```

```
        var postDir = r.ReadString();
        if (postDir != "")
            PostDirectional = new SqlString(postDir);
    }
}
```

Unlike *Write*, which reads from the member variables, *Read* writes them back. The *null* property is checked first, and that is followed by the building number, a check against the pre-directional, and so on—in exactly the same order as the values were written.

The final implementation prior to trying out the type is the *ToString* method. Although, as mentioned earlier, you ideally want to have *ToString* and *Parse* methods that are compatible with one another, that is not possible here. *ToString* is, however, quite simple to put together:

```
public override string ToString()
{
    return (
        BuildingNumber.Value + " " +
        (PreDirectional.IsNull ? "" : PreDirectional.Value + " ") +
        StreetName.Value + " " +
        StreetType.Value +
        (PostDirectional.IsNull ? "" : " " + PostDirectional.Value));
}
```

This method concatenates all the strings to produce the kind of text you normally find in an AddressLine column of a database.

After putting everything together and publishing, the type can be used:

```
DECLARE @t dbo.USAddressLine =
    dbo.USAddressLine::StandardLine('123', 'Contoso', 'ST');
SET @t.PostDirectional = 'SW';

SELECT
    @t.ToString() AS AddressLine,
    @t.BuildingNumber AS BuildingNumber,
    @t.StreetName AS StreetName,
    @t.StreetType AS StreetType;
GO

---

AddressLine         BuildingNumber  StreetName   StreetType
------------------- --------------- -----------  -----------
123 Contoso ST SW   123             Contoso      ST

(1 row(s) affected)
```

Once fully implemented, the type exposes the base data either as a string or as one of the constituent parts. The type implements built-in validation and can also implement other behaviors. (For example, it could internally tie into a geocoding engine.) Although more conservative practitioners might consider this to be a bad idea, this kind of design can add a lot of flexibility and functionality within the database.

SQLCLR user-defined aggregates

User-defined aggregates, like user-defined types, represent functionality available via SQLCLR that has no similarity to anything available in T-SQL. Although SQL Server ships with various aggregates—COUNT, SUM, AVG, and so on—the ability to write your own is powerful and creates an extreme amount of programmatic flexibility for complex development scenarios.

Creating a user-defined aggregate

User-defined aggregates are similar to user-defined types, with almost the same programming patterns and caveats. They are either structs or classes and must be binary formatted at various stages. The SSDT template for aggregates is shown in Listing 9-5.

LISTING 9-5 Generic template for a user-defined aggregate

```
[Serializable]
[Microsoft.SqlServer.Server.SqlUserDefinedAggregate(Format.Native)]
public struct SqlAggregate1
{
    public void Init()
    {
        // Put your code here
    }

    public void Accumulate(SqlString Value)
    {
        // Put your code here
    }

    public void Merge (SqlAggregate1 Group)
    {
        // Put your code here
    }

    public SqlString Terminate ()
    {
        // Put your code here
        return new SqlString (string.Empty);
    }

    // This is a place-holder member field
    public int _var1;
}
```

User-defined aggregates must implement each of four mandatory methods, which align with the life cycle of the type:

- When aggregation is about to begin, one instance of the type is instantiated for each group of rows (as determined by the GROUP BY clause or other factors, depending on the query plan) and *Init* is called. The job of *Init* is to initialize any member variables to a correct starting state. This step is most important for aggregates that internally use collection classes.

- For each row containing data to be aggregated, SQL Server calls the *Accumulate* method. This method consumes the data and adds it to the internal variables that are used to track the aggregation. The default input type is *SqlString*, but *Accumulate* can accept multiple parameters of any convertible SQL Server type. (As with functions and procedures, *SqlTypes* are usually recommended.)

- If two or more row groups are aggregated on separate threads in a parallel plan but all the aggregation belongs together in a single group, the partially aggregated data will be brought together by one or more calls to the *Merge* method. This method's job is to consume the other group's aggregated data and combine it with any locally aggregated data.

- Once all aggregation is finished, an aggregate must produce a scalar result. This is the job of the *Terminate* method.

Instances of a user-defined aggregate will be binary serialized at various points during processing, and the binary will be temporarily stored in tempdb. This is done primarily to reduce memory pressure in cases where many row groups, concurrent large aggregations, or both are running on a given server. Because of this, user-defined aggregates must be serializable and can implement either *Native* serialization—if only value types are used internally—or *UserDefined* serialization.

Once implemented and published, a user-defined aggregate can be used just like a built-in aggregate, in conjunction with a GROUP BY clause or partitioned (but not ordered) using the OVER clause. Note that, as with user-defined types, aggregates are bound to a schema; but unlike with types, a schema reference is required in all cases when using an aggregate.

The concatenate aggregate

A common request from SQL Server developers is a built-in aggregate that enables you to create comma-separated strings from strings stored in rows in the database. Although you can accomplish this task in a number of ways in T-SQL, most of your options for doing this are rather clunky as compared to the standard SQL aggregation and GROUP BY syntax. Implementing such an aggregate in C# is almost trivial, and a good example of the kind of thing that can be done using user-defined aggregates.

To begin with, the aggregate will need a place to store strings during accumulation. Although it could simply use an internal string and append to it each time a new row is accumulated, this approach is computationally expensive. Strings in .NET are immutable (unchangeable) once created, and modifying an existing string actually internally creates a new string. It's better to use a collection class:

```
private System.Collections.Generic.List<string> stringList;

public void Init()
{
    stringList = new System.Collections.Generic.List<string>();
}
```

Here the code is shown using the *List* generic collection class, typed for a collection of strings. Also shown is the implementation of the *Init* method, which simply instantiates the *stringList* local variable so that it will be ready for rows. Once this is done, *Accumulate* can be implemented:

```
public void Accumulate(SqlString Value)
{
    if (!(Value.IsNull))
        //prepend a comma on each string
        stringList.Add("," + Value.Value);
}
```

This method accepts a *SqlString*, and first does a null check; if a null is passed in, it will simply be ignored. If the input is non-null, a comma will be prepended. Later, when producing the final output string, the comma that prepends the first string in the list will be removed so that there are no extra commas.

Next is the *Merge* method:

```
public void Merge (Concatenate Group)
{
    foreach (string s in Group.stringList)
        this.stringList.Add(s);
}
```

Merge, when called, reads the values from the other aggregate's *stringList*, adding them to the local *stringList*. This is effectively the same as calling *Accumulate* one value at a time, and for more complex aggregates, an internal call to the *Accumulate* method itself might be a good idea. Once the values have been merged, the other aggregate will be disposed of, so there is no need to worry about removing it or its values from memory.

The final core method to implement is *Terminate*:

```
public SqlString Terminate ()
{
    if (stringList.Count == 0)
        return SqlString.Null;
    else
    {
        //remove the comma on the first string
        stringList[0] = stringList[0].Substring(1, stringList[0].Length - 1);
        return new SqlString(string.Concat(stringList.ToArray()));
    }
}
```

If *Init* was called but no non-null values were encountered, the internal collection will have zero elements and the aggregate can return a null to the caller. If, on the other hand, there is some data present, any prepending comma should be removed—this is done by taking a substring of the first element in the collection—and a concatenated string should be produced by using *String.Concat* and the *ToArray* method.

Because this aggregate uses a collection class, the defining attribute must be modified and the *IBinarySerialize* interface must be implemented:

```
[Serializable]
[Microsoft.SqlServer.Server.SqlUserDefinedAggregate(
    Format.UserDefined,
    MaxByteSize=-1,
    IsInvariantToDuplicates=false,
    IsInvariantToNulls=true
// This one does nothing!
//    IsInvariantToOrder=false
)]
public struct Concatenate : IBinarySerialize
```

As with the *SqlUserDefinedType* attribute, *SqlUserDefinedAggregate* includes the *Format* setting, which is set to *UserDefined*. *MaxByteSize* is specified as –1 (for up to 2 GB of data) because string arrays can grow arbitrarily large.

The next two options are set to protect the aggregation process by limiting which query plans can be chosen. *IsInvariantToDuplicates*, if set to *true*, means that a query plan that might aggregate duplicate values that are not present in the source data will not cause any data problems—consider, for example, COUNT(DISTINCT). In the case of string concatenation, that's not the case, so the option is set to *false*. *IsInvariantToNulls*, if set to *true*, allows the query optimizer to produce a plan that might result in additional nulls being aggregated. In the case of this aggregate, because it deals with nulls, that is not a problem, so it is set to *true*.

The *IsInvariantToOrder* option has been included on the *SqlUserDefinedAggregate* attribute since SQL Server 2005, and it has generated much talk and speculation. Alas, it never has been functional in any way, and Microsoft has never officially commented on it nor made a move to remove it. It is recommended that you not set it in your aggregates, in case it is one day enabled and causes unforeseen results.

The *IBinarySerialize Write* method follows:

```
public void Write(System.IO.BinaryWriter w)
{
    w.Write(stringList.Count);

    foreach (string s in stringList)
        w.Write(s);
}
```

This method first writes the number of elements in the list of strings, and then writes each string. *Read*, as in a user-defined type, reverses the operation:

```
public void Read(System.IO.BinaryReader r)
{
    Init();

    int count = r.ReadInt32();

    while (count > 0)
    {
        stringList.Add(r.ReadString());
        count--;
    }
}
```

Read first calls *Init*, because this is not automatically done prior to calling the *Read* method—only prior to calling *Accumulate*. Once the string list has been instantiated, the number of strings that was written is read in, and one call to *ReadString* is made per string. This number of *ReadString* calls should equal the number of calls that were made to *Write* for the same strings.

After publication, the aggregate can finally be tested:

```
SELECT dbo.Concatenate(theString) AS CSV
FROM
(
    VALUES
        ('abc'),
        ('def'),
        ('ghi')
) AS x (theString);
GO
```

```
---

CSV
------------
abc,def,ghi

(1 row(s) affected)
```

Derived table "x" uses the VALUES clause to create three rows with string values in a column called "theString." These values are passed to the *dbo.Concatenate* aggregate, and the output result is a comma-separated string, as expected.

Aggregates, in practice, are incredibly useful in a large number of T-SQL development scenarios. They can implement anything from simple tasks, such as the string manipulation shown here, to complex statistics algorithms and various exotic forms of data manipulation, such as packing data into custom interchange formats.

Transaction and concurrency

This section describes how SQL Server handles multiple sessions that interact with the database concurrently. It covers the classic ACID (atomicity, consistency, isolation, and durability) properties of transactions, locking and blocking, lock escalation, delayed durability, isolation levels, and deadlocks. This section focuses on working with disk-based tables; Chapter 10 extends the discussion to working with memory-optimized tables.

In my examples, I'll use a database called testdb and, within it, tables called T1 and T2. Run the following code to create the database and tables and to populate the tables with sample data:

```
SET NOCOUNT ON;
IF DB_ID(N'testdb') IS NULL CREATE DATABASE testdb;
GO
USE testdb;
GO
```

```
IF OBJECT_ID(N'dbo.T1', 'U') IS NOT NULL DROP TABLE dbo.T1;
IF OBJECT_ID(N'dbo.T2', 'U') IS NOT NULL DROP TABLE dbo.T2;
GO

CREATE TABLE dbo.T1
(
  keycol INT        NOT NULL PRIMARY KEY,
  col1   INT        NOT NULL,
  col2   VARCHAR(50) NOT NULL
);

INSERT INTO dbo.T1(keycol, col1, col2) VALUES
  (1, 101, 'A'),
  (2, 102, 'B'),
  (3, 103, 'C');

CREATE TABLE dbo.T2
(
  keycol INT        NOT NULL PRIMARY KEY,
  col1   INT        NOT NULL,
  col2   VARCHAR(50) NOT NULL
);

INSERT INTO dbo.T2(keycol, col1, col2) VALUES
  (1, 201, 'X'),
  (2, 202, 'Y'),
  (3, 203, 'Z');
```

Transactions described

A *transaction* is a unit of work that fulfils four properties that are commonly known by their acronym ACID. The four properties abbreviated in this acronym are atomicity, consistency, isolation, and durability.

The atomicity property is what most people have in mind when they think of transactions. It means that the transaction is treated as an all-or-nothing operation. Either all of the transaction's changes are applied or none are applied. By default, if you don't explicitly start a user transaction with a BEGIN TRAN command, each statement is handled as an autocommit transaction. If you want to change the default from autocommit mode to implicit-transactions mode (that is, the user will have to explicitly commit the transaction), turn on the session option IMPLICIT_TRANSACTIONS.

As an example, say you start a transaction and submit some changes by running the following code:

```
BEGIN TRAN;
  INSERT INTO dbo.T1(keycol, col1, col2) VALUES(4, 101, 'C');
```

Suppose a power failure occurs before you manage to submit the rest of the commit transaction for the changes. When you restart the system, SQL Server runs a recovery process that includes redo and undo phases. The redo phase involves rolling forward all changes that are recorded in the log since the last checkpoint. The undo phase rolls back all uncommitted changes, including the ones you just made, to make sure that the database isn't left in an inconsistent state.

Suppose there was no power failure, and you managed to submit the rest of the changes and commit the transaction by running the following code:

```
INSERT INTO dbo.T2(keycol, col1, col2) VALUES(4, 201, 'X');
COMMIT TRAN;
```

As soon as you get an acknowledgment back from SQL Server for the COMMIT TRAN command, the transaction is said to be *durable in its entirety*. I'll elaborate on the durability property shortly.

The consistency property refers to the state of the database. The database is considered to be in a consistent state before the transaction starts and after it completes. Once the transaction makes a change, the database state becomes inconsistent until you commit the transaction or roll it back.

In SQL Server, constraints are treated as immediate constraints—namely, they are checked at the end of each statement, even if the statement is part of a user transaction. SQL Server doesn't support deferred constraints, which are checked only when the transaction commits.

The isolation property means that SQL Server isolates inconsistent data generated by one transaction from other transactions. But what exactly *consistent data* means to your application is subjective to your application's needs. For instance, suppose you have two occurrences of the same query in one transaction. Does your application require that the reads be repeatable? If the answer is yes, the second read must return the rows you read previously unchanged. If the answer is no, it's okay if the second read returns the rows you read previously in a changed state. You can control the degree of isolation you get by setting your *isolation level* to the one that gives you the desired semantics.

Finally, the durability property ensures that when you commit the transaction, as soon as you get an acknowledgment back from the database, you are assured that the transaction completed and that it can be recovered if needed. The way SQL Server guarantees durability depends on the recovery model of your database. The recovery model is a database setting that determines the database's recoverability capabilities. The supported options are SIMPLE, BULK_LOGGED, and FULL. If the recovery model is FULL, it's enough for SQL Server to harden the changes to the log file upon commit. Hardening the changes means flushing the 60-KB log buffer to the log file on disk. If you're using the SIMPLE or BULK_LOGGED recovery models, bulk operations perform only minimal logging to support a rollback operation if needed. Therefore, when you commit a transaction, to guarantee durability, it's not enough for SQL Server to flush the log buffer; it also needs to flush dirty data pages from the buffer pool to the data files. As a result, commits can take longer under the SIMPLE and BULK_LOGGED recovery models.

SQL Server 2014 introduces a new feature called *delayed durability*. I'll cover this feature later in this section.

SQL Server doesn't support true nested transactions. It does allow you to nest BEGIN TRAN/ COMMIT TRAN statements and to name a transaction, but there's really only one transaction present at most. A ROLLBACK TRAN *<tran_name>* command (with the transaction name) is valid only when referring to the outermost transaction name. With every BEGIN TRAN command, SQL Server increases a counter, which can be queried via the @@trancount function. With every COMMIT TRAN command, SQL Server decreases the counter. The transaction actually commits only when the counter drops to 0.

Suppose you open a transaction and, within it, call a stored procedure. Within the stored procedure, you issue a BEGIN TRAN command, do some work, and then issue a COMMIT TRAN command. When the procedure finishes, you're still in an open transaction. If there's a failure that causes the transaction to roll back, all the transaction's changes are undone—the ones submitted both before and after the procedure call, and the ones submitted by the procedure.

Because SQL Server doesn't support nested transactions, there's no way, inside the stored procedure, for you to force an actual commit. However, if you need to be able to undo only the procedure's work in certain conditions, you can use a savepoint for this purpose. At the beginning of the stored procedure, you can check whether you're already inside a transaction by querying @@trancount. Store this information as a flag in a variable (call it @tranexisted). If you're not inside a transaction, issue a BEGIN TRAN to open one. If you're already inside a transaction, issue a SAVE TRAN <savepoint_name> command to mark a savepoint. If everything goes well in the procedure, you will issue a COMMIT TRAN command only if the procedure opened the transaction. If you need to undo the procedure's work, depending on whether the procedure opened a transaction or marked a savepoint, you'll issue a ROLLBACK TRAN command or ROLLBACK TRAN <savepoint_name> command, respectively.

The following code demonstrates how you can implement this strategy (normally this code will reside in a stored procedure):

```
-- BEGIN TRAN;

DECLARE @tranexisted AS INT = 0, @allisgood AS INT = 0;

IF @@trancount = 0
  BEGIN TRAN;
ELSE
BEGIN
  SET @tranexisted = 1;
  SAVE TRAN S1;
END;

-- ... some work ...

-- Need to rollback only inner work
IF @allisgood = 1
  COMMIT TRAN;
ELSE
  IF @tranexisted = 1
  BEGIN
    PRINT 'Rolling back to savepoint.';
    ROLLBACK TRAN S1;
  END;
  ELSE
  BEGIN
    PRINT 'Rolling back transaction.';
    ROLLBACK TRAN;
  END;

-- COMMIT TRAN;
```

You can use the commented BEGIN TRAN and COMMIT TRAN commands to test the code both with and without an existing transaction. The *@allisgood* flag allows you to test the code both when things go well (when the flag is set to 1, you don't want to undo the work) and when they don't (when the flag is set to 0, you want to undo the work).

Running the code as is represents a case where there's no transaction open when the procedure is executed, and things in the procedure don't go well. In this case, the code opens a transaction and later rolls it back. The code produces the following output:

```
Rolling back transaction.
```

Uncomment the BEGIN TRAN and COMMIT TRAN commands, and run the code again. This execution represents a case where a transaction is open when the procedure is executed and things in the procedure don't go well. This time, the code rolls back to the savepoint. The code generates the following output:

```
Rolling back to savepoint.
```

Locks and blocking

SQL Server supports different models to enforce the isolation semantics that you are after. The oldest one—which is still the default, in-the-box version of SQL Server for disk-based tables—is based on locking. In this model, there's only one version of a row. Your session needs to acquire locks to interact with the data, whether for write purposes or read purposes. If your session requests a lock on a resource (a row, page, or table) that is in conflict with a lock that another session is holding on the same resource, your session gets blocked. This means that you wait until either the other session releases the lock or a timeout that you defined expires.

An alternative model for disk-based tables is a row-versioning one, which is the default model in Microsoft Azure SQL Database (or just "SQL Database" for short). In this model, when you update or delete a row, SQL Server copies the older version of the row to a version store in tempdb and creates a link from the current version of the row to the older one. SQL Server can maintain multiple versions of the same row in such a linked list. This model is a patch on top of the locking model. Writers still use locks, but readers don't. When a session needs to read a resource, it doesn't request a lock. If the current version of the row is not the one the session is supposed to see under its current isolation level, SQL Server follows the linked list to retrieve an earlier version of the row for the session.

Table 9-2 shows a lock-compatibility matrix with some common locks that SQL Server uses.

As you can see in Table 9-2, an exclusive lock (X) is incompatible with all types of locks and vice versa. Writers are required to take an exclusive lock for all types of modifications. This is true for disk-based tables in both the locking and row-versioning models. A shared lock (S) is compatible with another shared lock. In the locking model, readers are required to take a shared lock to read a resource under most isolation levels. The exception is the Read Uncommitted isolation level, under which readers don't take shared locks.

TABLE 9-2 Lock compatibility

Requested mode	Granted mode					
	IS	S	U	IX	SIX	X
Intent shared (IS)	Yes	Yes	Yes	Yes	Yes	No
Shared (S)	Yes	Yes	Yes	No	No	No
Update (U)	Yes	Yes	No	No	No	No
Intent exclusive (IX)	Yes	No	No	Yes	No	No
Shared with intent exclusive (SIX)	Yes	No	No	No	No	No
Exclusive (X)	No	No	No	No	No	No

An update lock (U) is sort of a hybrid between shared and exclusive. Like a shared lock, an update lock is compatible with another shared lock. Like an exclusive lock, an update lock is incompatible with another update lock. This means that only one session at a time can hold an update lock on a resource. An example where SQL Server uses an update lock internally is to protect the access path in an index when searching for a row that needs to be modified. You can also request to use an update lock explicitly with a table hint in your query, like so:

```
SELECT ... FROM YourTable WITH (UPDLOCK) WHERE ...;
```

A classic use case for such an explicit hint is when you have a transaction that involves reading data, applying some calculations, and later writing to the data. If you want to ensure that only one session runs the flow at any given moment, you can achieve this by adding an UPDLOCK hint in the SELECT query that starts the process. This way, whoever issues the query first gets to run the flow. All the rest will have to wait. Later, I will explain how this method can help you prevent a phenomenon called *lost updates*.

The remaining locks in the lock-compatibility table are intent locks. There's an intent shared lock (IS), intent exclusive lock (IX), and shared with intent exclusive lock (SIX). The intent shared and intent exclusive locks will block requests for conflicting locks at the same granularity level, but not at lower levels. Shared with intent exclusive is like intent exclusive, but with the additional restrictions of a shared lock, including blocking conflicting locks at lower levels of granularity.

An example where SQL Server internally uses intent locks is to protect the hierarchy of resources above the one you actually need to interact with. For example, suppose you need to update a row as part of a transaction. Your session needs an exclusive lock to update that row. Suppose your session acquires the lock and applies the update, but your transaction is still open. Suppose at this point another session tries to obtain a shared lock on the entire table. Clearly there's a conflict. But it's not that straightforward for SQL Server to figure out that there's a conflict because the resources are different—one is a row, and the other is a table. To simplify the detection of such conflicts, before your session acquires a lock on a resource, it has to first acquire intent locks of the same kind on the upper levels of granularity. For example, to update a row, your session will have to first acquire an intent exclusive lock on the table and the page before it requests the exclusive lock on the row. Then, when another session tries to acquire a conflicting lock on the same table or page, it will be easy for SQL Server to detect the conflict.

The situation where your session requests a lock on a resource that is incompatible with an existing lock on the same resource is called *blocking*. When your session is blocked, it waits. By default, there's no limit to how long you'll wait. If you want to set a limit, you can do so in your session or at the client. In your session, you can set an option called LOCK_TIMEOUT to some value in milliseconds. The default is –1, meaning indefinitely. If this option is set, once the timeout expires you'll get error 1222. At the client, you can set a command timeout that will cause the client to terminate the request as soon as the timeout expires. But then you don't necessarily know why your request didn't finish on time. It could be blocking, but it could be for other reasons as well, like if the system is very slow.

Short-term blocking is normal in a system that relies on the locking model. However, if blocking causes long wait times, it becomes a problem. If users experience long waits on a regular basis, you need to reevaluate the model you're using. For more specific cases where blocking causes unusual delays, SQL Server gives you tools to troubleshoot the situation. For example, suppose you have a bug in your code that in certain conditions causes a transaction to remain open. Your session will keep holding any locks that are normally held until the end of the transaction, like exclusive ones. Until someone terminates your transaction, other sessions that try to acquire conflicting locks will be blocked. At some point, users will start complaining about the waits. Suppose you get the support call and need to troubleshoot the situation.

Before I demonstrate such a blocking situation, run the following code to initialize the row I will query in the demo:

```
UPDATE dbo.T1 SET col2 = 'Version 1' WHERE keycol = 2;
```

Open two connections; call them *connection 1* and *connection 2*. When I did so in my system, I got session ID 53 for the first and session ID 54 for the second.

Issue the following code from connection 1 to open a transaction, and modify the row in T1 with a new value:

```
SET NOCOUNT ON;
USE testdb;
GO
BEGIN TRAN;
  UPDATE dbo.T1 SET col2 = 'Version 2' WHERE keycol = 2;
```

To apply the update, the session acquires an intent exclusive lock on the table, an intent exclusive lock on the page, and an exclusive lock on the row.

Issue the following code from connection 2 to query all rows in T1:

```
SET NOCOUNT ON;
USE testdb;
GO
SELECT keycol, col1, col2 FROM dbo.T1;
```

The SELECT query is running under the default isolation level Read Committed. The session acquires an intent shared lock on the table and an intent shared lock on the page. As soon as it tries to acquire a shared lock on the row that is locked exclusively by the other session, the request is blocked. Now the user with connection 2 is waiting. After some time, the user opens a support call and you're tasked with troubleshooting the situation.

Open a new connection (call it *connection 3*) to troubleshoot the problem. You can use a number of dynamic management views (DMVs) and functions (DMFs) to troubleshoot blocking. To get lock information, query the view *sys.dm_tran_locks*, like so:

```
SET NOCOUNT ON;
USE testdb;

SELECT
  request_session_id        AS sid,
  resource_type             AS restype,
  resource_database_id      AS dbid,
  resource_description      AS res,
  resource_associated_entity_id AS resid,
  request_mode              AS mode,
  request_status            AS status
FROM sys.dm_tran_locks;
```

Here's the output I got on my system:

```
sid  restype    dbid  res             resid                 mode   status
----  ---------  -----  --------------  --------------------  -----  -------
51   DATABASE   6                     0                     S      GRANT
54   DATABASE   6                     0                     S      GRANT
53   DATABASE   6                     0                     S      GRANT
54   PAGE       6     1:73            72057594040549376     IS     GRANT
53   PAGE       6     1:73            72057594040549376     IX     GRANT
54   OBJECT     6                     245575913             IS     GRANT
53   OBJECT     6                     245575913             IX     GRANT
53   KEY        6     (61a06abd401c)  72057594040549376     X      GRANT
54   KEY        6     (61a06abd401c)  72057594040549376     S      WAIT
```

In an active system, lots of locks are acquired and released all the time. Typically, you won't just query all rows from the view; rather, you will add some filters and perform further manipulation. For example, you likely want to focus first on the locks with the status WAIT.

Observe that session 54 is waiting for a shared lock on a key (a row in an index) in database 6 (testdb). The resource ID and description are not very useful for figuring out exactly which resource is in conflict. Their relevance is in figuring out which session is holding a conflicting lock on the same resource. Observe that session 53 is granted with an exclusive lock on the same row. Now you have the blocking chain. Also, observe that both session 54 and session 53 obtained intent locks of the respective types on the table (OBJECT) and the page. Apply the OBJECT_NAME function to the resource ID of the table (245575913, in my case), and you will get back T1 as the name of the table that is in conflict.

To get information about the connections involved, query the *sys.dm_exec_connections* view (replacing the session IDs with the ones in your system):

```
SELECT * FROM sys.dm_exec_connections
WHERE session_id IN(53, 54);
```

Among the columns in this view, you will find the column *most_recent_sql_handle*. This column holds a binary handle you provide to the table function *sys.dm_exec_sql_text* to get the text of the last SQL batch that the connection executed. Use the APPLY operator to apply the function to each of the connections involved, like so:

```
SELECT C.session_id, ST.text
FROM sys.dm_exec_connections AS C
  CROSS APPLY sys.dm_exec_sql_text(most_recent_sql_handle) AS ST
WHERE session_id IN(53, 54);
```

I got the following output on my system:

```
session_id  text
----------- ------------------------------------------------
53          BEGIN TRAN;
              UPDATE dbo.T1 SET col2 = 'Version 2' WHERE keycol = 2;
54          SELECT keycol, col1, col2 FROM dbo.T1;
```

Session 53 is the blocking session. In our case, the text for this session includes the statement that caused the blocking situation. In practice, that's not necessarily going to be the case because the session likely will continue work. Session 54 is the blocked session. Clearly, the last thing it executed was the statement that is blocked. That's a critical piece of information during the troubleshooting process.

To get session-related information, query the view *sys.dm_exec_sessions*:

```
SELECT * FROM sys.dm_exec_sessions
WHERE session_id IN(53, 54);
```

Here you will find lots of useful information about the sessions involved, like the host, program, login name, NT user name, performance measures, state of set options, and isolation level.

To get information about the blocked request, you can query the *sys.dm_exec_requests* view, like so:

```
SELECT * FROM sys.dm_exec_requests
WHERE blocking_session_id > 0;
```

You can also find information about the blocked request in the *sys.dm_os_waiting_tasks* view:

```
SELECT * FROM sys.dm_os_waiting_tasks
WHERE blocking_session_id > 0;
```

Observe that in both cases you filter only the requests that are blocked.

Many people like to start the troubleshooting process by querying these views. Both views provide you the blocking session ID (53 in our case), wait type (LCK_M_S in our case, meaning a shared lock), wait time, and other information. Each of the views has some unique elements. For example, the *sys.dm_exec_requests* view provides the isolation level of the request, plan handle, and SQL handle. The *sys.dm_os_waiting_tasks* view is more informative about the resource in conflict with the *resource_description* column.

All the tools I described here are built-in tools in SQL Server. Adam Machanic created his own tool to troubleshoot blocking in the form of a stored procedure called *sp_WhoIsActive*. Many people find it useful and make it a standard tool in their system. You can find the stored procedure, with an explanation of how to use it, and licensing terms in Adam's blog here: *http://tinyurl.com/WhoIsActive*.

Back to our troubleshooting process; at this point, you know that session 53 is the blocking session and that its transaction is open and will remain so until someone terminates it. To terminate the user process associated with session 53 and the open transaction in this session, use the KILL command, like so:

```
KILL 53;
```

The change applied by the transaction in session 53 is undone. Back in connection 2, session 54 managed to obtain the shared lock it was waiting for and completed the query. The query generates the following output:

```
keycol  col1  col2
-------  ----  ----------
1        101   A
2        102   Version 1
3        103   C
4        101   C
```

As mentioned, you can use the LOCK_TIMEOUT session option to set a lock timeout in milliseconds. To try it with our example, execute the code in connection 1 again. (You'll first need to reconnect.) Then issue the following code in connection 2 to set a lock timeout of five seconds and run the query:

```
SET LOCK_TIMEOUT 5000;
SELECT keycol, col1, col2 FROM dbo.T1;
```

After five seconds, you get an error saying that the timeout expired:

```
Msg 1222, Level 16, State 51, Line 2
Lock request time out period exceeded.
```

Run the following code to revert back to the default indefinite timeout:

```
SET LOCK_TIMEOUT -1;
```

When you're done testing, close both connections.

Lock escalation

Every lock your transaction acquires is represented by a memory structure that uses approximately 100 bytes. Normally, your transaction starts by acquiring granular locks like row or page locks. But at some point, SQL Server will intervene with an escalation process. If it didn't, a transaction acquiring a very large number of locks would use large amounts of memory and take longer to complete because it takes time to allocate those memory structures. As soon as a single transaction obtains 5,000 locks against the same object, SQL Server attempts to escalate the fine-grained locks to a full-blown table lock. If SQL Server doesn't succeed in escalating the locks—for example, when another session is locking a row in the same table—it will keep trying again every additional 1,250 locks. Once SQL Server succeeds in the escalation, your transaction will lock the entire table.

The upside in lock escalation is clear—you use less memory, and the transaction finishes more quickly. The downside is that you're locking more than what you need, which affects the concurrency in your system. People might be blocked even when trying to access resources that are supposed to be accessible.

To demonstrate lock escalation, I'll use a table called TestEscalation, which you create and populate by running the following code:

```
USE testdb;
IF OBJECT_ID(N'dbo.TestEscalation', N'U') IS NOT NULL DROP TABLE dbo.TestEscalation;
GO

SELECT n AS col1, CAST('a' AS CHAR(200)) AS filler
INTO dbo.TestEscalation
FROM TSQLV3.dbo.GetNums(1, 100000) AS Nums;

CREATE UNIQUE CLUSTERED INDEX idx1 ON dbo.TestEscalation(col1);
```

Run the following transaction, which deletes 20,000 rows from the table and then checks how many present locks are associated with the current session ID:

```
BEGIN TRAN;

  DELETE FROM dbo.TestEscalation WHERE col1 <= 20000;

  SELECT COUNT(*)
  FROM sys.dm_tran_locks
  WHERE request_session_id = @@SPID
    AND resource_type <> 'DATABASE';

ROLLBACK TRAN;
```

The code reported that there is only one lock present, indicating that lock escalation took place.

Next, disable lock escalation and run the transaction again:

```
ALTER TABLE dbo.TestEscalation SET (LOCK_ESCALATION = DISABLE);

BEGIN TRAN;

  DELETE FROM dbo.TestEscalation WHERE col1 <= 20000;

  SELECT COUNT(*)
  FROM sys.dm_tran_locks
  WHERE request_session_id = @@SPID;

ROLLBACK TRAN;
```

This time, the code reported over 20,000 locks were present, indicating that lock escalation did not take place. You can also capture lock-escalation events using an Extended Events session with the *lock_escalation* event.

When you're done testing, run the following code for cleanup:

```
IF OBJECT_ID(N'dbo.TestEscalation', N'U') IS NOT NULL DROP TABLE dbo.TestEscalation;
```

Delayed durability

Recall the earlier discussion about the durability property of transactions. SQL Server uses a concept called *write-ahead logging* to optimize log writes. This means that it first writes log records to a 60-KB log buffer in cache. It flushes the log buffer when it's full, and also when a transaction commits to guarantee the transaction's durability property. In OLTP environments with intense workloads, you have lots of small transactions, each doing a little work that causes a small amount of writing to the transaction log. Such environments tend to have frequent nonfull, log-buffer flushes that might become a bottleneck in the system.

SQL Server 2014 introduces a feature called *delayed durability*, which you can use to relax the classic durability requirement at the cost of possibly losing data. When you commit a transaction under the delayed durability mode, SQL Server gives control back to you once it finishes writing the transaction log records to the log buffer, without flushing it. This feature allows your transactions to finish more quickly, reducing the bottleneck related to frequent log-buffer flushes. On the flipside, if there's a power failure, you lose all the changes that were written to the log buffer but weren't flushed, even for committed transactions.

> **Important** It is critical to understand that with delayed durability some data loss is possible. You should use this feature only if you can regenerate the data that is lost or you really don't care if it's lost.

You control the durability semantics that you are after by setting the database option DELAYED_ DURABILITY. You can set this option to one of three possible values:

- **Disabled**   All transactions are fully durable.

- **Forced**   All transactions are delayed durable.

- **Allowed**   By default, transactions are fully durable. But with the COMMIT TRAN command, you can specify the option WITH (DELAYED_DURABILITY = ON) to use delayed durability with that specific transaction. You can also control this option at the atomic-block level in natively compiled stored procedures. (See Chapter 10 for details.)

Environments with lots of small transactions are the ones that will benefit most from this feature. Environments running large transactions will see little, if any, impact. That's because in such environments most log flushes are the result of the log buffer getting full.

To demonstrate this feature and its impact on performance, I'll use a database called testdd and, within it, a table called T1. Run the following code to create the database and the table, and to set the DELAYED_DURABILITY option in the database to *Allowed*:

```
SET NOCOUNT ON;
USE master;
GO
IF DB_ID(N'testdd') IS NOT NULL DROP DATABASE testdd;
GO
CREATE DATABASE testdd;
ALTER DATABASE testdd SET DELAYED_DURABILITY = Allowed;
GO
USE testdd;
CREATE TABLE dbo.T1(col1 INT NOT NULL);
```

Before running each test, truncate the table to make sure it's empty:

```
TRUNCATE TABLE dbo.T1;
```

Run the following code to insert 100,000 rows into T1 in 100,000 fully durable transactions executing in autocommit mode:

```
DECLARE @i AS INT = 1;
WHILE @i <= 100000
BEGIN
  INSERT INTO dbo.T1(col1) VALUES(@i);
  SET @i += 1;
END;
```

It took this code 33 seconds to complete on my system.

Truncate the table before running the next test:

```
TRUNCATE TABLE dbo.T1;
```

Run the following code to insert 100,000 rows into T1 in 100,000 delayed durable transactions:

```
DECLARE @i AS INT = 1;
WHILE @i <= 100000
BEGIN
  BEGIN TRAN;
    INSERT INTO dbo.T1(col1) VALUES(@i);
  COMMIT TRAN WITH (DELAYED_DURABILITY = ON);
  SET @i += 1;
END;
```

This code completed in only two seconds on my system.

Again, truncate the table before running the next test:

```
TRUNCATE TABLE dbo.T1;
```

Run the following code to insert 100,000 rows into T1 in one large fully durable transaction:

```
BEGIN TRAN;
  DECLARE @i AS INT = 1;
  WHILE @i <= 100000
  BEGIN
    INSERT INTO dbo.T1(col1) VALUES(@i);
    SET @i += 1;
  END;
COMMIT TRAN;
```

It took this code one second to complete on my system.

Clear the table before the final test:

```
TRUNCATE TABLE dbo.T1;
```

Run the following code to insert 100,000 rows into T1 in one large delayed durable transaction:

```
BEGIN TRAN;
  DECLARE @i AS INT = 1;
  WHILE @i <= 100000
  BEGIN
    INSERT INTO dbo.T1(col1) VALUES(@i);
    SET @i += 1;
  END;
COMMIT TRAN WITH (DELAYED_DURABILITY = ON);
```

This code completed in one second on my system.

These tests confirm that the type of workload that will mainly benefit from the delayed durability feature is one with many small transactions.

Isolation levels

You use isolation levels to control what "consistent data" means to you. You can experience a number of classic phenomena when interacting with data in the database; each phenomenon is either possible or not depending on the isolation level you are running under. These phenomena are

- **Dirty reads**   A read of uncommitted data. One transaction changes data but does not commit the change before another transaction reads the same data. The second transaction ends up reading an inconsistent state of the data.

- **Lost updates**   Two transactions run the following flow in parallel: read data, make some calculations, and later update the data. With such a flow, one transaction might overwrite the other's update.

- **Nonrepeatable reads (also known as *inconsistent analysis*)**   In two separate queries within the same transaction, you get different values when reading the same rows. This can happen if a second session changed the data between the queries issued by the first session.

- **Phantoms**   In two separate queries within the same transaction using the same query filter, the second query returns rows that were not part of the result of the first query. This can happen if a second transaction inserts new rows that satisfy the first transaction's query filter in between its two queries. Those new rows are known as *phantom reads*.

Table 9-3 summarizes the isolation levels and the phenomena that are possible under each. I'll provide more specifics and demonstrate working under the different isolation levels shortly.

TABLE 9-3 Summary of isolation levels

Isolation	Dirty reads	Lost updates	Nonrepeatable reads	Phantoms	Concurrency model	Update conflict detection
Read Uncommitted	Yes	Yes	Yes	Yes	Pessimistic	No
Read Committed	No	Yes	Yes	Yes	Pessimistic	No
Repeatable Read	No	No	No	Yes	Pessimistic	No
Serializable	No	No	No	No	Pessimistic	No
Snapshot	No	No	No	No	Optimistic	Yes
Read Committed Snapshot	No	Yes	Yes	Yes	Optimistic	No

With disk-based tables, there are two isolation models available to you: locking and a mix of locking and row versioning. The former supports four isolation levels: Read Uncommitted, Read Committed, Repeatable Read, and Serializable. The latter supports two isolation levels: Read Committed Snapshot and Snapshot. The default, in-the-box version of SQL Server is Read Committed, and in the cloud platform (SQL Database) it is Read Committed Snapshot.

You can set the isolation level at either the session level or the query level for each table. You set the isolation level at the session level by issuing the following statement:

```
SET TRANSACTION ISOLATION LEVEL <isolation level>;
```

In this statement, *<isolation level>* can be one of the following: READ UNCOMMITTED, READ COMMITTED, REPEATABLE READ, SERIALIZABLE, or SNAPSHOT.

You set the isolation level at the query level for each table by using a table hint (READUNCOMMITTED, READCOMMITTED, REPEATABLEREAD, or SERIALIZABLE). The hint NOLOCK is equivalent to READUNCOMMITTED, and the hint HOLDLOCK is equivalent to SERIALIZABLE.

In the box version of SQL Server (as opposed to the cloud platform), you need to enable database flags in order to work with the Snapshot and Read Committed Snapshot isolation levels. I'll provide the specifics when describing these isolation levels.

Tip SQL Server also provides you with a table hint called READPAST. This hint causes your query to skip locked rows rather than being blocked or getting dirty reads. Make sure, though, that it makes sense for your application to use this hint. SQL Server supports this hint both with queries that retrieve data and with ones that modify data.

The following sections discuss the details of the different isolation levels and demonstrate working under them.

Read Uncommitted isolation level

There are two sides to the Read Uncommitted isolation level—one that most people are familiar with and another that many people aren't. The familiar side is that, unlike under the default Read Committed isolation level, under Read Uncommitted your session doesn't acquire a shared lock to read data. This means that if one session modifies data in a transaction and keeps the transaction open, another session running under the Read Uncommitted isolation level can read the uncommitted changes made by the first session. Because the reader doesn't acquire shared locks, there's no conflict with the writer's exclusive locks.

Before I demonstrate this behavior, first initialize the data by running the following code:

```
USE testdb;
UPDATE dbo.T1 SET col2 = 'Version 1' WHERE keycol = 2;
```

Open two connections. Run the following code from connection 1 to open a transaction, and modify a row with the value *Version 2* instead of the current value *Version 1*:

```
BEGIN TRAN;
  UPDATE dbo.T1 SET col2 = 'Version 2' WHERE keycol = 2;
  SELECT col2 FROM dbo.T1 WHERE keycol = 2;
```

Run the following code from connection 2 to set the session's isolation level to Read Uncommitted and read the data:

```
SET TRANSACTION ISOLATION LEVEL READ UNCOMMITTED;
SELECT col2 FROM dbo.T1 WHERE keycol = 2;
```

You get the following output:

```
col2
----------
Version 2
```

You got an uncommitted read, also known as a *dirty read*. Remember that another way to work under the Read Uncommitted isolation level is to use the NOLOCK hint in the query.

Run the following code from connection 1 to roll back the transaction:

```
ROLLBACK TRAN
```

Close both connections.

The less familiar, or dark, side of Read Uncommitted has to do with how the storage engine carries out the requests from the relational engine when SQL Server executes a query plan. The storage engine perceives the Read Uncommitted isolation level as a blanket approval to focus on speed, even at the cost of reduced consistency. As an example, when the storage engine processes an Index Scan operator (clustered or nonclustered) with an Ordered: False property, it tends to prefer an allocation-order scan of the data (using IAM pages) over an index-order scan (using the linked list). As a result, a reader can read the same row multiple times or skip rows if another writer causes page splits during that time. Under Read Committed, the storage engine prefers to use an index-order scan exactly to prevent such things from happening. I provide more details about such problems and demonstrate such behavior in Chapter 2.

As a result, using the Read Uncommitted isolation level is rarely a good thing. Sadly, many environments use it extensively, mainly in the form of NOLOCK hints in the queries, without realizing all the implications. Environments that suffer from performance problems that are related to locking and blocking should consider either using the row-versioning technology or the In-Memory OLTP engine.

As an example where using the Read Uncommitted isolation level could be a good thing, consider a data warehouse that absorbs changes only during the night in an Extract, Transform, and Load (ETL) process. Only queries that read data are submitted during the day. You want to remove the overhead of shared locks obtained by readers and allow the storage engine to use faster access methods. You can achieve this by setting the database to read-only mode, but then you won't allow SQL Server to automatically create statistics when needed. The Read Uncommitted isolation level gives you the performance advantages without preventing SQL Server from automatically creating statistics when needed. As long as you know with certainty the changes cannot happen while users are reading data, there's no risk.

Read Committed isolation level

Under the Read Committed isolation level, a session is required to obtain shared locks to read data. The session releases the shared lock as soon as it is done with the resource. It doesn't need to wait until the statement finishes, and certainly not until the transaction finishes. As a result, under this isolation level you can read only committed changes—hence the name *Read Committed*.

To see a demonstration of this behavior, open two connections. Run the following code from connection 1 to open a transaction and modify a row:

```
BEGIN TRAN;
  UPDATE dbo.T1 SET col2 = 'Version 2' WHERE keycol = 2;
  SELECT col2 FROM dbo.T1 WHERE keycol = 2;
```

Run the following code from connection 2 to set the session's isolation level to Read Committed (also the default) and read the data:

```
SET TRANSACTION ISOLATION LEVEL READ COMMITTED;
SELECT col2 FROM dbo.T1 WHERE keycol = 2;
```

At this point, the reader is blocked.

Run the following code from connection 1 to commit the transaction:

```
COMMIT TRAN;
```

The session in connection 1 releases the exclusive lock from the row, allowing the session in connection 2 to obtain the shared lock it was waiting for and read the data. You get the following output in connection 2:

```
col2
----------
Version 2
```

In connection 2, you waited in order to read the committed state of the data.

Run the following code to set the value of *col2* in the modified row back to '*Version 1*'.

```
UPDATE dbo.T1 SET col2 = 'Version 1' WHERE keycol = 2;
```

Close both connections.

The Read Committed isolation level does not try to prevent nonrepeatable reads. Suppose you query the same rows twice within the same transaction. Because you're not holding any locks between reads, another session can modify the rows during that time. Therefore, two different queries can get different states of the same rows.

The Read Committed isolation level does not try to prevent lost updates. Suppose you have two transactions running in parallel, both with flow that includes reading data, making calculations, and later updating the data. Both transactions read the same initial state of the data. Each transaction, based on its calculations, tries to write its own values to the data. One transaction will apply the update first and commit. The other transaction will apply the update last, overwriting the first transaction's update.

Repeatable Read isolation level

The Repeatable Read isolation level guarantees that once a query within a transaction reads rows, all subsequent queries in the same transaction will keep getting the same state of those rows. The way SQL Server achieves this behavior is by causing a reader to obtain shared locks on the target rows and to keep them until the end of the transaction. After you open a transaction and read some rows, any other session that tries to update those rows will be blocked until your transaction completes. Therefore, subsequent reads within your transaction are guaranteed to get the same state of those rows as in the first read.

To see a demonstration of a repeatable read, open two connections. Run the following code in connection 1 to set the session's isolation level to Repeatable Read, open a transaction, and read a row:

```
SET TRANSACTION ISOLATION LEVEL REPEATABLE READ;
BEGIN TRAN;
  SELECT col2 FROM dbo.T1 WHERE keycol = 2;
```

You get the following output:

```
col2
----------
Version 1
```

Try to update the same row from connection 2:

```
UPDATE dbo.T1 SET col2 = 'Version 2' WHERE keycol = 2;
```

You get blocked because you need an exclusive lock on the row, and you cannot get one while the other session is holding a shared lock on that row.

Back in connection 1, run the following code to query the row again and commit the transaction:

```
  SELECT col2 FROM dbo.T1 WHERE keycol = 2;
COMMIT TRAN;
```

You get the following output, which represents a repeatable read:

```
col2
----------
Version 1
```

Meanwhile, the writer obtained the exclusive lock it was waiting for, modified the row, and committed the transaction.

When you're done, run the following code for cleanup:

```
UPDATE dbo.T1 SET col2 = 'Version 1' WHERE keycol = 2;
```

Close both connections.

The Repeatable Read isolation level doesn't allow update conflicts. Suppose you have two transactions running in parallel, both with flow that includes reading data, making calculations, and later updating the data. Both sessions read the same initial state of the data after obtaining shared locks, and they keep the locks until the end of the transaction. Each transaction, based on its calculations, tries to update the data with its own values. To apply the update, both sessions request exclusive locks, each getting blocked by the other's shared locks. That's a deadlock. SQL Server detects the deadlock, typically within a few seconds. Once it does, it chooses one of the sessions as the deadlock victim and terminates its transaction, causing it to undo the work and release all locks. That session gets error 1205. Anticipating such errors, you can have error-handling code with retry logic. If your session is chosen as the deadlock victim, when you retry the transaction you start by reading the new state of the data and use it in your calculations before updating the data. This way, no update is lost.

If you get frequent deadlocks that are related to the prevention of lost updates, you should reevaluate your solution. An alternative solution is to use the Read Committed isolation level, and in those transactions where you want to prevent lost updates you add an explicit UPDLOCK hint in the query that reads the data. The session that reads the data first gets the update lock, and the session that gets there second is blocked already in the attempt to read the data. You cause a queuing of the transactions without the need for error-handling code with retry logic.

Serializable isolation level

The Serializable isolation level guarantees that once you query data within a transaction, you will keep working with the same state of the data, seeing only your own changes, until your transaction completes. In other words, transactions work with the data in a serializable fashion. Once a session opens a transaction and accesses data, it's as if it's the only one working with the data.

For example, if you issue the same query multiple times in the same transaction, all occurrences of the query get the exact same result sets (assuming the same transaction doesn't modify the data between the queries). Not only that, you're guaranteed to get repeatable reads like under the Repeatable Read isolation level. You're also guaranteed not to get phantom reads. Under the Repeatable Read isolation level, phantom reads are possible. Often people are surprised by this fact, but remember, the Repeatable Read isolation level guarantees only that once you read rows, subsequent reads will get the same state of the rows that you read previously. It's not supposed to guarantee you won't get new rows that were added between the reads.

Suppose that working under the Serializable isolation level you submit a query against the table T1 with the filter *col1 = 102* twice in the same transaction. You have an index on the filtered column. To guarantee serializable behavior, SQL Server uses key-range locks. This means that once you query data for the first time in a transaction, your session locks the range of keys in the index starting with the first qualifying key and ending with the key after the last qualifying one. Your session keeps the locks until the transaction completes. If another session tries to add, update, or delete rows that satisfy your query filter after you queried the data for the first time and before you complete the transaction, it gets blocked. This way, you get no phantom reads.

To see a demonstration of serializable behavior, first create an index on *col1* in T1 by running the following code:

```
CREATE INDEX idx_col1 ON dbo.T1(col1);
```

Open two connections. Run the following code in connection 1 to set the isolation level to Serializable, open a transaction, and query the rows in T1 where *col1* is equal to *102*:

```
SET TRANSACTION ISOLATION LEVEL SERIALIZABLE;
BEGIN TRAN;
  SELECT *
  FROM dbo.T1 WITH (INDEX(idx_col1))
  WHERE col1 = 102;
```

The query uses a hint to force the use of the index because the table is so small. This code generates the following output:

```
keycol  col1  col2
-------  -----  ----------
2       102    Version 1
```

In connection 2, run the following code to attempt to insert a new row into T1 with the value *102* in *col1*:

```
INSERT INTO dbo.T1(keycol, col1, col2) VALUES(5, 102, 'D');
```

If the code in connection 1 was running under the Repeatable Read isolation level, your insert would have been successful. However, the code in connection 1 is running under the Serializable isolation level, so your insert is blocked.

Back in connection 1, run the following code to execute the same query a second time and to commit the transaction:

```
SELECT *
FROM dbo.T1 WITH (INDEX(idx_col1))
  WHERE col1 = 102;
COMMIT TRAN;
```

You get the same output you got in the first execution of the query:

```
keycol  col1  col2
-------  -----  ----------
2        102    Version 1
```

Meanwhile, the INSERT statement in connection 2 completed.

When you're done, run the following code for cleanup:

```
DELETE FROM dbo.T1 WHERE keycol = 5;
DROP INDEX dbo.T1.idx_col1;
```

Close both connections.

Snapshot and Read Committed Snapshot isolation levels

The Snapshot and Read Committed Snapshot isolation levels are based on a model that mixes the use of locking and row versioning. Writers keep using exclusive locks as usual. In addition, when you update or delete a row, SQL Server copies the version before the change to a version store in tempdb and creates a link from the current version of the row to the older one. If you apply multiple updates to a row, SQL Server will keep adding more versions to the chain, placing the newest one in front of the others. SQL Server adds 14 bytes of versioning information to new rows that you insert. Readers don't take shared locks; rather, if the current version of the row is not the one they are supposed to see, they request an older committed version of the row from the version store.

The Snapshot isolation level gives you a transaction-level-consistent view of the data, plus it prevents lost updates by generating an "update conflict" error. The Read Committed Snapshot isolation level gives you a statement-level-consistent view of the data and doesn't attempt to prevent update conflicts. With this in mind, and by examining Table 9-3 that I provided earlier, identify which locking-based isolation levels are the closest parallels to the row-versioning-based ones. You will notice that Snapshot is closest to Serializable, and Read Committed Snapshot is closest to Read Committed.

A cleanup thread wakes up every minute and removes row versions that aren't needed anymore from the tail forward until getting to the first row version that is still needed. So, if you have long-running transactions, it increases the chances for long chains.

Under the row-versioning-based isolation levels, readers don't need to wait. The fact that they don't use shared locks reduces the overhead related to locking and tends to result in reduced blocking and deadlocking. The tradeoff is that readers might need to traverse linked lists to get to the correct row version, and writers need to write row versions to the version store. You need to make sure that you tune tempdb to cope with the increased load and that you do thorough testing before enabling row versioning in production.

Each of the row-versioning-based isolation levels requires you to turn on a respective database option to enable it. To allow the use of the Snapshot isolation level, you turn on the database flag ALLOW_SNAPSHOT_ISOLATION. This causes SQL Server to start versioning rows. To actually use the Snapshot isolation level, you also need to set the session's isolation level to SNAPSHOT. To work with the Read Committed Snapshot isolation level, you turn on the database option READ_COMMITTED_SNAPSHOT. Once you do, you change the semantics of the default Read Committed isolation level from locking-only-based semantics to semantics based on mixed locking and row versioning. Because enabling this database flag changes the default isolation level, you need exclusive access to the database to apply it. New connections will use the Read Committed Snapshot isolation level. Then, in cases where you want a reader to use shared locks, you add the table hint READCOMMITTEDLOCK.

To enable the use of the Snapshot isolation level in the testdb database, turn on the database option ALLOW_SNAPSHOT_ISOLATION ON, like so:

```
ALTER DATABASE testdb SET ALLOW_SNAPSHOT_ISOLATION ON;
```

Open two connections. Run the following code from connection 1 to open a transaction, update a row, and read the row:

```
BEGIN TRAN;
  UPDATE dbo.T1 SET col2 = 'Version 2' WHERE keycol = 2;
  SELECT col2 FROM dbo.T1 WHERE keycol = 2;
```

This code generates the following output:

```
col2
----------
Version 2
```

Query the view *sys.dm_tran_version_store* to see the row versions that currently reside in the version store:

```
SELECT * FROM sys.dm_tran_version_store;
```

You get one row version in the output.

Run the following code in connection 2 to set the session's isolation level to Snapshot, open a transaction, and query the row that was modified by connection 1:

```
SET TRANSACTION ISOLATION LEVEL SNAPSHOT;
BEGIN TRAN;
  SELECT col2 FROM dbo.T1 WHERE keycol = 2;
```

Remember that under Snapshot you get a transaction-level-consistent view of the data. This means that throughout the transaction you will get the last committed state of the data at the point in time when you issued the first statement within the transaction. You get the following output:

```
col2
----------
Version 1
```

Then, in connection 1, run the following code to commit the transaction and read the row:

```
COMMIT TRAN;
SELECT col2 FROM dbo.T1 WHERE keycol = 2;
```

You get the following output:

```
col2
----------
Version 2
```

Back in connection 2, run the following code to read the row again, still in the open transaction:

```
SELECT col2 FROM dbo.T1 WHERE keycol = 2;
```

You get the same state of the row you got in the previous query:

```
col2
----------
Version 1
```

If you were running under the Read Committed Snapshot isolation level, instead of getting 'Version 1', you would have got the new committed state 'Version 2'.

Finally, run the following code in connection 2 to commit the transaction and query the row again:

```
COMMIT TRAN;
SELECT col2 FROM dbo.T1 WHERE keycol = 2;
```

You get the following output:

```
col2
----------
Version 2
```

Run the following code to update the row back to the value 'Version 1':

```
UPDATE dbo.T1 SET col2 = 'Version 1' WHERE keycol = 2;
```

As mentioned, the Snapshot isolation level prevents lost updates by detecting update conflicts. As an example, in connection 1 run the following code to set the isolation level to Snapshot, open a transaction, and query a row:

```
SET TRANSACTION ISOLATION LEVEL SNAPSHOT;
BEGIN TRAN;
  SELECT col2 FROM dbo.T1 WHERE keycol = 2;
```

You get the following output:

```
col2
----------
Version 1
```

In connection 2, run the following code to update the same row:

```
UPDATE dbo.T1 SET col2 = 'Version 2' WHERE keycol = 2;
```

Back in connection 1, try to update the row too:

```
UPDATE dbo.T1 SET col2 = 'Version 3' WHERE keycol = 2;
```

SQL Server detects that someone else modified the row you're trying to update, and it generates error 3960, indicating that it detected an update conflict:

```
Msg 3960, Level 16, State 2, Line 7
Snapshot isolation transaction aborted due to update conflict. You cannot use snapshot isolation
to access table 'dbo.T1' directly or indirectly in database 'testdb' to update, delete, or
insert the row that has been modified or deleted by another transaction. Retry the transaction
or change the isolation level for the update/delete statement.
```

SQL Server terminates your transaction and undoes the work. Anticipating such conflicts, you can have error-handling code with retry logic. If you think about this, getting an "update conflict" error is better than getting a more generic deadlock error. Deadlocks can happen for all sorts of reasons, and perhaps you want to handle differently cases where an error is related to the prevention of lost updates and others.

Run the following code for cleanup:

```
UPDATE dbo.T1 SET col2 = 'Version 1' WHERE keycol = 2;
```

Close both connections.

Next, I'll demonstrate using the Read Committed Snapshot isolation level. Assuming you have exclusive access to the database, turn on the database option READ_COMMITTED_SNAPSHOT in testdb to change the semantics of the Read Committed isolation level to Read Committed Snapshot:

```
ALTER DATABASE testdb SET READ_COMMITTED_SNAPSHOT ON;
```

Open two connections. Both are now running under the Read Committed Snapshot isolation level by default. Run the following code in connection 1 to open a transaction, update a row, and then read that row:

```
BEGIN TRAN;
  UPDATE dbo.T1 SET col2 = 'Version 2' WHERE keycol = 2;
  SELECT col2 FROM dbo.T1 WHERE keycol = 2;
```

You get the following output:

```
col2
----------
Version 2
```

Run the following code in connection 2 to open a transaction and read the same row:

```
BEGIN TRAN;
  SELECT col2 FROM dbo.T1 WHERE keycol = 2;
```

You get the last committed state that was available when your statement started:

```
col2
----------
Version 1
```

Go back to connection 1, and run the following code to commit the transaction:

```
COMMIT TRAN;
```

Then, in connection 2, run the following code to query the row again and commit the transaction:

```
  SELECT col2 FROM dbo.T1 WHERE keycol = 2;
COMMIT TRAN;
```

You get the new state of the row that was last committed before you issued your statement:

```
col2
----------
Version 2
```

Remember that under the Snapshot isolation level in the same situation you got *Version 1*, because that isolation level gives you a transaction-level-consistent view of the data.

When you're done, run the following code for cleanup:

```
UPDATE dbo.T1 SET col2 = 'Version 1' WHERE keycol = 2;
```

Close both connections.

Run the following code to restore the testdb database to its default settings:

```
ALTER DATABASE testdb SET ALLOW_SNAPSHOT_ISOLATION OFF;
ALTER DATABASE testdb SET READ_COMMITTED_SNAPSHOT OFF;
```

Deadlocks

A *deadlock* is a combination of blocking situations that end up in a cycle. It can involve two or more sessions. For example, suppose that session X blocks session Y, session Y blocks session Z, and session Z blocks session X. SQL Server actively searches for deadlocks normally every five seconds. When it detects a deadlock, it reduces the interval between searches to as low as 100 milliseconds, depending on the frequency of the deadlocks. After some time with no deadlocks, it increases the interval to five seconds. Once SQL Server detects a deadlock, it chooses one of the sessions involved as the deadlock victim and terminates its transaction. That session gets error 1205; all the work within the transaction is undone and all locks are released.

SQL Server chooses the deadlock victim based on two criteria. You can set an option in your session called DEADLOCK_PRIORITY to a value in the range –10 to 10. SQL Server chooses the session with the lowest deadlock priority as the deadlock victim. In the case of ties in the priority, SQL Server estimates the amount of work involved in rolling back each of the transactions based on the information recorded in the transaction log and chooses the transaction that involves the least work. In the case of ties in the priority and the estimated amount of work, SQL Server chooses the victim randomly.

SQL Server provides you with a number of tools to troubleshoot deadlocks. Trace flags 1222 and 1204 cause SQL Server to write information about the deadlock to the error log. The trace-event Deadlock graph and the Extended Events event *xml_deadlock_report* (part of the default *system_health* session) can be used to produce a deadlock graph as an XML instance. The deadlock graph can be viewed graphically in Profiler and SSMS. You can also run a trace or an Extended Events session with the following events: *sql_statement_starting*, *sp_statement_starting*, or both as needed; *lock_deadlock*; and *lock_deadlock_chain*. The deadlock-chain event reports which session IDs were involved. You analyze the statement-starting events of the sessions involved, from the moment their transactions started until the deadlock event. This way, you can identify the sequence of statements that lead to the deadlock. The problem with running such a trace or Extended Events session is that it can be expensive if you run it for long periods.

In the following sections, I demonstrate a simple deadlock example, and then I describe the measures you can take to reduce deadlock occurrences. After that, I describe a more complex deadlock example involving a single table and a single statement submitted by each session.

Simple deadlock example

To see a demonstration of a simple deadlock, open two connections. Run the following code in connection 1 to open a transaction and update a row in T1:

```
BEGIN TRAN;
  UPDATE dbo.T1 SET col1 = col1 + 1 WHERE keycol = 2;
```

The session acquires an exclusive lock on the row.

Run the following code in connection 2 to open a transaction, and update a row in T2:

```
BEGIN TRAN;
  UPDATE dbo.T2 SET col1 = col1 + 1 WHERE keycol = 2;
```

The session acquires an exclusive lock on the row.

Back in connection 1, run the following code to try and query the row from T2 that the other session is locking and to commit the transaction:

```
  SELECT col1 FROM dbo.T2 WHERE keycol = 2;
COMMIT TRAN;
```

This session needs a shared lock to read the row but cannot obtain it while the other session is holding an exclusive lock on the same row. This session is blocked.

Run the following code in connection 2 to try and query the row from T1 that the other session is locking and to commit the transaction:

```
  SELECT col1 FROM dbo.T1 WHERE keycol = 2;
COMMIT TRAN;
```

This session also gets blocked. At this point, you have a deadlock. Within a few seconds, SQL Server detects the deadlock, chooses a deadlock victim based on the logic I described earlier, and terminates the victim's transaction. In my case, SQL Server chose the session in connection 2 as the victim. I got the following error in connection 2:

```
Msg 1205, Level 13, State 51, Line 5
Transaction (Process ID 54) was deadlocked on lock resources with another process and has been
chosen as the deadlock victim. Rerun the transaction.
```

Close both connections.

Measures to reduce deadlock occurrences

When deadlock occurrences are infrequent, you can use error-handling code with retry logic to retry the task when you get error 1205. But when deadlocks are frequent in the system, they can become a performance problem. It's not realistic to expect that you can eliminate all deadlock occurrences in the system; after all, they have a reason to exist. But you can certainly take measures to reduce their frequency.

A common cause of deadlocks that can be avoided is a lack of important indexes. If you don't have an index to support a query filter, SQL Server has to scan the entire table to get the qualifying rows. As it scans the table, it acquires locks even on rows you don't really need. As a result, you can run into conflicts that lead to a deadlock even though there's no real logical conflict between the sessions involved.

To see a demonstration of such a deadlock, open two connections. Run the following code from connection 1 to open a transaction and update the rows in T1 where *col1* is equal to *101*:

```
BEGIN TRAN;
  UPDATE dbo.T1 SET col2 = col2 + 'A' WHERE col1 = 101;
```

Run the following code from connection 2 to open a transaction and update the rows in T2 where *col1* is equal to *203*:

```
BEGIN TRAN;
  UPDATE dbo.T2 SET col2 = col2 + 'B' WHERE col1 = 203;
```

Run the following code from connection 1 to query the rows from T2 where *col1* is equal to *201*:

```
  SELECT col2 FROM dbo.T2 WHERE col1 = 201;
COMMIT TRAN;
```

You get blocked even though there's no real logical conflict.

Run the following code from connection 2 to query the rows from T1 where *col1* is equal to *103*:

```
  SELECT col2 FROM dbo.T1 WHERE col1 = 103;
COMMIT TRAN;
```

You get blocked again, even though there's no real logical conflict. At this point, SQL Server detects a deadlock. In my test, SQL Server terminated the transaction in connection 2, generating the following error:

```
Msg 1205, Level 13, State 51, Line 1
Transaction (Process ID 54) was deadlocked on lock resources with another process and has been
chosen as the deadlock victim. Rerun the transaction.
```

Run the following code to create the missing indexes:

```
CREATE INDEX idx_col1 ON dbo.T1(col1);
CREATE INDEX idx_col1 ON dbo.T2(col1);
```

Rerun the test, but first add the hint WITH(INDEX(idx_col1)) after the table name in both SELECT queries to force SQL Server to use the index. Normally, you do not need to do this. However, because the tables in our example are so small, the chances are that SQL Server will scan the whole table even with the index in place. This time, the test should complete with no conflicts.

In addition to using indexing, you can take other measures to reduce deadlock occurrences in your system. The order in which you access physical resources in the different transactions is important. For a deadlock to happen, you must access physical resources in different transactions in reverse order. For example, consider the simple deadlock example I presented earlier. In one transaction, you first modify T1 and then query T2, and in another transaction you first modify T2 and then query T1. If it's not critical to your application to perform the activities in a particular order, by accessing the objects in the same order in both transactions (say, T1 first and T2 second), you prevent the deadlock from happening.

Another aspect you should consider is the length of your transactions. The longer the transaction is, the greater likelihood you have of blocking, and therefore the greater likelihood you have for deadlocks. You should try to reduce the length of your transactions by pulling out activities that aren't really integral parts of the transaction.

Finally, another measure you should consider is changing the isolation level you're using. For example, suppose you're currently using the Read Committed isolation level. You have lots of concurrency problems, including deadlocks, and many of them involve writers and readers. Switching to a row-versioning-based isolation level like Read Committed Snapshot eliminates the conflicts that involve readers because readers don't acquire shared locks. This tends to result in an overall reduction of occurrences of blocking, and consequently a reduction in occurrences of deadlocks.

To recap, the four main measures you can take are adding supporting indexes, accessing objects in the same order, reducing the length of the transactions, and using a row-versioning-based isolation level.

Deadlock with a single table

When people think of deadlocks, they usually intuitively assume more than one table is involved and at least two different statements are submitted by each of the transactions. It's true that for a deadlock to happen at least two different sessions need to access at least two different physical resources in reverse order. But it could be that each side submits only one statement against the same table, and that the query plans for the two statements access at least two physical resources like different indexes in reverse order. Figure 9-25 illustrates such a deadlock.

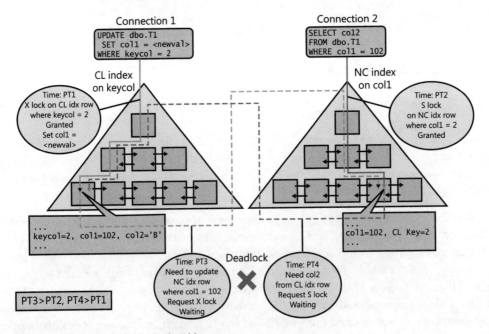

FIGURE 9-25 Deadlock with a single table.

There's a clustered index defined with *keycol* as the key and a nonclustered index defined with *col1* as the key. Connection 1 submits an UPDATE statement that modifies a row in T1 where *keycol* is equal to *2*, setting *col1* to some new value. At the same time, connection 2 submits a SELECT statement against T1, filtering the row where *col1* is equal to *102* and returning *col2* in the result. Observe that the UPDATE statement first updates the row in the clustered index (after acquiring an exclusive lock) and then tries to update the respective row in the nonclustered index (requesting an exclusive lock). The SELECT statement first finds the row in the nonclustered index (acquiring a shared lock) and, because *col2* is not part of the index, it then tries to look up the respective row in the clustered index (requesting a shared lock). It's a deadlock.

Obviously, it's much trickier to figure out how such a deadlock happened compared to ones that involve explicit transactions with multiple activities in each transaction. But even if you manage to figure out how a deadlock happened, usually you also want to reproduce it. You need to submit the activities from both sides simultaneously. The easiest way to get the timing right is to run two infinite loops from the two connections. Usually, after a few seconds you will see it happening.

Before I demonstrate such a deadlock, first run the following code to initialize values in the row in T1 where *keycol* is equal to *2*:

```
UPDATE dbo.T1 SET col1 = 102, col2 = 'B' WHERE keycol = 2;
```

Open two connections. Run the following code in connection 1 to execute an infinite loop that updates the row in each iteration, setting *col1* to *203* minus the current value. (This will cause the current value to alternate between 101 and 102.)

```
SET NOCOUNT ON;
WHILE 1 = 1
  UPDATE dbo.T1 SET col1 = 203 - col1 WHERE keycol = 2;
```

Run the following code in connection 2 to execute an infinite loop that queries the row in each iteration and returns the *col2* value. (An index hint is used because the table is so small.)

```
SET NOCOUNT ON;

DECLARE @i AS VARCHAR(10);
WHILE 1 = 1
  SET @i = (SELECT col2 FROM dbo.T1 WITH (index = idx_col1)
             WHERE col1 = 102);
```

When I ran this test, after a few seconds SQL Server detected a deadlock and terminated the transaction in connection 2, generating the following error:

```
Msg 1205, Level 13, State 51, Line 5
Transaction (Process ID 54) was deadlocked on lock resources with another process and has been
chosen as the deadlock victim. Rerun the transaction.
```

When thinking about what measures you can take to prevent this deadlock, remember there are four things to consider. Two of them are inapplicable here because each side submits only a single statement; you cannot reverse the order of access to the objects, and you cannot shorten the transaction. However, you still have two options. One option is to extend the index on *col1* to include *col2*.

This way, you prevent the need for the lookup in the SELECT statement, and therefore prevent the deadlock. The other option is to evaluate switching to a row-versioning-based isolation level. Under such an isolation level, readers don't acquire shared locks, which eliminates the possibility of a deadlock in our case. Obviously, you will not consider switching to a row-versioning-based isolation level just for this reason, but if you were evaluating the option anyway, that's one more reason that you add to the list.

When you're done testing, run the following code for cleanup:

```
USE testdb;

IF OBJECT_ID('dbo.T1', 'U') IS NOT NULL DROP TABLE dbo.T1;
IF OBJECT_ID('dbo.T2', 'U') IS NOT NULL DROP TABLE dbo.T2;
```

Close both connections.

Error handling

This section covers error handling in T-SQL using the TRY-CATCH construct. It compares error handling with and without the construct. It describes the available error functions and the THROW command. It also covers how to perform error handling in transactions and how to apply retry logic.

In my examples, I will use a table called Employees, which you create by running the following code:

```
USE tempdb;

IF OBJECT_ID(N'dbo.Employees', N'U') IS NOT NULL DROP TABLE dbo.Employees;

CREATE TABLE dbo.Employees
(
  empid   INT         NOT NULL,
  empname VARCHAR(25) NOT NULL,
  mgrid   INT         NULL,
  /* other columns */
  CONSTRAINT PK_Employees PRIMARY KEY(empid),
  CONSTRAINT CHK_Employees_empid CHECK(empid > 0),
  CONSTRAINT FK_Employees_Employees
    FOREIGN KEY(mgrid) REFERENCES dbo.Employees(empid)
)
```

The TRY-CATCH construct

The TRY-CATCH construct is a classic error-handling construct used by most modern programming languages. The implementation in SQL Server is basic, but if you're an experienced T-SQL developer, you really will appreciate it when you compare it to the legacy error-handling tools.

In old versions of SQL Server, before the introduction of the TRY-CATCH construct, the main tool you had to handle errors was the @@error function. This function tells you how the previous statement terminated. If the statement finished successfully, the function returns 0; if there was an error, the function returns the error number. There are a number of problems with handling errors based on this function. Almost every statement you run causes the value of the function to be overwritten. Therefore, you have to capture the function's value in a variable after every suspect statement that can generate an error in order not to lose the error number. This forces you to mix the usual code and the error-handling code, which is considered a bad practice because it hurts the maintainability and reusability of your error-handling code. In addition, when you are not using the TRY-CATCH construct, there are cases where nonsevere errors cause your batch (for example, procedure) to terminate. In such cases, if you have error-handling code within that batch, it doesn't have a chance to run and you have to deal with the error in the caller.

The TRY-CATCH construct addresses most of the inadequacies of the legacy error-handling tools. You specify your usual code in the TRY block and the error-handling code in the CATCH block. If code in the TRY block completes successfully, the CATCH block is skipped. If there's an error, SQL Server passes control to the first line of code in the CATCH block. As an example, run the following code to insert a new row into the Employees table:

```
SET NOCOUNT ON;

BEGIN TRY
  INSERT INTO dbo.Employees(empid, empname, mgrid)
    VALUES(1, 'Emp1', NULL);
  PRINT 'After INSERT';
END TRY
BEGIN CATCH
  PRINT 'INSERT failed';
  /* handle error */
END CATCH;
```

In the first execution of the code, the INSERT statement completes successfully. The next line of code in the TRY block is executed and the CATCH block is skipped. You get the following output:

```
After INSERT
```

Execute the code again. This time, the INSERT statement fails because of a primary-key violation error. SQL Server passes control to the CATCH block. You get the following output:

```
INSERT failed
```

In case you're curious about the proper use of the semicolon with the TRY-CATCH construct, be aware that you're supposed to place one only after the END CATCH keywords, like so:

```
BEGIN TRY
  ...
END TRY
BEGIN CATCH
  ...
END CATCH;
```

If you specify a semicolon after the BEGIN TRY or BEGIN CATCH clause, you won't get an error. However, in such a case, the semicolon isn't considered to be a terminator of these clauses; rather, it is a meaningless terminator of an empty statement. If you place a semicolon after END TRY, you will get an error. In short, the proper syntax is to place a semicolon only after the END CATCH keywords.

If an error is trapped by a TRY-CATCH construct, the error is not reported to the application. If an error happens within a stored procedure (or within any other module) but not within a TRY block, the error bubbles up until a TRY block is found. SQL Server passes control to the respective CATCH block. If no TRY block is found throughout the call stack, the error is reported to the application. SQL Server supports nesting TRY-CATCH constructs, so if you anticipate errors in the CATCH block, you can place the code within a nested TRY-CATCH construct. If an error happens in a CATCH block without a nested TRY-CATCH construct, the error is treated the same as when you are not using TRY-CATCH.

Most nonsevere errors that terminate the batch when you are not using TRY-CATCH don't terminate it and are trappable when you do use the construct. A conversion error is an example. However, there are still cases in which an error is not trappable with TRY-CATCH in the same batch. For example, compilation and binding errors—like referring to a table or column that doesn't exist—cannot be trappable in the same batch. However, such errors are trappable in the calling batch. So, if you're expecting such errors, make sure you encapsulate the code in a stored procedure and invoke the procedure from a TRY block. Also, some errors with severity 20 and up cause the SQL Server engine to stop processing the session and terminate the connection. Such errors obviously cannot be captured. Errors with severity 20 and up that don't disrupt the connection are trappable.

SQL Server supports a number of functions that provide error information and that you can query in the CATCH block:

- ERROR_NUMBER
- ERROR_MESSAGE
- ERROR_SEVERITY
- ERROR_STATE
- ERROR_LINE
- ERROR_PROCEDURE

Mostly, the functions are self-explanatory, returning the error number, message, severity, state, line number, and procedure name where the error happened. The procedure name is interesting, especially in cases where the error bubbles up. If the error doesn't happen in a procedure, the ERROR_PROCEDURE function returns a NULL. As for the ERROR_NUMBER function, unlike @@error it preserves its value throughout the CATCH block. That's unless you nest TRY-CATCH constructs—in which case, the function returns the error number of the innermost one.

A common practice with error handling is that you want to deal with certain errors in the current procedure but let the upper level in the call stack deal with the rest. Prior to SQL Server 2012, there was no tool you could use to rethrow the original error. The closest tool you had was the RAISERROR command, which raises a user-defined error based on the inputs you provide to it. The typical use of this function is to construct a message containing elements you obtain from the error functions, and then raise a user-defined error with that message. But then you need to add logic to the upper level to anticipate such a user-defined error and to extract the error information from that message. This sort of handling is quite awkward.

SQL Server 2012 introduced the THROW command to address this need. This command has two modes: one with parameters and one without. The former is just an alternative to using the RAISER-ROR command to raise a user-defined error. The latter is the more critical addition. Without parameters, the THROW command simply rethrows the original error.

As an example of typical error handling, the following code demonstrates a TRY-CATCH construct that issues an INSERT statement, traps errors, handles some of the errors, and rethrows the rest:

```
BEGIN TRY

  INSERT INTO dbo.Employees(empid, empname, mgrid) VALUES(2, 'Emp2', 1);
  -- Also try with empid = 0, 'A', NULL, 1/0
  PRINT 'After INSERT';

END TRY
BEGIN CATCH

  IF ERROR_NUMBER() = 2627
  BEGIN
    PRINT 'Handling PK violation...';
  END;
  ELSE IF ERROR_NUMBER() = 547
  BEGIN
    PRINT 'Handling CHECK/FK constraint violation...';
  END;
  ELSE IF ERROR_NUMBER() = 515
  BEGIN
    PRINT 'Handling NULL violation...';
  END;
  ELSE IF ERROR_NUMBER() = 245
  BEGIN
    PRINT 'Handling conversion error...';
  END;
  ELSE
  BEGIN
    PRINT 'Re-throwing error...';
    THROW;
  END;

  PRINT 'Error Number  : ' + CAST(ERROR_NUMBER() AS VARCHAR(10));
  PRINT 'Error Message : ' + ERROR_MESSAGE();
  PRINT 'Error Severity: ' + CAST(ERROR_SEVERITY() AS VARCHAR(10));
  PRINT 'Error State   : ' + CAST(ERROR_STATE() AS VARCHAR(10));
  PRINT 'Error Line    : ' + CAST(ERROR_LINE() AS VARCHAR(10));
  PRINT 'Error Proc    : ' + ISNULL(ERROR_PROCEDURE(), 'Not within proc');

END CATCH;
```

I use this code for illustration purposes. I issue PRINT statements so that you can see which parts of the code are activated.

When you execute this code for the first time, the INSERT statement finishes successfully and the CATCH block is skipped. You get the following output:

```
After INSERT
```

When you execute the code for the second time, the INSERT statement fails because of a primary-key violation and SQL Server passes control to the CATCH block. The error-handling code identifies the error as a primary-key violation error. You get the following output:

```
Handling PK violation...
Error Number  : 2627
Error Message : Violation of PRIMARY KEY constraint 'PK_Employees'. Cannot insert duplicate key
in object 'dbo.Employees'. The duplicate key value is (2).
Error Severity: 14
Error State   : 1
Error Line    : 4
Error Proc    : Not within proc
```

Try the code a few more times after changing the employee ID value you pass to the following options: 0, 'A', NULL, 10/0. The last one will cause a "divide by zero" error. This error isn't one of the errors you want to deal with in the current level; therefore, the code ends up rethrowing the error.

Errors in transactions

When an error happens in a transaction but not in a TRY block, there are two possible consequences as far as the transaction is concerned: either the error is minor enough (for example, a primary-key violation) that SQL Server leaves the transaction open and committable, or the error is severe enough (for example, a conversion error) that SQL Server aborts the transaction. In such a case, it's enough for you to query the @@*trancount* function to know what the transaction state is. If the function returns zero, there's no transaction open; if it returns a value greater than zero, the transaction is open and committable. In the latter case, you can decide what you want to do; you can either roll the transaction back or commit it. If you want all errors to cause the transaction to abort, turn on the session option XACT_ABORT.

When an error happens in a transaction within a TRY block, things are handled differently. An error that would normally cause a transaction to end outside of a TRY block causes it to enter an open but uncommittable state when it happens inside a TRY block. This state is also known as the *failed*, or *doomed*, state. When a transaction is in this state, you're not allowed to make any changes, but you are allowed to read data. You're not allowed to commit the transaction; rather, you eventually will have to roll it back before you can start applying changes in a new transaction. The advantage of this state compared to SQL Server ending your transaction is that you can read data that your transaction generated before you roll the transaction back.

Recall that when you turn on the session option XACT_ABORT, all errors that happen outside of a TRY block cause the transaction to abort. However, turning on this option has a different effect on errors that happen inside a TRY block; all errors cause the transaction to enter the open and uncommittable state.

When an error happens in a transaction within a TRY block, there are three possible consequences as far as the transaction is concerned. If the error is minor enough (for example, a primary-key violation), the transaction remains open and committable. If the error is more severe (for example, a conversion error) but not too severe, the transaction enters the open and uncommittable state. If the error is very severe, SQL Server might end the transaction. As mentioned, some errors with severity 20 and up cause the SQL Server engine to stop processing the session and terminate the connection, so you won't be able to trap those with a TRY-CATCH construct. You will have to deal with such errors in the caller. However, some errors with severity 20 and up don't disrupt the connection, and you will be able to trap them.

If you need to know the state of the transaction after trapping an error with a TRY-CATCH construct, it's not sufficient to query the @@*trancount* function. This function tells you only whether the transaction is open or not, not whether it's open and committable or open and uncommittable. To get this information, you query the XACT_STATE function. This function has three possible returned values: 0 means no open transaction, 1 means open and committable, and –1 means open and uncommittable.

The following code demonstrates how you might want to handle errors in transactions:

```
-- SET XACT_ABORT ON

BEGIN TRY

  BEGIN TRAN;
    INSERT INTO dbo.Employees(empid, empname, mgrid) VALUES(3, 'Emp3', 1);
    /* other activity */
  COMMIT TRAN;

  PRINT 'Code completed successfully.';

END TRY
BEGIN CATCH

  PRINT 'Error ' + CAST(ERROR_NUMBER() AS VARCHAR(10)) + ' found.';

  IF (XACT_STATE()) = -1
  BEGIN
      PRINT 'Transaction is open but uncommittable.';
      /* ...investigate data... */
      ROLLBACK TRAN; -- can only ROLLBACK
      /* ...handle the error... */
  END;
  ELSE IF (XACT_STATE()) = 1
```

```
    BEGIN
        PRINT 'Transaction is open and committable.';
        /* ...handle error... */
        COMMIT TRAN; -- or ROLLBACK
    END;
    ELSE
    BEGIN
        PRINT 'No open transaction.';
        /* ...handle error... */
    END;

END CATCH;

-- SET XACT_ABORT OFF
```

In the CATCH block, you query the XACT_STATE function. If the function returns –1, you can read data to investigate what you need, but then you have to roll the transaction back. If it returns 1, you can roll back or commit the transaction as you wish. If it returns 0, there's no transaction open, so there's no point in trying to commit or roll back the transaction. Such an attempt would result in an error. You can open a new transaction and apply changes if you like.

Run this code for the first time. The INSERT statement completes successfully, and you get the following output:

```
Code completed successfully.
```

Run this code for the second time. The INSERT statement fails because of a primary-key violation error, but it leaves the transaction open and committable. You get the following output:

```
Error 2627 found.
Transaction is open and committable.
```

Change the employee ID from 3 to 'abc', and run the code again. The INSERT statement fails because of a conversion error and causes the transaction to enter the open and uncommittable state. You get the following output:

```
Error 245 found.
Transaction is open but uncommittable.
```

Change the employee ID back to 3, uncomment the SET XACT_ABORT commands, and run the code again. The INSERT statement fails because of a primary-key violation error and causes the transaction to enter the open and uncommittable state. You get the following output:

```
Error 2627 found.
Transaction is open but uncommittable.
```

Retry logic

With certain kinds of errors, like deadlock and "update conflict" errors, a classic treatment involves applying retry logic. If your session is the one that got the error, once you end the transaction, the other session can continue work. There's a likelihood that if you retry the task, you will be successful. You can create a wrapper procedure that implements the retry logic and calls the procedure that handles the original task. The following code demonstrates what such a wrapper procedure might look like (*MyProc* is the procedure that handles the original task):

```
CREATE PROC dbo.MyProcWrapper(<parameters>)
AS
BEGIN
  DECLARE @retry INT = 10;

  WHILE (@retry > 0)
  BEGIN
    BEGIN TRY
      EXEC dbo.MyProc <parameters>;

      SET @retry = 0; -- finished successfully
    END TRY
    BEGIN CATCH
      SET @retry -= 1;

      IF (@retry > 0 AND ERROR_NUMBER() IN (1205, 3960)) -- errors for retry
      BEGIN
        IF XACT_STATE() <> 0
          ROLLBACK TRAN;
      END;
      ELSE
      BEGIN
        THROW; -- max # of retries reached or other error
      END;
    END CATCH;
  END;
END;
GO
```

In this example, the code sets the retry counter (*@retry* variable) to 10. If you want, you can parameterize this counter. The code enters a loop that keeps iterating while the retry counter is greater than zero. The code executes *MyProc* within a TRY block. If the procedure completes successfully, the code sets the retry counter to zero to prevent the loop from executing again. Otherwise, the code reduces the retry counter by one. If, after reducing the counter, there are retries left and the error is a deadlock or "update conflict" error, the code checks whether a transaction is open. If a transaction is open, the code rolls it back. If the retry counter drops to zero or the error is not a deadlock or "update conflict" error, the code rethrows the error to let the upper level deal with it.

This example demonstrates how to handle retry logic for deadlock and "update conflict" errors involving disk-based tables. The same pattern can be used to handle errors with memory-optimized tables. However, instead of looking for errors 1205 and 3960, you will look for error numbers 41302, 41305, 41325, and 41301, which represent update conflict, repeatable read validation, serializable validation, and dependent transaction aborted errors, respectively.

Conclusion

This chapter focused on some programmability constructs SQL Server supports, mainly the ones that involve queries. It covered dynamic SQL, user-defined functions, stored procedures, triggers, SQLCLR, transactions and concurrency, and error handling. The discussions in many cases focused on robust and efficient use of the code.

In-Memory OLTP

Microsoft SQL Server 2014 introduces the In-Memory OLTP feature. In-Memory OLTP can produce great increases in performance, but you need to understand that the increases are not primarily because the data is resident in memory. Rather, the increases come from leveraging the fact that the data is in memory and using different data structures and methods that make database operations much more efficient. This chapter will help you to understand these different structures and methods and how to use them to unlock the performance potential of In-Memory OLTP. I'll give a brief overview to help you understand the context, and then discuss the ways in which memory-optimized tables need to be handled differently when writing queries and designing systems.

In this chapter, I'll base my examples primarily on the AdventureWorks sample database, as extended to include memory-optimized tables. This database can be downloaded from *https://msftdbprodsamples.codeplex.com/releases/view/114491* and used on any server running a compatible version of SQL Server (SQL Server 2014 or newer Enterprise, Developer, or Eval edition).

In-Memory OLTP overview

The In-Memory OLTP system started out as a blue-sky project, where the SQL Server development team was challenged to wipe the slate clean and imagine what a database engine would look like if it were designed from scratch given today's business and hardware landscape. This blue-sky project became the development project that was code-named *Hekaton*. The team made several observations about the environment in modern computing:

- Commodity systems now support enough memory to keep an interesting data set in memory at all times. Previously, a database management system could pull only a small subset of data into memory at one time. This data would be manipulated and then evicted from memory to make room for other data. With commodity systems that can now hold hundreds of GB of main memory, we now can hold an interesting data set in memory at all times, without the need to evict data as before.

- Processor clock speed is no longer increasing. Although overall chip complexity continues to increase following Moore's Law, the clock speed has plateaued at around 3 GHz and hasn't moved from there in many years.

- On the other hand, the number of cores per socket is increasing. The additional complexity and power of modern CPU chips is being delivered in the form of more and more cores (both physical and virtual) per socket.

The implication of the latter two observations is that each execution stream will not move faster than it did years ago, but you have many more potential parallel execution streams to work with.

The In-Memory OLTP feature of SQL Server is a different implementation than traditional SQL Server. On one hand, it is a fully integrated part of the SQL engine; on the other hand, it is an entirely new execution engine. So what is In-Memory OLTP, and what makes it different from the rest of the SQL Server engine?

Data is always in memory

In the In-Memory OLTP environment, data is always in memory. There is no concept of paging subsets of the data in and out of memory. When a table is designated as *memory optimized*, its rows are never paged out. Although this is a significant change in behavior, it is only the start. After all, if you have sufficient memory on a traditional database server, you have no reason to evict pages from memory. You can, however, leverage this information to do things more wisely.

Because you know you'll never need to page data in and out of memory, you can eliminate a number of structures and features of the engine. Pages, for example, are structures whose purpose is to facilitate moving subsets of data in and out of memory. Because this system never does that, you can eliminate pages entirely. As shown in Figure 10-1, the in-memory data structure for a row in a memory-optimized table is simply the data storage for the columns themselves in native format, as well as a couple of timestamps for visibility and isolation purposes (which I'll get into more in the "Isolation" section) and an array of pointers used for index chains.

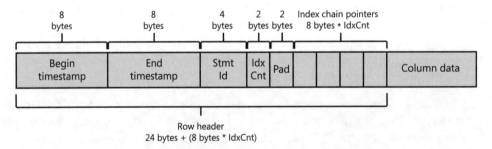

FIGURE 10-1 Memory-optimized table row format.

The begin and end timestamps are important for maintaining transaction isolation and consistency. The begin timestamp marks the time when the row version was created. Any transaction that started before this timestamp will not see this row version. The end timestamp marks the time when this row version was logically deleted. Transactions starting before this time but after the begin timestamp time will continue to see the row version so that a consistent view is provided. Transactions starting after the end timestamp time will not see this row version.

You can also dispense with the considerable infrastructure used to track which pages are in memory, which pages are in the buffer pool, where in the buffer pool a given page might be, whether the in-memory copy of the page has been modified (making it "dirty" and requiring that it eventually be flushed back out to disk), and so on. All that management just doesn't happen, which is a significant savings in processing effort and time.

It also means that a transaction against a memory-optimized table will never have to wait and go back on the scheduler queue because it's waiting for an IO to bring a needed page into memory.

Native compilation

This is another new innovation of In-Memory OLTP in SQL Server. In recognition of the stalled processor speed and the need to always get as much work out of every CPU cycle as possible, the In-Memory OLTP system also gives you the option to natively compile stored procedures that access only memory-optimized tables. Okay, so what does that mean?

First, the prerequisite: this capability will work only if you are creating a stored procedure and that stored procedure does *not* access any traditional row-based or column-based tables. The only tables that can be accessed in one of these procedures are memory-optimized tables. Also, note that the native compilation environment has a somewhat restricted T-SQL surface area, so at least for the first release, you might be required to do some workarounds if you encounter missing surface area. Some workarounds are trivial and don't really cost anything performance-wise. Others can be prohibitive, either in terms of implementation complexity or performance impact.

Now the payback: if you create a natively compiled stored procedure, the T-SQL source is run through the standard SQL Query Optimizer and then translated into C code, which is capable of accessing the memory structures containing the rows directly. This C code is then compiled and built into a dynamic-link library (DLL), which is loaded into the SQL process dynamically, in the same way that the fundamental data-access routines are built and loaded when you first create a table.

The result of all this is that when you execute a natively compiled stored procedure, instead of looking up the T-SQL source and executing it as a series of interpreted SQL operations with many context switches along the way, a natively compiled procedure is simply a function call in the engine context. There's not even a context switch. As discussed earlier, there's never a stall for IO either. When we get into the locking section, you'll discover there isn't any reason to stall while waiting on locks or latches. In short, when a natively compiled procedure starts executing, there isn't any reason for it to stop and wait for anything. Once it starts, it will generally run to completion without ever being stalled. This makes for an extremely efficient execution engine.

Lock and latch-free architecture

Another key facet of this architecture is that it is designed to be completely lock and latch free. Remember I discussed earlier that modern processors are delivering more and more cores per socket and that to exploit that processing power you need to enable an increasing number of parallel execution threads.

Latches are used to protect physical structures such as pages. As I mentioned, you don't use any pages for memory-optimized data, so you have no need for page latches. In addition to this, all row and index structures are engineered to be lock free, using an optimistic concurrency model.

Most database systems, including SQL Server, are designed with a pessimistic concurrency model. Fundamentally, this means the system assumes that if two threads try to access the same data structure, a conflict might occur that causes problems. To avoid that, systems designed with pessimistic concurrency use *locks*. The first thread to attempt access will be granted a lock on the structure, and others that have conflicting requests will block and wait until the first thread is finished. This model does a good job at guaranteeing consistency, but it has the unfortunate effect of leading to a lot of threads waiting for locks to be released. The SQL Server development team also discovered while profiling the SQL engine that a surprising number of CPU cycles were spent just acquiring and releasing locks and latches, even when there was never a conflict or wait.

Optimistic concurrency, on the other hand, assumes that in most cases there will not be a conflict that causes inconsistency, and thus you can get by without stalling threads. Concurrency is guaranteed by checking for actual write-write conflicts and, if a conflict is found, failing the second thread that attempts to modify the same data. I'll get into this in more detail in the "Commit validation errors" section.

The result of this is that you never have threads stalled waiting for locks or latches to be released. So, if the application is designed appropriately, you can have many execution threads running in parallel, making use of all cores in your system.

SQL Server integration

Perhaps the most unique feature of SQL Server In-Memory OLTP, compared to other in-memory offerings, is that it is fully integrated with the core database engine. You can decide on a table-by-table basis which tables should be memory optimized, which should stay in traditional row stores, and which should be in column stores. In this way, you have full control to put each piece of data in the most appropriate storage format, based on its usage and performance requirements.

So you will likely have a database that contains memory optimized, traditional tables and clustered column-store tables. You'll need to consider some implications of crossing those boundaries, and we'll get into those issues. On the positive side, you have the same tools to aid you in your tuning efforts.

Not only can databases have a mix of storage types, traditional row stores, memory optimized tables, and column stores, but tables containing such mixes behave like any other SQL table. The same syntax applies, the same connection methods are used, and the same management tools and utilities are used. Backup just works. AlwaysOn clusters and Availability Groups just work. As one of our early adopters said, "If you know SQL, you know Hekaton." This existing knowledge is a significant advantage compared to moving to a different platform, because you don't need to learn a completely new system for managing your data.

Creating memory-optimized tables

To create memory-optimized tables within a database, the database must first contain a special-purpose *Memory Optimized Data* filegroup. This filegroup will contain the data persisted for in-memory tables. The syntax is similar to FILESTREAM filegroups, with the exception of the *CONTAINS MEMORY_OPTIMIZED_DATA* option. The code to add a memory optimized data filegroup to the AdventureWorks database is shown in Listing 10-1.

LISTING 10-1 Creating a memory optimized data filegroup and container

```
ALTER DATABASE AdventureWorks2014
ADD FILEGROUP AdventureWorks2014_mod CONTAINS MEMORY_OPTIMIZED_DATA;
GO
ALTER DATABASE CURRENT ADD FILE
(NAME='AdventureWorks2014_mod',
 FILENAME='Q:\MOD_DATA\AdventureWorks2014_mod')
 TO FILEGROUP AdventureWorks2014_mod;
```

Note that you can add more than one container (using the ADD FILE syntax, just as you would for a FILESTREAM container). All data in memory-optimized tables must be read into memory before the database can be recovered and brought online, so you need to consider the speed with which that data can be read from storage. Having multiple containers will speed up database startup by enabling the engine to process all containers in parallel. To further optimize the startup, you should spread the IO load of the checkpoint files over multiple storage devices.

After you create the memory optimized data filegroup, you can proceed to create a memory-optimized data table. You'll see that the syntax for doing so (shown in Listing 10-2) is not significantly different from creating any other table, with the exception of some specific keywords.

LISTING 10-2 Creating a memory-optimized table

```
USE AdventureWorks2014;
GO

CREATE TABLE Sales.ShoppingCartItem_inmem
(
  ShoppingCartItemID int IDENTITY(1,1) NOT NULL,
  ShoppingCartID nvarchar(50) NOT NULL,
  Quantity int NOT NULL CONSTRAINT IMDF_ShoppingCartItem_Quantity  DEFAULT ((1)),
  ProductID int NOT NULL,
  DateCreated datetime2(7) NOT NULL
    CONSTRAINT IMDF_ShoppingCartItem_DateCreated  DEFAULT (sysdatetime()),
  ModifiedDate datetime2(7) NOT NULL
    CONSTRAINT IMDF_ShoppingCartItem_ModifiedDate  DEFAULT (sysdatetime()),
  CONSTRAINT IMPK_ShoppingCartItem_ShoppingCartItemID PRIMARY KEY NONCLUSTERED
    HASH (ShoppingCartItemID) WITH ( BUCKET_COUNT = 1048576),
  INDEX IX_CartDate NONCLUSTERED (DateCreated ASC),
  INDEX IX_ProductID NONCLUSTERED HASH (ProductID) WITH ( BUCKET_COUNT = 1048576)
) WITH ( MEMORY_OPTIMIZED = ON , DURABILITY = SCHEMA_ONLY );
```

```
GO

-- Insert the data from the original Sales.ShoppingCartItem table
-- to the new memory-optimized table

SET IDENTITY_INSERT Sales.ShoppingCartItem_inmem ON;

INSERT INTO Sales.ShoppingCartItem_inmem
    (ShoppingCartItemID, ShoppingCartID, Quantity, ProductID, DateCreated, ModifiedDate)
  SELECT ShoppingCartItemID, ShoppingCartID, Quantity, ProductID, DateCreated,
ModifiedDate
  FROM Sales.ShoppingCartItem;

SET IDENTITY_INSERT Sales.ShoppingCartItem_inmem OFF;
```

Much of this is familiar syntax. There are just a few things that are done differently:

- Constraints and indexes are always specified as part of the CREATE TABLE statement. This is because In-Memory OLTP in SQL Server 2014 does not permit tables to be altered after creation. So constraints or indexes cannot be added after the table creation.

- The last line contains two new options: *MEMORY_OPTIMIZED* and *DURABILITY*.

- *MEMORY_OPTIMIZED = ON* specifies that this is a memory-optimized table. Specifying *OFF* would result in a traditional table.

- *DURABILITY* has two options: *SCHEMA_AND_DATA* and *SCHEMA_ONLY*. The *SCHEMA_ONLY* option is a special-purpose table where only the schema is persisted across restarts, and no data is persisted. *DURABILITY = SCHEMA_AND_DATA* specifies normal, full-durability semantics apply to this table. *SCHEMA_ONLY* durability is appropriate for data that needs to be accessed using transactional semantics but that does not have long-term value. Examples include data at the midpoint of an Extract, Transform, and Load (ETL) stream, where the source is still available, or various caches such as the ASP.NET Session State Cache.

Creating indexes in memory-optimized tables

Indexes in memory-optimized tables in some ways are the same as any other indexes you've used for years. In other ways, however, they behave differently from the indexes you're familiar with. It helps to remember that these indexes are not disk-based structures—they are memory structures. Rather than using references to pages that contain data, these indexes are made up of pointers to data structures just like the structures in a program that might be querying the database.

Clustered vs. nonclustered indexes

Traditional tables use indexes that might be either clustered or nonclustered. *Clustered indexes* contain the primary copy of the data for the table. *Nonclustered indexes* contain a subset of the columns in the table that are used as the keys for that index, as well as containing optional additional columns that are copied into the nonclustered index structures to avoid the overhead of looking up the page in the clustered index.

In memory-optimized tables, there really is no concept of clustered versus nonclustered indexes because all indexes are simply pointers to the row structure in memory. Because all columns in the row are not stored in the index structure itself, all indexes on memory-optimized tables are considered to be nonclustered. Of course, the row structure has all the columns, so you can think of every index in a memory-optimized table as being a *covering index* (an index that has direct access to all columns needed for a query, whether included in the index key or not). This is because it will have access to the full row without any additional lookups.

Within the nonclustered indexes used on memory-optimized tables, there are two distinct types of indexes: B-tree based indexes, which use the syntax NONCLUSTERED, and hash indexes.

Nonclustered indexes

The primary index type for use in memory-optimized tables is nonclustered. These indexes are sometimes referred to as *range* indexes because, unlike hash indexes, they can be used to efficiently retrieve ranges of rows using inequality predicates rather than the exact key lookups that hash indexes are designed for. Of course, like the traditional B-trees we're more familiar with, nonclustered indexes can be used for exact key lookups, but they will not be as fast or efficient as hash indexes for that usage.

The syntax for creating a nonclustered index is simply this:

```
INDEX IX_CartDate NONCLUSTERED (DateCreated ASC)
```

You can find the context for this fragment near the end of the table definition shown earlier in Listing 10-2.

Note that all indexes in memory-optimized tables are created as part of the table, not added separately.

Nonclustered index structure

Nonclustered indexes on memory-optimized tables are different from traditional B-tree indexes in that their BW-Tree structure gives them the properties of being lock and latch free, and having variable sized pages that are always tightly packed, with no empty space.

Traditional B-tree indexes are subject to significant locking not only when an individual entry is being inserted, but also when the index needs to be rearranged. Entire ranges of the tree are commonly locked when pages need to be split or merged. BW-Tree indexes are capable of inserting pages without ever locking the structure, because they create new pages and simply switch the pointer to the page using the page-mapping table. Swapping the content of pages out also frees you from the need to create large empty pages with room for future insertions. Instead, you just create a new version of the page with the additional entry and replace the previous version of the page.

These characteristics gave rise to the name *BW-Tree*. As the team that invented the structure was looking for a name, they discussed the attributes: lock-free, latch-free, flash-friendly, and so on. Someone noted that it sounded like a list of current industry buzzwords that this design embodied. From this the BW-Tree (buzzword tree) was named.

The page-mapping table is the key to enabling these indexes to function without the need for locks or latches. The table provides a layer of indirection between the logical page ID within the index and the physical location of the page. Unlike traditional index pages, where the identity of the page and its physical location are bound in a one-to-one relationship, the page-mapping table gives you the ability to effectively replace the contents of an index page by swapping the physical pointer to a new copy of the index page without disrupting any of the pages that refer to it. This is diagrammed in Figure 10-2.

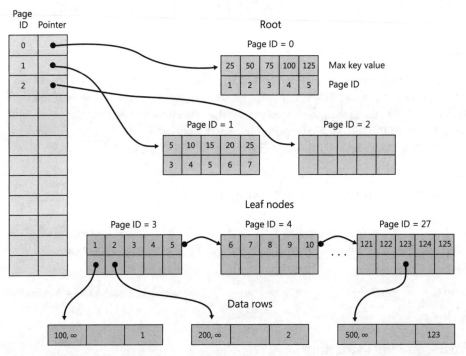

FIGURE 10-2 Nonclustered indexes.

The links between pages of the BW-Tree structure itself are all in the form of logical page IDs. These are then looked up via the page-mapping table. If you need to update a page in the index (to account for a page split or to insert a new value in the leaf nodes), you can simply build the new version of the page and change the entry in the page-mapping table to point to the new version of the page. Say you need to modify index page 101. You just create a new copy of page 101 and call it

101', with the new contents. You change the pointer in the mapping table entry for page 101 to point to the new copy, 101'. All references to page 101 still go to page 101—you just swapped the physical page pointed to by logical page number 101 with another physical page, atomically.

Each entry in an index page has a key value (in non-leaf pages, this is the high end of the range in the page in the next level of the index) and a payload. For non-leaf pages, the payload is a page ID. For leaf pages, the payload is a pointer to the actual row or rows that match the key value.

The leaf pages are linked to each other in the order of the scan for that index. So, if the index is defined based on a key ASCENDING, each page will link to the page with the next higher grouping of key values. For DESCENDING indexes, pages will link to the leaf page with the next lower grouping of key values. You should understand that, unlike they do in normal B-tree indexes, the links do not go in both directions. This means that if an index is defined in one direction, you cannot retrieve rows in the opposite order without going through a sort step, as you'll see a little later. Again, these links are done by page ID, not pointer, so that you can replace the contents of a page without having the change ripple through the whole structure. This linking of leaf nodes is what makes scans much more efficient—once you find the starting point of the scan, you simply follow the links between leaf pages until you reach the end point of the scan.

As with most B-tree structures, these indexes can grow and shrink as needed. This is different from the case with hash indexes where you need to pre-size the index for the expected cardinality of the table, as you will see when I discuss hash indexes later.

Nonclustered index behavior

Nonclustered indexes on memory-optimized tables behave similarly to traditional nonclustered/B-tree indexes, with some key differences, as described in the following sections.

Indexes are latch free

Unlike traditional B-tree indexes, the index structures used for memory-optimized tables use a slightly different structure based on BW-Trees. This structure enables these indexes to operate without any locks or latches. So two threads can insert adjacent rows into an index, even causing page splits, without blocking either thread. This is done in large part by means of the page-mapping table described earlier, which facilitates replacing the contents of an index page in a single atomic operation.

Indexes are single direction

Traditional indexes can be used to produce scans in either direction; however, nonclustered indexes in memory-optimized tables can be traversed only in one direction. So if you need to retrieve data in both directions, you will need to define an index for each direction; otherwise, the scans that are not in the same direction as the index will need a sort operator to reorder the result set.

For the following examples, you use the nonclustered index on *DateCreated*. Note that it is specified as ASC sort order.

```
INDEX IX_CartDate NONCLUSTERED (DateCreated ASC)
```

When the following query is run against this index, you can see that the query plan is able to do a simple index seek on the nonclustered index. This is because the query and the index both use the same sort direction (ascending). (See Figure 10-3.)

```
SELECT DateCreated
FROM Sales.ShoppingCartItem_inmem
WHERE DateCreated BETWEEN '20131101' AND '20131201'
ORDER BY DateCreated ASC;
```

Index Seek (NonClustered)
[ShoppingCartItem_inmem].[IX_CartDa…
Cost: 100 %

FIGURE 10-3 Query plan for an index seek ordered in the same direction as the index definition.

This query is the same as the preceding one, but with the opposite sort order.

```
SELECT DateCreated
FROM Sales.ShoppingCartItem_inmem
WHERE DateCreated BETWEEN '20131101' AND '20131201'
ORDER BY DateCreated DESC;
```

You can see in Figure 10-4 that because the query specified a sort order (DESC) that is not the same as the order specified for the index (ASC), the query plan needs to contain a sort operator, which adds to the cost of the query. Also, note that although both queries do the same index seek, because of the additional sort work needed, the seek now accounts for only 20 percent of the cost, meaning that the overall cost of the query has gone up five times the original cost.

Index Seek (NonClustered)
[ShoppingCartItem_inmem].[IX_CartDa…
Cost: 20 %

FIGURE 10-4 Query plan for in index seek ordered in the opposite direction from the index definition.

Indexes are covering

As with all indexes on memory-optimized tables, the index structures contain pointers directly to the full row structure, so it is not necessary (or indeed possible) to add included columns to the index to reduce lookups. Any lookup gets you to a structure that contains all columns for the row or rows. In that sense, all indexes are "covering," in that they directly give access to all columns in the table.

Hash indexes

Hash indexes are a new type of index for SQL Server. Hash indexes consist of a hash table, which is an array of pointers to the rows in memory. This array of pointers (*buckets*) is explicitly sized when the index is created.

Lookups are simply taking the key values for the set of key columns and running them through the hash function, which produces an offset in the array of pointers, which leads directly to the rows that match the hash value. The hash function is designed to spread the data as evenly and randomly across the hash buckets as possible. That means that there is explicitly no ordering within the structures of a hash index, unlike the natural ordering contained in a nonclustered index (whether on a traditional disk-based table or the style described earlier on a memory-optimized table). Of course, if there are far fewer distinct values than rows in the table, the hash function will not be able to spread the data appropriately. In the extreme case, a hash index on a TRUE | FALSE column would have only two buckets populated, regardless of how many rows were in the table. This would obviously not be a good choice. Ideally, there will be one row for each hash bucket. When multiple values hash to the same bucket, the query must follow index chain pointers to find the row needed by the query, which is not as efficient as a direct lookup of a single row.

Hash index structure

Hash indexes are structurally simple. Each hash index on a table consists of an array of hash buckets, which are memory pointers. Each bucket points to the first row that hashes to its offset in the array. For example, if you have a simple char(3) index on the Airport code, you take the key value for a row (say, SEA) and run it through the hash function. This results in an integer in the range of the number of hash buckets. If the index was created with eight buckets, every possible value hashes into a number between 0 and 7. Although it is recommended that you have at least as many buckets as you expect to have distinct key values, there is not a one-to-one mapping. There will likely be empty buckets and other buckets with more than one value in them. The overall design of hash functions is to spread the data as randomly as possible among the array of buckets provided.

As with nonclustered indexes, for each index on a table, there is a pointer in every row for index chains. When more than one row hashes to the same bucket, as in the case of duplicate values, or distinct values that hash to the same bucket, you use these pointers to chain from one row to the next, and so on, until you cover all the rows that hash to that bucket. (See Figure 10-5.)

Hash index on Name   Hash index on Airport

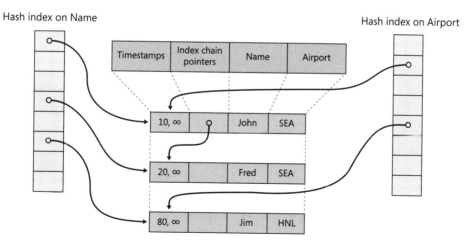

FIGURE 10-5 Hash indexes.

The syntax for creating a hash index (within the creation of the table itself) is similar to the syntax for the nonclustered index I discussed earlier and is taken from Listing 10-2:

```
INDEX IX_ProductID NONCLUSTERED HASH (ProductID) WITH (BUCKET_COUNT = 1048576)
```

Note the added *HASH* keyword as well as the additional clause *WITH (BUCKET_COUNT = 1048576)*. This last clause is what sizes the array of pointers that form the root of the hash index. It is critical to note that, at least in SQL Server 2014, this array cannot be resized once the index and table are created. Unlike nonclustered indexes, hash indexes cannot dynamically resize, and once they are created, the size of the bucket array cannot be changed. This restriction can have significant performance implications, so you need to think carefully about how big the table that this index is a part of will eventually grow.

Hash index behavior

Hash indexes have a specific purpose, which is to optimize exact key lookups. As you can see, they are extremely efficient at doing this. Because all the data structures involved in the hash index are in memory, the entire lookup process translates into directly following memory pointers.

If, however, you are doing a full table scan, the system must visit every hash bucket, whether it is empty or not, and then for each populated bucket, it will follow the index chain pointers of rows that hash to the same bucket.

Unlike B-trees, there is no inherent ordering of the data within hash indexes. That has a couple of practical implications. The first is that there is no way to leverage the index structures to efficiently find a range of values. If the query predicate does not give an exact value, the resulting query will perform a full table scan, filtering for rows between the given values.

It also means you can't leverage an index's structure to return an ordered set. Consider the following query:

```
SELECT ProductID, Name FROM Production.Product ORDER BY ProductID;
```

When run against the traditional AdventureWorks Production.Product table, this code results in the execution plan seen in Figure 10-6:

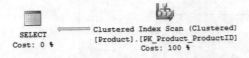

```
         SELECT              Clustered Index Scan (Clustered)
         Cost: 0 %           [Product].[PK_Product_ProductID]
                                       Cost: 100 %
```

FIGURE 10-6 Query plan for a traditional index.

Even though you specified that the results should be ordered by ProductID, there is no sort phase because the B-tree index is inherently ordered. In contrast, as seen in Figure 10-7, when the same query is run against the in-memory version of this same table, which has a hash index on ProductID, you see the following execution plan:

```
SELECT ProductID, Name FROM Production.Product_inmem ORDER BY ProductID;
```

FIGURE 10-7 Query plan for the hash index.

Note that after the index scan, you still need to do a sort, because the scan of a hash index does not produce ordered results automatically.

Where hash indexes work well

Hash indexes excel at single-point lookups, where you have an exact key for the lookup. In this case, the lookup is as simple as running the keys through the hash function and then following the pointer to the data. If more than one row hashes to the same bucket, the initial pointer takes you to the first row, and then you follow the continuation pointers in each row to the next in the chain of records that all hash to that bucket.

Most OLTP systems use the pattern of exact key lookups of one or a few rows in their most performance-critical logic. Think of inventory updates, where you need to find a part number and change the quantity on hand, a billing system that needs to record millions of cell-phone call records per day, or an ordering system where a single order and its line items are referenced repeatedly through the business process. In all these scenarios, you can see that these processes can be greatly sped up if you have an index structure that is optimized for this pattern of access.

Things to watch out for

As fast as hash indexes are when used properly, there are cases where they can be much less efficient and cause surprising performance issues. I'll go through a few scenarios and explain what happens to cause the problems.

Poorly configured bucket count   When a hash index is created, you are required to specify a bucket count. The bucket count should ideally be close to _1 – 2X_ the number of unique key values that are expected in the table. For example, if you have an index on part_no and expect 10,000 unique part numbers, you specify a BUCKET_COUNT of _10,000 – 20,000_. If you use a bucket count of 100, those 10,000 part numbers get spread across only 100 buckets. So, on average, every bucket will contain 100 rows. That means, in turn, that on average a lookup, which could be a one-pointer lookup, will need to go through 50 rows before the correct row is found. If the size is further off, the performance impact is even more severe.

The other impact of undersizing hash buckets relates to performing an insert. To insert a row in a hash index where there are collisions on the hash buckets, the system has to first find the proper insertion point. If the values are all duplicates, this isn't a big impact because you simply insert in the head of the chain. If, however, there are lots of hash collisions but NOT many duplicate values, you need to walk the chain of duplicates to find the proper place for this new value. The list is sorted by key value, so all entries for duplicate keys are grouped together within the list. New duplicates are inserted at the beginning of the group with the same key value.

Take the example of the following two tables, which is shown in Listing 10-3.

LISTING 10-3 Tables with different bucket counts

```
-- The first table has a bucket count of 8

CREATE TABLE dbo.tTable
(
    c INT NOT NULL,
    PRIMARY KEY NONCLUSTERED HASH (c) WITH ( BUCKET_COUNT = 8)
)
WITH ( MEMORY_OPTIMIZED = ON , DURABILITY = SCHEMA_ONLY );

-- The second table is identical except it has a bucket count of 2,000,000

CREATE TABLE dbo.tTable2
(
    c int NOT NULL,
    PRIMARY KEY NONCLUSTERED HASH (c) WITH ( BUCKET_COUNT = 2000000)
)
WITH ( MEMORY_OPTIMIZED = ON , DURABILITY = SCHEMA_ONLY );
```

Here you created two identical tables with a single column, which is a primary key (ensuring that there will be no duplicate values). The only difference between them is that the bucket count on the first table is 8, while the bucket count on the second is 2 million.

If you insert a modest number of rows—say, 10 or 20—you won't see much difference in execution time. If, however, you insert 100,000 rows in each table, you do see a large difference in execution time for inserting the batch of 100,000 rows. In fact, if you plot a number of points with varying numbers of rows inserted, the elapsed time becomes exponentially larger as the row count increases. (See Table 10-1.) You use nondurable tables to eliminate log growth or other IO issues, and you use natively compiled procedures to get as efficient an execution as possible:

```
CREATE PROCEDURE Fill_tTable
@iterations INT
WITH NATIVE_COMPILATION, SCHEMABINDING, EXECUTE AS OWNER
AS
BEGIN ATOMIC WITH
  (TRANSACTION ISOLATION LEVEL = SNAPSHOT,
   LANGUAGE = N'us_english');
DECLARE @i INT = 0;
WHILE (@i < @iterations)
BEGIN
  INSERT INTO dbo.tTable (C) VALUES (@i);
  SET @i += 1;
END;
END;
GO
```

```
CREATE PROCEDURE Fill_tTable2
@iterations INT
WITH NATIVE_COMPILATION, SCHEMABINDING, EXECUTE AS OWNER AS
BEGIN ATOMIC WITH
  (TRANSACTION ISOLATION LEVEL = SNAPSHOT,
   LANGUAGE = N'us_english')
  DECLARE @i INT = 0;
  WHILE (@i < @iterations)
  BEGIN
    INSERT INTO dbo.tTable2 (C) VALUES (@i);
    SET @i += 1;
  END;
END;
GO

EXEC Fill_tTable 100000;

EXEC Fill_tTable2 100000;
```

TABLE 10-1 Performance comparison of the two tables with different bucket counts

Table	CPU time	Elapsed time
tTable (bucket count 8)	10,625 ms	10,619 ms
tTable2 (bucket count 2,000,000)	124 ms	125 ms

Even in this trivial example, there is a significant difference in both CPU and elapsed times. In a more complex ETL load involving billions of rows, this becomes a significant performance issue.

You can determine the health of a hash index by querying the DMV sys.dm_db_xtp_hash_index_stats:

```
SELECT
    object_name(hs.object_id) AS [object name],
    hs.total_bucket_count,
    hs.empty_bucket_count,
    floor((cast(empty_bucket_count as float)/total_bucket_count) * 100) AS[empty_bucket_percent],
    hs.avg_chain_length,
    hs.max_chain_length
FROM sys.dm_db_xtp_hash_index_stats AS hs
    JOIN sys.indexes AS i
    ON hs.object_id=i.object_id AND hs.index_id=i.index_id;
```

This query produces the following results:

```
Object   total_bucket_   empty_bucket_   empty_bucket_   avg_chain_   max_chain_
Name     count           count           percent         length       length
-------  -------------   -------------   -------------   ----------   -----------
tTable   8               0               0               12500        12543
tTable2  33554432        33454455        99              1            2
```

Here you see that for the first table, there are no empty buckets, and the average hash collision chain is 12,500. This means that by the time this table was full, insertions had to scan through over 6,000 entries on average to find the proper insertion point. For the second table, in contrast, there are nearly 2 million empty buckets, and the average chain length is 1. With this query, you look at both the empty bucket percent and the average chain length. Ideally, you're looking for an empty bucket percent of over 30 percent and an average chain length in the single digits.

If the bucket count is oversized, the impacts are not nearly as severe, so it is always better to err on the side of oversizing. There are two impacts to oversizing:

- First, the hash buckets are each an 8-byte pointer, which consumes memory, so a dramatically oversized hash-bucket count will result in wasting memory. Because there is only one hash table per index, this is usually not a significant factor.

- The second impact comes into play when the query results in a table scan. Table scans are implemented by visiting each bucket in the index being scanned. The optimizer will choose the hash index with the lowest bucket count to scan, because that will minimize the number of buckets to be visited. If 90 percent of the buckets are empty because of an oversized hash table, the query will still need to visit every bucket, which slows down the query substantially. If you follow my recommendation that there be at least one nonclustered index on a table, this will not be a problem because the optimizer will choose the BW-Tree nonclustered index for the scan.

Query predicates that don't include all key columns   The hash function is a mathematical function, which takes all the key columns as input and produces an offset in the hash array. If the query predicate doesn't give all the columns, the function can't work, because it doesn't have all the required inputs. When this happens, the hash index can't be used. The result of this is usually a full table scan, so this error takes you from a direct pointer lookup to a full table scan, which has a disastrous effect on performance.

This situation, unfortunately, is easy to fall into because with traditional B-tree indexes, we're used to being able to specify the leading columns of an index and get a plan that uses an index seek. When this same query is run against a hash index, the result will be a table scan if not all key columns in the hash index are provided in the query predicate. It can easily produce a situation where a direct conversion from a traditional table to a memory-optimized table can result in decreased performance, when the original queries use only leading columns. In this case, it's better to either specify an index with fewer columns or add an additional index for the queries that cannot specify all key columns for the original index. You can see this approach in Listing 10-4, which produces the query plan shown in Figure 10-8.

LISTING 10-4 Illustration of the results of queries that specify only leading columns

```
CREATE TABLE dbo.IndexExample (
ID  INT NOT NULL IDENTITY(1,1) PRIMARY KEY NONCLUSTERED HASH WITH (BUCKET_COUNT=1024),
C1 INT NOT NULL,
C2 INT NOT NULL,
C3 INT NOT NULL,
C4 INT NOT NULL,

-- Nonclustered HASH index for columns C1 & C2
INDEX IX_HashExample NONCLUSTERED HASH
(
    C1, C2
)WITH ( BUCKET_COUNT = 1048576),

--Nonclustered (Bw-Tree) index for columns C3 & C4
INDEX IX_NonClusteredExample NONCLUSTERED
(
    C3, C4
)
)WITH ( MEMORY_OPTIMIZED = ON , DURABILITY = SCHEMA_AND_DATA );

GO
INSERT INTO dbo.IndexExample (C1, C2, C3, C4) VALUES (1,1,1,1);
INSERT INTO dbo.IndexExample (C1, C2, C3, C4) VALUES (2,2,2,2);

--The first query uses the leading column of the hash index
SELECT C1, C2 FROM dbo.IndexExample WHERE C1 = 1;

--The second query uses the leading column of the Bw-Tree index
SELECT C1, C2 FROM dbo.IndexExample WHERE c3 = 1;
```

SELECT * FROM [IndexExample] WHERE [C1]=@1

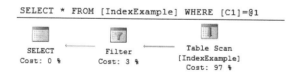

FIGURE 10-8 Plan resulting from querying the leading column of a hash index.

This is the plan you get when querying a hash index with a predicate that contains leading columns but not all the key columns from the hash index. Notice that even though there is an index on the table that includes this column, you are still doing a full table scan and then filtering rather than taking advantage of the index.

Unlike the previous example in Figure 10-8, when you query a BW-Tree index with only the leading column, and not all key columns, you can still seek using the index and avoid a full table scan. This is the behavior we're familiar with, and it results in the plan in Figure 10-9.

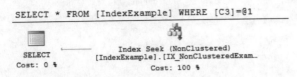

FIGURE 10-9 Plan resulting from querying the leading column of a nonclustered (BW-Tree) index.

This demonstrates clearly why simply doing a straight conversion from an existing disk-based table and application to a memory-optimized table can cause surprising and negative performance results. As fast as memory-optimized tables are, they usually can't make up for scanning millions of rows rather than doing a direct index seek. So you need to carefully consider your indexes in light of all the queries that can be done on a table.

New design patterns

So now, you understand that a hash index is much more efficient in cases where the query predicate includes all the index's key columns. You also understand that getting sorted output from a hash index will require extra steps to explicitly sort the output, and you know that if there are queries with predicates that do not include all the key columns of a hash index, this will result in very poor performance by causing a full table scan. So what do you do when you have a table that is queried in a performance-critical area of the application, using a predicate with three columns that results in a single-row lookup, *and* another frequent query that needs sorted output based on the first two columns?

If the performance of the BW-Tree index for exact-key lookups is acceptable, this is the simplest answer. Even though the hash index would be faster for those exact-key lookups, overall using a single BW-Tree index might be faster.

Another option if the exact-key lookup speed is critical is to define two indexes with the same key columns, one hash and one BW-Tree. The optimizer can then determine which index would most efficiently satisfy the query. Queries that require sorted output (in the same direction as the index), or that provide only leading columns, would be satisfied using the BW-Tree index.

If the exact-key queries dominate and sorted output is rarely required, it might be advantageous to define a single hash index with fewer key columns, to match the minimum number of columns provided in common query predicates. That way, you can use the hash to get the subset of rows that match those columns and then filter that set on the rest of the predicate.

In Listing 10-5, the optimizer chooses between two indexes based on the query predicates, even though the indexes have identical sets of key columns.

LISTING 10-5 Example of the optimizer choosing between indexes based on query attributes

```
CREATE TABLE dbo.tTable3
(
     C1 int NOT NULL,
     C2 int NOT NULL,
     C3 int NOT NULL,
     C4 int NOT NULL,
     PRIMARY KEY NONCLUSTERED HASH (C4)
        WITH ( BUCKET_COUNT = 2097152),
     INDEX HASH_IDX NONCLUSTERED HASH (C1, C2, C3)
        WITH ( BUCKET_COUNT = 2097152),
     INDEX NC_IDX NONCLUSTERED (C1, C2, C3)
) WITH ( MEMORY_OPTIMIZED = ON , DURABILITY = SCHEMA_AND_DATA );

GO


INSERT INTO dbo.tTable3 VALUES(1,1,1,1),(1,1,1,2),(1,1,1,3);
GO


-- Exact key lookup, will be satisfied by the hash index
SELECT C1, C2, C3, C4 FROM dbo.tTable3 WHERE C1 = 1 AND C2=1 AND C3=1;

-- Query with a range predicate will be satisfied by the BW-Tree index
SELECT C1, C2, C3, C4 FROM dbo.tTable3 WHERE C1 = 1 AND C2=1 AND C3 BETWEEN 0 AND 2;

-- Query on leading columns, will be satisfied by the BW-Tree index.
SELECT C1, C2, C3, C4 FROM dbo.tTable3 WHERE C1 = 1 AND C2=1;
```

Figure 10-10 illustrates the query plan for the first query, showing that when the predicate supplied all key columns and there was no ORDER BY clause, the optimizer chose the HASH_IDX index.

FIGURE 10-10 Plan for a query with exact matches on all key columns.

The next plan, which you can see in Figure 10-11, shows that when the same predicate is supplied but the third element is expressed as a range (BETWEEN), the optimizer will choose the BW-Tree index.

FIGURE 10-11 Plan for a query with a range predicate.

The final query, shown in Figure 10-12, will also generate a plan that uses a nonclustered index to find all the rows that satisfy a predicate that contains only some leading key columns.

FIGURE 10-12 Plan for a query with some leading key columns.

Execution environments

All transactions involving memory-optimized tables execute, at least in part, in a different environment than classic SQL transactions. As I've discussed, the In-Memory OLTP system is a distinct "engine within an engine." The In-Memory OLTP engine has some unique properties and semantics:

- Memory-optimized tables are always in memory, which means that transactions won't stall for IO, optimizer costing is somewhat different so that it accounts for all-memory access, and of course you need to have enough memory to hold all your memory-optimized data.

- Transactions on memory-optimized tables are all done using isolation semantics, which are entirely lock free. This is usually advantageous; however, there are some scenarios you'll need to be aware of.

Depending on how the query is executed, there are two different environments that can be used. The simpler of the two is known as *query interop*. This is where the query processing proceeds using the same layers of SQL Server as traditional queries, using the standard query engine. However, instead of using the layer that retrieves data from the buffer pool (or disk, if the page is not currently in buffer pool), these queries access the data directly in the In-Memory OLTP environment.

The second execution environment is via natively compiled procedures. This environment has the highest level of performance gains and execution efficiency; however, it does come with a greater number of restrictions, both in terms of T-SQL surface area, as well as transactional semantics.

Query interop

The query interop execution environment is used for ad hoc SQL queries as well as traditional stored procedures and other T-SQL modules. You can reference memory-optimized tables also from other modules like triggers, user-defined functions (UDFs), and so on. It really is nothing more than writing a T-SQL query against one or more memory-optimized tables. In this environment, you have the least amount of work to do to adapt to the In-Memory OLTP environment, because you do not need to port stored procedures to the more restrictive natively compiled surface area. This does not mean there is no work at all to do, but it means the work involved to port will be significantly smaller and simpler.

So, what are the considerations when using query interop?

Isolation

In-Memory OLTP currently offers a restricted set of isolation levels. Snapshot is the default isolation level, and Repeatable Read and Serializable isolation levels are supported. Read Uncommitted, Read Committed, and Read Committed Snapshot isolation levels are not supported with memory-optimized tables. Because the isolation level is set at a minimum at the transaction level, any transaction that involves a memory-optimized table cannot use any of the unsupported isolation levels. The entire transaction must run in the Snapshot, Repeatable Read, or Serializable isolation level.

In traditional SQL Server transactions, the default, and most common, isolation level is Read Committed. The Read Committed isolation level specifies that a transaction will see only data that has been committed, not any data that might be later rolled back. If such a transaction encounters a row that has been modified but not yet committed, the transaction will block until the update is resolved one way or the other. This is not possible in the lock-free environment of In-Memory OLTP.

Deadlocks and blocking

The following examples demonstrate the differences between traditional and in-memory environments.

TABLE 10-2 Example of a deadlock with traditional tables

Step	Transaction 1	Transaction 2

Setup	`--Setup the table`
	`USE AdventureWorks2014;`
	`GO`
	`IF (OBJECT_ID('dbo.T1') IS NOT NULL)`
	`  DROP TABLE dbo.T1;`
	
	`CREATE TABLE dbo.T1`
	`(`
	`  C1 INT NOT NULL PRIMARY KEY,`
	`  C2 INT NOT NULL`
	`);`
	
	`GO`
	`INSERT INTO dbo.T1(C1,C2) VALUES (1,1),(2,1);`
	`GO`	

1	`BEGIN TRANSACTION;`	
2		`BEGIN TRANSACTION;`
3	`UPDATE dbo.T1 SET C2 = 2` `WHERE C1 = 2;`	
4		`UPDATE dbo.T1 SET C2 = 3` `WHERE C1 = 1;`
5	`SELECT C2 FROM dbo.T1` `WHERE C1 = 1;`	
6		`SELECT C2 FROM dbo.T1` `WHERE C1 = 2;`
7	`COMMIT;`	
8		`COMMIT;`

In this example, you have a simple table and two transactions accessing it:

- In steps 1 and 2, Transactions 1 and 2 each begin.

- In step 3, Transaction 1 updates the row where *C1 = 2*, acquiring an exclusive (X) lock on that row.

- In step 4, Transaction 2 updates the row where *C1 = 1*, acquiring an X lock on that row.

- In step 5, Transaction 1 selects from the row where *C1 = 1* and blocks behind Transaction 2's X lock.

- In step 6, Transaction 2 selects from the row where *C1 = 2* and blocks behind Transaction 1's X lock.

This forms a classic deadlock, and one of the transactions will be chosen as the *victim* and aborted.

In contrast, Table 10-3 shows what happens when the sequence is run against a memory-optimized table.

TABLE 10-3 Example of a deadlock with memory-optimized tables

Step	Transaction 1	Transaction 2

Setup	`--Setup the table`
	`USE AdventureWorks2014;`
	`GO`
	
	`IF (OBJECT_ID(N'dbo.T1') IS NOT NULL)`
	`  DROP TABLE dbo.T1;`
	
	`CREATE TABLE dbo.T1`
	`(`
	`  C1 INT NOT NULL`
	`    PRIMARY KEY NONCLUSTERED HASH WITH (BUCKET_COUNT = 1024),`
	`  C2 INT NOT NULL`
	`)`
	`WITH (MEMORY_OPTIMIZED = ON);`
	
	`GO`
	`INSERT INTO dbo.T1(C1,C2) VALUES (1,1),(2,1);`
	`GO`	

1	`BEGIN TRANSACTION;`	
2		`BEGIN TRANSACTION;`

3	`UPDATE dbo.T1 WITH (SNAPSHOT)`
	`  SET C2 = 2`
	`WHERE C1 = 2;`	

4		`UPDATE dbo.T1 WITH (SNAPSHOT)`
		`  SET C2 = 3`
		`WHERE C1 = 1;`

5	`SELECT C2 FROM dbo.T1 WITH (SNAPSHOT)` `WHERE C1 = 1;`	
6		`SELECT C2 FROM dbo.T1 WITH (SNAPSHOT)` `WHERE C1 = 2;`

Step	Transaction 1	Transaction 2
7	COMMIT;	
8		COMMIT;

- In steps 1 and 2, Transactions 1 and 2 each begin.

- In step 2, Transaction 1 updates the row where *C1 = 2*, creating a new version of that row.

- In step 3, Transaction 2 updates the row where *C1 = 1*, creating a new version of that row.

- In step 4, Transaction 1 selects from the row where *C1 = 1* and sees the original version of that row (because Transaction 2 has not yet committed).

- In step 5, Transaction 2 selects from the row where *C1 = 2* and sees the original version of that row (because Transaction 1 has not yet committed).

Commit validation errors

When two transactions against a memory-optimized table have a write-write conflict, both transactions cannot be allowed to succeed. Instead, if a second transaction attempts to modify a row before the first transaction modifying the same row has committed, the second transaction updating the row will fail. This is very different behavior than the case of traditional tables, where one transaction will just block until the first update is complete.

Consider Table 10-4, where you create a memory-optimized table and then have two transactions attempting to modify the same row.

TABLE 10-4 Example of blocking versus commit error in a memory-optimized table

Step	Transaction 1	Transaction 2
| Setup | ```
--Setup the table
USE AdventureWorks2014;
GO
IF (OBJECT_ID('dbo.T1') IS NOT NULL)
  DROP TABLE dbo.T1;

CREATE TABLE dbo.T1
(
  C1 INT NOT NULL
    PRIMARY KEY NONCLUSTERED HASH WITH (BUCKET_COUNT = 1024),
  C2 INT NOT NULL
)
WITH (MEMORY_OPTIMIZED = ON);

GO
INSERT INTO dbo.T1(C1,C2) VALUES (1,1);
GO
``` | |
| 1 | BEGIN TRANSACTION; | |
| 2 | | BEGIN TRANSACTION; |
```

Step	Transaction 1	Transaction 2
3	UPDATE dbo.T1 WITH (SNAPSHOT) SET C2 = 2 WHERE C1 = 1;	
4		UPDATE dbo.T1 WITH (SNAPSHOT) SET C2 = 3 WHERE C1 = 1;
5	COMMIT;	
6		COMMIT;

- In steps 1 and 2, Transaction 1 and Transaction 2 issue BEGIN TRANSACTION statements starting the context.

- In step 3, Transaction 1 then updates a row in the database. This creates a new row version with a timestamp that is more recent than the start of either transaction.

- In step 4, Transaction 2 attempts to modify the same row. It detects that the row has been modified and that it is not yet committed. In this instance, the transaction cannot proceed, and Transaction 2 fails with the following error:

```
Msg 41302, Level 16, State 110, Line 8
The current transaction attempted to update a record that has been updated since this
transaction started. The transaction was aborted.
Msg 3998, Level 16, State 1, Line 8
Uncommittable transaction is detected at the end of the batch. The transaction is rolled
back.
The statement has been terminated.
```

Table 10-5 presents an example of the differences between the blocking behavior of traditional tables and the commit error that results for in-memory tables.

TABLE 10-5 Example of blocking versus commit error in a traditional table

Step	Transaction 1	Transaction 2

Setup	`--Setup the table`
	`USE AdventureWorks2014;`
	`GO`
	
	`IF (OBJECT_ID('dbo.T1') IS NOT NULL)`
	`  DROP TABLE dbo.T1;`
	
	`CREATE TABLE dbo.T1`
	`(`
	`  C1 INT NOT NULL PRIMARY KEY,`
	`  C2 INT NOT NULL`
	`);`
	
	`GO`
	`INSERT INTO dbo.T1(C1,C2) VALUES (1,1);`
	`GO`	

1	BEGIN TRANSACTION;	
2		BEGIN TRANSACTION;

Step	Transaction 1	Transaction 2

3	`UPDATE dbo.T1`
	`  SET C2 = 2`
	`WHERE C1 = 1;`	

4		`UPDATE dbo.T1`
		`  SET C2 = 3`
		`WHERE C1 = 1;`

5	`COMMIT;`	
6		`COMMIT;`

By contrast, if the same series of updates had been attempted against a non-memory-optimized table, the following happens:

- In steps 1 and 2, Transaction 1 and Transaction 2 issue BEGIN TRANSACTION statements starting the context.

- In step 3, Transaction 1 then updates a row in the database. It acquires an exclusive lock on the row.

- In step 4, Transaction 2 attempts to modify the same row, but it is blocked by Transaction 1's exclusive lock. It will stall and wait until Transaction 1 completes.

- In step 5, Transaction 1 completes by committing. This releases the lock on the row, and Transaction 2 proceeds with its update.

- In step 6, Transaction 2 completes by committing.

Note that in the case of the memory-optimized table, because Transaction 2's update would not complete, the value of C2 would be 2, as updated by Transaction 1. In the case of a traditional table, Transaction 2 would eventually succeed, so the final value of C2 would be 3.

To deal with these commit validation errors, transactions should be written with the same sort of logic that would be applied to deadlock retries, as shown in Listing 10-6.

LISTING 10-6 Retry logic for validation failures

```
-- number of retries - tune based on the workload
  DECLARE @retry INT = 10;

  WHILE (@retry > 0)
  BEGIN
    BEGIN TRY

      -- exec usp_my_native_proc @param1, @param2, ...

      --      or
```

```
    -- BEGIN TRANSACTION
    --   ...
    -- COMMIT TRANSACTION

    SET @retry = 0;
  END TRY
BEGIN CATCH
  SET @retry -= 1;

  IF (@retry > 0 AND error_number() in (41302, 41305, 41325, 41301, 1205))
  BEGIN
    -- These errors cannot be recovered and continued from.  The transaction must
    -- be rolled back and completely retried.
    -- The native proc will simply rollback when an error is thrown, so skip the
    -- rollback in that case.

    IF XACT_STATE() = -1
      ROLLBACK TRANSACTION;

    -- use a delay if there is a high rate of write conflicts (41302)
    -- length of delay should depend on the typical duration of conflicting
    -- transactions
    -- WAITFOR DELAY '00:00:00.001';
  END
  ELSE
  BEGIN
    -- insert custom error handling for other error conditions here

    -- throw if this is not a qualifying error condition
    THROW;
  END;
 END CATCH;
END;
```

Cross-database queries

With SQL Server 2014, you cannot execute a query that accesses a memory-optimized table and any table on another database, whether the database is in the same instance or in another instance. You can, however, use memory-optimized table variables in cross-database transactions.

Parallelism

Transactions that access memory-optimized tables in any way will not use parallel plans. This is a limitation of SQL Server 2014 that will likely be removed in a future release. These transactions will effectively have a Degree of Parallelism (MAXDOP) of 1. This can have severe implications for the performance of the queries, which in some cases can overwhelm the performance advantages of the memory-optimized tables. For example, if you are joining a memory-optimized table with a table based on a Clustered Column Store index, you would expect that these two technologies, which are each extremely fast in their own realms, would work very well together. Unfortunately, the column store performance design is based on high degrees of parallelism. Column stores are able to use all cores of the system in parallel to perform scans of huge data sets in a very short time. When a memory-optimized table is introduced to that query, the overall parallelism of the query is dropped to 1, and the performance of column store indexes is severely affected.

This is an extreme example of the performance effects of the current limitations of parallelism in In-Memory OLTP queries, but there are many other cases where the effect might still be felt, even if it is not nearly as pronounced. Fortunately, it is simple to detect when this might be the issue in a performance problem by looking at the query plan of the disk-based query and comparing it with the plan for the memory-optimized query.

You can see from the first plan that the parallel operator is used consistently throughout the plan, while in the second plan from the memory-optimized query, the plan is entirely based on serial operators.

You can also look at or search the XML representation of the query plan for the *<RelOp>* tags and look for the *Parallel* attribute:

```
<RelOp AvgRowSize="121" EstimateCPU="0.27821" EstimateIO="0" EstimateRebinds="0"
EstimateRewinds="0" EstimatedExecutionMode="Row" EstimateRows="22475.9" LogicalOp="Inner Join"
NodeId="4" Parallel="true" PhysicalOp="Hash Match" EstimatedTotalSubtreeCost="29.8961">
```

In a query with memory-optimized tables, this looks like the following:

```
<RelOp AvgRowSize="90" EstimateCPU="2.51839" EstimateIO="0" EstimateRebinds="0"
EstimateRewinds="0" EstimatedExecutionMode="Row" EstimateRows="99900" LogicalOp="Inner Join"
NodeId="7" Parallel="false" PhysicalOp="Hash Match" EstimatedTotalSubtreeCost="20.3456">
```

To validate that this is indeed the problem, you can execute the query on the disk-based tables, where performance is as expected, with the MAXDOP query hint set to 1, and see if the results are still consistent.

Cardinality and statistics

For the query optimizer to properly determine the optimum query plan, it needs the input of the estimated cardinality of the tables involved, as well as estimates for the number of rows in each table that will satisfy the query predicates. SQL Server will automatically create and update statistics to make sure the optimizer has accurate information to work with. There are heuristics for when an update gets triggered, because there is cost involved in building the new statistics.

In-Memory OLTP has some behaviors that are not what you might be used to in classic SQL. Some of them are fundamental to the architecture, and others are the result of limitations in SQL Server 2014 and will likely change in future releases.

Statistics and natively compiled procedures

Because natively compiled procedures are optimized via the SQL Server optimizer before the code is compiled into a DLL, they do not change when the data or statistics change. Outside of the memory-optimized OLTP environment, changing statistics would trigger a recompile of queries including stored procedures, but for natively compiled procedures, this does not occur.

> **Note** When setting up a new table to be memory optimized, if possible it is best to load data into the table before creating any natively compiled stored procedures that will access it. That way, the optimizer will have more valid data to work with, and the procedure will have a more optimum plan.

If the content of a table accessed by a natively compiled procedure changes sufficiently enough that performance starts to degrade, you might need to drop and re-create the stored procedure to force it to be recompiled with the current statistics.

Updating statistics

With SQL Server 2014, when statistics on a memory-optimized table are updated, the engine does not use sampling as it would for traditional tables. Instead, it will perform a full scan of the table or tables. Although this will generally give more accurate results, it will take significantly longer, which can cause some disruptions in performance.

ATOMIC blocks

Natively compiled procedures are required to consist of exactly one atomic block. It must encapsulate all of the T-SQL logic in the procedure.

An ATOMIC block is a new concept introduced in SQL Server 2014. It represents a set of statements that are all guaranteed to succeed or fail as a unit, atomically. ATOMIC blocks interact with SQL transactions in the following ways:

- If there is a current SQL transaction, the ATOMIC block will create a savepoint and join in the existing transaction.

- If there is no current transaction, the ATOMIC block will create one whose scope is the block itself.

- If there is an exception thrown by the block, the block is rolled back as a whole.

- If the block succeeds, the savepoint it created is committed, and if it created its own transaction, that transaction is committed.

You can think of the entire block being modeled as if it were a single statement. Thus, it is not possible to create, roll back, or commit transactions within that block. Any commits or rollbacks must be done outside of the context of an atomic block.

Natively compiled procedures

As I mentioned, natively compiled stored procedures are extremely efficient, because they are pre-compiled into DLLs and loaded into the engine context. Note that there is some overhead involved in transitioning between the interpreted environment you use for interop queries, or for stored procedures that do not access memory-optimized tables, and the natively compiled environment. For very small amounts of logic (single statement transactions, for example), you will likely find better performance by just performing the query directly in interop. However, the more logic you can execute within the context of a native procedure, the more benefit you will see.

To get the most out of natively compiled procedures, you should try to do as much business logic as possible within each invocation of a native procedure. One way to pass a large unit of work into a native procedure for processing entirely within the procedure is to pass in a set of rows in the form of a table-valued parameter (TVP).

TVPs

To be accessed from inside a natively compiled procedure, TVPs must be memory optimized. This presents a great advantage that goes beyond natively compiled procedures. Memory-optimized TVPs can be used by traditional T-SQL procedures in much the same way as temp tables can, and in many cases they are far more efficient because they don't need to be instantiated in tempdb. The syntax for creating a memory-optimized table type can be seen in the AdventureWorks sample mentioned earlier, which is shown in Listing 10-7.

LISTING 10-7 Memory-optimized table type

```
CREATE TYPE Sales.SalesOrderDetailType_inmem AS TABLE(
    OrderQty SMALLINT NOT NULL,
    ProductID INT NOT NULL,
    SpecialOfferID INT NOT NULL,
    LocalID INT NOT NULL,
    INDEX IX_ProductID NONCLUSTERED HASH
(
    ProductID
) WITH ( BUCKET_COUNT = 8),
    INDEX [IX_SpecialOfferID] NONCLUSTERED HASH
(
    SpecialOfferID
) WITH ( BUCKET_COUNT = 8)
)
WITH ( MEMORY_OPTIMIZED = ON );
```

This is then used in the calling of a native procedure, as shown in Listing 10-8.

LISTING 10-8 Using a table-valued parameter with a native procedure

```
-------------------------------------------------------------------------
-- Table Valued Parameters
-------------------------------------------------------------------------
-- Delete the old objects if they exist

IF (OBJECT_ID('Sales.usp_InsertSalesOrder_inmem') IS NOT NULL)
  DROP PROCEDURE Sales.usp_InsertSalesOrder_inmem;

IF (TYPE_ID('Sales.SalesOrderDetailType_inmem') IS NOT NULL)
  DROP TYPE Sales.SalesOrderDetailType_inmem;

-- Memory Optimized Table Type
CREATE TYPE Sales.SalesOrderDetailType_inmem AS TABLE(
    OrderQty SMALLINT NOT NULL,
    ProductID INT NOT NULL,
    SpecialOfferID INT NOT NULL,
    LocalID INT NOT NULL,
    INDEX IX_ProductID NONCLUSTERED HASH
(
    ProductID
) WITH ( BUCKET_COUNT = 8),
    INDEX [IX_SpecialOfferID] NONCLUSTERED HASH
(
    SpecialOfferID
) WITH ( BUCKET_COUNT = 8)
)
WITH ( MEMORY_OPTIMIZED = ON );

GO

--Using a table valued parameter with a native proc

CREATE PROCEDURE Sales.usp_InsertSalesOrder_inmem
  @SalesOrderID INT OUTPUT,
  @DueDate DATETIME2(7) NOT NULL,
  @CustomerID INT NOT NULL,
  @BillToAddressID INT NOT NULL,
  @ShipToAddressID INT NOT NULL,
  @ShipMethodID INT NOT NULL,
  @SalesOrderDetails Sales.SalesOrderDetailType_inmem READONLY,
  @Status TINYINT NOT NULL = 1,
  @OnlineOrderFlag BIT NOT NULL = 1,
  @PurchaseOrderNumber NVARCHAR(25) = NULL,
  @AccountNumber NVARCHAR(15) = NULL,
  @SalesPersonID INT NOT NULL = -1,
  @TerritoryID INT = NULL,
  @CreditCardID INT = NULL,
  @CreditCardApprovalCode VARCHAR(15) = NULL,
  @CurrencyRateID INT = NULL,
  @Comment NVARCHAR(128) = NULL
```

```sql
WITH NATIVE_COMPILATION, SCHEMABINDING, EXECUTE AS OWNER
AS
BEGIN ATOMIC WITH
  (TRANSACTION ISOLATION LEVEL = SNAPSHOT,
  LANGUAGE = N'us_english')
    DECLARE @OrderDate DATETIME2 NOT NULL = sysdatetime();
    DECLARE @SubTotal MONEY NOT NULL = 0;
    SELECT @SubTotal = ISNULL(SUM(p.ListPrice * (1 - so.DiscountPct)),0)
    FROM @SalesOrderDetails od
      JOIN Sales.SpecialOffer_inmem so ON od.SpecialOfferID=so.SpecialOfferID
      JOIN Production.Product_inmem p ON od.ProductID=p.ProductID;

    INSERT INTO Sales.SalesOrderHeader_inmem
    ( DueDate,
      Status,
      OnlineOrderFlag,
      PurchaseOrderNumber,
      AccountNumber,
      CustomerID,
      SalesPersonID,
      TerritoryID,
      BillToAddressID,
      ShipToAddressID,
      ShipMethodID,
      CreditCardID,
      CreditCardApprovalCode,
      CurrencyRateID,
      Comment,
      OrderDate,
      SubTotal,
      ModifiedDate)
    VALUES
    (
      @DueDate,
      @Status,
      @OnlineOrderFlag,
      @PurchaseOrderNumber,
      @AccountNumber,
      @CustomerID,
      @SalesPersonID,
      @TerritoryID,
      @BillToAddressID,
      @ShipToAddressID,
      @ShipMethodID,
      @CreditCardID,
      @CreditCardApprovalCode,
      @CurrencyRateID,
      @Comment,
      @OrderDate,
      @SubTotal,
      @OrderDate
    );
```

```
      SET @SalesOrderID = SCOPE_IDENTITY();

      INSERT INTO Sales.SalesOrderDetail_inmem
      (
        SalesOrderID,
        OrderQty,
        ProductID,
        SpecialOfferID,
        UnitPrice,
        UnitPriceDiscount,
        ModifiedDate
      )
      SELECT
        @SalesOrderID,
        od.OrderQty,
        od.ProductID,
        od.SpecialOfferID,
        p.ListPrice,
        p.ListPrice * so.DiscountPct,
        @OrderDate
      FROM @SalesOrderDetails od
      JOIN Sales.SpecialOffer_inmem so
      ON od.SpecialOfferID=so.SpecialOfferID
      JOIN Production.Product_inmem p ON od.ProductID=p.ProductID;

  END;
  GO
```

Here you see the parameter *@SalesOrderDetails* being passed in as the table variable type defined earlier, *Sales.SalesOrderDetailType_inmem*. It is then used to insert a whole block of rows into a memory-optimized table, using the INSERT INTO...SELECT FROM syntax. Without this capability, you would need to iterate through the set of rows in a wrapper procedure, calling a native procedure that inserted a single row for each individual row. That would have been far less efficient than using a TVP and accomplishing all of this logic in a single invocation.

Retry logic

We discussed earlier that there are situations where transactions will fail with validation errors, which are a new class of errors not seen outside of memory-optimized table logic and that need to be handled with retry logic similar to what might be used for deadlock retries. The two primary errors to be dealt with are write conflict errors (error 41302) and commit dependency failures (error 41301). In general, these are rare errors, but they should be handled properly to avoid unnecessary application failures. You can see an example of this retry logic in Listing 10-6.

Cross-container queries

The term *cross-container queries* refers to queries that access tables in the memory-optimized area as well as traditional disk-based tables. Because these two areas of the database engine use different methods to ensure consistency, some restrictions apply regarding the isolation levels that can be used.

Table 10-6 shows which isolation levels can be combined and which ones will not work successfully together.

TABLE 10-6 Cross-container isolation levels

Disk-based	Memory optimized	Usage comments
READCOMMITTED	SNAPSHOT	■ Baseline combination. Most cases that use READCOMMITTED will work here.
READCOMMITTED	REPEATABLEREAD/ SERIALIZABLE	■ Data migration. ■ In-memory only interop.
REPEATABLEREAD/ SERIALIZABLE	SNAPSHOT	■ Memory-optimized table access is INSERT ONLY. ■ Useful for data migration and, if there are no concurrent writes, on memory-optimized tables (for example, ETL).
SNAPSHOT	Any Isolation Level	Not supported.
REPEATABLEREAD/ SERIALIZABLE	REPEATABLEREAD/ SERIALIZABLE	Not supported.

Surface-area restrictions

The implementation of In-Memory OLTP in SQL Server 2014 has a number of restrictions in surface area, both in the Data Definition Language (DDL) for defining the schema and the Data Manipulation Language (DML) for accessing the tables. Although these restrictions are expected to ease over time, for now you need to deal with them. In some cases, there are ready workarounds. In other cases, there are somewhat cumbersome workarounds, and for some situations the limitations might make a specific operation or table not suitable for migration until the limitations are removed. In this section, I'll discuss some of the more significant limitations and strategies for dealing with them. You can find the full list of restrictions and pointers to documentation on them in Books Online at *http://msdn. microsoft.com/en-us/library/dn246937(v=sql.120).aspx*.

Table DDL

The following restrictions exist in SQL Server 2014 for table schema DDL:

- **Computed columns**   These are not supported for memory-optimized tables. You will need to remove them from the table definition and simulate their functionality in the select statements or procedures that retrieve data from the table.

- **Foreign-key constraints**   Because these are not supported, I recommend that application logic performing any update operation (insert, update, or delete) on a table with a critical relationship to another table be validated in application logic to avoid inconsistency. This validation can be done in the form of wrappers around the DML statement to validate consistency or it can be inline in the application code.

- **Check constraints**   Like foreign-key constraints, check constraints must be simulated in application code that wraps the update statement that could violate the condition.

- **Unique constraints**   These are not supported directly; however, all memory-optimized tables that have the durability of SCHEMA AND DATA must have a unique primary-key index. In many cases, this unique index will serve as a unique constraint.

- **ALTER TABLE**   Altering tables in any way is not supported in SQL Server 2014. If you want to change the definition of a table or its indexes, you need to unload, drop, re-create, and reload the table. This includes any change or addition to the indexes on the table.

- **Large Object (LOB) data types** (for example, *varchar(max)*, *image*, *xml*, *text*, and *ntext*)   Memory-optimized tables have a maximum row size of 8,060 bytes for all columns combined. Although you can have columns such as *varbinary(8000)*, you cannot use *(max)*, which would exceed the 8,060-byte limit. When a larger LOB is needed, it is often faster to chunk the column up in 8,000-byte records and reassemble on retrieval than to leave the data in a traditional table. For an example of how this can be done, you can look at the implementation of the ASP.NET Session State Cache using memory-optimized tables, which has been published on CodePlex at *https://msftdbprodsamples.codeplex.com/releases/view/125282*.

- **Clustered indexes**   This isn't a restriction as much as a need to have an understanding of how indexes work for these tables. Because the indexes on memory-optimized tables are all effectively pointers to the actual data, there is no distinction between clustered and nonclustered indexes. Because the row data doesn't physically reside in the index structure, all indexes on memory-optimized tables are NONCLUSTERED. They can be considered to be covering, because the index directly references all columns in the table.

DML

The natively compiled stored procedures in SQL Server 2014 have some restrictions with regard to the surface area that is available, which might require workarounds. In some cases, these restrictions might indicate that a given stored procedure would be better left running in interop mode. There are many cases where procedures can be split into a wrapper procedure in interop and an inner procedure that is natively compiled. The outer wrapper contains constructs that are unsupported inside natively compiled procedures, and an inner procedure that is natively compiled, to perform the most perf-sensitive logic. Here are some key constructs to consider:

- **Cursors**   These are not supported in natively compiled procedures. Instead, and as a general best practice, use set-based logic or a WHILE loop.

- **Subqueries**   Subqueries nested inside another query are not supported. Either rewrite the query or perform it in interop mode.

- **SELECT INTO**   The SELECT INTO syntax is not supported; however, it can be rewritten as INSERT INTO Table SELECT.

- **Cross-database transactions**   With SQL Server 2014, transactions that touch memory-optimized tables cannot access data in another database, regardless of whether they are local or remote.

- **EXECUTE, INSERT EXEC**   You cannot call a stored procedure from within a natively compiled procedure. In some cases, to comply with this restriction you must inline code that had been factored out.

- **Outer Join, Union**   Outer joins or unions must be implemented by aggregating smaller queries, usually using a local, memory-optimized table variable.

- **Disjunctions (OR, IN)**   These are not supported in natively compiled procedures. You must create queries for each of the cases and then aggregate the results.

Conclusion

You saw that the In-Memory OLTP system in SQL Server 2014 has the potential to speed up database operations dramatically—in some cases representing a game-changer to the business. However, this does not remove the need to understand the performance issues you're trying to solve and to figure out what bottlenecks are causing them. By understanding the ways in which this new environment behaves differently from traditional database tables, you can realize great gains.

Graphs and recursive queries

This chapter covers the treatment of specialized data structures called *graphs* in Microsoft SQL Server using T-SQL. People use different terms when they want to discuss a graph, like *hierarchy* and *tree*, but those terms are often used incorrectly. For this reason, the chapter starts with a terminology section describing graphs and their properties to clear up the confusion.

The treatment of graphs in a relational database management system (RDBMS) is far from trivial. I'll discuss the two main approaches. One is based on iterative or recursive logic—for example, using recursive queries. Another is based on materializing extra information in the database that describes the data structure—for example, using the HIERARCHYID data type.

Terminology

This chapter uses many terms to discuss graphs and how to manipulate them in SQL Server. This section provides definitions of important terms to make sure you understand them.

> **Note** The explanations in this section are based on definitions from the National Institute of Standards and Technology (NIST). I made some revisions and added some narrative to the original definitions to make them less formal and keep them relevant to the subject area (T-SQL).
>
> For more complete and formal definitions of graphs and related terms, refer to *http://www.nist.gov/dads/*.

Graphs

A *graph* is a set of items connected by *edges*. Each item is called a *vertex* or *node*. An edge is a connection between two nodes of a graph.

Graph is a catchall term for a data structure, and many scenarios can be represented as graphs—for example, employee organizational charts, bills of materials (BOMs), road systems, and so on. To narrow down the type of graph to a more specific case, you need to identify its properties:

- **Directed/Undirected** In a *directed graph* (also known as a *digraph*), the two nodes of an edge have a direction or order—as if one is the major node and the other is the minor node.

For example, in a BOM graph for coffee shop products, you might have nodes named Latte and Milk. Latte contains Milk, but you cannot turn that relationship around. The graph has an edge (a containment relationship) for the pair of nodes (Latte, Milk), but it has no edge for the pair (Milk, Latte).

In an *undirected graph*, each edge simply connects two nodes, with no particular order. For example, a road-system graph could have a road between Los Angeles and San Francisco. The edge (road) between the nodes (cities) Los Angeles and San Francisco can be expressed as either of the following: {Los Angeles, San Francisco} or {San Francisco, Los Angeles}.

- **Acyclic/Cyclic** An *acyclic graph* is a graph with no cycle—that is, no *path* that starts and ends at the same node. Examples include employee organizational charts and BOMs. A directed acyclic graph is also known as a *DAG*.

   If the graph has paths that start and end at the same node—as there usually are in road systems—the graph is not acyclic. In other words, the graph is *cyclic*.

Trees

A *tree* is a data structure accessed beginning at the *root* node. Each node is either a *leaf node* or an *internal node*. An internal node has one or more *child* nodes and is called the *parent* of its child nodes. All child nodes of the same node are *siblings*. A tree is an acyclic graph. Contrary to the appearance in a physical tree, the root is usually depicted at the top of the structure and the leaves are depicted at the bottom, as illustrated in Figure 11-1.

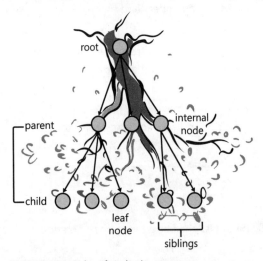

FIGURE 11-1 Roles of nodes in a tree.

A *forest* is a collection of one or more trees—for example, forum discussions can be represented as a forest in which each thread is a tree.

Hierarchies

Some scenarios can be described as *hierarchies* and modeled as directed acyclic graphs—for example, inheritance among types and classes in object-oriented programming and reports-to relationships in an employee organizational chart. In the former scenario, the edges of the graph locate the inheritance. Classes can inherit methods and properties from other classes (and possibly from multiple classes). In the latter scenario, the edges represent the reports-to relationship between employees. Note the directed, acyclic nature of these scenarios. The management chain of responsibility in a company cannot go around in circles, for example.

Scenarios

Throughout the chapter, I will use three scenarios: Employee Organizational Chart (tree, hierarchy); Bill of Materials, or BOM (DAG); and Road System (undirected cyclic graph). Note what distinguishes a (directed) rooted tree from a DAG. All trees are DAGs, but not all DAGs are trees. In a tree, an item can have at most one parent.

Employee organizational chart

The employee organizational chart I will use is depicted graphically in Figure 11-2.

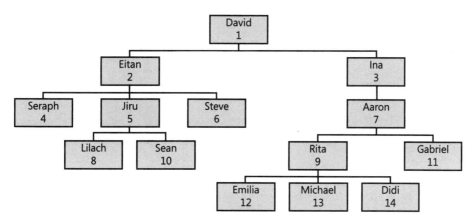

FIGURE 11-2 Employee organizational chart.

To create the Employees table and populate it with sample data, run the code in Listing 11-1. The contents of the Employees table are shown in Table 11-1.

LISTING 11-1 Data-definition language and sample data for the Employees table

```
SET NOCOUNT ON;
USE tempdb;
IF OBJECT_ID(N'dbo.Employees', 'U') IS NOT NULL DROP TABLE dbo.Employees;
GO
CREATE TABLE dbo.Employees
(
  empid    INT          NOT NULL CONSTRAINT PK_Employees PRIMARY KEY,
  mgrid    INT              NULL CONSTRAINT FK_Employees_Employees REFERENCES dbo.Employees,
  empname  VARCHAR(25) NOT NULL,
  salary   MONEY        NOT NULL,
  CHECK (empid <> mgrid)
);

INSERT INTO dbo.Employees(empid, mgrid, empname, salary) VALUES
  (1,  NULL, 'David'  , $10000.00),
  (2,  1,    'Eitan'  , $7000.00),
  (3,  1,    'Ina'    , $7500.00),
  (4,  2,    'Seraph' , $5000.00),
  (5,  2,    'Jiru'   , $5500.00),
  (6,  2,    'Steve'  , $4500.00),
  (7,  3,    'Aaron'  , $5000.00),
  (8,  5,    'Lilach' , $3500.00),
  (9,  7,    'Rita'   , $3000.00),
  (10, 5,    'Sean'   , $3000.00),
  (11, 7,    'Gabriel', $3000.00),
  (12, 9,    'Emilia' , $2000.00),
  (13, 9,    'Michael', $2000.00),
  (14, 9,    'Didi'   , $1500.00);

CREATE UNIQUE INDEX idx_unc_mgrid_empid ON dbo.Employees(mgrid, empid);
```

TABLE 11-1 Contents of Employees table

empid	mgrid	empname	salary
1	NULL	David	10000.0000
2	1	Eitan	7000.0000
3	1	Ina	7500.0000
4	2	Seraph	5000.0000
5	2	Jiru	5500.0000
6	2	Steve	4500.0000
7	3	Aaron	5000.0000
8	5	Lilach	3500.0000
9	7	Rita	3000.0000
10	5	Sean	3000.0000

empid	mgrid	empname	salary
11	7	Gabriel	3000.0000
12	9	Emilia	2000.0000
13	9	Michael	2000.0000
14	9	Didi	1500.0000

The Employees table represents a management hierarchy as an adjacency list, where the manager and employee represent the parent and child nodes, respectively.

Bill of materials (BOM)

I will use a BOM of coffee shop products, which is depicted graphically in Figure 11-3.

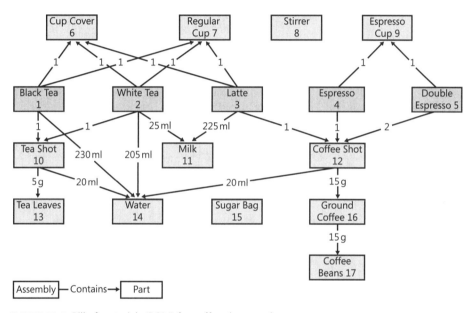

FIGURE 11-3 Bill of materials (BOM) for coffee shop products.

To create the Parts and BOM tables and populate them with sample data, run the code in Listing 11-2. The contents of the Parts and BOM tables are shown in Tables 11-2 and 11-3.

Notice that the first scenario (employee organizational chart) requires only one table because it is modeled as a tree; both an edge (manager, employee) and a node (employee) can be represented by the same row. The BOM scenario requires two tables because it is modeled as a DAG, where multiple paths can lead to each node. An edge (assembly, part) is represented by a row in the BOM table, and a node (part) is represented by a row in the Parts table.

LISTING 11-2 Data-definition language and sample data for the Parts and BOM tables

```
IF OBJECT_ID(N'dbo.BOM', N'U') IS NOT NULL DROP TABLE dbo.BOM;
IF OBJECT_ID(N'dbo.Parts', N'U') IS NOT NULL DROP TABLE dbo.Parts;
GO
CREATE TABLE dbo.Parts
(
  partid   INT          NOT NULL CONSTRAINT PK_Parts PRIMARY KEY,
  partname VARCHAR(25) NOT NULL
);

INSERT INTO dbo.Parts(partid, partname) VALUES
  ( 1, 'Black Tea'      ),
  ( 2, 'White Tea'      ),
  ( 3, 'Latte'          ),
  ( 4, 'Espresso'       ),
  ( 5, 'Double Espresso'),
  ( 6, 'Cup Cover'      ),
  ( 7, 'Regular Cup'    ),
  ( 8, 'Stirrer'        ),
  ( 9, 'Espresso Cup'   ),
  (10, 'Tea Shot'       ),
  (11, 'Milk'           ),
  (12, 'Coffee Shot'    ),
  (13, 'Tea Leaves'     ),
  (14, 'Water'          ),
  (15, 'Sugar Bag'      ),
  (16, 'Ground Coffee'  ),
  (17, 'Coffee Beans'   );

CREATE TABLE dbo.BOM
(
  partid     INT              NOT NULL CONSTRAINT FK_BOM_Parts_pid REFERENCES dbo.Parts,
  assemblyid INT                  NULL CONSTRAINT FK_BOM_Parts_aid REFERENCES dbo.Parts,
  unit       VARCHAR(3)   NOT NULL,
  qty        DECIMAL(8, 2) NOT NULL,
  CONSTRAINT UNQ_BOM_pid_aid UNIQUE(partid, assemblyid),
  CONSTRAINT CHK_BOM_diffids CHECK (partid <> assemblyid)
);

INSERT INTO dbo.BOM(partid, assemblyid, unit, qty) VALUES
  ( 1, NULL, 'EA',   1.00),
  ( 2, NULL, 'EA',   1.00),
  ( 3, NULL, 'EA',   1.00),
  ( 4, NULL, 'EA',   1.00),
  ( 5, NULL, 'EA',   1.00),
  ( 6,    1, 'EA',   1.00),
  ( 7,    1, 'EA',   1.00),
  (10,    1, 'EA',   1.00),
  (14,    1, 'mL', 230.00),
  ( 6,    2, 'EA',   1.00),
  ( 7,    2, 'EA',   1.00),
  (10,    2, 'EA',   1.00),
  (14,    2, 'mL', 205.00),
```

```
(11,    2, 'mL',   25.00),
( 6,    3, 'EA',    1.00),
( 7,    3, 'EA',    1.00),
(11,    3, 'mL',  225.00),
(12,    3, 'EA',    1.00),
( 9,    4, 'EA',    1.00),
(12,    4, 'EA',    1.00),
( 9,    5, 'EA',    1.00),
(12,    5, 'EA',    2.00),
(13,   10, 'g' ,    5.00),
(14,   10, 'mL',   20.00),
(14,   12, 'mL',   20.00),
(16,   12, 'g' ,   15.00),
(17,   16, 'g' ,   15.00);
```

TABLE 11-2 Contents of Parts table

partid	partname
1	Black Tea
2	White Tea
3	Latte
4	Espresso
5	Double Espresso
6	Cup Cover
7	Regular Cup
8	Stirrer
9	Espresso Cup
10	Tea Shot
11	Milk
12	Coffee Shot
13	Tea Leaves
14	Water
15	Sugar Bag
16	Ground Coffee
17	Coffee Beans

TABLE 11-3 Contents of BOM table

partid	assemblyid	unit	qty
1	NULL	EA	1.00
2	NULL	EA	1.00
3	NULL	EA	1.00
4	NULL	EA	1.00
5	NULL	EA	1.00
6	1	EA	1.00
7	1	EA	1.00
10	1	EA	1.00
14	1	mL	230.00
6	2	EA	1.00
7	2	EA	1.00
10	2	EA	1.00
14	2	mL	205.00
11	2	mL	25.00
6	3	EA	1.00
7	3	EA	1.00
11	3	mL	225.00
12	3	EA	1.00
9	4	EA	1.00
12	4	EA	1.00
9	5	EA	1.00
12	5	EA	2.00
13	10	g	5.00
14	10	mL	20.00
14	12	mL	20.00
16	12	g	15.00
17	16	g	15.00

The BOM represents a directed acyclic graph (DAG). It holds the parent and child node IDs in the *assemblyid* and *partid* attributes, respectively. The BOM also represents a *weighted* graph, where a weight or number is associated with each edge. In our case, that weight is the *qty* attribute that holds the quantity of the part within the assembly (the assembly of subparts). The *unit* attribute holds the unit of the *qty* (*EA* for each, *g* for gram, *mL* for milliliter, and so on).

Road system

The Road System scenario I will use refers to road systems for several major cities in the United States, and it is depicted graphically in Figure 11-4. In this scenario, I chose an International Air Transport Association (IATA) code to identify each city.

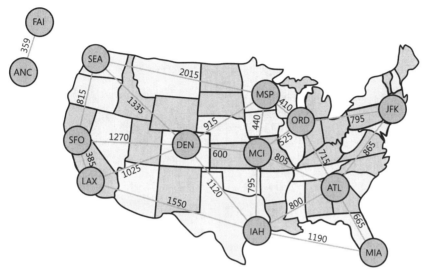

FIGURE 11-4 Road-system scenario.

To create the Cities and Roads tables and populate them with sample data, run the code in Listing 11-3. The contents of the Cities and Roads tables are shown in Tables 11-4 and 11-5.

LISTING 11-3 Data-definition language and sample data for the Cities and Roads tables

```
IF OBJECT_ID(N'dbo.Roads', N'U') IS NOT NULL DROP TABLE dbo.Roads;
IF OBJECT_ID(N'dbo.Cities', N'U') IS NOT NULL DROP TABLE dbo.Cities;
GO
CREATE TABLE dbo.Cities
(
  cityid  CHAR(3)     NOT NULL CONSTRAINT PK_Cities PRIMARY KEY,
  city    VARCHAR(30) NOT NULL,
  region  VARCHAR(30)     NULL,
  country VARCHAR(30) NOT NULL
);

INSERT INTO dbo.Cities(cityid, city, region, country) VALUES
  ('ATL', 'Atlanta', 'GA', 'USA'),
  ('ORD', 'Chicago', 'IL', 'USA'),
  ('DEN', 'Denver', 'CO', 'USA'),
  ('IAH', 'Houston', 'TX', 'USA'),
  ('MCI', 'Kansas City', 'KS', 'USA'),
  ('LAX', 'Los Angeles', 'CA', 'USA'),
  ('MIA', 'Miami', 'FL', 'USA'),
```

```
  ('MSP', 'Minneapolis', 'MN', 'USA'),
  ('JFK', 'New York', 'NY', 'USA'),
  ('SEA', 'Seattle', 'WA', 'USA'),
  ('SFO', 'San Francisco', 'CA', 'USA'),
  ('ANC', 'Anchorage', 'AK', 'USA'),
  ('FAI', 'Fairbanks', 'AK', 'USA');

CREATE TABLE dbo.Roads
(
  city1     CHAR(3) NOT NULL CONSTRAINT FK_Roads_Cities_city1 REFERENCES dbo.Cities,
  city2     CHAR(3) NOT NULL CONSTRAINT FK_Roads_Cities_city2 REFERENCES dbo.Cities,
  distance  INT     NOT NULL,
  CONSTRAINT PK_Roads PRIMARY KEY(city1, city2),
  CONSTRAINT CHK_Roads_citydiff CHECK(city1 < city2),
  CONSTRAINT CHK_Roads_posdist CHECK(distance > 0)
);

INSERT INTO dbo.Roads(city1, city2, distance) VALUES
  ('ANC', 'FAI',  359),
  ('ATL', 'ORD',  715),
  ('ATL', 'IAH',  800),
  ('ATL', 'MCI',  805),
  ('ATL', 'MIA',  665),
  ('ATL', 'JFK',  865),
  ('DEN', 'IAH', 1120),
  ('DEN', 'MCI',  600),
  ('DEN', 'LAX', 1025),
  ('DEN', 'MSP',  915),
  ('DEN', 'SEA', 1335),
  ('DEN', 'SFO', 1270),
  ('IAH', 'MCI',  795),
  ('IAH', 'LAX', 1550),
  ('IAH', 'MIA', 1190),
  ('JFK', 'ORD',  795),
  ('LAX', 'SFO',  385),
  ('MCI', 'ORD',  525),
  ('MCI', 'MSP',  440),
  ('MSP', 'ORD',  410),
  ('MSP', 'SEA', 2015),
  ('SEA', 'SFO',  815);
```

TABLE 11-4 Contents of Cities table

cityid	city	region	country
ANC	Anchorage	AK	USA
ATL	Atlanta	GA	USA
DEN	Denver	CO	USA
FAI	Fairbanks	AK	USA
IAH	Houston	TX	USA

cityid	city	region	country
JFK	New York	NY	USA
LAX	Los Angeles	CA	USA
MCI	Kansas City	KS	USA
MIA	Miami	FL	USA
MSP	Minneapolis	MN	USA
ORD	Chicago	IL	USA
SEA	Seattle	WA	USA
SFO	San Francisco	CA	USA

TABLE 11-5 Contents of Roads table

city1	city2	distance
ANC	FAI	359
ATL	IAH	800
ATL	JFK	865
ATL	MCI	805
ATL	MIA	665
ATL	ORD	715
DEN	IAH	1120
DEN	LAX	1025
DEN	MCI	600
DEN	MSP	915
DEN	SEA	1335
DEN	SFO	1270
IAH	LAX	1550
IAH	MCI	795
IAH	MIA	1190
JFK	ORD	795
LAX	SFO	385
MCI	MSP	440
MCI	ORD	525
MSP	ORD	410
MSP	SEA	2015
SEA	SFO	815

The Roads table represents an undirected cyclic weighted graph. Each edge (road) is represented by a row in the table. The attributes *city1* and *city2* are two city IDs representing the nodes of the edge. The weight in this case is the distance attribute, which holds the distance between the cities in miles. Note that the Roads table has a CHECK constraint (*city1* < *city2*) as part of its schema definition to reject attempts to enter the same edge twice (for example, {SEA, SFO} and {SFO, SEA}).

Having all the scenarios and sample data in place, let's go over the approaches to the treatment of graphs. I'll cover three main approaches: iterative/recursive, materialized path, and nested sets.

Iteration/recursion

Iterative approaches apply some form of loops or recursion. Many iterative algorithms traverse graphs. Some traverse graphs a node at a time and are usually implemented with cursors, but these are typically very slow. I will focus on algorithms that traverse graphs one level at a time using a combination of iterative or recursive logic and set-based queries. Given a set of nodes *P*, the *next level* refers to the set *C*, which consists of the children of the nodes in *P*. In my experience, implementations of iterative algorithms that traverse a graph one level at a time perform much better than the ones that traverse a graph one node at a time.

Using iterative solutions has several advantages over the other methods. First, you don't need to materialize any extra information describing the graph to the database other than the node IDs in the edges. In other words, you don't need to redesign your tables. The solutions traverse the graph by relying solely on the stored edge information—for example, (*mgrid, empid*), (*assemblyid, partid*), (*city1, city2*), and so on.

Second, most of the solutions that apply to trees also apply to the more generic digraphs. In other words, most solutions that apply to graphs where only one path can lead to a given node also apply to graphs where multiple paths may lead to a given node.

Finally, most of the solutions I will describe in this section support a virtually unlimited number of levels.

There are two ways to implement iterative solutions: with loops or with recursive common table expressions (CTEs). The core algorithms are similar in both cases. The use of loops can result in better performance because you have more control over the physical side of things. You can work with your own temporary tables, define your own indexing on them, and so on. Especially when you know what you're doing, you can achieve good performance. As for recursive CTEs, on the downside they give you very little control over the physical side of things. SQL Server does spool interim sets in internal work tables, but it gives you no control over their structure and indexing. On the upside, recursive CTEs are less verbose and more elegant.

If you want to encapsulate the logic of your loop-based solutions, you can use either multistatement, table-valued user-defined functions (UDFs) or stored procedures. From the user perspective,

UDFs are more convenient to work with because you query them like you query tables. However, stored procedures are much less restricted, and you can typically achieve better performance with them. For example, in stored procedures you can materialize and index interim sets in temporary tables, which have histograms. Multistatement, table-valued UDFs use table variables, which have no histograms. So, with temporary tables the query optimizer tends to produce better estimates, which in turn tend to lead to more efficient query plans. That said, I chose to use UDFs in my examples for the loop-based solutions because I want to focus on the algorithms and the clarity of the code. You can easily convert those to stored procedures with temporary tables if you like.

As for the solutions that use recursive CTEs, if you want to encapsulate their logic in a routine, you can use an inline (rather than a multistatement) table-valued UDF. There's no performance downside to this option because, from an optimization perspective, the use of inline UDFs is transparent. The code gets inlined by definition. In the examples of recursive CTEs in this chapter, I use ad hoc code with local variables in the following form:

```
DECLARE @input AS <data_type>;

<recursive_query>;
```

To encapsulate the logic in an inline UDF, simply use the following form:

```
CREATE FUNCTION <function_name>(@input AS <data_type>) RETURNS TABLE
AS
RETURN
  <recursive_query>;
```

Subgraph/descendants

Let's start with a classical request to return a subgraph (also known as *descendants*) of a given root in a digraph; for example, return all subordinates of a given employee. When the graph qualifies as a tree, the request is usually referred to as a *subtree*. The iterative algorithm is simple:

Input: @root

Algorithm:

- *set @lvl = 0; insert into table @Subs row for @root*

- *while there were rows in the previous level of employees:*

- *set @lvl += 1; insert into table @Subs rows for the next level (*mgrid *in (*empid *values in previous level))*

- *return @Subs*

Run the following code to create the *Subordinates1* UDF, which implements this algorithm.

```
-------------------------------------------------------------------
-- Function: Subordinates1, Descendants
--
-- Input    : @root INT: Manager id
--
-- Output   : @Subs Table: id and level of subordinates of
--                         input manager (empid = @root) in all levels
--
-- Process  : * Insert into @Subs row of input manager
--            * In a loop, while previous insert loaded more than 0 rows
--              insert into @Subs next level of subordinates
-------------------------------------------------------------------
IF OBJECT_ID(N'dbo.Subordinates1', N'TF') IS NOT NULL DROP FUNCTION dbo.Subordinates1;
GO
CREATE FUNCTION dbo.Subordinates1(@root AS INT) RETURNS @Subs TABLE
(
  empid INT NOT NULL PRIMARY KEY NONCLUSTERED,
  lvl   INT NOT NULL,
  UNIQUE CLUSTERED(lvl, empid)          -- Index will be used to filter level
)
AS
BEGIN
  DECLARE @lvl AS INT = 0;              -- Initialize level counter with 0

  -- Insert root node into @Subs
  INSERT INTO @Subs(empid, lvl)
    SELECT empid, @lvl FROM dbo.Employees WHERE empid = @root;

  WHILE @@rowcount > 0                  -- while previous level had rows
  BEGIN
    SET @lvl += 1;                      -- Increment level counter

    -- Insert next level of subordinates to @Subs
    INSERT INTO @Subs(empid, lvl)
      SELECT C.empid, @lvl
      FROM @Subs AS P                   -- P = Parent
        INNER JOIN dbo.Employees AS C   -- C = Child
          ON P.lvl = @lvl - 1           -- Filter parents from previous level
             AND C.mgrid = P.empid;

  END

  RETURN;
END
GO
```

The function accepts the *@root* input parameter, which is the ID of the requested subtree's root employee. The function returns the *@Subs* table variable, with all subordinates of employee with *ID = @root* in all levels. Besides containing the employee attributes, *@Subs* also has a column called *lvl* that keeps track of the level in the subtree (0 for the subtree's root and increasing from there by 1 in each iteration).

The function's code keeps track of the current level being handled in the *@lvl* local variable, which is initialized with zero.

The function's code first inserts into @*Subs* the row from Employees where *empid = @root*.

Then in a loop, while the last insert affects more than zero rows, the code increments the @*lvl* variable's value by one and inserts into @*Subs* the next level of employees—in other words, direct subordinates of the managers inserted in the previous level.

To insert the next level of employees into @*Subs*, the query in the loop joins @*Subs* (representing managers) with Employees (representing subordinates).

The *lvl* column is important because you can use it to isolate the managers that were inserted into @*Subs* in the last iteration. To return only subordinates of the previously inserted managers, the join condition filters from @*Subs* only rows where the *lvl* column is equal to the previous level (@*lvl – 1*).

To test the function, run the following code, which returns the subordinates of employee 3:

```
SELECT empid, lvl FROM dbo.Subordinates1(3) AS S;
```

This code generates the following output:

```
empid        lvl
-----------  -----------
3            0
7            1
9            2
11           2
12           3
13           3
14           3
```

You can verify that the output is correct by examining Figure 11-2 and following the subtree of the input root employee (*ID = 3*).

To get other attributes of the employees in addition to just the employee ID, you can either rewrite the function and add those attributes to the @*Subs* table or simply join the function with the Employees table, like so:

```
SELECT E.empid, E.empname, S.lvl
FROM dbo.Subordinates1(3) AS S
  INNER JOIN dbo.Employees AS E
    ON E.empid = S.empid;
```

You get the following output:

```
empid        empname                  lvl
-----------  ------------------------ -----------
3            Ina                      0
7            Aaron                    1
9            Rita                     2
11           Gabriel                  2
12           Emilia                   3
13           Michael                  3
14           Didi                     3
```

To limit the result set to leaf employees under the given root, simply add a filter with a NOT EXISTS predicate to select only employees that are not managers of other employees:

```
SELECT empid
FROM dbo.Subordinates1(3) AS P
WHERE NOT EXISTS
  (SELECT * FROM dbo.Employees AS C
   WHERE c.mgrid = P.empid);
```

This query returns employee IDs 11, 12, 13, and 14.

So far, you've seen a UDF implementation of a subtree under a given root, which contains a WHILE loop. The following code has the CTE solution, which contains no explicit loop:

```
DECLARE @root AS INT = 3;

WITH Subs AS
(
  -- Anchor member returns root node
  SELECT empid, empname, 0 AS lvl
  FROM dbo.Employees
  WHERE empid = @root

  UNION ALL

  -- Recursive member returns next level of children
  SELECT C.empid, C.empname, P.lvl + 1
  FROM Subs AS P
    INNER JOIN dbo.Employees AS C
      ON C.mgrid = P.empid
)
SELECT empid, empname, lvl FROM Subs;
```

This code generates the following output:

empid	empname	lvl
3	Ina	0
7	Aaron	1
9	Rita	2
11	Gabriel	2
12	Emilia	3
13	Michael	3
14	Didi	3

The solution applies logic similar to the UDF implementation. It's simpler in the sense that you don't need to explicitly define the returned table or filter the previous level's managers.

The first query in the CTE's body returns the row from Employees for the given root employee. It also returns zero as the level of the root employee. In a recursive CTE, a query that doesn't have any recursive references is known as an *anchor member*.

The second query in the CTE's body (following the UNION ALL operator) has a recursive reference to the CTE's name. This makes it a *recursive member*, and it is treated in a special manner.

The recursive reference to the CTE's name (*Subs*) represents the result set returned previously. The recursive member query joins the previous result set, which represents the managers in the previous level, with the Employees table to return the next level of employees. The recursive query also calculates the level value as the employee's manager level plus one. The first time that the recursive member is invoked, *Subs* stands for the result set returned by the anchor member (root employee). There's no explicit termination check for the recursive member; rather, it is invoked repeatedly until it returns an empty set. Thus, the first time it is invoked, it returns direct subordinates of the subtree's root employee. The second time it is invoked, *Subs* represents the result set of the first invocation of the recursive member (first level of subordinates), so it returns the second level of subordinates. The recursive member is invoked repeatedly until there are no more subordinates—in which case, it returns an empty set and recursion stops.

The reference to the CTE name in the outer query represents the unified result sets returned by the invocation of the anchor member and all the invocations of the recursive member.

As I mentioned earlier, using iterative logic to return a subgraph of a digraph where multiple paths might exist to a node is similar to returning a subtree. Run the following code to create the *PartsExplosion* function:

```
---------------------------------------------------------------------
-- Function: PartsExplosion, Parts Explosion
--
-- Input    : @root INT: assembly id
--
-- Output   : @PartsExplosion Table:
--               id and level of contained parts of input part
--               in all levels
--
-- Process  : * Insert into @PartsExplosion row of input root part
--            * In a loop, while previous insert loaded more than 0 rows
--              insert into @PartsExplosion next level of parts
---------------------------------------------------------------------
IF OBJECT_ID(N'dbo.PartsExplosion', N'TF') IS NOT NULL DROP FUNCTION dbo.PartsExplosion;
GO
CREATE FUNCTION dbo.PartsExplosion(@root AS INT) RETURNS @PartsExplosion Table
(
  partid INT            NOT NULL,
  qty    DECIMAL(8, 2)  NOT NULL,
  unit   VARCHAR(3)     NOT NULL,
  lvl    INT            NOT NULL,
  n      INT            NOT NULL IDENTITY, -- surrogate key
  UNIQUE CLUSTERED(lvl, n)                 -- Index will be used to filter lvl
)
AS
BEGIN
  DECLARE @lvl AS INT = 0;       -- Initialize level counter with 0

  -- Insert root node to @PartsExplosion
  INSERT INTO @PartsExplosion(partid, qty, unit, lvl)
    SELECT partid, qty, unit, @lvl
    FROM dbo.BOM
    WHERE partid = @root;
```

```
      WHILE @@rowcount > 0              -- while previous level had rows
      BEGIN
        SET @lvl = @lvl + 1;           -- Increment level counter

        -- Insert next level of subordinates to @PartsExplosion
        INSERT INTO @PartsExplosion(partid, qty, unit, lvl)
          SELECT C.partid, P.qty * C.qty, C.unit, @lvl
          FROM @PartsExplosion AS P  -- P = Parent
            INNER JOIN dbo.BOM AS C  -- C = Child
              ON P.lvl = @lvl - 1    -- Filter parents from previous level
                AND C.assemblyid = P.partid;
      END

    RETURN;
END
GO
```

The function accepts a part ID representing an assembly in a BOM, and it returns the parts explosion (the direct and indirect subitems) of the assembly. The implementation of the *PartsExplosion* function is similar to the implementation of the function *Subordinates1*. The row for the root part is inserted into the @*PartsExplosion* table variable (the function's output parameter). And then in a loop, while the previous insert returned rows, the next level parts are inserted into @*PartsExplosion*. A small addition here is specific to a BOM: calculating the quantity. The root part's quantity is simply the one stored in the part's row. The contained (child) part's quantity is the quantity of its containing (parent) item multiplied by its own quantity.

Run the following code to test the function, which returns the part explosion of *partid* 2 (White Tea):

```
SELECT P.partid, P.partname, PE.qty, PE.unit, PE.lvl
FROM dbo.PartsExplosion(2) AS PE
  INNER JOIN dbo.Parts AS P
    ON P.partid = PE.partid;
```

This code generates the following output:

```
partid  partname      qty      unit lvl
-------  ------------  -------  ---- ----
2        White Tea     1.00     EA   0
6        Cup Cover     1.00     EA   1
7        Regular Cup   1.00     EA   1
10       Tea Shot      1.00     EA   1
14       Water         205.00   mL   1
11       Milk          25.00    mL   1
13       Tea Leaves    5.00     g    2
14       Water         20.00    mL   2
```

You can check the correctness of this output by examining Figure 11-3.

Following is the CTE solution for the parts explosion, which, again, is similar to the subtree solution with the addition of the quantity calculation:

```
DECLARE @root AS INT = 2;

WITH PartsExplosion
AS
(
  -- Anchor member returns root part
  SELECT partid, qty, unit, 0 AS lvl
  FROM dbo.BOM
  WHERE partid = @root

  UNION ALL

  -- Recursive member returns next level of parts
  SELECT C.partid, CAST(P.qty * C.qty AS DECIMAL(8, 2)), C.unit, P.lvl + 1
  FROM PartsExplosion AS P
    INNER JOIN dbo.BOM AS C
      ON C.assemblyid = P.partid
)
SELECT P.partid, P.partname, PE.qty, PE.unit, PE.lvl
FROM PartsExplosion AS PE
  INNER JOIN dbo.Parts AS P
    ON P.partid = PE.partid;
```

A parts explosion might contain more than one occurrence of the same part because different parts in the assembly might contain the same subpart. For example, you can notice in the result of the explosion of *partid 2* that water appears twice because white tea contains 205 milliliters of water directly, and it also contains a tea shot, which in turn contains 20 milliliters of water. You might want to aggregate the result set by part and unit as follows:

```
SELECT P.partid, P.partname, PES.qty, PES.unit
FROM (SELECT partid, unit, SUM(qty) AS qty
      FROM dbo.PartsExplosion(2) AS PE
      GROUP BY partid, unit) AS PES
  INNER JOIN dbo.Parts AS P
    ON P.partid = PES.partid;
```

You get the following output:

```
partid  partname      qty      unit
------- ------------- -------- ----
2       White Tea     1.00     EA
6       Cup Cover     1.00     EA
7       Regular Cup   1.00     EA
10      Tea Shot      1.00     EA
13      Tea Leaves    5.00     g
11      Milk          25.00    mL
14      Water         225.00   mL
```

I won't get into issues with the grouping of parts that might contain different units of measurements here. Obviously, you'll need to deal with those by applying conversion factors.

As another example, the following code explodes part ID 5 (Double Espresso):

```
SELECT P.partid, P.partname, PES.qty, PES.unit
FROM (SELECT partid, unit, SUM(qty) AS qty
      FROM dbo.PartsExplosion(5) AS PE
      GROUP BY partid, unit) AS PES
  INNER JOIN dbo.Parts AS P
    ON P.partid = PES.partid;
```

This code generates the following output:

```
partid  partname          qty      unit
-------  ----------------  -------  ----
5        Double Espresso   1.00     EA
9        Espresso Cup      1.00     EA
12       Coffee Shot       2.00     EA
16       Ground Coffee     30.00    g
17       Coffee Beans      450.00   g
14       Water             40.00    mL
```

Going back to returning a subtree of a given employee, in some cases you might need to limit the number of returned levels. To achieve this, you need to make a minor addition to the original algorithm:

Input: @root, @maxlevels *(besides root)*

Algorithm:

- *set @lvl = 0; insert into table @Subs row for @root*

- *while there were rows in the previous level, and @lvl < @maxlevels:*

- *set @lvl += 1; insert into table @Subs rows for the next level (mgrid in (empid values in previous level))*

- *return @Subs*

Run the following code to create the *Subordinates2* function, which is a revision of *Subordinates1* that also supports a level limit:

```
------------------------------------------------------------------
-- Function: Subordinates2,
--           Descendants with optional level limit
--
-- Input   : @root       INT: Manager id
--           @maxlevels INT: Max number of levels to return
--
-- Output  : @Subs TABLE: id and level of subordinates of
--                        input manager in all levels <= @maxlevels
--
-- Process : * Insert into @Subs row of input manager
--           * In a loop, while previous insert loaded more than 0 rows
--             and previous level is smaller than @maxlevels
--             insert into @Subs next level of subordinates
------------------------------------------------------------------
```

```
IF OBJECT_ID(N'dbo.Subordinates2', N'TF') IS NOT NULL DROP FUNCTION dbo.Subordinates2;
GO
CREATE FUNCTION dbo.Subordinates2 (@root AS INT, @maxlevels AS INT = NULL) RETURNS @Subs TABLE
(
  empid INT NOT NULL PRIMARY KEY NONCLUSTERED,
  lvl   INT NOT NULL,
  UNIQUE CLUSTERED(lvl, empid)          -- Index will be used to filter level
)
AS
BEGIN
  DECLARE @lvl AS INT = 0;              -- Initialize level counter with 0

  -- Insert root node to @Subs
  INSERT INTO @Subs(empid, lvl)
    SELECT empid, @lvl FROM dbo.Employees WHERE empid = @root;

  WHILE @@rowcount > 0                  -- while previous level had rows
    AND (@lvl < @maxlevels              -- and haven't reached level limit
        OR @maxlevels IS NULL)
  BEGIN
    SET @lvl += 1;                      -- Increment level counter

    -- Insert next level of subordinates to @Subs
    INSERT INTO @Subs(empid, lvl)
      SELECT C.empid, @lvl
      FROM @Subs AS P                   -- P = Parent
        INNER JOIN dbo.Employees AS C -- C = Child
          ON P.lvl = @lvl - 1          -- Filter parents from previous level
            AND C.mgrid = P.empid;
  END

  RETURN;
END
GO
```

In addition to the original input, *Subordinates2* also accepts the *@maxlevels* input that indicates the maximum number of requested levels under *@root* to return. For no limit on levels, a NULL should be specified in *@maxlevels*.

The loop's condition, besides checking that the previous insert affected more than zero rows, also checks that the level limit wasn't reached (specifically, the *@lvl* variable is smaller than *@maxlevels* or is NULL). Except for these minor revisions, the function's implementation is the same as *Subordinates1*.

To test the function, run the following code that requests the subordinates of employee 3 in all levels (*@maxlevels* is NULL):

```
SELECT empid, lvl
FROM dbo.Subordinates2(3, NULL) AS S;
```

You get the following output:

```
empid       lvl
----------- -----------
3           0
7           1
```

9	2
11	2
12	3
13	3
14	3

To get only two levels of subordinates under employee 3, run the following code:

```
SELECT empid, lvl
FROM dbo.Subordinates2(3, 2) AS S;
```

This code generates the following output:

```
empid        lvl
-----------  -----------
3            0
7            1
9            2
11           2
```

To get only the second-level employees under employee 3, add a filter on the level:

```
SELECT empid
FROM dbo.Subordinates2(3, 2) AS S
WHERE lvl = 2;
```

You get the following output:

```
empid
-----------
9
11
```

Use caution regarding the MAXRECURSION hint

To limit levels using a CTE, you might be tempted to use the hint called MAXRECURSION, which raises an error and aborts when the number of invocations of the recursive member exceeds the input. However, MAXRECURSION was designed as a safety measure to avoid infinite recursion in cases where problems exist in the data or there are bugs in the code. When not specified, MAXRECURSION defaults to 100. You can specify MAXRECURSION 0 to have no limit, but be aware of the implications.

To test this approach, run the following code:

```
DECLARE @root AS INT = 3;

WITH Subs
AS
(
  SELECT empid, empname, 0 AS lvl
  FROM dbo.Employees
  WHERE empid = @root
```

```
    UNION ALL

    SELECT C.empid, C.empname, P.lvl + 1
    FROM Subs AS P
      INNER JOIN dbo.Employees AS C
        ON C.mgrid = P.empid
)
SELECT empid, empname, lvl FROM Subs
OPTION (MAXRECURSION 2);
```

This is the same subtree CTE shown earlier, with the addition of the MAXRECURSION hint, limiting recursive invocations to 2. This code generates the following output, including an error message:

```
empid       empname                  lvl
----------- ------------------------ -----------
3           Ina                      0
7           Aaron                    1
9           Rita                     2
11          Gabriel                  2
Msg 530, Level 16, State 1, Line 3
The statement terminated. The maximum recursion 2 has been exhausted before
    statement completion.
```

The code breaks as soon as the recursive member is invoked the third time. There are two reasons not to use the MAXRECURSION hint to logically limit the number of levels. First, an error is generated even though there's no logical error here. Second, there's no guarantee SQL Server will return any result set if an error is generated. In this particular case, a result set was returned, but this is not guaranteed to happen in other cases.

You can logically limit the number of levels by adding a predicate in the recursive query's ON clause, like so:

```
DECLARE @root AS INT = 3, @maxlevels AS INT = 2;

WITH Subs
AS
(
  SELECT empid, empname, 0 AS lvl
  FROM dbo.Employees
  WHERE empid = @root

  UNION ALL

  SELECT C.empid, C.empname, P.lvl + 1
  FROM Subs AS P
    INNER JOIN dbo.Employees AS C
      ON C.mgrid = P.empid
        AND lvl < @maxlevels
)
SELECT empid, empname, lvl
FROM Subs;
```

Ancestors/path

Requests for ancestors (also known as a *path*) of a given node are also common—for example, returning the chain of management for a given employee. Not surprisingly, the algorithms for returning ancestors using iterative logic are similar to those for returning a subgraph. Instead of traversing the graph starting with a given node and proceeding "downward" to child nodes, you start with a given node and proceed "upward" to parent nodes.

Run the following code to create the *Managers* function:

```
---------------------------------------------------------------------
-- Function: Managers, Ancestors with optional level limit
--
-- Input    : @empid INT : Employee id
--            @maxlevels : Max number of levels to return
--
-- Output   : @Mgrs Table: id and level of managers of
--                         input employee in all levels <= @maxlevels
--
-- Process  : * In a loop, while current manager is not null
--              and previous level is smaller than @maxlevels
--              insert into @Mgrs current manager,
--              and get next level manager
---------------------------------------------------------------------
IF OBJECT_ID(N'dbo.Managers', N'TF') IS NOT NULL DROP FUNCTION dbo.Managers;
GO
CREATE FUNCTION dbo.Managers
  (@empid AS INT, @maxlevels AS INT = NULL) RETURNS @Mgrs TABLE
(
  empid INT NOT NULL PRIMARY KEY,
  lvl   INT NOT NULL
)
AS
BEGIN
  IF NOT EXISTS(SELECT * FROM dbo.Employees WHERE empid = @empid)
    RETURN;

  DECLARE @lvl AS INT = 0;         -- Initialize level counter with 0

  WHILE @empid IS NOT NULL         -- while current employee has a manager
    AND (@lvl <= @maxlevels        -- and haven't reached level limit
         OR @maxlevels IS NULL)
  BEGIN
    -- Insert current manager to @Mgrs
    INSERT INTO @Mgrs(empid, lvl) VALUES(@empid, @lvl);
    SET @lvl += 1;                 -- Increment level counter
    -- Get next level manager
    SET @empid = (SELECT mgrid FROM dbo.Employees
                  WHERE empid = @empid);
  END

  RETURN;
END
GO
```

The function accepts an input employee ID (@empid) and, optionally, a level limit (@maxlevels), and it returns managers up to the requested number of levels from the input employee (if a limit was specified). The function first checks whether the input node ID exists and then breaks if it doesn't. It then initializes the @lvl counter to zero.

The function then enters a loop that iterates as long as @empid is not NULL (because NULL represents the root's manager ID) and the level limit hasn't been exceeded (if one was specified). The loop's body inserts the current employee ID along with the level counter into the @Mgrs output table variable, increments the level counter, and assigns the current employee's manager's ID to the @empid variable.

There are a couple of differences between this function and the subordinates function. This function uses a scalar subquery to get the manager ID in the next level, unlike the subordinates function, which used a join to get the next level of subordinates. The reason for the difference is that a given employee can have only one manager, whereas a manager can have multiple subordinates. Also, this function uses the expression @lvl <= @maxlevels to limit the number of levels, whereas the subordinates function used the expression @lvl < @maxlevels. The reason for the discrepancy is that this function doesn't have a separate INSERT statement to get the root employee and a separate one to get the next level of employees; rather, it has only one INSERT statement in the loop. Consequently, the @lvl counter here is incremented after the INSERT, whereas in the subordinates function it was incremented before the INSERT.

To test the function, run the following code:

```
SELECT empid, lvl
FROM dbo.Managers(8, NULL) AS M;
```

This code returns managers of employee 8 in all levels and generates the following output:

```
empid       lvl
----------- -----------
1           3
2           2
5           1
8           0
```

I should point out that in the ancestors/path case and in the subgraph/descendants case, the lvl column has different meanings. In the former case, lvl represents the distance from the starting descendant (subordinate). In the latter case, lvl represents the distance from the starting ancestor (root manager).

The CTE solution to returning ancestors is almost identical to the CTE solution to returning a subtree. The minor difference is that here the recursive member treats the CTE as the child part of the join and the Employees table as the parent part, whereas in the subtree solution the roles were the opposite. Run the following code to get the management chain of employee 8.

```
DECLARE @empid AS INT = 8;

WITH Mgrs
AS
(
  SELECT empid, mgrid, empname, 0 AS lvl
  FROM dbo.Employees
  WHERE empid = @empid

  UNION ALL

  SELECT P.empid, P.mgrid, P.empname, C.lvl + 1
  FROM Mgrs AS C
    INNER JOIN dbo.Employees AS P
      ON C.mgrid = P.empid
)
SELECT empid, mgrid, empname, lvl
FROM Mgrs;
```

This code generates the following output:

```
empid  mgrid  empname  lvl
------ ------ -------- ----
8      5      Lilach   0
5      2      Jiru     1
2      1      Eitan    2
1      NULL   David    3
```

To get only two levels of managers of employee 8 using the *Managers* function, run the following code:

```
SELECT empid, lvl
FROM dbo.Managers(8, 2) AS M;
```

You get the following output:

```
empid        lvl
-----------  -----------
2            2
5            1
8            0
```

And to return only the second-level manager, simply add a filter in the outer query, returning employee ID 2:

```
SELECT empid
FROM dbo.Managers(8, 2) AS M
WHERE lvl = 2;
```

To return two levels of managers for employee 8 with a CTE, simply add a predicate in the recursive query's ON clause, as shown in bold in the following example:

```
DECLARE @empid AS INT = 8, @maxlevels AS INT = 2;

WITH Mgrs
AS
(
  SELECT empid, mgrid, empname, 0 AS lvl
  FROM dbo.Employees
  WHERE empid = @empid

  UNION ALL

  SELECT P.empid, P.mgrid, P.empname, C.lvl + 1
  FROM Mgrs AS C
    INNER JOIN dbo.Employees AS P
      ON C.mgrid = P.empid
        AND lvl < @maxlevels
)
SELECT empid, mgrid, empname, lvl
FROM Mgrs;
```

See Also *Both the subgraph and path solutions presented here implement what can be considered "divide and conquer" or "reduce and conquer" algorithms. In the article "Divide and Conquer Halloween" (http://sqlmag.com/t-sql/divide-and-conquer-halloween), I describe further optimization aspects of such implementations.*

Subgraph/descendants with path enumeration

In the subgraph/descendants solutions, you might also want to generate for each node an enumerated path consisting of all node IDs in the path to that node, using some separator (such as '.'). For example, the enumerated path for employee 8 in the Organization Chart scenario is '.1.2.5.8.' because employee 5 is the manager of employee 8, employee 2 is the manager of 5, employee 1 is the manager of 2, and employee 1 is the root employee.

The enumerated path has many uses—for example, to sort the nodes from the graph in the output, to detect cycles, and to do other things that I'll describe later in the "Materialized path" section. Fortunately, you can make minor additions to the solutions I provided for returning a subgraph to calculate the enumerated path without any additional I/O.

The algorithm starts with the subtree's root node and, in a loop or recursive call, returns the next level. For the root node, the path is simply '.' + *node id* + '.'. For successive level nodes, the path is *parent's path* + *node id* + '.'.

Run the following code to create the *Subordinates3* function, which is the same as *Subordinates2* except for the addition of the enumerated path calculation.

```
-- -----------------------------------------------------------------
-- Function: Subordinates3,
--           Descendants with optional level limit
--           and path enumeration
--
-- Input   : @root      INT: Manager id
--           @maxlevels INT: Max number of levels to return
--
-- Output  : @Subs TABLE: id, level and materialized ancestors path
--                        of subordinates of input manager
--                        in all levels <= @maxlevels
--
-- Process : * Insert into @Subs row of input manager
--           * In a loop, while previous insert loaded more than 0 rows
--             and previous level is smaller than @maxlevels:
--             - insert into @Subs next level of subordinates
--             - calculate a materialized ancestors path for each
--               by concatenating current node id to parent's path
-- -----------------------------------------------------------------
IF OBJECT_ID(N'dbo.Subordinates3', N'TF') IS NOT NULL DROP FUNCTION dbo.Subordinates3;
GO
CREATE FUNCTION dbo.Subordinates3 (@root AS INT, @maxlevels AS INT = NULL) RETURNS @Subs TABLE
(
  empid INT          NOT NULL PRIMARY KEY NONCLUSTERED,
  lvl   INT          NOT NULL,
  path  VARCHAR(896) NOT NULL,
  UNIQUE CLUSTERED(lvl, empid)          -- Index will be used to filter level
)
AS
BEGIN
  DECLARE @lvl AS INT = 0;              -- Initialize level counter with 0

  -- Insert root node to @Subs
  INSERT INTO @Subs(empid, lvl, path)
    SELECT empid, @lvl, '.' + CAST(empid AS VARCHAR(10)) + '.'
    FROM dbo.Employees WHERE empid = @root;

  WHILE @@rowcount > 0                  -- while previous level had rows
    AND (@lvl < @maxlevels              -- and haven't reached level limit
         OR @maxlevels IS NULL)
  BEGIN
    SET @lvl += 1;                      -- Increment level counter

    -- Insert next level of subordinates to @Subs
    INSERT INTO @Subs(empid, lvl, path)
      SELECT C.empid, @lvl, P.path + CAST(C.empid AS VARCHAR(10)) + '.'
      FROM @Subs AS P                   -- P = Parent
        INNER JOIN dbo.Employees AS C -- C = Child
          ON P.lvl = @lvl - 1           -- Filter parents from previous level
            AND C.mgrid = P.empid;
  END

  RETURN;
END
GO
```

Run the following code to return all subordinates of employee 1 and their paths:

```
SELECT empid, lvl, path
FROM dbo.Subordinates3(1, NULL) AS S;
```

This code generates the following output:

```
empid       lvl          path
----------- ------------ -------------------
1           0            .1.
2           1            .1.2.
3           1            .1.3.
4           2            .1.2.4.
5           2            .1.2.5.
6           2            .1.2.6.
7           2            .1.3.7.
8           3            .1.2.5.8.
9           3            .1.3.7.9.
10          3            .1.2.5.10.
11          3            .1.3.7.11.
12          4            .1.3.7.9.12.
13          4            .1.3.7.9.13.
14          4            .1.3.7.9.14.
```

With both the *lvl* and *path* values, you can easily return output that graphically shows the hierarchical relationships of the employees in the subtree:

```
SELECT E.empid, REPLICATE(' | ', lvl) + empname AS empname
FROM dbo.Subordinates3(1, NULL) AS S
  INNER JOIN dbo.Employees AS E
    ON E.empid = S.empid
ORDER BY path;
```

The query joins the subtree returned from the *Subordinates3* function with the Employees table based on employee ID match. From the function, you get the *lvl* and *path* values, and from the table, you get other employee attributes of interest, such as the employee name. You generate an indentation before the employee name by replicating a string (in this case, ' | ') *lvl* times and concatenating the employee name to it. Sorting the employees by the *path* column produces a correct hierarchical sort (topological sort), which requires a child node to appear later than its parent node—or, in other words, it requires a child node to have a higher sort value than its parent node. By definition, a child's path is greater than a parent's path because it is prefixed with the parent's path. Following is the output of this query:

```
empid       empname
---  ------  ------------------------
1            David
2            | Eitan
4            | | Seraph
5            | | Jiru
10           | | | Sean
8            | | | Lilach
6            | | Steve
3            | Ina
7            | | Aaron
```

```
11            | | | Gabriel
9             | | | Rita
12            | | | | Emilia
13            | | | | Michael
14            | | | | Didi
```

Similarly, you can add a path calculation to the subtree CTE, as shown in bold in the following example:

```
DECLARE @root AS INT = 1;

WITH Subs
AS
(
  SELECT empid, empname, 0 AS lvl,
    -- Path of root = '.' + empid + '.'
    CAST('.' + CAST(empid AS VARCHAR(10)) + '.' AS VARCHAR(MAX)) AS path
  FROM dbo.Employees
  WHERE empid = @root

  UNION ALL

  SELECT C.empid, C.empname, P.lvl + 1,
    -- Path of child = parent's path + child empid + '.'
    CAST(P.path + CAST(C.empid AS VARCHAR(10)) + '.' AS VARCHAR(MAX))
  FROM Subs AS P
    INNER JOIN dbo.Employees AS C
      ON C.mgrid = P.empid
)
SELECT empid, REPLICATE(' | ', lvl) + empname AS empname
FROM Subs
ORDER BY path;
```

 Note Corresponding columns between an anchor member and a recursive member of a CTE must match in both data type and size. That's why I converted the path strings in both to the same data type and size: VARCHAR(MAX).

Sorting

Sorting is a presentation request that generally is used by the client rather than the server. This means you might want the sorting of hierarchies to take place on the client. In this section, however, I'll present server-side sorting techniques with T-SQL that you can use when you prefer to handle sorting on the server.

A *topological sort* of a DAG is defined as one that provides a child with a higher sort value than its parent. Occasionally, I will refer to a topological sort informally as a *correct hierarchical sort*. More than one way of ordering the items in a DAG can qualify as correct. You might or might not care about the order among siblings. If the order among siblings doesn't matter to you, you can achieve sorting by constructing an enumerated path for each node, as described in the previous section, and sort the nodes by that path.

Remember that the enumerated path is a character string made of the IDs of the ancestors leading to the node, using some separator. This means that siblings are sorted by their node IDs. Because the path is character based, you get character-based sorting of IDs, which might be different than the integer sorting. For example, employee ID 11 sorts lower than its sibling with ID 9 (*'.1.3.7.11.'* < *'.1.3.7.9.'*), even though 9 is less than 11. You can guarantee that sorting by the enumerated path produces a topological sort, but it doesn't guarantee the order of siblings. If you need such a guarantee, you need a different solution.

For optimal sorting flexibility, you might want to guarantee the following:

1. A topological sort—that is, a sort in which a child has a higher sort value than its parent's.

2. Siblings are sorted in a requested order (for example, by *empname* or by *salary*).

3. Integer sort values are generated rather than lengthy strings.

In the enumerated path solution, requirement 1 is met. Requirement 2 is not met because the path is made of node IDs and is character based; making a comparison of characters and sorting among characters is based on collation properties, yielding different comparison and sorting behavior than with integers. Requirement 3 is not met because the solution orders the results by the path, which is lengthy compared to an integer value. To meet all three requirements, you can still make use of a path for each node, but with several differences:

- Instead of using node IDs, the path is constructed from values that represent a position (row number) among nodes based on a requested order (for example, *empname* or *salary*).

- Instead of using a character string with varying lengths for each level in the path, use a binary string with a fixed length for each level.

- Once the binary paths are constructed, calculate integer values representing path order (row numbers) and, ultimately, use those to sort the hierarchy.

The core algorithm to traverse the subtree is maintained, but the paths are constructed differently, based on the binary representation of row numbers. The implementation uses CTEs and the ROW_NUMBER function.

Run the following code to return the subtree of employee 1, with siblings sorted by *empname* (as shown in bold) with indentation:

```
DECLARE @root AS INT = 1;

WITH Subs
AS
(
  SELECT empid, empname, 0 AS lvl,
    -- Path of root is 1 (binary)
    CAST(CAST(1 AS BINARY(4)) AS VARBINARY(MAX)) AS sort_path
  FROM dbo.Employees
  WHERE empid = @root

  UNION ALL
```

```
SELECT C.empid, C.empname, P.lvl + 1,
  -- Path of child = parent's path + child row number (binary)
  P.sort_path + CAST(ROW_NUMBER() OVER(PARTITION BY C.mgrid ORDER BY C.empname) AS BINARY(4))
FROM Subs AS P
  INNER JOIN dbo.Employees AS C
    ON C.mgrid = P.empid
)
SELECT empid,
  ROW_NUMBER() OVER(ORDER BY sort_path) AS sortval, REPLICATE(' | ', lvl) + empname AS empname
FROM Subs
ORDER BY sortval;
```

This code generates the following output:

```
empid  sortval  empname
------ -------- --------------------
1      1        David
2      2        | Eitan
5      3        | | Jiru
8      4        | | | Lilach
10     5        | | | Sean
4      6        | | Seraph
6      7        | | Steve
3      8        | Ina
7      9        | | Aaron
11     10       | | | Gabriel
9      11       | | | Rita
14     12       | | | | Didi
12     13       | | | | Emilia
13     14       | | | | Michael
```

The anchor member query returns the root, with the integer 1 converted to BINARY(4), and then returns VARBINARY(MAX) as the binary path. The recursive member query calculates the row number of an employee among siblings based on *empname* ordering and concatenates that row number converted to BINARY(4) to the parent's path.

> **Tip** I used BINARY(4) as the target type for each element in the sort path; however, you can use a smaller size to minimize the length of the path. Just remember that you compute row numbers that are partitioned by the manager. So ask yourself how many direct subordinates at most you can have per manager. For example, if the answer is "Never more than 100," BINARY(1) is sufficient. If it's 1,000, BINARY(2) would be sufficient.

The outer query calculates row numbers to generate the sort values based on the binary path order, and it sorts the subtree by those sort values, adding indentation based on the calculated level.

If you want siblings sorted in a different way, you need to change only the ORDER BY list of the ROW_NUMBER function in the recursive member query. The following code has the revision that sorts siblings by *salary* (as shown in bold):

```
DECLARE @root AS INT = 1;

WITH Subs
AS
(
  SELECT empid, empname, salary, 0 AS lvl,
    -- Path of root = 1 (binary)
    CAST(CAST(1 AS BINARY(4)) AS VARBINARY(MAX)) AS sort_path
  FROM dbo.Employees
  WHERE empid = @root

  UNION ALL

  SELECT C.empid, C.empname, C.salary, P.lvl + 1,
    -- Path of child = parent's path + child row number (binary)
    P.sort_path + CAST(ROW_NUMBER() OVER(PARTITION BY C.mgrid ORDER BY C.salary) AS BINARY(4))
  FROM Subs AS P
    INNER JOIN dbo.Employees AS C
      ON C.mgrid = P.empid
)
SELECT empid, salary, ROW_NUMBER() OVER(ORDER BY sort_path) AS sortval,
  REPLICATE(' | ', lvl) + empname AS empname
FROM Subs
ORDER BY sortval;
```

This code generates the following output:

```
empid  salary      sortval  empname
------ ----------  -------  --------------------
1      10000.00    1        David
2      7000.00     2        | Eitan
6      4500.00     3        | | Steve
4      5000.00     4        | | Seraph
5      5500.00     5        | | Jiru
10     3000.00     6        | | | Sean
8      3500.00     7        | | | Lilach
3      7500.00     8        | Ina
7      5000.00     9        | | Aaron
9      3000.00     10       | | | Rita
14     1500.00     11       | | | | Didi
12     2000.00     12       | | | | Emilia
13     2000.00     13       | | | | Michael
11     3000.00     14       | | | Gabriel
```

Note If you need to sort siblings by a single integer sort column (for example, by *empid*), you can construct the binary sort path from the sort column values themselves instead of row numbers based on that column.

Cycles

Cycles in graphs are paths that begin and end at the same node. In some scenarios, cycles are natural (for example, road systems). If you have a cycle in what's supposed to be an acyclic graph, it might indicate a problem in your data. Either way, you need a way to identify cycles. If a cycle indicates a problem in the data, you need to identify the problem and fix it. If cycles are natural, you don't want to endlessly keep returning to the same point while traversing the graph.

Cycle detection with T-SQL can be a complex and expensive task. However, I'll show you a simple technique to detect cycles with reasonable performance, relying on path enumeration, which I discussed earlier. For demonstration purposes, I'll use this technique to detect cycles in the tree represented by the Employees table, but you can apply this technique to forests as well and also to more generic graphs, as I will demonstrate later.

Suppose that Didi (*empid* 14) is unhappy with her location in the company's management hierarchy. Didi also happens to be the database administrator and has full access to the Employees table. Didi runs the following code, making her the manager of the CEO and introducing a cycle:

```
UPDATE dbo.Employees SET mgrid = 14 WHERE empid = 1;
```

The Employees table currently contains the following cycle of employee IDs:

```
1 3 7 9 14 1
```

As a baseline, I'll use one of the solutions I covered earlier, which constructs an enumerated path. In my examples, I'll use a CTE solution, but of course you can apply the same logic to the UDF solution that uses loops.

A cycle is detected when you follow a path leading to a given node if its parent's path already contains the child node ID. You can keep track of cycles by maintaining a *cycle* column, which contains 0 if no cycle is detected and 1 if one is detected. In the anchor member of the solution CTE, the *cycle* column value is simply the constant 0 because, obviously, the root level has no cycle. In the recursive member's query, use a LIKE predicate to check whether the parent's path contains the child node ID. Return 1 if it does and 0 otherwise. Note the importance of the dots at both the beginning and end of both the path and the pattern—without the dots, you get an unwanted match for employee ID *n* (for example, *n* = 3) if the path contains employee ID *nm* (for example, *m* = 15, *nm* = 315). The following code returns a subtree with an enumerated path calculation and has the addition of the *cycle* column calculation, as indicated in bold:

```
DECLARE @root AS INT = 1;

WITH Subs
AS
(
  SELECT empid, empname, 0 AS lvl,
    CAST('.' + CAST(empid AS VARCHAR(10)) + '.' AS VARCHAR(MAX)) AS path,
    -- Obviously root has no cycle
    0 AS cycle
  FROM dbo.Employees
  WHERE empid = @root
```

```
    UNION ALL

    SELECT C.empid, C.empname, P.lvl + 1,
      CAST(P.path + CAST(C.empid AS VARCHAR(10)) + '.' AS VARCHAR(MAX)),
      -- Cycle detected if parent's path contains child's id
      CASE WHEN P.path LIKE '%.' + CAST(C.empid AS VARCHAR(10)) + '.%' THEN 1 ELSE 0 END
    FROM Subs AS P
      INNER JOIN dbo.Employees AS C
        ON C.mgrid = P.empid
)
SELECT empid, empname, cycle, path
FROM Subs;
```

If you run this code, it always breaks after 100 levels (the default MAXRECURSION value) because cycles are detected but not avoided. You need to avoid cycles—in other words, don't pursue paths for which cycles are detected. To achieve this, simply add a filter to the recursive member that returns a child only if its parent's *cycle* value is 0, as shown in bold in the following example:

```
DECLARE @root AS INT = 1;

WITH Subs AS
(
  SELECT empid, empname, 0 AS lvl,
    CAST('.' + CAST(empid AS VARCHAR(10)) + '.' AS VARCHAR(MAX)) AS path,
    -- Obviously root has no cycle
    0 AS cycle
  FROM dbo.Employees
  WHERE empid = @root

  UNION ALL

  SELECT C.empid, C.empname, P.lvl + 1,
    CAST(P.path + CAST(C.empid AS VARCHAR(10)) + '.' AS VARCHAR(MAX)),
    -- Cycle detected if parent's path contains child's id
    CASE WHEN P.path LIKE '%.' + CAST(C.empid AS VARCHAR(10)) + '.%' THEN 1 ELSE 0 END
  FROM Subs AS P
    INNER JOIN dbo.Employees AS C
      ON C.mgrid = P.empid
        AND P.cycle = 0 -- do not pursue path for parent with cycle
)
SELECT empid, empname, cycle, path
FROM Subs;
```

This code generates the following output:

```
empid  empname  cycle  path
------ -------- ------ ----------------
1      David    0      .1.
2      Eitan    0      .1.2.
3      Ina      0      .1.3.
7      Aaron    0      .1.3.7.
9      Rita     0      .1.3.7.9.
11     Gabriel  0      .1.3.7.11.
12     Emilia   0      .1.3.7.9.12.
13     Michael  0      .1.3.7.9.13.
```

```
14    Didi     0    .1.3.7.9.14.
1     David    1    .1.3.7.9.14.1.
4     Seraph   0    .1.2.4.
5     Jiru     0    .1.2.5.
6     Steve    0    .1.2.6.
8     Lilach   0    .1.2.5.8.
10    Sean     0    .1.2.5.10.
```

Notice in the output that the second time employee 1 was reached, a cycle was detected for it, and the path was not pursued any further. In a cyclic graph, that's all the logic you usually need to add. In our case, the cycle indicates a problem with the data that needs to be fixed. To isolate only the cyclic path (in our case, *.1.3.7.9.14.1.*), simply add the filter *cycle = 1* to the outer query, as shown in bold here:

```
DECLARE @root AS INT = 1;

WITH Subs AS
(
  SELECT empid, empname, 0 AS lvl,
    CAST('.' + CAST(empid AS VARCHAR(10)) + '.' AS VARCHAR(MAX)) AS path,
    -- Obviously root has no cycle
    0 AS cycle
  FROM dbo.Employees
  WHERE empid = @root

  UNION ALL

  SELECT C.empid, C.empname, P.lvl + 1,
    CAST(P.path + CAST(C.empid AS VARCHAR(10)) + '.' AS VARCHAR(MAX)),
    -- Cycle detected if parent's path contains child's id
    CASE WHEN P.path LIKE '%.' + CAST(C.empid AS VARCHAR(10)) + '.%' THEN 1 ELSE 0 END
  FROM Subs AS P
    INNER JOIN dbo.Employees AS C
      ON C.mgrid = P.empid
        AND P.cycle = 0
)
SELECT path FROM Subs WHERE cycle = 1;
```

Now that the cyclic path has been identified, you can fix the data by running the following code:

```
UPDATE dbo.Employees SET mgrid = NULL WHERE empid = 1;
```

Materialized path

So far, I presented solutions where paths were computed when the code was executed. In the materialized path solution, the paths are stored so that they need not be computed repeatedly. You basically store an enumerated path and a level for each node of the tree in two additional columns. The solution works optimally with trees and forests. Theoretically, you could use this approach with the more generic DAGs that can have multiple paths leading to each node. However, because this solution needs to store the path and level values per node and the path that leads to it, maintaining the extra information can be both complex and expensive.

This approach has two main advantages over the iterative/recursive approach. Queries are simpler and set based (without relying on recursive CTEs). Also, queries typically perform much faster because they can rely on the indexing of the path.

However, now that you have two additional attributes in the table, you need to keep them in sync with the tree as it undergoes changes. The cost of modifications determines whether it's reasonable to synchronize the path and level values with every change in the tree. For example, what is the effect of adding a new leaf to the tree? I like to refer to the effect of such a modification informally as the *shake effect*. Fortunately, as I will elaborate on shortly, the shake effect of adding new leaves is minor. Also, the effect of dropping or moving a small subtree is typically not significant.

The enumerated path can get lengthy when the tree is deep—in other words, when there are many levels of managers. SQL Server limits the size of index keys to 900 bytes. To achieve the performance benefits of an index on the path column, you must limit the size of that column to 900 bytes. If you need the index key list to include other columns besides *path*, like (*lvl, path*), the total length cannot exceed 900 bytes. Before you become concerned by this fact, try thinking in practical terms: 900 bytes is enough for trees with hundreds of levels. Will your tree ever reach more levels than that?

Maintaining data

First run the following code to create the Employees table with the new *lvl* and *path* columns:

```
IF OBJECT_ID(N'dbo.Employees', N'U') IS NOT NULL DROP TABLE dbo.Employees;
GO
CREATE TABLE dbo.Employees
(
  empid    INT          NOT NULL,
  mgrid    INT          NULL    ,
  empname  VARCHAR(25)  NOT NULL,
  salary   MONEY        NOT NULL,
  lvl      INT          NOT NULL,
  path     VARCHAR(896) NOT NULL
);

CREATE UNIQUE CLUSTERED INDEX idx_depth_first ON dbo.Employees(path);
CREATE UNIQUE INDEX idx_breadth_first ON dbo.Employees(lvl, path);
ALTER TABLE dbo.Employees ADD CONSTRAINT PK_Employees PRIMARY KEY NONCLUSTERED(empid);

ALTER TABLE dbo.Employees
  ADD CONSTRAINT FK_Employees_Employees
    FOREIGN KEY(mgrid) REFERENCES dbo.Employees(empid);
```

Observe the definition of the indexes that the code creates. The index idx_depth_first can be useful for depth-first types of requests like returning a subtree and sorting. Assuming there might be large subtrees in the requests, it becomes important for the index to be a covering one; therefore, I made this index a clustered index. The index idx_breadth_first can be useful for breadth-first types of requests like returning an entire level. The index created on the *empid* column to support the primary key constraint will naturally support queries that need to filter an employee based on the employee's ID.

To handle modifications in a tree, it's recommended that you use stored procedures that also take care of the *lvl* and *path* values. Alternatively, you can use triggers, and their logic will be very similar to that shown in the following stored procedures.

Adding employees who manage no one (leaves)

Let's start with handling inserts. The logic of the insert procedure is simple. If the new employee is a root employee (that is, the manager ID is NULL), its level is 0, and its path is '.' + *employee id* + '.'. Otherwise, its level is the parent's level plus 1, and its path is *parent path* + *employee* id + '.'. As you probably can figure out, the shake effect here is minor. You don't need to make any changes to other employees, and to calculate the new employee's *lvl* and *path* values, you need only to query the employee's parent.

Run the following code to create the *AddEmp* stored procedure and populate the Employees table with sample data:

```
---------------------------------------------------------------------
-- Stored Procedure: AddEmp,
--    Inserts into the table a new employee who manages no one
---------------------------------------------------------------------
IF OBJECT_ID(N'dbo.AddEmp', N'P') IS NOT NULL DROP PROC dbo.AddEmp;
GO
CREATE PROC dbo.AddEmp
  @empid   INT,
  @mgrid   INT,
  @empname VARCHAR(25),
  @salary  MONEY
AS

SET NOCOUNT ON;

-- Handle case where the new employee has no manager (root)
IF @mgrid IS NULL
  INSERT INTO dbo.Employees(empid, mgrid, empname, salary, lvl, path)
    VALUES(@empid, @mgrid, @empname, @salary,
      0, '.' + CAST(@empid AS VARCHAR(10)) + '.');
-- Handle subordinate case (non-root)
ELSE
  INSERT INTO dbo.Employees(empid, mgrid, empname, salary, lvl, path)
    SELECT @empid, @mgrid, @empname, @salary, lvl + 1, path + CAST(@empid AS VARCHAR(10)) + '.'
    FROM dbo.Employees
    WHERE empid = @mgrid;
GO

EXEC dbo.AddEmp
  @empid = 1, @mgrid = NULL, @empname = 'David', @salary = $10000.00;
EXEC dbo.AddEmp
  @empid = 2, @mgrid = 1, @empname = 'Eitan', @salary = $7000.00;
EXEC dbo.AddEmp
  @empid = 3, @mgrid = 1, @empname = 'Ina', @salary = $7500.00;
EXEC dbo.AddEmp
  @empid = 4, @mgrid = 2, @empname = 'Seraph', @salary = $5000.00;
```

```
EXEC dbo.AddEmp
  @empid = 5, @mgrid = 2, @empname = 'Jiru', @salary = $5500.00;
EXEC dbo.AddEmp
  @empid = 6, @mgrid = 2, @empname = 'Steve', @salary = $4500.00;
EXEC dbo.AddEmp
  @empid = 7, @mgrid = 3, @empname = 'Aaron', @salary = $5000.00;
EXEC dbo.AddEmp
  @empid = 8, @mgrid = 5, @empname = 'Lilach', @salary = $3500.00;
EXEC dbo.AddEmp
  @empid = 9, @mgrid = 7, @empname = 'Rita', @salary = $3000.00;
EXEC dbo.AddEmp
  @empid = 10, @mgrid = 5, @empname = 'Sean', @salary = $3000.00;
EXEC dbo.AddEmp
  @empid = 11, @mgrid = 7, @empname = 'Gabriel', @salary = $3000.00;
EXEC dbo.AddEmp
  @empid = 12, @mgrid = 9, @empname = 'Emilia', @salary = $2000.00;
EXEC dbo.AddEmp
  @empid = 13, @mgrid = 9, @empname = 'Michael', @salary = $2000.00;
EXEC dbo.AddEmp
  @empid = 14, @mgrid = 9, @empname = 'Didi', @salary = $1500.00;
```

Run the following query to examine the resulting contents of Employees:

```
SELECT empid, mgrid, empname, salary, lvl, path
FROM dbo.Employees
ORDER BY path;
```

You get the following output:

```
empid  mgrid  empname  salary     lvl  path
------ ------ -------- ---------- ---- --------------
1      NULL   David    10000.00   0    .1.
2      1      Eitan    7000.00    1    .1.2.
4      2      Seraph   5000.00    2    .1.2.4.
5      2      Jiru     5500.00    2    .1.2.5.
10     5      Sean     3000.00    3    .1.2.5.10.
8      5      Lilach   3500.00    3    .1.2.5.8.
6      2      Steve    4500.00    2    .1.2.6.
3      1      Ina      7500.00    1    .1.3.
7      3      Aaron    5000.00    2    .1.3.7.
11     7      Gabriel  3000.00    3    .1.3.7.11.
9      7      Rita     3000.00    3    .1.3.7.9.
12     9      Emilia   2000.00    4    .1.3.7.9.12.
13     9      Michael  2000.00    4    .1.3.7.9.13.
14     9      Didi     1500.00    4    .1.3.7.9.14.
```

Moving a subtree

Moving a subtree is a bit tricky. A change in someone's manager affects the row for that employee and for all of his or her subordinates. The inputs are the root of the subtree and the new parent (manager) of that root. The level and path values of all employees in the subtree are going to be affected. So you need to be able to isolate that subtree and also figure out how to revise the level and path values of all the subtree's members. To isolate the affected subtree, you join the row for the root (R) with the Employees table (E) based on *E.path LIKE R.path + '%'*. To calculate the revisions in level and path, you need access to the rows of both the old manager of the root (OM) and the new one (NM). The new level value for all nodes is their current level value plus the difference in levels between the new manager's level and the old manager's level. For example, if you move a subtree to a new location so that the difference in levels between the new manager and the old one is 2, you need to add 2 to the level value of all employees in the affected subtree. Similarly, to amend the path value of all nodes in the subtree, you need to remove the prefix containing the root's old manager's path and substitute it with the new manager's path. This can be achieved by using the STUFF function.

Run the following code to create the *MoveSubtree* stored procedure, which implements the logic I just described:

```
---------------------------------------------------------------------
-- Stored Procedure: MoveSubtree,
--    Moves a whole subtree of a given root to a new location
--    under a given manager
---------------------------------------------------------------------
IF OBJECT_ID(N'dbo.MoveSubtree', N'P') IS NOT NULL DROP PROC dbo.MoveSubtree;
GO
CREATE PROC dbo.MoveSubtree
  @root  INT,
  @mgrid INT
AS

SET NOCOUNT ON;

BEGIN TRAN;
  -- Update level and path of all employees in the subtree (E)
  -- Set level =
  --    current level + new manager's level - old manager's level
  -- Set path =
  --    in current path remove old manager's path
  --    and substitute with new manager's path
  UPDATE E
    SET lvl  = E.lvl + NM.lvl - OM.lvl,
        path = STUFF(E.path, 1, LEN(OM.path), NM.path)
  FROM dbo.Employees AS E          -- E = Employees    (subtree)
    INNER JOIN dbo.Employees AS R  -- R = Root         (one row)
      ON R.empid = @root
        AND E.path LIKE R.path + '%'
    INNER JOIN dbo.Employees AS OM -- OM = Old Manager (one row)
      ON OM.empid = R.mgrid
    INNER JOIN dbo.Employees AS NM -- NM = New Manager (one row)
      ON NM.empid = @mgrid;

  -- Update root's new manager
  UPDATE dbo.Employees SET mgrid = @mgrid WHERE empid = @root;
COMMIT TRAN;
GO
```

The implementation of this stored procedure is simplistic and is provided for demonstration purposes. Good behavior is not guaranteed for invalid parameter choices. To make this procedure more robust, you should also check the inputs to make sure that attempts to make someone his or her own manager or to generate cycles are rejected. For example, you can achieve this by using an EXISTS predicate with a SELECT statement that first generates a result set with the new paths and making sure that the employees' IDs do not appear in their managers' paths.

To test the procedure, first examine the tree before moving the subtree:

```
SELECT empid, REPLICATE(' | ', lvl) + empname AS empname, lvl, path
FROM dbo.Employees
ORDER BY path;
```

You get the following output:

```
empid       empname               lvl  path
----------- --------------------- ---- -------------
1           David                 0    .1.
2            | Eitan              1    .1.2.
4            | | Seraph           2    .1.2.4.
5            | | Jiru             2    .1.2.5.
10           | | | Sean           3    .1.2.5.10.
8            | | | Lilach         3    .1.2.5.8.
6            | | Steve            2    .1.2.6.
3            | Ina                1    .1.3.
7            | | Aaron            2    .1.3.7.
11           | | | Gabriel        3    .1.3.7.11.
9            | | | Rita           3    .1.3.7.9.
12           | | | | Emilia       4    .1.3.7.9.12.
13           | | | | Michael      4    .1.3.7.9.13.
14           | | | | Didi         4    .1.3.7.9.14.
```

Then run the following code to move Aaron's subtree under Sean:

```
BEGIN TRAN;

  EXEC dbo.MoveSubtree
  @root  = 7,
  @mgrid = 10;

  -- After moving subtree
  SELECT empid, REPLICATE(' | ', lvl) + empname AS empname, lvl, path
  FROM dbo.Employees
  ORDER BY path;

ROLLBACK TRAN; -- rollback used in order not to apply the change
```

 Note The change is rolled back for demonstration only, so the data is the same at the start of each test script.

Examine the result tree to verify that the subtree moved correctly.

```
empid      empname                    lvl  path
---------- -------------------------- ---- -------------------
1          David                      0    .1.
2          | Eitan                    1    .1.2.
4          | | Seraph                 2    .1.2.4.
5          | | Jiru                   2    .1.2.5.
10         | | | Sean                 3    .1.2.5.10.
7          | | | | Aaron              4    .1.2.5.10.7.
11         | | | | | Gabriel          5    .1.2.5.10.7.11.
9          | | | | | Rita             5    .1.2.5.10.7.9.
12         | | | | | | Emilia         6    .1.2.5.10.7.9.12.
13         | | | | | | Michael        6    .1.2.5.10.7.9.13.
14         | | | | | | Didi           6    .1.2.5.10.7.9.14.
8          | | | Lilach               3    .1.2.5.8.
6          | | Steve                  2    .1.2.6.
3          | Ina                      1    .1.3.
```

Removing a subtree

Removing a subtree is a simple task. You just delete all employees whose path value has the subtree's root path as a prefix.

To test this solution, first examine the current state of the tree by running the following query:

```
SELECT empid, REPLICATE(' | ', lvl) + empname AS empname, lvl, path
FROM dbo.Employees
ORDER BY path;
```

You get the following output:

```
empid      empname              lvl  path
---------- -------------------- ---- ------------
1          David                0    .1.
2          | Eitan              1    .1.2.
4          | | Seraph           2    .1.2.4.
5          | | Jiru             2    .1.2.5.
10         | | | Sean           3    .1.2.5.10.
8          | | | Lilach         3    .1.2.5.8.
6          | | Steve            2    .1.2.6.
3          | Ina                1    .1.3.
7          | | Aaron            2    .1.3.7.
11         | | | Gabriel        3    .1.3.7.11.
9          | | | Rita           3    .1.3.7.9.
12         | | | | Emilia       4    .1.3.7.9.12.
13         | | | | Michael      4    .1.3.7.9.13.
14         | | | | Didi         4    .1.3.7.9.14.
```

Issue the following code, which first removes Aaron and his subordinates and then displays the resulting tree:

```
BEGIN TRAN;

  DELETE FROM dbo.Employees
  WHERE path LIKE
```

```
    (SELECT M.path + '%'
     FROM dbo.Employees as M
     WHERE M.empid = 7);


  -- After deleting subtree
  SELECT empid, REPLICATE(' | ', lvl) + empname AS empname, lvl, path
  FROM dbo.Employees
  ORDER BY path;

ROLLBACK TRAN; -- rollback used in order not to apply the change
```

You get the following output:

```
empid       empname            lvl   path
----------- ---------------    ----  -----------
1           David              0     .1.
2           | Eitan            1     .1.2.
4           | | Seraph         2     .1.2.4.
5           | | Jiru           2     .1.2.5.
10          | | | Sean         3     .1.2.5.10.
8           | | | Lilach       3     .1.2.5.8.
6           | | Steve          2     .1.2.6.
3           | Ina              1     .1.3.
```

Querying

Querying data in the materialized path solution is simple and elegant. For subtree-related requests, the optimizer can always use a clustered or covering index that you create on the *path* column. If you create a nonclustered, noncovering index on the *path* column, the optimizer can still use it if the query is selective enough.

Let's review typical requests from a tree. For each request, I'll provide a sample query followed by its output.

Return the subtree with a given root:

```
SELECT REPLICATE(' | ', E.lvl - M.lvl) + E.empname
FROM dbo.Employees AS E
  INNER JOIN dbo.Employees AS M
    ON M.empid = 3 -- root
       AND E.path LIKE M.path + '%'
ORDER BY E.path;
```

```
Ina
 | Aaron
 | | Gabriel
 | | Rita
 | | | Emilia
 | | | Michael
 | | | Didi
```

The query joins two instances of Employees. One represents the managers (*M*) and is filtered by the given root employee. The other represents the employees in the subtree (*E*). The subtree is identified using the following logical expression in the join condition, *E.path LIKE M.path* + '%', which identifies a subordinate if it contains the root's path as a prefix. Indentation is achieved by replicating a string ('| ') as many times as the employee's level within the subtree. The output is sorted by the path of the employee.

This query generates the execution plan shown in Figure 11-5.

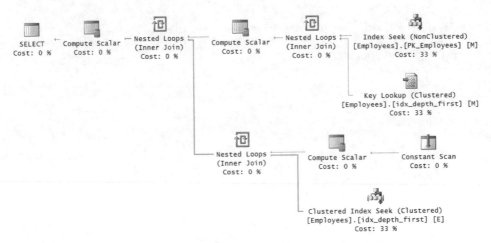

FIGURE 11-5 Execution plan for the custom materialized path subtree query.

The first Index Seek operator in the plan and the associated Key Lookup are in charge of retrieving the row for the filtered employee (*empid* 3). The second Index Seek operator in the plan performs a range scan in the index on the *path* attribute to retrieve the requested subtree of employees. Because the *path* attribute represents topological sorting, an index on *path* ensures that all members of the same subtree are stored contiguously in the leaf level of the index. Therefore, a request for a subtree is processed with a simple range scan in the index, touching only the nodes that, in fact, are members of the requested subtree.

To exclude the subtree's root (top-level manager) from the output, simply add an underscore before the percent sign in the LIKE pattern:

```
SELECT REPLICATE(' | ', E.lvl - M.lvl - 1) + E.empname
FROM dbo.Employees AS E
  INNER JOIN dbo.Employees AS M
    ON M.empid = 3
      AND E.path LIKE M.path + '_%'
ORDER BY E.path;

Aaron
 | Gabriel
 | Rita
 | | Emilia
 | | Michael
 | | Didi
```

With the additional underscore in the LIKE condition, an employee is returned only if its path starts with the root's path and has at least one subsequent character.

To return leaf nodes under a given root (including the root itself if it is a leaf), add a NOT EXISTS predicate to identify only employees who are not managers of another employee:

```
SELECT E.empid, E.empname
FROM dbo.Employees AS E
  INNER JOIN dbo.Employees AS M
    ON M.empid = 3
      AND E.path LIKE M.path + '%'
WHERE NOT EXISTS
  (SELECT *
   FROM dbo.Employees AS E2
   WHERE E2.mgrid = E.empid);
```

```
empid       empname
----------- --------
11          Gabriel
12          Emilia
13          Michael
14          Didi
```

To return a subtree with a given root, limiting the number of levels under the root, add a filter that limits the level difference between the employee and the root:

```
SELECT REPLICATE(' | ', E.lvl - M.lvl) + E.empname
FROM dbo.Employees AS E
  INNER JOIN dbo.Employees AS M
    ON M.empid = 3
      AND E.path LIKE M.path + '%'
WHERE E.lvl - M.lvl <= 2
ORDER BY E.path;
```

```
Ina
 | Aaron
 | | Gabriel
 | | Rita
```

To return only the nodes exactly *n* levels under a given root, use an equal to operator (=) to identify the specific level difference instead of a less than or equal to (<=) operator:

```
SELECT E.empid, E.empname
FROM dbo.Employees AS E
  INNER JOIN dbo.Employees AS M
    ON M.empid = 3
      AND E.path LIKE M.path + '%'
WHERE E.lvl - M.lvl = 2;
```

```
empid       empname
----------- --------
11          Gabriel
9           Rita
```

To return the management chain of a given node, you use a query similar to the subtree query, with one small difference: you filter a specific employee ID rather than filtering a specific manager ID:

```
SELECT REPLICATE(' | ', M.lvl) + M.empname
FROM dbo.Employees AS E
  INNER JOIN dbo.Employees AS M
    ON E.empid = 14
        AND E.path LIKE M.path + '%'
ORDER BY E.path;
```

```
David
 | Ina
 | | Aaron
 | | | Rita
 | | | | Didi
```

You get all managers whose paths are a prefix of the given employee's path.

Note that requesting a subtree and requesting the ancestors have an important difference in performance, even though they look very similar. For each query, either *M.path* or *E.path* is a constant. If *M.path* is constant, *E.path* LIKE *M.path* + '%' enables the plan to use the index on *path* efficiently, because the predicate asks for all paths with a given prefix and all qualifying rows appear in a consecutive section in the index. If *E.path* is constant, the plan does not use the index efficiently, because the predicate asks for all prefixes of a given path and all qualifying rows do not appear in a consecutive section in the index. The subtree query can seek within the index to the first path that meets the filter, and then perform a range scan until it gets to the last path that meets the filter. In other words, only the relevant paths in the index are accessed. Conversely, in the ancestors query, *all* paths must be scanned to check whether they match the filter. In large tables, this approach translates to a slow query. To handle ancestor requests more efficiently, you can create a function that accepts an employee ID as input, splits its path, and returns a table with the path's node IDs in separate rows. You can join this table with the tree and use index seek operations for the specific employee IDs in the path. The split function uses the auxiliary table Nums from the sample database TSQLV3.

Run the following code to create the *SplitPath* function:

```
IF OBJECT_ID(N'dbo.SplitPath', N'IF') IS NOT NULL DROP FUNCTION dbo.SplitPath;
GO
CREATE FUNCTION dbo.SplitPath(@empid AS INT) RETURNS TABLE
AS
RETURN
  SELECT ROW_NUMBER() OVER(ORDER BY n) AS pos,
    CAST(SUBSTRING(path, n + 1, CHARINDEX('.', path, n + 1) - n - 1) AS INT) AS empid
  FROM dbo.Employees
    INNER JOIN TSQLV3.dbo.Nums
      ON empid = @empid
          AND n < LEN(path)
          AND SUBSTRING(path, n, 1) = '.';
GO
```

You can find details on the logic behind the split technique that the function implements in Chapter 3, "Multi-table queries."

To test the function, run the following code, which splits employee 14's path:

```
SELECT pos, empid FROM dbo.SplitPath(14);
```

This code generates the following output:

```
pos   empid
----  ------
1     1
2     3
3     7
4     9
5     14
```

To get the management chain of a given employee, join the table returned by the function with the Employees table, like so:

```
SELECT REPLICATE(' | ', lvl) + empname
FROM dbo.SplitPath(14) AS SP
  INNER JOIN dbo.Employees AS E
    ON E.empid = SP.empid
ORDER BY path;
```

When presenting information from a tree or a subtree, a common need is to present the nodes in topological sort order (parent before child). Because the *path* column already gives you topological sorting, you can simply sort the rows by *path*. Having an index on the *path* column means that the optimizer can satisfy the request with an index order scan as opposed to needing to apply a sort operation. As shown earlier, the indentation of nodes can be achieved by replicating a string *lvl* times. For example, the following query presents the employees in topological sort order:

```
SELECT REPLICATE(' | ', lvl) + empname
FROM dbo.Employees
ORDER BY path;
```

This code generates the following output:

```
David
 | Eitan
 | | Seraph
 | | Jiru
 | | | Sean
 | | | Lilach
 | | Steve
 | Ina
 | | Aaron
 | | | Gabriel
 | | | Rita
 | | | | Emilia
 | | | | Michael
 | | | | Didi
```

The execution plan for this query is shown in Figure 11-6. Notice that the clustered index created on the *path* column is scanned in an ordered fashion.

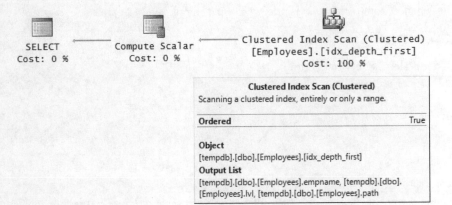

FIGURE 11-6 Execution plan for a custom materialized path sorting query.

Materialized path with the HIERARCHYID data type

SQL Server supports a CLR-based data type called HIERARCHYID that you can use to represent graphs. This type provides a built-in implementation for the materialized path model. Like the custom materialized path model, it works ideally for trees. As with the custom model, the HIERARCHYID values provide topological ordering, positioning a node in a certain place in the tree with respect to other nodes. Besides providing topological sorting, the HIERARCHYID paths position each node under a certain path of ancestors and in a certain place with respect to siblings. The HIERARCHYID paths differ from the custom model's paths in two main ways. First, the custom model's paths are made of the actual node IDs, whereas the HIERARCHYID paths are made of internally generated values. Second, the custom model's path is character based, whereas the HIERARCHYID paths are binary. One of the major benefits I found with the HIERARCHYID type paths is that they tend to be more economical compared to the custom model's paths. The encoding of the paths in the HIERARCHYID data type cannot exceed 892 bytes, but this limit shouldn't present a problem for most trees. Also, you typically want to index the paths, sometimes adding other columns to the key list, and index keys are limited to 900 bytes anyway.

> **Note** The HIERARCHYID data type is a proprietary feature in SQL Server. If you care about the portability of your solution, you might prefer to stick to the custom model. That's because it relies on basic language elements that are supported by virtually all SQL-based dialects: a character string column, an integer column, and the LIKE predicate. Still, it is worthwhile to be familiar with the HIERARCHYID data type for two main reasons:
>
> 1. You might need to maintain existing solutions that already use it.
> 2. There are features in SQL Server that use this data type, like the FileTable feature.

The HIERARCHYID type provides the following set of methods and properties that help you maintain and query the tree: *GetLevel*, *GetRoot*, *GetAncestor*, *GetDescendant*, *GetReparentedValue*, *IsDescendantOf*, *ToString*, *Parse*, *Read*, and *Write*. I will describe the methods and properties in the context of the tasks where they need to be used.

> **Note** I should mention several points about working with the HIERARCHYID type in terms of case sensitivity.
>
> - As a T-SQL type identifier, HIERARCHYID is always case insensitive, like any T-SQL keyword.
>
> - The method names associated with this type, like *GetAncestor()*, are always case sensitive, like any CLR identifier, whether they are static methods or not.
>
> - HIERARCHYID/hierarchyid, when used to identify the CLR class of a static method, as in *hierarchyid::GetRoot()*, is case sensitive or case insensitive according to the current database context. When the current database is case sensitive, lowercase must be used to identify the CLR class of a static method.
>
> - I chose to write the T-SQL type as HIERARCHYID for typographical reasons, but lowercase *hierarchyid* is the most portable choice for code.

Like I did with the custom model, I will use an employee organizational chart to demonstrate working with the HIERARCHYID type. Run the following code to create the Employees table, along with indexes similar to the ones used in the custom model to support typical queries:

```
IF OBJECT_ID(N'dbo.Employees', N'U') IS NOT NULL DROP TABLE dbo.Employees;
GO
CREATE TABLE dbo.Employees
(
  empid   INT NOT NULL,
  hid     HIERARCHYID NOT NULL,
  lvl AS hid.GetLevel() PERSISTED,
  empname VARCHAR(25) NOT NULL,
  salary  MONEY       NOT NULL
);

CREATE UNIQUE CLUSTERED INDEX idx_depth_first ON dbo.Employees(hid);
CREATE UNIQUE INDEX idx_breadth_first ON dbo.Employees(lvl, hid);
ALTER TABLE dbo.Employees ADD CONSTRAINT PK_Employees PRIMARY KEY NONCLUSTERED(empid);
```

In addition to the *hid* column that holds the path, the table has a computed *persisted* column based on the *GetLevel* method applied to the *hid* column. As its name implies, the method returns the level of the node in the tree—in other words, the distance from the root.

As a reminder, besides the obvious index on the *empid* column that supports queries requesting a particular employee, the code creates two other indexes. It creates one for depth-first requests like returning a subtree, and presenting the nodes in topological sort order. It also creates another one for breadth-first requests like returning an entire level.

Notice that the Employees table does not include an attribute for the manager ID. With the HIERARCHYID type, you can easily address requests that would normally require such an attribute. Consequently, there's no need for a self-referencing foreign key either.

Maintaining data

Whenever you need to apply changes to the tree, such as adding new leaf nodes or moving a subtree, you want to make sure you produce new HIERARCHYID values or adjust existing ones correctly. The HIERARCHYID type's methods and properties can help you with such tasks. Also, note that the type itself does not enforce the validity of your tree—that's your responsibility. For example, if you do not enforce the uniqueness of the HIERARCHYID values with a constraint, the type itself won't reject attempts to insert multiple rows with the same HIERARCHYID value. Also, it is your responsibility to develop a process that prevents concurrent sessions that perform tree maintenance tasks from producing conflicting (the same) HIERARCHYID values for different nodes. I will explain how this can be achieved.

I will demonstrate techniques for adding employees who manage no one (leaf nodes) and for moving a subtree. I'll leave other tasks—such as dropping a subtree and changing a manager—as exercises because those apply similar techniques to the ones I will cover.

Adding employees

The task of adding a new employee who manages no one requires you to produce a HIERARCHYID value for the new node that positions it correctly within the tree and then insert the new employee row into the table. Run the following code to create a stored procedure called *AddEmp* that implements this task:

```
---------------------------------------------------------------------
-- Stored Procedure: AddEmp,
--    Inserts into the table a new employee who manages no one
---------------------------------------------------------------------
IF OBJECT_ID(N'dbo.AddEmp', N'P') IS NOT NULL DROP PROC dbo.AddEmp;
GO
CREATE PROC dbo.AddEmp
  @empid   AS INT,
  @mgrid   AS INT,
  @empname AS VARCHAR(25),
  @salary  AS MONEY
AS

DECLARE
  @hid            AS HIERARCHYID,
  @mgr_hid        AS HIERARCHYID,
  @last_child_hid AS HIERARCHYID;

BEGIN TRAN
```

```
IF @mgrid IS NULL
  SET @hid = hierarchyid::GetRoot();
ELSE
BEGIN
  SET @mgr_hid = (SELECT hid FROM dbo.Employees WITH (UPDLOCK) WHERE empid = @mgrid);
  SET @last_child_hid = (SELECT MAX(hid) FROM dbo.Employees
                         WHERE hid.GetAncestor(1) = @mgr_hid);
  SET @hid = @mgr_hid.GetDescendant(@last_child_hid, NULL);
END

INSERT INTO dbo.Employees(empid, hid, empname, salary)
  VALUES(@empid, @hid, @empname, @salary);

COMMIT TRAN
GO
```

The procedure accepts as inputs all attributes of the new employee (employee ID, manager ID, employee name, and salary). It then applies logic to generate the HIERARCHYID value of the new employee and store it in the variable *@hid*. Finally, the procedure uses the new HIERARCHYID value, *@hid*, in the new row it inserts into the Employees table.

The procedure's code first checks whether the input employee is the root employee (that is, manager ID is NULL). In such a case, the code calculates the employee's path with the static method *hierarchyid::GetRoot*. As you can imagine, the purpose of this method is to produce the path for the tree's root node. In terms of the binary value that actually represents the path, this method simply returns an empty binary string (0x). You could, if you wanted, replace the static method call with the constant 0x, but with the method call the code is clearer and more self-explanatory.

The next section of the procedure's code (the ELSE block of the IF statement) handles an input employee that is not the root employee. To calculate a path for an employee that is not the root employee, you can invoke the *GetDescendant* method applied to the HIERARCHYID value of the employee's manager. The code retrieves the manager's HIERARCHYID value, puts it into the *@mgr_hid* variable, and later applies the *GetDescendant* method to it.

The *GetDescendant* method accepts two input HIERARCHYID values and returns a HIERARCHYID value that is positioned under the node it is applied to and between the input left and right nodes. If both inputs are NULL, the method simply generates a value below the parent node. If the left input is not NULL, the method generates a value greater than the left input. If the right input is not NULL, the method generates a value less than the right input. Note that the method has no knowledge of other values in your tree; all it cares about is the value to which it is applied and the two input values. If you call the method twice and in both cases apply it to the same value with the same inputs, you get the same output back. It is your responsibility to prevent such conflicts.

A simple technique to achieve this is to run the code in a transaction (as in the *AddEmp* procedure) and specify the UPDLOCK hint in the query that retrieves the manager's path. Remember that an update lock can be held by only one process on the same resource at a time. This hint allows only one session to request a new HIERARCHYID value under the same manager. This simple technique will guarantee that distinct HIERARCHYID values are generated by each process.

You need to be specific about where to position the new node with respect to other siblings under the same manager. For example, the inputs to the stored procedure could be the IDs of two employees between which you want to position the new employee, and the stored procedure could retrieve their HIERARCHYID values and provide those as the left and right values to the *GetDescendant* method. For this implementation, I decided that I'll simply position the new employee right after the last child under the target manager. This strategy, coupled with the use of the UPDLOCK described earlier, is always safe in the sense that HIERARCHYID values of employees will never conflict. If you choose to implement a solution that allows specifying the left and right employees, the responsibility to prevent conflicts is now yours.

To apply my chosen strategy, immediately after a query that retrieves the path of the target manager, another query retrieves the maximum path among the existing subordinates of the manager, and the result is stored in the *@last_child_hid* variable. The method *GetAncestor* helps identify direct subordinates of the target manager. The method is applied to a HIERARCHYID value of a node, and it returns the HIERARCHYID value of an ancestor that is *n* levels up, where *n* is provided as input. For *n=1*, you get the node's parent. So all employees for whom *GetAncestor(1)* returns the path of the manager are direct subordinates of the manager.

Once you have the path of the manager stored in the *@mgr_hid* variable and the path of the manager's last direct subordinate is stored in the variable *@last_child_hid*, you can generate the input employee's path with the expression *@hid.GetDescendant(@last_child_hid, NULL)*. Once the path for the input employee is generated, you can insert the employee's row into the Employees table and commit the transaction. Committing the transaction releases the update lock held on the manager's row, allowing those who want to add other subordinates under that manager to generate new HIERARCHYID values.

Run the following code to populate the Employees table with sample data:

```
EXEC dbo.AddEmp @empid =  1, @mgrid = NULL, @empname = 'David'  , @salary = $10000.00;
EXEC dbo.AddEmp @empid =  2, @mgrid =    1, @empname = 'Eitan'  , @salary = $7000.00;
EXEC dbo.AddEmp @empid =  3, @mgrid =    1, @empname = 'Ina'    , @salary = $7500.00;
EXEC dbo.AddEmp @empid =  4, @mgrid =    2, @empname = 'Seraph' , @salary = $5000.00;
EXEC dbo.AddEmp @empid =  5, @mgrid =    2, @empname = 'Jiru'   , @salary = $5500.00;
EXEC dbo.AddEmp @empid =  6, @mgrid =    2, @empname = 'Steve'  , @salary = $4500.00;
EXEC dbo.AddEmp @empid =  7, @mgrid =    3, @empname = 'Aaron'  , @salary = $5000.00;
EXEC dbo.AddEmp @empid =  8, @mgrid =    5, @empname = 'Lilach' , @salary = $3500.00;
EXEC dbo.AddEmp @empid =  9, @mgrid =    7, @empname = 'Rita'   , @salary = $3000.00;
EXEC dbo.AddEmp @empid = 10, @mgrid =    5, @empname = 'Sean'   , @salary = $3000.00;
EXEC dbo.AddEmp @empid = 11, @mgrid =    7, @empname = 'Gabriel', @salary = $3000.00;
EXEC dbo.AddEmp @empid = 12, @mgrid =    9, @empname = 'Emilia' , @salary = $2000.00;
EXEC dbo.AddEmp @empid = 13, @mgrid =    9, @empname = 'Michael', @salary = $2000.00;
EXEC dbo.AddEmp @empid = 14, @mgrid =    9, @empname = 'Didi'   , @salary = $1500.00;
```

Run the following query to present the contents of the Employees table:

```
SELECT hid, hid.ToString() AS path, lvl, empid, empname, salary
FROM dbo.Employees
ORDER BY hid;
```

The *ToString* method returns a canonical representation of the path, using slashes to separate the values at each level. This query generates the following output:

```
hid         path        lvl     empid   empname   salary
---------   ----------  ------  ------  --------  ---------
0x          /           0       1       David     10000.00
0x58        /1/         1       2       Eitan     7000.00
0x5AC0      /1/1/       2       4       Seraph    5000.00
0x5B40      /1/2/       2       5       Jiru      5500.00
0x5B56      /1/2/1/     3       8       Lilach    3500.00
0x5B5A      /1/2/2/     3       10      Sean      3000.00
0x5BC0      /1/3/       2       6       Steve     4500.00
0x68        /2/         1       3       Ina       7500.00
0x6AC0      /2/1/       2       7       Aaron     5000.00
0x6AD6      /2/1/1/     3       9       Rita      3000.00
0x6AD6B0    /2/1/1/1/   4       12      Emilia    2000.00
0x6AD6D0    /2/1/1/2/   4       13      Michael   2000.00
0x6AD6F0    /2/1/1/3/   4       14      Didi      1500.00
0x6ADA      /2/1/2/     3       11      Gabriel   3000.00
```

This output gives you a sense of the logic that the *GetDescendant* method applies to calculate the values. The root (empty binary string) is represented by the canonical path /. The first child under a node obtains its HIERARCHYID from a call to *GetDescendant* with two NULL inputs. The result is the parent's canonical path plus 1/. So the path of the first child of the root becomes /1/.

If you add someone to the right of an existing child and under that child's parent, the new child's *hid* is obtained by a call to *GetDescendant* with the existing child's *hid* as the left input and NULL as the right input. The new *path* value is like the existing child's value but with a rightmost number that is greater by one. So, for example, the value under / and to the right of /1/ would be /2/. Similarly, the value under /1/ and to the right of /1/1/ would be /1/2/.

If you add someone under a certain parent and to the left of an existing child, the left input to *GetDescendant* is NULL, and the new *path* value will be like the existing child's but with a rightmost number that is less by one. So, for example, the value under /1/ and to the left of /1/1/ would be /1/0/. Similarly, the value under /1/ and to the left of /1/0/ would be /1/–1/.

If you add someone under a certain parent and provide two of that parent's existing children's *hid* values as inputs to *GetDescendant*, the resulting *path* matches the existing children's paths except for the last number. If the last numbers in the existing children's paths aren't consecutive, the last number of the new child's path will be one greater than that of the left child. For example, when the method is applied to the parent /1/1/ and the input children are /1/1/1/ and /1/1/4/, you get /1/1/2/. If the last path numbers of the input children are consecutive, you get the last number of the left child, followed by .1 (read "dot one"). For example, when the method is applied to the parent /1/1/ and the input children's paths are /1/1/1/ and /1/1/2/, you get /1/1/1.1/. Similarly, when the method is applied to the parent /1/2.1/3/4/5/ and the input children are /1/2.1/3/4/5/2.1.3.4/ and /1/2.1/3/4/5/2.1.3.5/, you get /1/2.1/3/4/5/2.1.3.4.1/, and so on. As you might realize, the paths are simpler and shorter if you add new nodes either to the right of the last child or to the left of the first child.

Later in the chapter, in the section "Normalizing HIERARCHYID values," I'll explain how you can normalize paths when they become too lengthy.

Moving a subtree

The HIERARCHYID type supports a method called *GetReparentedValue* that helps in calculating new paths when you need to move a whole subtree to a new location in the tree. The method is applied to the HIERARCHYID value of a node that you want to reparent, but it doesn't perform the actual reparenting. It simply returns a new value you can then use to overwrite the existing path. The method accepts two inputs (call them *@old_root* and *@new_root*) and returns a new value with the target node's path where the *@new_root* prefix replaces the *@old_root* prefix. It's as simple as that.

> **Note** When you call *GetReparentedValue* on a HIERARCHYID *h*, the path of *@old_root* must be a prefix of *h*'s path. If it is not, you'll get an exception of type *HierarchyIdException*.

For example, if you apply the *GetReparentedValue* method to a HIERARCHYID whose canonical path is /1/1/2/3/2/, providing /1/1/ as the old root and /2/1/4/ as the new root, you get a HIERARCHYID whose canonical path is /2/1/4/2/3/2/. By the way, you can cast a canonical path representation to the HIERARCHYID data type by using the CAST function or the static method *hierarchyid::Parse*. You can test the aforementioned example by using the *GetReparentedValue* with constants, like so:

```
SELECT CAST('/1/1/2/3/2/' AS HIERARCHYID).GetReparentedValue('/1/1/', '/2/1/4/').ToString();
```

You get the path /2/1/4/2/3/2/ as output.

With this in mind, consider the task to create a stored procedure called *MoveSubtree* that accepts two inputs called *@empid* and *@new_mgrid*. The stored procedure's purpose is to move the subtree of employee *@empid* under *@new_mgrid*. The stored procedure can implement the task in three steps:

1. Store the existing paths of the employees represented by *@new_mgrid* and *@empid* in variables. (Call them *@new_mgr_hid* and *@old_root*, respectively.)

2. Apply the *GetDescendant* method to *@new_mgr_hid*, providing the maximum among the new manager's existing subordinates (or NULL if there are none) as left input, to get a new path under the target manager for employee *@empid*. Store the new path in a variable. (Call it *@new_root*.)

3. Update the *hid* value of all descendants of the employee represented by *@empid* (including itself) to *hid.GetReparentedValue(@old_root, @new_root)*. To identify all descendants of a node, you can check the value of the method *IsDescendantOf* on each *hid* in the table. This method returns 1 when the node it is applied to is a descendant of the input node and 0 otherwise.

Run the following code to create the *MoveSubtree* stored procedure, which implements the preceding steps:

```
----------------------------------------------------------------------
-- Stored Procedure: MoveSubtree,
--   Moves a whole subtree of a given root to a new location
--   under a given manager
----------------------------------------------------------------------
IF OBJECT_ID(N'dbo.MoveSubtree', N'P') IS NOT NULL DROP PROC dbo.MoveSubtree;
GO
CREATE PROC dbo.MoveSubtree
  @empid    AS INT,
  @new_mgrid AS INT
AS

DECLARE
  @old_root    AS HIERARCHYID,
  @new_root    AS HIERARCHYID,
  @new_mgr_hid AS HIERARCHYID;

BEGIN TRAN

  SET @new_mgr_hid = (SELECT hid FROM dbo.Employees WITH (UPDLOCK)
                        WHERE empid = @new_mgrid);
  SET @old_root = (SELECT hid FROM dbo.Employees
                     WHERE empid = @empid);

  -- First, get a new hid for the subtree root employee that moves
  SET @new_root = @new_mgr_hid.GetDescendant
    ((SELECT MAX(hid)
      FROM dbo.Employees
      WHERE hid.GetAncestor(1) = @new_mgr_hid),
     NULL);

  -- Next, reparent all descendants of employee that moves
  UPDATE dbo.Employees
    SET hid = hid.GetReparentedValue(@old_root, @new_root)
  WHERE hid.IsDescendantOf(@old_root) = 1;

COMMIT TRAN
GO
```

Notice that the code uses an explicit transaction, and as the first step when querying the target manager's row, the statement obtains an update lock on that row. Much like in the *AddEmp* procedure discussed earlier, this technique guarantees that only one subtree is moved under a given target manager at a time, which prevents conflicts in the newly generated HIERARCHYID values.

To test the *MoveSubtree* procedure, run the following code, moving the subtree of employee 5 (Jiru) under employee 9 (Rita):

```
SELECT empid, REPLICATE(' | ', lvl) + empname AS empname, hid.ToString() AS path
FROM dbo.Employees
ORDER BY hid;

BEGIN TRAN

  EXEC dbo.MoveSubtree
    @empid    = 5,
    @new_mgrid = 9;

  SELECT empid, REPLICATE(' | ', lvl) + empname AS empname, hid.ToString() AS path
  FROM dbo.Employees
  ORDER BY hid;

ROLLBACK TRAN
```

The code presents the before and after states of the data, and because this is just a demonstration, it runs the activity in a transaction so that the changes won't be committed. Following are the outputs of this code showing that the subtree was moved correctly:

```
empid       empname                 path
----------- ----------------------- ------------
1           David                   /
2           | Eitan                 /1/
4           | | Seraph              /1/1/
5           | | Jiru                /1/2/
8           | | | Lilach            /1/2/1/
10          | | | Sean              /1/2/2/
6           | | Steve               /1/3/
3           | Ina                   /2/
7           | | Aaron               /2/1/
9           | | | Rita              /2/1/1/
12          | | | | Emilia          /2/1/1/1/
13          | | | | Michael         /2/1/1/2/
14          | | | | Didi            /2/1/1/3/
11          | | | Gabriel           /2/1/2/


empid       empname                 path
----------- ----------------------- ------------
1           David                   /
2           | Eitan                 /1/
4           | | Seraph              /1/1/
6           | | Steve               /1/3/
3           | Ina                   /2/
7           | | Aaron               /2/1/
9           | | | Rita              /2/1/1/
12          | | | | Emilia          /2/1/1/1/
13          | | | | Michael         /2/1/1/2/
14          | | | | Didi            /2/1/1/3/
5           | | | | Jiru            /2/1/1/4/
8           | | | | | Lilach        /2/1/1/4/1/
10          | | | | | Sean          /2/1/1/4/2/
11          | | | Gabriel           /2/1/2/
```

Querying

As with the custom materialized path solution, querying data in the built-in materialized path solution that is based on the HIERARCHYID data type is simple and elegant. With the depth-first and breadth-first indexes in place, you can enable SQL Server's optimizer to handle certain types of requests efficiently.

I won't cover all possible requests against the tree here because there are so many. Instead, I'll show a sample of the common ones. As I did before, I'll provide a sample query for each request followed by its output.

Subgraph/descendants

Return the subtree of employee 3, limiting the number of levels under the input employee to 3:

```
SELECT E.empid, E.empname
FROM dbo.Employees AS M
  INNER JOIN dbo.Employees AS E
    ON M.empid = 3
      AND E.hid.IsDescendantOf(M.hid) = 1
WHERE E.lvl - M.lvl <= 3;
```

The query uses the *IsDescendantOf* method. Recall that this method returns 1 if the node to which it is applied is a descendant of the input node and 0 otherwise. The query joins two instances of the Employees table: one representing the input manager (M) and one representing the subordinates (E). The predicate in the ON clause filters only one row from the instance M—the one for employee 3—and returns all employees from E that are descendants of the employee in M. The predicate in the WHERE clause filters only employees that are up to three levels below the employee in M.

This query generates the following output:

```
empid       empname
----------- ------------------------
3           Ina
7           Aaron
9           Rita
12          Emilia
13          Michael
14          Didi
11          Gabriel
```

The execution plan of this query is shown in Figure 11-7.

The first Index Seek operator in the plan (the top one) is responsible for returning the row for employee 3 from the index on the *empid* column. A Compute Scalar operator (the second one) then calculates the upper boundary point of the HIERARCHYID values of the requested subtree by invoking an internal method called *DescendantLimit*, storing the result in the variable *Expr1002*. Recall that because the HIERARCHYID values give you topological sorting, an index on the *hid* column arranges all members of the same subtree together. The second Index Seek operator in the plan (the bottom one) performs a range scan in the index on *hid* based on the predicate: *E.hid >= M.hid AND*

E.hid <= *Expr1002*. This plan is pretty much as good as it can get for this kind of request because SQL Server ends up scanning only the members of the applicable subtree.

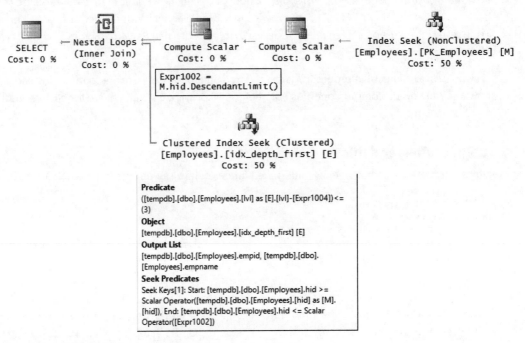

FIGURE 11-7 Execution plan for a HIERARCHYID subtree query.

Ancestors/path

Next, I'll explain how to handle a request to return all managers in the path leading to a certain employee. You can implement a solution that is similar to the one used to handle the subtree request. Instead of filtering the row representing the one manager (from an instance M of Employees) and then returning the attributes of all qualifying subordinates (from an instance E), you filter the row representing the one employee and then return the attributes of all qualifying managers. For example, the following query returns all managers of employee 14, direct or indirect:

```
SELECT M.empid, M.empname
FROM dbo.Employees AS M
  INNER JOIN dbo.Employees AS E
    ON E.empid = 14
      AND E.hid.IsDescendantOf(M.hid) = 1;
```

This query generates the following output:

```
empid       empname
----------- -------------------------
1           David
3           Ina
7           Aaron
9           Rita
14          Didi
```

Although this query is similar to the one that implemented the subtree request, it cannot be optimized as efficiently. That's because members of the same path do not reside in a consecutive range in the index.

Children/direct subordinates

Next, I'll describe how to handle a request to get direct subordinates of an employee. To handle this request, you can use a similar join form as in the previous queries. Filter the one row representing the employee whose subordinates you want from an instance (M) of the Employees table and return all employees (from another instance, E) whose parent is the employee filtered from M. A node's parent is its ancestor one level up, and the *GetAncestor* method with input value 1 returns the parent HIERARCHYID value. As an example of finding direct subordinates, the following query returns direct subordinates of employee 2:

```
SELECT E.empid, E.empname
FROM dbo.Employees AS M
  INNER JOIN dbo.Employees AS E
    ON M.empid = 2
      AND E.hid.GetAncestor(1) = M.hid;
```

This code generates the following output:

```
empid       empname
----------- ------------------------
4           Seraph
5           Jiru
6           Steve
```

Leaf nodes

You can also use the *GetAncestor* method with input value 1 to identify leaf nodes. Leaf nodes, or employees who manage no one, are employees that do not appear as the parent of other employees. This logic can be implemented with a NOT EXISTS predicate, like so:

```
SELECT empid, empname
FROM dbo.Employees AS M
WHERE NOT EXISTS
  (SELECT * FROM dbo.Employees AS E
    WHERE E.hid.GetAncestor(1) = M.hid);
```

This code generates the following output:

```
empid       empname
----------- ------------------------
4           Seraph
8           Lilach
10          Sean
6           Steve
12          Emilia
13          Michael
14          Didi
11          Gabriel
```

Presentation

Finally, to present the hierarchy of employees so that a subordinate appears under and to the right of its manager, use the following query:

```
SELECT REPLICATE(' | ', lvl) + empname AS empname, hid.ToString() AS path
FROM dbo.Employees
ORDER BY hid;
```

Recall that the HIERARCHYID data type gives you topological sorting, so all you need to do to get the desired presentation ordering is to order by the *hid* attribute. Indentation is achieved by replicating a string *lvl* times. This query generates the following output:

```
empname                 path
--------------------    ----------
David                   /
 | Eitan                /1/
 | | Seraph             /1/1/
 | | Jiru               /1/2/
 | | | Lilach           /1/2/1/
 | | | Sean             /1/2/2/
 | | Steve              /1/3/
 | Ina                  /2/
 | | Aaron              /2/1/
 | | | Rita             /2/1/1/
 | | | | Emilia         /2/1/1/1/
 | | | | Michael        /2/1/1/2/
 | | | | Didi           /2/1/1/3/
 | | | Gabriel          /2/1/2/
```

The execution plan of this query is shown in Figure 11-8.

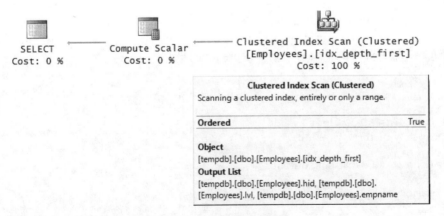

FIGURE 11-8 Execution plan for a HIERARCHYID sorting query.

You can see that the optimizer efficiently processed the request with an ordered scan of the index on the *hid* column.

Further aspects of working with HIERARCHYID

This section covers further aspects of working with the HIERARCHYID data type. I'll explain the circumstances in which paths can get lengthy and provide you with a solution to normalize them. I'll show you how to convert a representation of a tree as an adjacency list to one that is based on the HIERARCHYID data type. Finally, I'll show you how you can use the HIERARCHYID data type to sort separated lists of values.

Normalizing HIERARCHYID values

When you use the HIERARCHYID data type to represent trees, in certain cases the paths can become long. With very deep trees, this is natural because the HIERARCHYID value represents a path of all nodes leading to the current node, starting with the root. However, in certain cases, even when the tree is not very deep, the path can become long. First I'll explain the circumstances in which this can happen, and then I'll provide a solution to normalizing the values, making them shorter. Note that in this section, the word *normalizing* does not refer to database normalization.

HIERARCHYID values can become long when you keep adding new nodes between existing nodes whose canonical paths have consecutive last numbers. For example, say you have nodes with canonical paths /1/ and /2/ and you add a node between them. You get a new value whose canonical path is /1.1/. Now add a value between /1.1/ and /2/, and you get /1.2/. Now add a value between /1.1/ and /1.2/, and you get /1.1.1/. As you see, if you keep adding nodes between existing nodes in this manner, you can get lengthy paths (which represent lengthy HIERARCHYID values) even when the tree is not deep.

If order among siblings is not important, you can always make sure to add new child nodes after the last existing child or before the first one; this way, the paths are more economical. But when order among siblings matters, you can't control this. If you must frequently add new nodes between existing ones, you might end up with very long HIERARCHYID values. In such a case, you can periodically run a procedure, which I will provide here, that normalizes the HIERARCHYID values for the whole graph, making them shorter.

Run the following code to create a new version of the *AddEmp* stored procedure:

```
---------------------------------------------------------------------
-- Stored Procedure: AddEmp,
--    Inserts into the table a new employee who manages no one
---------------------------------------------------------------------
IF OBJECT_ID(N'dbo.AddEmp', N'P') IS NOT NULL DROP PROC dbo.AddEmp;
GO
CREATE PROC dbo.AddEmp
  @empid      AS INT,
  @mgrid      AS INT,
  @leftempid  AS INT,
  @rightempid AS INT,
  @empname    AS VARCHAR(25) ,
  @salary     AS MONEY = 1000
AS
```

```
DECLARE @hid AS HIERARCHYID;

IF @mgrid IS NULL
  SET @hid = hierarchyid::GetRoot();
ELSE
  SET @hid = (SELECT hid FROM dbo.Employees WHERE empid = @mgrid).GetDescendant
    ( (SELECT hid FROM dbo.Employees WHERE empid = @leftempid),
      (SELECT hid FROM dbo.Employees WHERE empid = @rightempid) );

INSERT INTO dbo.Employees(empid, hid, empname, salary)
  VALUES(@empid, @hid, @empname, @salary);
GO
```

This version accepts the IDs of the two child employees between which you want to add the new one.

Next, run the following code, which truncates the Employees table and populates it with data in such a manner that lengthy paths are produced:

```
TRUNCATE TABLE dbo.Employees;

EXEC dbo.AddEmp @empid =  1, @mgrid = NULL, @leftempid = NULL, @rightempid = NULL,
    @empname = 'A';
EXEC dbo.AddEmp @empid =  2, @mgrid =    1, @leftempid = NULL, @rightempid = NULL,
    @empname = 'B';
EXEC dbo.AddEmp @empid =  3, @mgrid =    1, @leftempid =    2, @rightempid = NULL,
    @empname = 'C';
EXEC dbo.AddEmp @empid =  4, @mgrid =    1, @leftempid =    2, @rightempid =    3,
    @empname = 'D';
EXEC dbo.AddEmp @empid =  5, @mgrid =    1, @leftempid =    4, @rightempid =    3,
    @empname = 'E';
EXEC dbo.AddEmp @empid =  6, @mgrid =    1, @leftempid =    4, @rightempid =    5,
    @empname = 'F';
EXEC dbo.AddEmp @empid =  7, @mgrid =    1, @leftempid =    6, @rightempid =    5,
    @empname = 'G';
EXEC dbo.AddEmp @empid =  8, @mgrid =    1, @leftempid =    6, @rightempid =    7,
    @empname = 'H';
EXEC dbo.AddEmp @empid =  9, @mgrid =    8, @leftempid = NULL, @rightempid = NULL,
    @empname = 'I';
EXEC dbo.AddEmp @empid = 10, @mgrid =    8, @leftempid =    9, @rightempid = NULL,
    @empname = 'J';
EXEC dbo.AddEmp @empid = 11, @mgrid =    8, @leftempid =    9, @rightempid =   10,
    @empname = 'K';
EXEC dbo.AddEmp @empid = 12, @mgrid =    8, @leftempid =   11, @rightempid =   10,
    @empname = 'J';
EXEC dbo.AddEmp @empid = 13, @mgrid =    8, @leftempid =   11, @rightempid =   12,
    @empname = 'L';
EXEC dbo.AddEmp @empid = 14, @mgrid =    8, @leftempid =   13, @rightempid =   12,
    @empname = 'M';
EXEC dbo.AddEmp @empid = 15, @mgrid =    8, @leftempid =   13, @rightempid =   14,
    @empname = 'N';
EXEC dbo.AddEmp @empid = 16, @mgrid =    8, @leftempid =   15, @rightempid =   14,
    @empname = 'O';
EXEC dbo.AddEmp @empid = 17, @mgrid =    8, @leftempid =   15, @rightempid =   16,
    @empname = 'P';
```

```
EXEC dbo.AddEmp @empid = 18, @mgrid =    8, @leftempid =   17, @rightempid =   16,
    @empname = 'Q';
EXEC dbo.AddEmp @empid = 19, @mgrid =    8, @leftempid =   17, @rightempid =   18,
    @empname = 'E';
EXEC dbo.AddEmp @empid = 20, @mgrid =    8, @leftempid =   19, @rightempid =   18,
    @empname = 'S';
EXEC dbo.AddEmp @empid = 21, @mgrid =    8, @leftempid =   19, @rightempid =   20,
    @empname = 'T';
```

Then run the following code to show the current HIERARCHYID values and their canonical paths:

```
SELECT empid, REPLICATE(' | ', lvl) + empname AS emp, hid, hid.ToString() AS path
FROM dbo.Employees
ORDER BY hid;
```

You get the following output:

```
empid  emp        hid                  path
------  --------   ------------------   -----------------------
1      A          0x                   /
2      | B        0x58                 /1/
4      | D        0x62C0               /1.1/
6      | F        0x6316               /1.1.1/
8      | H        0x6318B0             /1.1.1.1/
9      | | I      0x6318B580           /1.1.1.1/1/
11     | | K      0x6318B62C           /1.1.1.1/1.1/
13     | | L      0x6318B63160         /1.1.1.1/1.1.1/
15     | | N      0x6318B6318B         /1.1.1.1/1.1.1.1/
17     | | P      0x6318B6318C58       /1.1.1.1/1.1.1.1.1/
19     | | E      0x6318B6318C62C0     /1.1.1.1/1.1.1.1.1.1/
21     | | T      0x6318B6318C6316     /1.1.1.1/1.1.1.1.1.1.1/
20     | | S      0x6318B6318C6340     /1.1.1.1/1.1.1.1.1.2/
18     | | Q      0x6318B6318C68       /1.1.1.1/1.1.1.1.2/
16     | | O      0x6318B6318D         /1.1.1.1/1.1.1.2/
14     | | M      0x6318B631A0         /1.1.1.1/1.1.2/
12     | | J      0x6318B634           /1.1.1.1/1.2/
10     | | J      0x6318B680           /1.1.1.1/2/
7      | G        0x631A               /1.1.2/
5      | E        0x6340               /1.2/
3      | C        0x68                 /2/
```

As you can see, even though the tree is only three levels deep, some of the HIERARCHYID values became quite long because of the insertion order of children.

The solution that normalizes the values involves the following steps:

1. Define a CTE called *EmpsRN* that calculates for each node a row number, partitioned by parent and ordered by current *hid* value.

2. Define a recursive CTE called *EmpPaths* that iterates through the levels of the tree, starting with the root node and proceeding to the next level of children in each iteration. Use this CTE to construct a new canonical path for the nodes. The root should be assigned the path /, and for each node in the next level the path is obtained by concatenating the parent's path, the current node's row number from the previous step, and another / character.

3. Join the Employees table with the *EmpPaths* CTE, and update the existing *hid* values with new ones converted from the canonical paths generated in the previous step.

Here's the code that performs this normalization process:

```
WITH EmpsRN AS
(
  SELECT empid, hid, ROW_NUMBER() OVER(PARTITION BY hid.GetAncestor(1) ORDER BY hid) AS rownum
  FROM dbo.Employees
),
EmpPaths AS
(
  SELECT empid, hid, CAST('/' AS VARCHAR(900)) AS path
  FROM dbo.Employees
  WHERE hid = hierarchyid::GetRoot()

  UNION ALL

  SELECT C.empid, C.hid, CAST(P.path + CAST(C.rownum AS VARCHAR(20)) + '/' AS VARCHAR(900))
  FROM EmpPaths AS P
    INNER JOIN EmpsRN AS C
      ON C.hid.GetAncestor(1) = P.hid
)
UPDATE E
  SET hid = CAST(EP.path AS HIERARCHYID)
FROM dbo.Employees AS E
  INNER JOIN EmpPaths AS EP
    ON E.empid = EP.empid;
```

Now query the data after normalization:

```
SELECT empid, REPLICATE(' | ', lvl) + empname AS emp, hid, hid.ToString() AS path
FROM dbo.Employees
ORDER BY hid;
```

As you can see in the output, you get nice compact paths:

```
empid       emp        hid      path
----------- ---------- -------- --------
1           A          0x       /
2            | B       0x58     /1/
4            | D       0x68     /2/
6            | F       0x78     /3/
8            | H       0x84     /4/
9            |  | I    0x8560   /4/1/
11           |  | K    0x85A0   /4/2/
13           |  | L    0x85E0   /4/3/
15           |  | N    0x8610   /4/4/
17           |  | P    0x8630   /4/5/
19           |  | E    0x8650   /4/6/
21           |  | T    0x8670   /4/7/
20           |  | S    0x8688   /4/8/
18           |  | Q    0x8698   /4/9/
16           |  | O    0x86A8   /4/10/
14           |  | M    0x86B8   /4/11/
12           |  | J    0x86C8   /4/12/
```

```
10            |  | J  0x86D8  /4/13/
7             |  G     0x8C   /5/
5             |  E     0x94   /6/
3             |  C     0x9C   /7/
```

Convert a parent-child representation to HIERARCHYID

This section explains how to convert an existing representation of a tree that is based on an adjacency list (parent-child relationships) to one that is based on the HIERARCHYID data type.

Run the following code to create and populate the EmployeesOld table that implements an adjacency-list representation of an employee tree:

```
IF OBJECT_ID(N'dbo.EmployeesOld', N'U') IS NOT NULL DROP TABLE dbo.EmployeesOld;
IF OBJECT_ID(N'dbo.EmployeesNew', N'U') IS NOT NULL DROP TABLE dbo.EmployeesNew;
GO
CREATE TABLE dbo.EmployeesOld
(
  empid    INT                    CONSTRAINT PK_EmployeesOld PRIMARY KEY,
  mgrid    INT            NULL CONSTRAINT FK_EmpsOld_EmpsOld REFERENCES dbo.EmployeesOld,
  empname VARCHAR(25)  NOT NULL,
  salary   MONEY         NOT NULL
);
CREATE UNIQUE INDEX idx_unc_mgrid_empid ON dbo.EmployeesOld(mgrid, empid);

INSERT INTO dbo.EmployeesOld(empid, mgrid, empname, salary) VALUES
  (1,  NULL, 'David',  $10000.00),
  (2,  1,    'Eitan',   $7000.00),
  (3,  1,    'Ina',     $7500.00),
  (4,  2,    'Seraph',  $5000.00),
  (5,  2,    'Jiru',    $5500.00),
  (6,  2,    'Steve',   $4500.00),
  (7,  3,    'Aaron',   $5000.00),
  (8,  5,    'Lilach',  $3500.00),
  (9,  7,    'Rita',    $3000.00),
  (10, 5,    'Sean',    $3000.00),
  (11, 7,    'Gabriel', $3000.00),
  (12, 9,    'Emilia' , $2000.00),
  (13, 9,    'Michael', $2000.00),
  (14, 9,    'Didi',    $1500.00);
```

Run the following code to create the target EmployeesNew table that will represent the employee tree using HIERARCHYID values:

```
CREATE TABLE dbo.EmployeesNew
(
  empid    INT          NOT NULL,
  hid      HIERARCHYID NOT NULL,
  lvl AS hid.GetLevel() PERSISTED,
  empname VARCHAR(25) NOT NULL,
  salary   MONEY        NOT NULL
);
```

The task is now to query the EmployeesOld table that contains the source data, calculate HIERARCHYID values for the employees, and populate the target EmployeesNew table. This task can be achieved in a similar manner to normalizing existing HIERARCHYID values as described earlier. You apply the following steps:

1. Define a CTE called *EmpsRN* that calculates for each node a row number partitioned by *mgrid*, ordered by the attributes that should determine order among siblings—for example, *empid*.

2. Define a recursive CTE called *EmpPaths* that iterates through the levels of the tree, starting with the root node and proceeding to the next level of children in each iteration. Use this CTE to construct a new canonical path for the nodes. The root should be assigned the path /, and for each node in the next level the path is obtained by concatenating the parent's path, the current node's row number from the previous step, and another / character.

3. Insert into the target table EmployeesNew the employee rows along with their newly generated HIERARCHYID values from the *EmpPaths* CTE.

Here's the code that performs this conversion process:

```
WITH EmpsRN AS
(
  SELECT empid, mgrid, empname, salary,
    ROW_NUMBER() OVER(PARTITION BY mgrid ORDER BY empid) AS rn
  FROM dbo.EmployeesOld
),
EmpPaths AS
(
  SELECT empid, mgrid, empname, salary,
    CAST('/' AS VARCHAR(900)) AS cpath
  FROM dbo.EmployeesOld
  WHERE mgrid IS NULL

  UNION ALL

  SELECT C.empid, C.mgrid, C.empname, C.salary,
    CAST(cpath + CAST(C.rn AS VARCHAR(20)) + '/' AS VARCHAR(900))
  FROM EmpPaths AS P
    INNER JOIN EmpsRN AS C
      ON C.mgrid = P.empid
)
INSERT INTO dbo.EmployeesNew WITH (TABLOCK) (empid, empname, salary, hid)
  SELECT empid, empname, salary, CAST(cpath AS HIERARCHYID) AS hid
  FROM EmpPaths;
```

Run the following code to create the recommended indexes to support typical queries:

```
CREATE UNIQUE CLUSTERED INDEX idx_depth_first ON dbo.EmployeesNew(hid);
CREATE UNIQUE INDEX idx_breadth_first ON dbo.EmployeesNew(lvl, hid);
ALTER TABLE dbo.EmployeesNew ADD CONSTRAINT PK_EmployeesNew PRIMARY KEY NONCLUSTERED(empid);
```

Run the following code to present the contents of the EmployeesNew table after the conversion:

```
SELECT REPLICATE(' | ', lvl) + empname AS empname, hid.ToString() AS path
FROM dbo.EmployeesNew
ORDER BY hid;
```

You get the following output:

```
empname                 path
--------------------    ----------
David                   /
 | Eitan                /1/
 | | Seraph             /1/1/
 | | Jiru               /1/2/
 | | | Lilach           /1/2/1/
 | | | Sean             /1/2/2/
 | | Steve              /1/3/
 | Ina                  /2/
 | | Aaron              /2/1/
 | | | Rita             /2/1/1/
 | | | | Emilia         /2/1/1/1/
 | | | | Michael        /2/1/1/2/
 | | | | Didi           /2/1/1/3/
 | | | Gabriel          /2/1/2/
```

Sorting separated lists of values

Some applications store information about arrays and lists of numbers in the form of character strings with separated lists of values. I won't get into a discussion here regarding whether such representation of data is really appropriate. Instead, I'll address a certain need involving such representation. Sometimes you don't have control over the design of certain systems, and you need to provide solutions to requests using the existing design.

The request at hand involves sorting such lists, but based on the numeric values of the elements and not by their character representation. For example, consider the lists '13,41,17' and '13,41,3'. If you sort the lists based on the character representation of the elements, the former would be returned before the latter because the character '1' is considered smaller than the character '3'. You want the second string to sort before the first because the number 3 is smaller than the number 17.

A special case of the problem is sorting IP addresses represented as character strings. In this special case, you have an assurance that each string always has exactly four elements, and the length of each element never exceeds three digits. I'll first cover this special case and then discuss the more generic one.

Run the following code to create the IPs table, and populate it with some sample IP addresses:

```
IF OBJECT_ID(N'dbo.IPs', N'U') IS NOT NULL DROP TABLE dbo.IPs;
GO
-- Creation script for table IPs
CREATE TABLE dbo.IPs
(
  ip varchar(15) NOT NULL,
  CONSTRAINT PK_IPs PRIMARY KEY(ip),
  -- CHECK constraint that validates IPs
  CONSTRAINT CHK_IP_valid CHECK
  (
      -- 3 periods and no empty octets
      ip LIKE '_%._%._%._%'
    AND
      -- not 4 periods or more
      ip NOT LIKE '%.%.%.%.%'
    AND
      -- no characters other than digits and periods
      ip NOT LIKE '%[^0-9.]%'
    AND
      -- not more than 3 digits per octet
      ip NOT LIKE '%[0-9][0-9][0-9][0-9]%'
    AND
      -- NOT 300 - 999
      ip NOT LIKE '%[3-9][0-9][0-9]%'
    AND
      -- NOT 260 - 299
      ip NOT LIKE '%2[6-9][0-9]%'
    AND
      -- NOT 256 - 259
      ip NOT LIKE '%25[6-9]%'
  )
);
GO


-- Sample data
INSERT INTO dbo.IPs(ip) VALUES
  ('131.107.2.201'),
  ('131.33.2.201'),
  ('131.33.2.202'),
  ('3.107.2.4'),
  ('3.107.3.169'),
  ('3.107.104.172'),
  ('22.107.202.123'),
  ('22.20.2.77'),
  ('22.156.9.91'),
  ('22.156.89.32');
```

I'll first describe one of the solutions I had for this need without using the HIERARCHYID data type.

An IP address must be one of 81 (3^4) possible patterns in terms of the number of digits in each octet (assuming we are talking about IPv4). You can write a query that produces all possible patterns that a LIKE predicate would recognize, representing each digit with an underscore. You can use an auxiliary table of numbers (like the Nums table in the TSQLV3 database) that has three numbers for the three possible octet lengths. By joining four instances of the Nums table, you get the 81 possible variations of the four octet sizes. You can then construct the LIKE patterns representing the IP addresses and, using the numbers from the Nums table, calculate the starting position and length of each octet.

Run the following code to create and query the view IPPatterns, which implements this logic:

```
IF OBJECT_ID(N'dbo.IPPatterns', N'V') IS NOT NULL DROP VIEW dbo.IPPatterns;
GO
CREATE VIEW dbo.IPPatterns
AS

SELECT
  REPLICATE('_', N1.n) + '.' + REPLICATE('_', N2.n) + '.'
    + REPLICATE('_', N3.n) + '.' + REPLICATE('_', N4.n) AS pattern,
  N1.n AS l1, N2.n AS l2, N3.n AS l3, N4.n AS l4,
  1 AS s1, N1.n+2 AS s2, N1.n+N2.n+3 AS s3, N1.n+N2.n+N3.n+4 AS s4
FROM TSQLV3.dbo.Nums AS N1 CROSS JOIN TSQLV3.dbo.Nums AS N2
  CROSS JOIN TSQLV3.dbo.Nums AS N3 CROSS JOIN TSQLV3.dbo.Nums AS N4
WHERE N1.n <= 3 AND N2.n <= 3 AND N3.n <= 3 AND N4.n <= 3;
GO

SELECT pattern, l1, l2, l3, l4, s1, s2, s3, s4 FROM dbo.IPPatterns;
```

When you query the view, you get the possible IP patterns and the starting position and length of each pattern, as shown here in abbreviated form:

```
pattern           l1  l2  l3  l4  s1  s2  s3  s4
---------------   --- --- --- --- --- --- --- ---
_._._._           1   1   1   1   1   3   5   7
_._._.__          1   1   1   2   1   3   5   7
_._._.___         1   1   1   3   1   3   5   7
_._.__._          1   1   2   1   1   3   5   8
_._.__.__         1   1   2   2   1   3   5   8
_._.__.___        1   1   2   3   1   3   5   8
_._.___._         1   1   3   1   1   3   5   9
_._.___.__        1   1   3   2   1   3   5   9
_._.___.___       1   1   3   3   1   3   5   9
_.__._._          1   2   1   1   1   3   6   8
_.__._.__         1   2   1   2   1   3   6   8
_.__._.___        1   2   1   3   1   3   6   8
_.__.__._         1   2   2   1   1   3   6   9
_.__.__.__        1   2   2   2   1   3   6   9
_.__.__.___       1   2   2   3   1   3   6   9
_.__.___._        1   2   3   1   1   3   6   10
_.  .__.___.__    1   2   3   2   1   3   6   10
_.__.___.___      1   2   3   3   1   3   6   10
_.___._._         1   3   1   1   1   3   7   9
_.___._.__        1   3   1   2   1   3   7   9
...
```

Of course, you can implement similar logic to create the possible patterns for IP addresses of IPv6.

Now you can write a query that joins the IPs table with the IPPatterns view based on a match between the IP address and the IP pattern. This way you identify the IP pattern for each IP address, along with the measures indicating the starting position and length of each octet. You can then specify four expressions in the ORDER BY clause that apply the SUBSTRING function to extract the octets and cast the character-string representation of the octet to a numeric one. Here's what the query looks like:

```
SELECT ip
FROM dbo.IPs
  INNER JOIN dbo.IPPatterns
    ON ip LIKE pattern
ORDER BY
  CAST(SUBSTRING(ip, s1, 11) AS TINYINT),
  CAST(SUBSTRING(ip, s2, 12) AS TINYINT),
  CAST(SUBSTRING(ip, s3, 13) AS TINYINT),
  CAST(SUBSTRING(ip, s4, 14) AS TINYINT);
```

This query generates the following output:

```
ip
---------------
3.107.2.4
3.107.3.169
3.107.104.172
22.20.2.77
22.107.202.123
22.156.9.91
22.156.89.32
131.33.2.201
131.33.2.202
131.107.2.201
```

The problem with this solution is that it's not very efficient, and it doesn't work in the more generic cases of lists where you have an unknown number of elements.

Interestingly, the canonical representation of HIERARCHYID values is also a separated list of numbers. Within a level, you can have values separated by dots, and between levels the values are separated by slashes. With this in mind, you can handle the task at hand by concatenating a slash before and after the IP address, and then sorting the rows after converting the result to the HIERARCHYID data type, like so:

```
SELECT ip
FROM dbo.IPs
ORDER BY CAST('/' + ip + '/' AS HIERARCHYID);
```

This solution works just as well with the more generic case of the problem. To demonstrate this, first create and populate the table T1 by running the following code:

```
IF OBJECT_ID(N'dbo.T1', N'U') IS NOT NULL DROP TABLE dbo.T1;
GO
CREATE TABLE dbo.T1
(
  id  INT         NOT NULL IDENTITY PRIMARY KEY,
  val VARCHAR(500) NOT NULL
);
```

```
INSERT INTO dbo.T1(val) VALUES
  ('100'),
  ('7,4,250'),
  ('22,40,5,60,4,100,300,478,19710212'),
  ('22,40,5,60,4,99,300,478,19710212'),
  ('22,40,5,60,4,99,300,478,9999999'),
  ('10,30,40,50,20,30,40'),
  ('7,4,250'),
  ('-1'),
  ('-2'),
  ('-11'),
  ('-22'),
  ('-123'),
  ('-321'),
  ('22,40,5,60,4,-100,300,478,19710212'),
  ('22,40,5,60,4,-99,300,478,19710212');
```

As you can see, the lists in the table have varying numbers of elements. Note that because the separator used in these lists is a comma, you need to replace the separators by slashes or dots before converting to the HIERARCHYID data type. Here's the solution query that sorts the lists by the numeric values of the elements:

```
SELECT id, val
FROM dbo.T1
ORDER BY CAST('/' + REPLACE(val, ',', '/') + '/' AS HIERARCHYID);
```

This query generates the following output:

```
id          val
----------- ----------------------------------
13          -321
12          -123
11          -22
10          -11
9           -2
8           -1
7           7,4,250
2           7,4,250
6           10,30,40,50,20,30,40
14          22,40,5,60,4,-100,300,478,19710212
15          22,40,5,60,4,-99,300,478,19710212
5           22,40,5,60,4,99,300,478,9999999
4           22,40,5,60,4,99,300,478,19710212
3           22,40,5,60,4,100,300,478,19710212
1           100
```

Note that you can create a computed persisted column in the table based on this expression and index that column. Such an index can support a request to sort the data without the need for an explicit sort operation in the query's execution plan.

Nested sets

The nested sets solution is one of the most beautiful solutions I've seen for modeling trees.

 More Info Joe Celko has extensive coverage of the nested sets model in his writings. You can find Joe Celko's coverage of nested sets in his book *Joe Celko's Trees and Hierarchies in SQL for Smarties, Second Edition* (Morgan Kaufmann, 2012).

The main advantages of the nested sets solution are simple and fast queries, which I'll describe later, and no level limit. Unfortunately, however, with large data sets the solution's practicality is usually limited to static trees. For dynamic environments that incur frequent changes, the solution is limited to small trees (or forests of small trees).

Instead of representing a tree as an adjacency list (parent-child relationship), this solution models the tree relationships as nested sets. A parent is represented in the nested sets model as a containing set, and a child is represented as a contained set. Set containment relationships are represented with two integer values assigned to each set: left and right. For all sets, a set's left value is smaller than all contained sets' left values, and a set's right value is higher than all contained sets' right values. Naturally, this containment relationship is transitive in terms of *n*-level relationships (ancestor/descendant). The queries are based on these nested sets relationships. Logically, it's as if a set spreads two arms around all its contained sets.

Assigning left and right values

Figure 11-9 provides a graphical visualization of the Employees tree with the left and right values assigned to each employee.

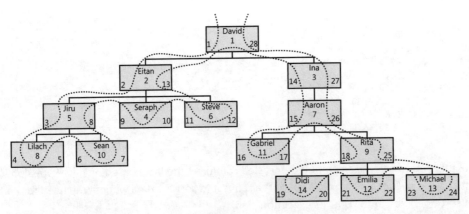

FIGURE 11-9 Employees hierarchy as nested sets.

The curved line that walks the tree represents the order of assignment of the left and right values. Note that the model allows you to choose in which order you assign values to siblings. In this particular case, I chose to traverse siblings by employee name order.

You start with the root, traversing the tree counterclockwise. Every time you enter a node, you increment a counter and set it as the node's left value. Every time you leave a node, you increment the counter and set it as the node's right value. This algorithm can be implemented to the letter as an iterative or recursive routine that assigns each node with left and right values. However, such an implementation requires traversing the tree one node at a time, which can be very slow. I'll show an algorithm that traverses the tree one level at a time, which is faster. The core algorithm is based on logic I discussed earlier in the chapter, traversing the tree one level at a time and calculating binary sort paths. To understand this algorithm, examine Figure 11-10.

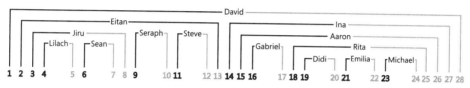

FIGURE 11-10 The nested sets model.

The figure illustrates each employee as spreading two arms around its subordinates. Left and right values can now be assigned to the different arms by simply incrementing a counter from left to right. Keep this illustration in mind—it's the key to understanding the solution I will present.

Again, the baseline is the original algorithm that traverses a subtree one level at a time and constructs a binary sort path based on a desired ordering of siblings (for example, *empname, empid*).

> **Note** For good performance, you should create an index on the parent ID and sort columns—for example, *(mgrid, empname, empid)*.

Instead of generating one row for each node (as was the case in the earlier solutions for generating sort values based on a binary path), you generate two rows by cross-joining each level with an auxiliary table that has two numbers: $n=1$ represents the left arm, and $n=2$ represents the right arm. The binary paths are still constructed from row numbers, but in this case the arm number is taken into consideration in addition to the other sort elements (for example, *empname, empid, n*). The query that returns the next level of subordinates returns the subordinates of the left arm only—again, cross-joined with two numbers ($n=1$, $n=2$) to generate two arms for each node.

The following code is the CTE implementation of this algorithm. The purpose of this code is to generate two binary sort paths for each employee that are later used to calculate left and right values. Before you run this code, make sure you have the original Employees table in the tempdb database. If you don't, rerun the code in Listing 11-1 first:

```
-- Create index to speed sorting siblings by empname, empid
CREATE UNIQUE INDEX idx_unc_mgrid_empname_empid ON dbo.Employees(mgrid, empname, empid);
GO
```

```
DECLARE @root AS INT = 1;

-- CTE with two numbers: 1 and 2
WITH TwoNums AS
(
  SELECT n FROM (VALUES(1),(2)) AS D(n)
),
-- CTE with two binary sort paths for each node:
--    One smaller than descendants sort paths
--    One greater than descendants sort paths
SortPath AS
(
  SELECT empid, 0 AS lvl, n, CAST(CAST(n AS BINARY(4)) AS VARBINARY(MAX)) AS sort_path
  FROM dbo.Employees CROSS JOIN TwoNums
  WHERE empid = @root

  UNION ALL

  SELECT C.empid, P.lvl + 1, TN.n,
    P.sort_path + CAST(
      ( -1 + ROW_NUMBER() OVER(PARTITION BY C.mgrid
                          -- *** determines order of siblings ***
                          ORDER BY C.empname, C.empid)) / 2 * 2 + TN.n
    AS BINARY(4))
  FROM SortPath AS P
    INNER JOIN dbo.Employees AS C
      ON P.n = 1
         AND C.mgrid = P.empid
    CROSS JOIN TwoNums AS TN
)
SELECT empid, lvl, n, sort_path FROM SortPath
ORDER BY sort_path;
```

This code generates the following output:

```
empid  lvl  n  sort_path
------ ---- -- --------------------------------------------
1      0    1  0x00000001
2      1    1  0x0000000100000001
5      2    1  0x000000010000000100000001
8      3    1  0x00000001000000010000000100000001
8      3    2  0x00000001000000010000000100000002
10     3    1  0x00000001000000010000000100000003
10     3    2  0x00000001000000010000000100000004
5      2    2  0x000000010000000100000002
4      2    1  0x000000010000000100000003
4      2    2  0x000000010000000100000004
6      2    1  0x000000010000000100000005
6      2    2  0x000000010000000100000006
2      1    2  0x0000000100000002
3      1    1  0x0000000100000003
7      2    1  0x000000010000000300000001
11     3    1  0x00000001000000030000000100000001
11     3    2  0x00000001000000030000000100000002
9      3    1  0x00000001000000030000000100000003
```

```
14   4   1   0x00000001000000030000000100000003000000001
14   4   2   0x00000001000000030000000100000003000000002
12   4   1   0x00000001000000030000000100000003000000003
12   4   2   0x00000001000000030000000100000003000000004
13   4   1   0x00000001000000030000000100000003000000005
13   4   2   0x00000001000000030000000100000003000000006
9    3   2   0x000000010000000300000001000000004
7    2   2   0x000000010000000300000002
3    1   2   0x0000000100000004
1    0   2   0x00000002
```

TwoNums is the auxiliary table with two numbers representing the two arms. Of course, if you want to, you can use a real Nums table instead of generating a virtual one.

Two sort paths are generated for each node. The left one is represented by $n=1$, and the right one is represented by $n=2$. Notice that for a given node, the left sort path is smaller than all left sort paths of subordinates, and the right sort path is greater than all right sort paths of subordinates. The sort paths are used to generate the left and right values in Figure 11-10. You need to generate left and right integer values to represent the nested sets relationships between the employees. To assign the integer values to the arms (*sortval*), use the ROW_NUMBER function based on *sort_path* order. Finally, to return one row for each employee containing the left and right integer values, group the rows by employee and level and return the *MIN(sortval)* as the left value and *MAX(sortval)* as the right value. Here's the complete solution to generate left and right values, followed by its output:

```
DECLARE @root AS INT = 1;

-- CTE with two numbers: 1 and 2
WITH TwoNums AS
(
  SELECT n FROM (VALUES(1),(2)) AS D(n)
),
-- CTE with two binary sort paths for each node:
--   One smaller than descendants sort paths
--   One greater than descendants sort paths
SortPath AS
(
  SELECT empid, 0 AS lvl, n, CAST(CAST(n AS BINARY(4)) AS VARBINARY(MAX)) AS sort_path
  FROM dbo.Employees CROSS JOIN TwoNums
  WHERE empid = @root

  UNION ALL

  SELECT C.empid, P.lvl + 1, TN.n,
    P.sort_path + CAST(
      (-1 + ROW_NUMBER() OVER(PARTITION BY C.mgrid
                              -- *** determines order of siblings ***
                              ORDER BY C.empname, C.empid)) / 2 * 2 + TN.n
      AS BINARY(4))
  FROM SortPath AS P
    INNER JOIN dbo.Employees AS C
      ON P.n = 1
        AND C.mgrid = P.empid
    CROSS JOIN TwoNums AS TN
),
```

```
-- CTE with Row Numbers Representing sort_path Order
Sort AS
(
  SELECT empid, lvl, ROW_NUMBER() OVER(ORDER BY sort_path) AS sortval
  FROM SortPath
),
-- CTE with Left and Right Values Representing
-- Nested Sets Relationships
NestedSets AS
(
  SELECT empid, lvl, MIN(sortval) AS lft, MAX(sortval) AS rgt
  FROM Sort
  GROUP BY empid, lvl
)
SELECT empid, lvl, lft, rgt FROM NestedSets
ORDER BY lft;
```

empid	lvl	lft	rgt
1	0	1	28
2	1	2	13
5	2	3	8
8	3	4	5
10	3	6	7
4	2	9	10
6	2	11	12
3	1	14	27
7	2	15	26
11	3	16	17
9	3	18	25
14	4	19	20
12	4	21	22
13	4	23	24

Remember the tip I provided earlier concerning the target type of each element in the sort path as a function of the maximum number of children that a single parent can have. I use BINARY(4) in my examples, but remember that you can use a smaller size in some cases.

In the opening paragraph of the "Nested sets" section, I mentioned that this solution is not adequate for large dynamic trees (trees that incur frequent changes). Suppose you stored left and right values in two additional columns in the Employees table. Note that you won't need the *mgrid* column in the table anymore because the two additional columns with the left and right values are sufficient to answer requests for subordinates, ancestors, and so on. Consider the shake effect of adding a node to the tree. For example, take a look at Figures 11-9 and 11-10 and try to figure out the effect of adding a new subordinate to Steve.

Steve has left and right values of 11 and 12, respectively. The new node should get left and right values of 12 and 13, respectively. Steve's right value—and in fact all left and right values in the tree that are greater than or equal to 12—should be increased by two. On average, at least half the nodes in the tree must be updated every time a new node is inserted. As you can see here, the shake effect is dramatic. That's why the nested sets solution is adequate for a large tree only if it's static or if you need to run queries against a static snapshot of the tree periodically.

Nested sets can provide reasonably good performance with dynamic trees that are small (or forests of small trees)—for example, when maintaining forum discussions where each thread is a small independent tree in a forest. You can implement a solution that synchronizes the left and right values of the tree with every change. You can achieve this by using stored procedures or even triggers, as long as the cost of modification is small enough to be bearable. I won't even get into variations of the nested sets model that maintain gaps between the values (that is, one that leaves room to insert new leaves without as much work), because they are all ultimately limited.

To generate a table of employees (EmployeesNS) with the employee ID, employee name, salary, level, left values, and right values, join the outer query of the CTE solution and use a SELECT INTO statement. Run the following code to create this as the EmployeesNS table with siblings ordered by *empname, empid*:

```
DECLARE @root AS INT = 1;

WITH TwoNums AS
(
  SELECT n FROM (VALUES(1),(2)) AS D(n)
),
SortPath AS
(
  SELECT empid, 0 AS lvl, n, CAST(CAST(n AS BINARY(4)) AS VARBINARY(MAX)) AS sort_path
  FROM dbo.Employees CROSS JOIN TwoNums
  WHERE empid = @root

  UNION ALL

  SELECT C.empid, P.lvl + 1, TN.n,
    P.sort_path + CAST(
      (-1 + ROW_NUMBER() OVER(PARTITION BY C.mgrid
                    -- *** determines order of siblings ***
                    ORDER BY C.empname, C.empid)) / 2 * 2 + TN.n
      AS BINARY(4))
  FROM SortPath AS P
    INNER JOIN dbo.Employees AS C
      ON P.n = 1
        AND C.mgrid = P.empid
    CROSS JOIN TwoNums AS TN
),
Sort AS
(
  SELECT empid, lvl, ROW_NUMBER() OVER(ORDER BY sort_path) AS sortval
  FROM SortPath
),
NestedSets AS
(
  SELECT empid, lvl, MIN(sortval) AS lft, MAX(sortval) AS rgt
  FROM Sort
  GROUP BY empid, lvl
)
```

```
SELECT E.empid, E.empname, E.salary, NS.lvl, NS.lft, NS.rgt
INTO dbo.EmployeesNS
FROM NestedSets AS NS
  INNER JOIN dbo.Employees AS E
    ON E.empid = NS.empid;

CREATE UNIQUE CLUSTERED INDEX idx_uc_lft ON dbo.EmployeesNS(lft);
ALTER TABLE dbo.EmployeesNS ADD PRIMARY KEY NONCLUSTERED(empid);
```

In the nested sets model, the left attribute gives you a topological sort order. For this reason, the code creates an index on the *lft* column.

Querying

The EmployeesNS table models a tree of employees as nested sets. Querying is simple, elegant, and fast for the most part (assuming you have an index on the *lft* column).

In the following section, I'll present common requests against a tree and the query solution for each, followed by the output of the query.

Return the subtree of a given root:

```
SELECT C.empid, REPLICATE(' | ', C.lvl - P.lvl) + C.empname AS empname
FROM dbo.EmployeesNS AS P
  INNER JOIN dbo.EmployeesNS AS C
    ON P.empid = 3
        AND C.lft BETWEEN P.lft AND P.rgt
ORDER BY C.lft;
```

```
empid        empname
-----------  ------------------
3            Ina
7            | Aaron
11           | | Gabriel
9            | | Rita
14           | | | Didi
12           | | | Emilia
13           | | | Michael
```

The query joins two instances of EmployeesNS. One represents the parent (*P*) and is filtered by the given root. The other represents the child (*C*). The two are joined based on the child's left being between the parent's left and right values.

> **Important** You might be tempted to use the predicate *C.lft >= P.lft AND C.rgt <= P.rgt* because it's a bit more intuitive than *C.lft BETWEEN P.lft AND P.rgt*. Both have the same logical meaning in the nested sets model. However, the latter can be optimized much more efficiently in terms of the index access method because it's based on only one range predicate and not on two like the former.

Indentation of the output is achieved by subtracting the parent level from the child level and replicating the ' | ' string that number of times. The output is sorted by the child's left value, which by definition represents topological sorting, and the desired sort of siblings. This subtree query is used as the baseline for most of the following queries.

If you want to exclude the subtree's root node from the output, simply use greater than (>) and less than (<) operators instead of BETWEEN. To the subtree query, add a filter that returns only nodes where the child's level minus the parent's level is smaller than or equal to the requested number of levels under the root.

Return the subtree of a given root, limiting two levels of subordinates under the root:

```
SELECT C.empid, REPLICATE(' | ', C.lvl - P.lvl) + C.empname AS empname
FROM dbo.EmployeesNS AS P
  INNER JOIN dbo.EmployeesNS AS C
    ON P.empid = 3
       AND C.lft BETWEEN P.lft AND P.rgt
WHERE C.lvl - P.lvl <= 2
ORDER BY C.lft;
```

```
empid       empname
----------- ----------------
3           Ina
7            | Aaron
11           |  | Gabriel
9            |  | Rita
```

Return leaf nodes under a given root:

```
SELECT C.empid, C.empname
FROM dbo.EmployeesNS AS P
  INNER JOIN dbo.EmployeesNS AS C
    ON P.empid = 3
       AND C.lft BETWEEN P.lft AND P.rgt
WHERE C.rgt - C.lft = 1;
```

```
empid       empname
----------- ---------
11          Gabriel
14          Didi
12          Emilia
13          Michael
```

A leaf node is a node for which the right value is greater than the left value by 1 (no subordinates). Add this filter to the subtree query's WHERE clause. As you can see, the nested sets solution allows for dramatically faster identification of leaf nodes than other solutions that use a NOT EXISTS predicate.

Return the count of subordinates of each node:

```
SELECT empid, (rgt - lft - 1) / 2 AS cnt, REPLICATE(' | ', lvl) + empname AS empname
FROM dbo.EmployeesNS
ORDER BY lft;
```

```
empid  cnt  empname
------ ---- --------------------
1      13   David
2      5    | Eitan
5      2    | | Jiru
8      0    | | | Lilach
10     0    | | | Sean
4      0    | | Seraph
6      0    | | Steve
3      6    | Ina
7      5    | | Aaron
11     0    | | | Gabriel
9      3    | | | Rita
14     0    | | | | Didi
12     0    | | | | Emilia
13     0    | | | | Michael
```

Because each node accounts for exactly two *lft* and *rgt* values and, in our implementation, no gaps exist, you can calculate the count of subordinates by accessing the subtree's root alone. The count is $(rgt - lft - 1) / 2$.

Return all ancestors of a given node:

```
SELECT P.empid, P.empname, P.lvl
FROM dbo.EmployeesNS AS P
  INNER JOIN dbo.EmployeesNS AS C
    ON C.empid = 14
       AND C.lft BETWEEN P.lft AND P.rgt;
```

```
empid  empname  lvl
------ -------- ----
1      David    0
3      Ina      1
7      Aaron    2
9      Rita     3
14     Didi     4
```

The ancestors query is almost identical to the subtree query. The nested sets relationships remain the same. The only difference is that here you filter a specific child-node ID, whereas in the subtree query you filtered a specific parent-node ID. Unfortunately, though, from a performance perspective, the path/ancestors query cannot be optimized as well as the subgraph/descendants query because ancestors do not reside in a consecutive range in the index leaf.

When you're done querying the EmployeesNS table, run the following code for cleanup:

```
DROP TABLE dbo.EmployeesNS;
```

Transitive closure

The transitive closure of a directed graph G is the graph with the same nodes as G and with an edge connecting each pair of nodes that are connected by a path (not necessarily containing just one edge) in G. The transitive closure helps answer a number of questions immediately, without the need to explore paths in the graph. For example, is David a manager of Aaron (directly or indirectly)? If the transitive closure of the Employees graph contains an edge from David to Aaron, he is. Does Double Espresso contain water? Can I drive from Los Angeles to New York? If the input graph contains the edges (a, b) and (b, c), a and c have a transitive relationship. The transitive closure contains the edges (a, b), (b, c), and also (a, c). If David is the direct manager of Ina and Ina is the direct manager of Aaron, David transitively is a manager of Aaron, or Aaron transitively is a subordinate of David.

Problems related to transitive closure deal with specialized cases of transitive relationships. An example is the "shortest path" problem, where you're trying to determine the shortest path between two nodes. For example, what's the shortest path between Los Angeles and New York?

In this section, I will describe iterative/recursive solutions for transitive closure and shortest-path problems.

> **Note** The performance of some solutions I will show (specifically those that use recursive CTEs) degrades exponentially as the input graph grows. I'll present them for demonstration purposes because they are fairly simple and natural. They are adequate for small graphs. Some efficient algorithms for transitive closure–related problems (for example, Floyd's and Warshall's algorithms) can be implemented as "level at a time" (breadth-first) iterations. For details on those, refer to *http://www.nist.gov/dads/*. I'll show efficient solutions that can be applied to larger graphs.

Directed acyclic graph

The first problem I will discuss is generating a transitive closure of a directed acyclic graph (DAG). Later, I'll show you how to deal with undirected and cyclic graphs as well. Whether the graph is directed or undirected doesn't really complicate the solution significantly, but dealing with cyclic graphs does. The input DAG I will use in my example is the BOM I used earlier in the chapter, which you create by running the code in Listing 11-2.

The code that generates the transitive closure of the BOM is somewhat similar to solutions for the subgraph problem (that is, the parts explosion). Specifically, you traverse the graph one level at a time (or, more accurately, you are using breadth-first search techniques). However, instead of returning only a root node here, the anchor member returns all first-level relationships in the BOM. In most graphs, this simply means all existing source/target pairs. In our case, this means all assembly/part pairs where the assembly is not NULL. The recursive member joins the CTE representing the previous level or parent (*P*) with the BOM representing the next level or child (*C*). It returns the original product ID (*P*) as the source and the child product ID (*C*) as the target. The outer query returns the distinct assembly/part pairs. Keep in mind that multiple paths might lead to a part in the BOM, but you need to return each unique pair only once.

Run the following code to generate the transitive closure of the BOM:

```
WITH BOMTC AS
(
  -- Return all first-level containment relationships
  SELECT assemblyid, partid
  FROM dbo.BOM
  WHERE assemblyid IS NOT NULL

  UNION ALL

  -- Return next-level containment relationships
  SELECT P.assemblyid, C.partid
  FROM BOMTC AS P
    INNER JOIN dbo.BOM AS C
      ON C.assemblyid = P.partid
)
-- Return distinct pairs that have
-- transitive containment relationships
SELECT DISTINCT assemblyid, partid
FROM BOMTC;
```

This code generates the following output:

```
assemblyid  partid
----------  ----------
1           6
1           7
1           10
1           13
1           14
2           6
2           7
2           10
2           11
2           13
2           14
3           6
3           7
3           11
3           12
3           14
3           16
3           17
4           9
4           12
4           14
4           16
4           17
5           9
5           12
5           14
5           16
```

5	17
10	13
10	14
12	14
12	16
12	17
16	17

This solution eliminates duplicate edges found in the BOMTC by applying a DISTINCT clause in the outer query. A more efficient solution is to avoid getting duplicates altogether by using a NOT EXISTS predicate in the query that runs repeatedly; such a predicate would filter newly found edges that do not appear in the set of edges that were already found. However, such an implementation can't use a CTE because the recursive member in the CTE has access only to the immediate previous level, rather than to all previous levels obtained thus far. Instead, you can use a UDF or a stored procedure that invokes the query that runs repeatedly in a loop and inserts each obtained level of nodes into a work table. Run the following code to create the *BOMTC* UDF, which implements this logic:

```
IF OBJECT_ID(N'dbo.BOMTC', N'TF') IS NOT NULL DROP FUNCTION dbo.BOMTC;
GO
CREATE FUNCTION BOMTC() RETURNS @BOMTC TABLE
(
  assemblyid INT NOT NULL,
  partid     INT NOT NULL,
  PRIMARY KEY (assemblyid, partid)
)
AS
BEGIN
  INSERT INTO @BOMTC(assemblyid, partid)
    SELECT assemblyid, partid
    FROM dbo.BOM
    WHERE assemblyid IS NOT NULL

  WHILE @@rowcount > 0
    INSERT INTO @BOMTC(assemblyid, partid)
      SELECT P.assemblyid, C.partid
      FROM @BOMTC AS P
        INNER JOIN dbo.BOM AS C
          ON C.assemblyid = P.partid
      WHERE NOT EXISTS
        (SELECT * FROM @BOMTC AS P2
         WHERE P2.assemblyid = P.assemblyid
         AND P2.partid = C.partid);

  RETURN;
END
GO
```

Query the function to get the transitive closure of the BOM:

```
SELECT assemblyid, partid FROM BOMTC();
```

If you want to return all paths in the BOM, along with the distance in levels between the parts, you use a similar algorithm with a few additions and revisions. You calculate the distance the same way you calculated the level value in the subgraph/subtree solutions. That is, the anchor assigns a constant distance of 1 for the first level, and the recursive member simply adds one in each iteration. Also, the path calculation is similar to the one used in the subgraph/subtree solutions. The anchor generates a path made of '.' + source_id + '.' + target_id + '.'. The recursive member generates it as *parent's path* + *target_id* + '.'. Finally, the outer query simply returns all paths (without applying DISTINCT in this case).

Run the following code to generate all possible paths in the BOM and their distances:

```
WITH BOMPaths AS
(
  SELECT assemblyid, partid, 1 AS distance, -- distance in first level is 1
    -- path in first level is .assemblyid.partid.
    '.' + CAST(assemblyid AS VARCHAR(MAX)) +
    '.' + CAST(partid      AS VARCHAR(MAX)) + '.' AS path
  FROM dbo.BOM
  WHERE assemblyid IS NOT NULL

  UNION ALL

  SELECT P.assemblyid, C.partid,
    -- distance in next level is parent's distance + 1
    P.distance + 1,
    -- path in next level is parent_path.child_partid.
    P.path + CAST(C.partid AS VARCHAR(MAX)) + '.'
  FROM BOMPaths AS P
    INNER JOIN dbo.BOM AS C
      ON C.assemblyid = P.partid
)
-- Return all paths
SELECT assemblyid, partid, distance, path
FROM BOMPaths;
```

You get the following output:

assemblyid	partid	distance	path
1	6	1	.1.6.
2	6	1	.2.6.
3	6	1	.3.6.
1	7	1	.1.7.
2	7	1	.2.7.
3	7	1	.3.7.
4	9	1	.4.9.
5	9	1	.5.9.
1	10	1	.1.10.
2	10	1	.2.10.
2	11	1	.2.11.
3	11	1	.3.11.
3	12	1	.3.12.
4	12	1	.4.12.
5	12	1	.5.12.
10	13	1	.10.13.
1	14	1	.1.14.

2	14	1	.2.14.
10	14	1	.10.14.
12	14	1	.12.14.
12	16	1	.12.16.
16	17	1	.16.17.
12	17	2	.12.16.17.
5	14	2	.5.12.14.
5	16	2	.5.12.16.
5	17	3	.5.12.16.17.
4	14	2	.4.12.14.
4	16	2	.4.12.16.
4	17	3	.4.12.16.17.
3	14	2	.3.12.14.
3	16	2	.3.12.16.
3	17	3	.3.12.16.17.
2	13	2	.2.10.13.
2	14	2	.2.10.14.
1	13	2	.1.10.13.
1	14	2	.1.10.14.

To isolate only the shortest paths, add a second CTE (BOMRnk) that computes rank values that are partitioned by assembly and part, and ordered by the distance within each partition. In the outer query, filter only the rows with a rank of 1.

Run the following code to produce the shortest paths in the BOM:

```
WITH BOMPaths AS -- All paths
(
  SELECT assemblyid, partid, 1 AS distance,
    '.' + CAST(assemblyid AS VARCHAR(MAX)) +
    '.' + CAST(partid    AS VARCHAR(MAX)) + '.' AS path
  FROM dbo.BOM
  WHERE assemblyid IS NOT NULL

  UNION ALL

  SELECT P.assemblyid, C.partid, P.distance + 1,
    P.path + CAST(C.partid AS VARCHAR(MAX)) + '.'
  FROM BOMPaths AS P
    INNER JOIN dbo.BOM AS C
      ON C.assemblyid = P.partid
),
BOMRnk AS -- Rank paths
(
  SELECT *, RANK() OVER(PARTITION BY assemblyid, partid ORDER BY distance) AS rnk
  FROM BOMPaths
)
-- Shortest path for each pair
SELECT assemblyid, partid, distance, path
FROM BOMRnk
WHERE rnk = 1;
```

This code generates the following output:

assemblyid	partid	distance	path
1	6	1	.1.6.
1	7	1	.1.7.
1	10	1	.1.10.
1	13	2	.1.10.13.
1	14	1	.1.14.
2	6	1	.2.6.
2	7	1	.2.7.
2	10	1	.2.10.
2	11	1	.2.11.
2	13	2	.2.10.13.
2	14	1	.2.14.
3	6	1	.3.6.
3	7	1	.3.7.
3	11	1	.3.11.
3	12	1	.3.12.
3	14	2	.3.12.14.
3	16	2	.3.12.16.
3	17	3	.3.12.16.17.
4	9	1	.4.9.
4	12	1	.4.12.
4	14	2	.4.12.14.
4	16	2	.4.12.16.
4	17	3	.4.12.16.17.
5	9	1	.5.9.
5	12	1	.5.12.
5	14	2	.5.12.14.
5	16	2	.5.12.16.
5	17	3	.5.12.16.17.
10	13	1	.10.13.
10	14	1	.10.14.
12	14	1	.12.14.
12	16	1	.12.16.
12	17	2	.12.16.17.
16	17	1	.16.17.

Undirected cyclic graph

Even though transitive closure is defined for a directed graph, you can also define and generate it for undirected graphs where each edge represents a two-way relationship. In my examples, I will use the Roads graph, which you create and populate by running the code in Listing 11-3. To see a visual representation of Roads, examine Figure 11-4. To apply the transitive-closure and shortest-path solutions to Roads, first convert it to a digraph by generating two directed edges from each existing edge:

```
SELECT city1 AS from_city, city2 AS to_city FROM dbo.Roads
UNION ALL
SELECT city2, city1 FROM dbo.Roads
```

For example, the edge (*JFK, ATL*) in the undirected graph appears as two edges, (*JFK, ATL*) and (*ATL, JFK*), in the digraph. The former represents the road from New York to Atlanta, and the latter represents the road from Atlanta to New York.

Because Roads is a cyclic graph, you also need to use the cycle-detection logic I described earlier in the chapter to avoid traversing cyclic paths. Armed with the techniques to generate a digraph out of an undirected graph and to detect cycles, you have all the tools you need to produce the transitive closure of Roads.

Run the following code to generate the transitive closure of Roads:

```
WITH Roads2 AS -- Two rows for each pair (from-->to, to-->from)
(
  SELECT city1 AS from_city, city2 AS to_city FROM dbo.Roads
  UNION ALL
  SELECT city2, city1 FROM dbo.Roads
),
RoadPaths AS
(
  -- Return all first-level reachability pairs
  SELECT from_city, to_city,
    -- path is needed to identify cycles
    CAST('.' + from_city + '.' + to_city + '.' AS VARCHAR(MAX)) AS path
  FROM Roads2

  UNION ALL

  -- Return next-level reachability pairs
  SELECT F.from_city, T.to_city, CAST(F.path + T.to_city + '.' AS VARCHAR(MAX))
  FROM RoadPaths AS F
    INNER JOIN Roads2 AS T
      -- if to_city appears in from_city's path, cycle detected
      ON CASE WHEN F.path LIKE '%.' + T.to_city + '.%'
              THEN 1 ELSE 0 END = 0
        AND F.to_city = T.from_city
)
-- Return Transitive Closure of Roads
SELECT DISTINCT from_city, to_city
FROM RoadPaths;
```

The *Roads2* CTE creates the digraph out of Roads. The *RoadPaths* CTE returns all possible source/target pairs (and has a big performance penalty), and it avoids returning and pursuing a path for which a cycle is detected. The outer query returns all distinct source/target pairs, shown next.

from	to	from	to	from	to	from	to	from	to
ANC	FAI	IAH	LAX	LAX	SEA	MSP	JFK	SEA	ORD
ATL	DEN	IAH	MCI	LAX	SFO	MSP	LAX	SEA	SFO
ATL	IAH	IAH	MIA	MCI	ATL	MSP	MCI	SFO	ATL
ATL	JFK	IAH	MSP	MCI	DEN	MSP	MIA	SFO	DEN
ATL	LAX	IAH	ORD	MCI	IAH	MSP	ORD	SFO	IAH
ATL	MCI	IAH	SEA	MCI	JFK	MSP	SEA	SFO	JFK
ATL	MIA	IAH	SFO	MCI	LAX	MSP	SFO	SFO	LAX
ATL	MSP	JFK	ATL	MCI	MIA	ORD	ATL	SFO	MCI
ATL	ORD	JFK	DEN	MCI	MSP	ORD	DEN	SFO	MIA
ATL	SEA	JFK	IAH	MCI	ORD	ORD	IAH	SFO	MSP
ATL	SFO	JFK	LAX	MCI	SEA	ORD	JFK	SFO	ORD
DEN	ATL	JFK	MCI	MCI	SFO	ORD	LAX	SFO	SEA
DEN	IAH	JFK	MIA	MIA	ATL	ORD	MCI		
DEN	JFK	JFK	MSP	MIA	DEN	ORD	MIA		
DEN	LAX	JFK	ORD	MIA	IAH	ORD	MSP		
DEN	MCI	JFK	SEA	MIA	JFK	ORD	SEA		
DEN	MIA	JFK	SFO	MIA	LAX	ORD	SFO		
DEN	MSP	LAX	ATL	MIA	MCI	SEA	ATL		
DEN	ORD	LAX	DEN	MIA	MSP	SEA	DEN		
DEN	SEA	LAX	IAH	MIA	ORD	SEA	IAH		
DEN	SFO	LAX	JFK	MIA	SEA	SEA	JFK		
FAI	ANC	LAX	MCI	MIA	SFO	SEA	LAX		
IAH	ATL	LAX	MIA	MSP	ATL	SEA	MCI		
IAH	DEN	LAX	MSP	MSP	DEN	SEA	MIA		
IAH	JFK	LAX	ORD	MSP	IAH	SEA	MSP		

Here, as well, you can use loops instead of a recursive CTE to optimize the solution, as demonstrated earlier with the BOM scenario. Run the following code to create the *RoadsTC* UDF, which returns the transitive closure of Roads using loops:

```
IF OBJECT_ID(N'dbo.RoadsTC', N'TF') IS NOT NULL DROP FUNCTION dbo.RoadsTC;
GO
CREATE FUNCTION dbo.RoadsTC() RETURNS @RoadsTC TABLE
(
  from_city VARCHAR(3) NOT NULL,
  to_city   VARCHAR(3) NOT NULL,
  PRIMARY KEY (from_city, to_city)
)
AS
BEGIN
  DECLARE @added as INT;

  INSERT INTO @RoadsTC(from_city, to_city)
    SELECT city1, city2 FROM dbo.Roads;

  SET @added = @@rowcount;

  INSERT INTO @RoadsTC
    SELECT city2, city1 FROM dbo.Roads

  SET @added = @added + @@rowcount;

  WHILE @added > 0 BEGIN
```

```
    INSERT INTO @RoadsTC
      SELECT DISTINCT TC.from_city, R.city2
      FROM @RoadsTC AS TC
        INNER JOIN dbo.Roads AS R
          ON R.city1 = TC.to_city
      WHERE NOT EXISTS
        (SELECT * FROM @RoadsTC AS TC2
          WHERE TC2.from_city = TC.from_city
            AND TC2.to_city = R.city2)
        AND TC.from_city <> R.city2;

    SET @added = @@rowcount;

    INSERT INTO @RoadsTC
      SELECT DISTINCT TC.from_city, R.city1
      FROM @RoadsTC AS TC
        INNER JOIN dbo.Roads AS R
          ON R.city2 = TC.to_city
      WHERE NOT EXISTS
        (SELECT * FROM @RoadsTC AS TC2
          WHERE TC2.from_city = TC.from_city
            AND TC2.to_city = R.city1)
        AND TC.from_city <> R.city1;

    SET @added = @added + @@rowcount;
  END
  RETURN;
END
GO


-- Use the RoadsTC UDF
SELECT from_city, to_city FROM dbo.RoadsTC();
GO
```

Run the following query to get the transitive closure of Roads:

```
SELECT from_city, to_city FROM dbo.RoadsTC();
```

To return all paths and distances, use similar logic to the one used in the digraph solution in the previous section. The difference here is that the distance is not just a level counter—it is the sum of the distances along the route from one city to the other.

Run the following code to return all paths and distances in Roads:

```
WITH Roads2 AS
(
  SELECT city1 AS from_city, city2 AS to_city, distance FROM dbo.Roads
  UNION ALL
  SELECT city2, city1, distance FROM dbo.Roads
),
RoadPaths AS
(
  SELECT from_city, to_city, distance,
    CAST('.' + from_city + '.' + to_city + '.' AS VARCHAR(MAX)) AS path
  FROM Roads2
```

```
UNION ALL

  SELECT F.from_city, T.to_city, F.distance + T.distance,
    CAST(F.path + T.to_city + '.' AS VARCHAR(MAX))
  FROM RoadPaths AS F
    INNER JOIN Roads2 AS T
      ON CASE WHEN F.path LIKE '%.' + T.to_city + '.%'
              THEN 1 ELSE 0 END = 0
          AND F.to_city = T.from_city
)
-- Return all paths and distances
SELECT from_city, to_city, distance, path
FROM RoadPaths;
```

Finally, to return shortest paths in Roads, use the same logic as the digraph shortest-paths solution. Run the following code to return shortest paths in Roads:

```
WITH Roads2 AS
(
  SELECT city1 AS from_city, city2 AS to_city, distance FROM dbo.Roads
  UNION ALL
  SELECT city2, city1, distance FROM dbo.Roads
),
RoadPaths AS
(
  SELECT from_city, to_city, distance,
    CAST('.' + from_city + '.' + to_city + '.' AS VARCHAR(MAX)) AS path
  FROM Roads2

  UNION ALL

  SELECT F.from_city, T.to_city, F.distance + T.distance,
    CAST(F.path + T.to_city + '.' AS VARCHAR(MAX))
  FROM RoadPaths AS F
    INNER JOIN Roads2 AS T
      ON CASE WHEN F.path LIKE '%.' + T.to_city + '.%'
              THEN 1 ELSE 0 END = 0
          AND F.to_city = T.from_city
),
RoadsRnk AS -- Rank paths
(
  SELECT *, RANK() OVER(PARTITION BY from_city, to_city ORDER BY distance) AS rnk
  FROM RoadPaths
)
-- Return shortest paths and distances
SELECT from_city, to_city, distance, path
FROM RoadsRnk
WHERE rnk = 1;
```

You get the following output:

```
from_city  to_city  distance      path
---------  -------  -----------   ------------------------
ANC        FAI      359           .ANC.FAI.
ATL        IAH      800           .ATL.IAH.
ATL        JFK      865           .ATL.JFK.
ATL        MCI      805           .ATL.MCI.
ATL        MIA      665           .ATL.MIA.
ATL        ORD      715           .ATL.ORD.
DEN        IAH      1120          .DEN.IAH.
DEN        LAX      1025          .DEN.LAX.
DEN        MCI      600           .DEN.MCI.
DEN        MSP      915           .DEN.MSP.
DEN        SEA      1335          .DEN.SEA.
DEN        SFO      1270          .DEN.SFO.
IAH        LAX      1550          .IAH.LAX.
IAH        MCI      795           .IAH.MCI.
IAH        MIA      1190          .IAH.MIA.
JFK        ORD      795           .JFK.ORD.
LAX        SFO      385           .LAX.SFO.
MCI        MSP      440           .MCI.MSP.
MCI        ORD      525           .MCI.ORD.
MSP        ORD      410           .MSP.ORD.
MSP        SEA      2015          .MSP.SEA.
SEA        SFO      815           .SEA.SFO.
FAI        ANC      359           .FAI.ANC.
IAH        ATL      800           .IAH.ATL.
JFK        ATL      865           .JFK.ATL.
MCI        ATL      805           .MCI.ATL.
MIA        ATL      665           .MIA.ATL.
ORD        ATL      715           .ORD.ATL.
IAH        DEN      1120          .IAH.DEN.
LAX        DEN      1025          .LAX.DEN.
MCI        DEN      600           .MCI.DEN.
MSP        DEN      915           .MSP.DEN.
SEA        DEN      1335          .SEA.DEN.
SFO        DEN      1270          .SFO.DEN.
LAX        IAH      1550          .LAX.IAH.
MCI        IAH      795           .MCI.IAH.
MIA        IAH      1190          .MIA.IAH.
ORD        JFK      795           .ORD.JFK.
SFO        LAX      385           .SFO.LAX.
MSP        MCI      440           .MSP.MCI.
ORD        MCI      525           .ORD.MCI.
ORD        MSP      410           .ORD.MSP.
SEA        MSP      2015          .SEA.MSP.
SFO        SEA      815           .SFO.SEA.
SEA        ORD      2425          .SEA.MSP.ORD.
SEA        JFK      3220          .SEA.MSP.ORD.JFK.
ORD        SEA      2425          .ORD.MSP.SEA.
ORD        DEN      1125          .ORD.MCI.DEN.
ORD        IAH      1320          .ORD.MCI.IAH.
ORD        LAX      2150          .ORD.MCI.DEN.LAX.
ORD        SFO      2395          .ORD.MCI.DEN.SFO.
MSP        IAH      1235          .MSP.MCI.IAH.
SFO        IAH      1935          .SFO.LAX.IAH.
SFO        MIA      3125          .SFO.LAX.IAH.MIA.
MIA        LAX      2740          .MIA.IAH.LAX.
```

MIA	SFO	3125	.MIA.IAH.LAX.SFO.
LAX	MIA	2740	.LAX.IAH.MIA.
LAX	ATL	2350	.LAX.IAH.ATL.
SFO	MCI	1870	.SFO.DEN.MCI.
SFO	MSP	2185	.SFO.DEN.MSP.
SFO	ORD	2395	.SFO.DEN.MCI.ORD.
SFO	ATL	2675	.SFO.DEN.MCI.ATL.
SFO	JFK	3190	.SFO.DEN.MCI.ORD.JFK.
SEA	IAH	2455	.SEA.DEN.IAH.
SEA	MCI	1935	.SEA.DEN.MCI.
SEA	ATL	2740	.SEA.DEN.MCI.ATL.
SEA	MIA	3405	.SEA.DEN.MCI.ATL.MIA.
MSP	LAX	1940	.MSP.DEN.LAX.
MSP	SFO	2185	.MSP.DEN.SFO.
MCI	LAX	1625	.MCI.DEN.LAX.
MCI	SEA	1935	.MCI.DEN.SEA.
MCI	SFO	1870	.MCI.DEN.SFO.
LAX	MCI	1625	.LAX.DEN.MCI.
LAX	MSP	1940	.LAX.DEN.MSP.
LAX	ORD	2150	.LAX.DEN.MCI.ORD.
LAX	JFK	2945	.LAX.DEN.MCI.ORD.JFK.
IAH	SEA	2455	.IAH.DEN.SEA.
ORD	MIA	1380	.ORD.ATL.MIA.
MIA	JFK	1530	.MIA.ATL.JFK.
MIA	MCI	1470	.MIA.ATL.MCI.
MIA	ORD	1380	.MIA.ATL.ORD.
MIA	MSP	1790	.MIA.ATL.ORD.MSP.
MIA	DEN	2070	.MIA.ATL.MCI.DEN.
MIA	SEA	3405	.MIA.ATL.MCI.DEN.SEA.
MCI	MIA	1470	.MCI.ATL.MIA.
JFK	IAH	1665	.JFK.ATL.IAH.
JFK	MIA	1530	.JFK.ATL.MIA.
IAH	JFK	1665	.IAH.ATL.JFK.
SEA	LAX	1200	.SEA.SFO.LAX.
MSP	ATL	1125	.MSP.ORD.ATL.
MSP	JFK	1205	.MSP.ORD.JFK.
MSP	MIA	1790	.MSP.ORD.ATL.MIA.
MCI	JFK	1320	.MCI.ORD.JFK.
LAX	SEA	1200	.LAX.SFO.SEA.
JFK	MCI	1320	.JFK.ORD.MCI.
JFK	MSP	1205	.JFK.ORD.MSP.
JFK	SEA	3220	.JFK.ORD.MSP.SEA.
JFK	DEN	1920	.JFK.ORD.MCI.DEN.
JFK	LAX	2945	.JFK.ORD.MCI.DEN.LAX.
JFK	SFO	3190	.JFK.ORD.MCI.DEN.SFO.
IAH	MSP	1235	.IAH.MCI.MSP.
IAH	ORD	1320	.IAH.MCI.ORD.
IAH	SFO	1935	.IAH.LAX.SFO.
DEN	ORD	1125	.DEN.MCI.ORD.
DEN	ATL	1405	.DEN.MCI.ATL.
DEN	MIA	2070	.DEN.MCI.ATL.MIA.
DEN	JFK	1920	.DEN.MCI.ORD.JFK.
ATL	MSP	1125	.ATL.ORD.MSP.
ATL	DEN	1405	.ATL.MCI.DEN.
ATL	SEA	2740	.ATL.MCI.DEN.SEA.
ATL	SFO	2675	.ATL.MCI.DEN.SFO.
ATL	LAX	2350	.ATL.IAH.LAX.

To satisfy multiple requests for the shortest paths between two cities, you might want to materialize the result set in a table and index it, like so:

```
WITH Roads2 AS
(
  SELECT city1 AS from_city, city2 AS to_city, distance FROM dbo.Roads
  UNION ALL
  SELECT city2, city1, distance FROM dbo.Roads
),
RoadPaths AS
(
  SELECT from_city, to_city, distance,
    CAST('.' + from_city + '.' + to_city + '.' AS VARCHAR(MAX)) AS path
  FROM Roads2

  UNION ALL

  SELECT F.from_city, T.to_city, F.distance + T.distance,
    CAST(F.path + T.to_city + '.' AS VARCHAR(MAX))
  FROM RoadPaths AS F
    INNER JOIN Roads2 AS T
      ON CASE WHEN F.path LIKE '%.' + T.to_city + '.%'
             THEN 1 ELSE 0 END = 0
        AND F.to_city = T.from_city
),
RoadsRnk AS -- Rank paths
(
  SELECT *, RANK() OVER(PARTITION BY from_city, to_city ORDER BY distance) AS rnk
  FROM RoadPaths
)
-- Return shortest paths and distances
SELECT from_city, to_city, distance, path
INTO dbo.RoadPaths
FROM RoadsRnk
WHERE rnk = 1;

CREATE UNIQUE CLUSTERED INDEX idx_uc_from_city_to_city
  ON dbo.RoadPaths(from_city, to_city);
```

Once the result set is materialized and indexed, a request for the shortest path between two cities can be satisfied instantly. This is practical and advisable when information changes infrequently. As is often the case, there is a trade-off between up to date and fast. The following query requests the shortest path between Los Angeles and New York:

```
SELECT from_city, to_city, distance, path FROM dbo.RoadPaths
WHERE from_city = 'LAX' AND to_city = 'JFK';
```

This query generates the following output:

```
from_city to_city distance    path
--------- ------- ----------- ----------------------
LAX       JFK     2945        .LAX.DEN.MCI.ORD.JFK.
```

A more efficient solution to the shortest-paths problem uses loops instead of recursive CTEs. It is more efficient for reasons similar to the ones described earlier; that is, in each iteration of the loop you have access to all previously spooled data and not just to the immediate previous level. You create a function called *RoadsTC* that returns a table variable called *@RoadsTC*. The table variable has the attributes *from_city*, *to_city*, *distance*, and *route*, which are self-explanatory. The function's code first inserts into *@RoadsTC* a row for each (*city1, city2*) and (*city2, city1*) pair from the table Roads. The code then enters a loop that iterates as long as the previous iteration inserted rows to *@RoadsTC*. In each iteration of the loop, the code inserts new routes that extend the existing routes in *@RoadsTC*. New routes are added only if the source and destination do not appear already in *@RoadsTC* with the same distance or a shorter distance. Run the following code to create the *RoadsTC* function.

```
IF OBJECT_ID(N'dbo.RoadsTC', N'TF') IS NOT NULL DROP FUNCTION dbo.RoadsTC;
GO
CREATE FUNCTION dbo.RoadsTC() RETURNS @RoadsTC TABLE
(
  uniquifier INT        NOT NULL IDENTITY,
  from_city  VARCHAR(3) NOT NULL,
  to_city    VARCHAR(3) NOT NULL,
  distance   INT        NOT NULL,
  route      VARCHAR(MAX) NOT NULL,
  PRIMARY KEY (from_city, to_city, uniquifier)
)
AS
BEGIN
  DECLARE @added AS INT;

  INSERT INTO @RoadsTC
    SELECT city1 AS from_city, city2 AS to_city, distance, '.' + city1 + '.' + city2 + '.'
    FROM dbo.Roads;

  SET @added = @@rowcount;

  INSERT INTO @RoadsTC
    SELECT city2, city1, distance, '.' + city2 + '.' + city1 + '.'
    FROM dbo.Roads;

  SET @added = @added + @@rowcount;

  WHILE @added > 0 BEGIN
    INSERT INTO @RoadsTC
      SELECT DISTINCT TC.from_city, R.city2, TC.distance + R.distance, TC.route + city2 + '.'
      FROM @RoadsTC AS TC
        INNER JOIN dbo.Roads AS R
          ON R.city1 = TC.to_city
      WHERE NOT EXISTS
        (SELECT * FROM @RoadsTC AS TC2
          WHERE TC2.from_city = TC.from_city
            AND TC2.to_city = R.city2
            AND TC2.distance <= TC.distance + R.distance)
        AND TC.from_city <> R.city2;

    SET @added = @@rowcount;
```

```
    INSERT INTO @RoadsTC
      SELECT DISTINCT TC.from_city, R.city1, TC.distance + R.distance, TC.route + city1 + '.'
      FROM @RoadsTC AS TC
        INNER JOIN dbo.Roads AS R
          ON R.city2 = TC.to_city
      WHERE NOT EXISTS
        (SELECT * FROM @RoadsTC AS TC2
         WHERE TC2.from_city = TC.from_city
           AND TC2.to_city = R.city1
           AND TC2.distance <= TC.distance + R.distance)
        AND TC.from_city <> R.city1;

    SET @added = @added + @@rowcount;
  END
  RETURN;
END
GO
```

The function might return more than one row for the same source and target cities. To return shortest paths and distances, use the following query:

```
SELECT from_city, to_city, distance, route
FROM (SELECT from_city, to_city, distance, route,
        RANK() OVER (PARTITION BY from_city, to_city ORDER BY distance) AS rnk
      FROM dbo.RoadsTC() AS F) AS RTC
WHERE rnk = 1;
```

This solution applies logic similar to the CTE-based solution to filter the shortest paths. The derived table query assigns a rank value (*rnk*) to each row, based on *from_city, to_city* partitioning and *distance* ordering. This means that shortest paths are assigned with the rank value 1. The outer query filters only the shortest paths (*rnk = 1*).

When you're done querying the RoadPaths table, don't forget to drop it:

```
DROP TABLE dbo.RoadPaths;
```

Conclusion

This chapter covered the treatment of graphs. I presented iterative/recursive solutions as well as ones that materialize extra information about the relationships in the graph.

The main advantage of the iterative/recursive solutions is that you don't need to materialize and maintain any additional attributes—the graph manipulation is based on the stored edge attributes. The materialized path solution materializes an enumerated path and possibly also the level for each node and path that leads to it. You can either maintain your own custom materialized path or use SQL Server's proprietary HIERARCHYID data type.

In the materialized path solution, the maintenance of the additional information is not very expensive, and you benefit from simple and fast set-based queries. The nested sets solution materializes left and right values representing set containment relationships and possibly the level as well. This is probably the most elegant solution of those I presented, and it also allows for simple and fast queries. However, maintaining the materialized information is expensive, so typically this solution is practical for either static trees or small dynamic trees.

In the last section, I presented solutions to transitive-closure and shortest-path problems.

Because this chapter concludes the book, I'd like to leave you with a final thought. If you ask me what the most important thing is that I hope you get from this book, I'd say it is the importance of paying special attention to fundamentals. Do not underestimate them or take them lightly. Spend time on identifying, focusing on, and perfecting fundamental techniques. When you are faced with a tough problem, solutions will flow naturally.

"Matters of great concern should be treated lightly."

"Matters of small concern should be treated seriously."

—*Hagakure, The Book of the Samurai* by Yamamoto Tsunetomo

The meaning of these sayings is not what appears on the surface. The book goes on to explain:

"Among one's affairs there should not be more than two or three matters of what one could call great concern. If these are deliberated upon during ordinary times, they can be understood. Thinking about things previously and then handling them lightly when the time comes is what this is all about. To face an event and solve it lightly is difficult if you are not resolved beforehand, and there will always be uncertainty in hitting your mark. However, if the foundation is laid previously, you can think of the saying, 'Matters of great concern should be treated lightly,' as your own basis for action."

Index

Symbols

= (equality) operator
    cardinality estimates for, 110, 113–114, 561
    equi joins, 230–231
> (greater than) operator, cardinality estimates for, 561
< (less than) operator, cardinality estimates for, 561

A

absolute frequencies, 476–479
absolute percentages, 476–479
absolute values, computing, 323–324
access methods. *See also* scans; seeks
    allocation order scan safety issues, 65–76
    allocation order scans vs. index order scans, 65
    clustered index seek + range scan, 93–94
    cost associations of, 57
    covering nonclustered index seek + range scan, 94–97
    dm_db_index_usage_stats function, 135–136
    index order scan issues. *See* index order scans
    index seek, 49. *See also* Index Seek operator
    logical reads as performance metric for, 57
    nonclustered index seek + range scan + lookups, 81–90
    ordered clustered index scans, 62–63
    ordered covering nonclustered index scans, 63–65
    Read Uncommitted isolation level, 68–69, 78, 81
    table scan/unordered clustered index scan, 57–60
    unordered covering nonclustered index scans, 60–62
    unordered nonclustered index scans + lookups, 91–93
acyclic graphs, 708. *See also* directed acyclic graphs (DAGs)
add outer rows logical processing phase, 4–5, 13
ADO.NET context connection strings with SQLCLR, 603–605
Affinity Mask setting, 175, 177
AFTER DDL triggers, 579–581
AFTER DML triggers, 575–578, 581–583

AFTER UPDATE triggers, 575–578
aggregate calculations, custom
    carry-along-sort solutions, 326–327
    cursors for, 314–315
    FOR XML string concatenation, 317–319
    hierarchical levels of aggregation. *See* grouping sets
    modes, 324–327
    overview of, 313–314
    pivoting for, 315–316, 318–319
    products, 322–324
    SELECT @local_variable method, 319–322
    user-defined. *See* SQLCLR user-defined aggregates
aggregate functions
    AVG. *See* averages, AVG window function
    cardinality overestimations, effects of, 100
    cardinality underestimations, effects of, 99
    COUNT. *See* COUNT function
    cumulative aggregate function plans, 274–275
    expected frequency calculations with, 504–505
    limitations of, 261–262
    parallelism inhibited by certain, 179
    scalar aggregates, 179
    subquery inputs prohibited, 17
    SUM. *See* SUM function; SUM OVER window function
    window functions. *See* aggregate window functions
aggregate window functions
    packing interval solutions, 466–468
    similarity to grouped functions, 260
aggregation
    custom calculations of. *See* aggregate calculations, custom
    functions for. *See* aggregate functions
    persisting with grouping sets, 334–337
    user-defined. *See* SQLCLR user-defined aggregates
aliases, column
    ensuring uniqueness in queries with, 204
    inline vs. external, for derived tables, 205
    in ORDER BY clauses, 14, 20
    referencing, 8, 17
    reuse with APPLY operator, 222–224
ALL variant of UNION operator, 37–38, 250
all-at-once operations, 17–18

N

R

T

About the authors

ITZIK BEN-GAN is a mentor for and co-founder of SolidQ. A SQL Server Microsoft MVP (Most Valuable Professional) since 1999, Itzik has delivered numerous training events around the world focused on T-SQL querying, query tuning, and programming. Itzik has authored several T-SQL books as well as articles for *SQL Server Pro*, *SolidQ Journal*, and MSDN. Itzik's speaking activities include TechEd, SQLPASS, SQL Server Connections, SolidQ events, and various user groups around the world. Itzik is the author of SolidQ's Advanced T-SQL Querying, Programming and Tuning, and T-SQL Fundamentals courses, along with being a primary resource within the company for its T-SQL-related activities.

DEJAN SARKA, MCT and SQL Server MVP, is an independent consultant, trainer, and developer focusing on database and business intelligence applications. His specialties are advanced topics like data modeling, data mining, and data quality. On these tough topics, he works and researches together with SolidQ and the Data Quality Institute. He is the founder of the Slovenian SQL Server and .NET Users Group. Dejan Sarka is the main author or coauthor of 11 books about databases and SQL Server, with more to come. He also has developed and is continuing to develop many courses and seminars for SolidQ and Microsoft. He has been a regular speaker at many conferences worldwide for more than 15 years, including Microsoft TechEd, PASS Summit, and others.

ADAM MACHANIC is a Boston-based SQL Server developer, writer, and speaker. He focuses on large-scale data warehouse performance and development, and he is the author of the award-winning SQL Server monitoring stored procedure *sp_WhoIsActive*. Adam has written for numerous websites and magazines, including *SQLblog*, *Simple Talk*, *Search SQL Server*, *SQL Server Professional*, *CoDe*, and *VSJ*. He has also contributed to several books on SQL Server, including *SQL Server 2008 Internals* (Microsoft Press, 2009) and *Expert SQL Server 2005 Development* (Apress, 2007). Adam regularly speaks at conferences and training events on a variety of SQL Server topics. He is a Microsoft Most Valuable Professional (MVP) for SQL Server, a Microsoft Certified IT Professional (MCITP), and an alumnus of the INETA North American Speakers Bureau.

KEVIN FARLEE has over 25 years in the industry, in both database and storage-management software. In his current role as a Storage Engine Program Manager on the Microsoft SQL Server team, he brings these threads together. His current projects include the SQL Server Project "Hekaton" In-Memory OLTP feature.

From technical overviews to drilldowns on special topics, get *free* ebooks from Microsoft Press at:

www.microsoftvirtualacademy.com/ebooks

Download your free ebooks in PDF, EPUB, and/or Mobi for Kindle formats.

Look for other great resources at Microsoft Virtual Academy, where you can learn new skills and help advance your career with free Microsoft training delivered by experts.

Microsoft Press

Now that you've read the book...

Tell us what you think!

Was it useful?
Did it teach you what you wanted to learn?
Was there room for improvement?

Let us know at http://aka.ms/tellpress

Your feedback goes directly to the staff at Microsoft Press,
and we read every one of your responses. Thanks in advance!

 Microsoft